序 言

　　「學科能力測驗」開辦至今，已經有十六年的歷史。再加上另外舉行的兩次補考，一共有十八份珍貴的英文試題。這些試題內容，是命題教授們的心血結晶，每一道題目都具有代表性，非常重要。這些題目是未來考生們準備學測時，不可或缺的參考資料。

　　「學科能力測驗」實施以來，考試的題型和方向大抵已有脈絡可循。就題型來說，選擇題部分沒有太大的變動；而非選擇題部分，則可能出現簡答題、中翻英、看圖說故事等。至於出題方向，考生要特別注意近半年來的重大新聞議題；要應付層出不窮的新聞考題，多做最新試題是不二法門，像「劉毅英文家教班」的學生，每週都參加模擬考試，每次考試都考世界最新動態的相關文章，不管學測題目再怎麼變，「劉毅英文家教班」的學生，永遠是最後的贏家。

　　「歷屆大學學測英文試題詳解」，特別將歷屆學測英文試題全部收錄在內，且針對每一道題目，都有最完善的講解，讀者們不需另外花時間查字典。編者的目標，就是幫助考生們以最有效率的方式，研讀最重要的資料。另外，本書還附上「電腦統計歷屆學測單字和成語」，考生們只要善加利用這些資料，並在考前將常考的單字及片語背熟，就能把英文這一科，變成幫助你得高分的秘密武器。

　　本書編校製作過程嚴謹，但仍恐有疏失之處，尚祈各界先進不吝指正。

編者 謹識

目 錄

九十八年大學入學學科能力測驗試題
英文考科

第壹部份：選擇題（佔 72 分）

一、詞彙（佔 15 分）

說明：第 1 至 15 題，每題選出最適當的一個選項，標示在答案卡之「**選擇題答案區**」。每題答對得 1 分，答錯不倒扣。

1. Steve's description of the place was so _____ that I could almost picture it in my mind.
   (A) bitter　　　(B) vivid　　　(C) sensitive　　　(D) courageous

2. When people feel uncomfortable or nervous, they may _____ their arms across their chests as if to protect themselves.
   (A) toss　　　(B) fold　　　(C) veil　　　(D) yield

3. The doors of these department stores slide open _____ when you approach them. You don't have to open them yourself.
   (A) necessarily　(B) diligently　(C) automatically (D) intentionally

4. Nicole is a _____ language learner. Within a short period of time, she has developed a good command of Chinese and Japanese.
   (A) convenient　(B) popular　　(C) regular　　　(D) brilliant

5. With rising oil prices, there is an increasing _____ for people to ride bicycles to work.
   (A) permit　　(B) instrument　(C) appearance　(D) tendency

6. This information came from a very _____ source, so you don't have to worry about being cheated.
   (A) reliable　　(B) flexible　　(C) clumsy　　　(D) brutal

7. We hope that there will be no war in the world and that all people live in peace and _____ with each other.

    (A) complaint   (B) harmony   (C) mission   (D) texture

8. To have a full discussion of the issue, the committee spent a whole hour _____ their ideas at the meeting.

    (A) depositing   (B) exchanging   (C) governing   (D) interrupting

9. While adapting to western ways of living, many Asian immigrants in the US still try hard to _____ their own cultures and traditions.

    (A) volunteer   (B) scatter   (C) preserve   (D) motivate

10. With the worsening of global economic conditions, it seems wiser and more _____ to keep cash in the bank rather than to invest in the stock market.

    (A) sensible   (B) portable   (C) explicit   (D) anxious

11. Under the _____ of newly elected president Barack Obama, the US is expected to turn a new page in politics and economy.

    (A) adoption   (B) fragrance   (C) identity   (D) leadership

12. Rapid advancement in motor engineering makes it _____ possible to build a flying car in the near future.

    (A) individually (B) narrowly   (C) punctually   (D) technically

13. When you take photos, you can move around to shoot the target object from different _____.

    (A) moods   (B) trends   (C) angles   (D) inputs

14. Students were asked to _____ or rewrite their compositions
    based on the teacher's comments.

　　(A) revise　　　(B) resign　　　(C) refresh　　　(D) remind

15. Besides lung cancer, another _____ of smoking is wrinkles, a
    premature sign of aging.

　　(A) blessing　　(B) campaign　　(C) consequence　　(D) breakthrough

二、綜合測驗（佔 15 分）

說明： 第 16 至 30 題，每題一個空格，請依文意選出最適當的一個選項，標
　　　 示在答案卡之「選擇題答案區」。每題答對得 1 分，答錯不倒扣。

　　　Art Fry was a researcher in the 3M Company. He was bothered by
a small irritation every Sunday as he sang in the church choir. That is,
after he ___16___ his pages in the hymn book with small bits of paper,
the small pieces would invariably fall out all over the floor. One day,
an idea ___17___ Art Fry. He remembered a kind of glue developed by
a colleague that everyone thought ___18___ a failure because it did not
stick very well. He then coated the glue on a paper sample and found
that it was not only a good bookmark, but it was great for writing notes.
It would stay in place ___19___ you wanted it to. Then you could remove
it ___20___ damage. The resulting product was called the Post-it, one of
3M's most successful office products.

16. (A) marked　　　(B) tore　　　(C) served　　　(D) took

17. (A) threw at　　　　　　　　　(B) occurred to
　　(C) looked down upon　　　　　(D) came up with

18. (A) is　　　　　(B) was　　　　(C) will be　　　(D) has been

19. (A) despite that   (B) rather than   (C) as long as   (D) no matter what

20. (A) into   (B) out of   (C) within   (D) without

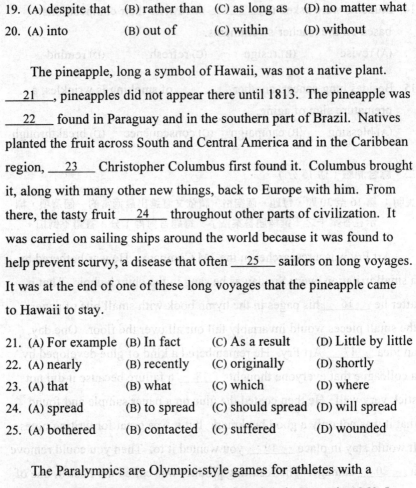

The pineapple, long a symbol of Hawaii, was not a native plant.
   21   , pineapples did not appear there until 1813. The pineapple was
   22   found in Paraguay and in the southern part of Brazil. Natives
planted the fruit across South and Central America and in the Caribbean
region,   23   Christopher Columbus first found it. Columbus brought
it, along with many other new things, back to Europe with him. From
there, the tasty fruit   24   throughout other parts of civilization. It
was carried on sailing ships around the world because it was found to
help prevent scurvy, a disease that often   25   sailors on long voyages.
It was at the end of one of these long voyages that the pineapple came
to Hawaii to stay.

21. (A) For example (B) In fact   (C) As a result   (D) Little by little

22. (A) nearly   (B) recently   (C) originally   (D) shortly

23. (A) that   (B) what   (C) which   (D) where

24. (A) spread   (B) to spread   (C) should spread (D) will spread

25. (A) bothered   (B) contacted   (C) suffered   (D) wounded

The Paralympics are Olympic-style games for athletes with a
disability. They were organized for the first time in Rome in 1960. In
Toronto in 1976, the idea of putting together different disability groups
   26   sports competitions was born. Today, the Paralympics are
sports events for athletes from six different disability groups. They
emphasize the participants' athletic achievements   27   their physical
disability. The games have grown in size gradually. The number of

athletes ___28___ in the Summer Paralympic Games has increased from 400 athletes from 23 countries in 1960 to 3,806 athletes from 136 countries in 2004.

　　The Paralympic Games have always been held in the same year as the Olympic Games. Since the Seoul 1988 Paralympic Games and the Albertville 1992 Winter Paralympic Games, they have also ___29___ in the same city as the Olympics. On June 19, 2001, an agreement was signed between the International Olympic Committee and the International Paralympics Committee to keep this ___30___ in the future. From the 2012 bid onwards, the city chosen to host the Olympic Games will also host the Paralympics.

26. (A) for　　　　(B) with　　　　(C) as　　　　(D) on
27. (A) in terms of　(B) instead of　(C) at the risk of　(D) at the cost of
28. (A) participate　(B) participated　(C) participating　(D) to participate
29. (A) taken turns　(B) taken place　(C) taken off　　(D) taken over
30. (A) piece　　　(B) deadline　　(C) date　　　(D) practice

三、文意選填（佔 10 分）

說明：　第 31 至 40 題，每題一個空格，請依文意在文章後所提供的 (A) 到(J) 選項中分別選出最適當者，並將其英文字母代號標示在答案卡之「選擇題答案區」。每題答對得 1 分，答錯不倒扣。

　　Familiar fables can be narrated differently or extended in interesting and humorous ways. The end of the famous fable of "The Tortoise and the Hare" is well known to all: the tortoise wins the race against the hare. The moral lesson is that slow and steady wins the race. We all have grown up with this popular version, but the ___31___ fable can be

extended with different twists. At the request of the hare, a second race
is ___32___ and this time, the hare runs without taking a rest and wins.
The moral lesson is that ___33___ and consistent will always beat slow
and steady. Then it is the tortoise that ___34___ the hare to a third race
along a different route in which there is a river just before the final
destination. This time, the tortoise wins the race because the hare
cannot swim. The moral lesson is "First ___35___ your strengths, and
then change the playing field to suit them."

But the story continues. Both ___36___ know their own drawbacks
and limitations very well; therefore, they jointly decide to have one last
race—not to decide who the winner or loser is, but just for their own
pleasure and satisfaction. The two ___37___ as a team. Firstly, the hare
carries the tortoise on its back to the river. Then, the tortoise carries the
hare and swims to the ___38___ bank of the river. Lastly, the hare carries
the tortoise again on its back. Thus they reach the ___39___ line together.
Overall, many moral lessons from the last match are highlighted. The
most obvious one is the importance of ___40___. Another moral which
also means a great deal is "competition against situations rather than
against rivals."

(A) arranged   (B) challenges   (C) competitors   (D) cooperate
(E) fast   (F) finishing   (G) identify   (H) opposite
(I) same   (J) teamwork

四、閱讀測驗（佔 32 分）

說明： 第 41 至 56 題，每題請分別根據各篇文章之文意選出最適當的一個選
項，標示在答案卡之「選擇題答案區」。每題答對得 2 分，答錯不倒扣。

41-44 為題組

To Whom It May Concern:

Your address was forwarded to us by Why Bother Magazine. All of us here think The International Institute of Not Doing Much is the best organization in the world. You know how to avoid unnecessary activities!

We closely followed the advice in your article. First, we replaced all our telephones with carrier pigeons. Simply removing the jingle of telephones and replacing them with the pleasant sounds of birds has had a remarkable effect on everyone. Besides, birds are cheaper than telephone service. After all, we are a business. We have to think of the bottom line. As a side benefit, the birds also fertilize the lawn outside the new employee sauna.

Next, we sold the computers off to Stab, Grab, Grit, and Nasty, a firm of lawyers nearby. Our electricity bill went way down. Big savings! The boss is impressed. We have completely embraced paper technology. Now that we all use pencils, doodling is on the increase, and the quality of pencilwomanship is impressive, as you can tell from my handwriting in this letter. By the way, if you can, please send this letter back to us. We can erase and reuse it. Just tie it to Maggie's leg and she'll know where to take it.

Now it's very calm and quiet here. You can notice the difference. No more loud chatter on the telephones! All we hear is the scratching of pencil on paper, the sound of pigeons, and the delivery of inter-office correspondence by paper airplane.

Wonderful! I've always wanted to work for an insurance company ever since I was a little girl. Now it's perfect.

Sincerely yours,
Eleanor Lightly
Spokeswoman and Company Hair Stylist
ABC Activity Insurance: Insure against overdoing it

41. Which of the following best describes the life the author is leading?

    (A) A simple, slow-paced life.

    (B) A life of hard work and security.

    (C) A religious, peasant-like life.

    (D) A life away from paper and pencils.

42. Where is Eleanor's letter sent to?

    (A) Why Bother Magazine.

    (B) ABC Activity Insurance Company.

    (C) Stab, Grab, Grit, and Nasty Law Firm.

    (D) The International Institute of Not Doing Much.

43. Which of the following is practiced in the author's company?

    (A) Replacing the manual work system with modern technology.

    (B) Turning off lights in the daytime to save electricity.

    (C) Recycling paper resources whenever possible.

    (D) Buying birds and pets as company for the staff.

44. What is true about **Maggie**?

    (A) She works as a manager in the author's company.

    (B) She sometimes helps fertilize the lawn outside the sauna.

    (C) She often helps with inter-office correspondence using e-mail.

    (D) Her handwriting has improved a lot after entering the company.

45-48 為題組

    The Galápagos Islands are the Pacific island paradise where Darwin's theory of evolution was born. They are places filled with giant tree lizards, sandy beaches, and tropical plants. Now they will be famous for one more thing: the world's first green airport.

　　This group of islands off the coast of Ecuador has recently contracted Argentine Corporación America to manage the redevelopment of the airport on the island of Baltra. It is estimated that US$20 million is needed to complete **the project** by 2009. The new development has several important features: use of wind and solar energy, passive heating and cooling systems, as well as concrete runways in place of asphalt, which has a greater carbon footprint during its production cycle. This new development couldn't be coming at a better time for the Galápagos, which were added to an environmental "danger list" in 2007.

　　Pacific islands like the Galápagos, Easter Island, and Tahiti, have economies that are driven almost completely by tourism. However, some people think these are "unsustainable models of development." The number of visitors to the Galápagos rose more than 250% from 1990 to 2006, while the number of commercial flights to the area rose 193% from 2001 to 2006. These increases put great stress on the islands' resources and environment. Air travel is especially criticized for exhausting natural resources and causing environmental damage. Thus, efforts are being made to reduce the environmental impact of the tourism industry. The greening of airports is just one of these attempts.

45. What is this article mainly about?
    (A) The problems of Darwin's theory.
    (B) The background of building a green airport.
    (C) The history of the Galápagos Islands.
    (D) The ease of transportation to the Pacific islands.

46. Where will the world's first green airport be built?

    (A) In Tahiti.   (B) In Argentina.

    (C) In Baltra.   (D) In the United States.

47. What is true about the Galápagos Islands?

    (A) They are located near Ecuador in the Pacific Ocean.

    (B) They have had a great increase in population since 2001.

    (C) They will invest US$20 million to promote their tourism.

    (D) They have become one of the most dangerous places in the world.

48. What does **the project** in the second paragraph refer to?

    (A) The plan to build a green airport.

    (B) The research on the production of solar energy.

    (C) The task of calculating a carbon footprint.

    (D) The study on the exhaustion of natural resources.

49-52 為題組

According to popular folklore, many animals are smarter than they appear. Dogs bark before earthquakes; cattle predict rainfall by sitting on the ground. But cattle may have another hidden talent in telling which way is north.

Small animals such as mole rats living underground are known for the use of magnetism to navigate. Dr. Begall and her colleagues wanted to know whether larger mammals also have the ability to perceive magnetic fields. They investigated this possibility by studying images of thousands of cattle captured on Google Earth, a website that stitches together satellite photographs to produce an image of the Earth's surface.

Grazing animals are known to orient themselves in a way that minimizes wind chill from the north and maximizes the warmth of the sun when they are cold. The researchers therefore had to study a lot of cows grazing in lots of different places at different times of day, in order to average out these factors and see whether cattle could act like compass needles.

The researchers concluded that cattle do generally orient themselves in a north-south direction. This north-south preference has also been noted in flies, termites and honeybees. But unfortunately, even the high resolution of Google Earth is not powerful enough to tell which end of the cow is its head, and which its tail. The researchers were therefore unable to answer their research questions of whether cattle prefer to look north or south, and whether that differs in the northern and southern hemispheres.

49. What is the article mainly about?
   (A) The usefulness of Google Earth.
   (B) Whether cattle are superior to other animals.
   (C) Animals' sensitivity to natural disasters.
   (D) Whether cattle behave like compass needles.

50. Which of the following factors might affect Dr. Begall's research result?
   (A) Rainfall.　(B) Earthquakes.　(C) Location.　(D) Cost.

51. What is the major finding of Dr. Begall's study?
   (A) Cattle point north-south.
   (B) Magnetism can't be studied scientifically.
   (C) Animals prefer to look south.
   (D) Google Earth is a reliable research tool.

52. Why couldn't the researchers get the answer to their research
    questions?

    (A) Many cattle in their study were sitting on the ground.

    (B) The cattle constantly change directions to avoid wind chill.

    (C) There is magnetic difference between the two hemispheres.

    (D) They couldn't tell a cow's head from its tail in the satellite
        pictures.

53-56 為題組

Children normally have a distrust of new foods. But it's the parents'
job to serve a variety of foods and expose their children to healthy dieting
habits.

Some simple strategies can help even the pickiest eater learn to like
a more varied diet. First of all, you don't have to send children out of
the kitchen. With hot stoves, boiling water and sharp knives at hand, it
is understandable that parents don't want children in the kitchen when
they're making dinner. But studies suggest that involving children in
meal preparation is an important first step in getting them to try new
foods. In one study, nearly 600 children from kindergarten to sixth
grade took part in a nutrition curriculum intended to get them to eat
more vegetables and whole grains. The researchers found that children
who had cooked their own foods were more likely to eat those foods in
the cafeteria than children who had not. Kids don't usually like
radishes, but if kids cut them up and put them in the salad, they will
love the dish.

Another strategy is not to diet in front of your children. Kids are tuned into their parents' eating preferences and are far more likely to try foods if they see their mother or father eating them. Given this powerful effect, parents who are trying to lose weight should be careful of how their dieting habits can influence a child's perceptions about food and healthful eating. In one study of 5-year-old girls about dieting, one child noted that dieting involved drinking chocolate milkshakes, because her mother was using Slim-Fast drinks. Another child said dieting meant "you fix food but you don't eat it." By exposing young children to **erratic** dieting habits, parents may be putting them at risk for eating disorders.

53. What is the main purpose of this article?
    (A) To explain what causes children's eating disorder.
    (B) To teach children about the meal preparation process.
    (C) To advocate the importance of vegetables and whole grains.
    (D) To inform parents how they can help their children like varied foods.

54. Which of the following groups will eat more balanced meals?
    (A) The children who help cook food.
    (B) The children whose parents are on a diet.
    (C) The children who do not love radishes.
    (D) The children whose parents work in a cafeteria.

55. What does **erratic** in the last sentence imply?
    (A) Obvious.   (B) Healthful.
    (C) Dishonest.   (D) Inappropriate.

56. Which of the following is true about Slim-Fast?

   (A) It is children's favorite food.

   (B) It looks like a chocolate milkshake.

   (C) It contains a variety of vegetables.

   (D) It is intended for slim, fast people.

第貳部份：非選擇題（佔 28 分）

一、翻譯題（佔 8 分）

說明：1. 請將以下兩題中文譯成正確而通順達意的英文，並將答案寫在「答案卷」上。

　　　2. 請依序作答，並標明題號。每題僅能譯成一個英文句子。每題 4 分，共 8 分。

1. 大部分學生不習慣自己解決問題，他們總是期待老師提供標準答案。

2. 除了用功讀書獲取知識外，學生也應該培養獨立思考的能力。

二、英文作文（佔 20 分）

說明：1. 依提示在「答案卷」上寫一篇英文作文。

　　　2. 文長 120 個單詞（words）左右。

提示：

請根據右方圖片的場景，描述整個事件發生的前因後果。文章請分兩段，第一段說明之前發生了什麼事情，並根據圖片內容描述現在的狀況；第二段請合理說明接下來可能會發生什麼事，或者未來該做些什麼。

98年度學科能力測驗英文科試題詳解

第壹部分：單選題

一、詞彙：

1. (**B**) Steve's description of the place was so <u>vivid</u> that I could almost picture it in my mind.

史蒂夫對這個地方的描述很<u>生動</u>，以致於我幾乎能在腦海中想像。

(A) bitter ('bɪtɚ) *adj.* 苦的

(B) *vivid* ('vɪvɪd) *adj.* 生動的

(C) sensitive ('sɛnsətɪv) *adj.* 敏感的

(D) courageous (kə'redʒəs) *adj.* 勇敢的

description (dɪ'skrɪpʃən) *n.* 描述   picture ('pɪktʃɚ) *v.* 想像

2. (**B**) When people feel uncomfortable or nervous, they may <u>fold</u> their arms across their chests as if to protect themselves.

當人覺得不舒服或緊張時，可能會將雙臂<u>交叉</u>在胸前，就好像在保護自己。

(A) toss (tɔs) *v.* 投擲   (B) *fold* (fold) *v.* 交叉

(C) veil (vel) *v.* 以面紗罩住   (D) yield (jild) *v.* 生產；屈服

nervous ('nɜvəs) *adj.* 緊張的   chest (tʃɛst) *n.* 胸部   *as if* 好像

3. (**C**) The doors of these department stores slide open <u>automatically</u> when you approach them. You don't have to open them yourself.

當你走近這些百貨公司的門時，它們會<u>自動</u>滑開。你不必自己打開它們。

(A) necessarily ('nɛsə,sɛrəlɪ) *adv.* 必定

(B) diligently ('dɪlədʒəntlɪ) *adv.* 勤勉地

(C) *automatically* (,ɔtə'mætɪkl̩ɪ) *adv.* 自動地

(D) intentionally (ɪn'tɛnʃənlɪ) *adv.* 故意地

slide (slaɪd) *v.* 滑   approach (ə'protʃ) *v.* 接近；走近

4. (**D**) Nicole is a <u>brilliant</u> language learner. Within a short period of time, she has developed a good command of Chinese and Japanese.
妮可是一個<u>聰明的</u>語言學習者。在短時間內,她已能精通中文和日文。

    (A) convenient (kən'vinjənt) *adj.* 方便的

    (B) popular ('pɑpjələ) *adj.* 受歡迎的

    (C) regular ('rɛgjələ) *adj.* 規律的

    (D) ***brilliant*** ('brɪljənt) *adj.* 聰明的

period ('pɪrɪəd) *n.* 期間   develop (dɪ'vɛləp) *v.* 培養
command (kə'mænd) *n.* 運用自如的能力
have a good command of 精通

5. (**D**) With rising oil prices, there is an increasing <u>tendency</u> for people to ride bicycles to work.
由於油價上漲,所以大家騎腳踏車上班的<u>趨勢</u>也增加了。

    (A) permit ('pɜmɪt) *n.* 許可證

    (B) instrument ('ɪnstrəmənt) *n.* 儀器;樂器

    (C) appearance (ə'pɪrəns) *n.* 外表

    (D) ***tendency*** ('tɛndənsɪ) *n.* 趨勢;傾向

rising ('raɪzɪŋ) *adj.* 上漲的

6. (**A**) This information came from a very <u>reliable</u> source, so you don't have to worry about being cheated.
這個消息來源很<u>可靠</u>,所以你不必擔心被騙。

    (A) ***reliable*** (rɪ'laɪəbḷ) *adj.* 可靠的

    (B) flexible ('flɛksəbḷ) *adj.* 有彈性的

    (C) clumsy ('klʌmzɪ) *adj.* 笨拙的   (D) brutal ('brutḷ) *adj.* 殘忍的

source (sors) *n.* 來源   cheat (tʃit) *v.* 欺騙

7. (**B**) We hope that there will be no war in the world and that all people live in peace and <u>harmony</u> with each other.
我們希望世界上沒有戰爭,所有人可以和平而<u>且和諧</u>地相處。

    (A) complaint (kəm'plent) *n.* 抱怨   (B) ***harmony*** ('hɑrmənɪ) *n.* 和諧

    (C) mission ('mɪʃən) *n.* 任務   (D) texture ('tɛkstʃə) *n.* 質地

peace (pis) *n.* 和平

8. (**B**) To have a full discussion of the issue, the committee spent a whole
hour <u>exchanging</u> their ideas at the meeting.

為了充分討論這個議題，委員會在會議中花了一整個小時<u>交換</u>他們
的想法。

(A) deposit〔dɪ'pɑzɪt〕v. 存（款）

(B) *exchange*〔ɪks'tʃendʒ〕v. 交換

(C) govern〔'gʌvən〕v. 統治　(D) interrupt〔͵ɪntə'rʌpt〕v. 打斷

issue〔'ɪʃu〕n. 議題　committee〔kə'mɪtɪ〕n. 委員會

meeting〔'mitɪŋ〕n. 會議

9. (**C**) While adapting to western ways of living, many Asian immigrants
in the US still try hard to <u>preserve</u> their own cultures and
traditions. 在適應西方生活方式的同時，很多在美國的亞洲移民，
依然很努力地想<u>保存</u>自己的文化及傳統。

(A) volunteer〔͵vɑlən'tɪr〕v. 自願從事

(B) scatter〔'skætə〕v. 散播　(C) *preserve*〔prɪ'zɝv〕v. 保存

(D) motivate〔'motə͵vet〕v. 激勵

adapt to 適應　western〔'wɛstən〕adj. 西方的

Asian〔'eʃən〕adj. 亞洲的　immigrant〔'ɪməgrənt〕n. 移民

culture〔'kʌltʃə〕n. 文化　tradition〔trə'dɪʃən〕n. 傳統

10. (**A**) With the worsening of global economic conditions, it seems wiser
and more <u>sensible</u> to keep cash in the bank rather than to invest
in the stock market.

隨著全球經濟情況的惡化，把現金存在銀行而非投資股票市場，
似乎是比較<u>明智的</u>。

(A) *sensible*〔'sɛnsəbḷ〕adj. 明智的

(B) portable〔'portəbḷ〕adj. 可攜帶的

(C) explicit〔ɪk'splɪsɪt〕adj. 明白的；清晰的

(D) anxious〔'æŋkʃəs〕adj. 焦慮的

worsen〔'wɝsṇ〕v. 使惡化　global〔'globḷ〕adj. 全球的

economic〔͵ikə'nɑmɪk〕adj. 經濟的　*rather than* 而不是

invest〔ɪn'vɛst〕v. 投資　*stock market* 股票市場

11. (**D**) Under the <u>leadership</u> of newly elected president Barack Obama,
the US is expected to turn a new page in politics and economy.
在新當選的總統巴拉克・歐巴馬的<u>領導</u>之下，一般預料美國會在
政治及經濟上，開啓嶄新的一頁。

(A) adoption (ə'dapʃən) *n.* 採用；領養
(B) fragrance ('fregrəns) *n.* 芳香
(C) identity (aɪ'dɛntətɪ) *n.* 身分
(D) ***leadership*** ('lidɚ,ʃɪp) *n.* 領導

newly ('njulɪ) *adv.* 最近；新近　　elect (ɪ'lɛkt) *v.* 選舉
turn (tɜn) *v.* 翻（頁）　　politics ('palə,tɪks) *n.* 政治
economy (ɪ'kanəmɪ) *n.* 經濟

12. (**D**) Rapid advancement in motor engineering makes it <u>technically</u>
possible to build a flying car in the near future.
在汽車工程上的迅速進步，使得在不久的將來，在<u>技術上</u>可能能
夠建造可以飛行的汽車。

(A) individually (,ɪndə'vɪdʒʊəlɪ) *adv.* 個別地
(B) narrowly ('nærolɪ) *adv.* 勉強地；狹窄地
(C) punctually ('pʌŋktʃʊəlɪ) *adv.* 準時地
(D) ***technically*** ('tɛknɪkḷɪ) *adv.* 技術上

rapid ('ræpɪd) *adj.* 快速的
advancement (əd'vænsmənt) *n.* 進步
motor ('motɚ) *adj.* 汽車的
engineering (,ɛndʒə'nɪrɪŋ) *n.* 工程學
flying ('flaɪɪŋ) *adj.* 會飛的

13. (**C**) When you take photos, you can move around to shoot the target
object from different <u>angles</u>.
當你在拍照的時候，可以四處移動，從不同的<u>角度</u>來拍攝目標物。

(A) mood (mud) *n.* 心情　　(B) trend (trɛnd) *n.* 趨勢
(C) ***angle*** ('æŋgḷ) *n.* 角度　　(D) input ('ɪn,pʊt) *n.* 輸入

take photos 拍照　　shoot (ʃut) *v.* 拍攝
target ('targɪt) *n.* 目標　　object ('abdʒɪkt) *n.* 物體；對象

14. (**A**) Students were asked to <u>revise</u> or rewrite their compositions based on the teacher's comments.

學生被要求根據老師的評論，來<u>修正</u>或重寫他們的作文。

(A) *revise* (rɪ'vaɪz) *v.* 修正；改正

(B) resign (rɪ'zaɪn) *v.* 辭職

(C) refresh (rɪ'frɛʃ) *v.* 使恢復精神

(D) remind (rɪ'maɪnd) *v.* 提醒

rewrite (ri'raɪt) *v.* 重寫　　composition (ˌkɑmpə'zɪʃən) *n.* 作文

based on 根據　　comment ('kɑmɛnt) *n.* 評論

15. (**C**) Besides lung cancer, another <u>consequence</u> of smoking is wrinkles, a premature sign of aging.

除了肺癌之外，另一項吸煙的<u>後果</u>就是皺紋，這是一種提早老化的徵兆。

(A) blessing ('blɛsɪŋ) *n.* 幸福

(B) campaign (kæm'pen) *n.* 宣傳活動

(C) *consequence* ('kɑnsəˌkwɛns) *n.* 後果

(D) breakthrough ('brekˌθru) *n.* 突破

lung cancer 肺癌　　wrinkle ('rɪŋkl̩) *n.* 皺紋

premature (ˌprimə'tjur) *adj.* 過早的

sign (saɪn) *n.* 徵兆　　aging ('edʒɪŋ) *n.* 老化

二、綜合測驗：

　　Art Fry was a researcher in the 3M Company. He was bothered by a small irritation every Sunday as he sang in the church choir. That is, after he <u>marked</u> his pages in the hymn book with small bits of paper, the
　　　　16
small pieces would invariably fall out all over the floor. One day, an idea <u>occurred to</u> Art Fry.
　17

　　雅特・富萊是 3M 公司的研究員。他每週日在教會唱詩班唱聖歌時，都會受到一件小事情的困擾。那就是，他用小紙片在歌本中標示頁數之後，這些小紙片必定會掉出來，掉得滿地都是。有一天，雅特・富萊想到了一個主意。

> researcher (rɪˈsɝtʃə) *n.* 研究員；調查員
> bother (ˈbɑðə) *v.* 困擾；煩惱 (= *trouble*)
> irritation (ˌɪrəˈteʃən) *n.* 令人煩躁的事物 (= *annoyance* ; *nuisance*)
> choir (kwaɪr) *n.* 唱詩班　　*that is* 也就是 (= *namely*)
> hymn (hɪm) *n.* 讚美詩；聖歌　　bit (bɪt) *n.* 一小片
> invariably (ɪnˈvɛrɪəblɪ) *adv.* 不變地；必定 (= *always*)
> *fall out* 掉落外面　　*all over* 到處　　floor (flor) *n.* 地板

16. (**A**) 依句意，他用小紙片「標示」頁數，故本題選 (A) *marked*「做記號；標示」。(B) tear「撕毀；撕破」，(C) serve「服務」，(D) take「帶走」，均不合句意。

17. (**B**) *sth.* ***occur to*** *sb.* 某人想到某事【以事物爲主詞】
   = *sth.* ***strike*** *sb.*【83 年學測考過】
   (A) throw　*v.* 投擲【通常以人爲主詞，「對準~」丟，介系詞用 at】
   (C) look down upon　輕視
   (D) *sb.* come up with *sth.* 想到【以人爲主詞】

He remembered a kind of glue developed by a colleague that everyone
thought <u>was</u> a failure because it did not stick very well.　He then coated the
　　　　18
glue on a paper sample and found that it was not only a good bookmark, but
it was great for writing notes.　It would stay in place <u>as long as</u> you wanted
　　　　　　　　　　　　　　　　　　　　　　　　　　19
it to.　Then you could remove it <u>without</u> damage.　The resulting product
　　　　　　　　　　　　　　　20
was called the Post-it, one of 3M's most successful office products.
他記得一位同事曾經研發出一種黏膠，每個人都覺得很失敗，因爲黏不牢。後來，他把那種黏膠塗在一張樣品紙上，發現這樣不只是很棒的書籤，當便條紙也很方便。紙條可以黏在你想要的地方，想黏多久就黏多久。然後你把它撕下來也不會有損傷。這樣子而產生的產品被稱爲「便利貼」，是 3M 最成功的辦公室產品之一。

> glue (glu) *n.* 黏膠　　develop (dɪˈvɛləp) *v.* 研發
> colleague (ˈkɑlig) *n.* 同事 (= *coworker*)
> failure (ˈfeljə) *n.* 失敗品　　stick (stɪk) *v.* 黏貼

coat〔kot〕v. 塗在～上　　sample〔'sæmpl〕n. 樣品
bookmark〔'buk,mark〕n. 書籤　　note〔not〕n. 便條；紙條
stay〔ste〕v. 保持　　*in place* 在正確的位置；在適當的位置
remove〔rɪ'muv〕v. 除去　　damage〔'dæmɪdʒ〕n. 損害
resulting〔rɪ'zʌltɪŋ〕adj. 因而產生的（= *consequent*）
product〔'pradəkt , 'pradʌkt〕n. 產品　　post〔post〕v. 張貼

18. (**B**) that everyone thought…a failure 是形容詞子句，修飾先行詞 glue，
子句中 that 為關代，代替 glue，everyone thought 為插入語，空格
中缺動詞，且依事實為過去式，故選 (B) *was*。

19. (**C**) 依句意，你想要紙條黏多久，它就黏多久，選 (C) *as long as*「和～
一樣久」【也可作「只要」解，93 年學測考過】。而 (A) despite〔dɪ'spaɪt〕
prep. 儘管，為介系詞，不可加連接詞 that，(B) rather than「而非」，
(D) no matter what「無論什麼」，均不合句意。

20. (**D**) 依句意，撕下來「沒有」損傷，選 (D) *without*。

　　The pineapple, long a symbol of Hawaii, was not a native plant.
<u>In fact</u>, pineapples did not appear there until 1813.　The pineapple was
　　21
<u>originally</u> found in Paraguay and in the southern part of Brazil.　Natives
　22
planted the fruit across South and Central America and in the Caribbean
region, <u>where</u> Christopher Columbus first found it.
　　　　23
　　長久以來鳳梨都是夏威夷的象徵，但它並非夏威夷土生土長的植物。事實
上，直到 1813 年鳳梨才出現在那裡。鳳梨最初是在巴拉圭和巴西南部被發現
的。當地人種植鳳梨，遍及中南美洲和加勒比海地區，哥倫布初次發現鳳梨，
就是在那裡。

　　　pineapple〔'paɪn,æpl〕n. 鳳梨　　symbol〔'sɪmbl〕n. 象徵
　　　Hawaii〔hə'waɪjə , hə'wajə〕n. 夏威夷【夏威夷州的首府為火奴魯魯
　　　（Honolulu〔,hanə'lulə , ,hanə'lulu〕），又名檀香山】

native (ˈnetɪv) *adj.* 本土的；土產的　*n.* 當地人；原住民

Paraguay (ˈpærə,gwe) *n.* 巴拉圭【南美中部內陸國家，首都為亞森松

　(Asuncion (,ɑsun'sjon))】　　southern (ˈsʌðən) *adj.* 南方的

Brazil (brəˈzɪl) *n.* 巴西【南美洲最大的國家，首都為巴西利亞

　(Brasilia (brəˈzɪljə))】　　across (əˈkrɔs) *prep.* 橫越

South America 南美洲　　***Central America*** 中美洲

Caribbean (,kærəˈbiən , kəˈrɪbjən) *adj.* 加勒比海的【在中美、南美

　和西印度群島之間的海域】　　region (ˈridʒən) *n.* 地區

Christopher Columbus 哥倫布【1451-1506，中世紀義大利航海家，

　在 1492 年發現美洲新大陸】

21. (**B**) (A) for example　例如

　　　(B) ***in fact*** 事實上【91、95 年指考考過】

　　　(C) as a result　因此

　　　(D) little by little　逐漸地

22. (**C**) (A) nearly (ˈnɪrlɪ) *adv.* 將近；幾乎

　　　(B) recently (ˈrisn̩tlɪ) *adv.* 最近

　　　(C) ***originally*** (əˈrɪdʒənlɪ) *adv.* 最初地【95 學測考過】

　　　(D) shortly (ˈʃɔrtlɪ) *adv.* 不久

23. (**D**) 前後二句話之間缺少連接詞和副詞，故空格應填入關係副詞，表示

　　　地方，選 (D) ***where***。【常考，83、89、92 學測，93、94 指考考過】

Columbus brought it, along with many other new things, back to Europe
with him.　From there, the tasty fruit <u>spread</u> throughout other parts of
　　　　　　　　　　　　　　　　　　24
civilization.　It was carried on sailing ships around the world because it
was found to help prevent scurvy, a disease that often <u>bothered</u> sailors on
　　　　　　　　　　　　　　　　　　　　　　　　　　　　25
long voyages.　It was at the end of one of these long voyages that the
pineapple came to Hawaii to stay.

哥倫布帶著它，以及其他許多新的東西，回到了歐洲。從那裡，這種美味的水果傳遍了文明世界的其他地區。鳳梨被大帆船載到世界各地，因爲它被發現有助於避免壞血病，這種疾病在長途旅行中經常困擾著船員。就在這些長途旅行結束後，鳳梨來到了夏威夷，就生存下來了。

> ***along with*** 以及　　tasty（'testɪ）*adj.* 好吃的
> throughout（θruˋaʊt）*prep.* 遍及（= *all over*）
> civilization（ˌsɪvḷaɪˋzeʃən）*n.* 文明；文明世界
> ***sailing ship*** 大帆船　　prevent（prɪˋvɛnt）*v.* 避免；預防
> scurvy（'skɝvɪ）*n.* 壞血病【因缺乏維他命 C 而導致的疾病】
> disease（dɪˋziz）*n.* 疾病　　sailor（'selɚ）*n.* 水手；船員
> voyage（'vɔɪˑɪdʒ）*n.* 旅程（= *journey*）
> end（ɛnd）*n.* 結束　　***at the end of*** ~ 在~結束時

24. (**A**) 空格之前 the tasty fruit 爲主詞，故空格應填入動詞，根據事實，時態應爲過去式，故本題選 (A) ***spread*** 「傳播；散播」。

25. (**A**) (A) ***bother***（'bɑðɚ）*v.* 困擾；煩惱
　　　(B) contact（'kɑntækt）*v.* 聯絡
　　　(C) suffer（'sʌfɚ）*v.* 遭受；受苦【主詞通常爲人】
　　　(D) wound（wund）*v.* 傷害【一般指「武器」傷害人，不用於疾病】

　　The Paralympics are Olympic-style games for athletes with a disability. They were organized for the first time in Rome in 1960. In Toronto in 1976, the idea of putting together different disability groups <u>for</u> sports competitions
26
was born.
　　殘障奧運會是奧運形式的比賽，是給殘障運動員參加的。殘障運動會第一次是在 1960 年，於羅馬舉辦。1976 年，在多倫多，開始有了將不同的殘障團體聚集起來參加運動比賽的想法。

> Paralympics（ˌpærəˋlɪmpɪks）*n.* 殘障奧運會（= *Paralympic Games*）
> 【Para (plegic)（下身麻痹的）+ (O)lympics（奧運會）】

Olympic (o'lɪmpɪk) *adj.* 奧運會的　　game (gem) *n.* 比賽
athlete ('æθlit) *n.* 運動員
disability (,dɪsə'bɪlətɪ) *n.* 無能力；殘障
organize ('ɔrgən,aɪz) *v.* 籌畫；舉辦　　***for the first time*** 第一次
Rome (rom) *n.* 羅馬　　Toronto (tə'rɑnto) *n.* 多倫多
put together 使集合　　sports (sports) *adj.* 運動的
competition (,kɑmpə'tɪʃən) *n.* 競爭；比賽

26. (**A**) 依句意，「爲了」參加運動比賽，介系詞用 *for*，選 (A)。

Today, the Paralympics are sports events for athletes from six different
disability groups. They emphasize the participants' athletic achievements
<u>instead of</u> their physical disability. The games have grown in size gradually.
　27
The number of athletes <u>participating</u> in the Summer Paralympic Games has
　　　　　　　　　　　　28
increased from 400 athletes from 23 countries in 1960 to 3,806 athletes
from 136 countries in 2004.

現在，殘障奧運會，是給來自六個不同殘障團體的運動員參加的。他們強調的
是參賽者的體育成績，而不是他們身體的殘障。這些比賽的規模逐漸擴大。參
加夏季殘障奧運會的人數，已經從 1960 年的 23 國，400 名運動員，增加到 2004
年的 136 國，3,806 人。

sports events 運動競賽項目
emphasize ('ɛmfə,saɪz) *v.* 強調
participant (pə'tɪsəpənt) *n.* 參加者
athletic (æθ'lɛtɪk) *adj.* 運動競賽的；體育的
achievements (ə'tʃivmənts) *n. pl.* 成就
physical ('fɪzɪkl̩) *adj.* 身體的
grow (gro) *v.* 增大　　size (saɪz) *n.* 大小；規模
gradually ('grædʒʊəlɪ) *adv.* 逐漸地
number ('nʌmbɚ) *n.* 人數　　increase (ɪn'kris) *v.* 增加

27. (**B**) 依句意，選 (B) *instead of*「而不是」。而 (A) in terms of「以～觀點；就～而言」，(C) at the risk of「冒～危險」，(D) at the cost of「以～爲代價」，均不合句意。

28. (**C**) 原句爲：The number of athletes <u>who participate</u> in...，關代 who 可省略，並須將動詞 participate 改成現在分詞 *participating*，故選 (C)。　　participate〔par'tɪsə,pet〕v. 參加
【這種類似的題目，從 93 年到 98 年已經連考了 6 年，可參考「文法寶典」p.457】

The Paralympic Games have always been held in the same year as the Olympic Games. Since the Seoul 1988 Paralympic Games and the Albertville 1992 Winter Paralympic Games, they have also <u>taken place</u> in the same city
29
as the Olympics. On June 19, 2001, an agreement was signed between the International Olympic Committee and the International Paralympics Committee to keep this <u>practice</u> in the future. From the 2012 bid onwards,
30
the city chosen to host the Olympic Games will also host the Paralympics.

殘障奧運會一直是和奧運會在同一年舉行。自從 1988 年漢城殘障奧運會及 1992 年阿爾伯特維爾的多季殘障奧運會以來，都是和奧運會在同一個城市舉辦。在 2001 年 6 月 19 日，國際奧委會和國際殘障奧委會之間已經簽定協議，以後要持續這樣做。自從大家爭取主辦 2012 年奧運會以來，獲選主辦奧運會的城市，也將主辦殘障奧運會。

hold〔hold〕v. 舉行　　Seoul〔sol〕n. 首爾【韓國首都】
Albertville〔ˈælbɚtˈvɪl〕n. 阿爾伯特維爾【位於剛果】
agreement〔əˈgrimənt〕n. 協議　　sign〔saɪn〕v. 簽名於；簽署
committee〔kəˈmɪtɪ〕n. 委員會
bid〔bɪd〕n. 出價；投標；努力爭取
onwards〔ˈɑnwɚdz〕adv. 向前；向前進（= *onward*）
from ~ onwards 從～以後　　host〔host〕v. 主辦

29. (**B**) 依句意，選 (B) *take place*「舉行」【96年指考考過】。而 (A) take turns 「輪流」，(C) take off「脫掉；起飛」，(D) take over「接管」，均不 合句意。

30. (**D**) 依句意，「要繼續這樣做」，也就是要持續這種「做法」，選 (D) *practice* 「習俗；做法」【89年學測也考過，作「(醫師的)業務」解，】。而 (A) piece「一件；一片」，(B) deadline ('dɛd,laɪn) *n.* 截止日期，(C) date 「日期；約會」，均不合句意。

三、文意選填：

　　Familiar fables can be narrated differently or extended in interesting and humorous ways. The end of the famous fable of "The Tortoise and the Hare" is well known to all: the tortoise wins the race against the hare. The moral lesson is that slow and steady wins the race. We all have grown up with this popular version, but the [31](I) same fable can be extended with different twists.

　　耳熟能詳的寓言故事，可以用不同的方式來闡述，或者用有趣而詼諧的方式來作延伸。「龜兔賽跑」這則有名的寓言故事，大家都非常清楚它的結局：烏龜跑贏了兔子。它在道德上的教訓是，緩慢與穩健才能贏得比賽。我們都是聽這個大眾化的版本長大的，然而同樣的寓言可以延伸出不同的意外發展。

> fable ('febḷ) *n.* 寓言　　narrate (næ'ret) *v.* 敘述
> extend (ɪk'stɛnd) *v.* 延伸　　humorous ('hjumərəs) *adj.* 幽默的
> tortoise ('tɔrtəs) *n.* 烏龜　　hare (hɛr) *n.* 野兔
> race (res) *n.* 賽跑　　moral ('mɔrəl) *adj.* 道德上的　*n.* 寓意
> steady ('stɛdɪ) *adj.* 穩定的；踏實的
> *grow up* 成長　　popular ('pɑpjələ) *adj.* 大眾化的
> version ('vɝʒən) *n.* 版本
> twist (twɪst) *n.* 意外發展；意外轉折

　　At the request of the hare, a second race is [32](A) arranged and this time, the hare runs without taking a rest and wins. The moral lesson is that [33](E) fast and consistent will always beat slow and steady.　Then it is the tortoise that [34](B) challenges the hare to a third race along a different route in which there is a river just before the final destination.　This time, the tortoise wins the race because the hare cannot swim.　The moral lesson is "First [35](G) identify your strengths, and then change the playing field to suit them."

在兔子的要求下，他們安排了第二次賽跑，而這次，兔子完全沒有休息地跑完並且贏了。這次的道德教訓是，迅速且一致，永遠勝過緩慢與穩健。接著，換烏龜向兔子挑戰第三次的賽跑，這次的路線不同，在終點前有一條河流。這次，烏龜贏了賽跑，因為兔子不會游泳。而道德教訓是，「先分析出你的優勢，再依你的優勢來變更適合的比賽場地。」

> ***at the request of*** 在～的要求下　　arrange〔əˋrendʒ〕*v.* 安排
> ***take a rest*** 休息　　consistent〔kənˋsɪstənt〕*adj.* 始終如一的
> beat〔bit〕*v.* 擊敗　　challenge〔ˋtʃælɪndʒ〕*v.* 向…挑戰
> route〔rut , raʊt〕*n.* 路線　　destination〔͵dɛstəˋneʃən〕*n.* 目的地
> ***final destination*** 終點　　identify〔aɪˋdɛntə͵faɪ〕*v.* 確認；分辨
> strength〔strɛŋθ〕*n.* 優勢；長處
> ***playing field*** 遊戲場；操場　　suit〔sut〕*v.* 使合適

But the story continues.　Both [36](C) competitors know their own drawbacks and limitations very well; therefore, they jointly decide to have one last race—not to decide who the winner or loser is, but just for their own pleasure and satisfaction.　The two [37](D) cooperate as a team.　Firstly, the hare carries the tortoise on its back to the river.　Then, the tortoise carries the hare and swims to the [38](H) opposite bank of the river.　Lastly, the hare carries the tortoise again on its back.　Thus they reach the [39](F) finishing line together.

　　然而故事還沒結束。雙方對手都非常明白自己的短處和侷限；因此，他們共同決定舉行最後一次賽跑——並非要分出誰輸誰贏，只是他們自己覺得好玩有趣。他們兩人一組協力合作。首先，兔子將烏龜背在背上跑到河邊。然後，烏龜背著兔子游到河的對岸。最後，兔子再將烏龜背回背上。就這樣，他們一起抵達終點線。

competitor〔kəm'pɛtətə〕n. 對手

drawback〔'drɔ,bæk〕n. 劣勢；短處

limitation〔,lɪmə'teʃən〕n. 限度；侷限

jointly〔'dʒɔɪntlɪ〕adv. 共同地　　winner〔'wɪnə〕n. 優勝者

loser〔'luzə〕n. 失敗者　　pleasure〔'plɛʒə〕n. 樂趣

satisfaction〔,sætɪs'fækʃən〕n. 樂趣；愉快

cooperate〔ko'ɑpə,ret〕v. 合作

firstly〔'fɜstlɪ〕adv. 首先　　opposite〔'ɑpəzɪt〕adj. 對面的

bank〔bæŋk〕n. 岸　　lastly〔'læstlɪ〕adv. 最後

thus〔ðʌs〕adv. 如此；以此方式　　*finishing line* 終點線

Overall, many moral lessons from the last match are highlighted. The most obvious one is the importance of [40](J) teamwork. Another moral which also means a great deal is "competition against situations rather than against rivals."

整體而言，最後一場比賽中，有很多被人所強調的道德教訓。最明顯的一個，就是團隊合作的重要性。另一個也非常重要的寓意則是，「要與情勢競爭，而非對手。」

overall〔'ovə,ɔl〕adv. 大體上

match〔mætʃ〕n. 比賽　　highlight〔'haɪ,laɪt〕v. 強調

obvious〔'ɑbvɪəs〕adj. 明顯的

teamwork〔'tim,wɜk〕n. 協調合作

a great deal 非常　　competition〔,kɑmpə'tɪʃən〕n. 競爭

rather than 而不是　　rival〔'raɪvl̩〕n. 敵手

四、閱讀測驗：

41-44 為題組

To Whom It May Concern:

　　Your address was forwarded to us by Why Bother Magazine. All of us here think The International Institute of Not Doing Much is the best organization in the world. You know how to avoid unnecessary activities!

敬啓者：

　　你的地址是由「何必煩惱雜誌」轉寄給我們的。我們這裡的所有人都認爲「做得不多國際協會」是世界上最好的組織。你們知道如何避免不必要的活動！

concern〔 kən'sɜn 〕v. 與…有關
to whom it may concern 敬啓者（用作正式信件的開頭）
address〔 ə'drɛs 〕n. 地址　　forward〔'fɔrwəd 〕v. 轉寄
bother〔'baðə 〕v. 煩惱　　international〔,ɪntə'næʃənḷ 〕adj. 國際的
institute〔'ɪnstə,tut 〕n. 協會
organization〔,ɔrgənə'zeʃən 〕n. 組織　　avoid〔 ə'vɔɪd 〕v. 避免
unnecessary〔 ʌn'nɛsə,sɛrɪ 〕adj. 不必要的
activity〔 æk'tɪvətɪ 〕n. 活動

We closely followed the advice in your article. First, we replaced all our telephones with carrier pigeons. Simply removing the jingle of telephones and replacing them with the pleasant sounds of birds has had a remarkable effect on everyone. Besides, birds are cheaper than telephone service. After all, we are a business. We have to think of the bottom line. As a side benefit, the birds also fertilize the lawn outside the new employee sauna.

　　我們非常仔細地遵循你們文章中的建議。首先，我們用信鴿取代我們所有的電話。僅僅用鳥類美妙的聲音代替，除去電話的鈴響聲，就給予我們每個人驚人的影響。此外，鳥比電話服務便宜。畢竟，我們是做生意的。我們必須考慮到收益。鳥類還有另一個好處，牠們還可以使新蓋好的員工三溫暖外面的草地肥沃。

closely〔'klɔslɪ 〕adv. 仔細地　　advice〔 əd'vaɪs 〕n. 建議
article〔'artɪkḷ 〕n. 文章　　replace〔 rɪ'ples 〕v. 取代
carrier〔'kærɪə 〕n. 信差　　pigeon〔'pɪdʒɪn 〕n. 鴿子
carrier pigeon 信鴿　　simply〔'sɪmplɪ 〕adv. 僅僅；只是
remove〔 rɪ'muv 〕v. 除去　　jingle〔'dʒɪŋgḷ 〕n. 叮噹聲；鈴響聲
pleasant〔'plɛzn̩t 〕adj. 令人愉快的
remarkable〔 rɪ'markəbḷ 〕adj. 驚人的

effect〔ɪ'fɛkt〕n. 影響　　**after all** 畢竟
bottom〔'bɑtəm〕n. 底部　　***bottom line*** 帳本底線；純收益
side〔saɪd〕adj. 附加的　　benefit〔'bɛnəfɪt〕n. 利益；好處
fertilize〔'fɝtḷ,aɪz〕v. 使肥沃　　lawn〔lɔn〕n. 草地
employee〔,ɛmplɔɪ'i〕n. 員工；受雇者
sauna〔'saʊnə〕n. 三溫暖澡堂

Next, we sold the computers off to Stab, Grab, Grit, and Nasty, a firm of lawyers nearby. Our electricity bill went way down. Big savings! The boss is impressed. We have completely embraced paper technology. Now that we all use pencils, doodling is on the increase, and the quality of pencilwomanship is impressive, as you can tell from my handwriting in this letter. By the way, if you can, please send this letter back to us. We can erase and reuse it. Just tie it to ***Maggie***'s leg and she'll know where to take it.

　　其次，我們廉價出售電腦給「刺傷、搶奪、砂礫和討人厭」，這是一間附近的法律事務所。我們的電費帳單減少很多。老闆很感動。我們完全採用紙張科技。由於我們全部都使用鉛筆，所以有愈來愈多人在胡亂塗寫，這種與一般不同的字跡品質，十分令人印象深刻，你可以從這封信中看得出來我的筆跡。順便一提，如果可以的話，請你把這封信寄還給我們。我們可以把這封信擦掉，然後再重新使用。只要把這封信綁在**瑪姬**的腿上，她知道要帶去哪裡。

sell off 廉售　　stab〔stæb〕n. 刺傷
grab〔græb〕n. 搶奪　　grit〔grɪt〕n. 砂礫
nasty〔'næstɪ〕n. 討人厭的東西
firm〔fɝm〕n. 公司；商行　　lawyer〔'lɔjə〕n. 律師
firm of lawyers 法律事務所（ = *law firm* ）
go down 下降；減少　　way〔we〕adv. 非常
saving〔'sevɪŋ〕n. 節省　　impressed〔ɪm'prɛst〕adj. 深受感動的
completely〔kəm'plitlɪ〕adv. 完全地　　embrace〔ɪm'bres〕v. 採用
technology〔tɛk'nɑlədʒɪ〕n. 科技　　***now that*** 由於
doodle〔'dudḷ〕v. 塗鴉；胡亂塗寫　　increase〔'ɪnkris〕n. 增加
on the increase 增加中　　quality〔'kwɑlətɪ〕n. 品質

pencilwomanship〔ˈpɛnslˈwumənˌʃɪp〕 *n.* 別於一般的字跡【字典上查不到這個字，在此是作者反諷寫法，原本的寫法是 penmanship〔ˈpɛnmənˌʃɪp〕 *n.* 筆跡；字跡】

impressive〔ɪmˈprɛsɪv〕 *adj.* 令人印象深刻的

handwriting〔ˈhændˌraɪtɪŋ〕 *n.* 筆跡　　***by the way*** 順便一提

erase〔ɪˈres〕 *v.* 擦掉　　reuse〔riˈjuz〕 *v.* 再使用

tie〔taɪ〕 *v.* 繫；綁

Now it's very calm and quiet here. You can notice the difference. No more loud chatter on the telephones! All we hear is the scratching of pencil on paper, the sound of pigeons, and the delivery of inter-office correspondence by paper airplane.

現在，這裡非常平靜和安靜。你會注意到不同之處。再也沒有講電話時的大聲喧嘩！所有我們聽到的只有紙上鉛筆劃寫的聲音、鴿子的聲音和部門之間互相用紙飛機通信的傳遞聲。

calm〔kɑm〕 *adj.* 平靜的　　notice〔ˈnotɪs〕 *v.* 注意

loud〔laʊd〕 *adj.* 大聲的　　chatter〔ˈtʃætɚ〕 *n.* 嘮叨

scratch〔skrætʃ〕 *v.* 潦草書寫　　delivery〔dɪˈlɪvərɪ〕 *n.* 傳遞

inter-office〔ˈɪntɚˌɔfɪs〕 *n.* 部門之間

correspondence〔ˌkɔrəˈspɑndəns〕 *n.* 通信

Wonderful! I've always wanted to work for an insurance company ever since I was a little girl. Now it's perfect.

>Sincerely yours,
>Eleanor Lightly
>Spokeswoman and Company Hair Stylist
>ABC Activity Insurance: Insure against overdoing it

太棒了！自從我是小女孩時，就一直想要在一家保險公司工作。現在，非常完美。

>艾麗娜‧萊特利　敬上
>發言人及公司的髮型設計師
>ABC 活動保險：保證避免做得過多

insurance (ɪnˈʃʊrəns) n. 保險　　sincerely (sɪnˈsɪrlɪ) adv. 誠摯地
spokeswoman (ˈspoksˌwʊmən) n. (女) 發言人
stylist (ˈstaɪlɪst) n. 設計師　　insure (ɪnˈʃʊr) v. 保證
overdo (ˈovəˈdu) v. 做得過多

41. (**A**) 下列何者最能描述作者所過的生活？
　　(A) 簡單、慢步調的<u>生活。</u>　　(B) 努力工作及有安全感的生活。
　　(C) 嚴謹、務農的生活。　　(D) 遠離紙和鉛筆的生活。

　　lead (lid) v. 過 (生活)　　slow-paced (ˈsloˌpest) adj. 慢步調的
　　security (sɪˈkjurətɪ) n. 安全 (感)
　　religious (rɪˈlɪdʒəs) adj. 虔誠的；嚴謹的
　　peasant (ˈpɛznt) n. 農夫

42. (**D**) 艾麗娜的信寄到哪裡？
　　(A) 何必煩惱雜誌。　　(B) ABC 活動保險公司。
　　(C) 刺傷、搶奪、砂礫和討人厭法律事務所。
　　(D) <u>做得不多國際協會。</u>

43. (**C**) 下列何者在作者的公司實行？
　　(A) 用現代科技取代手工。　　(B) 白天關燈以節省電力。
　　(C) <u>無論何時儘可能回收紙資源。</u>
　　(D) 為員工購買鳥類和寵物來作伴。

　　practice (ˈpræktɪs) v. 實行　　***turn off*** 關掉
　　recycle (riˈsaɪkl̩) v. 回收　　resource (rɪˈsors) n. 資源
　　company (ˈkʌmpənɪ) n. 陪伴；同伴　　staff (stæf) n. 員工；職員

44. (**B**) 關於**瑪姬**下列何者為真？
　　(A) 她在作者的公司擔任經理。
　　(B) <u>她有時幫助三溫暖外面的草地施肥。</u>
　　(C) 她時常使用電子郵件幫助部門之間的通信。
　　(D) 在進入公司之後，她的努力工作改善很多。

　　hardworking (ˈhardˌwɜkɪŋ) n. 努力工作
　　improve (ɪmˈpruv) v. 改善

<u>45-48 為題組</u>

The Galápagos Islands are the Pacific island paradise where Darwin's theory of evolution was born.　They are places filled with giant tree lizards, sandy beaches, and tropical plants.　Now they will be famous for one more thing: the world's first green airport.

加拉巴戈群島是太平洋島嶼的天堂，達爾文的進化論在這裡誕生。這些地方充滿了大蜥蜴、沙灘以及熱帶植物。現在它還將因全球首座綠色機場而聞名於世。

> ***Galápagos Islands*** 加拉巴戈群島【是由十多個火山口所形成，是太平洋東部的一個群島，也是激發達爾文寫下物種起源的地方】
> Pacific〔pəˋsɪfɪk〕*adj.* 太平洋的　　paradise〔ˋpærəˏdaɪs〕*n.* 天堂
> Darwin〔ˋdɑrwɪn〕*n.* 達爾文【1809-1882，英國的生物學家，也是進化論的創立者】　　theory〔ˋθɪərɪ〕*n.* 理論
> evolution〔ˏɛvəˋluʃən〕*n.* 進化　　giant〔ˋdʒaɪənt〕*adj.* 巨大的
> lizard〔ˋlɪzəd〕*n.* 蜥蜴　　sandy〔ˋsændɪ〕*adj.* 覆蓋著沙的
> tropical〔ˋtrɑpɪkl〕*adj.* 熱帶（地區）的

This group of islands off the coast of Ecuador has recently contracted Argentine Corporación America to manage the redevelopment of the airport on the island of Baltra.　It is estimated that US$20 million is needed to complete **the project** by 2009.　The new development has several important features: use of wind and solar energy, passive heating and cooling systems, as well as concrete runways in place of asphalt, which has a greater carbon footprint during its production cycle.　This new development couldn't be coming at a better time for the Galápagos, which were added to an environmental "danger list" in 2007.

厄瓜多外海的這個群島，近來與阿根廷的 Corporación America 建築公司簽約，著手巴特拉島機場的重新規劃。據估計要在 2009 年前完成這項計劃，需要兩千萬美元。這項新的開發有幾個重要特徵：應用風力、太陽能、被動式的加熱及冷卻系統，以及用混凝土的飛機跑道來代替柏油跑道，因為柏油跑道在建造的過程中，會產生大量的碳足跡。加拉巴戈在 2007 年被列入環境「受威脅名單」，這項新發展對它而言，再也找不到更適當的時機了。

coast〔kost〕n. 海岸　　Ecuador〔'ɛkwə,dɔr〕n. 厄瓜多【南美洲西北部的一個國家，於1809年8月10日時脫離西班牙的統治獨立建國。由於赤道橫貫了厄瓜多的國境，再加上在西班牙文中「厄瓜多」的意思就是「赤道」，因此該國又擁有「赤道國」的別稱】

recently〔'risn̩tlɪ〕adv. 近來

contract〔kən'trækt〕v. 簽訂（合約）

Argentine〔'ɑrdʒɛn,taɪn〕adj. 阿根廷的

redevelopment〔,ridɪ'vɛləpmənt〕n. 重新規劃；重新建設

estimate〔'ɛstə,met〕v. 估計　　complete〔kəm'plit〕v. 完成

project〔'prɑdʒɛkt〕n. 規劃；計劃

development〔dɪ'vɛləpmənt〕n. 發展；開發

feature〔'fitʃə〕n. 特徵　　solar〔'solə〕adj. 太陽的

solar energy 太陽能　　passive〔'pæsɪv〕adj. 被動的；消極的

heating〔'hitɪŋ〕adj. 加熱的　　cooling〔'kulɪŋ〕adj. 冷卻的

system〔'sɪstəm〕n. 系統　　*as well as* 以及；連同

concrete〔'kɑnkrit〕adj. 混凝土製的

runway〔'rʌn,we〕n.（飛機的）跑道

in place of 代替　　asphalt〔'æsfɔlt〕n. 瀝青；柏油

carbon〔'kɑrbən〕n. 碳　　footprint〔'fut,prɪnt〕n. 足跡

carbon footprint 碳足跡【指每個人、每個國家或每家公司日常釋放的溫室氣體數量（以二氧化碳即 CO_2 的影響為單位），用以衡量人類活動對環境的影響。】　　production〔prə'dʌkʃən〕n. 生產；製造

cycle〔'saɪkl̩〕n. 循環　　*add to* 增加

environmental〔ɪn,vaɪrən'mɛntl̩〕adj. 環境的

danger〔'dendʒə〕n. 危險

Pacific islands like the Galápagos, Easter Island, and Tahiti, have economies that are driven almost completely by tourism. However, some people think these are "unsustainable models of development." The number of visitors to the Galápagos rose more than 250% from 1990 to 2006, while the number of commercial flights to the area rose 193% from 2001 to 2006. These increases put great stress on the islands' resources and environment. Air travel is especially criticized for exhausting natural resources and causing environmental damage. Thus, efforts are being made to reduce the environmental impact of the tourism industry. The greening of airports is just one of these attempts.

　　像是加拉巴戈群島、復活節島、大溪地島等太平洋島嶼，它們的經濟完全靠旅遊業來推動。然而，有些人認為這些是「無法維持的發展模式」。從 1990 年到 2006 年，加拉巴戈群島觀光客的數目，提高了超過百分之兩百五十。而從 2001 年到 2006 年，飛往這個區域的商業班機，上升了百分之一百九十三。這些增加，對這些島嶼的資源與環境帶來了極大的壓力，尤其空中運輸被批評消耗了天然資源，也造成環境的損害。因此，他們正在努力降低觀光業對環境所造成的衝擊。蓋一座環保的機場只是其中之一而已。

> ***Easter Island*** 復活節島【是南太平洋中的一個島嶼，位於智利以西外海】
> Tahiti〔tɑ'hiti〕*n.* 大溪地島【法國法屬波里尼西亞最大島嶼，位於南太平洋東部】
> economy〔ɪ'kɑnəmɪ〕*n.* 經濟（制度）　　drive〔draɪv〕*v.* 驅動；推動
> completely〔kəm'plitlɪ〕*adv.* 完全地　　tourism〔'turɪzm̩〕*n.* 旅遊業
> unsustainable〔͵ʌnsə'stenəbl̩〕*adj.* 無法維持的
> model〔'mɑdl̩〕*n.* 模式；模型　　rise〔raɪz〕*v.* 上升
> commercial〔kə'mɝʃəl〕*adj.* 商業的　　flight〔flaɪt〕*n.* 班機；飛行
> stress〔strɛs〕*n.* 壓力　　resource〔rɪ'sors〕*n.* 資源
> criticize〔'krɪtə͵saɪz〕*v.* 批評　　exhaust〔ɪg'zɔst〕*v.* 耗盡
> effort〔'ɛfət〕*n.* 努力　　reduce〔rɪ'djus〕*v.* 降低
> impact〔'ɪmpækt〕*n.* 衝擊　　***tourism industry*** 觀光業
> greening〔'grinɪŋ〕*n.* 綠化　　attempt〔ə'tɛmpt〕*n.* 努力；嘗試

45.(**B**) 這篇文章主題為何？

(A) 達爾文理論的問題。

(B) <u>建造一座綠色機場的相關資料。</u>

(C) 加拉巴戈群島的歷史。

(D) 到太平洋島嶼舒適的交通。

> background〔'bæk͵graʊnd〕*n.* 背景；（為了解某問題所需的）資料
> history〔'hɪstrɪ〕*n.* 歷史　　ease〔iz〕*n.* 舒適
> transportation〔͵trænspɚ'teʃən〕*n.* 運輸

46. (**C**) 全世界第一座綠色機場將於何處建造？
   (A) 大溪地島。 (B) 阿根廷。
   (C) 巴特拉島。 (D) 美國。

47. (**A**) 有關加拉巴戈群島，下列何者爲眞？
   (A) 位於太平洋接近厄瓜多的地方。
   (B) 自從 2001 年起人口急速成長。
   (C) 將投資兩千萬美元來促進觀光業。
   (D) 已成爲全世界最危險的地方之一。

   locate（'loket）v. 使位於　　increase（'ınkris）n. 增加
   population（,pɑpjə'leʃən）n. 人口　　invest（ın'vɛst）v. 投資
   promote（prə'mot）v. 提升；促進

48. (**A**) 第二段中所提到的這項計劃，指的是什麼？
   (A) 建造綠色機場的計劃。
   (B) 生產太陽能的研究。
   (C) 計算碳足跡的任務。
   (D) 耗盡天然資源的研究。

   refer to ~ 意指~　　research（'risɚtʃ, rı'sɚtʃ）n. 研究
   task（tæsk）n. 任務　　calculate（'kælkjə,let）v. 計算
   exhaustion（ıg'zɔstʃən）n. 耗盡

49-52 爲題組

According to popular folklore, many animals are smarter than they appear. Dogs bark before earthquakes; cattle predict rainfall by sitting on the ground. But cattle may have another hidden talent in telling which way is north.

根據民間相傳的習俗，很多的動物都比牠們顯現出的要聰明。狗兒在地震前會吠叫；牛藉由坐在地面預測降雨。但是，牛可能有另一項天賦在於分辨哪裡是北方。

popular ('pɑpjələ) *adj.* 民眾的

folklore ('foklor) *n.* (民間) 習俗；故事

appear (ə'pɪr) *v.* 表現　　bark (bɑrk) *v.* 吠叫

cattle ('kætḷ) *n.* 牛；牲口　　predict (prɪ'dɪkt) *v.* 預測

rainfall ('ren,fɔl) *n.* 降雨　　hidden ('hɪdṇ) *adj.* 隱藏的

talent ('tælənt) *n.* 天賦　　tell (tɛl) *v.* 辨識出

Small animals such as mole rats living underground are known for the use of magnetism to navigate. Dr. Begall and her colleagues wanted to know whether larger mammals also have the ability to perceive magnetic fields. They investigated this possibility by studying images of thousands of cattle captured on Google Earth, a website that stitches together satellite photographs to produce an image of the Earth's surface.

住在地面下的小動物像是鼴鼠，以運用磁性來行走而為人所知。畢果博士和她的同事們想要知道，是否較大的哺乳類動物也有能力察覺磁場。他們藉由研究數以千計在 Google Earth，一個結合衛星照片來產生地球表面圖像的網站，上頭所網羅的牛隻影像來調查這樣的可能性。

mole rat ('mol ,ræt) *n.* 鼴鼠

underground ('ʌndə,graʊnd) *adv.* 地面下

magnetism ('mægnə,tɪzm) *n.* 磁性

navigate ('nævə,get) *v.* 行走；航行

colleague ('kɑlig) *n.* 同事　　mammal ('mæmḷ) *n.* 哺乳動物

perceive (pə'siv) *v.* 察覺　　***magnetic field*** 磁場

investigate (ɪn'vɛstə,get) *v.* 調查

possibility (,pɑsə'bɪlətɪ) *n.* 可能性

capture ('kæptʃə) *v.* 網羅；捕獲；擄獲

Google ('guɡḷ) *n.* 谷歌【世界知名搜尋引擎】

website ('wɛb,saɪt) *n.* 網站　　stitch (stɪtʃ) *v.* 結合；縫 (合)

satellite ('sætḷ,aɪt) *n.* 衛星

produce (prə'djus) *v.* 產生；製作

image ('ɪmɪdʒ) *n.* 影像　　surface ('sɝfɪs) *n.* 表面

Grazing animals are known to orient themselves in a way that minimizes wind chill from the north and maximizes the warmth of the sun when they are cold. The researchers therefore had to study a lot of cows grazing in lots of different places at different times of day, in order to average out these factors and see whether cattle could act like compass needles.

草食性動物為人所知的一點，就是在寒冷時，可為自己找出一條北方冷風減至最低，又是陽光最溫暖的路徑。因此研究人員必須在一天不同的時刻，研究很多在各不同地點吃草的牛隻，以使得這些因素達到平衡，並且弄清牛隻是否會表現得像羅盤上的磁針。

　　grazing〔'grezɪŋ〕adj. 吃草的　　orient〔'orɪˌɛnt〕v. 定位；朝東
　　minimize〔'mɪnəˌmaɪz〕v. 使～減到最小　　chill〔tʃɪl〕n. 寒意
　　maximize〔'mæksəˌmaɪz〕v. 使～達到最高限度
　　warmth〔wɔrmθ〕n. 溫暖　　*average out* 使～達到平衡
　　factor〔'fæktɚ〕n. 因素；結果　　act〔ækt〕v. 表現得
　　compass needle　（羅盤上的）磁針

The researchers concluded that cattle do generally orient themselves in a north-south direction. This north-south preference has also been noted in flies, termites and honeybees. But unfortunately, even the high resolution of Google Earth is not powerful enough to tell which end of the cow is its head, and which its tail. The researchers were therefore unable to answer their research questions of whether cattle prefer to look north or south, and whether that differs in the northern and southern hemispheres.

研究人員定論牛隻的確大致上以南北方向為牠們自己訂出方位。這種南北向的偏好已在蒼蠅、白蟻以及蜜蜂身上也被發現到。但不幸地，即使 Google Earth 的解析度高，還是不夠強到能分辨哪一端是乳牛的頭部，而哪一端是牠的尾巴。研究人員因此無法回答他們所研究的，牛隻偏好朝北或朝南的問題，以及是否這在北半球及南半球有所不同。

conclude (kən'klud) v. 下結論

generally ('dʒɛnərəlɪ) adv. 大致上　　　**in~direction** 以~方向

preference ('prɛfərəns) n. 喜好；優先選擇

note (not) v. 發現　　　termite ('tɝmaɪt) n. 白蟻

honeybee ('hʌnɪ,bi) n. 蜜蜂

resolution (,rɛzə'luʃən) n. 解析

powerful ('paʊəfəl) adj. 強而有力的　　　end (ɛnd) n. 末端

prefer to~ 偏好於~　　　differ ('dɪfə) v. 使~不同

hemisphere ('hɛməs,fɪr) n. 半球

49. (**D**) 本篇文章主要是關於什麼？

(A) 谷歌地球的益處。

(B) 牛隻是否比其他動物優越。

(C) 動物對於自然災害的靈敏度。

(D) 牛隻是否表現出像羅盤上的磁針。

50. (**C**) 下列哪一項因素可能影響到畢果博士的研究結果？

(A) 降雨。　　　　　　　　(B) 地震。

(C) 位置。　　　　　　　　(D) 花費。

51. (**A**) 何者是畢果博士研究的主要發現？

(A) 牛隻指向南北方。

(B) 無法以科學的方法研究磁力。

(C) 動物偏好看向南方。

(D) 谷歌地球是可靠的搜尋工具。

52. (**D**) 研究人員為何無法得到他們所研究問題的答案？

(A) 他們研究中的許多牛隻都坐在地上。

(B) 牛隻為了避開寒風而不斷地改變方向。

(C) 兩個半球的磁力不同。

(D) 在衛星照片上他們無法辨識出乳牛的頭部和尾巴。

53-56 為題組

Children normally have a distrust of new foods. But it's the parents' job to serve a variety of foods and expose their children to healthy dieting habits. 孩子們對陌生的食物通常有些不信任。但是,提供多樣化的食物使孩子有健康的飲食習慣,是父母的職責。

> normally (ˈnɔrml̩ɪ) adv. 正常地;通常
> distrust (dɪsˈtrʌst) n. 不信任   serve (sɜv) v. 供應;提供
> **a variety of** 多樣的   **expose…to** 使…接觸

Some simple strategies can help even the pickiest eater learn to like a more varied diet. First of all, you don't have to send children out of the kitchen. With hot stoves, boiling water and sharp knives at hand, it is understandable that parents don't want children in the kitchen when they're making dinner. But studies suggest that involving children in meal preparation is an important first step in getting them to try new foods. In one study, nearly 600 children from kindergarten to sixth grade took part in a nutrition curriculum intended to get them to eat more vegetables and whole grains. The researchers found that children who had cooked their own foods were more likely to eat those foods in the cafeteria than children who had not. Kids don't usually like radishes, but if kids cut them up and put them in the salad, they will love the dish.

一些簡單的技巧,可以幫助即使是最挑嘴的人,去喜歡更多元化的飲食。首先,無需將孩子趕出廚房。由於有熱爐、滾水、與尖刀,家長做晚餐時,不喜歡孩子待在廚房,是可以理解的。然而研究指出,讓孩子願意嘗試新食物重要的第一步,便是讓孩子參與料理的準備。在一項研究中,將近 600 位幼稚園至小學六年級的學童,參與了一堂營養學課程,目的是為了讓他們吃更多蔬菜與全麥類食物。研究員發現,自己親手料理的孩子相較於其他的孩子,更會去吃自助吧上的食物。孩子通常不愛紅蘿蔔,但若他們將紅蘿蔔切好放入沙拉,他們便會喜歡這道菜。

strategy (ˈstrætədʒɪ) n. 策略；計謀　　picky (ˈpɪkɪ) adj. 挑剔的
varied (ˈvɛrɪd) adj. 各樣的　　stove (stov) n. 火爐
boiling (ˈbɔɪlɪŋ) adj. 沸騰的　　sharp (ʃɑrp) adj. 鋒利的
at hand 在手邊　　understandable (ˌʌndəˈstændəbḷ) adj. 可理解的
suggest (səˈdʒɛst) v. 建議；提議
involve (ɪnˈvɑlv) v. 使參與；包含
preparation (ˌprɛpəˈreʃən) n. 準備
kindergarten (ˈkɪndəˌgɑrtṇ) n. 幼稚園　　**take part in** 參加
nutrition (njuˈtrɪʃən) n. 營養
curriculum (kəˈrɪkjələm) n. 學校課程　　**intend to** 企圖
whole (hol) adj. 完全的；全部的　　grain (gren) n. 穀物；穀粒
researcher (rɪˈsɝtʃə) n. 研究人員　　cook (kʊk) v. 烹飪
be likely to 可能　　cafeteria (ˌkæfəˈtɪrɪə) n. 自助餐廳
radish (ˈrædɪʃ) n. 大菜；紅皮的小蘿蔔

Another strategy is not to diet in front of your children. Kids are tuned into their parents' eating preferences and are far more likely to try foods if they see their mother or father eating them. Given this powerful effect, parents who are trying to lose weight should be careful of how their dieting habits can influence a child's perceptions about food and healthful eating. In one study of 5-year-old girls about dieting, one child noted that dieting involved drinking chocolate milkshakes, because her mother was using Slim-Fast drinks. Another child said dieting meant "you fix food but you don't eat it." By exposing young children to **erratic** dieting habits, parents may be putting them at risk for eating disorders.

　　另一個技巧是不要在你的孩子面前節食。孩子會發展出與父母相同的飲食偏好，而且更可能去嘗試，他們看到母親或父親吃的食物。鑒於這強大效果，如果家長正在減肥，應注意他們的飲食習慣，可能影響孩子對食物與健康飲食的看法。在一項針對五歲女孩關於減肥的研究中，一位孩童表示節食的飲食中包含喝巧克力奶昔，因爲她的母親正在使用速纖（Slim-Fast）飲品。另一位孩童說，節食是「煮食物，卻不吃。」讓小朋友暴露在不正常的減肥習慣中的家長，可能會讓他們的小孩有飲食失調的風險。

diet（'daɪət）v. 實行節食　　tune（tjun）v. 使與⋯一致
preference（'prɛfərəns）n. 偏好　　effect（ɪ'fɛkt）n. 作用；效果
influence（'ɪnfluəns）v. 起作用；影響
perception（pə'sɛpʃən）n. 觀念；看法
healthful（'hɛlθfəl）adj. 有益健康的　　note（not）v. 提到
milkshake（,mɪlk'ʃek）n. 奶昔
slim（slɪm）adj. 苗條的　　fix（fɪks）v. 準備飯菜
erratic（ə'rætɪk）adj. 不穩定的；無規律的
at risk 處於危險中　　disorder（dɪs'ɔrdə）n. 混亂；無秩序

53.（**D**）本文主旨為何？
(A) 解釋造成孩子飲食失調的原因。
(B) 教導孩子料理食物的流程。
(C) 提倡蔬菜與全麥類食物的重要性。
(D) 告知家長他們如何幫助孩子喜歡多元的食物。

54.（**A**）下列哪一組的飲食會更均衡？
(A) 幫忙料理的孩子。
(B) 家長正在節食的孩子。
(C) 不愛吃紅蘿蔔的孩子。
(D) 家長在自助餐廳工作的孩子。
on a diet 節食

55.（**D**）最後一句的 erratic 暗示甚麼？
(A) 明顯的。　　　　　　　(B) 健康的。
(C) 不誠實的。　　　　　　(D) 不恰當的。

56.（**B**）下列關於速纖（Slim-Fast）的敘述，何者正確？
(A) 孩子最愛的食物。　　　(B) 看起來像巧克力奶昔。
(C) 包含多種水果。　　　　(D) 給希望快速減重的人使用。

第貳部分：非選擇題

一、翻譯題

1. Most students are not $\left\{\begin{array}{l}\text{used}\\\text{accustomed}\end{array}\right\}$ to solving problems themselves,

   and always expect the teacher to $\left\{\begin{array}{l}\text{give}\\\text{provide}\end{array}\right\}$ the $\left\{\begin{array}{l}\text{standard}\\\text{correct}\end{array}\right\}$ answer.

2. $\left\{\begin{array}{l}\text{Besides}\\\text{In addition to}\\\text{Aside from}\\\text{Other than}\end{array}\right\}$ studying hard to $\left\{\begin{array}{l}\text{gain}\\\text{acquire}\end{array}\right\}$ knowledge,

   students should also develop $\left\{\begin{array}{l}\text{the ability to think independently.}\\\text{independent thinking ability.}\end{array}\right.$

   solve〔sɑlv〕*v.* 解決
   aside from 除此之外　　knowledge〔'nɑlɪdʒ〕*n.* 知識
   independently〔ˌɪndɪ'pɛndəntlɪ〕*adv.* 獨立地

二、英文作文：

【範例1】

The Earthquake

I never thought it'd happen to me. We've all seen poor people lose their homes, or even worse, their lives, to earthquakes. We sympathize with them, but at the same time are glad it didn't happen to us. Well, I can't be glad anymore. My house has been torn apart, and I'm lucky to just be alive.

It's not safe here anymore. Debris and aftershocks are still a danger. Plus, the refugee camp is way too crowded. Therefore, I plan on moving to my parents' for a while. The news says it'll take at least a year to get everything back on track here. I can't wait that long, so I have to start a new life somewhere else. Hopefully, a place without earthquakes.

sympathize (ˈsɪmpəˌθaɪz) v. 同情

at the same time 同時　　tear (tɛr) v. 撕開；扯破

debris (dəˈbri) n. 殘骸；碎片　　aftershock (ˈæftəˌʃɑk) n. 餘震

refugee (ˌrɛfjʊˈdʒi) n. 難民　　crowded (ˈkraʊdɪd) adj. 擁擠的

hopefully (ˈhopfəlɪ) adv. 但願

apology (əˈpɑlədʒɪ) n. 道歉　　digital (ˈdɪdʒɪt!) adj. 數位的

extra (ˈɛkstrə) adv. 特別地；格外地

crowd (kraʊd) n. 群眾；人群

get out of hand 變得難以控制　　*take a picture* 拍照

bump into 撞上　　space (spes) n. 空間

bend down 彎下腰　　*let alone* 更不用說 (= *not to mention*)

search (sɜtʃ) v. 搜尋　　avail (əˈvel) n. 效用；效力

to no avail 徒勞無功 (= *in vain*)

precious (ˈprɛʃəs) adj. 珍貴的　　definitely (ˈdɛfənɪtlɪ) adv. 一定

compensate (ˈkɑmpənˌset) v. 賠償；彌補

memory (ˈmɛmərɪ) n. 回憶　　*make it up* 彌補

【範例 2】

The Earthquake

An earthquake happened off the east coast three days ago. It reached 6.8 on the Richter scale, and took over a thousand lives. More than five thousand people are now living in refugee camps, with another four thousand yet to be found. Many refugees are going back to their homes to scavenge for what little is left, or to look for missing family members. It is a disastrous sight.

Donations and rescue teams are coming in, but what's more important is to get the wounded better medical attention. The refugees need to be moved quickly, too, for fear of a large aftershock. Many have lost their lives, but it is no time to mourn. It is time to take care of the living.

reach (ritʃ) v. 到達　　***Richter Scale*** (衡量地震)芮氏規模
take (tek) v. 奪取　　refugee (ˌrɛfjuˈdʒi) n. 難民
scavenge (ˈskævɪndʒ) v. 在…中搜尋有用之物
disastrous (dɪzˈæstrəs) adj. 悲慘的
donation (doˈneʃən) n. 捐款;捐贈物
wounded (ˈwundɪd) n. 受傷者
medical (ˈmɛdɪkl̩) adj. 醫療的
aftershock (ˈæftɚˌʃɑk) n. 餘震　　mourn (morn) v. 哀悼

98 年度學科能力測驗英文試題修正意見

題　號	題　　目	修　正　意　見
第 16－20 題 第 5 行	He then *coated* the glue on a paper.... → He then *put* the glue on a paper....	「在紙上塗上黏膠」，不是 *coat the glue on a paper* 而是 *put the glue on a paper*，因為 coat 是「在…塗上」，在此不合句意。
第 31－40 題 第 5 行	___32___ *and this time*, ... → ___32___ and, this time, ...	this time 為插入語，前後須有逗點。
第 31－40 題 選項 (F)	(F) *finishing* → (F) *finish*	「終點線」是 *finish line*，不是 *finishing line*（誤）。
第 42 題	Where *is* Eleanor's letter sent to? → Where *was* Eleanor's letter sent to?	依句意為過去式，故 *is* 須改為 *was*。
第 44 題 (D)	Her handwriting *has improved* a lot after entering the company. → Her handwriting *improved* a lot after entering the company. 或 Her handwriting has improved a lot *since she entered* the company.	after entering the company 是過去的時間，故動詞 *has improved* 須改為過去式 *improved*；也可保留 has improved，但須將後半句改為 *since she entered* the company。
第 45－48 題 第二段第 5 行	*has* a greater... → *creates* a greater...	依句意，應是「產生」碳足跡，故 *has* 須改為 *creates*。create 一般當「創造」講，在這裡作「產生」解。
第 46 題 (C)	*In* Baltra. → *On* Baltra.	Baltra 是一座島，在島上，介系詞須用 on。在第二段第 2 行也出現：on the island of Baltra。
第 49－52 題 第 4 行	...are known for *the* use of... → ...are known for *their* use of...	依句意，應是「牠們」使用…，故須將 the 改為 their。
第 53－56 題 第一段第 2 行 第三段第 3 行 及第 7 行	...*dieting* habits → *eating* habits 或 *dietary* habits	「飲食習慣」應說成：*eating habits* 或 *dietary habits*，而不是 *dieting habits*（節食習慣）。
第 53 題 (A)	To...eating *disorder*. → To...eating *disorders*.	disorder（疾病）為可數名詞，故 *disorder* 須改為 *disorders*。

98 年學測英文科考題出題來源

題　　號	出　　　　　處
一、詞彙 第 1～15 題	所有各題對錯答案的選項，均出自「高中常用 7000 字」。
二、綜合測驗 第 16～20 題	改編自 Top 100 inspiring anecdotes and wisdom，便利貼的由來。
第 21～25 題	出自 Social Studies for Kids，關於鳳梨為什麼會傳到夏威夷的由來（Pineapples Arrive in Hawaii）的文章。
第 26～30 題	改編自國際傷殘奧運委員會，關於傷殘奧運 Paralympic Games 的介紹。
三、文意選填 第 31～40 題	出自於 William's Tales。在 "Parables and Fables"一文中，作者改寫龜兔賽跑的結局及其帶來的寓意。
四、閱讀測驗 第 41～44 題	改編自 International Institute of Not Doing Much 的一封信，關於回歸純樸、步調緩慢的生活。
第 45～48 題	出自 triplepundit，對於加拉巴哥群島有著全世界第一座綠色機場的介紹，以及其帶來的環境問題（Galapagos Islands Get World's First "Green" Airport）的文章。
第 49～52 題	出自倫敦風水網（Feng Shui London），INTERESTING ARTICLES ON FENG SHUI RELATED SUBJECTS（與風水相關的有趣小文章）一文。
第 53～56 題	改編自紐約時報 2008 年 9 月 14 日健康版，有關父母要如何讓小孩不偏食的報導。

Post-it Notes

The 3M Company encourages creativity from its employees. The company allows its researchers to spend 15 percent of their time on any project that interests them. This attitude has brought fantastic benefits not only to the employees but to the 3M Company itself Many times, a spark of an idea turned into a successful product has boosted 3M's profits tremendously.

Some years ago, a scientist in 3M's commercial office took advantage of this 15 percent creative time. This scientist, Art Fry, came up with an idea for one of 3M's best-selling products. It seems that Art Fry dealt with a small irritation every Sunday as he sang in the church choir. After marking his pages in the hymnal with small bits of paper, the small pieces would invariably fall out all over the floor.

Suddenly, an idea struck Fry. He remembered an adhesive developed by a colleague that everyone thought was a failure because it did not stick very well. "I coated the adhesive on a paper sample," Fry recalls, "and I found that it was not only a good bookmark, but it was great for writing notes. It will stay in place as long as you want it to, and then you can remove it without damage." Yes, Art Fry hit the jackpot. The resulting product was called Post-it! and has become one of 3M's most successful office products.

【98 年學測】綜合測驗：21-25 出題來源

Pineapples Arrive in Hawaii

The pineapple, long a symbol of Hawaii, did not originate there. Even though Polynesians lived on Hawaii for a great many years, the pineapple is not native to the Hawaiian Islands. In fact, pineapples did not appear there until 1813. Don Francisco de Paula y Marin, a Spanish advisor to King Kamehameha, brought the famous fruits back with him.

The pineapple is originally to be found in Paraguay and in the southern part of Brazil. Natives spread the fruit throughout South American and Central America and into the Caribbean region, including the West Indies, where Christopher Columbus first found them. The pineapple's original name was anana, which meant "excellent fruit" in one of the Caribbean native languages. European explorers called it the "Pine of the Indies." When the fruit traveled to English-speaking countries, the word "apple" was added. (Historians aren't really sure why this happened. Many believe that it was to associate the "Pine of the Indies" with the "apple," another fruit that people really enjoyed. Nonetheless, the suffix "apple" stuck, giving us the English word pineapple.)

Columbus brought it, along with many other new things, back to Europe with him. From there, the tasty fruit spread throughout other parts of civilization. It was carried on sailing ships around the world because it was found to, like oranges, help prevent scurvy, a devastating disease that often afflicted sailors on long voyages. It was at the end of one of these long voyages that the pineapple came to Hawaii to stay. On January 11, 1813, pineapples were first planted there.

The familiar name of Dole came into the picture in 1901, when James Drummond Dole planted his first pineapples near Wahiawa. He also founded the Hawaiian Pineapple Company. Just six years later, he opened another cannery, in Iwilei. The pineapple industry was off and running.

Graphics courtesy of ClipArt.com

Paralympic Games

In 1948, Sir Ludwig Guttmann organized a sports competition involving World War II veterans with a spinal cord injury in Stoke Mandeville, England. Four years later, competitors from the Netherlands joined the games and an international movement was born. Olympic style games for athletes with a disability were organized for the first time in Rome in 1960, now called Paralympics. In Toronto in 1976, other disability groups were added and the idea of merging together different disability groups for international sport competitions was born. In the same year, the first Paralympic Winter Games took place in Sweden.

Today, the Paralympics are elite sport events for athletes from six different disability groups. They emphasize, however, the participants' athletic achievements rather than their disability. The movement has grown dramatically since its first days. The number of athletes participating in Summer Paralympic Games has increased from 400 athletes from 23 countries in Rome in 1960 to 3806 athletes from 136 countries in Athens in 2004.

The Paralympic Games have always been held in the same year as the Olympic Games. Since the Seoul 1988 Paralympic Games and the Albertville 1992 Winter Paralympic Games they have also taken place at the same venues as the Olympics. On 19 June 2001, an agreement was signed between IOC and IPC securing this practice for the future. From the 2012 bid process onwards, the host city chosen to host the Olympic Games will be obliged to also host the Paralympics.

The Chinese city of <u>Beijing</u> will host the next 2008 Paralympic Games, whereas the Winter Paralympics 2010 will be in <u>Vancouver</u>, Canada. <u>London</u> will host the Paralympics in 2012 and Sochi will be the host of the 2014 Winter Paralympics.

【98 年學測】文意選填：31-40 出題來源

Parables and Fables

Recently, I chanced to view an interesting Article based on the famous fable of 'The Tortoise and the Hare'. Its end is well known to all that the tortoise wins the race against the hare. The moral lesson is as 'A slow and steady wins the race.' We all have grown up with hearing this popular version, but the same fable is extended in a different twist. The second race is arranged with the request of the hare and this time, the hare wins and moral lesson is as 'Fast and consistent will always beat the slow and steady.' Further, the tortoise challenges the hare for the third race with a different route where there is a river just before final destination. This time, the tortoise wins the race and moral lesson is as 'First identify your core competency and then change the playing field to suit your core competency.' But the story still continues. Both the competitors know their own drawbacks and limitations very well and therefore they jointly decide to do the last race again; not to decide any winner or loser, but just for their own pleasure and satisfaction. Both co-operate each other as a team. Firstly, the hare carries the tortoise on its back up to the river. Then, the tortoise carries the hare and swims to the opposite bank of the river. And, lastly the hare carries the tortoise again on its back. Thus they reach the finishing line together. Overall to say, many moral lessons from the last match are highlighted. They may be named as team work, to harness individual's capacity for greater success, to face the adverse situations with collective decisions, qualities of a good leadership, ability of turning failure to success, changing of strategy to try something different and the last very important to compete against situations rather than rivals.

Above Article has inspired me to try any other familiar fable to be narrated differently or extended interestingly and humorously or twisted in an anti-climax mode of end. I have preferred a story 'A smart crow' to try it with other than above three options. I have made up my mind, now, to fabricate a post discussion of the episode of the above story in form of conversation among the crows. But before that, let us overview this story in its original text that we had read in our primers of our primary education years. It is as below:

Slow Office

To Whom It May Concern:

Your address was forwarded to us by Why Bother Magazine. The staff here salute you. The International Institute of Not Doing Much is the best organization in the world. You people know how to avoid unnecessary activity!

We followed the recommendations in your article to the letter. First, we replaced all our telephones with carrier pigeons. Simply removing the jangle of telephones and replacing them with the pleasant sounds of bird life has had a remarkable effect on everyone. However, we are a business. We have to think of the bottom line. Telephone service was more expensive than the birds. As a side benefit, they fertilize the lawn beyond the new employee sauna.

Next, we sold the computers off to Stab, Grab, Grit, and Nasty, a firm of lawyers nearby. Our electricity bill went way down. Big savings! The boss is impressed. We have completely embraced paper technology. Now that we all use pencils, doodling is on the increase, and the quality of pencilwomanship is impressive— as you can tell from this letter. By the way, when you can make the effort, please send back this letter back to us. We can erase and reuse it. Just tie it to Maggie's leg and she'll know where to take it.

Now it's very calm and quiet here. You can notice the difference. No more loud chatter on the telephones! All we hear is the scratching of pencil on paper; the sound of pigeons, and the delivery of inter-office correspondence by paper airplane.

Wonderful! I've always wanted to work for an insurance company ever since I was a little girl. Now it's perfect.

Yours truly,
Eleanor Lightly
Spokeswoman and Company Hair Stylist
Activity Insurance: Insure against overdoing it
(Sign our no-claim waiver for a lower premium)

【98 年學測】閱讀測驗：45-48 出題來源

Galapagos Islands Get World's First "Green" Airport

The Galápagos Islands are the Pacific island paradise where Darwin's theory of evolution was born. It is a place filled with iguanas the size of small Fords, sandy beaches, and tropical flora. Now it will be famous for one more thing: the world's first green airport.

The archipelago off the coast of Ecuador has recently contracted Argentine Corporación America to manage the redevelopment of the airport on the island of Baltra, an estimated US\$ 20 million project to be completed in 2009. Several highlights of the new development are the utilization of wind and solar energy, passive heating and cooling systems, as well as concrete tarmacs as opposed to asphalt, which are claimed to have a greater carbon footprint during its production cycle. (Note: links appear in Spanish)

This new development couldn't be coming at a better time for the Galápagos archipelago, which last year was added to Unesco's environmental "danger list." For Pacific islands like the Galápagos, Easter Island, or Tahiti, economies are driven almost completely by tourism. However, people like Dr. Graham Watkins, executive director of Charles Darwin Foundation, think these are "unsustainable models of development."

According to an article in the New York Times earlier this year, the number of visitors to the Galápagos rose more than 250% from 1990 to 2006, while the number of commercial flights to the area has risen 193% from 2001 to 2006. As the Galápagos' popularity as a tourist destination increases, these types of rises impose serious strains on its resources and environment. The new green airport will allow the archipelago to be more efficient and self-sustaining with the amount of resources it consumes to accommodate such high numbers of visitors.

Air travel has often been reviled for its unsustainability, though recently practices like carbon offsetting have sought to reduce the overall environmental impact of the industry. The greening of airports is yet another one of those attempts. Nearly two years ago, Boston's Logan airport received LEED-certification for its use of low-flow faucets, waterless toilets, and energy saving features.

【98 年學測】閱讀測驗：49-52 出題來源

INTERESTING ARTICLES ON FENG SHUI RELATED SUBJECTS

Like compass needles, cows point north-south

ACCORDING to popular folklore, many animals are smarter than they appear. Dogs bark before earthquakes; chimpanzees know the right herbs to deal with intestinal worms; cattle predict rainfall by sitting on the ground. But cows, in particular, may have a hidden talent that far outweighs any meteorological skills. It appears they know which way is north.

Sabine Begall of the University of Duisburg-Essen in Germany and her colleagues became interested in animal magnetism when they were working on mole rats—blind animals that live underground and use magnetism to navigate. In a paper published in this week's Proceedings of the National Academy of Sciences, they looked at whether larger mammals also have the ability to perceive magnetic fields. They did so by studying images of thousands of cattle captured on Google Earth, a website that stitches together high-resolution satellite photographs to produce a simulacrum of the Earth's surface.

It was not merely a matter of looking for a few fuzzy blobs in fields and recording which way they were pointing. Grazing animals are known to orient themselves in a way that minimises wind chill and maximises the warmth of the sun when they are cold. Dr Begall and her colleagues therefore had to study a lot of cows grazing in lots of different places at different times of day, in order to average out these other factors and see whether there was a residual tendency for cattle to act like compass needles. They were also able to use data collected by colleagues in the Czech Republic on the grazing behaviour of roe and red deer.

The researchers concluded that cattle do generally align themselves in a north-south direction. Moreover, at high latitudes—where the geographical and magnetic poles are perceptibly separate from one another—it was to the magnetic pole that the animals pointed. Unfortunately, even the high resolution of Google Earth is not good enough to tell routinely which end of a cow is its head, and which its tail. Dr Begall was therefore unable to answer the vexed questions of whether cows prefer to look north or south, and whether that differs in the northern and southern hemispheres.

Food Mistakes Parents Make

"I think parents feel like it's their job to just make their children eat something," Ms. Worobey said. "But it's really their job to serve a variety of healthy foods and get their children exposed to foods."

A series of simple meal-time strategies can help even the pickiest eater learn to like a more varied diet. Here's a look at six common mistakes parents make when feeding their children.

Sending children out of the kitchen With hot stoves, boiling water and sharp knives at hand, it is understandable that parents don't want children in the kitchen when they're making dinner. But studies suggest that involving children in meal preparation is an important first step in getting them to try new foods.

Researchers at Teachers College at <u>Columbia University</u> studied how cooking with a child affects the child's eating habits. In one study, nearly 600 children from kindergarten to sixth grade took part in a nutrition curriculum intended to get them to eat more vegetables and whole grains. Some children, in addition to having lessons about healthful eating, took part in cooking workshops. The researchers found that children who had cooked their own foods were more likely to eat those foods in the cafeteria, and even ask for seconds, than children who had not had the cooking class.

When children are involved in meal preparation, "they come to at least try the food," said Isobel Contento, professor of nutrition education at Teachers College and a co-author of the study. "Kids don't usually like radishes, but we found that if kids cut up radishes and put them in the salad, they love the radishes."

九十八年度學科能力測驗（英文考科）

大考中心公佈答案

題號	答案	題號	答案	題號	答案
1	B	21	B	41	A
2	B	22	C	42	D
3	C	23	D	43	C
4	D	24	A	44	B
5	D	25	A	45	B
6	A	26	A	46	C
7	B	27	B	47	A
8	B	28	C	48	A
9	C	29	B	49	C
10	A	30	D	50	C
11	D	31	I	51	A
12	D	32	A	52	D
13	C	33	E	53	D
14	C	34	B	54	A
15	C	35	G	55	D
16	A	36	C	56	B
17	B	37	D		
18	B	38	H		
19	C	39	F		
20	D	40	J		

98 年度學測英文考科非選擇題評分原則

閱卷召集人：殷允美 教授（政治大學英文系）

　　九十八學年度學科能力測驗英文考科的非選擇題題型共有兩大題：第一大題是翻譯題，考生需將兩個中文句子譯成正確而通順達意的英文，這個題型與過去幾年相同，兩題合計八分。第二大題為英文作文，但與往年的看圖作文不太一樣，在引導的方式略作改變，僅提供考生單張照片，希望給考生更多的寫作發揮空間。今年考生需依提供的照片，寫一篇 120 個單詞（words）左右的作文。作文滿分為二十分。

　　至於閱卷籌備工作，在正式閱卷前，於 2 月 2 日先召開評分標準訂定會議，由正副召集人及協同主持人共十四人，參閱了 100 本約 4000 多份的答案卷，經過一天的討論，訂定評分標準，選出合適的樣本，編製了閱卷參考手冊，供閱卷委員共同參考，以確保閱卷之公平性。

　　2 月 3 日上午 9:00 到 11:00 間，140 多位大學教授，分為 12 組進行試閱會議，討論評分時應注意的事項及評分標準，再根據閱卷參考手冊的樣卷，分別評分。在試閱會議之後（11:00），正副召集人及協同主持人進行第一次評分標準確定會議以確定評分原則，經會議確認後才開始正式的閱卷。不同於往年，為求慎重起見，今年特別於下午三點加開第二次評分標準確定會議，以求整體評分標準更為一致。

　　關於評分標準，在翻譯題部分，每題總分 4 分，分四小部分，每部分 1 分，每個錯誤扣 0.5 分。英文作文的評分標準是依據內容（5 分）、組織（5 分）、文法句構（4 分）、字彙拼字（4 分）、體例（2 分）五個項目給分。若字數不足，則總分扣 1 分。

依慣例，每份答案卷皆經過兩位委員分別評分，最後以二人之平均分數計算。如果第一閱與第二閱委員的分數在翻譯題部分的差距大於 2 分，或在作文題部分差距大於 5 分，則由第三位主閱（正副召集人或協同主持人）評分。

今年的翻譯題的句型與詞彙，皆為高中生應該熟習的，評量的重點在於考生是否能運用熟悉的字詞（比如：解決問題 solve problems、期待 expect、提供 provide、標準答案 standard answers、獲取知識 gain/obtain/get knowledge、培養 develop、獨立思考 independent thinking、能力 ability 等）與基本句型翻譯成正確且達意的英文句子（如：be used to、in addition to/besides 的用法）。所測驗之詞彙都屬於大考中心詞彙表四級內之詞彙，中等程度以上的考生如果能使用正確句型並注意拼字，應能得到理想的分數。但在選取樣卷時發現，很多考生對於像 Most students 這樣的名詞詞組（noun phrase）的用法都無法掌握；另外，考生對於名詞單複數以及冠詞（the）的使用，及多音節字（如 independent）的掌握仍有待加強。

英文作文部分，照片內容為「斷垣殘壁中有個人撿拾物品」，學生可將其定位為地震過後、戰亂轟炸過後、甚或地方沒落後的破落景象，希望給學生更大的發揮空間。本題評量學生描述照片的能力；同時也要求學生提供合理的「前因」，並提出合理的後續發展或因應措施。不但能同時評量學生「過去式、現在式、未來式」的語法能力，也同時評量學生「描述事件」、「談論問題並解決問題」等英文寫作能力，評量層面相當廣，但亦具挑戰性。由試閱樣本顯示：大多數學生描述的是地震的情境，偶有考生以第一人稱敘述事情經過。在第二段部分，很多考生提到的解決方式大多由政府或慈善機構協助居民重建家園。

九十八學年度學科能力測驗總級分與各科成績標準一覽表

考　科	頂標	前標	均標	後標	底標
國　文	14	13	11	10	8
英　文	13	11	8	5	4
數　學	11	9	6	4	3
社　會	14	13	11	9	8
自　然	12	11	9	7	6
總級分	60	55	46	37	29

※ 五項標準之計算，均不含缺考生（總級分之計算不含五科都缺考的考生）
　之成績，計算方式如下：
　　頂標：成績位於第88百分位數之考生成績
　　前標：成績位於第75百分位數之考生成績
　　均標：成績位於第50百分位數之考生成績
　　後標：成績位於第25百分位數之考生成績
　　底標：成績位於第12百分位數之考生成績

九十八學年度學科能力測驗英文科各級分人數累計表

	級分	人　數	百分比 (%)	累計人數	累計百分比 (%)
英 文	15	4,895	3.51	139,512	100.00
	14	8,541	6.12	134,617	96.49
	13	8,890	6.37	126,076	90.37
	12	10,168	7.29	117,186	84.00
	11	9,629	6.90	107,018	76.71
	10	10,930	7.83	97,389	69.81
	9	10,481	7.51	86,459	61.97
	8	11,946	8.56	75,978	54.46
	7	11,145	7.99	64,032	45.90
	6	12,053	8.64	52,887	37.91
	5	11,274	8.08	40,834	29.27
	4	14,649	10.50	29,560	21.19
	3	12,190	8.74	14,911	10.69
	2	2,631	1.89	2,721	1.95
	1	83	0.06	90	0.06
	0	7	0.01	7	0.01

九十八學年度學科能力測驗
總級分人數百分比累計表（違規處理前）

總級分	人數	百分比	累計人數	累計百分比
75	109	0.08	140,007	100.00
74	226	0.16	139,898	99.92
73	297	0.21	139,672	99.76
72	437	0.31	139,375	99.55
71	551	0.39	138,938	99.24
70	700	0.50	138,387	98.84
69	815	0.58	137,687	98.34
68	961	0.69	136,872	97.76
67	1,144	0.82	135,911	97.07
66	1,361	0.97	134,767	96.26
65	1,574	1.12	133,406	95.29
64	1,744	1.25	131,832	94.16
63	1,967	1.40	130,088	92.92
62	2,246	1.60	128,121	91.51
61	2,351	1.68	125,875	89.91
60	2,619	1.87	123,524	88.23
59	2,764	1.97	120,905	86.36
58	3,052	2.18	118,141	84.38
57	3,240	2.31	115,089	82.20
56	3,343	2.39	111,849	79.89
55	3,539	2.53	108,506	77.50
54	3,600	2.57	104,967	74.97
53	3,946	2.82	101,367	72.40
52	4,066	2.90	97,421	69.58
51	4,080	2.91	93,355	66.68
50	4,186	2.99	89,275	63.76
49	4,224	3.02	85,089	60.77
48	4,460	3.19	80,865	57.76
47	4,364	3.12	76,405	54.57
46	4,358	3.11	72,041	51.46
45	4,284	3.06	67,683	48.34
44	4,163	2.97	63,399	45.28
43	4,102	2.93	59,236	42.31
42	3,970	2.84	55,134	39.38
41	3,855	2.75	51,164	36.54
40	3,650	2.61	47,309	33.79

總級分	人數	百分比	累計人數	累計百分比
39	3,338	2.38	43,659	31.18
38	3,063	2.19	40,321	28.80
37	2,922	2.09	37,258	26.61
36	2,802	2.00	34,336	24.52
35	2,499	1.78	31,534	22.52
34	2,339	1.67	29,035	20.74
33	2,256	1.61	26,696	19.07
32	2,153	1.54	24,440	17.46
31	2,088	1.49	22,287	15.92
30	2,063	1.47	20,199	14.43
29	1,990	1.42	18,136	12.95
28	1,936	1.38	16,146	11.53
27	1,930	1.38	14,210	10.15
26	1,857	1.33	12,280	8.77
25	1,740	1.24	10,423	7.44
24	1,679	1.20	8,683	6.20
23	1,472	1.05	7,004	5.00
22	1,296	0.93	5,532	3.95
21	1,073	0.77	4,236	3.03
20	854	0.61	3,163	2.26
19	681	0.49	2,309	1.65
18	487	0.35	1,628	1.16
17	362	0.26	1,141	0.81
16	228	0.16	779	0.56
15	129	0.09	551	0.39
14	74	0.05	422	0.30
13	45	0.03	348	0.25
12	45	0.03	303	0.22
11	37	0.03	258	0.18
10	30	0.02	221	0.16
9	25	0.02	191	0.14
8	25	0.02	166	0.12
7	37	0.03	141	0.10
6	19	0.01	104	0.07
5	22	0.02	85	0.06
4	27	0.02	63	0.04
3	17	0.01	36	0.03
2	14	0.01	19	0.01
1	3	0.00	5	0.00
0	2	0.00	2	0.00

註：累計百分比＝從 0 到該級分的累計人數／（報名人數－五科均缺考人數）

九十八學年度學科能力測驗
原始分數與級分對照表

科目	國文	英文	數學	社會	自然
級距	5.94	6.25	5.97	8.56	7.91
級分	分 數 區 間				
15	83.17 - 108.00	87.51 - 100.00	83.59 - 100.00	119.85 - 144.00	110.75 - 128.00
14	77.23 - 83.16	81.26 - 87.50	77.62 - 83.58	111.29 - 119.84	102.84 - 110.74
13	71.29 - 77.22	75.01 - 81.25	71.65 - 77.61	102.73 - 111.28	94.93 - 102.83
12	65.35 - 71.28	68.76 - 75.00	65.68 - 71.64	94.17 - 102.72	87.02 - 94.92
11	59.41 - 65.34	62.51 - 68.75	59.71 - 65.67	85.61 - 94.16	79.11 - 87.01
10	53.47 - 59.40	56.26 - 62.50	53.74 - 59.70	77.05 - 85.60	71.20 - 79.10
9	47.53 - 53.46	50.01 - 56.25	47.77 - 53.73	68.49 - 77.04	63.29 - 71.19
8	41.59 - 47.52	43.76 - 50.00	41.80 - 47.76	59.93 - 68.48	55.38 - 63.28
7	35.65 - 41.58	37.51 - 43.75	35.83 - 41.79	51.37 - 59.92	47.47 - 55.37
6	29.71 - 35.64	31.26 - 37.50	29.86 - 35.82	42.81 - 51.36	39.56 - 47.46
5	23.77 - 29.70	25.01 - 31.25	23.89 - 29.85	34.25 - 42.80	31.65 - 39.55
4	17.83 - 23.76	18.76 - 25.00	17.92 - 23.88	25.69 - 34.24	23.74 - 31.64
3	11.89 - 17.82	12.51 - 18.75	11.95 - 17.91	17.13 - 25.68	15.83 - 23.73
2	5.95 - 11.88	6.26 - 12.50	5.98 - 11.94	8.57 - 17.12	7.92 - 15.82
1	0.01 - 5.94	0.01 - 6.25	0.01 - 5.97	0.01 - 8.56	0.01 - 7.91
0	0.00 - 0.00	0.00 - 0.00	0.00 - 0.00	0.00 - 0.00	0.00 - 0.00

級分計算方式如下：

1. 級距：以各科到考考生，計算其原始得分前百分之一考生（取整數，小數無條件進位）的平均原始得分，再除以 15，並取至小數第二位，第三位四捨五入。

2. 本測驗之成績採級分制，原始得分 0 分為 0 級分，最高為 15 級分，缺考以 0 級分計。各級分與原始得分、級距之計算方式詳見簡章第 10 頁。

九十七年大學入學學科能力測驗試題
英文考科

第壹部份：單一選擇題

一、詞彙（15%）

說明：第1至15題，每題選出最適當的一個選項，標示在答案卡之「選擇題答案區」。每題答對得1分，答錯不倒扣。

1. Amy did not _____ changes in the course schedule and therefore missed the class.

   (A) arrest　　　(B) alarm　　　(C) notice　　　(D) delay

2. It is not easy for old people to _____ their backs, so they need help when their backs itch.

   (A) label　　　(B) scratch　　　(C) lighten　　　(D) squeeze

3. Mary is suffering from a stomachache and needs to eat food which is easy to _____.

   (A) launch　　　(B) invade　　　(C) adopt　　　(D) digest

4. Since our classroom is not air-conditioned, we have to _____ the heat during the hot summer days.

   (A) consume　　　(B) tolerate　　　(C) recover　　　(D) promote

5. Sue is so _____ that she always breaks something when she is shopping at a store.

   (A) religious　　　(B) visual　　　(C) clumsy　　　(D) intimate

6. Ann enjoyed going to the flower market. She believed that the _____ of flowers refreshed her mind.

   (A) instance　　　(B) dominance　　　(C) appliance　　　(D) fragrance

7. The profits of Prince Charles's organic farm go to _____ to help
   the poor and the sick.
   (A) charities   (B) bulletins   (C) harvests   (D) rebels

8. Jack was given the rare _____ of using the president's office,
   which made others quite jealous.
   (A) mischief   (B) privilege   (C) involvement (D) occupation

9. This new computer is obviously _____ to the old one because it
   has many new functions.
   (A) technical   (B) suitable   (C) superior   (D) typical

10. Simon loves his work. To him, work always comes first, and family
    and friends are _____.
    (A) secondary   (B) temporary   (C) sociable   (D) capable

11. Although your plans look good, you have to be _____ and
    consider what you can actually do.
    (A) dramatic   (B) realistic   (C) stressful   (D) manageable

12. Built under the sea in 1994, the _____ between England and
    France connects the UK more closely with mainland Europe.
    (A) waterfall   (B) temple   (C) tunnel   (D) channel

13. This tour package is very appealing, and that one looks _____
    attractive. I don't know which one to choose.
    (A) equally   (B) annually   (C) merely   (D) gratefully

14. Hseu Fang-yi, a young Taiwanese dancer, recently _____ at
    Lincoln Center in New York and won a great deal of praise.
    (A) performed   (B) pretended   (C) postponed   (D) persuaded

15. The police searched the house of the suspect _____. They almost
    turned the whole house upside down.
    (A) relatively   (B) thoroughly   (C) casually   (D) permanently

二、綜合測驗（15％）

說明：　第 16 至 30 題，每題一個空格，請依文意選出最適當的一個選項，標
　　　　示在答案卡之「選擇題答案區」。每題答對得 1 分，答錯不倒扣。

What is so special about green tea? The Chinese and Indians
___16___ it for at least 4,000 years to treat everything from headache to
depression. Researchers at Purdue University recently concluded that a
compound in green tea ___17___ the growth of cancer cells. Green tea is
also helpful ___18___ infection and damaged immune function. The
secret power of green tea is its richness in a powerful anti-oxidant.

Green tea and black tea come from the same plant. Their ___19___ is
in the processing. Green tea is dried but not fermented, and this shorter
processing gives it a lighter flavor than black tea. It also helps retain the
tea's beneficial chemicals. That is ___20___ green tea is so good for
health. The only reported negative effect of drinking green tea is a
possible allergic reaction and insomnia due to the caffeine it contains.

16. (A) would use　　(B) are using　　(C) had used　　(D) have been using
17. (A) looks after　　(B) slows down　　(C) takes over　　(D) turns out
18. (A) for　　　　　(B) from　　　　　(C) at　　　　　(D) inside
19. (A) weight　　　　(B) purpose　　　　(C) difference　　(D) structure
20. (A) whether　　　(B) whenever　　　(C) what　　　　(D) why

A wise woman traveling in the mountains found a precious stone.
The next day she met another traveler who was hungry. The wise woman
generously opened her bag to ___21___ her food with the traveler. When
the hungry traveler saw the precious stone, he asked her to give it to him.
The woman did ___22___ without hesitation. The traveler left, rejoicing.
If he sold the stone, he thought, he ___23___ enough money for the rest

of his life. But in a few days he came back to find the woman. When he found her, he said, "I know how valuable this stone is, but I'm giving it back to you, ____24____ that you can give me something even more precious. You gave me the stone without asking for anything ____25____. Please teach me what you have in your heart that makes you so generous."

21. (A) give   (B) bring   (C) share   (D) earn
22. (A) so   (B) such   (C) as   (D) thus
23. (A) had   (B) had had   (C) would have   (D) would have had
24. (A) hope   (B) hoping   (C) hoped   (D) to hope
25. (A) on leave   (B) by surprise (C) off record   (D) in return

Prague, the capital of the Czech Republic, is a very beautiful city. Situated on both banks of the winding River Vltava, Prague is like one big open-air museum. ____26____ some six hundred years of architecture nearly untouched by natural disaster or war, the city retains much of its medieval appearance. ____27____ you go, there are buildings in Romanic, Baroque, and Rococo styles that were popular hundreds of years ago. All of them successfully ____28____ the destruction of postwar redevelopment and remained unchanged. While the Iron Curtain was still in place under the communist government, Prague was ____29____ visited by foreigners. Since the 1990s, ____30____, all that has changed. Prague is now one of the most popular tourist attractions in Europe.

26. (A) For   (B) With   (C) Upon   (D) Along
27. (A) Since   (B) Before   (C) Whatever   (D) Wherever
28. (A) escaped   (B) featured   (C) defended   (D) inspired
29. (A) ever   (B) seldom   (C) nearly   (D) wholly
30. (A) afterwards (B) therefore   (C) however   (D) furthermore

三、文意選填（10％）

說明：第 31 至 40 題，每題一個空格，請依文意在文章後所提供的 (A) 到(J)
選項中分別選出最適當者，並將其英文字母代號標示在答案卡之「選
擇題答案區」。每題答對得 1 分，答錯不倒扣。

One day, a guru foresaw in a vision what he would be in his next
life. Then he called his favorite disciple and asked him, "What would
you do to thank me for all you have received from me?" The disciple
said he would do whatever his guru asked him to do. Having received
this ___31___ , the guru said, "Then this is what I'd like you to do for
me. I've just ___32___ that I'll die very soon and I'm going to be reborn
as a pig. Do you see that sow eating garbage there in the yard? I'm
going to be the fourth piglet of its next litter. You'll ___33___ me by a
mark on my brow. After that sow gives birth, find the fourth piglet with
a mark on its brow and, with one ___34___ of your knife, slaughter it.
I'll then be ___35___ from a pig's life. Will you do this for me?"

The disciple felt sad to hear this, but he agreed to do as he was told.
Soon after their ___36___ , the guru died and the sow did have a litter of
four little pigs. Then the disciple ___37___ his knife and picked out the
little pig with a mark on its brow. When he was about to cut its throat,
the little pig suddenly ___38___ , "Stop!" Before the disciple could
recover from the ___39___ of hearing the little pig speak in a human
voice, it continued, "Don't kill me. I want to live on as a pig. When I
asked you to kill me, I didn't know what a pig's life would be ___40___ .
It's great! Just let me go."

(A) shock   (B) conversation   (C) like   (D) promise
(E) released   (F) screamed   (G) learned   (H) recognize
(I) stroke   (J) sharpened

四、閱讀測驗（32%）

說明：第 41 至 56 題，每題請分別根據各篇文章之文意選出最適當的一個選項，標示在答案卡之「選擇題答案區」。每題答對得 2 分，答錯不倒扣。

41-44 為題組

Howler monkeys are named for the long loud cries, or howls, that they make every day. They are the loudest land animal and their howls can be heard three miles away through dense forests. Male howler monkeys use their loud voices to fight for food, mates, or territory. Everyone starts and ends the day by howling to check out where their nearest competitors are.

Interestingly, when there are few howler monkeys in an area, the howling routine takes on a different pattern. In Belize, where howler monkeys were newly reintroduced into a wildlife sanctuary, the howler monkeys were heard only a few times a week rather than every day. Apparently, with plenty of space and no other howler monkeys around, there was no need to check on the whereabouts of their competitors. At the sanctuary, keepers now use recorded howler sounds from a distance so that the monkeys feel the need to make the territorial calls as they would do in the wild. In the future when the population grows, there will be no need for the recording because the howler monkeys will have more reason to check in with the neighbors to define their own territories.

41. Why do howler monkeys howl?
    (A) To claim their territory.
    (B) To check how popular they are.
    (C) To tell others they are going to leave.
    (D) To show friendliness to their neighbors.

42. Why did the howler monkeys in Belize howl less often?
    (A) They lived too close to each other.
    (B) There was enough food for all of them.
    (C) There were no other competitors around.
    (D) They were not used to the weather there.

43. Why do the keepers at the sanctuary use recorded howls?
   (A) To prevent the howler monkeys from getting homesick.
   (B) To help howler monkeys maintain their howling ability.
   (C) To trick the monkeys into the belief that there is plenty of
       space around.
   (D) To teach the monkeys how to make the loudest cries to scare
       people away.

44. According to the passage, which of the following is true about
   howler monkeys?
   (A) They howl most often at noon.
   (B) They originally came from Belize.
   (C) People can hear their howls three miles away.
   (D) Female monkeys howl to protect their babies.

45-48 為題組

After the creation of the Glacier National Park in Montana, the
growing number of park visitors increased the need for roads. Eventually,
the demand for a road across the mountains led to the building of the
Going-to-the-Sun Road.

The construction of the Going-to-the-Sun Road was a huge task.
After 11 years of work, the final section of the road was completed in
1932. The road is considered **an engineering feat**. Even today, visitors
to the park marvel at how such a road could have been built. It is one of
the most scenic roads in North America. The construction of the road
has changed the way visitors experience the Glacier National Park.
Visitors now can drive over sections of the park that previously took
days of horseback riding to see.

Just across the border, in Canada, is the Waterton Lakes National
Park. In 1931, members of the Rotary Clubs of Alberta and Montana

suggested joining the two parks as a symbol of peace and friendship between the two countries. In 1932, the United States and Canadian governments renamed the parks the Waterton-Glacier International Peace Park, the world's first. More recently, the parks have received several international honors. They were named as a World Heritage Site in 1995. This international recognition highlights the importance of this area, not just to the United States and Canada, but to the entire world.

45. What made it necessary to build a road through the Glacier National Park?
    (A) There were too many parks in Montana.
    (B) The park was not sunny enough for visitors.
    (C) The existing mountain roads were destroyed.
    (D) More visitors were interested in going to the park.

46. How has the Going-to-the-Sun Road influenced the way people experience the Glacier National Park?
    (A) The scenery along the road is too beautiful for visitors to drive carefully.
    (B) It has become a marvelous experience for people to ride horses on this road.
    (C) The road has allowed people to see more of the park in a shorter period of time.
    (D) The transportation on the road was so difficult that few people could really enjoy the trip.

47. What does "**an engineering feat**" mean?
    (A) A big success in construction.
    (B) A magical building machine.
    (C) A great disaster for the travelers.
    (D) An enjoyable process for engineers.

48. What is special about the Waterton-Glacier International Peace Park?
  (A) It is where the glacier runs to the lake.
  (B) It is the first park funded by the whole world.
  (C) It is a special park built to protect wild animals.
  (D) It is composed of two parks located in two countries.

49-52 為題組

Ice sculpting is a difficult process. First, ice must be carefully selected so that it is suitable for sculpting. Its ideal material is pure, clean water with high clarity. It should also have the minimum amount of air bubbles. Perfectly clear ice blocks weighing 140 kg and measuring 100cm× 50cm×25cm are available from the Clinebell Company in Colorado. Much larger clear blocks are produced in Europe and Canada or harvested from a frozen river in Sweden. These large ice blocks are used for large ice sculpting events and for building ice hotels.

Another difficulty in the process of ice sculpting is time control. The temperature of the environment affects how quickly the piece must be completed to avoid the effects of melting. If the sculpting does not take place in a cold environment, then the sculptor must work quickly to finish his piece. The tools used for sculpting also affect when the task can be accomplished. Some sculptures can be completed in as little as ten minutes if power tools are used. Ice sculptors also use razor-sharp chisels that are specifically designed for cutting ice. The best ice chisels are made in Japan, a country that, along with China, has a long tradition of magnificent ice sculptures.

Ice sculptures are used as decorations in some cuisines, especially in Asia. When holding a dinner party, some large restaurants or hotels will use an ice sculpture to decorate the table. For example, in a wedding banquet it is common to see a pair of ice-sculpted swans that represent the union of the new couple.

49. What kind of ice is ideal for sculpting?
    (A) Ice from ice hotels.
    (B) Ice from clean water.
    (C) Ice with lots of bubbles in it.
    (D) Ice weighing over 100 kilograms.

50. Why is ice sculpting difficult?
    (A) It is hard to control the size and shape of the ice.
    (B) The right theme for ice sculpting is not easy to find.
    (C) The appropriate tools are only available in some countries.
    (D) It is not easy to find the right kind of ice and work environment.

51. What is paragraph 3 mainly about?
    (A) The uses of ice sculptures.
    (B) The places where ice is sculpted.
    (C) The quality of ice sculptures.
    (D) The origin of ice sculpting parties.

52. Which of the following statements is true about the process of sculpting ice?
    (A) It takes more time to carve with razor-sharp chisels.
    (B) It can be finished in 10 minutes if the right tools are used.
    (C) Larger blocks of ice from Sweden are easier to handle for sculptors.
    (D) The carver must work fast in a cold environment to avoid catching cold.

53-56 為題組

If you touch your finger to a hot stove, you know it's going to hurt. However, if you convince yourself beforehand that the pain won't be so bad, you might not suffer as much. According to a recent study, the part of your brain that reacts to severe pain is largely the same part that reacts to expectation of pain.

Researchers in this study worked with 10 volunteers, ages 24 to 46. Each volunteer wore a device that gave out 20-second-long pulses of heat to the right leg. There were three levels of heat, producing mild, moderate, or strong pain. During training, the volunteers would first hear a tone, followed by a period of silence, and then feel a heat pulse. They then learned to associate the length of the silent pause with the intensity of the upcoming heat pulse. The longer the pause, the stronger the heat pulse would be, causing more severe pain.

A day or two later, the real experiment began. The researchers found that the parts of the brain involved in learning, memory, emotion, and touch became more active as the volunteers expected higher levels of pain. These were mainly the same areas that became active when participants actually felt pain. Interestingly, when the volunteers expected only mild or moderate pain but experienced severe pain, they reported feeling 28 percent less pain than when they expected severe pain and actually got it.

The new study emphasizes that pain has both physical and psychological elements. Understanding how pain works in the mind and brain could eventually give doctors tools for helping people cope with painful medical treatments.

53. What is the main idea of the passage?
    (A) We should learn to be sensitive to pain.
    (B) Our feeling of pain is decided by our environment.
    (C) How people feel pain remains unknown to scientists.
    (D) Our reaction to pain is closely related to our expectation of pain.

54. Which of the following is true about the pulses of heat in the study?
    (A) Each heat pulse lasted for 20 seconds.
    (B) The pulses were given to the arms of the volunteers.
    (C) Different devices gave out different levels of heat pulses.
    (D) There were two levels of heat intensity given to the volunteers.

55. How did the volunteers learn to expect different levels of heat?
    (A) From the loudness of the tone they heard.
    (B) From the instruction given to them by the researchers.
    (C) From the color of a light flashing on the device they wore.
    (D) From the length of the pause between a tone and the heat pulse.

56. According to the passage, what may be the author's advice to a doctor before a surgery?
    (A) To provide the patient with more pain killers.
    (B) To talk to the patient and ease his/her worries.
    (C) To give the patient strong heat pulses beforehand.
    (D) To emphasize the possible severe pain to the patient.

第貳部份：非選擇題

一、翻譯題（8％）

說明：1. 請將以下兩個中文句子譯成正確、通順、達意的英文，並將答案寫
        在「答案卷」上。
      2. 請依序作答，並標明題號。每題4分，共8分。

1. 聽音樂是一個你可以終生享受的嗜好。
2. 但能彈奏樂器可以為你帶來更多的喜悅。

二、英文作文（20％）

說明：1. 依提示在「答案卷」上寫一篇英文作文。
      2. 文長 120 個單詞（words）左右。

提示：你（英文名字必須假設為 George 或 Mary）向朋友（英文名字必須
     假設為 Adam 或 Eve）借了一件相當珍貴的物品，但不慎遺失，一
     時又買不到替代品。請寫一封信，第一段說明物品遺失的經過，第
     二段則表達歉意並提出可能的解決方案。

請注意：為避免評分困擾，請使用上述提示的 George 或 Mary 在信末署名，
       不得使用自己真實的中文或英文姓名。

97年度學科能力測驗英文科試題詳解

第壹部分：單選題

一、詞彙：

1. (**C**) Amy did not <u>notice</u> changes in the course schedule and therefore missed the class.
   愛咪沒有<u>注意到</u>課表的變動，因而錯過這堂課。
   (A) arrest〔ə'rɛst〕v. 逮捕　(B) alarm〔ə'lɑrm〕v. 使驚慌
   (C) **notice**〔'notɪs〕v. 注意到　(D) delay〔dɪ'le〕v. 延遲；耽擱
   course〔kors〕n. 課程　schedule〔'skɛdʒul〕n. 時間表
   miss〔mɪs〕v. 錯過；缺（席、課）

2. (**B**) It is not easy for old people to <u>scratch</u> their backs, so they need help when their backs itch.
   對老人來說，要<u>抓</u>自己的背不太容易，所以當他們背部發癢的時候，會需要幫忙。
   (A) label〔'lebl̩〕v. 貼標籤於　(B) **scratch**〔skrætʃ〕v. 抓（癢）
   (C) lighten〔'laɪtn̩〕v. 照亮　(D) squeeze〔skwiz〕v. 擠壓
   itch〔ɪtʃ〕v. 癢

3. (**D**) Mary is suffering from a stomachache and needs to eat food which is easy to <u>digest</u>.
   瑪莉胃痛，所以必須吃容易<u>消化</u>的食物。
   (A) launch〔lɔntʃ〕v. 發射
   (B) invade〔ɪn'ved〕v. 入侵
   (C) adopt〔ə'dɑpt〕v. 採用；領養
   (D) **digest**〔daɪ'dʒɛst〕v. 消化
   suffer〔'sʌfɚ〕v. 受苦；罹患
   stomachache〔'stʌmək‚ek〕n. 胃痛

4. (**B**) Since our classroom is not air-conditioned, we have to <u>tolerate</u> the heat during the hot summer days.

因爲我們的教室沒有裝冷氣，所以我們必須忍受炎熱夏天的暑氣。

(A) consume (kən'sum) *v.* 消耗

(B) ***tolerate*** ('talə,ret) *v.* 忍受

(C) recover (rɪ'kʌvɚ) *v.* 恢復

(D) promote (prə'mot) *v.* 升遷；提倡；促銷

air-conditioned ('ɛrkən'dɪʃənd) *adj.* 裝有冷氣機的

heat (hit) *n.* 熱；暑氣

5. (**C**) Sue is so <u>clumsy</u> that she always breaks something when she is shopping at a store.

蘇很<u>笨拙</u>，她在商店裡購物的時候，老是打破東西。

(A) religious (rɪ'lɪdʒəs) *adj.* 虔誠的

(B) visual ('vɪʒʊəl) *adj.* 視覺的

(C) ***clumsy*** ('klʌmzɪ) *adj.* 笨拙的

(D) intimate ('ɪntəmɪt) *adj.* 親密的

6. (**D**) Ann enjoyed going to the flower market. She believed that the <u>fragrance</u> of flowers refreshed her mind.

安喜歡去花市。她認爲花的<u>香味</u>可以讓她提神。

(A) instance ('ɪnstəns) *n.* 實例

(B) dominance ('damənəns) *n.* 權勢；支配

(C) appliance (ə'plaɪəns) *n.* 器具；用品

(D) ***fragrance*** ('fregrəns) *n.* 香味

refresh (rɪ'frɛʃ) *v.* 使提神

7. (**A**) The profits of Prince Charles's organic farm go to <u>charities</u> to help the poor and the sick.

查理斯王子的有機農場的利潤，是要捐給<u>慈善機構</u>去幫助窮人及病人。

(A) ***charity*** ('tʃærətɪ) *n.* 慈善機構

(B) bulletin ('bʊlətɪn) *n.* 佈告

(C) harvest (ˈhɑrvɪst) *n.* 收穫；收成

(D) rebel (ˈrɛbl̩) *n.* 叛徒

profit (ˈprɑfɪt) *n.* 利潤　　organic (ɔrˈgænɪk) *adj.* 有機的

go to 被給予　　***the poor*** 窮人 (= *poor people*)

the sick 生病的人 (= *sick people*)

8. (**B**) Jack was given the rare privilege of using the president's office, which made others quite jealous.
傑克得到使用董事長辦公室稀有的特權，使得其他人相當嫉妒。

    (A) mischief (ˈmɪstʃɪf) *n.* 惡作劇

    (B) ***privilege*** (ˈprɪvl̩ɪdʒ) *n.* 特權

    (C) involvement (ɪnˈvɑlvmənt) *n.* 牽連

    (D) occupation (ˌɑkjəˈpeʃən) *n.* 職業

rare (rɛr) *adj.* 罕見的；稀有的　　president (ˈprɛzədənt) *n.* 董事長

jealous (ˈdʒɛləs) *adj.* 嫉妒的

9. (**C**) This new computer is obviously superior to the old one because it has many new functions.
這台新電腦明顯地比舊的好，因為它有許多新的功能。

    (A) technical (ˈtɛknɪkl̩) *adj.* 技術上的

    (B) suitable (ˈsutəbl̩) *adj.* 適合的

    (C) ***superior*** (səˈpɪrɪɚ) *adj.* 較優秀的

    (D) typical (ˈtɪpɪkl̩) *adj.* 典型的

obviously (ˈɑbvɪəslɪ) *adv.* 顯然　　function (ˈfʌŋkʃən) *n.* 功能

10. (**A**) Simon loves his work. To him, work always comes first, and family and friends are secondary. 賽門熱愛他的工作。對他來說，工作總是第一優先，家人和朋友是第二順序。

    (A) ***secondary*** (ˈsɛkəndˌɛrɪ) *adj.* (重要性、順序) 第二位的；次要的

    (B) temporary (ˈtɛmpəˌrɛrɪ) *adj.* 暫時的

    (C) sociable (ˈsoʃəbl̩) *adj.* 善交際的

    (D) capable (ˈkepəbl̩) *adj.* 有能力的

11. (**B**) Although your plans look good, you have to be <u>realistic</u> and consider what you can actually do. 雖然你的計畫看起來很不錯，但你必須<u>實際</u>一點，想想你真正可以做到的。

 (A) dramatic〔drə'mætɪk〕*adj.* 戲劇性的

 (B) *realistic*〔,riə'lɪstɪk〕*adj.* 現實的；實際的

 (C) stressful〔'strɛsfəl〕*adj.* 壓力大的

 (D) manageable〔'mænɪdʒəbl̩〕*adj.* 易於管理的

 consider〔kən'sɪdɚ〕*v.* 仔細考慮 actually〔'æktʃʊəlɪ〕*adv.* 實際上

12. (**C**) Built under the sea in 1994, the <u>tunnel</u> between England and France connects the UK more closely with mainland Europe. 1994 年在英國和法國之間建造於海底的<u>隧道</u>，使英國與歐洲大陸更緊密地連結在一起。

 (A) waterfall〔'wɔtɚ,fɔl〕*n.* 瀑布

 (B) temple〔'tɛmpl̩〕*n.* 寺廟

 (C) *tunnel*〔'tʌnl̩〕*n.* 隧道；地道

 (D) channel〔'tʃænl̩〕*n.* 海峽；頻道

 connect〔kə'nɛkt〕*v.* 連接 *the UK* 英國 (= *the United Kingdom*)

 closely〔'kloslɪ〕*adv.* 緊密地 mainland〔'men,lænd〕*n.* 大陸

 mainland Europe 歐洲大陸

13. (**A**) This tour package is very appealing, and that one looks <u>equally</u> attractive. I don't know which one to choose. 這個套裝行程非常令人心動，而那個看起來也<u>相同地</u>吸引人。我不知道該選那一個。

 (A) *equally*〔'ikwəlɪ〕*adv.* 同樣地；相等地

 (B) annually〔'ænjuəlɪ〕*adv.* 每年；每年一次地

 (C) merely〔'mɪrlɪ〕*adv.* 僅僅

 (D) gratefully〔'gretfəlɪ〕*adv.* 感激地

 tour package 套裝行程

 appealing〔ə'pilɪŋ〕*adj.* 吸引人的；令人心動的

 attractive〔ə'træktɪv〕*adj.* 吸引人的

14. (**A**) Hseu Fang-yi, a young Taiwanese dancer, recently <u>performed</u> at Lincoln Center in New York and won a great deal of praise.

許芳宜是一位年輕的台灣舞者，最近在紐約的林肯中心<u>表演</u>，贏得了許多讚揚。

(A) ***perform*** (pəˋfɔrm) v. 表演
(B) pretend (prɪˋtɛnd) v. 假裝
(C) postpone (postˋpon) v. 拖延；延遲
(D) persuade (pəˋswed) v. 說服

recently (ˋrisn̩tlɪ) adv. 最近　　***a great deal*** 相當多的
praise (prez) n. 稱讚

15. (**B**) The police searched the house of the suspect <u>thoroughly</u>. They almost turned the whole house upside down.

警方<u>徹底地</u>搜索嫌疑犯的家裡。他們幾乎把整個房子翻得亂七八糟。

(A) relatively (ˋrɛlətɪvlɪ) adv. 相對地；相當地
(B) ***thoroughly*** (ˋθɝolɪ) adv. 徹底地
(C) casually (ˋkæʒʊəlɪ) adv. 偶然地
(D) permanently (ˋpɝmənəntlɪ) adv. 永久地

search (sɝtʃ) v. 搜查；搜索　　suspect (ˋsʌspɛkt) n. 嫌疑犯
upside down 混亂地；雜亂地

二、綜合測驗：

What is so special about green tea? The Chinese and Indians <u>have been using</u> it for at least 4,000 years to treat everything from headache to
　16
depression. Researchers at Purdue University recently concluded that a compound in green tea <u>slows down</u> the growth of cancer cells. Green tea is
　　　　　　　　　　　　　　17
also helpful <u>for</u> infection and damaged immune function. The secret power
　　　　　　　18
of green tea is its richness in a powerful anti-oxidant.

綠茶有何特別之處？中國人和印度人一直使用綠茶，來治療小至頭痛，大至憂鬱症的病，已經至少有四千年之久。最近，普渡大學的研究人員斷定，綠茶中有種化合物，能減緩癌細胞的生長。綠茶也有助於治療傳染病，以及免疫功能受損。綠茶的神秘力量，就在於它富含一種強效的抗氧化劑。

> Indian〔'ɪndɪən〕n. 印度人　　***at least*** 至少
> treat〔trit〕v. 治療　　headache〔'hɛd,ek〕n. 頭痛
> depression〔dɪ'prɛʃən〕n. 沮喪；憂鬱症
> researcher〔rɪ'sɜtʃə〕n. 研究人員　　Purdue〔pə'dju〕n. 普渡
> ***Purdue University*** 普渡大學【位於美國印地安那州】
> recently〔'risn̩tlɪ〕adv. 最近
> conclude〔kən'klud〕v. 下結論；斷定
> compound〔'kɑmpaʊnd〕n. 化合物　　growth〔groθ〕n. 生長
> cell〔sɛl〕n. 細胞　　***cancer cell*** 癌細胞
> infection〔ɪn'fɛkʃən〕n. 感染；傳染病
> damaged〔'dæmɪdʒd〕adj. 受損的　　immune〔ɪ'mjun〕adj. 免疫的
> function〔'fʌŋkʃən〕n. 功能；作用　　secret〔'sikrɪt〕adj. 秘密的
> power〔'paʊə〕n. 力量　　richness〔'rɪtʃnɪs〕n. 豐富
> powerful〔'paʊəfəl〕adj. 強有力的；有功效的
> anti-oxidant〔,æntɪ'ɑksədn̩t〕n. 抗氧化劑

16. (**D**) 由 for at least 4,000 years（持續至少四千年）可知，動作由過去持續到現在，須用「現在完成式」，如果強調該動作仍在進行中，則可用「現在完成進行式」，故選 (D) ***have been using***。

17. (**B**) 依句意，選 (B) ***slows down***「減緩」。而 (A) look after「照顧」，(C) take over「接管」，(D) turn out「結果（是）」，均不合句意。

18. (**A**) ***be helpful for*** 有助於

　　Green tea and black tea come from the same plant. Their <u>difference</u> is 19 in the processing. Green tea is dried but not fermented, and this shorter processing gives it a lighter flavor than black tea. It also helps retain the tea's beneficial chemicals. That is <u>why</u> green tea is so good for health. 20

The only reported negative effect of drinking green tea is a possible allergic reaction and insomnia due to the caffeine it contains.

　　綠茶與紅茶來自於同樣的植物。它們的不同在於處理的過程。綠茶是被曬乾而非發酵，而這種較短的處理過程，使它比紅茶的味道更清淡。這種處理方式也保留了茶中有益的化學物質。這就是爲什麼綠茶會有益健康的原因。據說喝綠茶唯一的負面影響就是，由於綠茶含有咖啡因，所以可能會引起過敏反應與失眠。

> **black tea** 紅茶　　plant (plænt) *n.* 植物
> process ('prasɛs) *v.* 處理　　dry (draɪ) *v.* 使乾燥；曬乾
> ferment (fə'mɛnt) *v.* 使發酵　　light (laɪt) *adj.* 清淡的
> flavor ('flevɚ) *n.* 味道；風味　　retain (rɪ'ten) *v.* 保持；保留
> beneficial (,bɛnə'fɪʃəl) *adj.* 有益的
> chemical ('kɛmɪkḷ) *n.* 化學物質　　**be good for** 對…有益
> health (hɛlθ) *n.* 健康　　report (rɪ'port) *v.* 報導；報告；說
> negative ('nɛgətɪv) *adj.* 負面的　　effect (ɪ'fɛkt) *n.* 影響
> allergic (ə'lɝdʒɪk) *adj.* 過敏的　　reaction (rɪ'ækʃən) *n.* 反應
> insomnia (ɪn'samnɪə) *n.* 失眠　　**due to** 由於
> caffeine ('kæfiɪn) *n.* 咖啡因　　contain (kən'ten) *v.* 包含

19. (**C**)　依句意，選 (C) *difference*「不同」。而 (A) weight (wet) *n.* 重量，
　　(B) purpose ('pɝpəs) *n.* 目的，(D) structure ('strʌktʃɚ) *n.* 構造，
　　均不合句意。

20. (**D**)　這就是「爲什麼」綠茶會有益健康的原因，故選 (D) *why*。

　　A wise woman traveling in the mountains found a precious stone. The next day she met another traveler who was hungry. The wise woman generously opened her bag to <u>share</u> her food with the traveler. When the
　　　　　　　　　　　　　　　　　21
hungry traveler saw the precious stone, he asked her to give it to him. The woman did <u>so</u> without hesitation. The traveler left, rejoicing. If he sold
　　　　　22
the stone, he thought, he <u>would have</u> enough money for the rest of his life.
　　　　　　　　　　　　　　　　23

　　一位很有智慧的女士在山裡旅行時，發現了一顆寶石。隔天，她遇見另一位飢餓的旅行者。這位有智慧的女士很慷慨地打開她的背包，與那位旅行者分享她的食物。當飢餓的旅行者看見那顆寶石時，他要求她把寶石給他。女士毫不猶豫就這麼做了。旅行者離開了，非常高興。他想，如果他把寶石賣了，他就有足夠的錢可以過下半輩子了。

> precious (ˈprɛʃəs) *adj.* 珍貴的　**precious stone** 寶石
> generously (ˈdʒɛnərəslɪ) *adv.* 大方地；慷慨地
> hesitation (ˌhɛzəˈteʃən) *n.* 猶豫；遲疑
> **without hesitation** 毫不猶豫；毫不遲疑
> rejoice (rɪˈdʒɔɪs) *v.* 高興；慶幸 (= be glad；be pleased)

21. (**C**) 依句意，女士與他「分享」食物，選 (C) *share*。(A) 應改成 give her
　　　　 food *to* the traveler，(B) bring「帶來」，(D) earn「賺得」，均不合。

22. (**A**) 空格前動詞 did 之後需要代名詞作受詞，代替前面 give it to him
　　　　 這件事，故本題選 (A) *so*。(B) such 也可當代名詞，但指的是「這
　　　　 樣的人、事、物」，在此用法不合。(C) 和 (D) 則無此用法。

23. (**C**) 前句 If 子句為條件句，若以旅行者本人第一人稱來說，應說成：If
　　　　 I sell the stone, I will have enough money for the rest of my life.
　　　　 而在文章裡，將這句話改成第三人稱單數、過去式，即成為：If he
　　　　 sold the stone, he would have enough money for the rest of his
　　　　 life.，故本題選 (C) *would have*。

But in a few days he came back to find the woman.　When he found her,
he said, "I know how valuable this stone is, but I'm giving it back to you,
hoping that you can give me something even more precious.　You gave me
　24
the stone without asking for anything in return. Please teach me what you
　　　　　　　　　　　　　　　　　　　　　 25
have in your heart that makes you so generous."

但是在幾天之內，他又回去找那位女士。當他找到她時，他說：「我知道這顆寶
石非常價值，但是我要把它還給妳，希望妳能夠給我別的更珍貴的東西。妳給

我這顆寶石，完全沒有要求任何東西作為回報。請教導我，妳心中有什麼能讓妳如此慷慨大方。」

　　valuable (ˈvæljəbḷ) adj. 有價值的

24. (**B**) 空格原本應為 I'm…to you, *and hope* that you can…，省略連接詞 and，則將 hope 改成分詞，故本題選 (B) *hoping*。

25. (**D**) (A) on leave 休假中
　　　　　(B) 要用 *take* ~ by surprise 使~驚訝；偷襲~
　　　　　(C) 要用 off *the* record 不留記錄的；非正式的
　　　　　(D) *in return* 作為回報

　　　Prague, the capital of the Czech Republic, is a very beautiful city. Situated on both banks of the winding River Vltava, Prague is like one big open-air museum. <u>With</u> some six hundred years of architecture nearly
　　　　　　　　　　　　　26
untouched by natural disaster or war, the city retains much of its medieval appearance.

　　布拉格，捷克首都，是一座非常美麗的都市。布拉格位於蜿蜒的伏爾塔瓦河兩岸，它就像一座龐大的露天博物館。布拉格有大約六百年歷史的建築物，幾乎都沒有被天災或戰爭所破壞，這座都市保留了許多中世紀的風貌。

　　　　Prague〔 prɑg , preg〕n. 布拉格【捷克首都】
　　　　capital (ˈkæpətḷ) n. 首都　　Czech〔 tʃɛk〕adj. 捷克的
　　　　republic〔 rɪˈpʌblɪk〕n. 共和國
　　　　situated (ˈsɪtʃu͵etɪd) adj. 位於~的 (= *located*)
　　　　bank〔 bæŋk〕n. 河岸　　winding (ˈwaɪndɪŋ) adj. 蜿蜒的
　　　　Vltava n. 伏爾塔瓦河【捷克最長的河流】
　　　　open-air adj. 戶外的；露天的　　some〔 sʌm〕adv. 大約【與數詞連用】
　　　　architecture (ˈɑrkə͵tɛktʃɚ) n. 建築物；建築樣式
　　　　untouched〔 ʌnˈtʌtʃt〕adj. 未被碰到的；未受影響的
　　　　natural disaster 天然災害　　retain〔 rɪˈten〕v. 保留 (= *keep*)
　　　　medieval (͵midɪˈivḷ) adj. 中世紀的
　　　　appearance〔 əˈpɪrɪəns〕n. 外表；外貌

26.(**B**) 表示「具有」，介系詞用 *With*，選 (B)。

Wherever you go, there are buildings in Romanic, Baroque, and Rococo
　　27
styles that were popular hundreds of years ago. All of them successfully
escaped the destruction of postwar redevelopment and remained unchanged.
　28
無論你走到那裡，都有數百年前非常流行的古羅馬式、巴洛克式、洛可可式風
格的建築物。所有建築物都成功地逃過了戰後重建的破壞，而依然保持不變。

> Romanic (ro'mænɪk) *adj.* 古羅馬的
> Baroque (bə'rok) *adj.* 巴洛克式的【十七世紀起源於羅馬，之後風行
> 　　全歐洲的一種奇異、過度裝飾的建築、美術和音樂風格】
> Rococo (rə'koko) *adj.* 洛可可式的【十八世紀以法國為中心所盛行的
> 　　一種華麗的建築、美術和音樂風格】　　style (staɪl) *n.* 風格
> destruction (dɪ'strʌkʃən) *n.* 破壞
> postwar (post'wɔr) *adj.* 戰後的【post = after】
> redevelopment (,ridɪ'vɛləpmənt) *n.* 重新開發
> remain (rɪ'men) *v.* 仍然；保持
> unchanged (ʌn'tʃendʒd) *adj.* 不變的

27.(**D**) 依句意「無論你走到那裡」，選 (C) *Wherever*。

28.(**A**) 依句意，所有的建築物都維持不變，當然是「逃過」了破壞，故
　　　　選 (A) *escaped*。
　　　　而 (B) feature「以～為特色」，(C) defend「保護；保衛」，
　　　　(D) inspire「啓發；激勵」，句意均不合。

While the Iron Curtain was still in place under the communist government,
Prague was seldom visited by foreigners. Since the 1990s, however, all that
　　　　　　　　　29　　　　　　　　　　　　　　　　　　　30
has changed. Prague is now one of the most popular tourist attractions in
Europe.

在共產政府統治之下，鐵幕還存在時，布拉格很少有外國人造訪。然而，自從一九九〇年代以來，所有的一切都改變了。布拉格現在是全歐洲最受歡迎的旅遊景點之一。

> iron（ˈaɪən）n. 鐵　　curtain（ˈkɜtṇ）n. 窗簾；布幕
> ***Iron Curtain*** 鐵幕【在政治上與思想上，劃分東歐共產國家和西歐諸國的界線】　　***be in place*** 在一定的位置上
> communist（ˈkɑmjʊnɪst）adj. 共產主義的
> tourist（ˈtʊrɪst）adj. 旅遊的；觀光的
> attraction（əˈtrækʃən）n. 吸引人之物；名勝

29.（ **B** ）依句意，鐵幕還存在，一定「很少」有外國人造訪，選 (B) *seldom*。
　　而 (A) ever「曾經」(用於疑問、否定、條件句)，(C) nearly「幾乎」，
　　(D) wholly「完全地」，均不合句意。

30.（ **C** ）前句說到外國人很少，後句則說一切都改變了，可知語氣有所轉折，
　　故本題選 (C) *however*「然而」。
　　而 (A) afterwards「後來」，(B) therefore「因此」，(D) furthermore
　　「此外」，均不合句意。

三、文意選填：

　　One day, a guru foresaw in a vision what he would be in his next life. Then he called his favorite disciple and asked him, "What would you do to thank me for all you have received from me?" The disciple said he would do whatever his guru asked him to do.

　　有一天，有個印度上師在幻象中，預知到他來世會變成什麼。然後他叫他最喜愛的弟子過來，並問他：「對於所有你從我這邊學到的東西，你要怎麼答謝我呢？」這位弟子說，他願意做所有上師要求他做的事。

> guru（ˈguru）n. (印度教的) 宗教教師；上師
> foresee（fɔrˈsi）v. 預知　　vision（ˈvɪʒən）n. 幻象
> ***next life*** 來生　　favorite（ˈfevərɪt）adj. 最喜愛的
> disciple（dɪˈsaɪpḷ）n. 門徒；弟子　　receive（rɪˈsiv）v. 接受；得到

Having received this ³¹**(D) promise** , the guru said, "Then this is what I'd like you to do for me. I've just ³²**(G) learned** that I'll die very soon and I'm going to be reborn as a pig. Do you see that sow eating garbage there in the yard? I'm going to be the fourth piglet of its next litter. You'll ³³**(H) recognize** me by a mark on my brow. After that sow gives birth, find the fourth piglet with a mark on its brow and, with one ³⁴**(I) stroke** of your knife, slaughter it. I'll then be ³⁵**(E) released** from a pig's life. Will you do this for me?"

得到這個承諾之後，上師說：「那麼這就是我要你為我做的事。我剛得知我很快就要死了，而且我來生會是一隻豬。你看到那頭正在豬圈裡吃剩菜的母豬了嗎？我會是牠下一胎的第四隻小豬。你會從我額頭上的記號認出我。在那隻母豬生產之後，找到額頭上有記號的第四隻小豬，用你的刀給牠一擊，把牠殺了。然後我就可以從豬的生活中解脫了。你會為我做這件事嗎？」

promise〔'pramɪs〕n. 承諾　　***would like*** 想要

learn〔lɝn〕v. 得知　　reborn〔ri'bɔrn〕adj. 再生的；重生的

sow〔sau〕n. 母豬　　garbage〔'garbɪdʒ〕n. 垃圾；剩菜

yard〔jard〕n.（家畜等的）圈欄　　piglet〔'pɪglɪt〕n. 小豬

litter〔'lɪtɚ〕n.（豬、狗等）一胎所生的小豬、小狗

recognize〔'rɛkəg,naɪz〕v. 認出

mark〔mark〕n. 記號　　brow〔brau〕n. 眉毛；額頭

give birth 生產　　stroke〔strok〕n. 一擊

knife〔naɪf〕n. 刀子　　slaughter〔'slɔtɚ〕v. 宰殺

release〔rɪ'lis〕v. 釋放；使脫離

The disciple felt sad to hear this, but he agreed to do as he was told. Soon after their ³⁶**(B) conversation**, the guru died and the sow did have a litter of four little pigs. Then the disciple ³⁷**(J) sharpened** his knife and picked out the little pig with a mark on its brow.

聽到這個，這位弟子感到很難過，不過他同意照被吩咐的話去做。在他們談完話不久後，上師過世了，而母豬真的生了四隻小豬。然後這位弟子將他的刀磨利，並且挑出了額頭上有記號的那隻小豬。

have〔hev〕v. 生育　　sharpen〔'ʃarpən〕v. 使銳利；磨（刀）

pick out 辨認出；挑出

When he was about to cut its throat, the little pig suddenly [38](F) screamed, "Stop!" Before the disciple could recover from the [39](A) shock of hearing the little pig speak in a human voice, it continued, "Don't kill me. I want to live on as a pig. When I asked you to kill me, I didn't know what a pig's life would be [40](C) like. It's great! Just let me go."

當他正要割牠的喉嚨時，這隻小豬突然放聲大叫：「住手！」在這位弟子還沒從聽到小豬會說人話的這個驚嚇中恢復過來之前，牠繼續說：「不要殺我。我想要繼續當一隻豬。當我要求你殺我時，我並不知道豬的生活會是什麼樣子。真是快活極了！把我放開，讓我走。」

> ***be about to*** 即將　　throat〔θrot〕*n.* 喉嚨
> suddenly〔'sʌdṇlɪ〕*adv.* 突然地　　scream〔skrim〕*v.* 尖叫
> recover〔rɪ'kʌvɚ〕*v.* 恢復　　shock〔ʃɑk〕*n.* 震驚
> voice〔vɔɪs〕*n.* 聲音　　continue〔kən'tɪnju〕*v.* 繼續說
> ***live on*** 繼續活著　　like〔laɪk〕*prep.* 像⋯的
> great〔gret〕*adj.* 很棒的

四、閱讀測驗：

41-44 為題組

Howler monkeys are named for the long loud cries, or howls, that they make every day. They are the loudest land animal and their howls can be heard three miles away through dense forests. Male howler monkeys use their loud voices to fight for food, mates, or territory. Everyone starts and ends the day by howling to check out where their nearest competitors are.

吼猴是因為牠們每天都發出長而響亮的叫聲，或吼聲而得名。牠們是聲音最大的陸地動物，其吼叫聲能穿過密林，傳到三哩之外的地方。公的吼猴利用吼叫聲來爭奪食物、伴侶及領土。每個成員，藉由吼叫確認最接近牠們的對手位置，來開始和結束一天的生活。

> howler〔'haʊlɚ〕*n.* 咆哮者
> ***howler monkey*** 吼猴，產地為中南美洲，喜活動於樹林的中、低層。
> dense〔dɛns〕*adj.* 濃密的　　male〔mel〕*adj.* 公的　　***fight for*** 爭奪
> mate〔met〕*n.* 配偶　　territory〔'tɛrə,torɪ〕*n.* 領土
> competitor〔kəm'pɛtətɚ〕*n.* 對手；競爭者

Interestingly, when there are few howler monkeys in an area, the howling routine takes on a different pattern. In Belize, where howler monkeys were newly reintroduced into a wildlife sanctuary, the howler monkeys were heard only a few times a week rather than every day. Apparently, with plenty of space and no other howler monkeys around, there was no need to check on the whereabouts of their competitors. At the sanctuary, keepers now use recorded howler sounds from a distance so that the monkeys feel the need to make the territorial calls as they would do in the wild. In the future when the population grows, there will be no need for the recording because the howler monkeys will have more reason to check in with the neighbors to define their own territories.

有趣的是，當一個地區裡只有少數幾隻吼猴時，日常的吼叫模式會不一樣。最近在貝里斯，吼猴被重新引進一個野生動物保護區，這些吼猴變成一週只叫幾次而不是天天吼叫。顯然，空間大且沒有其他的吼猴在旁時，牠們不需要去確認競爭者的位置。現在，在保護區內，管理員在一段距離外，播放錄製好的吼猴聲音，讓猴子們覺得，有必要發出宣示領土的叫聲，就跟牠們在野外一樣。當未來族群數量增加時，就不需要這些錄音了，因為這些吼猴將更有理由，讓牠們的鄰居知道牠們的存在，以界定自己的領土範圍。

routine (ru'tin) *n.* 慣例　　pattern ('pætən) *n.* 模式
newly ('njulɪ) *adv.* 最近
reintroduce (,riɪntrə'djus) *v.* 重新引進
wildlife ('waɪld,laɪf) *adj.* 野生動物的
sanctuary ('sæŋktʃu,ɛrɪ) *n.* (動物) 保護區
apparently (ə'pærəntlɪ) *adv.* 顯然　　***plenty of*** 很多
whereabouts (,hwɛrə'baʊts) *n.* 下落；去向
keeper ('kipə) *n.* 管理員　　recorded (rɪ'kɔrdɪd) *adj.* 錄音的
distance ('dɪstəns) *n.* 距離　　territorial (,tɛrə'torɪəl) *adj.* 領土的
call (kɔl) *n.* 叫聲　　wild (waɪld) *n.* 野外
population (,pɑpjə'leʃən) *n.* 族群　　reason ('rizn̩) *n.* 理由；動機
check in with *sb.* 讓某人知道你的存在 (*= let sb. know you're there*)
【此成語美國人常用，但字典上查不到】　　define (dɪ'faɪn) *v.* 界定

41. (**A**) 為什麼吼猴要吼叫？

(A) 宣示牠們的領域。　　　　(B) 確認牠們有多受歡迎。

(C) 告訴別人牠們要離開了。　(D) 向牠們的鄰居們表示友善。

claim〔klem〕v. 宣稱　　　popular〔'pɑpjələ〕adj. 受歡迎的
friendliness〔'frɛndlınıs〕n. 友善

42. (**C**) 為什麼貝里斯的吼猴們較不常吼叫？

(A) 牠們彼此居住得太近了。

(B) 有足夠的食物供給牠們全部。

(C) 附近沒有其他的競爭者。

(D) 牠們不習慣那裡的天氣。

43. (**B**) 為什麼保護區的管理員們使用錄音的吼叫聲？

(A) 防止吼猴們想家。

(B) 幫助吼猴們維持牠們吼叫的能力。

(C) 欺騙猴子們相信有很充分的空間。

(D) 教導猴子們如何吼出最大的叫聲來嚇走人們。

prevent〔prı'vɛnt〕v. 防止

homesick〔'hom,sık〕adj. 想家的

maintain〔men'ten〕v. 維持　　ability〔ə'bılətı〕n. 能力

trick〔trık〕v. 欺騙　　　belief〔bə'lif〕n. 確信；信念

44. (**C**) 根據本文，下列關於吼猴的敘述，何者正確？

(A) 牠們最常在中午吼叫。

(B) 牠們最初來自貝里斯。

(C) 人們在三哩外能聽見牠們的吼聲。

(D) 母猴以吼叫來保護牠們的小孩。

originally〔ə'rıdʒənlı〕adv. 最初　　mile〔maıl〕n. 哩
female〔'fimel〕adj. 母的　　protect〔prə'tɛkt〕v. 保護

45-48 為題組

After the creation of the Glacier National Park in Montana, the growing number of park visitors increased the need for roads. Eventually, the demand for a road across the mountains led to the building of the Going-to-the-Sun Road.

在蒙大拿州的「冰河國家公園」設立後，園內遊客數目的成長增加了對道路的需求。最後，對於山間道路的要求造就了「向陽大道」的建設。

> creation (krɪ'eʃən) *n.* 創造　　glacier ('gleʃɚ) *n.* 冰河
> ***Glacier National Park*** 冰河國家公園
> Montana (mɑn'tænə) *n.* 蒙大拿州【美國西北部一州】
> eventually (ɪ'vɛntʃʊəlɪ) *adv.* 最後；終於
> increase (ɪn'kris) *v.* 增加　　demand (dɪ'mænd) *n.* 要求
> ***lead to*** 致使；造就　　***Going-to-the-Sun Road*** 向陽大道

The construction of the Going-to-the-Sun Road was a huge task. After 11 years of work, the final section of the road was completed in 1932. The road is considered **an engineering feat**. Even today, visitors to the park marvel at how such a road could have been built. It is one of the most scenic roads in North America. The construction of the road has changed the way visitors experience the Glacier National Park. Visitors now can drive over sections of the park that previously took days of horseback riding to see.

「向陽大道」的建築是一項浩大的任務。歷時十一年工程後，最後的路段於一九三二年完工。此路被視為一工程偉業。甚至現今，園內的遊客對如此的道路是如何得以被建造感到驚嘆。它是北美沿途景致最佳的公路之一。此路的興建改變了遊客體驗冰河國家公園的方式。遊客現在可以開車遊覽數個地區，這在昔日需騎馬數日才能走完。

> huge (hjudʒ) *adj.* 巨大的　　task (tæsk) *n.* 工作；任務
> section ('sɛkʃən) *n.* 地區　　complete (kəm'plit) *v.* 完成
> consider (kən'sɪdɚ) *v.* 認為

engineering (͵ɛndʒə'nɪrɪŋ) n. 工程學

feat (fit) n. 偉業；功績　　marvel ('mɑrvl̩) v. 驚嘆 < at >

scenic ('sinɪk) adj. 風景優美的

construction (kən'strʌkʃən) n. 建設

experience (ɪk'spɪrɪəns) v. 體驗

previously ('privɪəslɪ) adv. 以前　　*horseback riding* 騎馬

Just across the border, in Canada, is the Waterton Lakes National Park. In 1931, members of the Rotary Clubs of Alberta and Montana suggested joining the two parks as a symbol of peace and friendship between the two countries. In 1932, the United States and Canadian governments renamed the parks the Waterton-Glacier International Peace Park, the world's first. More recently, the parks have received several international honors. They were named as a World Heritage Site in 1995. This international recognition highlights the importance of this area, not just to the United States and Canada, but to the entire world.

邊界的對岸，就是加拿大的「華特頓湖國家公園」。在一九三一年，亞伯頓省和蒙大拿州的扶輪社員建議結合兩座公園，以做爲兩國和平及友誼的象徵。在一九三二年，美國與加拿大政府重新命名此一公園爲「華特頓冰河國際和平公園」，這是世界創舉。更在最近，此公園獲得幾項國際殊榮。它們在一九九五年被命名爲「世界遺產」地點之一。此項國際認可凸顯了此一地區的重要性，不只對於美國與加拿大，而是對於全世界。

border ('bordɚ) n. 邊界　　*Waterton Lake* 華特頓湖

member ('mɛmbɚ) n. 會員　　rotary ('rotərɪ) adj. 旋轉的

Rotary Club 扶輪社【以服務社會和促進世界和平爲目的之國際團體】

Alberta (æl'bɝtə) n. 亞伯頓省【加拿大西部一省】

suggest (sə'dʒɛst) v. 建議　　join (dʒɔɪn) v. 結合

symbol ('sɪmbl̩) n. 象徵　　rename (rɪ'nem) v. 重新命名

receive (rɪ'siv) v. 獲得　　honor ('ɑnɚ) n. 榮譽

heritage ('hɛrətɪdʒ) n. 遺產　　site (saɪt) n. 地點

World Heritage 世界遺產【一項由聯合國支持，聯合國教科文組織負責執行的計畫，以保存對全世界均有自然或文化價值的事物為目的。世界遺產分為自然遺產、文化遺產，和文化與自然雙重遺產】

recognition (ˌrɛkəgˈnɪʃən) n. 認同；認可

highlight (ˈhaɪˌlaɪt) v. 使重要；突顯

entire (ɪnˈtaɪr) adj. 整個的

45. (**D**) 什麼使得穿越冰河國家道路的興建成為必要？

(A) 蒙大拿州有太多的公園。

(B) 遊客認為園內陽光不夠充足。

(C) 現有的山路被毀壞。

(D) 更多的遊客對於入園感興趣。

necessary (ˈnɛsəˌsɛrɪ) adj. 必要的

sunny (ˈsʌnɪ) adj. 陽光充足的

existing (ɪgˈzɪstɪŋ) adj. 現有的   destroy (dɪˈstrɔɪ) v. 毀壞

46. (**C**) 「向陽大道」如何影響人們體驗冰河國家公園的方式？

(A) 沿途的風景太優美，使得遊客無法小心開車。

(B) 在此路上騎馬，成為人們一個很棒的經驗。

(C) 此路使得人們在更短的時間內看到公園的更多樣貌。

(D) 路上的交通太艱困，很少人能真正盡興遊玩。

influence (ˈɪnfluəns) v. 影響   marvelous (ˈmɑrvləs) adj. 很棒的

allow (əˈlau) v. 使能夠   period (ˈpɪrɪəd) n. 期間

transportation (ˌtrænspɚˈteʃən) n. 運輸系統

47. (**A**) 工程偉業的意思為何？

(A) 建設上的大舉成功。   (B) 神奇的建設器械。

(C) 旅客的浩劫。   (D) 工程師建築過程中的愉快時光。

magical (ˈmædʒɪkḷ) adj. 神奇的   disaster (dɪzˈæstɚ) n. 災難

enjoyable (ɪnˈdʒɔɪəbḷ) adj. 令人愉悅的

process (ˈprɑsɛs) n. 過程

48. (**D**) 關於華特頓冰河國際和平公園，有什麼特殊之處？

　　(A) 它是冰河流向湖泊之處。

　　(B) 它是第一座由全世界出資的公園。

　　(C) 它是一座為保護野生動物而建的特殊公園。

　　(D) <u>它是由位於兩個國家的兩個公園所組成。</u>

　　fund〔fʌnd〕*v.* 提供資金　　protect〔prə'tɛkt〕*v.* 保護

　　compose〔kəm'poz〕*v.* 組成　　***be composed of*** 由～組成

　　located〔lo'ketɪd〕*adj.* 位於～的

<u>49-52 為題組</u>

　　Ice sculpting is a difficult process. First, ice must be carefully selected so that it is suitable for sculpting. Its ideal material is pure, clean water with high clarity. It should also have the minimum amount of air bubbles. Perfectly clear ice blocks weighing 140 kg and measuring 100 cm × 50 cm × 25 cm are available from the Clinebell Company in Colorado. Much larger clear blocks are produced in Europe and Canada or harvested from a frozen river in Sweden. These large ice blocks are used for large ice sculpting events and for building ice hotels.

　　冰雕是一種艱難的過程。首先，必須要仔細挑選冰，以便於適合拿來做雕刻。理想的原料是具有高純度純淨、乾淨的水。它也應該要有最少量的氣泡。在科羅拉多州的克萊貝爾公司，可以提供重一百四十公斤，長 100 公分、寬 50 公分、高 25 公分的完全純淨的冰磚。在歐洲和加拿大有生產更大型乾淨的冰磚，或是也可從瑞典結冰的河川獲得。這些大型的冰磚被用於大型的冰雕活動，以及用來建造冰雕飯店。

　　　　sculpt〔skʌlpt〕*v.* 雕刻　　process〔'prɑsɛs〕*n.* 過程

　　　　suitable〔'sutəbḷ〕*adj.* 適合的　　ideal〔aɪ'diəl〕*adj.* 理想的

　　　　material〔mə'tɪrɪəl〕*n.* 原料；材料

　　　　pure〔pjʊr〕*adj.* 純粹的；乾淨的

　　　　clarity〔'klærətɪ〕*n.* (液體)清澈透明；純度

　　　　minimum〔'mɪnəməm〕*adj.* 最小的　　amount〔ə'maʊnt〕*n.* 量

bubble〔'bʌbḷ〕*n.* 氣泡　　perfectly〔'pɜˋfɪktlɪ〕*adv.* 完美地；完全地
block〔blɑk〕*n.* 磚　　weigh〔we〕*v.* 有…重量
measure〔'mɛʒɚ〕*v.* 有…（長、寬、高）
available〔ə'veləbḷ〕*adj.* 可獲得的
Colorado〔͵kɑlə'rædo〕*n.* 科羅拉多州（美國西部的一州，首府丹佛）
produce〔prə'dus〕*v.* 生產　　harvest〔'hɑrvɪst〕*v.* 獲得
frozen〔'frozn〕*adj.* 結凍的；結冰的　　Sweden〔'swidn〕*n.* 瑞典
event〔ɪ'vɛnt〕*n.* 大事；活動

Another difficulty in the process of ice sculpting is time control. The temperature of the environment affects how quickly the piece must be completed to avoid the effects of melting. If the sculpting does not take place in a cold environment, then the sculptor must work quickly to finish his piece. The tools used for sculpting also affect when the task can be accomplished. Some sculptures can be completed in as little as ten minutes if power tools are used. Ice sculptors also use razor-sharp chisels that are specifically designed for cutting ice. The best ice chisels are made in Japan, a country that, along with China, has a long tradition of magnificent ice sculptures.

在製作冰雕的過程中，另一項困難就是時間的控制。環境的溫度會影響作品必須要多快完成，以避免融化。如果不能在冰冷的環境中雕刻，那麼雕刻家就必須很快地完成他的作品。用來雕刻的工具也會影響這項任務完成的時間。如果使用電動工具，就可以在短短的十分鐘內完成一些雕刻。冰雕家也會使用剃刀般銳利的鑿子，這些鑿子是專為冰雕而設計的。最好的冰雕鑿子是日本製造的，日本和中國一樣，擁有悠久的壯麗冰雕傳統。

difficulty〔'dɪfə͵kʌltɪ〕*n.* 困難　　temperature〔'tɛmpərətʃɚ〕*n.* 溫度
environment〔ɪn'vaɪrənmənt〕*n.* 環境　　affect〔ə'fɛkt〕*v.* 影響
piece〔pis〕*n.* 一件（雕刻）；作品　　complete〔kəm'plit〕*v.* 完成
avoid〔ə'bɪɔv〕*v.* 避免　　effect〔ɪ'fɛkt〕*n.* 影響；結果
melt〔mɛlt〕*v.* 融化　　***take place*** 發生
sculptor〔'skʌlptɚ〕*n.* 雕刻家　　task〔tæsk〕*n.* 任務
accomplish〔ə'kɑmplɪʃ〕*v.* 完成　　***power tool*** 電動工具

razor-sharp ('rezə⋏ʃɑrp) adj. (剃刀般) 銳利的

chisel ('tʃɪzl̩) n. 鑿子　specifically (spɪ'sɪfɪklɪ) adv. 特別地

design (dɪ'zaɪn) v. 設計　*along with* 連同

tradition (trə'dɪʃən) n. 傳統

magnificent (mæg'nɪfəsn̩t) adj. 壯麗的

　　Ice sculptures are used as decorations in some cuisines, especially in Asia. When holding a dinner party, some large restaurants or hotels will use an ice sculpture to decorate the table. For example, in a wedding banquet it is common to see a pair of ice-sculpted swans that represent the union of the new couple.

　　在一些菜餚中，冰雕也被用來當作裝飾品，特別是在亞洲。有些大型餐廳或飯店，在舉行晚餐派對時，會用冰雕來裝飾餐桌。例如，在喜宴中，常會看到一對用冰雕成的天鵝，來代表一對新婚夫妻的結合。

decoration (ˌdɛkə'reʃən) n. 裝飾 (品)

cuisine (kwɪ'zin) n. 菜餚　Asia ('eʃə,'eʒə) n. 亞洲

hold (hold) v. 舉行　decorate ('dɛkə,ret) v. 裝飾

banquet ('bæŋkwɪt) n. 盛宴　*wedding banquet* 喜宴

common ('kɑmən) adj. 平常的；常見的　　*a pair of* 一對

swan (swɑn) n. 天鵝　represent (ˌrɛprɪ'zɛnt) v. 代表；表示

union ('junjən) n. 結合　couple ('kʌpl̩) n. 夫妻

49. (**B**) 哪一種冰最適合做冰雕？

(A) 來自冰雕飯店的冰。　　(B) 來自乾淨的水的冰。

(C) 有很多氣泡在裡面的冰。　(D) 重量超過一百公斤的冰。

50. (**D**) 為什麼冰雕很困難？

(A) 很難控制冰的大小和形狀。

(B) 不容易找到合適的冰雕主題。

(C) 適當的工具只有在某些國家可以獲得。

(D) 不容易找到適合的冰和工作環境。

right (raɪt) adj. 適合的　theme (θim) n. 主題

appropriate (ə'proprɪɪt) adj. 適當的

51. (**A**) 第三段主要是關於什麼？

(A) 冰雕的用途。　　　　　(B) 冰雕的地點。

(C) 冰雕的品質。　　　　　(D) 冰雕派對的起源。

origin (ˈɔrədʒɪn) n. 起源

52. (**B**) 關於冰雕的過程，下列敘述何者為真？

(A) 用銳利的鑿子雕刻要花比較多的時間。

(B) 如果使用合適的工具，可以在十分鐘之內完成。

(C) 來自瑞典較大型的冰磚，對雕刻家而言比較容易處理。

(D) 雕刻師在冰冷的環境中，必須要快速地工作，以免感冒。

carve (kɑrv) v. 雕刻　　　handle (ˈhændl̩) v. 處理

carver (ˈkɑrvɚ) n. 雕刻師　　***catch cold*** 感冒

53-56 為題組

If you touch your finger to a hot stove, you know it's going to hurt.
However, if you convince yourself beforehand that the pain won't be so bad,
you might not suffer as much. According to a recent study, the part of your
brain that reacts to severe pain is largely the same part that reacts to
expectation of pain.

如果用你的手指去碰熱爐子，你知道那會痛。不過，如果你事先說服自己，
其實沒那麼痛的話，可能感覺就真的不會那麼強烈。根據一份最近的研究指出，
人類反應強烈疼痛，與預期疼痛的大腦區塊，其實差不多是同一塊。

stove (stov) n. 爐子　　　convince (kənˈvɪns) v. 使信服

beforehand (bɪˈforˌhænd) adv. 預先

suffer (ˈsʌfɚ) v. 受苦　　　react (rɪˈækt) v. 反應

severe (səˈvɪr) adj. 嚴重的

largely (ˈlɑrdʒlɪ) adv. 大部分地

expectation (ˌɛkspɛkˈteʃən) n. 預期

Researchers in this study worked with 10 volunteers, ages 24 to 46. Each volunteer wore a device that gave out 20-second-long pulses of heat to the right leg. There were three levels of heat, producing mild, moderate, or strong pain. During training, the volunteers would first hear a tone, followed by a period of silence, and then feel a heat pulse. They then learned to associate the length of the silent pause with the intensity of the upcoming heat pulse. The longer the pause, the stronger the heat pulse would be, causing more severe pain.

研究專家實驗的對象為，十位年齡層在二十四到四十六歲之間的自願受測者。每一位受測者，都會在右腳戴上一次發熱二十秒的熱脈衝裝置。熱度共分為輕度、中度及重度疼痛等三種強度。在訓練過程當中，受測者會先聽到一聲提示音，接著會靜止無聲，然後才會感覺到一段熱脈衝。於是他們就會瞭解，暫停無聲的時間長度，與隨之而來的熱脈衝強度之間的相對關係。暫停時間越久，熱脈衝的強度就越強，疼痛的程度也隨之加深。

> ***work with*** 與～共事　　device (dɪˈvaɪs) *n.* 裝置；器具
> ***give out*** 發出　　pulse (pʌls) *n.* 律動；拍子
> mild (maɪld) *adj.* 輕度的　　moderate (ˈmɑdərɪt) *adj.* 中度的
> tone (ton) *n.* 樂音　　***heat pulse*** 熱脈衝　　learn (lɝn) *v.* 得知
> ***associate with*** 將（物、人）與～聯想在一起
> intensity (ɪnˈtɛnsətɪ) *n.* 強度
> upcoming (ˈʌpˌkʌmɪŋ) *adj.* 即將來臨的

A day or two later, the real experiment began. The researchers found that the parts of the brain involved in learning, memory, emotion, and touch became more active as the volunteers expected higher levels of pain. These were mainly the same areas that became active when participants actually felt pain. Interestingly, when the volunteers expected only mild or moderate pain but experienced severe pain, they reported feeling 28 percent less pain than when they expected severe pain and actually got it.

一兩天之後，開始進行眞正的實驗。研究專家發現，當受測者預期強度較強的疼痛時，負責處理學習、情緒以及觸覺的大腦區塊，會變得比較活躍。當受測者眞正感覺到疼痛的時候，主要也是這些區塊會有活躍的反應。有趣的是，當受測者只預期輕度或中度的疼痛，但眞正經歷的卻是強烈疼痛的時候，他們說，比預期和眞正經歷重度疼痛的時候，疼痛的程度還少了百分之二十八。

involved (ɪn'vɑlvd) *adj.* 涉及～的　　emotion (ɪ'moʃən) *n.* 情緒
active ('æktɪv) *adj.* 活躍的；旺盛的
mainly ('menlɪ) *adv.* 主要地
participant (pə'tɪsəpənt) *n.* 參與者

The new study emphasizes that pain has both physical and psychological elements. Understanding how pain works in the mind and brain could eventually give doctors tools for helping people cope with painful medical treatments.

這項新的研究強調，疼痛與生理和心理因素都有關。瞭解心智與大腦如何對疼痛反應，最後可以提供醫生方法，協助病患應付會有疼痛感覺的治療。

emphasize ('ɛmfə,saɪz) *v.* 強調
physical ('fɪzɪkl̩) *adj.* 生理的
psychological (,saɪkə'lɑdʒɪkl̩) *adj.* 心理的
element ('ɛləmənt) *n.* 要素；元素　　work (wɝk) *v.* 產生影響
eventually (ɪ'vɛntʃuəlɪ) *adv.* 最後　　tool (tul) *n.* 手段
cope with 處理　　medical ('mɛdɪkl̩) *adj.* 醫學的
treatment ('tritmənt) *n.* 治療

53. (**D**) 本文主旨爲何？

(A) 我們應該學著對疼痛敏感。

(B) 我們對疼痛的感覺是由環境決定的。

(C) 人們如何感覺疼痛對科學家而言還是未知數。

(D) 我們對疼痛的反應和我們所預期的疼痛息息相關。

sensitive ('sɛnsətɪv) *adj.* 敏感的

54.（**A**）在這份研究當中，關於熱脈衝的敘述何者正確？

　　(A) 每一次的熱脈衝持續二十秒。

　　(B) 脈衝會施打在受測者的手臂上。

　　(C) 不同的裝置會產生不同強度的熱脈衝。

　　(D) 會對受測者施打兩種強度的熱脈衝。

55.（**D**）自願者如何知道不同程度的熱度？

　　(A) 從他們聽到的提示音大小。

　　(B) 從研究專家給的指示。

　　(C) 從他們戴的裝置上的閃爍顏色。

　　(D) 從提示音與熱脈衝之間的暫停長度。

　　flashing〔'flæʃɪŋ〕*n.* 閃爍

56.（**B**）根據本文，作者可能會在醫生施行手術之前給予什麼建議？

　　(A) 給病人更多的止痛藥。

　　(B) 和病人說話以消除他們的憂慮。

　　(C) 事先給病人重度的熱脈衝。

　　(D) 對病人強調可能產生的劇烈疼痛。

第貳部分：非選擇題

一、翻譯題

1. Listening to music is a hobby that you can enjoy <u>for your whole life / forever</u>.

2. But being able to play a musical instrument can bring you (much) more <u>joy/ happiness / pleasure</u>.

二、英文作文：

An Apology Letter to Eve

February 2, 2008

Dear Eve,

I'll be honest with you. I lost your digital camera at the concert last night. I promised I'd be extra careful with it, and I was. *However*, there were so many people yesterday, and the crowd got out of hand. When I was taking pictures, people kept bumping into me. The camera fell out of my hand, and there wasn't even space to bend down, let alone look for it. I stayed after the concert and searched, but to no avail.

Please forgive me. You don't know how sorry I am. I know you had precious pictures in there, not to mention the camera itself. I definitely will pay for a new camera. Just give me some time. And to compensate for the pictures and memories, let me take you out to wherever you want. *Again*, I'm truly sorry for what happened, and hope that I can make it up to you.

Your friend,
George

apology〔ə'pɑlədʒɪ〕*n.* 道歉　　digital〔'dɪdʒɪtl̩〕*adj.* 數位的
extra〔'ɛkstrə〕*adv.* 特別地；格外地
crowd〔kraʊd〕*n.* 群衆；人群
get out of hand 變得難以控制　　***take a picture*** 拍照
bump into 撞上　　space〔spes〕*n.* 空間
bend down 彎下腰　　***let alone*** 更不用說（= *not to mention*）
search〔sɜtʃ〕*v.* 搜尋　　avail〔ə'vel〕*n.* 效用；效力
to no avail 徒勞無功（= *in vain*）
precious〔'prɛʃəs〕*adj.* 珍貴的　　definitely〔'dɛfənɪtlɪ〕*adv.* 一定
compensate〔'kɑmpən‚set〕*v.* 賠償；彌補
memory〔'mɛmərɪ〕*n.* 回憶　　***make it up*** 彌補

97 年度學科能力測驗英文試題修正意見

　　本次「學測」考題出得很漂亮，符合知識性、趣味性、教育性，以及生活化的命題原則，像作文題目「寫一封道歉信」，就兼具教育性及生活化。試題中的錯誤，是有史以來最少的一次。改編英文文章不容易，完全沒有錯誤實在很難，此次考題值得我們喝采。

題　號	題　　　目	修　正　意　見
第 41－44 題 第 3 行	*Everyone* starts… everyone 和 every one 不一樣。在大考中心參考的原文："Small Mammals: Black Howler Monkeys" 中，寫成 Every-one 也不對，在下列網站中，可以查到：http://nationalzoo.si.edu/Animals/SmallMammals/Exhibits/HowlerMonkeys/LoudestAnimal/default.cfm	應改爲：*Every one* starts…. * everyone = everybody = every person 是指「每一個人」，而 *every one* 是指「**每一個**」，未必是人，在此是指「猴子」，文章中的 every one 是 every one *of the howler monkeys* 的省略。every one 強調 one 的意思。
第 48 題 (A)	It is…run *to* the lake.	應改爲：It is…run *into* the lake. *「流入」應該是 *run into*，不是 *run to*。
第 52 題 (C)	…easier to *handle for sculptors*.	應改爲：…easier *for sculptors to handle*. * 不定詞的意義上的主詞 for sculptors 應放在 to handle 的前面。
第 56 題 (A)	…more *pain killers*.	應改爲：…more *painkillers*. * painkiller ('pen,kılə) n. 止痛藥是一個字，無論在所有字典上或網路上，都是一個字。

97 年學測英文科考題出題來源

題　號	出　　　　處
一、詞彙 第 1～15 題	所有各題的對錯答案的選項，均出自「高中常用 7000 字」，除了第 15 題非答案的選項 (A) relatively，在「高中常用 7000 字」裡面是形容詞或名詞 relative。
二、綜合測驗 第 16～20 題	改編自 About.com 網站上 "The Miracle of Green Tea"（綠茶的奇蹟） http://chinesefood.about.com/library/weekly/aa011400a.htm
第 21～25 題	引用美國寓言故事 "The Wise Woman's Stone"，加以改編。 www.ignitespirit.com/article.asp?ID=188
第 26～30 題	改編自 "The Rough Guide to Prague 5" 一書的前言。
三、文意選填 第 31～40 題	改編自印度的民間故事 "Living Like a Pig"。
四、閱讀測驗 第 41～44 題	改編自 Small Mammals: Black Howler Monkeys 　　　　　The Loudest Animal in the New World 出自美國華盛頓 Smithsonian 國家動物園的網站對於 Howler monkeys 的介紹。
第 45～48 題	改編自 Glacier National Park Information Page（冰河國家公園的簡介網頁）中的 Going-to-the-Sun Road History（「向陽大道」的歷史）。
第 49～52 題	出自維基百科（Wikipedia, the free encyclopedia）冰雕（Ice Sculpture）介紹中的 "The Raw Material"（冰雕的原料）。
第 53～56 題	出自 Science News for Kinds 網站，有關大腦處理痛覺（Pain Expectations）的文章。 http://www.sciencenewsforkids.org/articles/20050914/Note2.asp
英文作文	出自 2008 年 1 月 19 日中國大陸「全國碩士學位研究生入學考試英語試題」第三部份寫作測驗： You have just come back from Canada and found a music CD in your luggage that you forgot to return to Bob, your landlord there. Write him a letter to 1) make an apology, and 2) suggest a solution

九十七年度學科能力測驗（英文考科）

大考中心公佈答案

題號	答案	題號	答案	題號	答案
1	C	21	C	41	A
2	B	22	A	42	C
3	D	23	C	43	B
4	B	24	B	44	C
5	C	25	D	45	D
6	D	26	B	46	C
7	A	27	D	47	A
8	B	28	A	48	D
9	C	29	B	49	B
10	A	30	C	50	D
11	B	31	D	51	A
12	C	32	G	52	B
13	A	33	H	53	D
14	A	34	I	54	A
15	B	35	E	55	D
16	D	36	B	56	B
17	B	37	J		
18	A	38	F		
19	C	39	A		
20	D	40	C		

九十七學年度學科能力測驗
英文科各級分人數累計表

級分	人數	百分比（％）	累計人數	累計百分比（％）
15	8629	5.87	147085	100.00
14	14225	9.67	138456	94.13
13	14760	10.04	124231	84.46
12	13573	9.23	109471	74.43
11	11370	7.73	95898	65.20
10	11433	7.77	84528	57.47
9	10665	7.25	73095	49.70
8	9332	6.34	62430	42.44
7	9834	6.69	53098	36.10
6	9842	6.69	43264	29.41
5	10255	6.97	33422	22.72
4	10822	7.36	23167	15.75
3	10607	7.21	12345	8.39
2	1683	1.14	1738	1.18
1	48	0.03	55	0.04
0	7	0.00	7	0.00

九十六年大學入學學科能力測驗試題
英文考科

第壹部份：單一選擇題

一、詞彙（15％）

說明：　第 1 至 15 題，每題選出最適當的一個選項，標示在答案卡之「選擇題答案區」。每題答對得 1 分，答錯不倒扣。

1. The movie director adapted this year's bestseller into a hit and made a _____.
   (A) fortune　　(B) request　　(C) companion　　(D) decision

2. Wang Chien-ming, the Yankees' best pitcher last year, already showed his great _____ for baseball when he was still a teenager.
   (A) response　　(B) reluctance　　(C) permission　　(D) potential

3. Although Jeffery had to keep two part-time jobs to support his family, he never _____ his studies.　In fact, he graduated with honors.
   (A) neglected　　(B) segmented　　(C) financed　　(D) diminished

4. If it is too cold in this room, you can _____ the air conditioner to make yourself feel comfortable.
   (A) fasten　　(B) adjust　　(C) defeat　　(D) upload

5. This course will provide students with a solid _____ for research. It is highly recommended for those who plan to go to graduate school.
   (A) admission　　(B) circulation　　(C) foundation　　(D) extension

6. Peter is now living on a _____ of NT$100 per day.　He cannot afford any recreational activities.
   (A) division　　(B) guidance　　(C) measure　　(D) budget

7. Amy succeeded in _____ for a raise though her boss didn't agree to increase her salary at first.
   (A) compensating   (B) negotiating
   (C) substituting   (D) advertising

8. Ms. Li's business _____ very quickly. She opened her first store two years ago; now she has fifty stores all over the country.
   (A) discouraged   (B) transferred
   (C) stretched   (D) expanded

9. Ruth is a very _____ person. She cannot take any criticism and always finds excuses to justify herself.
   (A) shameful   (B) innocent   (C) defensive   (D) outgoing

10. It's a pity that you have to leave so soon. I _____ hope that you will come back very soon.
    (A) sincerely   (B) scarcely   (C) reliably   (D) obviously

11. We human beings may live without clothes, but food and air are _____ to our life.
    (A) magnificent   (B) essential   (C) influential   (D) profitable

12. The manager _____ without hesitation after he had been offered a better job in another company.
    (A) retreated   (B) revived   (C) removed   (D) resigned

13. Many important legal _____ concerning the tragic incident have now been preserved in the museum.
    (A) distributions   (B) formations
    (C) documents   (D) constructions

14. I'm not sure exactly how much scholarship you'll receive, but it will _____ cover your major expenses.
    (A) recently   (B) roughly   (C) frankly   (D) variously

15. Tom was very ill a week ago, but now he looks healthy.　We are
＿＿＿＿＿ by his quick recovery.

   (A) amazed　　(B) convinced　　(C) advised　　(D) confirmed

二、綜合測驗（15％）

說明： 第 16 至 30 題，每題一個空格，請依文意選出最適當的一個選項，標
示在答案卡之「選擇題答案區」。每題答對得 1 分，答錯不倒扣。

   All dogs deserve to look and feel their best.　After a spa treatment
at Happy Puppy, dogs come home ＿＿16＿＿ pampered and relaxed.　At
Happy Puppy, your dog can enjoy a half day of care and then be taken
to the salon at naptime.　Here all the dogs are given a bath using
professional shampoo and conditioners in a massaging tub.　Their
relaxing bath will be ＿＿17＿＿ a full fluff dry and brush-out.　When you
arrive for pick-up, your dog will be well-exercised and beautiful.

   You can also bring your dog to Happy Puppy and wash it yourself.
We supply everything, ＿＿18＿＿ waist-high tubs, shampoo, and towels.
This service is available seven days a week during normal operating
hours.

   ＿＿19＿＿ Happy Puppy is a relatively new service, we benefit from
more than 20 years of experience in breeding and caring for dogs.　We
are completely ＿＿20＿＿ to helping dogs enjoy a full and active life.
Our well-trained staff will provide the best possible service for you and
your dog.

16. (A) will feel　　(B) to feel　　(C) have felt　　(D) feeling
17. (A) counted on　(B) followed by　(C) turned into　(D) started with
18. (A) concerning　(B) showing　　(C) including　　(D) relating
19. (A) Although　　(B) Because　　(C) Once　　　(D) Until
20. (A) devoted　　(B) determined　　(C) delighted　　(D) directed

   India is shrinking.　A new analysis of satellite-based data has given
precisely the rate ＿＿21＿＿ which the country is losing size as it pushes

northward against the Himalayas. According to the analysis, the ___22___ between India's southern and northern tips shrinks by 2 cm every year. As India's size decreases, the thickness of the Himalayas increases. ___23___ the shrinking continues, India will disappear in 200 million years. There would only be a vast mountain range along the southern coast of China.

The Indian plate's ___24___ movement is not new. However, this cannot be treated as a trivial finding in science. A movement of ___25___ a few millimeters (mm) of the earth's crust is a sign of possible earthquakes. Such dangers are now obvious in India, where the movement of the plate continues.

21. (A) by   (B) in   (C) of   (D) at
22. (A) height   (B) distance   (C) geography   (D) landscape
23. (A) If   (B) For   (C) Unless   (D) Though
24. (A) wayward   (B) downward   (C) northward   (D) outward
25. (A) yet   (B) even   (C) rather   (D) indeed

Whenever I set foot on the soil of Rwanda, a country in east-central Africa, I feel as if I have entered paradise: green hills, red earth, sparkling rivers and mountain lakes. Herds of goats and cows ___26___ enormous horns graze the lush green fields. Although located close to the equator, Rwanda's "thousand hills," ___27___ from 1,500 m to 2,500 m in height, ensure that the temperature is pleasant all year around. And being a tiny country, everything in Rwanda is ___28___ in a few hours and the interesting spots can be explored comfortably in a couple of weeks. But ___29___, Rwanda is a symbol of the triumph of the human spirit over evil. Though it was once known to the world for the 1994 tribal conflict that resulted in about one million deaths, Rwanda has ___30___ the mass killing. Now it is healing and prospering and greets visitors with open arms.

26. (A) into　　　(B) with　　　(C) for　　　(D) from
27. (A) differing　(B) wandering　(C) ranging　(D) climbing
28. (A) off the record　(B) beyond doubt　(C) in touch　(D) within reach
29. (A) worst of all　(B) for that matter　(C) above all　(D) at most
30. (A) survived　(B) transformed　(C) recovered　(D) endangered

三、文意選填（10％）

說明： 第 31 至 40 題，每題一個空格，請依文意在文章後所提供的 (A) 到(J)
　　　 選項中分別選出最適當者，並將其英文字母代號標示在答案卡之「選
　　　 擇題答案區」。每題答對得 1 分，答錯不倒扣。

An old man who lived in a small side street of Mumbai had to put up with the nuisance of boys playing cricket and making a lot of noise outside his house, at night.

One evening when the boys were particularly ___31___, he went out to talk to them. He explained that he had just retired and was happiest when he could see or hear boys playing his ___32___ game, cricket. He would therefore give them 25 rupees each week to play in the street at night. The boys were thrilled, for they could hardly believe that they were being paid to do something they ___33___!

At the end of the first two weeks, the boys came to the old man's house, and went away ___34___ with their 25 rupees. The third week when they came back, however, the old man said he had ___35___ money and sent them away with only 15 rupees. The fourth week, the man said he had not yet received his ___36___ from the government and gave them only 10 rupees. The boys were very ___37___, but there was not much they could do about it.

At the end of the fifth week, the boys came back again and knocked at the old man's house, waiting for their ___38___. Slowly, the door opened and the old man appeared. He apologized that he could not afford to pay them 25 rupees as he had ____39____, but said he would give them five rupees each week without fail.

This was really too much for the boys. "You expect us to play seven days a week for ____40____ five rupees!" they yelled. "No way!"

They stormed away and never played on the street again.

(A) disappointed　(B) enjoyed　(C) favorite　(D) happily
(E) merely　　　　(F) noisy　　(G) paycheck　(H) promised
(I) reward　　　　(J) run out of

四、閱讀測驗（32％）

說明：第 41 至 56 題，每題請分別根據各篇文章之文意選出最適當的一個選項，標示在答案卡之「選擇題答案區」。每題答對得 2 分，答錯不倒扣。

41-44 為題組

Most American kids love Halloween treats, but a bucket of Halloween candy can be a dentist's nightmare. Some parents try to get rid of half of the candy after their children go to bed, but dentists say parents also need to separate the good kinds of treats from the bad.

It is not exactly what a child eats that truly matters, but how much time it stays in his mouth. According to pediatric dentist Dr. Kaneta Lott, the most damaging stuff is something that is sticky or very hard and thus stays in the mouth for a long time. This is because we all have bacteria in our mouths. When we eat, the bacteria take our food as their food and produce an acid that destroys the surface of the teeth, causing cavities to form. The longer the food stays in the mouth, the more likely cavities will develop. Therefore, potato chips are worse than candy because they get stuck between teeth. For the same reason, raisins and crackers are not the best choice. Hard candies take a long time to consume and are also a bad choice for Halloween treats.

If children really love candy, dentists recommend that they eat chocolate instead. Unlike hard candies, chocolate dissolves quickly in the mouth. Besides, chocolate contains tannins, which help to kill some of the bacteria in the mouth. But no matter what a child eats, brushing after each meal is still the best way to fight cavities.

41. What is the main purpose of this passage?
    (A) To discuss how cavities can be treated.
    (B) To point out the problems with Halloween celebrations.
    (C) To tell parents what sweets are less damaging to their children's teeth.
    (D) To teach parents the meaning of Halloween candies for their children.

42. Why are hard candies especially bad for teeth?
    (A) They may break the child's teeth.
    (B) They contain too much sugar.
    (C) They help bacteria to produce tannins.
    (D) They stay in the mouth for a long time.

43. According to the passage, which of the following is a better choice for Halloween treats?
    (A) Chocolate.　　(B) Crackers.　　(C) Raisins.　　(D) Potato chips.

44. According to the passage, which of the following is true of tannins?
    (A) They are produced when the bacteria digest the food.
    (B) They help to get rid of some bacteria in the mouth.
    (C) They help chocolate to dissolve more quickly.
    (D) They destroy the surface of the teeth.

45-48 為題組

The largest television network in America is not ABC, CBS, or Fox. Nor is it one of the cable networks such as CNN, which carries only news and news stories. It is not ESPN, the all-sports cable network, or even MTV, which is famous for its music videos. Rather it is PBS, Public Broadcasting System, a non-profit public broadcasting TV service.

PBS has 349 member television stations in the U.S. and some member stations by cable in Canada.

　　PBS only attracts a minority of all TV viewers, about 2 percent. The industry leader, NBC, however, attracts 11 percent of viewers. But the growth of public television in the past two decades has been dramatic. This is especially noteworthy when one considers that public television stations must often survive on very limited budgets, on viewers' donations, and on private foundations and some governmental funding.

　　The level of quality of PBS programs, whether in national and international news, entertainment, or education, is excellent. Almost a whole generation of children throughout the world is familiar with Sesame Street and the characters of The Muppet Show. PBS is especially well known for the quality of its many educational TV programs. Over 95 percent of all public television stations have tele-courses. These courses are accepted and supported by more than 1,800 colleges and universities throughout the US. Each year, over a quarter of a million students take courses this way.

45. According to this article, PBS received part of its funding from
   _____.
   (A) private organizations   (B) public schools
   (C) advertising agencies   (D) other television stations

46. What is PBS most famous for?
   (A) Cable services.   (B) Generous donations.
   (C) Educational programs.   (D) Live news broadcasts.

47. Which of the following is true about public television stations?
   (A) The majority of their viewers are minority people.
   (B) Ninety-five percent of their programs are tele-courses.
   (C) They are shrinking in number because they make no profits.
   (D) Their courses are accepted by many universities in America.

48. Which of the following has the highest percentage of viewers?

(A) ABC　　　(B) PBS　　　(C) NBC　　　(D) Fox

49-52 為題組

Last week Jay McCarroll and The HSUS (The Humane Society of the United States) made a bold fur-free statement on the runway, marking **a new chapter** for the fashion industry and animal protection. The encouraging response to McCarroll's show confirmed that change is happening in fashion.

McCarroll has good reasons for rejecting fur. Each year, tens of millions of animals, including dogs and cats, needlessly suffer and die to fuel the fur industry. But what did Jay McCarroll use in place of fur? "I have patchwork pieces that contain all sorts of combinations of fabrics. The rest is cotton, nylon, polyester...you name it. I even have some stuff made out of bamboo/cotton blend. Anything but fur and leather," he told *Fashion Wire Daily.*

"So many people want to protect animals and live their lives without causing unnecessary cruelty. More than two thirds of Americans have pets, and we share a bond with animals every day. Saying no to fur can help millions of animals, and we want to show our respect to leading designers like Jay who embrace compassion as the fashion," said Michael Markarian, executive vice president of The HSUS. "It is great to see leaders in the fashion industry recognizing that the animals need their fur more than we do."

49. Which of the following is true about Jay McCarroll?

(A) He is a famous fashion designer.

(B) He is the executive vice president of the HSUS.

(C) He is an editor of *Fashion Wire Daily.*

(D) He is the head of an animal protection organization.

50. What does "**a new chapter**" in line 3, paragraph 1 mean?
　　(A) A new unit of a book.
　　(B) The beginning of a new trend.
　　(C) The latest issue of a magazine.
　　(D) A newly established organization.

51. Which of the following is NOT recommended for clothing by Jay McCarroll?
　　(A) Polyester.　(B) Bamboo.　(C) Leather.　(D) Patchwork pieces.

52. What do we learn from this passage?
　　(A) Human beings depend emotionally on animals.
　　(B) Fashion can go hand in hand with compassion for life.
　　(C) Fur is more effective than bamboo/cotton blend for clothing.
　　(D) Fur is more expensive than other materials for fashion designers.

53-56 為題組

　　Twenty years ago, most experts believed that differences in how boys and girls behaved were mainly due to differences in how they were treated by their parents, teachers, and friends. It's hard to **cling to** that belief today. Recent research has shown that there are biological differences between boys and girls. Understanding these differences is important in raising and educating children.

　　For example, girls are born with more sensitive hearing than boys, and the difference increases as kids grow up. So when a grown man speaks to a girl in what he thinks is a normal voice, she may hear it as yelling. Conversely, boys who appear to be inattentive in class may just be sitting too far away to hear the teacher.

　　Likewise, girls are better in their expression of feelings. Studies reveal that negative emotions are seated in an area of the brain called the amygdala. Girls develop an early connection between this area and the cerebral cortex, enabling them to talk about their feelings. In boys these links develop later. So if you ask a troubled adolescent boy to tell you what his feelings are, he often cannot say much.

Dr. Sax, a proponent of single-sex education, points out that keeping boys and girls separate in the classroom has yielded striking educational, social, and interpersonal benefits. Therefore, parents and teachers should try to recognize, understand, and make use of the biological differences that make a girl a girl, and a boy a boy.

53. What is the main idea of the passage?
    (A) Boys tend to pay less attention in class than girls.
    (B) Girls are better than boys in their ability to detect sounds.
    (C) Boys and girls behave differently because of biological differences.
    (D) Single-sex schools are not good because they keep boys and girls separate.

54. Why do girls express negative feelings better than boys?
    (A) Girls are more emotional than boys.
    (B) Girls have more brain cells than boys.
    (C) The amygdala is located in different areas of the brain for boys and girls.
    (D) The links between certain parts of the brain develop earlier in girls than in boys.

55. Which of the following does the author believe?
    (A) Girls need more training in communication.
    (B) Boys and girls should be educated in different ways.
    (C) Parents should pay more attention to boys.
    (D) Sex differences should be ignored in education.

56. What does the phrase "**cling to**" in the first paragraph mean?
    (A) maintain　　(B) abandon　　(C) evaluate　　(D) challenge

第貳部份：非選擇題

一、翻譯題（8%）

說明：1. 請將以下兩個中文句子譯成正確、通順、達意的英文，並將答案寫在「答案卷」上。

2. 請依序作答，並標明題號。每題 4 分，共 8 分。

1. 如果我們只為自己而活，就不會真正地感到快樂。

2. 當我們開始為他人著想，快樂之門自然會開啟。

二、英文作文（20%）

說明：1. 依提示在「答案卷」上寫一篇英文作文。

2. 文長 100 個單詞（words）左右。

提示：請以下面編號 1 至 4 的四張圖畫內容為藍本，依序寫一篇文章，描述女孩與貓之間的故事。你也可以發揮想像力，自己選定一個順序，編寫故事。請注意，故事內容務必涵蓋四張圖意，力求情節完整、前後發展合理。

96年度學科能力測驗英文科試題詳解

第壹部分：單選題

一、詞彙：

1. (**A**) The movie director adapted this year's bestseller into a hit and made a <u>fortune</u>. 這位電影導演將今年的暢銷書，改編成一部成功的電影，賺了一<u>大筆錢</u>。

(A) ***fortune*** (ˈfɔrtʃən) *n.* 財富
(B) request (rɪˈkwɛst) *n.* 請求
(C) companion (kəmˈpænjən) *n.* 同伴
(D) decision (dɪˈsɪʒən) *n.* 決定

director (dəˈrɛktə) *n.* 導演
adapt (əˈdæpt) *v.* 改編

> ***adapt sth. into*** a hit (將某物改編成作品) 是 turn *sth.* into a hit (使某物變成暢銷作品) 的變體。

bestseller (ˈbɛstˈsɛlə) *n.* 暢銷書
hit (hɪt) *n.* 成功的作品【hit 的主要意思是「打擊」】
make a fortune 賺一大筆錢

2. (**D**) Wang Chien-ming, the Yankees' best pitcher last year, already showed his great <u>potential</u> for baseball when he was still a teenager. 洋基隊去年的最佳投手王建民，在他十幾歲的時候，就已經表現出在棒球方面很有<u>潛力</u>。

(A) response (rɪˈspɑns) *n.* 反應
(B) reluctance (rɪˈlʌktəns) *n.* 不情願
(C) permission (pəˈmɪʃən) *n.* 許可
(D) ***potential*** (pəˈtɛnʃəl) *n.* 潛力

Yankees (ˈjæŋkɪz) *n.* 洋基隊　　pitcher (ˈpɪtʃə) *n.* 投手
show (ʃo) *v.* 表現　　teenager (ˈtin,edʒə) *n.* 十幾歲的小孩

3. (**A**) Although Jeffery had to keep two part-time jobs to support his family, he never <u>neglected</u> his studies. In fact, he graduated with honors.

雖然傑佛瑞必須兼兩份差來養家，但他從未<u>疏忽</u>學業。事實上，他還以優等成績畢業了。

(A) ***neglect*** ﹝ nɪˈglɛkt ﹞ *v.* 疏忽　　(B) segment ﹝ˈsɛgmənt﹞ *v.* 分開
(C) finance ﹝ fəˈnæns ﹞ *v.* 資助　　(D) diminish ﹝ dəˈmɪnɪʃ ﹞ *v.* 減少

although ﹝ ɔlˈðo ﹞ *conj.* 雖然　　　keep ﹝ kip ﹞ *v.* 保有
part-time ﹝ˈpɑrtˈtaɪm ﹞ *adj.* 兼職的
support ﹝ səˈport ﹞ *v.* 供養
study ﹝ˈstʌdɪ ﹞ *n.* 學業　　　***in fact*** 事實上
graduate with honors 以優等成績畢業

4. (**B**) If it is too cold in this room, you can <u>adjust</u> the air conditioner to make yourself feel comfortable.

如果房間裡面太冷，你可以<u>調整</u>冷氣機，讓你自己覺得舒適。

(A) fasten ﹝ˈfæsn̩ ﹞ *v.* 綁緊　　　　(B) ***adjust*** ﹝ əˈdʒʌst ﹞ *v.* 調整
(C) defeat ﹝ dɪˈfit ﹞ *v.* 打敗　　　　(D) upload ﹝ ʌpˈlod ﹞ *v.* 上傳

air conditioner 冷氣機
comfortable ﹝ˈkʌmfətəbl̩ ﹞ *adj.* 舒適的

5. (**C**) This course will provide students with a solid <u>foundation</u> for research. It is highly recommended for those who plan to go to graduate school.

這個課程會提供學生研究方面的穩固<u>基礎</u>。非常推薦給那些計畫要唸研究所的學生。

(A) admission ﹝ ədˈmɪʃən ﹞ *n.* 入學
(B) circulation ﹝ˌsɝkjəˈleʃən ﹞ *n.* 循環
(C) ***foundation*** ﹝ faʊnˈdeʃən ﹞ *n.* 基礎
(D) extension ﹝ ɪkˈstɛnʃən ﹞ *n.* 延長

course ﹝ kors ﹞ *n.* 課程　　　provide ﹝ prəˈvaɪd ﹞ *v.* 提供
solid ﹝ˈsɑlɪd ﹞ *adj.* 穩固的　　research ﹝ rɪˈsɝtʃ ﹞ *n.* 研究
highly ﹝ˈhaɪlɪ ﹞ *adv.* 非常　　　recommend ﹝ˌrɛkəˈmɛnd ﹞ *v.* 推薦
graduate school 研究所

6. (**D**) Peter is now living on a <u>budget</u> of NT$100 per day.　He cannot afford any recreational activities.

彼特現在每天靠著一百塊的<u>生活費</u>過活。他負擔不起任何娛樂活動的費用。

(A) division〔dəˋvɪʒən〕n. 劃分

(B) guidance〔ˋgaɪdn̩s〕n. 指示

(C) measure〔ˋmɛʒɚ〕n. 測量　　(D) *budget*〔ˋbʌdʒɪt〕n. 生活費

live on 靠…過活　　per〔pɚ〕prep. 每

afford〔əˋford〕v. 負擔得起　　recreational〔ˌrɛkrɪˋeʃən̩l〕adj. 娛樂的

7. (**B**) Amy succeeded in <u>negotiating</u> for a raise though her boss didn't agree to increase her salary at first.

雖然愛咪的老闆一開始不同意幫她加薪，但她最後還是<u>談判</u>成功了。

(A) compensate〔ˋkɑmpənˌset〕v. 賠償

(B) *negotiate*〔nɪˋgoʃɪˌet〕v. 談判

(C) substitute〔ˋsʌbstəˌtjut〕v. 替換

(D) advertise〔ˋædvɚˌtaɪz〕v. 登廣告

succeed〔səkˋsid〕v. 成功　　raise〔rez〕n. 增加（薪水）

though〔ðo〕conj. 雖然　　boss〔bɔs〕n. 老闆

agree〔əˋgri〕v. 同意　　increase〔ɪnˋkris〕v. 增加

salary〔ˋsælərɪ〕n. 薪水　　*at first* 最初；一開始

8. (**D**) Ms. Li's business <u>expanded</u> very quickly.　She opened her first store two years ago; now she has fifty stores all over the country.

李小姐的事業<u>擴張</u>得非常迅速。她兩年前開了第一間店；現在她在全國有五十間店。

(A) discourage〔dɪsˋkɝɪdʒ〕v. 使沮喪

(B) transfer〔trænsˋfɝ〕v. 轉移　　(C) stretch〔strɛtʃ〕v. 延伸

(D) *expand*〔ɪkˋspænd〕v. 擴張

business〔ˋbɪznɪs〕n. 事業　　quickly〔ˋkwɪklɪ〕adv. 迅速地

open〔ˋopən〕v. 使開張　　*all over the country* 全國

9. (**C**) Ruth is a very <u>defensive</u> person. She cannot take any criticism and always finds excuses to justify herself.

露絲是個<u>防衛心</u>很<u>重</u>的人。她無法接受任何批評,而且總是找理由為她自己辯護。

(A) shameful ('ʃemfəl) *adj.* 可恥的

(B) innocent ('ɪnəsn̩t) *adj.* 清白的

(C) *defensive* (dɪ'fɛnsɪv) *adj.* 自我防禦心理的

(D) outgoing ('aʊt,goɪŋ) *adj.* 外向的

criticism ('krɪtə,sɪzəm) *n.* 批評　　excuse (ɪk'skjus) *n.* 理由

justify ('dʒʌstə,faɪ) *v.* 為…辯護

10. (**A**) It's a pity that you have to leave so soon. I <u>sincerely</u> hope that you will come back very soon.

可惜你這麼快就要離開。我<u>衷心地</u>希望你很快就能回來。

(A) *sincerely* (sɪn'sɪrlɪ) *adv.* 衷心地

(B) scarcely ('skɛrslɪ) *adv.* 幾乎不

(C) reliably (rɪ'laɪəblɪ) *adv.* 可靠地

(D) obviously ('ɑbvɪəslɪ) *adv.* 顯然地

pity ('pɪtɪ) *n.* 可惜的事

11. (**B**) We human beings may live without clothes, but food and air are <u>essential</u> to our life.

我們人類生存也許可以沒有衣服,但對我們的生活而言,食物和空氣卻是<u>非常重要的</u>。

(A) magnificent (mæg'nɪfəsn̩t) *adj.* 雄偉的

(B) *essential* (ə'sɛnʃəl) *adj.* 非常重要的

(C) influential (,ɪnflʊ'ɛnʃəl) *adj.* 有影響力的

(D) profitable ('prɑfɪtəbl̩) *adj.* 有利的

human being 人類　　clothes (kloðz) *n. pl.* 衣服

12. (**D**) The manager <u>resigned</u> without hesitation after he had been offered a better job in another company.

當另一家公司提供更好的職位給這位經理之後,他毫不猶豫地<u>辭職</u>。

(A) retreat ﹝ rɪ'trit ﹞ v. 撤退　　(B) revive ﹝ rɪ'vaɪv ﹞ v. 復活

(C) remove ﹝ rɪ'muv ﹞ v. 移除　　(D) *resign* ﹝ rɪ'zaɪn ﹞ v. 辭職

manager ﹝'mænɪdʒɚ﹞ n. 經理

hesitation ﹝ˌhɛzə'teʃən﹞ n. 猶豫

without hesitation 毫不猶豫地　　offer ﹝'ɔfɚ﹞ v. 提供

13. (**C**) Many important legal <u>documents</u> concerning the tragic incident have now been preserved in the museum.

許多和這件悲劇有關的重要法律<u>文件</u>，現在都被保存在博物館裡。

(A) distribution ﹝ˌdɪstrə'bjuʃən﹞ n. 分配

(B) formation ﹝ fɔr'meʃən ﹞ n. 形成

(C) *document* ﹝'dɑkjəmənt﹞ n. 文件

(D) construction ﹝ kən'strʌkʃən ﹞ n. 建築物

legal ﹝'ligl̩﹞ adj. 法律的

concerning ﹝ kən'sɝnɪŋ ﹞ prep. 關於 (= *about*)

tragic ﹝'trædʒɪk﹞ adj. 悲劇的　　incident ﹝'ɪnsədənt﹞ n. 事件

preserve ﹝ prɪ'zɝv ﹞ v. 保存　　museum ﹝ mju'ziəm ﹞ n. 博物館

14. (**B**) I'm not sure exactly how much scholarship you'll receive, but it will <u>roughly</u> cover your major expenses.

我並不是很確定你會得到多少獎學金，但<u>大約</u>夠用來付你主要的支出。

(A) recently ﹝'risn̩tlɪ﹞ adv. 最近　　(B) *roughly* ﹝'rʌflɪ﹞ adv. 大約

(C) frankly ﹝'fræŋklɪ﹞ adv. 坦白地

(D) variously ﹝'vɛrɪəslɪ﹞ adv. 各式各樣地

not exactly 並不；並沒有　　scholarship ﹝'skɑlɚˌʃɪp﹞ n. 獎學金

receive ﹝ rɪ'siv ﹞ v. 得到　　cover ﹝'kʌvɚ﹞ v. 夠付

major ﹝'medʒɚ﹞ adj. 主要的　　expense ﹝ ɪk'spɛns ﹞ n. 費用；開支

15. (**A**) Tom was very ill a week ago, but now he looks healthy. We are <u>amazed</u> by his quick recovery.

湯姆一個星期前還病得很重，但是現在看起來很健康。他的迅速康復<u>使</u>我們感到<u>驚訝</u>。

(A) *amaze* ﹝ ə'mez ﹞ v. 使驚訝　　(B) convince ﹝ kən'vɪns ﹞ v. 使相信

(C) advise ﹝ əd'vaɪz ﹞ v. 建議　　(D) confirm ﹝ kən'fɝm ﹞ v. 證實

ill ﹝ ɪl ﹞ adj. 生病的　　recovery ﹝ rɪ'kʌvərɪ ﹞ n. 康復

二、綜合測驗：

All dogs deserve to look and feel their best. After a spa treatment at Happy Puppy, dogs come home <u>feeling</u> pampered and relaxed. At Happy
                                                            16
Puppy, your dog can enjoy a half day of care and then be taken to the salon at naptime. Here all the dogs are given a bath using professional shampoo and conditioners in a massaging tub. Their relaxing bath will be <u>followed by</u> a
                                                                               17
full fluff dry and brush-out. When you arrive for pick-up, your dog will be well-exercised and beautiful.

　　所有的狗都應該擁有最佳的外貌以及感受。經過 Happy Puppy 的溫泉療程後，小狗能帶著被寵愛以及放鬆的心情回家。在 Happy Puppy，你的小狗可以享受半天的照顧，接著在午睡時間被帶去美容沙龍。在這裡，我們會在按摩浴缸裡，用專業的洗髮精和潤髮乳，來幫所有小狗洗澡。在輕鬆的沐浴之後，我們會把小狗的毛吹蓬吹乾，然後再加以梳理。當你到這裡接小狗時，你的小狗會是充分運動過，而且美麗的。

> deserve〔dɪˈzɝv〕v. 應得　　spa〔spɑ〕n. 溫泉；水療
> treatment〔ˈtritmənt〕n. 治療；療程
> pampered〔ˈpæmpɚd〕adj. 嬌寵的；滿足的
> salon〔səˈlɑn〕n. 美容美髮沙龍
> naptime〔ˈnæptaɪm〕n. 午睡時間；休息時間
> professional〔prəˈfɛʃən̩〕adj. 專業的；一流的
> shampoo〔ʃæmˈpu〕n. 洗髮精　　conditioner〔kənˈdɪʃənɚ〕n. 潤髮乳
> massage〔məˈsɑʒ〕n. 按摩　　tub〔tʌb〕n. 浴缸
> *massaging tub* 按摩浴缸　　fluff〔flʌf〕n. 蓬鬆毛
> dry〔draɪ〕n. 乾燥　　brush〔brʌʃ〕n. 用刷子的拂拭
> *brush-out* 用刷狗毛的刷子刷過；梳理
> *pick-up* 接送　　*well-exercised* 運動後精神飽滿的

16. (**D**) 前面已有主要動詞 come，且空格前並無連接詞，故須用現在分詞，選
　　　 (D) *feeling*。

17. (**B**) 依句意，選 (B) *be followed by*「接著就是」。而 (A) count on「依賴」，
　　　 (C) be turned into「被轉變成」，(D) start with「以…開始」，均不合
　　　 句意。

You can also bring your dog to Happy Puppy and wash it yourself.　We
supply everything, <u>including</u> waist-high tubs, shampoo, and towels.　This
　　　　　　　　　18
service is available seven days a week during normal operating hours.

　　你也可以把你的小狗帶來 Happy Puppy，然後自己幫牠洗澡。我們提供
一切用品，包括高度及腰的浴缸、洗髮精，以及毛巾。在正常營業時間內，一
週七天皆可使用這項服務。

　　　　supply〔sə'plaɪ〕v. 提供　　　waist〔west〕n. 腰
　　　　waist-high tub 高度及腰的浴缸　　towel〔'tauəl〕n. 毛巾
　　　　available〔ə'veləbḷ〕adj. 可利用的　　normal〔'nɔrmḷ〕adj. 正常的
　　　　operating hours 營業時間

18.（**C**）依句意，選 (C) ***including***〔ɪn'kludɪŋ〕prep. 包括。而 (A) concerning
　　　　　〔kən'sɜnɪŋ〕prep. 關於，(B) show〔ʃo〕v. 顯示，(D) relate〔rɪ'let〕v.
　　　　　使有關聯，均不合句意。

<u>Although</u> Happy Puppy is a relatively new service, we benefit from
　　19
more than 20 years of experience in breeding and caring for dogs.　We are
completely <u>devoted</u> to helping dogs enjoy a full and active life.　Our
　　　　　　20
well-trained staff will provide the best possible service for you and your dog.

　　雖然 Happy Puppy 是很新的服務，但是我們從二十多年的養育以及照顧小
狗的經驗中獲得許多好處。我們全心致力於幫助小狗過著圓滿而活躍的生活。
我們訓練有素的員工，將會為您與您的愛狗提供最棒的服務。

　　　　relatively〔'rɛlətɪvlɪ〕adv. 相當
　　　　benefit from 自…中獲益　　breeding〔'bridɪŋ〕n. 養育；配種
　　　　completely〔kəm'plitlɪ〕adv. 完全地
　　　　active〔'æktɪv〕adj. 活躍的　　***well-trained*** 訓練有素的
　　　　staff〔stæf〕n. 全體工作人員
　　　　possible〔'pɑsəbḷ〕adj. 可能限度的；盡可能的

19.（**A**）依句意，選 (A) ***Although***「雖然」。而 (B) 因為，(C) 一旦，(D) 直到，
　　　　　不合句意。

20.（ **A** ）依句意，選 (A) *be devoted to +V-ing*「致力於…」。

　　而 (B) be determined to V.「決心…；決定…」, (C) be delighted to V.「很高興能…」, (D) be directed to + N.「針對…；把注意力集中在…」，用法與句意均不合。

　　India is shrinking.　A new analysis of satellite-based data has given precisely the rate <u>at</u> which the country is losing size as it pushes northward
　　　　　　　　　　　　　21
against the Himalayas.　According to the analysis, the <u>distance</u> between
　　　　　　　　　　　　　　　　　　　　　　　　　　22
India's southern and northern tips shrinks by 2 cm every year.

　　印度正在逐漸縮小中。一項新的衛星資料分析，已經精確地得知，當印度向北推擠喜馬拉雅山脈時，其縮小的速度。根據這項分析，印度南北端的距離，每年縮短兩公分。

India（'ɪndɪə）n. 印度　　shrink（ʃrɪŋk）v. 縮小
analysis（ə'næləsɪs）n. 分析　　satellite（'sætḷ,aɪt）n.（人造）衛星
base（bes）v. 以…為根據；以…為基礎　　data（'detə）n. pl. 資料
give（gɪv）v.（計算、分析等）產生…結果
precisely（prɪ'saɪslɪ）adv. 正確地；準確地　　lose（luz）v. 減少
size（saɪz）n. 大小；尺寸　　**push against** 推
northward（'nɔrθwəd）adv. 向北；朝北
the Himalayas（ðə hɪ'mɑljəz）n. 喜馬拉雅山脈
southern（'sʌðən）adj. 南方的　　northern（'nɔrðən）adj. 北方的
tip（tɪp）n. 尖端　　by 表「差距」。

21.（ **D** ）表示「以…速度」，介系詞用 *at*，選 (D)。

22.（ **B** ）印度南北端的「距離」，每年縮短兩公分，選 (B) *distance*（'dɪstəns）n. 距離。而 (A) height（haɪt）n. 高度，(C) geography（dʒɪ'ɑgrəfɪ）n. 地理；地形，(D) landscape（'lænd,skep）n. 風景，均不合句意。

As India's size decreases, the thickness of the Himalayas increases.　<u>If the</u>
　　　　　　　　　　　　　　　　　　　　　　　　　　　　　　　　23
shrinking continues, India will disappear in 200 million years.　There would only be a vast mountain range along the southern coast of China.

當印度的面積縮小時，喜馬拉雅山脈的厚度就增加了。如果縮小的情況一直持續，那麼再過兩億年，印度就會消失。在中國南方沿岸，就會只有龐大的山脈。

decrease (dɪ'kris) v. 減少

thickness ('θɪknɪs) n. 厚度；密度【在此指山脈的高度】

increase (ɪn'kris) v. 增加　　disappear (ˏdɪsə'pɪr) v. 消失

vast (væst) adj. 巨大的　　range (rendʒ) n. 山脈

mountain range 山脈　　along (ə'lɔŋ) prep. 沿著；鄰近

coast (kost) n. 海岸

23. (**A**) 依句意，選 (A) ***If***「如果」。而 (B) for「為了」，(C) unless「除非」，
(D) though「雖然」，均不合句意。

The Indian plate's <u>northward</u> movement is not new.　However, this
　　　　　　　　　　24

cannot be treated as a trivial finding in science.　A movement of <u>even</u> a few
　　　　　　　　　　　　　　　　　　　　　　　25

millimeters (mm) of the earth's crust is a sign of possible earthquakes.　Such
dangers are now obvious in India, where the movement of the plate continues.

　　印度板塊北移的情況，並不是第一次出現。然而，這不能被看成是微不足道的科學發現。地殼的移動，即使只有幾公釐，也可能是地震的徵兆。這樣的危險在印度是很明顯的，因為這裡的板塊持續在移動。

Indian ('ɪndɪən) adj. 印度的　　plate (plet) n. 板塊

movement ('muvmənt) n. 移動

new (nju) adj. 從未有過的；第一次出現的　　***be treated as*** 被視為

trivial ('trɪvɪəl) adj. 瑣碎的；微不足道的；不重要的

finding ('faɪndɪŋ) n. 發現　　millimeter ('mɪləˏmitə) n. 公釐 (= *mm*)

earth (ɜθ) n. 地球　　crust (krʌst) n. 地殼

sign (saɪn) n. 跡象；徵兆；預兆　　earthquake ('ɜθˏkwek) n. 地震

obvious ('ɑbvɪəs) adj. 明顯的　　continue (kən'tɪnju) v. 繼續

24. (**C**) 由第一段第二句…as it pushes ***northward*** against the Himalayas. 可
知，應選 (C) ***northward*** ('nɔrθwəd) adj. 向北的。而 (A) wayward
('wewəd) adj. 不聽話的；任性的，(B) downward ('daʊnwəd) adj.
向下的，(D) outward ('aʊtwəd) adj. 向外的，均不合句意。

25. (**B**) 依句意，地殼的移動，「即使」只有幾公釐，也可能是地震的徵兆，選 (B) *even*。而 (A) yet「然而；但是；尚（未）」，(C) rather（'ræðɚ）*adv.* 相當地，(D) indeed（ɪn'did）*adv.* 的確；真正地，均不合句意。

Whenever I set foot on the soil of Rwanda, a country in east-central Africa, I feel as if I have entered paradise: green hills, red earth, sparkling rivers and mountain lakes. Herds of goats and cows <u>with</u> enormous horns
　　　　　　　　　　　　　　　　　　　　　　　　　　　　　　　　26
graze the lush green fields.

　　每當我踏上盧安達的土地，這個位於非洲中東部的國家，我就覺得自己好像進入了天堂：綠色的山坡、紅色的土地、閃閃發光的河流，以及高山的湖泊。頭上長著大角的山羊和乳牛，成群地在青草茂盛的綠色原野上吃草。

　　　　set foot on 腳踏入；到達；造訪　　soil（sɔɪl）*n.* 土壤；土地
　　　　Rwanda（ru'ɑndə）*n.* 盧安達【非洲東部的共和國】
　　　　east-central（'ist,sɛntrəl）*adj.* 中東部的　　Africa（'æfrɪkə）*n.* 非洲
　　　　as if 就好像　　paradise（'pærə,daɪs）*n.* 天堂；樂園
　　　　hill（hɪl）*n.* 小山；山丘　　earth（ɝθ）*n.* 大地；土壤
　　　　sparkling（'spɑrklɪŋ）*adj.* 閃耀的；發光的
　　　　mountain lake 高山湖泊　　herd（hɝd）*n.*（獸）群
　　　　herds of 成群的　　goat（got）*n.* 山羊
　　　　cow（kaʊ）*n.* 母牛　　enormous（ɪ'nɔrməs）*adj.* 巨大的
　　　　horn（hɔrn）*n.*（牛、山羊等的）角　　graze（grez）*v.* 吃草
　　　　lush（lʌʃ）*adj.* 蔥翠的；茂盛的　　field（fild）*n.* 原野

26. (**B**) 表示「具有」，介系詞用 ***with***，選 (B)。

Although located close to the equator, Rwanda's "thousand hills," <u>ranging</u>
　　　　　　　　　　　　　　　　　　　　　　　　　　　　　　27
from 1,500 m to 2,500 m in height, ensure that the temperature is pleasant all

year around. And being a tiny country, everything in Rwanda is <u>within reach</u>
　　　　　　　　　　　　　　　　　　　　　　　　　　　　　　　　28
in a few hours and the interesting spots can be explored comfortably in a

couple of weeks.

雖然位於赤道附近，不過盧安達的「千山之地」，海拔從 1500 公尺到 2500 公尺
都有，能確保其終年氣溫宜人。由於盧安達是個很小的國家，所以這裡的一切，
都可在幾個小時內到達，而且可以在幾週內，悠閒地探索境內有趣的景點。

locate〔'loket , lo'ket〕*v.* 使位於　　equator〔ɪ'kwetə〕*n.* 赤道
height〔haɪt〕*n.* 高度；海拔　　ensure〔ɪn'ʃur〕*v.* 確保；保證
temperature〔'tɛmprətʃə〕*n.* 溫度
pleasant〔'plɛznt〕*adj.* 令人愉快的
all year around 一年到頭；整年（= *all the year round*）
tiny〔'taɪnɪ〕*adj.* 微小的　　spot〔spɑt〕*n.* 地點
explore〔ɪk'splor〕*v.* 探險；探測；實地查看
comfortably〔'kʌmfətəblɪ〕*adv.* 舒適地；輕鬆地；悠閒地
a couple of 幾個

27.（**C**）依句意，選 (C) *ranging*。
range from A *to* B （範圍）從 A 到 B 都有
而 (A) differ〔'dɪfə〕*v.* 不同，(B) wander〔'wɑndə〕*v.* 徘徊；流浪，
(D) climb〔klaɪm〕*v.* 爬，均不合句意。

28.（**D**）依句意，選 (D) *within reach*「在能輕易到達的距離內」。
reach〔ritʃ〕*n.* 伸手可及的範圍；能輕易到達的距離
而 (A) off the record「不留在記錄的；非正式的；不可公開的」，
(B) beyond doubt「無疑地」，(C) in touch「（與…）接觸；（與…）取
得聯繫」，句意均不合。

But above all, Rwanda is a symbol of the triumph of the human spirit over
　　　29
evil.　Though it was once known to the world for the 1994 tribal conflict
that resulted in about one million deaths, Rwanda has survived the mass
　　　　　　　　　　　　　　　　　　　　　　　　　30
killing.　Now it is healing and prospering and greets visitors with open arms.
但是，最重要的是，盧安達是人類精神戰勝邪惡的象徵。雖然全世界都知道，
盧安達於 1994 年發生部落衝突，造成了大約一百萬人死亡，但盧安達已經安然
度過那場大屠殺。現在它正在復原而且日漸繁榮，並張開雙臂，熱烈歡迎遊客。

symbol〔ˈsɪmbḷ〕n. 象徵　　triumph〔ˈtraɪəmf〕n. 勝利；征服＜over＞
spirit〔ˈspɪrɪt〕n. 精神　　over〔ˈovɚ〕prep. 勝過
evil〔ˈivḷ〕n. 邪惡；罪惡　　once〔wʌns〕adv. 從前；曾經
be known to 被…知道　　**the world** 世人
tribal〔ˈtraɪbḷ〕adj. 部落的　　conflict〔ˈkɑnflɪkt〕n. 衝突
result in 造成；導致　　mass〔mæs〕adj. 大量的
killing〔ˈkɪlɪŋ〕n. 殺害；屠殺　　heal〔hil〕v. 痊癒
prosper〔ˈprɑspɚ〕v. 興盛；繁榮；成功　　greet〔grit〕v. 迎接
visitor〔ˈvɪzɪtɚ〕n. 遊客；觀光客
with open arms 張開著雙臂；熱烈地（歡迎等）

29.（**C**）依句意，選 (C) *above all*「最重要的是」。而 (A) worst of all「最糟的
　　　　是」，(B) for that matter「關於那件事；說到那件事；進一步說」（用
　　　　於補述前面的話），(D) at most「最多；充其量」，均不合句意。

30.（**A**）依句意，選 (A) *survive*〔səˈvaɪv〕v. 自…中生還；熬過；順利度過。
　　　　而 (B) transform〔trænsˈfɔrm〕v. 轉變，(C) recover〔rɪˈkʌvɚ〕v. 恢復；
　　　　復原，(D) endanger〔ɪnˈdendʒɚ〕v. 使…陷於危險中；危及，均不合
　　　　句意。

三、文意選填：

　　An old man who lived in a small side street of Mumbai had to put
up with the nuisance of boys playing cricket and making a lot of noise
outside his house, at night.

　　有位老人住在孟買的小巷道裡，他晚上必須忍受一群討厭的男孩子玩板
球，而且在他家外面製造一堆噪音。

Mumbai〔mʌmˈbaɪ〕n. 孟買（是印度馬哈拉施特拉邦的首府，是印度最大
　　的城市，也是商業、金融、電影娛樂中心。孟買的英文名本來叫「Bombay」，
　　但印度政府於 1995 年 11 月 22 日決定恢復傳統的名稱「Mumbai」。）
side street 巷道　　*put up with* 忍受
nuisance〔ˈnusṇs〕n. 討厭的人（東西）　　cricket〔ˈkrɪkɪt〕n. 板球

One evening when the boys were particularly ³¹(F) noisy, he went out to talk to them. He explained that he had just retired and was happiest when he could see or hear boys playing his ³²(C) favorite game, cricket. He would therefore give them 25 rupees each week to play in the street at night. The boys were thrilled, for they could hardly believe that they were being paid to do something they ³³(B) enjoyed!

　　有一天晚上，當那些男孩子特別吵的時候，他走出去跟他們講話。他解釋說，他剛退休，而且當他可以看到或聽到，有男孩子在打他最喜歡的板球的時候最開心。因此，他願意一星期付他們 25 元盧比，請他們晚上在街上打球。那些男孩很興奮，因為他們幾乎沒辦法相信，有人會付錢讓他們從事自己喜歡的運動。

> particularly〔pɚˈtɪkjələˌlɪ〕adv. 特別地；尤其
> noisy〔ˈnɔɪzɪ〕adj. 吵雜的　　retire〔rɪˈtaɪr〕v. 退休
> favorite〔ˈfevərɪt〕adj. 最喜愛的　　therefore〔ˈðɛrˌfor〕adv. 因此
> rupee〔ruˈpi〕n. 盧比　　thrilled〔ˈθrɪld〕adj. 興奮的；激動的
> hardly〔ˈhɑrdlɪ〕adv. 幾乎不

At the end of the first two weeks, the boys came to the old man's house, and went away ³⁴(D) happily with their 25 rupees. The third week when they came back, however, the old man said he had ³⁵(J) run out of money and sent them away with only 15 rupees. The fourth week, the man said he had not yet received his ³⁶(G) paycheck from the government and gave them only 10 rupees. The boys were very ³⁷(A) disappointed, but there was not much they could do about it.

　　前兩個禮拜結束的時候，那些男孩子來到老人的家，拿了錢之後，開心地離開。然而，當他們第三個禮拜過來的時候，老人說他已經沒錢了，後來用 15 元盧比打發他們走。第四個禮拜的時候，老人說他還沒收到政府發的薪水支票，所以只給了 10 元盧比。那些男孩子非常失望，不過他們也莫可奈何。

> happily〔ˈhæpɪlɪ〕adv. 高興地
> *run out of* 用完　　*send away* 趕走
> receive〔rɪˈsiv〕v. 收到　　paycheck〔ˈpeˌtʃɛk〕n. 薪水支票
> *not yet* 還沒；尚未　　government〔ˈgʌvɚnmənt〕n. 政府
> disappointed〔ˌdɪsəˈpɔɪntɪd〕adj. 失望的

At the end of the fifth week, the boys came back again and knocked at the old man's house, waiting for their [38](I) reward. Slowly, the door opened and the old man appeared. He apologized that he could not afford to pay them 25 rupees as he had [39](H) promised, but said he would give them five rupees each week without fail.

第五個禮拜過去了，那些男孩打完球之後，回來敲老人的門，等著領他們的獎賞。門慢慢地打開，老人出現在他們眼前。老人覺得很抱歉，因為他已經付不起他當初所承諾的 25 元盧比。不過，他說他一定會每個禮拜給他們五元盧比。

　　reward (rɪ'wɔrd) n. 報酬；獎賞　　appear (ə'pɪr) v. 出現
　　apologize (ə'palə,dʒaɪz) v. 道歉；認錯
　　afford (ə'ford) v. 負擔得起
　　promise ('pramɪs) v. 承諾　　*without fail* 必定

This was really too much for the boys. "You expect us to play seven days a week for [40](E) merely five rupees!" they yelled. "No way!"

對那些男孩子而言，他們真的受夠了。他們大叫著說：「你期望我們打一個禮拜的球，然後只給我們五元盧比！不可能！」

　　too much for *sb.* 受不了　　expect (ɪk'spɛkt) v. 期待；期望
　　merely ('mɪrlɪ) *adv.* 僅僅；單單　　yell (jɛl) v. 大叫；大吼
　　no way 絕對不行

They stormed away and never played on the street again.
他們一哄而散，然後再也不在這條街上打球。

　　storm (stɔrm) v. 猛衝

四、閱讀測驗：

41-44 為題組

Most American kids love Halloween treats, but a bucket of Halloween candy can be a dentist's nightmare. Some parents try to get rid of half of the candy after their children go to bed, but dentists say parents also need to separate the good kinds of treats from the bad.

　　大部分的美國小孩都很愛萬聖節的糖果，但是一桶萬聖節糖果可能會是牙醫的惡夢。有些家長試著趁小孩睡著後，丟掉一半的糖果，但是牙醫說，家長還得把好的糖果和壞的糖果分開。

> treat〔trit〕*n.* 示好的食物、飲料等，在此指「萬聖節要來的糖果」。
> bucket〔'bʌkɪt〕*n.* 桶子　　　dentist〔'dɛntɪst〕*n.* 牙醫
> nightmare〔'naɪt,mɛr〕*n.* 惡夢　　***get rid of*** 丟棄
> separate〔'sɛpə,ret〕*v.* 分開

It is not exactly what a child eats that truly matters, but how much time it stays in his mouth. According to pediatric dentist Dr. Kaneta Lott, the most damaging stuff is something that is sticky or very hard and thus stays in the mouth for a long time. This is because we all have bacteria in our mouths. When we eat, the bacteria take our food as their food and produce an acid that destroys the surface of the teeth, causing cavities to form. The longer the food stays in the mouth, the more likely cavities will develop. Therefore, potato chips are worse than candy because they get stuck between teeth. For the same reason, raisins and crackers are not the best choice. Hard candies take a long time to consume and are also a bad choice for Halloween treats

　　真正重要的，並不是小孩吃了什麼，而是吃的停留在他嘴巴裡多久。根據小兒科牙醫 Kaneta Lott 的說法，傷害最大的是非常黏或是硬的東西，因爲它們會在嘴巴裡停留很久。這是因爲我們的嘴巴裡都有細菌。當我們吃東西時，細菌會把我們的食物當作牠們的食物，並製造出會破壞牙齒表面的酸，使蛀牙形成。食物在嘴巴裡停留越久，就越有可能會形成蛀牙。因此，洋芋片比糖果還糟，因爲它們會卡在牙縫。同理可證，葡萄乾和餅乾也不是最好的選擇。硬的糖果要花很長的時間吃，所以也不是萬聖節糖果的好選擇。

> ***not exactly*** 並不　　　truly〔'trulɪ〕*adv.* 真正地
> matter〔'mætɚ〕*v.* 有關係；關係重要
> pediatric〔,pidɪ'ætrɪk〕*adj.* 小兒科的
> damaging〔'dæmɪdʒɪŋ〕*adj.* 有害的　　　stuff〔stʌf〕*n.* 東西；物質

sticky（ˈstɪkɪ）*adj.* 黏黏的　　hard（hɑrd）*adj.* 硬的

thus（ðʌs）*adv.* 因此　　bacteria（bækˈtɪrɪə）*n. pl.* 細菌

acid（ˈæsɪd）*n.*【化學】酸　　destroy（dɪˈstrɔɪ）*v.* 破壞

surface（ˈsɝfɪs）*n.* 表面　　cavity（ˈkævətɪ）*n.* 蛀牙

form（fɔrm）*v.* 形成　　develop（dɪˈvɛləp）*v.* 發展；形成

potato chip 洋芋片　　stuck（stʌk）*adj.* 卡住的

raisin（ˈrezn̩）*n.* 葡萄乾　　cracker（ˈkrækɚ）*n.* 餅乾

consume（kənˈsum）*v.* 將…吃完

If children really love candy, dentists recommend that they eat chocolate instead. Unlike hard candies, chocolate dissolves quickly in the mouth. Besides, chocolate contains tannins, which help to kill some of the bacteria in the mouth. But no matter what a child eats, brushing after each meal is still the best way to fight cavities.

如果孩子真的很愛吃糖果，牙醫建議他們不如換吃巧克力。巧克力與硬的糖果不同，它會迅速溶解在嘴裡。除此之外，巧克力含有丹寧酸，有助於殺掉一些嘴裡的細菌。但是不管孩子吃什麼，每餐飯後刷牙仍是對抗蛀牙的最好方法。

recommend（ˌrɛkəˈmɛnd）*v.* 建議　　instead（ɪnˈstɛd）*adv.* 替換

unlike（ʌnˈlaɪk）*prep.* 與…不同；不像　　dissolve（dɪˈzɑlv）*v.* 溶解

tannin（ˈtænɪn）*n.*【化學】單寧酸　　*no matter what* 無論什麼

brush（brʌʃ）*v.* 刷；刷牙　　meal（mil）*n.* 餐

41.（**C**）本文的主旨是？

　　(A) 討論如何治療蛀牙。

　　(B) 點出慶祝萬聖節的問題。

　　(C) 告訴家長哪些甜食對小孩牙齒的傷害比較小。

　　(D) 教導家長萬聖節糖果對他們小孩的意義。

main（men）*adj.* 主要的　　purpose（ˈpɝpəs）*n.* 目的

passage（ˈpæsɪdʒ）*n.*（文章的）一段；一節

treat（trit）*v.* 治療　　*point out* 指出

celebration（ˌsɛləˈbreʃən）*n.* 慶祝

sweets（swits）*n. pl.* 甜食

42. (**D**) 為什麼硬的糖果對牙齒特別不好？

　　(A) 它們可能會使小孩的牙齒斷掉。

　　(B) 它們含有太多糖份。

　　(C) 它們協助細菌產生單寧酸。

　　(D) 它們停留在嘴巴裡很長一段時間。

　　break〔brek〕*v.* 使斷掉

　　contain〔kən'ten〕*v.* 含有；包含

　　sugar〔'ʃugɚ〕*n.* 糖

43. (**A**) 根據本文，下列何者比較適合用來當萬聖節糖果？

　　(A) 巧克力。　　　　　　(B) 餅乾。

　　(C) 葡萄乾。　　　　　　(D) 洋芋片。

44. (**B**) 根據本文，下列關於丹寧酸的敘述，何者正確？

　　(A) 它們是在細菌消化食物時產生。

　　(B) 它們協助去除掉嘴裡的一些細菌。

　　(C) 它們協助巧克力更快地溶解。

　　(D) 它們破壞牙齒的表面。

　　digest〔daɪ'dʒɛst〕*v.* 消化　　　***get rid of*** 除去

45-48 為題組

　　The largest television network in America is not ABC, CBS, or Fox. Nor is it one of the cable networks such as CNN, which carries only news and news stories.　It is not ESPN, the all-sports cable network, or even MTV, which is famous for its music videos.　Rather it is PBS, Public Broadcasting System, a non-profit public broadcasting TV service.　PBS has 349 member television stations in the U.S. and some member stations by cable in Canada.

　　美國最大的電視網不是「美國廣播公司」、「哥倫比亞廣播系統」或是「福克斯電視台」。也不是只播報新聞或新聞報導的有線電視網，像是「有線新聞電視網」。它不是全體育有線電視網的「娛樂體育節目電視網」，或甚至是以音樂錄影帶聞名的「音樂電視節目」。而是「公視」，公共廣播系統，它是非營利的公共廣播電視服務。美國公視有三百四十九個電視台分部，還有一些有線電視台分佈在加拿大。

network ('nɛt,wɜk) n. 電視網

ABC 美國廣播公司 (= *American Broadcasting Company*)

CBS 哥倫比亞廣播系統 (= *Columbia Broadcasting System*)

Fox ('faks) n. 美國福克斯電視台

cable ('kebḷ) n. 有線電視

CNN 有線新聞電視網 (= *Cable News Network*)

carry ('kærɪ) v. 傳達；報導

ESPN 娛樂體育節目電視網 (= *Entertainment and Sports Programs Network*)

MTV 音樂電視節目 (= *Music Television*)

video ('vɪdɪ,o) n. 錄影帶　　rather ('ræðæ) adv. 而是

PBS 公視 (= *Public Broadcasting System*)

non-profit (,nan'prafɪt) adj. 非營利的

member ('mɛmbæ) n. 分部；支部

PBS only attracts a minority of all TV viewers, about 2 percent. The industry leader, NBC, however, attracts 11 percent of viewers. But the growth of public television in the past two decades has been dramatic. This is especially noteworthy when one considers that public television stations must often survive on very limited budgets, on viewers' donations, and on private foundations and some governmental funding.

「公視」只吸引所有電視觀眾群中的少數，大約百分之二。然而，這個產業中的領導者，「國家廣播公司」，吸引了百分之十一的觀眾。但是在過去二十年，公共電視的成長一直都很戲劇化。特別值得注意的是，當一個人想到公共電視台時，一定會想到要在非常有限的預算、觀眾的捐贈、私人的捐款和一些政府資金的協助之下，才能生存。

attract (ə'trækt) v. 吸引　　minority (mə'nɔrətɪ) n. 少數

viewer ('vjuæ) n. 觀眾　　percent (pæ'sɛnt) n. 百分比

industry ('ɪndʌstrɪ) n. 產業

NBC 國家廣播公司 (= *National Broadcasting Company*)

growth〔 groθ 〕 *n.* 成長　　decade〔'dɛked 〕 *n.* 十年
dramatic〔 drə'mætɪk 〕 *adj.* 戲劇性的
noteworthy〔'not,wɝðɪ 〕 *adj.* 值得注意的
survive〔 sə'vaɪv 〕 *v.* 生存；活下來
limited〔'lɪmɪtɪd 〕 *adj.* 有限的　　budget〔'bʌdʒɪt 〕 *n.* 預算
donation〔 do'neʃən 〕 *n.* 捐贈　　private〔'praɪvɪt 〕 *adj.* 私人的
foundation〔 faʊn'deʃən 〕 *n.* 基金；捐款
governmental〔,gʌvən'mɛntḷ 〕 *adj.* 政府的
funding〔'fʌndɪŋ 〕 *n.* 基金；資金

The level of quality of PBS programs, whether in national and international news, entertainment, or education, is excellent. Almost a whole generation of children throughout the world is familiar with Sesame Street and the characters of The Muppet Show. PBS is especially well known for the quality of its many educational TV programs. Over 95 percent of all public television stations have tele-courses. These courses are accepted and supported by more than 1,800 colleges and universities throughout the US. Each year, over a quarter of a million students take courses this way.

　　無論是本國或國際性的新聞、娛樂節目或是教育節目，「公視」的品質水準都是極好的。幾乎全世界一整個時代的小孩子，都對「芝麻街」和「大青蛙布偶秀」的角色非常熟悉。「公視」最有名的，是許多電視教育節目的品質。百分之九十五以上的公共電視台，都有電視教學課程。全美國有超過一千八百所大專院校都接受和支持這些課程。每年，有超過二十五萬的學生用這種方式選修課程。

level〔'lɛvḷ 〕 *n.* 水準；等級　　quality〔'kwɑlətɪ 〕 *n.* 品質
entertainment〔,ɛntə'tenmənt 〕 *n.* 娛樂
generation〔,dʒɛnə'reʃən 〕 *n.* 一代　　familiar〔 fə'mɪljə 〕 *adj.* 熟悉的
sesame〔'sɛsəmɪ 〕 *n.* 芝麻　　character〔'kærɪktə 〕 *n.* 角色
tele-course〔'tɛlə,kɔrs 〕 *n.* 電視教學課程
support〔 sə'port 〕 *v.* 支持　　quarter〔'kwɔrtə 〕 *n.* 四分之一
take〔 tek 〕 *v.* 修（課程）

45. (**A**) 根據這篇文章，公視有部分資金是從＿＿＿＿＿＿得來。

    (A) <u>私人機構。</u>   (B) 公立學校。

    (C) 廣告公司。   (D) 其他電視台。

    organization (ˌɔrgənəˈzeʃən) n. 機構

    advertising (ˈædvɚˌtaɪzɪŋ) n. 廣告

    agency (ˈedʒənsɪ) n. 代理機構

46. (**C**) 公視最有名的是什麼？

    (A) 有線服務。   (B) 慷慨的捐贈。

    (C) <u>教育節目。</u>   (D) 現場新聞播報。

    generous (ˈdʒɛnərəs) adj. 慷慨的   live (laɪv) adj. 現場的

47. (**D**) 關於公視，下列何者為眞？

    (A) 它們大多數的觀眾是少數民族。

    (B) 它們百分之九十五的節目是電視教學課程。

    (C) 它們的數量正在減少當中，因為它們沒有獲利。

    (D) <u>美國很多大學接受它們的課程。</u>

    minority (maɪˈnɔrətɪ) adj. 少數的   people (ˈpipl̩) n. 民族

    shrink (ʃrɪŋk) v. 減少

48. (**C**) 下列何者有最高百分比的觀眾？

    (A) 美國廣播公司。   (B) 公視。

    (C) <u>國家廣播公司。</u>   (D) 福克斯電視台。

<u>49-52 為題組</u>

Last week Jay McCarroll and The HSUS (The Humane Society of the United States) made a bold fur-free statement on the runway, marking **a new chapter** for the fashion industry and animal protection. The encouraging response to McCarroll's show confirmed that change is happening in fashion.

上週，傑麥凱羅和美國人道協會，一起在伸展台上發表了拒用皮草的大膽聲明，這為時尚界和動物保護行動寫下新的一章。對麥凱羅這場秀的鼓勵性回應，證實時尚正在改變。

humane﹝hju'men﹞*adj.* 人道的　　society﹝sə'saɪətɪ﹞*n.* 協會
bold﹝bold﹞*adj.* 大膽的　　fur﹝fʒ﹞*n.* 皮毛；皮草
fur-free 拒用皮草　　statement﹝'stetmənt﹞*n.* 聲明
runway﹝'rʌn,we﹞*n.* 伸展台　　mark﹝mɑrk﹞*v.* 標上；寫上
chapter﹝'tʃæptə﹞*n.*（人生或歷史的）重要章節
industry﹝'ɪndʌstrɪ﹞*n.* 業；界　　protection﹝prə'tɛkʃən﹞*n.* 保護
encouraging﹝ɪn'kʒɪdʒɪŋ﹞*adj.* 鼓勵的
response﹝rɪ'spɑns﹞*n.* 回應　　confirm﹝kən'fʒm﹞*v.* 證實

McCarroll has good reasons for rejecting fur. Each year, tens of
millions of animals, including dogs and cats, needlessly suffer and die to
fuel the fur industry. But what did Jay McCarroll use in place of fur? "I
have patchwork pieces that contain all sorts of combinations of fabrics.
The rest is cotton, nylon, polyester...you name it. I even have some stuff
made out of bamboo/cotton blend. Anything but fur and leather," he told
Fashion Wire Daily.

　　麥凱羅有充分的理由要拒用皮草。每年，有數千萬的動物，包括狗和貓，
為了使皮草業繼續營運，而受到不必要的傷害或死亡。但是傑麥凱羅要用什麼
東西來代替皮草呢？「我用一塊一塊的東西拼縫起來，它們包含各式各樣的布
料組合。其餘部分則是棉、尼龍、聚酯纖維…應有盡有。甚至有些布是用竹子
和棉混紡而成的。除了皮草和皮革以外的任何東西」，他告訴流行線上日報。

good﹝gud﹞*adj.* 充分的　　reject﹝rɪ'dʒɛkt﹞*v.* 拒絕
needlessly﹝'nidlɪslɪ﹞*adv.* 不必要地　　suffer﹝'sʌfə﹞*v.* 受傷
fuel﹝'fjuəl﹞*v.* 保持…的進行　　***in place of*** 取代；代替
patchwork﹝'pætʃ,wʒk﹞*n.* 拼湊成的東西
piece﹝pis﹞*n.* 片；塊；部分　　contain﹝kən'ten﹞*v.* 包含
sort﹝sort﹞*n.* 種類　　combination﹝,kɑmbə'neʃən﹞*n.* 組合
fabric﹝'fæbrɪk﹞*n.* 布料；織品　　rest﹝rɛst﹞*n.* 其餘之物
cotton﹝'kɑtn̩﹞*n.* 棉　　nylon﹝'naɪlɑn﹞*n.* 尼龍
polyester﹝'pɑlɪ,ɛstə﹞*n.* 聚酯纖維
you name it 凡是你想到的；應有盡有

stuff〔stʌf〕*n.* 原料；布匹　　*make out of* 用…製成
bamboo〔bæmˈbu〕*n.* 竹子
blend〔blɛnd〕*n.* 混合製品；混紡
anything but 除～之外的任何東西　　leather〔ˈlɛðɚ〕*n.* 皮革
wire〔waɪr〕*n.* 電線　　daily〔ˈdelɪ〕*n.* 日報

"So many people want to protect animals and live their lives without causing unnecessary cruelty. More than two thirds of Americans have pets, and we share a bond with animals every day. Saying no to fur can help millions of animals, and we want to show our respect to leading designers like Jay who embrace compassion as the fashion," said Michael Markarian, executive vice president of The HSUS. "It is great to see leaders in the fashion industry recognizing that the animals need their fur more than we do."

「有非常多人想要保護動物，並過著無須造成不必要的殘忍行為的生活。超過三分之二的美國人有養寵物，而且我們每天都跟動物有聯繫。向皮草說不，可以幫助數百萬的動物，所以我們要向像傑這樣的一流設計師致敬，因為他採納同情心作為時尚的一部分」，麥克馬卡林說，他是美國人道協會的執行副總。「看到時尚界的領導者承認，動物比我們還需要牠們的皮，是件很棒的事」。

live〔lɪv〕*v.* 過…的生活
unnecessary〔ʌnˈnɛsə,sɛrɪ〕*adj.* 不必要的
cruelty〔ˈkruəltɪ〕*n.* 殘忍的行為　　*two thirds of* 三分之二的
pet〔pɛt〕*n.* 寵物　　share〔ʃɛr〕*v.* 共同具有
bond〔bɑnd〕*n.* 關聯；聯繫　　show〔ʃo〕*v.* 表示
respect〔rɪˈspɛkt〕*n.* 敬意　　leading〔ˈlidɪŋ〕*adj.* 一流的
designer〔dɪˈzaɪnɚ〕*n.* 設計師
embrace〔ɪmˈbres〕*v.* 接受；採取
compassion〔kəmˈpæʃən〕*n.* 同情心；憐憫
executive〔ɪgˈzɛkjutɪv〕*adj.* 執行的　　vice〔vaɪs〕*adj.* 副的
president〔ˈprɛzədənt〕*n.* 總裁　　leader〔ˈlidɚ〕*n.* 領導者
recognize〔ˈrɛkəg,naɪz〕*v.* 承認

49. (**A**) 關於傑麥凱羅，下列何者正確？

　　(A) 他是著名的時尚設計師。

　　(B) 他是美國人道協會的執行副總裁。

　　(C) 他是流行線上日報的編輯。

　　(D) 他是動物保護組織的會長。

　　editor ('ɛdɪtə) *n.* 編輯　　head (hɛd) *n.* 領袖；會長

　　organization (ˌɔrgənə'zeʃən) *n.* 組織

50. (**B**) 在第一段第三行的 **a new chapter** 意思是？

　　(A) 一本書的新單元。　　　　(B) 一種新趨勢的開始。

　　(C) 一本雜誌的最新議題。　　(D) 一個最近設立的組織。

　　unit ('junɪt) *n.* 單元　　trend (trɛnd) *n.* 趨勢

　　latest ('letɪst) *adj.* 最新的　　issue ('ɪʃju) *n.* 議題

　　newly ('njulɪ) *adv.* 最近　　established (ə'stæblɪʃt) *adj.* 已設立的

51. (**C**) 傑麥凱羅不推薦用下列哪一項來做衣服？

　　(A) 聚酯纖維。　　　　　　　(B) 竹子。

　　(C) 皮革。　　　　　　　　　(D) 拼湊起來的東西。

　　recommend (ˌrɛkə'mɛnd) *v.* 推薦

　　clothing ('kloðɪŋ) *n.* 衣服

52. (**B**) 我們可以從本文得知什麼？

　　(A) 人類在情感上依賴動物。

　　(B) 時尚可與對生物的同情並存。

　　(C) 用皮草來做衣服的效果比竹棉混紡還好。

　　(D) 對時尚設計師來說，皮草比其他布料還貴。

　　human being 人類　　depend (dɪ'pɛnd) *v.* 依賴

　　emotionally (ɪ'moʃənḷɪ) *adv.* 情感上

　　go hand in hand with 並存

　　life (laɪf) *n.* 生物　　effective (ə'fɛktɪv) *adj.* 有效的

　　material (mə'tɪrɪəl) *n.* 材料；布料

53-56 為題組

Twenty years ago, most experts believed that differences in how boys and girls behaved were mainly due to differences in how they were treated by their parents, teachers, and friends. It's hard to **cling to** that belief today. Recent research has shown that there are biological differences between boys and girls. Understanding these differences is important in raising and educating children.

二十年前，大部分專家相信男女的行為差異，主要是由於父母、老師及朋友對待他們的方式不同所造成的。現在則很難再堅持這樣的想法。最近的研究顯示，男女之間存在著生物學上的差異。了解這些差異對教養小孩很重要。

expert (ˈɛkspɜt) n. 專家　　difference (ˈdɪfərəns) n. 差異
behave (bɪˈhev) v. 行為　　mainly (ˈmenlɪ) adv. 主要地
due to 由於 (= *thanks to* = *owing to* = *on account of* = *because of* = *as a result of*)　　treat (trit) v. 對待
cling to 執著；堅守　　belief (bɪˈlif) n. 想法；信念
recent (ˈrisn̩t) adj. 最近的
research (ˈrisɜtʃ ; rɪˈsɜtʃ) n. 研究
biological (ˌbaɪəˈlɑdʒɪkl̩) adj. 生物 (學) 的
understand (ˌʌndɚˈstænd) v. 了解
raise (rez) v. 養育 (= *bring up*)

For example, girls are born with more sensitive hearing than boys, and the difference increases as kids grow up. So when a grown man speaks to a girl in what he thinks is a normal voice, she may hear it as yelling. Conversely, boys who appear to be inattentive in class may just be sitting too far away to hear the teacher.

例如，女生的聽覺天生比男生敏銳，這樣的差異會隨著小孩的成長而增加。所以，當成年男子以他認為正常的聲音對女孩說話時，她可能覺得聽起來像是在吼叫。相反地，課堂上顯得不太專心的男孩，可能只是因為坐得太遠，無法聽到老師說話。

sensitive (ˈsɛnsətɪv) *adj.* 敏感的
hearing (ˈhɪrɪŋ) *n.* 聽覺；聽力
increase (ɪnˈkris) *v.* 增加　　kid (kɪd) *n.* 小孩
grown (gron) *adj.* 成年的　　normal (ˈnɔrml̩) *adj.* 正常的
voice (vɔɪs) *n.* 聲音　　yell (jɛl) *v.* 吼叫
conversely (kənˈvɜslɪ) *adv.* 反過來；在另一方面
inattentive (ˌɪnəˈtɛntɪv) *adj.* 不注意的　　*in class* 課堂上
too ~ to… 太～而不能…

Likewise, girls are better in their expression of feelings. Studies reveal that negative emotions are seated in an area of the brain called the amygdala. Girls develop an early connection between this area and the cerebral cortex, enabling them to talk about their feelings. In boys these links develop later. So if you ask a troubled adolescent boy to tell you what his feelings are, he often cannot say much.

同樣地，女生較善於表達情感。研究顯示，負面的情緒位於腦部一個稱為扁桃體的區域，女生的大腦皮質很早便和這個區域發展出連結，讓她們能談論自己的感受。男生在這方面的連結則較晚發展，所以如果你要一個憂慮的青春期少年告訴你他的感受，他通常說不出什麼。

likewise (ˈlaɪkˌwaɪz) *adv.* 同樣地
expression (ɪkˈsprɛʃən) *n.* 表達
feeling (ˈfilɪŋ) *n.* 情感　　reveal (rɪˈvil) *v.* 顯示；揭露
negative (ˈnɛgətɪv) *adj.* 負面的；消極的
emotion (ɪˈmoʃən) *n.* 情緒；情感　　seat (sit) *v.* 位於
amygdala (əˈmɪgdələ) *n.* 扁桃體　　develop (dɪˈvɛləp) *v.* 發展
connection (kəˈnɛkʃən) *n.* 連結
cerebral (ˈsɛrəbrəl) *adj.* 大腦的
cortex (ˈkɔrtɛks) *n.* (腦或其他器官的) 皮層；大腦皮質
enable (ɪnˈebl̩) *v.* 使能夠　　link (lɪŋk) *n.* 連結
troubled (ˈtrʌbl̩d) *adj.* 憂慮的；煩惱的
adolescent (ˌædl̩ˈɛsn̩t) *adj.* 青春期的

Dr. Sax, a proponent of single-sex education, points out that keeping boys and girls separate in the classroom has yielded striking educational, social, and interpersonal benefits. Therefore, parents and teachers should try to recognize, understand, and make use of the biological differences that make a girl a girl, and a boy a boy.

塞克斯博士是單一性別教育的支持者，他指出男女分開在不同教室上課，能產生顯著的教育、社會、和人際關係上的益處。因此，父母和老師應該嘗試去認同、理解，並利用生物學上的差異——它讓男生成為男生，女生成為女生。

proponent (prə'ponənt) n. 支持者
single-sex ('sɪŋgḷ'sɛks) adj. 單一性別的　　**point out** 指出
separate ('sɛprɪt) adj. 分開的　　yield (jild) v. 產生
striking ('straɪkɪŋ) adj. 顯著的
educational (,ɛdʒʊ'keʃənḷ) adj. 教育的
social ('soʃəl) adj. 社會的
interpersonal (,ɪntə'pɜsənḷ) adj. 人際的
benefit ('bɛnəfɪt) n. 利益
recognize ('rɛkəg,naɪz) v. 承認；認同；辨識
make use of 利用

53. (**C**) 本文主旨為何？
　　(A) 課堂上男生容易比女生更不專心。
　　(B) 女生察覺聲音的能力比男生更好。
　　(C) 男女之間行為的差異是由於生物學上的差異。
　　(D) 單一性別的學校不好，因為它們把男女分開。

tend to 傾向　　**pay attention** 專心
detect (dɪ'tɛkt) v. 察覺

54. (**D**) 爲何女生比男生更善於表達負面情感？

　　(A) 女生比男生更多愁善感。

　　(B) 女生的腦細胞比男生多。

　　(C) 男女的扁桃體位在腦部不同的區域。

　　(D) <u>腦部特定部位的連結，女生發展得比男生早。</u>

　　emotional〔ɪˋmoʃənḷ〕*adj.* 多愁善感的

　　cell〔sɛl〕*n.* 細胞　　locate〔loˋket〕*v.* 座落；位於

55. (**B**) 作者相信下列何者？

　　(A) 女生在溝通方面需要更多訓練。

　　(B) <u>男生跟女生應該用不同的方式教育。</u>

　　(C) 父母親應該更注意男生。

　　(D) 教育時，應該忽略性別差異。

　　training〔ˋtrenɪŋ〕*n.* 訓練

　　communication〔kəˏmjunəˋkeʃən〕*n.* 溝通

　　ignore〔ɪgˋnor〕*v.* 忽視

56. (**A**) 第一段中的片語 **cling to** 意思爲何？

　　(A) <u>堅持。</u>　　(B) 放棄。　　(C) 評估。　　(D) 挑戰。

　　maintain〔menˋten〕*v.* 堅持；維持　　abandon〔əˋbændən〕*v.* 放棄

　　evaluate〔ɪˋvæljuˏet〕*v.* 評估　　challenge〔ˋtʃælɪndʒ〕*v.* 挑戰

第貳部分：非選擇題

一、翻譯題

1. If we only live for ourselves, we will not $\begin{cases} \text{truly } \begin{cases} \text{feel} \\ \text{be} \end{cases} \text{happy.} \\ \text{feel true happiness.} \end{cases}$

2. When we $\begin{cases} \text{begin} \\ \text{start} \end{cases}$ $\begin{cases} \text{thinking} \\ \text{to think} \end{cases}$ for others, the $\begin{cases} \text{gate} \\ \text{door} \end{cases}$ to happiness will open naturally.

二、英文作文：

Jane's New Pet

One day, Jane was playing in the park. She was very happy to find a little cat to play with. When she went home, she took the cat with her. She didn't know that all of the cat's brothers and sisters were following her.

Jane asked her mother if she could keep the cat as a pet. Her mother was not happy because she thought a pet would cause a lot of trouble. But Jane promised that she would take care of the cat well. Finally her mother agreed.

Unfortunately for Jane, all of the cats moved into her house and made a big mess. They scratched the sofa and broke a lamp. Their muddy feet made the floor dirty. Poor Jane. She will have to clean up the mess or her mother will be very angry.

pet (pɛt) n. 寵物　　follow ('falo) v. 跟隨
keep (kip) v. 飼養　　cause (kɔz) v. 造成；引起
trouble ('trʌbḷ) n. 麻煩的事
promise ('pramɪs) v. 承諾；答應
finally ('faɪnḷɪ) adv. 最後
agree (ə'gri) v. 同意　　*take care of* 照顧
unfortunately (ʌn'fɔrtʃənɪtlɪ) adv. 不幸地；遺憾地
move (muv) v. 搬家；遷移　　mess (mɛs) n. 混亂；亂七八糟
scratch (skrætʃ) v. 抓傷　　break (brek) v. 打破；弄壞
lamp (læmp) n. 燈　　muddy ('mʌdɪ) adj. 沾滿泥的
floor (flor) n. 地板　　dirty ('dɜtɪ) adj. 髒的
poor (pur) adj. 可憐的　　*clean up* 把…打掃乾淨；清理
or (ɔr) conj. 否則　　angry ('æŋgrɪ) adj. 生氣的

96 年度學科能力測驗英文試題修正意見

題　號	題　　　目	修　正　意　見
第 2 題	...last year, *already* showed his great....	將 already 去掉，或改成 ...last year, *had already* showed his great.... * already 在此應和完成式連用。
第 5 題	...solid foundation *for research*.	應改成...solid foundation *in research skills*.或 ...solid foundation *in research techniques*. 句意較清楚。
第 14 題	...how much *scholarship*....	...how much *scholarship money*.... 或 ...how *large a scholarship*.... * scholarship 應加冠詞 a，只能說 how large，不能說 how much；如要用 how much，scholarship 後須加 money。
第 26－30 題 第七行	And *being* a tiny country, everything in Rwanda....	And *because it is* a tiny country, everything in Rwanda.... * 這句話是明顯的錯誤，因為前後主詞不一致，故分詞構句中的主詞 it 不可省略，改成子句較佳。
第 31－40 題 第三行	...his *house, at night*.	...his *house at night*. * 不需要逗點，句尾的 at night 前面加個逗點很奇怪。
第 45－48 題 第一段 第四行	Rather it is PBS, *Public Broadcasting System*,....	Rather it is PBS, *the Public Broadcasting Service*,.... * 專有名詞不加冠詞，但公共建築、機關的名稱前，應加定冠詞 the。(詳見「文法寶典」p.218) 公共電視台 PBS 中的 S 是 Service，不是 System。
第 45 題	..., PBS *received* part of its....	..., PBS *receives* part of its.... * 整篇文章都是現在式，怎麼突然出現一個過去式動詞？表示不變的事實，應用現在式。
第 49－52 題 第二段 第六行	...out of *bamboo/cotton* blend.	...out of *a bamboo/cotton* blend. * blend (混合製品；混紡) 為可數名詞，前面須加冠詞 a。
第 52 題	(C)...than *bamboo/cotton* blend for clothing.	(C)...than *a bamboo/cotton* blend for clothing.

96 年學測英文科考題出題來源

題　　號	出　　　　　　　　處
一、詞彙 第 1～15 題	答案關鍵字完全出自大考中心 91 年 6 月 30 日新修訂的「高中常用 7000 字」，如果是以前舊版的，就沒有第 4 題 (D) upload（上傳）這個字。
二、綜合測驗 第 16～20 題 第 21～25 題 第 26～30 題	www.happytaildogcpa.com ；www.thedogspa.co.uk http://www.hindutantimes.com From agony to ecstasy, Travel & indulgence, *The Australian*, Oct. 07, 2006 http://www.theaustralian.news.com.au/story/0,20867, 20532195-5002031,00.html
三、文意選填 第 31～40 題	http://dimdima.com/khazana/stories/showstory.asp? q_title=Master+of+the+Game
四、閱讀測驗 第 41～44 題 第 45～48 題 第 49～52 題 第 53～56 題	CNN News, 30/10/2006 A pediatric dentist's tricks for the treat night Bodenstein, J. H., Daun-Barausch, E., & Stevenson, D. K. (1996). *American life and institutions*. Deutsch: Klett http://en.wikipedia.org/wiki/PBS Jay McCarroll and the HSUS make a bold fur-free statement on the runway www.hsus.org http://www.enotalone.com/article/4316.html

九十六年度學科能力測驗（英文考科）
大考中心公佈答案

題號	答案	題號	答案	題號	答案
1	A	21	D	41	C
2	D	22	B	42	D
3	A	23	A	43	A
4	B	24	C	44	B
5	C	25	B	45	A
6	D	26	B	46	C
7	B	27	C	47	D
8	D	28	D	48	C
9	C	29	C	49	A
10	A	30	A	50	B
11	B	31	F	51	C
12	D	32	C	52	B
13	C	33	B	53	C
14	B	34	D	54	D
15	A	35	J	55	B
16	D	36	G	56	A
17	B	37	A		
18	C	38	I		
19	A	39	H		
20	A	40	E		

九十六學年度學科能力測驗
英文科各級分人數累計表

級分	人數	百分比（%）	累計人數	累計百分比（%）
15	4928	3.28	150360	100.00
14	8956	5.96	145432	96.72
13	10212	6.79	136476	90.77
12	11814	7.86	126264	83.97
11	11008	7.32	114450	76.12
10	12320	8.19	103442	68.80
9	11752	7.82	91122	60.60
8	12972	8.63	79370	52.79
7	12507	8.32	66398	44.16
6	14039	9.34	53891	35.84
5	12857	8.55	39852	26.50
4	14570	9.69	26995	17.95
3	10336	6.87	12425	8.26
2	2036	1.35	2089	1.39
1	48	0.03	53	0.04
0	5	0.00	5	0.00

九十五年大學入學學科能力測驗試題
英文考科

第壹部份：單選題（佔 72 分）

一、詞彙（佔 15 分）

說明：第 1 至 15 題，每題選出最適當的一個選項，標示在答案卡之「選擇題答案區」。每題答對得 1 分，答錯不倒扣。

1. If we can _____ to, we will take a vacation abroad in the summer.
   (A) pay　　　　(B) move　　　　(C) expose　　　　(D) afford

2. A _____ mistake found in parenthood is that parents often set unrealistic goals for their children.
   (A) terrific　　(B) common　　(C) straight　　(D) favorable

3. Some words, such as "sandwich" and "hamburger," were _____ the names of people or even towns.
   (A) originally　(B) ideally　　(C) relatively　　(D) sincerely

4. Have you ever _____ how the ancient Egyptians created such marvelous feats of engineering as the pyramids?
   (A) concluded　(B) wondered　(C) admitted　　(D) persuaded

5. Mr. Johnson was disappointed at his students for having a passive learning _____.
   (A) result　　　(B) progress　　(C) attitude　　(D) energy

6. Anne dreaded giving a speech before three hundred people; even thinking about it made her _____.
   (A) passionate　(B) anxious　　(C) ambitious　　(D) optimistic

7. I had to _____ Jack's invitation to the party because it conflicted with an important business meeting.
   (A) decline　　(B) depart　　(C) devote　　(D) deserve

8. Selling fried chicken at the night market doesn't seem to be a decent business, but it is actually quite _____.

    (A) plentiful   (B) precious   (C) profitable   (D) productive

9. The passengers _____ escaped death when a bomb exploded in the subway station, killing sixty people.

    (A) traditionally   (B) valuably   (C) loosely   (D) narrowly

10. Jerry didn't _____ his primary school classmate Mary until he listened to her self-introduction.

    (A) acquaint   (B) acquire   (C) recognize   (D) realize

11. With the completion of several public _____ projects, such as the MRT, commuting to work has become easier for people living in the suburbs.

    (A) transportation (B) traffic   (C) travel   (D) transfer

12. With a good _____ of both Chinese and English, Miss Lin was assigned the task of oral interpretation for the visiting American delegation.

    (A) writing   (B) program   (C) command   (D) impression

13. I am studying so hard for the forthcoming entrance exam that I do not have the _____ of a free weekend to rest.

    (A) luxury   (B) license   (C) limitation   (D) strength

14. Kim was completely _____ after jogging in the hot sun all afternoon; she had little energy left.

    (A) kicked out   (B) handed out (C) worn out   (D) put out

15. When Jason failed to pay his bill, the network company _____ his Internet connection.

    (A) cut off   (B) cut back   (C) cut short   (D) cut down

二、**綜合測驗**（佔 15 分）

說明：　第 16 至 30 題，每題一個空格，請依文意選出最適當的一個選項，標
　　　　示在答案卡之「選擇題答案區」。每題答對得 1 分，答錯不倒扣。

Dear Son,

　　I am very happy to hear that you are doing well in school.
However, I am very concerned with the way you ___16___ money.
I understand that college students like to ___17___ parties,
movies, and lots of activities, but you also have to learn how to
do without certain things. After all, you must live within a
limited budget.

　　___18___ the extra money you want for this month, I am
sorry that I have decided not to send it to you because I think it
is time for you to learn how to live without my help. If I give
you a hand every time you have problems with money now,
what will you do when you no longer have me to support you?
Besides, I remember telling you I used to have two part-time
jobs when I was in college just to ___19___. So, if you need
money now, you should try either finding a job or cutting down
on your ___20___.

　　I understand it is not easy to live on your own. But learning
to budget your money is the first lesson you must learn to be
independent. Good luck, son. And remember: never spend more
than you earn.

Love,
Mom

---

16. (A) manage　　　(B) restrict　　　(C) charge　　　(D) deposit
17. (A) indulge in　　(B) dwell in　　　(C) attend to　　(D) apply to
18. (A) Regarded　　　　　　　　　　(B) To regard
　　(C) Being regarded　　　　　　　(D) Regarding

19. (A) catch up   (B) get my way
     (C) keep in touch   (D) make ends meet
20. (A) spirit   (B) expenses   (C) savings   (D) estimate

There are two kinds of heroes: heroes who shine in the face of great danger, who perform an ___21___ act in a difficult situation, and heroes who live an ordinary life like us, who do their work ___22___ by many of us, but who ___23___ a difference in the lives of others.

Heroes are selfless people who perform extraordinary acts. The mark of heroes is not necessarily the result of their action, but ___24___ they are willing to do for others and for their chosen cause. ___25___ they fail, their determination lives on for others to follow. The glory lies not in the achievement but in the sacrifice.

21. (A) annoying   (B) interfering   (C) amazing   (D) inviting
22. (A) noticing   (B) noticeable   (C) noticed   (D) unnoticed
23. (A) make   (B) do   (C) tell   (D) count
24. (A) what   (B) who   (C) those   (D) where
25. (A) Not until   (B) Even if   (C) As if   (D) No sooner than

Fans of professional baseball and football argue continually over which is America's favorite sport. Though the figures on attendance for each vary with every new season, certain ___26___ remain the same. To begin with, football is a quicker, more physical sport, and football fans enjoy the emotional involvement they feel while watching. Baseball, on the other hand, seems more mental, like chess, and ___27___ those fans that prefer a quieter, more complicated game. ___28___ , professional football teams usually play no more than fourteen games a year. Baseball teams, however, play ___29___ every day for six months. Finally, football fans seem to love the half-time activities, the marching bands, and the pretty cheerleaders. ___30___ , baseball fans are more content to concentrate on the game's finer details and spend the breaks between innings filling out their own private scorecards.

26. (A) agreements　　　　　　　(B) arguments
　　(C) accomplishments　　　　(D) arrangements
27. (A) attracted　(B) is attracted　(C) attract　(D) attracts
28. (A) In addition　(B) As a result　(C) In contrast　(D) To some extent
29. (A) hardly　(B) almost　(C) somehow　(D) rarely
30. (A) Even so　　　　　　　　(B) For that reason
　　(C) On the contrary　　　　(D) By the same token

三、文意選填（佔 10 分）

說明：第 31 至 40 題，每題一個空格，請依文意在文章後所提供的 (A) 到(J)
　　　選項中分別選出最適當者，並將其英文字母代號標示在答案卡之「選
　　　擇題答案區」。每題答對得 1 分，答錯不倒扣。

　　Good health is not something you are able to buy, nor can you get
it back with a quick ___31___ to a doctor. Keeping yourself healthy has
to be your own ___32___. If you mistreat your body by keeping bad
habits, ___33___ symptoms of illness, and ignoring common health rules,
even the best medicine can be of little use.

　　Nowadays health specialists ___34___ the idea of wellness for
everybody. Wellness means ___35___ the best possible health within
the limits of your body. One person may need fewer calories than
another. Some people might prefer a lot of ___36___ exercise to more
challenging exercise. While one person enjoys playing seventy-two
holes of golf a week, another would rather play three sweaty, competitive
games of tennis.

　　Understanding the needs of your body is the ___37___. Everyone
runs the risk of accidents, and no one can be sure of avoiding ___38___
disease. Nevertheless, poor diet, stress, a bad working environment,
and carelessness can ___39___ good health. By changing your habits or
the conditions surrounding you, you can ___40___ the risk or reduce the
damage of disease.

(A) ruin　　　　(B) visit　　　　(C) neglecting　　(D) lower
(E) easier　　　(F) responsibility　(G) chronic　　　(H) key
(I) promote　　(J) achieving

四、閱讀測驗（佔 32 分）

說明： 第 41 至 56 題，每題請分別根據各篇文章之文意選出最適當的一個選項，標示在答案卡之「選擇題答案區」。每題答對得 2 分，答錯不倒扣。

41-44 為題組

Who is more stressed out—the Asian teenager or the American teenager? Surprise. The American teen wins this contest. According to a recent study, almost three-quarters of American high school juniors said they felt stress at least once a week, some almost daily. Fewer than half of Japanese and Taiwanese eleventh graders reported feeling stress that often.

The phenomenon of stress is the constant interaction between mind and body. And the influence of one upon the other can be either positive or negative. What can the mind do to the body? Studies have proved that watching funny movies can reduce pain and promote healing. Conversely, worry can give a person an ulcer, high blood pressure, or even a heart attack.

The mind and body work together to produce stress, which is a bodily response to a stimulus, a response that disturbs the body's normal physiological balance. However, stress is not always bad. For example, a stress reaction can sometimes save a person's life by releasing hormones that enable a person to react quickly and with greater energy in a dangerous situation. In everyday situations, too, stress can provide that extra push needed to do something difficult. But too much stress often injures both the mind and the body. How can stress be kept under control? *Learn to Lighten Up and Live Longer*, the best seller of the month, has several good suggestions. So, grab a copy and start learning how you can reduce stress in your life.

41. What is the writer's main purpose for writing this passage?
    (A) To find who are the most stressed out teenagers.
    (B) To explain that stress is a mental problem.
    (C) To inform the reader how to reduce stress.
    (D) To promote a book about reducing stress.

42. The underlined word **ulcer** in the second paragraph refers to a
    particular kind of
    (A) mental illness.　　　　　　(B) physical problem.
    (C) spiritual healing.　　　　　(D) physiological treatment.

43. According to the passage, which of following is a positive effect of
    stress?
    (A) Watching funny movies.
    (B) Doing relaxing exercise.
    (C) Avoiding difficult things successfully.
    (D) Reacting quickly in risky situations.

44. Which of the following is TRUE according to the passage?
    (A) Taiwanese teens experience more stress than American teens.
    (B) Stress is a state too complicated to be kept under full control.
    (C) *Learn to Lighten Up and Live Longer* is a popular book.
    (D) Stress is always more positive than harmful to the body.

45-48 為題組

　　Tea was the first brewed beverage. The Chinese emperor Shen
Nung in 2737 B.C. introduced the drink. Chinese writer Lu Yu wrote
in A.D. 780 that there were "tens of thousands" of teas. Chinese tea
was introduced to Japan in A.D. 800. It was then introduced to Europe
in the early 1600s, when trade began between Europe and the Far East.
At that time, China was the main supplier of tea to the world. Then in
1834, tea cultivation began in India and spread to Sri Lanka, Thailand,
Burma, and other areas of Southeast Asia. Today, Java, South Africa,
South America, and areas of the Caucasus also produce tea.

　　There are three kinds of tea: black, green, and oolong. Most
international tea trading is in black tea. Black tea preparation consists
mainly of picking young leaves and leaf buds on a clear sunny day and
letting the leaves dry for about an hour in the sun. Then, they are lightly
rolled and left in a fermentation room to develop scent and a red color.

Next, they are heated several more times. Finally, the leaves are dried in a basket over a charcoal fire. Green tea leaves are heated in steam, rolled, and dried. Oolong tea is prepared similarly to black tea, but without the fermentation time.

Three main varieties of tea—Chinese, Assamese, and Cambodian— have distinct characteristics. The Chinese variety, a strong plant that can grow to be 2.75 meters high, can live to be 100 years old and survives cold winters. The Assamese variety can grow 18 meters high and lives about 40 years. The Cambodian tea tree grows five meters tall.

Tea is enjoyed worldwide as a refreshing and stimulating drink. Because so many people continue to drink the many varieties of tea, it will probably continue as the world's most popular drink.

45. In the early 1600s, tea was introduced to Europe due to
   (A) revolution.　　　　　　　　(B) marriage.
   (C) business.　　　　　　　　　(D) education.

46. According to the passage, which of following is the most popular tea around the world?
   (A) Green tea.　　　　　　　　(B) Black tea.
   (C) Oolong tea.　　　　　　　　(D) European tea.

47. According to the passage, which of the following is TRUE about tea preparation?
   (A) Black tea leaves need to be picked on a cloudy day.
   (B) Green tea leaves need to be heated over a charcoal fire.
   (C) The preparation of oolong tea is similar to that of black tea.
   (D) Oolong tea leaves need to be heated in steam before they are rolled.

48. Which of the following statements can be inferred from the passage?
    (A) People drink tea to become rich and healthy.
    (B) Java developed tea cultivation earlier than India.
    (C) Tea plants can grow for only a short period of time.
    (D) People drink tea because of its variety and refreshing effect.

49-52 為題組

Astronauts often work 16 hours a day on the space shuttle in order to complete all the projects set out for the mission. From space, astronauts study the geography, pollution, and weather patterns on Earth. They take many photographs to record their observations. Also, astronauts <u>conduct</u> experiments on the shuttle to learn how space conditions, such as microgravity, affect humans, animals, plants, and insects. Besides working, regular exercise is essential to keep the astronauts healthy in microgravity.

Astronauts sometimes go outside the shuttle to work. They are protected by a space suit from the radiation of the Sun. Meanwhile, the space suit provides necessary oxygen supply and keeps the astronauts from feeling the extreme heat or cold outside the shuttle.

When the mission is over, the crew members get ready to return to Earth. The shuttle does not use its engines for a landing. It glides through the atmosphere. When the shuttle touches the land, a drag parachute opens to steady the aircraft, get the speed right, and help the brakes on the landing-gear wheels to bring it to a complete stop.

49. The passage is mainly about
    (A) how astronauts fly the space shuttle.
    (B) how a space mission is completed.
    (C) how a space shuttle is constructed.
    (D) how far astronauts travel in space.

50. The underlined word **conduct** in the first paragraph is closest in meaning to

    (A) behave.   (B) instruct.   (C) serve as.   (D) carry out.

51. According to the passage, which of the following is NOT true?

    (A) The astronauts need a space suit to work outside the shuttle.

    (B) The astronauts keep themselves warm in a space suit.

    (C) The astronauts need a space suit to survive in space.

    (D) The astronauts can hardly breathe in a space suit.

52. A parachute needs to be opened because it can

    (A) slow down the shuttle.

    (B) stop the shuttle from falling.

    (C) make the shuttle get closer to Earth.

    (D) help the shuttle glide through the atmosphere.

53-56 為題組

    Joy Hirsch, a neuroscientist in New York, has recently found evidence that children and adults don't use the same parts of the brain when learning a second language. He used an instrument called an MRI (magnetic resonance imaging) to study the brains of two groups of bilingual people. One group consisted of those who had learned a second language as children. The other consisted of people who learned their second language later in life. People from both groups were placed inside the MRI scanner. This allowed Hirsch to see which parts of the brain were getting more blood and were more active. He asked people from both groups to think about what they had done the day before, first in one language and then the other. They couldn't speak out loud, because any movement would disrupt the scanning.

    Hirsch looked specifically at two language centers in the brain—Broca's area, believed to control speech production, and Wernicke's area, thought to process meaning. He found that both groups of people used the same part of Wernicke's area no matter what language they were speaking. But how they used Broca's area was different.

People who learned a second language as children used the same region in Broca's area for both languages. People who learned a second language later in life used a special part of Broca's area for their second language—near the one activated for their native tongue.

How does Hirsch explain this difference? He believes that, when language is first being programmed in young children, their brains may mix all languages into the same area. But once that programming is complete, a different part of the brain must take over a new language. Another possibility is simply that we may acquire languages differently as children than we do as adults. Hirsch thinks that mothers teach a baby to speak by using different methods such as touch, sound, and sight. And that's very different from sitting in a high school class.

53. The purpose of this passage is to
   (A) explain how people become bilingual.
   (B) explain how to be a better second language learner.
   (C) describe research into the brains of bilingual people.
   (D) describe the best ways to acquire languages at different ages.

54. In the study, the subjects were placed inside the MRI scanner to
   (A) observe the activities of the brains when they used languages.
   (B) observe the movements of the brains when they spoke out loud.
   (C) describe the functions of the areas of the brains when they slept.
   (D) describe the best areas of the brains for learning second languages.

55. The language center in the brain that is believed to control speech production is called
   (A) MRI.   (B) native tongue.
   (C) Wernicke's area.   (D) Broca's area.

56. According to the passage, which of the following is TRUE for bilingual people?

(A) Those who spoke different languages used the same part of Wernicke's area.

(B) Those who spoke different languages always used the same part of Broca's area.

(C) Those who spoke the same language never used Broca's area and Wernicke's area.

(D) Those who spoke different languages always used different parts of Wernicke's area.

第貳部份：非選擇題（佔 28 分）

一、翻譯題（佔 8 分）

說明： 1. 請將以下兩個中文句子譯成正確、通順、達意的英文，並將答案寫在「答案卷」上。

2. 請依序作答，並標明題號。每題 4 分，共 8 分。

1. 一般人都知道閱讀對孩子有益。

2. 老師應該多鼓勵學生到圖書館借書。

二、英文作文（佔 20 分）

說明： 1. 依提示在「答案卷」上寫一篇英文作文。

2. 文長 100 個單詞（words）左右。

提示： 根據下列連環圖畫的內容，將圖中女子、小狗與大猩猩（gorilla）之間所發生的事件作一合理的敘述。

95年度學科能力測驗英文科試題詳解

第壹部分：單選題

一、詞彙：

1. (**D**) If we can <u>afford</u> to, we will take a vacation abroad in the summer.
   如果<u>負擔得起</u>，我們將在夏天時出國度假。
   (A) pay〔pe〕v. 支付
   (B) move〔muv〕v. 移動；搬家
   (C) expose〔ɪk'spoz〕v. 暴露
   (D) *afford*〔ə'fɔrd〕v. 負擔得起
   take a vacation 度假　　abroad〔ə'brɔd〕adv. 到國外

2. (**B**) A <u>common</u> mistake found in parenthood is that parents often set unrealistic goals for their children.
   在親子關係中，一個<u>常見的</u>錯誤是，父母常會為他們的孩子設定不切實際的目標。
   (A) terrific〔tə'rɪfɪk〕adj. 很棒的
   (B) *common*〔'kɑmən〕adj. 常見的
   (C) straight〔stret〕adj. 直的
   (D) favorable〔'fevərəbl̩〕adj. 有利的
   parenthood〔'pɛrənt,hud〕n. 親子關係；父母的身分
   set〔sɛt〕v. 設定　　unrealistic〔,ʌnrɪə'lɪstɪk〕adj. 不切實際的
   goal〔gol〕n. 目標

3. (**A**) Some words, such as "sandwich" and "hamburger," were <u>originally</u> the names of people or even towns.
   有些字，像是「三明治」和「漢堡」，<u>本來</u>是人名，或甚至是鎮名。
   (A) *originally*〔ə'rɪdʒən̩lɪ〕adv. 本來
   (B) ideally〔aɪ'diəlɪ〕adv. 理想地
   (C) relatively〔'rɛlətɪvlɪ〕adv. 相對地
   (D) sincerely〔sɪn'sɪrlɪ〕adv. 衷心地
   such as 像是　　sandwich〔'sændwɪtʃ〕n. 三明治
   hamburger〔'hæmbɝgɚ〕n. 漢堡　　town〔taun〕n. 城鎮

4. (**B**) Have you ever <u>wondered</u> how the ancient Egyptians created such marvelous feats of engineering as the pyramids?

你是否曾<u>想知道</u>，古埃及人是如何創造像金字塔這樣，如此令人驚嘆的工程壯舉？

(A) conclude〔kən'klud〕v. 下結論
(B) ***wonder***〔'wʌndɚ〕v. 想知道
(C) admit〔əd'mɪt〕v. 承認
(D) persuade〔pɚ'swed〕v. 說服

ancient〔'enʃənt〕*adj.* 古代的　　　Egyptian〔ɪ'dʒɪpʃən〕*n.* 埃及人
creat〔krɪ'et〕v. 創造　　　marvelous〔'mɑrvḷəs〕*adj.* 令人驚嘆的
feat〔fit〕*n.* 功績；豐功偉業　　　engineering〔‚ɛndʒə'nɪrɪŋ〕*n.* 工程
pyramid〔'pɪrəmɪd〕*n.* 金字塔

5. (**C**) Mr. Johnson was disappointed at his students for having a passive learning <u>attitude</u>.

學生消極的學習<u>態度</u>令強森先生感到失望。

(A) result〔rɪ'zʌlt〕*n.* 結果
(B) progress〔'prɑgrɛs〕*n.* 進步
(C) ***attitude***〔'ætə‚tjud〕*n.* 態度
(D) energy〔'ɛnɚdʒɪ〕*n.* 活力

disappointed〔‚dɪsə'pɔɪntɪd〕*adj.* 失望的
passive〔'pæsɪv〕*adj.* 消極的；被動的

6. (**B**) Anne dreaded giving a speech before three hundred people; even thinking about it made her <u>anxious</u>.

安對於要面對三百個人發表演說感到害怕，光是想到就讓她<u>焦慮不安</u>。

(A) passionate〔'pæʃənɪt〕*adj.* 熱情的
(B) ***anxious***〔'æŋkʃəs〕*adj.* 焦慮的；不安的
(C) ambitious〔æm'bɪʃəs〕*adj.* 有野心的
(D) optimistic〔‚ɑptə'mɪstɪk〕*adj.* 樂觀的

dread〔drɛd〕v. 害怕　　　speech〔spitʃ〕*n.* 演說
give a speech 發表演說

7. (**A**) I had to <u>decline</u> Jack's invitation to the party because it conflicted with an important business meeting.

我必須拒絕傑克的派對邀請，因為它和一個重要的業務會議衝突了。

(A) *decline* (dɪ'klaɪn) v. 拒絕
(B) depart (dɪ'part) v. 離開
(C) devote (dɪ'vot) v. 奉獻
(D) deserve (dɪ'zɜv) v. 應得

invitation (ˌɪnvə'teʃən) n. 邀請　　conflict (kən'flɪkt) v. 衝突

8. (**C**) Selling fried chicken at the night market doesn't seem to be a decent business, but it is actually quite <u>profitable</u>.

在夜市賣炸雞似乎不是很好的行業，但實際上是相當有利潤的。

(A) plentiful ('plɛntɪfəl) adj. 豐富的
(B) precious ('prɛʃəs) adj. 珍貴的
(C) *profitable* ('prafɪtəbl̩) adj. 有利的
(D) productive (prə'dʌktɪv) adj. 有生產力的

fried chicken 炸雞　　*night market* 夜市
seem (sim) v. 似乎　　decent ('disn̩t) adj. 不錯的
business ('bɪznɪs) n. 行業；生意　　actually ('æktʃuəlɪ) adv. 實際上
quite (kwaɪt) adv. 相當

9. (**D**) The passengers <u>narrowly</u> escaped death when a bomb exploded in the subway station, killing sixty people.

當炸彈在地鐵站裡爆炸，造成六十人死亡時，這些乘客勉強死裡逃生。

(A) traditionally (trə'dɪʃənl̩ɪ) adv. 傳統上
(B) valuably ('væljuəblɪ) adv. 昂貴地
(C) loosely ('luslɪ) adv. 寬鬆地
(D) *narrowly* ('nærolɪ) adv. 勉強地

passenger ('pæsn̩dʒə) n. 乘客
escape (ə'skep) v. 逃脫；逃過　　bomb (bam) n. 炸彈
explode (ɪk'splod) v. 爆炸　　subway ('sʌbˌwe) n. 地下鐵
subway station 地鐵站

10. (**C**) Jerry didn't <u>recognize</u> his primary school classmate Mary until he listened to her self-introduction.
傑瑞直到聽了瑪麗的自我介紹，才<u>認出</u>她是他的小學同學。

(A) acquaint〔ə'kwent〕v. 使認識
(B) acquire〔ə'kwaɪr〕v. 獲得
(C) *recognize*〔'rɛkəg,naɪz〕v. 認出
(D) realize〔'rɪə,laɪz〕v. 了解；知道

primary〔'praɪ,mɛrɪ〕adj. 初級的　　*primary school* 小學
not…until～ 直到～才…
self-introduction〔,sɛlf,ɪntrə'dʌkʃən〕n. 自我介紹

11. (**A**) With the completion of several public <u>transportation</u> projects, such as the MRT, commuting to work has become easier for people living in the suburbs. 隨著幾個大眾運輸計劃的完成，例如大眾捷運系統，對住在郊區的人而言，通勤上班更便利了。

(A) *transportation*〔,trænspə'teʃən〕n. 運輸
(B) traffic〔'træfɪk〕n. 交通　　(C) travel〔'trævḷ〕v. 旅行
(D) transfer〔træns'fɝ〕v. 轉移；轉車

with〔wɪð〕prep. 隨著　　completion〔kəm'pliʃən〕n. 完成
public〔'pʌblɪk〕adj. 大眾的　　project〔'prɑdʒɛkt〕n. 計劃
MRT 大眾捷運系統 (= *Mass Rapid Transit*)
commute〔kə'mjut〕v. 通勤　　suburbs〔'sʌbɝbz〕n. pl. 郊區

12. (**C**) With a good <u>command</u> of both Chinese and English, Miss Lin was assigned the task of oral interpretation for the visiting American delegation.
林小姐<u>精通</u>中英文，所以被指派擔任美國訪問團的口譯員。

(A) writing〔'raɪtɪŋ〕n. 寫
(B) program〔'progræm〕n. 計劃；節目
(C) *command*〔kə'mænd〕n. (對語言) 運用自如的能力
　　good command of 精通 (語言)
(D) impression〔ɪm'prɛʃən〕n. 印象

assign〔ə'saɪn〕v. 指派　　task〔tæsk〕n. 工作
oral〔'orəl〕adj. 口頭的　　interpretation〔ɪn,tɝprɪ'teʃən〕n. 口譯
visiting〔'vɪzɪtɪŋ〕adj. 訪問的　　delegation〔,dɛlə'geʃən〕n. 代表團

13. (**A**)　I am studying so hard for the forthcoming entrance exam that I do not have the <u>luxury</u> of a free weekend to rest.
　　　　爲了即將到來的入學考試，我很努力用功，所以我不<u>奢望</u>有空閒的週末可以休息。

　　　　(A) *luxury* (ˈlʌkʃərɪ) *n.* 奢望；奢侈的事
　　　　(B) license (ˈlaɪsn̩s) *n.* 許可證
　　　　(C) limitation (ˌlɪməˈteʃən) *n.* 限制
　　　　(D) strength (strɛŋθ) *n.* 力量

　　　　forthcoming (ˈforθˈkʌmɪŋ) *adj.* 即將到來的
　　　　entrance (ˈɛntrəns) *n.* 入學
　　　　free (fri) *adj.* 空閒的　　　rest (rɛst) *v.* 休息

14. (**C**)　Kim was completely <u>worn out</u> after jogging in the hot sun all afternoon; she had little energy left.
　　　　金姆在大太陽底下慢跑一整個下午後，完全<u>筋疲力竭</u>了，幾乎沒剩多少力氣。

　　　　(A) kick out　開除；解雇
　　　　(B) hand out　分發；分配
　　　　(C) *worn out*　筋疲力竭的
　　　　(D) put out　熄滅

　　　　completely (kəmˈplitlɪ) *adv.* 完全地
　　　　jog (dʒɑg) *v.* 慢跑　　　little (ˈlɪtl̩) *adj.* 幾乎沒有的
　　　　energy (ˈɛnədʒɪ) *n.* 氣力；活力　　　leave (liv) *v.* 剩下

15. (**A**)　When Jason failed to pay his bill, the network company <u>cut off</u> his Internet connection.
　　　　當傑森沒有繳帳單時，網路公司就<u>切斷</u>了他的網際網路連結。

　　　　(A) *cut off*　切斷　　　　　　　(B) cut back　減少
　　　　(C) cut short　縮短　　　　　　(D) cut down　削減；減少

　　　　fail to V. 未能~　　　bill (bɪl) *n.* 帳單
　　　　network (ˈnɛtˌwɜk) *n.* 網路
　　　　Internet (ˈɪntəˌnɛt) *n.* 網際網路
　　　　connection (kəˈnɛkʃən) *n.* 連結

二、綜合測驗：

Dear Son,

I am very happy to hear that you are doing well in school. However, I am very concerned with the way you <u>manage</u> money. I understand that
16
college students like to <u>indulge in</u> parties, movies, and lots of activities,
17
but you also have to learn how to do without certain things. After all, you must live within a limited budget.

親愛的兒子：

聽到你在學校的功課很好，我很高興。不過，我非常關心你用錢的方式。我知道大學生都喜歡沉迷於派對、電影，以及許多活動，但你也必須學習如何做取捨。畢竟，你必須用有限的預算過活。

> ***do well*** 表現好；考得好　　however（haʊˈɛvə）*adv.* 然而
> concerned（kənˈsɝnd）*adj.* 關心的；擔心的　　way（we）*n.* 方式
> ***lots of*** 很多　　activity（ækˈtɪvətɪ）*n.* 活動
> ***do without*** 省去；不用　　certain（ˈsɝtn）*adj.* 某些
> ***after all*** 畢竟　　within（wɪðˈɪn）*prep.* 在…之內
> limited（ˈlɪmɪtɪd）*adj.* 有限的　　budget（ˈbʌdʒɪt）*n.* 預算

16. (**A**) 依句意，選 (A) *manage*（ˈmænɪdʒ）*v.* 管理。而 (B) restrict（rɪˈstrɪkt）*v.* 限制，(C) charge（tʃɑrdʒ）*v.* 收費，(D) deposit（dɪˈpɑzɪt）*v.* 存（款），均不合句意。

17. (**A**) 依句意，選 (A) *indulge in*「沉迷於」。而 (B) dwell in「居住在」，(C) attend to「注意聽；專心於；照料」，(D) apply to「適用於」，均不合句意。

<u>Regarding</u> the extra money you want for this month, I am sorry that I
18
have decided not to send it to you because I think it is time for you to learn how to live without my help. If I give you a hand every time you have problems with money now, what will you do when you no longer have me to support you? Besides, I remember telling you I used to have

two part-time jobs when I was in college just to <u>make ends meet</u>. So, if
19
you need money now, you should try either finding a job or cutting down
on your <u>expenses</u>.
20

關於你這個月想多要的錢，很抱歉，我已經決定不要寄給你，因為我認為，是該讓你學會，如何不靠我的幫助來過活的時候了。如果現在你每次有金錢方面的問題時，我都幫助你，那麼當我不再資助你時，你該怎麼辦？而且，我記得我告訴過你，當我唸大學時，有兩份兼差的工作，才能使收支平衡。所以，如果你現在需要錢，你就應該試著找份工作，或是減少開支。

extra〔ˈɛkstrə〕*adj.* 額外的　　*give sb.* *a hand* 幫忙某人
no longer 不再　　support〔səˈport〕*v.* 支持；資助
besides〔bɪˈsaɪdz〕*adv.* 此外　　*used to V.* 以前～
part-time〔ˈpɑrtˈtaɪm〕*adj.* 兼差的
either A *or* B　A 或 B；不是 A 就是 B　　*cut down on* 減少

18. (**D**) 空格應填一介系詞，且依句意，選 (D) *regarding*〔rɪˈgɑrdɪŋ〕*prep.*
關於 (= *concerning* = *respecting* = *about*)。而 (A)(B)(C) 的 regard
〔rɪˈgɑrd〕*v.* 認為，則不合句意。

19. (**D**) 依句意，選 (D) *make ends meet*「使收支平衡；量入為出」(= *make both ends meet*)。而 (A) catch up「趕上」，(B) get *one's* way「隨心所欲；為所欲為」(= *get one's own way*)，(C) keep in touch「保持聯絡」，均不合句意。

20. (**B**) 依句意，你應該試著找份工作，或是減少「開支」，選 (B) *expenses*
〔ɪkˈspɛnsɪz〕*n. pl.* 開支；花費。而 (A) spirit〔ˈspɪrɪt〕*n.* 精神，(C)
savings〔ˈsevɪŋz〕*n.* 儲金；存款，(D) estimate〔ˈɛstəmɪt〕*n.* 估計，均不合句意。

I understand it is not easy to live on your own. But learning to budget
your money is the first lesson you must learn to be independent. Good
luck, son. And remember: never spend more than you earn.

Love,
Mom

我知道自力更生並不容易。但是學習把錢編列預算，是你想獨立時，必須學習的第一課。兒子，祝你好運。而且要記得：絕對不要花超過你所賺的。

愛你的，

媽媽

> *on one's own* 獨立地；靠自己的力量
> budget〔'bʌdʒɪt〕v. 編…的預算
> independent〔͵ɪndɪ'pɛndənt〕adj. 獨立的　　earn〔ɝn〕v. 賺

There are two kinds of heroes: heroes who shine in the face of great danger, who perform an <u>amazing</u> act in a difficult situation, and heroes
21

who live an ordinary life like us, who do their work <u>unnoticed</u> by many of
22

us, but who <u>make</u> a difference in the lives of others.
23

英雄有兩種：一種是面對危險能大放異彩，而且在困難的情況中也能表現出色的英雄；另一種英雄和我們一樣過著平凡的生活，我們當中有許多人都不會注意到他們的工作，但他們會對別人的生活產生影響。

> hero〔'hɪro〕n. 英雄　　shine〔ʃaɪn〕v. 發光；出色；大放異彩
> *in the face of*~　面對~　　perform〔pɚ'fɔrm〕v. 執行；做
> act〔ækt〕n. 行為；舉動　　situation〔͵sɪtʃu'eʃən〕n. 情況
> *live a~life* 過著~的生活　　ordinary〔'ɔrdn͵ɛrɪ〕adj. 普通的

21. (**C**) 依句意，選 (C) *amazing*〔ə'mezɪŋ〕adj. 驚人的。而 (A) annoying
〔ə'nɔɪɪŋ〕adj. 煩人的；令人討厭的，(B) interfering〔͵ɪntɚ'fɪrɪŋ〕adj.
干涉的；妨礙的，(D) inviting〔ɪn'vaɪtɪŋ〕adj. 誘人的，均不合句意。

22. (**D**) 依句意，他們做的工作是「不被人所注意的」，為否定且被動，故
應選 (D) *unnoticed*〔ʌn'notɪst〕adj. 不被注意的。而 (A) noticing
為主動進行式，(B) noticeable〔'notɪsəbl̩〕adj. 值得注意的；明顯的，
(C) noticed 為肯定被動，均不合。

23. (**A**) *make a difference* 產生差別；有影響

Heroes are selfless people who perform extraordinary acts. The mark of heroes is not necessarily the result of their action, but <u>what</u> they are
24
willing to do for others and for their chosen cause. <u>Even if</u> they fail, their
25
determination lives on for others to follow. The glory lies not in the achievement but in the sacrifice.

英雄是無私的、表現出非凡行為的人。英雄的標準，未必是根據他們行動的結果，而是他們為了別人，以及為了自己所選擇的目標，願意去做的事情。即使他們失敗了，他們的決心會持續下去，為他人所仿效。這份榮耀不在於他們的成就，而在於他們的犧牲。

> selfless ('sɛlflɪs) adj. 無私的 (= *unselfish*)
> extraordinary (ɪk'strɔrdn̩‚ɛrɪ) adj. 非凡的
> mark (mɑrk) n. 標記；標準
> necessarily ('nɛsə‚sɛrəlɪ) adv. 必然地
> **not necessarily** 未必；不一定   **not** A **but** B 不是 A 而是 B
> result (rɪ'zʌlt) n. 結果   action ('ækʃən) n. 行動
> willing ('wɪlɪŋ) adj. 願意的   chosen ('tʃozn̩) adj. 選擇的
> cause (kɔz) n. 原因；目標   determination (dɪ‚tɜmə'neʃən) n. 決心
> **live on** 持續；繼續   follow ('fɑlo) v. 遵循；仿效
> glory ('glorɪ) n. 榮耀   **lie in** 在於
> achievement (ə'tʃivmənt) n. 成就   sacrifice ('sækrə‚faɪs) n. 犧牲

24. (**A**) 空格所指的是他們願意做「的事情」，應該用 the thing(s) which，結合成複合關代，則成 *what*，故選 (A)。

25. (**B**) 依句意，「即使」他們失敗了，選 (B) *Even if*。而 (A) not until「直到」，(C) as if「好像；彷彿」，(D) no sooner~than…「一~就…」，均不合句意。

Fans of professional baseball and football argue continually over which is America's favorite sport. Though the figures on attendance for each vary with every new season, certain <u>arguments</u> remain the same. To
26

begin with, football is a quicker, more physical sport, and football fans enjoy the emotional involvement they feel while watching. Baseball, on the other hand, seems more mental, like chess, and <u>attracts</u> those fans that
27
prefer a quieter, more complicated game.

美國的職業棒球迷和職業美式足球迷一直在爭論，何者才是美國最受歡迎的運動。雖然這兩種運動的觀眾出席人數，會隨著每一個新球季而不同，但某些論點仍然是相同的。首先，美式足球是速度較快、較需要體力的運動，而足球迷們喜歡在觀賞球賽時，所感受到的情感投入。而另一方面，棒球似乎比較屬於心理戰，就像下棋一樣，因此所吸引的球迷們，偏愛較安靜、較複雜的比賽。

fan (fæn) n. (球) 迷
professional (prə'fɛʃn̩l) adj. 職業的
football ('fut,bɔl) n. 美式足球　　argue ('ɑrgju) v. 爭論
continually (kən'tɪnjuəlɪ) adv. 持續地　　figure ('fɪgɚ) n. 數字
attendance (ə'tɛndəns) n. 出席　　vary ('vɛrɪ) v. 改變；不同
season ('sizn̩) n. 季節；球季　　certain ('sɝtn̩) adj. 某些
remain (rɪ'men) v. 仍然；依然　　*to begin with* 首先
physical ('fɪzɪkl̩) adj. 身體的
emotional (ɪ'moʃn̩l) adj. 情感的
involvement (ɪn'vɑlvmənt) n. 投入
on the other hand 另一方面　　mental ('mɛntl̩) adj. 心理的
chess (tʃɛs) n. 西洋棋　　prefer (prɪ'fɝ) v. 比較喜歡
complicated ('kɑmplə,ketɪd) adj. 複雜的

26. (**B**) 依句意，某些「論點」仍然是相同的，選 (B) *argument* ('ɑrgjəmənt)
　　　 n. 論點。而 (A) agreement (ə'grimənt) n. 同意；意見一致，(C)
　　　 accomplishment (ə'kɑmplɪʃmənt) n. 成就，(D) arrangement
　　　 (ə'rendʒmənt) n. 安排，均不合句意。

27. (**D**) 這句話的主詞是 Baseball，第一個動詞為 seems，而 and 之後要接
　　　 第二個動詞，同樣應為第三人稱單數現在式，故選 (D) *attracts*。
　　　 attract (ə'trækt) v. 吸引

<u>In addition</u>, professional football teams usually play no more than fourteen
　　28
games a year. Baseball teams, however, play <u>almost</u> every day for six
　　　　　　　　　　　　　　　　　　　　29
months. Finally, football fans seem to love the half-time activities, the
marching bands, and the pretty cheerleaders. <u>On the contrary</u>, baseball
　　　　　　　　　　　　　　　　　　　　　　　30
fans are more content to concentrate on the game's finer details and spend
the breaks between innings filling out their own private scorecards.

此外，職業美式足球隊一年的比賽通常只有十四場。然而，職業棒球隊六個月
裡面，幾乎天天有比賽。最後，足球迷似乎很喜歡中場休息的活動，像樂隊的
行進和美麗的啦啦隊長等。相反地，棒球迷就比較滿足於專心在比賽的細節上，
而且他們在局與局之間的休息時間時，都在填寫自己個人的計分卡。

　　no more than 不過；只；僅（ = *only ; simply ; merely* ）
　　half-time（'hæf,taɪm ）*n.* 上下半場之間的休息時間；中場休息
　　march（ mɑrtʃ ）*v.* 行軍；行進　　band（ bænd ）*n.* 樂隊
　　pretty（'prɪtɪ ）*adj.* 漂亮的　　cheerleader（'tʃɪr,lidɚ ）*n.* 啦啦隊隊長
　　content（ kən'tɛnt ）*adj.* 滿足的
　　concentrate（'kɑnsn̩,tret ）*v.* 專心＜ *on* ＞
　　fine（ faɪn ）*adj.* 細微的　　detail（'ditel ）*n.* 細節
　　break（ brek ）*n.* 休息　　inning（'ɪnɪŋ ）*n.*（ 棒球的 ）局
　　fill out 填寫　　private（'praɪvɪt ）*adj.* 私人的；個人的
　　scorecard（'skor,kɑrd ）*n.*（ 高爾夫等的 ）計分卡；選手一覽表（ 用以
　　　記錄選手的表現 ）

28. (**A**) 根據句意，接下來是第二組的比較，故轉承語選 (A) *In addition*
　　　「此外」。故 (B) as a result「因此」，(C) contrast（'kɑntræst ）*n.*
　　　對比，in contrast「對比之下」，(D) extent（ ɪk'stɛnt ）*n.* 程度，
　　　to some extent「到某種程度；有幾分」，句意均不合。

29. (**B**) 依句意，職棒「幾乎」天天有比賽，選 (B) *almost*。而(A) hardly
　　　「幾乎不」，(C) somehow（'sʌm,haʊ ）*adv.* 以某種方法；不知怎麼地，
　　　(D) rarely（'rɛrlɪ ）*adv.* 很少地，均不合句意。

30. (C) 空格置於足球迷和棒球迷的比較之間，應有對比之意，故選 (C) *On the contrary*「相反地」。而 (A) even so「即使如此」，(B) for that reason「為了那個理由」，(D) token (ˈtokən) *n.* 表徵，by the same token「此外；同樣地」，句意均不合。

三、文意選填：

Good health is not something you are able to buy, nor can you get it back with a quick ³¹(B) visit to a doctor. Keeping yourself healthy has to be your own ³²(F) responsibility. If you mistreat your body by keeping bad habits, ³³(C) neglecting symptoms of illness, and ignoring common health rules, even the best medicine can be of little use.

良好的健康不是你可以買得到的東西，也不是你趕快去看醫生，就可以恢復的。保持身體健康，必須是你自己的責任。如果你一直用壞習慣去虐待你的身體，忽略疾病的症狀，輕忽一般的健康守則，就算給你最好的藥，都沒有什麼用。

health (hɛlθ) *n.* 健康　　*be able to V.* 能夠～
get ~ back 恢復～　　quick (kwɪk) *adj.* 快速的
visit (ˈvɪzɪt) *n.* 拜訪；就診　　keep (kip) *v.* 保持；維持
healthy (ˈhɛlθɪ) *adj.* 健康的　　own (on) *adj.* (某人) 自己的
responsibility (rɪ,spɑnsəˈbɪlətɪ) *n.* 責任
mistreat (mɪsˈtrit) *v.* 虐待　　habit (ˈhæbɪt) *n.* 習慣
neglect (nɪˈglɛkt) *v.* 忽視　　symptom (ˈsɪmptəm) *n.* 症狀
illness (ˈɪlnɪs) *n.* 疾病　　ignore (ɪgˈnor) *v.* 忽視
common (ˈkɑmən) *adj.* 一般的　　rule (rul) *n.* 規則
medicine (ˈmɛdəsn̩) *n.* 藥　　*be of little use* 沒什麼用

Nowadays health specialists ³⁴(I) promote the idea of wellness for everybody. Wellness means ³⁵(J) achieving the best possible health within the limits of your body. One person may need fewer calories than another. Some people might prefer a lot of ³⁶(E) easier exercise to more challenging exercise. While one person enjoys playing seventy-two holes of golf a week, another would rather play three sweaty, competitive games of tennis.

現在健康專家都提倡全民健康的概念。良好的健康的意思是，在你的身體限制之下，達到可能的最佳健康狀態。有人需要的熱量，可能少於其他人。有些人比較喜歡簡單一點的運動，勝於比較具有挑戰性的運動。有人喜歡一週打七十二洞（四場）的高爾夫球，而有人則寧願打三場讓人汗流浹背，且競爭激烈的網球。

nowadays (ˈnaʊəˌdez) adv. 現在　　specialist (ˈspɛʃəlɪst) n. 專家

promote (prəˈmot) v. 提倡　　wellness (ˈwɛlnɪs) n. 良好的健康

achieve (əˈtʃiv) v. 達到　　possible (ˈpɑsəbḷ) adj. 可能做到的

within (wɪðˈɪn) prep. 在～之內　　limit (ˈlɪmɪt) n. 限制

calory (ˈkælərɪ) n. 卡路里 (= *calorie*) (熱量的單位)

prefer (prɪˈfɝ) v. 較喜歡　***prefer*** A ***to*** B　喜歡 A 勝於 B

exercise (ˈɛksəˌsaɪz) n. 運動

challenging (ˈtʃælɪndʒɪŋ) adj. 有挑戰性的

hole (hol) n. 洞　　golf (gɔlf) n. 高爾夫球

would rather V. 寧願～

sweaty (ˈswɛtɪ) adj. 使人流汗的

competitive (kəmˈpɛtətɪv) adj. 競爭的

tennis (ˈtɛnɪs) n. 網球

Understanding the needs of your body is the [37](H) key.　Everyone runs the risk of accidents, and no one can be sure of avoiding [38](G) chronic disease.　Nevertheless, poor diet, stress, a bad working environment, and carelessness can [39](A) ruin good health.　By changing your habits or the conditions surrounding you, you can [40](D) lower the risk or reduce the damage of disease.

了解你身體的需求是關鍵。每個人都冒著發生意外的危險，但沒有人有把握避免慢性疾病。然而，差勁的飲食、壓力、不良的工作環境，以及粗心大意，都會破壞良好健康。藉由改變你的習慣或是周遭的環境，就可以降低生病的風險，或減少疾病帶來的損害。

understand (ˌʌndəˈstænd) v. 了解　　need (nid) n. 需要

key (ki) n. 關鍵　　run (rʌn) v. 冒 (危險)

risk (rɪsk) n. 危險；風險　***run the risk of*** 冒～的危險

accident〔'æksədənt〕n. 意外　　**be sure of** 確實；有把握

avoid〔ə'vɔɪd〕v. 避免　　chronic〔'krɑnɪk〕adj. 慢性的

disease〔dɪ'ziz〕n. 疾病　　nevertheless〔‚nɛvəðə'lɛs〕adv. 然而

poor〔pʊr〕adj. 差勁的　　diet〔'daɪət〕n. 飲食

stress〔strɛs〕n. 壓力　　environment〔ɪn'vaɪrənmənt〕n. 環境

carelessness〔'kɛrlɪsnɪs〕n. 粗心　　ruin〔'rʊɪn〕v. 破壞

change〔tʃendʒ〕v. 改變　　condition〔kən'dɪʃən〕n. 情況

surround〔sə'raʊnd〕v. 圍繞　　lower〔'loə〕v. 降低

reduce〔rɪ'djus〕v. 減少　　damage〔'dæmɪdʒ〕n. 損害

四、閱讀測驗：

41-44 為題組

　　Who is more stressed out—the Asian teenager or the American teenager? Surprise. The American teen wins this contest. According to a recent study, almost three-quarters of American high school juniors said they felt stress at least once a week, some almost daily. Fewer than half of Japanese and Taiwanese eleventh graders reported feeling stress that often.

　　誰的壓力比較大——亞洲的青少年還是美國的青少年？真令人驚訝。美國的青少年在這項比賽中獲勝了。根據最近的一項研究指出，有將近四分之三的美國高二學生表示，他們每週至少會有一次感到壓力大，而有些人則幾乎天天都覺得壓力大。但是日本和台灣的高二學生，那麼常感到壓力大的，卻不到二分之一。

be stressed out 緊張；感到有壓力　　teenager〔'tin‚edʒə〕n. 青少年

surprise〔sə'praɪz〕interj. 真令人驚訝！　　teen〔tin〕n. 青少年

contest〔'kɑntɛst〕n. 比賽　　**according to** 根據

recent〔'risn̩t〕adj. 最近的　　**three-quarters** 四分之三的

junior〔'dʒunjə〕n. 高二學生　　stress〔strɛs〕n. 壓力；緊張

at least 至少　　**once a week** 每週一次

half〔hæf〕n. 一半；二分之一　　Japanese〔‚dʒæpə'niz〕adj. 日本的

Taiwanese〔‚taɪwɑ'niz〕adj. 台灣的　　grader〔'gredə〕n. ⋯⋯年級學生

an eleventh grader 高二學生【美國的學制與亞洲國家不同，他們的
　　十一年級，大約等於台灣的高二】

report〔rɪ'port〕v. 報告；說

The phenomenon of stress is the constant interaction between mind and body. And the influence of one upon the other can be either positive or negative. What can the mind do to the body? Studies have proved that watching funny movies can reduce pain and promote healing. Conversely, worry can give a person an ulcer, high blood pressure, or even a heart attack.

壓力的現象，是身心不斷交互作用下的產物。而一方對另一方的影響，可能是正面或負面的。心能對身體做什麼呢？研究證明，看有趣的電影能夠減輕痛苦，並促進身體康復。相反地，憂慮可能會使人有潰瘍、高血壓，或甚至是心臟病發作。

phenomenon (fə'namə,nan) *n.* 現象
constant ('kanstənt) *adj.* 持續不斷的
interaction (,ıntə'ækʃən) *n.* 交互作用　**mind** (maınd) *n.* 心；精神
influence ('ınfluəns) *n.* 影響　***either* A *or* B** 不是 A 就是 B
positive ('pazətıv) *adj.* 正面的　**negative** ('nɛgətıv) *adj.* 負面的
prove (pruv) *v.* 證明　**funny** ('fʌnı) *adj.* 有趣的
reduce (rı'djus) *v.* 減輕；減少　**pain** (pen) *n.* 痛苦
promote (prə'mot) *v.* 促進　**healing** ('hilıŋ) *n.* 治療；康復
conversely (kən'vɜslı) *adv.* 相反地　**worry** ('wɜı) *n.* 憂慮
ulcer ('ʌlsə) *n.* 潰瘍　***high blood pressure*** 高血壓
heart attack 心臟病發作

The mind and body work together to produce stress, which is a bodily response to a stimulus, a response that disturbs the body's normal physiological balance. However, stress is not always bad. For example, a stress reaction can sometimes save a person's life by releasing hormones that enable a person to react quickly and with greater energy in a dangerous situation.

在身心的共同作用下產生了壓力，壓力是身體對刺激的反應，而這種反應會干擾身體的正常生理平衡。但是，壓力不一定是壞事。舉例來說，壓力的反應有時可以救人一命，這種反應會使人體釋放出荷爾蒙，讓人在危險的狀態下，可以快速反應，而且擁有較大的力氣。

produce (prə'djus) v. 產生　　bodily ('badılı) adj. 身體的
response (rı'spans) n. 反應　　stimulus ('stımjələs) n. 刺激
disturb (dı'stɝb) v. 干擾　　normal ('norml) adj. 正常的
physiological (,fızıə'ladʒıkl) adj. 生理上的
balance ('bæləns) n. 平衡　　*not always* 不一定
reaction (rı'ækʃən) n. 反應　　release (rı'lis) v. 釋放
hormone ('hormon) n. 荷爾蒙　　enable (ın'ebl) v. 使能夠
react (rı'ækt) v. 反應　　energy ('ɛnədʒı) n. 力量
situation (,sıtʃu'eʃən) n. 狀態

In everyday situations, too, stress can provide that extra push needed to do something difficult. But too much stress often injures both the mind and the body. How can stress be kept under control? *Learn to Lighten Up and Live Longer*, the best seller of the month, has several good suggestions. So, grab a copy and start learning how you can reduce stress in your life.

在日常的工作中也是如此，壓力可以提供從事困難工作所需的額外精力。但是壓力太大常會使身心受創。怎樣才能把壓力控制好呢？本月暢銷書「學會放輕鬆才能活得久」有幾個好建議。所以，趕快去找一本來看，然後開始學習如何減輕你的生活壓力。

situation (,sıtʃu'eʃən) n. 工作　　provide (prə'vaıd) v. 提供
extra ('ɛkstrə) adj. 額外的　　push (puʃ) n. 精力；進取的精神
injure ('ındʒɚ) v. 使受傷　　lighten ('laıtṇ) v. (心情、精神) 變輕鬆
lighten up 放輕鬆　　*best seller* 暢銷書
several ('sɛvərəl) adj. 幾個的　　suggestion (sə'dʒɛstʃən) n. 建議
grab (græb) v. 抓取；匆忙地做　　copy ('kapı) n. 本；冊

41. (**D**) 作者寫這篇文章的主要目的是？
　　(A) 查出哪些青少年的壓力最大。
　　(B) 解釋壓力是一種心理問題。
　　(C) 告訴讀者如何減輕壓力。
　　(D) <u>推銷一本關於減輕壓力的書。</u>

main (men) adj. 主要的　　purpose ('pɝpəs) n. 目的
explain (ık'splen) v. 解釋　　mental ('mɛntḷ) adj. 心理的
inform (ın'fɔrm) v. 告訴　　promote (prə'mot) v. 推銷

42. (**B**) 第二段中畫底線的字 "**ulcer**"，指的是一種特殊的 _____
   (A) 心理疾病。
   (B) 身體的問題。
   (C) 精神上的治療。
   (D) 生理的治療。

   underlined (ˌʌndɚˈlaɪnd) *adj.* 畫底線的　　refer (rɪˈfɝ) *v.* 指
   particular (pɚˈtɪkjəlɚ) *adj.* 特殊的　　illness (ˈɪlnɪs) *n.* 疾病
   physical (ˈfɪzɪkḷ) *adj.* 身體的　　spiritual (ˈspɪrɪtʃuəl) *adj.* 精神上的
   treatment (ˈtritmənt) *n.* 治療

43. (**D**) 根據本文，下列何者是壓力所造成的正面影響？
   (A) 看有趣的電影。
   (B) 做放鬆的運動。
   (C) 成功地逃避困難的事。
   (D) 在危險的狀態下快速反應。

   relaxing (rɪˈlæksɪŋ) *adj.* 令人放鬆的　　avoid (əˈvɔɪd) *v.* 逃避
   successfully (səkˈsɛsfəlɪ) *adv.* 成功地　　risky (ˈrɪskɪ) *adj.* 危險的

44. (**C**) 根據本文，下列何者正確？
   (A) 台灣青少年所經歷的壓力，比美國青少年還大。
   (B) 壓力是一種很複雜的狀態，所以無法完全掌控。
   (C) 「學會放輕鬆才能活得久」是一本很受歡迎的書。
   (D) 壓力對身體而言，總是利多於弊。

   experience (ɪkˈspɪrɪəns) *v.* 經歷；體會　　state (stet) *n.* 狀態
   complicated (ˈkɑmpləˌketɪd) *adj.* 複雜的
   popular (ˈpɑpjələ) *adj.* 受歡迎的
   positive (ˈpɑzətɪv) *adj.* 正面的；有用的
   harmful (ˈhɑrmfəl) *adj.* 有害的

45-48 為題組

　　Tea was the first brewed beverage. The Chinese emperor Shen Nung
in 2737 B.C. introduced the drink. Chinese writer Lu Yu wrote in A.D. 780
that there were "tens of thousands" of teas. Chinese tea was introduced to
Japan in A.D. 800. It was then introduced to Europe in the early 1600s,
when trade began between Europe and the Far East. At that time, China
was the main supplier of tea to the world. Then in 1834, tea cultivation

began in India and spread to Sri Lanka, Thailand, Burma, and other areas of Southeast Asia. Today, Java, South Africa, South America, and areas of the Caucasus also produce tea.

　　茶是第一種釀造的飲料。西元前二七三七年，中國的皇帝神農氏（炎帝）讓茶問世。西元七八〇年，根據中國作家陸羽的記載，茶有數萬種之多。中國的茶在西元八〇〇年引進日本。之後，在十七世紀初引進歐洲，當時歐洲和遠東地區開始進行貿易。在那時候，中國是全世界茶的主要供應國。隨後，於一八三四年，印度開始栽種茶，然後傳到斯里蘭卡、泰國、緬甸，還有其他東南亞地區。現在，爪哇、南非、南美，還有高加索山脈的一些區域，也都有產茶。

> brewed〔brud〕adj. 釀造的　　beverage〔ˈbɛvrɪdʒ〕n. 飲料
> emperor〔ˈɛmpərɚ〕n. 皇帝
> **Shen Nung** 神農氏（又稱炎帝，在位 140 年，因生長於姜水，故姓姜，生於新石器時代晚期，他製作農耕用具，並教導人民從事農業生產。）
> introduce〔ˌɪntrəˈdjus〕v. 介紹；引進；使問世
> **Lu Yu** 陸羽（字鴻漸，是我國第一位著茶經而將茶藝發揚光大的人，後世經營茶業者奉之為「茶神」。）
> trade〔tred〕n. 貿易；交易　　**the Far East** 遠東
> supplier〔səˈplaɪɚ〕n. 供應者
> spread〔sprɛd〕v. 散播；散布
> cultivation〔ˌkʌltəˈveʃən〕n.（土地的）耕作；（作物的）栽種
> Sri Lanka〔ˌsriˈlæŋkə〕n. 斯里蘭卡（位於印度東南方，舊稱錫蘭）
> Burma〔ˈbɝmə〕n. 緬甸
> Java〔ˈdʒɑvə〕n. 爪哇（印尼共和國的主要島嶼）
> Caucasus〔ˈkɔkəsəs〕n. 高加索山脈（位於俄國西南部，介於黑海跟裏海之間的山脈）

　　There are three kinds of tea: black, green, and oolong. Most international tea trading is in black tea. Black tea preparation consists mainly of picking young leaves and leaf buds on a clear sunny day and letting the leaves dry for about an hour in the sun. Then, they are lightly rolled and left in a fermentation room to develop scent and a red color. Next, they are heated several more times. Finally, the leaves are dried in a basket over a charcoal fire. Green tea leaves are heated in steam, rolled, and dried. Oolong tea is prepared similarly to black tea, but without the fermentation time.

茶有三種：紅茶、綠茶，以及烏龍茶。大部份的國際貿易茶品是紅茶。紅茶主要的製作過程包含，在晴朗的日子裡，採收茶的嫩葉和葉芽，並在太陽底下曝曬大約一小時，使葉子乾燥。然後，把葉子稍微捲起來，放在發酵室裡，培養香氣以及紅的顏色。接下來，再加熱數次。最後，把葉子裝在籃子裡面，用炭火加熱。綠茶的葉子用蒸氣加熱、捲製，然後乾燥。烏龍茶的製作方法跟紅茶類似，但是不需要經過發酵。

oolong ('ulɔŋ) *n.* 烏龍茶　　　trading ('tredɪŋ) *n.* 貿易
preparation (ˌprɛpə'reʃən) *n.* 準備；製作
mainly ('menlɪ) *adv.* 主要地　　　*leaf bud* 葉芽
lightly ('laɪtlɪ) *adv.* 輕輕地；稍微地　　roll (rol) *v.* 捲製
fermentation (ˌfɝmən'teʃən) *n.* 發酵
scent (sɛnt) *n.* 香味　　dry (draɪ) *v.* 使乾燥
charcoal ('tʃar،kol) *n.* 木炭　　　steam (stim) *n.* 蒸氣

Three main varieties of tea—Chinese, Assamese, and Cambodian—have distinct characteristics. The Chinese variety, a strong plant that can grow to be 2.75 meters high, can live to be 100 years old and survives cold winters. The Assamese variety can grow 18 meters high and lives about 40 years. The Cambodian tea tree grows five meters tall.

茶的種類主要有三種：中國的、阿薩姆的、以及柬埔寨的，各具特色。中國茶的茶樹很堅韌，可以長到二點七五公尺高，樹齡可達一百歲，並且可以耐嚴寒的冬天。阿薩姆的茶樹，可以長到十八公尺高，樹齡可達四十歲。柬埔寨的茶樹，可以長到五公尺高。

variety (və'raɪətɪ) *n.* 種類；多樣性
Assamese (ˌæsə'miz) *adj.* 阿薩姆的【阿薩姆（Assam）是印度東北部的一省，以產紅茶聞名。】　　Cambodian (kæm'bodɪən) *adj.* 柬埔寨的【柬埔寨（Cambodia）為中南半島南部的一國，後更名高棉，首都金邊。】
distinct (dɪ'stɪŋkt) *adj.* 個別的；不同的　survive (sə'vaɪv) *v.* 存活

Tea is enjoyed worldwide as a refreshing and stimulating drink. Because so many people continue to drink the many varieties of tea, it will probably continue as the world's most popular drink.

因爲茶可以提神而且具有刺激性，所以全世界有很多人在喝。由於有很多人持續在喝許多不同種類的茶，因此它仍舊會是全世界最受歡迎的飲料。

worldwide (ˈwɝldˈwaɪd) *adj.* 遍及全世界的
refreshing (rɪˈfrɛʃɪŋ) *adj.* 提神的
stimulating (ˈstɪmjəˌletɪŋ) *adj.* 刺激的；鼓勵的

45. (C) 在十七世紀初，茶被引進歐洲的原因是 _____
  (A) 革命。   (B) 婚姻。
  (C) 貿易。   (D) 教育。
  revolution (ˌrɛvəˈluʃən) *n.* 革命

46. (B) 根據本文，以下何者是世界上最受歡迎的茶？
  (A) 綠茶。   (B) 紅茶。
  (C) 烏龍茶。   (D) 歐洲茶。

47. (C) 根據本文，關於茶的製作過程，下列何者正確？
  (A) 紅茶的葉子需要在陰天的時候採收。
  (B) 綠茶的葉子需要用炭火加熱。
  (C) 烏龍茶的製作過程和紅茶很類似。
  (D) 烏龍茶的葉子在捲製之前要先用蒸氣加熱。

48. (D) 從本文中，我們可以推論出下列哪一項敘述？
  (A) 人們爲了變富有以及增進健康而喝茶。
  (B) 爪哇栽種茶的時間比印度更早。
  (C) 茶樹只能生長一段短暫的期間。
  (D) 人們喝茶的原因是因爲它的多樣性，以及提神的效果。

<u>49-52 為題組</u>

Astronauts often work 16 hours a day on the space shuttle in order to complete all the projects set out for the mission. From space, astronauts study the geography, pollution, and weather patterns on Earth. They take many photographs to record their observations. Also, astronauts **conduct** experiments on the shuttle to learn how space conditions, such as microgravity, affect humans, animals, plants, and insects. Besides working, regular exercise is essential to keep the astronauts healthy in microgravity.

太空人在太空梭裡，通常一天工作十六小時，以完成這趟任務要進行的計畫。太空人從太空中研究地球的地理、污染，和天氣型態。他們拍了很多照片，來記錄他們的觀察。此外，太空人在太空梭上做實驗，以了解太空的情況，像是無重力狀態，對人類、動物、植物，和昆蟲有何影響。要使太空人在無重力狀態下保持健康，除了工作以外，規律的運動也是不可或缺的。

astronaut (ˈæstrə͵nɔt) n. 太空人　　*space shuttle* 太空梭 (= *shuttle*)
in order to V. 為了～　　complete (kəmˈplit) v. 完成
project (ˈprɑdʒɛkt) n. 計畫　　*set out* 開始；著手進行
mission (ˈmɪʃən) n. 任務　　geography (dʒiˈɑgrəfɪ) n. 地理
pollution (pəˈluʃən) n. 污染　　pattern (ˈpætən) n. 型態
photograph (ˈfotə͵græf) n. 照片　　record (rɪˈkɔrd) v. 記錄
observation (͵ɑbzəˈveʃən) n. 觀察
conduct (kənˈdʌkt) v. 進行；做
experiment (ɪkˈspɛrəmənt) n. 實驗
condition (kənˈdɪʃən) n. 狀態；情況
microgravity (͵maɪkroˈgrævətɪ) n. 無重力狀態
affect (əˈfɛkt) v. 影響　　human (ˈhjumən) n. 人類
insect (ˈɪnsɛkt) n. 昆蟲
essential (əˈsɛnʃəl) adj. 不可或缺的；必要的

Astronauts sometimes go outside the shuttle to work. They are protected by a space suit from the radiation of the Sun. Meanwhile, the space suit provides necessary oxygen supply and keeps the astronauts from feeling the extreme heat or cold outside the shuttle.

太空人有時候會走出太空梭工作。太空衣保護他們免於受到太陽的輻射。
同時，太空衣提供必要的氧氣供應，並且保護太空人，免於受到太空梭
外的酷熱或嚴寒。

suit〔sut〕n. 成套的衣服；套裝　　*space suit* 太空衣
radiation〔,redɪ'eʃən〕n. 輻射　　meanwhile〔'min,hwaɪl〕adv. 同時
provide〔prə'vaɪd〕v. 提供　　necessary〔'nɛsə,sɛrɪ〕adj. 必要的
oxygen〔'ɑksədʒən〕adj. 氧氣的　　n. 氧氣
supply〔sə'plaɪ〕n. 供給；供應　　extreme〔ɪk'strim〕adj. 極度的

When the mission is over, the crew members get ready to return to
Earth. The shuttle does not use its engines for a landing. It glides through
the atmosphere. When the shuttle touches the land, a drag parachute
opens to steady the aircraft, get the speed right, and help the brakes on the
landing-gear wheels to bring it to a complete stop.

當任務結束時，全體工作人員準備回到地球。太空梭不是用它的引擎著陸。
它滑行穿越大氣層。當太空梭接觸到陸地時，會張開拖曳降落傘，以穩定機體，
調整好速度，並幫助起落架輪子上的煞車，來讓太空梭完全停止。

crew〔kru〕n.（飛機或宇宙飛船的）全體機組員
member〔'mɛmbɚ〕n. 成員　　engine〔'ɛndʒən〕n. 引擎
landing〔'lændɪŋ〕n. 著陸　　glide〔glaɪd〕v. 滑行
atmosphere〔'ætməs,fɪr〕n. 大氣層　　drag〔dræg〕n. 拖曳
parachute〔'pærə,ʃut〕n. 降落傘　　steady〔'stɛdɪ〕v. 使穩固
aircraft〔'ɛr,kræft〕n. 飛行器；航空器　　brake〔brek〕n. 煞車
landing-gear〔'lændɪŋ'gɪr〕n. 起落架
complete〔kəm'plit〕adj. 完全的

49.（ **B** ）本文主要是關於
(A) 太空人如何駕駛太空梭。
(B) 如何完成太空任務。
(C) 如何建造太空梭。
(D) 太空人在太空中航行多遠。

fly〔flaɪ〕v. 駕駛（飛機、太空船）　　construct〔kən'strʌkt〕v. 建造

50.(**D**) 在第一段中，畫底線的字 **conduct** 意思最接近
　　 (A) 行為舉止。　　　　　　 (B) 教導。
　　 (C) 充當。　　　　　　　　 (D) 實行。
　　 underline〔͵ʌndəˋlaɪn〕v. 在（字等）下面畫線
　　 behave〔bɪˋhev〕v. 行為舉止　　 instruct〔ɪnˋstrʌkt〕v. 教導
　　 serve as 充當

51.(**D**) 根據本文，下列何者不正確？
　　 (A) 太空人需要太空衣才能在太空梭外工作。
　　 (B) 太空人穿太空衣保暖。
　　 (C) 太空人需要太空衣才能在太空中生存。
　　 (D) 太空人在太空衣中幾乎無法呼吸。
　　 survive〔səˋvaɪv〕v. 生存　　 hardly〔ˋhɑrdlɪ〕adv. 幾乎不
　　 breathe〔brið〕v. 呼吸

52.(**A**) 降落傘必須被打開，因為它可以
　　 (A) 減緩太空梭的速度。　　　 (B) 阻止太空梭免於落下。
　　 (C) 讓太空梭更接近地球。　　 (D) 幫助太空梭滑行穿越大氣層。

53-56 為題組

　　Joy Hirsch, a neuroscientist in New York, has recently found evidence that children and adults don't use the same parts of the brain when learning a second language. He used an instrument called an MRI (magnetic resonance imaging) to study the brains of two groups of bilingual people. One group consisted of those who had learned a second language as children. The other consisted of people who learned their second language later in life.

　　喬依賀須是紐約的神經科學專家，他最近發現一項證據，證明在學習第二種語言時，孩童與成人所使用的大腦部位，並不相同。他使用一種叫做 MRI（核磁共振）的儀器，來研究兩組雙語人士的大腦。一組是由幼年就學習第二國語言的人所組成的。另一組則是由較晚才學第二國語言的人所組成的。

neuroscientist (ˌnjuro'saɪəntɪst) *n.* 神經科學專家
evidence ('ɛvədəns) *n.* 證據　　　adult (ə'dʌlt) *n.* 成人
instrument ('ɪnstrəmənt) *n.* 儀器
MRI 核磁共振的儀器 (= *magnetic resonance imaging*)
magnetic (mæg'nɛtɪk) *adj.* 磁石的　　　resonance ('rɛzṇəns) *n.* 共振
image ('ɪmɪdʒ) *v.* 描繪影像　　　bilingual (baɪ'lɪŋgwəl) *adj.* 雙語的
consist of ~ 由~組成

People from both groups were placed inside the MRI scanner.　This allowed Hirsch to see which parts of the brain were getting more blood and were more active.　He asked people from both groups to think about what they had done the day before, first in one language and then the other.　They couldn't speak out loud, because any movement would disrupt the scanning.

兩組人員都被放進核磁共振的掃瞄裝置當中。這麼做讓賀須觀察到，腦中哪一部份得到的血液量較多、較活躍。他叫兩組人員回想一下，前一天做過的事，先用一種語言回想，再用第二種。他們不能大聲說出來，因為任何移動都會中斷掃瞄的進行。

scanner ('skænɚ) *n.* 掃瞄器　　　blood (blʌd) *n.* 血液
active ('æktɪv) *adj.* 活躍的　　　***speak out*** 說出來
movement ('muvmənt) *n.* 移動　　　disrupt (dɪs'rʌpt) *v.* 中斷
scanning ('skænɪŋ) *n.* 掃瞄

Hirsch looked specifically at two language centers in the brain — Broca's area, believed to control speech production, and Wernicke's area, thought to process meaning.　He found that both groups of people used the same part of Wernicke's area no matter what language they were speaking. But how they used Broca's area was different.

賀須特別查看腦中的兩個語言中心——白洛嘉腦迴區，一般認為它控制語言的產生，以及沃聶克區，一般認為它處理語言的含意。他發現兩組人，無論說的是什麼語言，都使用沃聶克同一個區塊。但是他們使用白洛嘉區的方法就不同了。

specifically (spɪ'sɪfɪkḷɪ) *adv.* 特別地
Broca's area 白洛嘉腦迴區 (大腦的左前區)
production (prə'dʌkʃən) *n.* 產生
Wernicke's area 沃聶克區　　　***no matter what*** 無論哪一個

　　People who learned a second language as children used the same
region in Broca's area for both languages. People who learned a second
language later in life used a special part of Broca's area for their second
language—near the one activated for their native tongue.

　　從小就學第二種語言的人，說兩種語言時，都用白洛嘉的同一個區塊。較
晚才學習第二語言者，講第二種語言時，用的是白洛嘉特定的一區──很靠近
說母語時所啓動的區域。

region (ˈridʒən) *n.* 區域　　activate (ˈæktəˌvet) *v.* 啓動
tongue (tʌŋ) *n.* 語言　　***native tongue*** 母語

　　How does Hirsch explain this difference? He believes that, when
language is first being programmed in young children, their brains may
mix all languages into the same area. But once that programming is
complete, a different part of the brain must take over a new language.
Another possibility is simply that we may acquire languages differently as
children than we do as adults. Hirsch thinks that mothers teach a baby to
speak by using different methods such as touch, sound, and sight. And
that's very different from sitting in a high school class.

　　賀須如何來解釋此差異？他認爲當語言第一次輸入到幼童的腦中時，他們
的大腦會把所有的語言混合在同一區域。但是一旦此輸入過程完成之後，就會
由不同的腦區來接掌新的語言。另一種可能性就是，孩童跟成人學語言的方式
根本就不相同。賀須認爲母親們使用如觸碰、聲音和視覺等，不同的方法，來
教嬰兒說話。而這種教法，跟坐在高中教室裏學習是不一樣的。

explain (ɪkˈsplen) *v.* 解釋　　difference (ˈdɪfərəns) *n.* 差異
program (ˈprogræm) *v.* 輸入程式　　once (wʌns) *conj.* 一旦
complete (kəmˈplit) *adj.* 完成的　　***take over*** 接掌
possibility (ˌpɑsəˈbɪlətɪ) *n.* 可能性
acquire (əˈkwaɪr) *v.* 獲得；學會　　method (ˈmɛθəd) *n.* 方式
sight (saɪt) *n.* 視覺　　***be different from***~ 和~不同

53. (**C**) 本文主旨爲
　　(A) 解釋人們如何會說雙語。　　(B) 解釋如何把第二種語言說得更好。
　　(C) 描述雙語人士腦部的研究。
　　(D) 描述不同年紀學語言的最佳方式。
　　research (ˈrisɜtʃ) *n.* 研究

54. (**A**) 本研究中，實驗對象被置於核磁共振儀器來

    (A) 觀察使用語言時腦中的活動。

    (B) 觀察大聲說話時腦中的活動。

    (C) 描述睡覺時腦中各區的功能。

    (D) 描述學第二種語言時，最適用的大腦區域。

    subject (′sʌbdʒɪkt) *n.* 實驗對象

    observe (əb′zɝv) *v.* 觀察   function (′fʌŋkʃən) *n.* 功能

55. (**D**) 一般認為腦中控制語言產生的中心是

    (A) 核磁共振儀器。   (B) 母語。

    (C) 沃聶克區。   (D) 白洛嘉區。

56. (**A**) 根據本文，有關雙語人士何者正確？

    (A) 說不同語言時，都使用沃聶克的同一區。

    (B) 說不同語言時，都使用白洛嘉的同一區。

    (C) 從不使用白洛嘉區和沃聶克區，來說同一種語言。

    (D) 總是使用沃聶克的不同區域，來說不同的語言。

第貳部分：非選擇題

一、翻譯題

1. People know that reading is { helpful / advantageous / beneficial / good / useful } for children.

2. Teachers should encourage their students to { borrow / check out / take out / get } books from the library.

二、英文作文：

A Romantic Surprise

A young woman is in her kitchen, stir-frying meat and vegetables. Her obedient dog is sitting patiently behind her, enjoying the smell, hoping for some! Suddenly, there is a terrifying growling noise! The startled woman turns and jumps in fright. She drops a plate of food and screams out, "Oh, my God!" A big hairy gorilla is coming at her.

Strangely, the dog is unafraid and starts eating the food happily. Meanwhile, the ferocious-looking gorilla takes off his head. What a surprise! It was a mask! The person underneath the costume is her husband. He smiles and offers her a beautiful bouquet of flowers. He says sweetly, "Happy April Fool's Day, honey. I love you!" The woman felt relieved and overwhelmed with joy. What a big gorilla surprise!

romantic〔ro'mæntɪk〕*adj.* 浪漫的　　stir-fry〔'stɜ,fraɪ〕*v.* 炒（菜）

meat〔mit〕*n.* 肉　　obedient〔ə'bidɪənt〕*adj.* 順從的；聽話的

patiently〔'peʃəntlɪ〕*adv.* 有耐心地　　smell〔smɛl〕*n.* 氣味；香味

suddenly〔'sʌdn̩lɪ〕*adv.* 突然地　　terrifying〔'tɛrə,faɪɪŋ〕*adj.* 可怕的

growling〔'graʊlɪŋ〕*adj.* 咆哮的　　noise〔nɔɪz〕*n.* 聲音

startled〔'stɑrtl̩d〕*adj.* 吃驚的；驚嚇的　　jump〔dʒʌmp〕*v.* 跳

fright〔fraɪt〕*n.* 驚嚇；恐怖　　drop〔drɑp〕*v.* 使掉落

plate〔plet〕*n.* 盤子；一盤的份量　　*scream out* 尖聲喊叫說

hairy〔'hɛrɪ〕*adj.* 毛茸茸的　　gorilla〔gə'rɪlə〕*n.* 大猩猩

come at 攻擊；衝向　　strangely〔'strendʒlɪ〕*adv.* 奇怪的是

unafraid〔,ʌnə'fred〕*adj.* 不怕的

meanwhile〔'min,hwaɪl〕*adv.* 同時；於此時

ferocious〔fə'roʃəs〕*adj.* 兇猛的　　*take off* 拿下

mask〔mæsk〕*n.* 面具　　underneath〔,ʌndə'niθ〕*prep.* 在…之下

costume〔'kɑstjum〕*n.* 服裝　　offer〔'ɔfə〕*v.* 給予；提供

bouquet〔bu'ke〕*n.* 花束　　sweetly〔'switlɪ〕*adv.* 甜蜜地；親切地

April Fool's Day 愚人節

95 年度學科能力測驗英文試題修正意見

題　號	題　　目	修　正　意　見
第 18 題	..., I am sorry *that*	..., I am sorry, **but** * 在此 I am sorry, but.... 源自 I wish I could, but....。
第 41 題	(A) To *find who are* the most stressed out teenagers.	(A) To **find out who** the most stressed out teenagers **are**. * 根據句意，應用 find out「找出」；名詞子句要用敘述句形式。
第 45－48 題 第一行	... Shen Nung *in 2737 B.C. introduced the drink.*	... Shen Nung **introduced the drink in 2737 B.C.**
第 49－52 題 第二段 第二行	*Meanwhile*, the space suit....	**In addition**, the space suit.... * 根據句意，是「此外（還有）」的意思。
第 49－52 題 第二段倒數 第二行	... provides necessary oxygen supply....	...provides **the** necessary oxygen supply.... * 指定的，應加定冠詞。
第 54 題	(A) ... of *the* brains.... (B) ... of *the* brains.... (C) ... of *the* brains.... (D) ... of the *brains* for learning *second languages*.	(A) ... of **their** brains.... (B) ... of **their** brains.... (C) ... of **their** brains.... * 根據句意，應用 their。 (D) ... of the **brain** for learning **a second language**.

九十五年度學科能力測驗（英文考科）
大考中心公佈答案

題號	答案	題號	答案	題號	答案
1	D	21	C	41	D
2	B	22	D	42	B
3	A	23	A	43	D
4	B	24	A	44	C
5	C	25	B	45	C
6	B	26	B	46	B
7	A	27	D	47	C
8	C	28	A	48	D
9	D	29	B	49	B
10	C	30	C	50	D
11	A	31	B	51	D
12	C	32	F	52	A
13	A	33	C	53	C
14	C	34	I	54	A
15	A	35	J	55	D
16	A	36	E	56	A
17	A	37	H		
18	D	38	G		
19	D	39	A		
20	B	40	D		

九十五學年度學科能力測驗
英文科各級分人數累計表

級分	人　　數	百分比（%）	累計人數	累計百分比（%）
15	5417	3.43	157745	100.00
14	9353	5.93	152328	96.57
13	10146	6.43	142975	90.64
12	12020	7.62	132829	84.20
11	11601	7.35	120809	76.58
10	12893	8.17	109208	69.23
9	12280	7.78	96315	61.06
8	13753	8.72	84035	53.27
7	13711	8.69	70282	44.55
6	15057	9.55	56571	35.86
5	13332	8.45	41514	26.32
4	14737	9.34	28182	17.87
3	11152	7.07	13445	8.52
2	2225	1.41	2293	1.45
1	61	0.04	68	0.04
0	7	0.00	7	0.00

九十四年大學入學學科能力測驗試題
英文考科

第壹部份：單選題

一、詞彙（15％）

說明：第1至15題，每題選出最適當的一個選項，標示在答案卡之「選擇題答案區」。每題答對得1分，答錯不倒扣。

1. As computers are getting less expensive, they are _____ used in schools and offices today.
   (A) widely　　(B) expectedly　(C) consciously　(D) influentially

2. Mr. Chang always tries to answer all questions from his students. He will not _____ any of them even if they may sound stupid.
   (A) reform　　(B) depress　　(C) ignore　　(D) confirm

3. Irene does not throw away used envelopes. She _____ them by using them for taking telephone messages.
   (A) designs　　(B) recycles　　(C) disguises　　(D) manufactures

4. Cheese, powdered milk, and yogurt are common milk _____.
   (A) produces　(B) products　(C) productions　(D) productivities

5. Although he is a chef, Roberto _____ cooks his own meals.
   (A) rarely　　(B) bitterly　　(C) naturally　　(D) skillfully

6. Due to the yearly bonus system, the 100 _____ positions in this high-tech company have attracted many applicants from around the island.
   (A) loyal　　(B) evident　　(C) typical　　(D) vacant

7. If you want to borrow magazines, tapes, or CDs, you can visit the library. They are all _____ there.
   (A) sufficient　(B) marvelous　(C) impressive　(D) available

8. The fire in the fireworks factory in Changhua set off a series of powerful _____ and killed four people.

(A) explosions　(B) extensions　(C) inspections　(D) impressions

9. A good government official has to _____ the temptation of money and make the right decision.

(A) consist　(B) insist　(C) resist　(D) persist

10. The drug dealer was _____ by the police while he was selling cocaine to a high school student.

(A) threatened　(B) endangered

(C) demonstrated　(D) arrested

11. The rise of oil prices made scientists search for new energy resources to _____ oil.

(A) apply　(B) replace　(C) inform　(D) persuade

12. Without much contact with the outside world for many years, John found many technological inventions _____ to him.

(A) natural　(B) common　(C) foreign　(D) objective

13. The medicine you take for a cold may cause _____; try not to drive after you take it.

(A) incident　(B) violence　(C) bacteria　(D) drowsiness

14. To gain more _____, some legislators would get into violent physical fights so that they may appear in TV news reports.

(A) publicity　(B) reputation

(C) significance　(D) communication

15. To live an efficient life, we have to arrange the things to do in order of _____ and start with the most important ones.

(A) authority　(B) priority　(C) regularity　(D) security

二、綜合測驗（15％）

說明： 第16至30題，每題一個空格，請依文意選出最適當的一個選項，標示
在答案卡之「選擇題答案區」。每題答對得1分，答錯不倒扣。

Experts say that creativity by definition means going against the
tradition and breaking the rules. To be creative, you must dare ___16___,
and courageously express your own outlook and ___17___ what makes
you unique.

But does our society encourage children to break the rules? I'm
afraid the answer is no. The famous film director Ang Lee recalls his
father's disappointment with him when he was young. ___18___ a small
child, he would pick up a broom and pretend to be playing guitar for the
entertainment of family guests. Then, when he was studying film in
college, he would exhaust himself just for a performance tour. His father,
___19___ always hoped that he would get a PhD and become a professor,
___20___ with a scoff: "What is all this nonsense?!" But it later turned
out that it was exactly his courage to "rebel" and to express his own ideas
that marks his films with distinct creativity.

16. (A) rebel　　　　(B) to rebel　　　(C) rebelling　　(D) be rebelled
17. (A) take pride in　(B) fall short of　(C) get out of　　(D) keep up with
18. (A) Since　　　　(B) For　　　　　(C) To　　　　　(D) As
19. (A) who　　　　 (B) while　　　　 (C) that　　　　　(D) when
20. (A) relieved　　　(B) relaxed　　　 (C) relied　　　　(D) reacted

European politicians are trying to get the UK Government to make
cigarette companies print photos on the packets. These photos will
show ___21___ smoking damages your health. The shocking pictures
include images of smoke-damaged lungs and teeth, with reminders in
large print that smokers die younger.

The picture ___22___ have been used in Canada for the last four years. It has been very successful and has led to a 44% ___23___ in smokers wanting to kick the habit. At the moment EU tobacco manufacturers only have to put written health warnings on cigarette packets ___24___ the dangers of smoking.

The aim of the campaign is to remind people of the damage the deadly weed does to their body. It is believed that this would be to the best interest of all people, ___25___ teens who might be tempted to start smoking. These dreadful photos may change the impression among teenagers that smoking is cool and sexy.

21. (A) when   (B) how   (C) where   (D) what
22. (A) symbols   (B) warnings   (C) commercials   (D) decorations
23. (A) increase   (B) change   (C) portion   (D) drop
24. (A) highlight   (B) highlights   (C) highlighting (D) highlighted
25. (A) in fact   (B) rather than   (C) regarding   (D) especially

Do plants have feelings? There is currently no reason to believe that plants experience pain, because they are devoid of central nervous systems and brains. Animals are able to feel pain ___26___ they can use it for self-protection. ___27___ , if you touch something hot and feel pain, you will learn from this ___28___ that you should not touch that item in the future. On the other hand, plants cannot move ___29___ and do not need to learn to avoid certain things, so this sensation would be unnecessary. From a physiological standpoint, plants are completely different from animals. They cannot feel pain. Therefore, ___30___ animals' body parts, many fruits and vegetables can be harvested over and over again without dying.

26. (A) although　　(B) because　　(C) when　　(D) so that
27. (A) In contrast　(B) Before long　(C) For example　(D) To begin with
28. (A) discomfort　(B) prescription　(C) enjoyment　(D) satisfaction
29. (A) from door to door　　　　(B) from place to place
　　(C) from top to toe　　　　　(D) from case to case
30. (A) as with　　(B) for　　　(C) unlike　　(D) except for

三、文意選填（10％）

說明： 第31至40題，每題一個空格，請依文意在文章後所提供的 (A) 到(J)
　　　選項中分別選出最適當者，並將其英文字母代號標示在答案卡之「選
　　　擇題答案區」。每題答對得 1 分，答錯不倒扣。

Falling in love is always magical. It feels eternal as if love will last
____31____. We naively believe that somehow we are ____32____ from the
problems our parents had. We are assured that we are destined to live
happily ever after.

But as the magic fades and daily life ____33____, it happens that men,
forgetting that men and women are supposed to be different, continue to
expect women to think and react the way men do; women, ____34____,
expect men to feel and behave the way women do. ____35____ taking time
to understand and respect each other, we become demanding, resentful,
judgmental, and intolerant.

____36____, our relationships are filled with unnecessary disagreements
and conflicts. Somehow, problems creep in, resentments build, and
communication ____37____. Mistrust increases and rejection and repression
surface. The magic of love is then lost.

Very ____38____ people are able to grow in love. Yet, it does happen.
____39____ men and women are able to respect and accept their differences,
love has a chance to blossom. Love is, ____40____, magical, and it
certainly can last if we remember our differences and respect each other.

(A) breaks down   (B) Consequently   (C) similarly   (D) indeed
(E) few   (F) forever   (G) Instead of   (H) takes over
(I) free   (J) As long as

四、閱讀測驗（32％）

說明：第 41 至 56 題，每題請分別根據各篇文章之文意選出最適當的一個
選項，標示在答案卡之「選擇題答案區」。每題答對得 2 分，答錯
不倒扣。

41-44 為題組

For many years, I was convinced that my suffering was due to my
size. I believed that when the weight disappeared, it would take old
wounds, hurts, and rejections with it.

Many weight-conscious people also mistakenly believe that changing
our bodies will fix *everything*. Perhaps our worst mistake is believing
that being thin equals being loved, being special, and being cherished.
We fantasize about what it will be like when we reach the long-awaited
goal. We work very hard to realize this dream. Then, at last, we find
ourselves there.

But we often gain back what we have lost. Even so, we continue
to believe that next time it will be different. Next time, we will keep it
off. Next time, being thin will finally fulfill its promise of everlasting
happiness, self-worth, and, of course, love.

It took me a long while to realize that there was something more
for me to learn about beauty. Beauty standards vary with culture. In
Samoa a woman is not considered attractive unless she weighs more
than 200 pounds. More importantly, if it's happiness that we want, why
not put our energy there rather than on the size of our body? Why not
look inside? Many of us strive hard to change our body, but in vain.

We have to find a way to live comfortably inside our body and make friends with and cherish ourselves. When we change our attitudes toward ourselves, the whole world changes.

41. The passage tries to highlight the importance of _____.
    (A) body size　　　　　　　　(B) attitudes toward life
    (C) culture difference　　　　　(D) different beauty standards

42. What does the word "*everything*" in paragraph 2 mean?
    (A) All the problems.　　　　　(B) All the properties.
    (C) The whole world.　　　　　(D) The absolute truth.

43. What can be inferred about the author?
    (A) The author is a Samoan.
    (B) The author succeeded in losing weight.
    (C) The author has been troubled by her/his weight.
    (D) The author probably got wounded in wars or accidents.

44. According to the author, what is the common view of those who have lost some weight first and gained it back later?
    (A) They feel angry about the regained weight.
    (B) They are indifferent to the regained weight.
    (C) They feel optimistic about future plans on weight control.
    (D) They think they should give up their future plans on weight control.

45-48 為題組

On December 26, 2003, the worst earthquake in more than a decade devastated Bam, a historic city in Iran. At least 25,000 people died in the quake—nearly a third of the city's population. And thousands more were left homeless, hungry, and grieving.

Bam was a city of mud-brick houses, old monuments and an ancient castle. But nearly everything crumbled in the disaster. One reason the earthquake caused such damage was that Bam's buildings were made mostly from baked mud. These buildings collapsed in heaps of dust and sand.

Bam was best known for its 2,000-year-old castle built out of mud, straw, and the trunks of palm trees. The castle was so big that it was once the city of Bam itself. Public dwellings lined its ground level; a marketplace and two mosques also fit comfortably inside.

Bam once blossomed as a trading post on the Silk Road. In the 16th and 17th centuries, treasures from the Far East were carried along the road into the capital cities of Europe. Fifty years ago, teams of architects began restoring the historic treasures of the city. Ever since, thousands of visitors have come to admire them.

In the face of this tragedy, food and other supplies from around the world landed in the provincial capital of Kerman on Sunday. With such support, spiritual leader Ayatollah Ali Khamenei vowed, "We will rebuild Bam stronger than before."

45. This passage is most likely taken from a(n) _____.
   (A) newspaper 　　　　　　(B) history textbook
   (C) book review 　　　　　　(D) magazine on international trade

46. What was Bam most famous for?
   (A) Beautiful palm trees.
   (B) Frequent earthquakes.
   (C) An old mud and straw castle.
   (D) Treasures from the Far East.

47. The use of baked mud for buildings explains _____.
   (A) why the earthquake occurred
   (B) why Bam collected so many treasures
   (C) why Bam developed into a trading post
   (D) why the earthquake caused such damage

48. Which of the following is CORRECT about the earthquake in Bam?
   (A) About 50,000 people survived the earthquake.
   (B) Not many countries sent food and supplies to Bam.
   (C) The 2003 earthquake was the first one in its history.
   (D) The city of Bam would be deserted after the earthquake.

49-52 為題組

Jet lag, caused by traveling between time zones, is becoming a common problem for frequent travelers: for 49 per cent it is only a nuisance and for 45 percent it is a real problem. It is caused by disruption to the internal biological clock, and may lead to digestive problems, tiredness, and sleep disruption.

Generally speaking, our biological clock is slightly disturbed if we just move into the next time zone, but jet lag becomes a problem once we have passed through three or four time zones. The body takes about one day to get over each hour of time difference. But the seriousness of jet lag problems also depends on our direction of travel. If we go north or south, we won't notice any difference, because there is usually no time zone change. However, if we travel west we will be in advance of ourselves as far as our internal clock is concerned, and problems may arise. A west-to-east journey, on the other hand, makes us late compared to the local time. It often demands even greater effort in adjustment since we are not quick enough to catch up with the new time schedule. Therefore, a trip from New York to Los Angeles often causes fewer problems than a Los Angeles-New York trip.

49. A traveler who suffers from jet lag has problems in _____.
　　(A) adjusting his biological clock
　　(B) knowing the direction of a jet
　　(C) knowing the distance of his flight
　　(D) getting used to the weather of a new place

50. If one travels across three time zones, he needs about _____ hours
　　to get over his jet lag problem.
　　(A) 24　　　　　　(B) 36　　　　　　(C) 48　　　　　　(D) 72

51. A person may suffer the most serious case of jet lag when he takes
　　a _____ journey.
　　(A) east-to-west　　　　　　(B) west-to-east
　　(C) north-to-south　　　　　(D) south-to-north

52. The main purpose of the passage is to _____.
　　(A) explain the cause of jet lag problems
　　(B) teach us how to avoid jet lag problems
　　(C) explain the differences between time zones
　　(D) show the ways to lessen the degree of jet lag problems

53-56 為題組

　　Originally from tropical South America, the red fire ant gained entry
to the United States through the port of Mobile, Alabama in the late
1930s on cargo ships, but the first colony of the red ants was not found
until 1942 by a 13-year-old boy in his backyard.

　　It immediately began to thrive in the new land and colonies spread
quickly throughout the southeastern states. By 1975 the red imported
fire ant had colonized over 52 million hectares of the United States. Now,
it has infested more than 275 million hectares in the country.

Red imported fire ants build mounds in any type of soil. They also make mounds indoors. Each nest used to have but one queen, but now many mounds are often found with multiple queens. With multiple queens at work, its population increases rapidly. It's common to find a nest with over 25,000 workers.

Red imported fire ants can cause a number of problems. They construct their colonies on precious farmland, invading crops while searching for insects underground. They also like to make their mounds in sunny areas, heavily infesting lawns and pastures. They can quickly strip fruit trees of their fruit. Small birds such as baby quails are fair game to the expanding colony. They appear to be attracted to electromagnetic fields and attack electrical insulation or wire connections. They can cause electrical shorts, fires, and other damage to electrical equipment. Worst of all, their stings can be fatal to livestock and humans.

53. When was the first nest of the red ant found in the United States?
    (A) In 1930s.　　(B) In 1942.　　(C) In 1975.　　(D) After 1975.

54. Which of the following is TRUE according to the article?
    (A) Each nest of the red ant has one queen.
    (B) The red ant was originally found in North America.
    (C) The red ant can reproduce young ants very quickly.
    (D) The red ant does not build mounds inside the house.

55. What kinds of problems can the red ant cause?
    (A) Health, social, and agricultural.
    (B) Health, social, and environmental.
    (C) Social, environmental, and agricultural.
    (D) Health, agricultural, and environmental.

56. What is the purpose of the article?
    (A) To ask for help to kill the red ant.
    (B) To urge people to protect the red ant.
    (C) To provide information about the red ant.
    (D) To seek help from the government to control the red ant.

第貳部份：非選擇題

一、翻譯題（8％）

說明：1. 請將以下兩個中文句子譯成正確、通順、達意的英文，並將答案寫
       在「答案卷」上。
      2. 請依序作答，並標明題號。每題 4 分，共 8 分。

1. 人類對外太空所知非常有限，但長久以來我們對它卻很感興趣。
2. 太空科技的快速發展，使我們得以探索它的奧秘。

二、英文作文（20％）

說明：1. 依提示在「答案卷」上寫一篇英文作文。
      2. 文長 120 個單詞（words）左右。

提示：請根據以下三張連環圖畫的內容，以 "In the English class last
      week,..." 開頭，將圖中主角所經歷的事件作一合理的敘述。

94年度學科能力測驗英文科試題詳解

第壹部分：單選題

一、詞彙：

1. (**A**) As computers are getting less expensive, they are <u>widely</u> used in schools and offices today.
   由於電腦越來越便宜，因此現在學校和公司都<u>廣泛地</u>使用電腦。

   (A) *widely* ('waɪdlɪ) *adv.* 廣泛地
   (B) expectedly (ɪk'spɛktɪdlɪ) *adv.* 預期地
   (C) consciously ('kɑnʃəslɪ) *adv.* 有意識地
   (D) influentially (ˌɪnfluˈɛnʃəlɪ) *adv.* 有影響地
   office ('ɔfɪs) *n.* 辦公室；公司

2. (**C**) Mr. Chang always tries to answer all questions from his students. He will not <u>ignore</u> any of them even if they may sound stupid.
   張先生總是試著回答學生所有的問題。即使有些問題可能聽起來很蠢，他也不會<u>忽視</u>任何一個。

   (A) reform (rɪ'fɔrm) *v.* 改革　　　(B) depress (dɪ'prɛs) *v.* 使沮喪
   (C) *ignore* (ɪg'nor) *v.* 忽視　　　(D) confirm (kən'fɜm) *v.* 證實
   even if 即使　　sound (saʊnd) *v.* 聽起來
   stupid ('stjupɪd) *adj.* 愚蠢的

3. (**B**) Irene does not throw away used envelopes. She <u>recycles</u> them by using them for taking telephone messages.
   艾琳不會丟掉用過的信封。她會<u>再利用</u>它們來記錄電話留言。

   (A) design (dɪ'zaɪn) *v.* 設計
   (B) *recycle* (ri'saɪk!) *v.* 再利用；回收
   (C) disguise (dɪs'gaɪz) *v.* 偽裝
   (D) manufacture (ˌmænjə'fæktʃɚ) *v.* 製造
   throw away 丟掉　　used (juzd) *adj.* 用過的
   envelope ('ɛnvəˌlop) *n.* 信封　　take (tek) *v.* 記錄
   message ('mɛsɪdʒ) *n.* 訊息；留言

4. (**B**) Cheese, powdered milk, and yogurt are common milk <u>products</u>.
乳酪、奶粉和優格都是常見的乳製品。

    (A) produce ('pradjus) n. 農產品 (prə'djus) v. 生產；製造

    (B) *product* ('pradəkt) n. 製品；產品

    (C) production (prə'dʌkʃən) n. 生產；製造

    (D) productivity (,prodʌk'tɪvətɪ) n. 生產力

    cheese (tʃiz) n. 乳酪   powdered ('paʊdəd) adj. 粉末狀的

    powdered milk 奶粉   yogurt ('jogət) n. 優格 (= *yoghurt*)

    common ('kamən) adj. 常見的

5. (**A**) Although he is a chef, Roberto <u>rarely</u> cooks his own meals.
雖然羅伯特是主廚，但是他很少煮飯給自己吃。

    (A) *rarely* ('rɛrlɪ) adv. 很少地

    (B) bitterly ('bɪtəlɪ) adv. 痛苦地；猛烈地

    (C) naturally ('nætʃərəlɪ) adv. 自然地

    (D) skillfully ('skɪlfəlɪ) adv. 巧妙地

    chef (ʃɛf) n. 主廚   meal (mil) n. 一餐

6. (**D**) Due to the yearly bonus system, the 100 <u>vacant</u> positions in this high-tech company have attracted many applicants from around the island.
由於有年度的分紅制度，這家高科技公司的一百個職缺，吸引了許多來自本島各處的應徵者。

    (A) loyal ('lɔɪəl) adj. 忠心的

    (B) evident ('ɛvədənt) adj. 明顯的

    (C) typical ('tɪpɪkl) adj. 典型的

    (D) *vacant* ('vekənt) adj. 空缺的

    due to 由於   yearly ('jɪrlɪ) adj. 每年的

    bonus ('bonəs) n. 紅利   position (pə'zɪʃən) n. 職位；工作

    high-tech ('haɪ'tɛk) adj. 高科技的

    applicant ('æpləkənt) n. 應徵者

    around (ə'raʊnd) prep. 在…四處

7. (**D**) If you want to borrow magazines, tapes, or CDs, you can visit
the library.　They are all <u>available</u> there.

如果你想要借雜誌、錄音帶或是雷射唱片，你可以去這家圖書館。
在那裡<u>可以借到</u>所有的東西。

(A) sufficient〔 səˈfɪʃənt〕 *adj.* 足夠的

(B) marvelous〔ˈmɑrvḷəs〕 *adj.* 令人驚歎的；很棒的

(C) impressive〔 ɪmˈprɛsɪv〕 *adj.* 令人印象深刻的

(D) ***available***〔 əˈveləbḷ〕 *adj.* 可獲得的

tape〔 tep〕 *n.* 錄音帶　　***CD*** 雷射唱片（ = *compact disc* ）

visit〔ˈvɪzɪt〕 *v.* 去

8. (**A**) The fire in the firworks factory in Changhua set off a series of
powerful <u>explosions</u> and killed four people.

彰化的爆竹工廠大火，引發了一連串的大<u>爆炸</u>，並且造成四個人
喪生。

(A) ***explosion***〔 ɪkˈsploʒən〕 *n.* 爆炸

(B) extension〔 ɪkˈstɛnʃən〕 *n.* 延長；（ 電話 ）分機

(C) inspection〔 ɪnˈspɛkʃən〕 *n.* 檢查

(D) impression〔 ɪmˈprɛʃən〕 *n.* 印象

fireworks〔ˈfaɪrˌwɝks〕 *n.pl.* 煙火　　***set off*** 引發；開始

series〔ˈsiriz〕 *n.* 一連串　　***a series of*** 一連串的

powerful〔ˈpaʊəfəl〕 *adj.* 強烈的；強大的　　kill〔 kɪl〕 *v.* 使喪生

9. (**C**) A good government official has to <u>resist</u> the temptation of money
and make the right decision.

一位好的政府官員必須要<u>抗拒</u>金錢的誘惑，並且做出正確的決定。

(A) consist〔 kənˈsɪst〕 *v.* 組成　　***consist of*** 由～組成

(B) insist〔 ɪnˈsɪst〕 *v.* 堅持

(C) ***resist***〔 rɪˈzɪst〕 *v.* 抵抗；抗拒

(D) persist〔 pəˈsɪst〕 *v.* 堅持；持續

official〔 əˈfɪʃəl〕 *n.* 公務員；官員

temptation〔 tɛmpˈteʃən〕 *n.* 誘惑　　decision〔 dɪˈsɪʒən〕 *n.* 決定

10. (**D**) The drug dealer was <u>arrested</u> by the police while he was selling cocaine to a high school student.

這名毒販在賣古柯鹼給一位高中生時，被警方<u>逮捕</u>。

(A) threaten〔'θrɛtn̩〕v. 威脅

(B) endanger〔ɪn'dendʒɚ〕v. 使危險；危及

(C) demonstrate〔'dɛmən͵stret〕v. 證明；示威遊行

(D) *arrest*〔ə'rɛst〕v. 逮捕

drug〔drʌg〕n. 毒品　　dealer〔'dilɚ〕n. 商人

cocaine〔ko'ken〕n. 古柯鹼

11. (**B**) The rise of oil prices made scientists search for new energy resources to <u>replace</u> oil.

石油的價格上漲，促使科學家去尋找新的能源來<u>代替</u>石油。

(A) apply〔ə'plaɪ〕v. 申請；應徵；應用

(B) *replace*〔rɪ'ples〕v. 代替

(C) inform〔ɪn'fɔrm〕v. 通知

(D) persuade〔pɚ'swed〕v. 說服

rise〔raɪz〕n. 上升；上漲　　scientist〔'saɪəntɪst〕n. 科學家

search for 尋找　　energy〔'ɛnɚdʒɪ〕n. 能量

resource〔rɪ'sors〕n. 資源

12. (**C**) Without much contact with the outside world for many years, John found many technological inventions <u>foreign</u> to him.

多年來，約翰不太和外界接觸，因此他發現自己對於許多科技上的發明感到很<u>陌生</u>。

(A) natural〔'nætʃərəl〕adj. 自然的

(B) common〔'kɑmən〕adj. 一般的；常見的

(C) *foreign*〔'fɔrɪn〕adj. 陌生的

(D) objective〔əb'dʒɛktɪv〕adj. 客觀的

contact〔'kɑntækt〕n. 接觸；聯絡

technological〔͵tɛknə'lɑdʒɪkl̩〕adj. 科技的

invention〔ɪn'vɛnʃən〕n. 發明

13. (**D**) The medicine you take for a cold may cause <u>drowsiness</u>; try not to drive after you take it.

你吃的感冒藥可能會使你<u>想睡</u>；所以不要在服藥之後開車。

(A) incident (ˈɪnsədənt) *n.* 事件

(B) violence (ˈvaɪələns) *n.* 暴力

(C) bacteria (bækˈtɪrɪə) *n. pl.* 細菌 (單數是 bacterium (bækˈtɪrɪəm))

(D) *drowsiness* (ˈdrauzɪnɪs) *n.* 睡意；想睡

cause (kɔz) *v.* 導致；引起

14. (**A**) To gain more <u>publicity</u>, some legislators would get into violent physical fights so that they may appear in TV news reports.

為了讓自己更<u>出名</u>，有些立法委員會捲入激烈的肢體衝突，這樣子他們就可以出現在電視新聞報導中。

(A) *publicity* (pʌbˈlɪsətɪ) *n.* 知名度；出名

(B) reputation (ˌrɛpjəˈteʃən) *n.* 名聲 (reputation 不可跟 more 連用，故不選)

(C) significance (sɪgˈnɪfəkəns) *n.* 意義；重要性

(D) communication (kəˌmjunəˈkeʃən) *n.* 溝通

gain (gen) *v.* 獲得   legislator (ˈlɛdʒɪsˌletə) *n.* 立法委員

get into 陷入 (某種狀態)   violent (ˈvaɪələnt) *adj.* 暴力的；激烈的

physical (ˈfɪzɪkl̩) *adj.* 身體的   fight (faɪt) *n.* 打架

physical fight 打架；肢體衝突 (*cf.* verbal fight 吵架)

appear (əˈpɪr) *v.* 出現   report (rɪˈport) *n.* 報導

15. (**B**) To live an efficient life, we have to arrange the things to do in order of <u>priority</u> and start with the most important ones.

為了過有效率的生活，我們必須要依照<u>優先</u>順序安排要做的事情，並且從最重要的事情開始做起。

(A) authority (əˈθɔrətɪ) *n.* 權威

(B) *priority* (praɪˈɔrətɪ) *n.* 優先

(C) regularity (ˌrɛgjəˈlærətɪ) *n.* 規則；規律

(D) security (sɪˈkjurətɪ) *n.* 安全

efficient (ɪˈfɪʃənt) *adj.* 有效率的

arrange (əˈrendʒ) *v.* 安排   *in order of* 按～順序

二、綜合測驗：

Experts say that creativity by definition means going against the tradition and breaking the rules. To be creative, you must dare <u>to rebel</u>, 16 and courageously express your own outlook and <u>take pride in</u> what makes 17 you unique.

專家指出，根據定義，創造力的意思就是要違反傳統，打破成規。想要有創意，你必須要敢反抗，要勇於表達自己的看法，並且以自己的特色為榮。

> expert（'ɛkspɝt）*n.* 專家　　creativity（ˌkrie'tɪvətɪ）*n.* 創造力
> definition（ˌdɛfə'nɪʃən）*n.* 定義　　***by definition*** 根據定義
> ***go against*** 違背；違反　　tradition（trə'dɪʃən）*n.* 傳統
> break（brek）*v.* 打破；違反　　rule（rul）*n.* 規則；慣例
> creative（krɪ'etɪv）*adj.* 有創造力的　　dare（dɛr）*v.* 敢
> courageously（kə'redʒəslɪ）*adv.* 勇敢地
> express（ɪk'sprɛs）*v.* 表達　　outlook（'aʊtˌlʊk）*n.* 看法
> unique（ju'nik）*adj.* 獨特的；特有的

16. (**B**) dare「敢」，因位於助動詞 must 之後，在此是一般動詞，其後須接不定詞，故選 (B) ***to rebel***。　　rebel（rɪ'bɛl）*v.* 反叛；反抗

17. (**A**) 依句意，選 (A) ***take pride in***「以…為榮」。而 (B) fall short of「未達…；不足…」，(C) get out of「離開」，(D) keep up with「趕上」，均不合句意。

But does our society encourage children to break the rules? I'm afraid the answer is no. The famous film director Ang Lee recalls his father's disappointment with him when he was young. <u>As</u> a small child, he would 18 pick up a broom and pretend to be playing guitar for the entertainment of family guests. Then, when he was studying film in college, he would exhaust himself just for a performance tour.

　　但是我們的社會有鼓勵小孩打破成規嗎？恐怕答案是否定的。知名的電影導演李安想起自己年輕時，父親對他很失望。他小的時候，會拿起掃帚，假裝在彈吉他，來娛樂家裡的客人。然後當他在大學裡研讀電影時，他會為了巡迴演出，而把自己弄得筋疲力盡。

> encourage (ɪn'kɝɪdʒ) v. 鼓勵　　　film (fɪlm) n. 電影
> director (də'rɛktɚ) n. 導演　　　recall (rɪ'kɔl) v. 記起；想起
> disappointment (ˌdɪsə'pɔɪntmənt) n. 失望　　***pick up*** 拿起
> broom (brum) n. 掃帚　　　pretend (prɪ'tɛnd) v. 假裝
> guitar (gɪ'tɑr) n. 吉他　　　entertainment (ˌɛntɚ'tenmənt) n. 娛樂
> guest (gɛst) n. 客人　　　exhaust (ɪg'zɔst) v. 使筋疲力盡
> performance (pɚ'fɔrməns) n. 表演　　　tour (tur) n. 巡迴演出

18. (**D**) 依句意，選 (D) ***As a small child***「小時候」。

His father, <u>who</u> always hoped that he would get a PhD and become a
　　　　　　19
professor, <u>reacted</u> with a scoff: "What is all this nonsense?!" But it later
　　　　　20
turned out that it was exactly his courage to "rebel" and to express his own
ideas that marks his films with distinct creativity.

他那一直希望他能拿到博士學位，然後當個教授的爸爸，以嘲笑的語氣回應說：「這些亂七八糟的東西是在做什麼？！」但是後來的結果是，就是因為他有「反抗」和表達自己想法的勇氣，才使他的電影具有獨特的創意。

> PhD ('piˌetʃ'di) n. 博士學位 (= *Ph.D.*)
> professor (prə'fɛsɚ) n. 教授　　　scoff (skɔf) n. 嘲笑；嘲弄
> nonsense ('nɑnsɛns) n. 愚昧的行為；無聊的事
> later ('letɚ) adv. 後來　　　***turn out*** 結果
> exactly (ɪg'zæktlɪ) adv. 正是　　　courage ('kɝɪdʒ) n. 勇氣
> mark (mɑrk) v. 使具有…特色；使…很顯著
> distinct (dɪ'stɪŋkt) adj. 不同的；獨特的

19. (**A**) 空格應填一關代，引導形容詞子句，先行詞為人，關代可用 who 或
　　　 that，但因前有逗點，不能用 that，故選 (A) ***who***。

20. (**D**) 依句意，他的父親以嘲笑的態度「回應」，故選 (D) **react** 〔 rɪˋækt 〕 *v.*
回應；反應。而 (A) relieve 〔 rɪˋliv 〕 *v.* 減輕；緩和，(B) relax
〔 rɪˋlæks 〕 *v.* 放鬆，(C) rely 〔 rɪˋlaɪ 〕 *v.* 依賴，均不合句意。

    European politicians are trying to get the UK Government to make
cigarette companies print photos on the packets. These photos will show
<u>how</u> smoking damages your health. The shocking pictures include images
  21
of smoke-damaged lungs and teeth, with reminders in large print that
smokers die younger.

    歐洲的政治人物正在努力，想要促使英國政府，強制要求香煙公司將照片
印在包裝上。這些照片將會說明，抽煙會如何危害健康。這些可怕的照片包括
因為抽煙而受損的肺部與牙齒的影像，以及用大寫的字提醒大家，抽煙的人會
比較早死。

      European 〔 ͵jurəˋpiən 〕 *adj.* 歐洲的
      politician 〔 ͵pɑləˋtɪʃən 〕 *n.* 政治人物   *try to V.* 努力～
      get 〔 gɛt 〕 *v.* 使   make 〔 mek 〕 *v.* (強制地) 使… (做～)
      cigarette 〔 ˋsɪgə͵rɛt 〕 *n.* 香煙   print 〔 prɪnt 〕 *v.* 印刷   *n.* 印刷之物
      photo 〔 ˋfoto 〕 *n.* 照片   packet 〔 ˋpækɪt 〕 *n.* 小包；小盒
      show 〔 ʃo 〕 *v.* 說明；證明   damage 〔 ˋdæmɪdʒ 〕 *v.* 損害
      shocking 〔 ˋʃɑkɪŋ 〕 *adj.* 使人震驚的；可怕的
      image 〔 ˋɪmɪdʒ 〕 *n.* 影像；畫像   lung 〔 lʌŋ 〕 *n.* 肺
      reminder 〔 rɪˋmaɪndɚ 〕 *n.* 提醒之物；起提醒作用的東西
      in large print 用大寫字母印刷   *die young* 早死

21. (**B**) 依句意，抽煙會「如何」危害健康，選 (B) **how**。

    The picture <u>warnings</u> have been used in Canada for the last four years.
          22
It has been very successful and has led to a 44% <u>increase</u> in smokers
                  23
wanting to kick the habit. At the moment EU tobacco manufacturers only
have to put written health warnings on cigarette packets <u>highlighting</u> the
                          24
dangers of smoking.

　　加拿大在過去四年來，已經採用這些具警告意味的圖片。這樣做很有效，而且已經使得想戒煙的人，增加了百分之四十四。目前歐盟的香煙製造商，只需要在香煙的包裝上，印書面的健康警告標語，來強調吸煙的危險即可。

last〔læst〕*adj.* 過去的　　*lead to* 導致；造成
kick〔kɪk〕*v.* 踢　　*kick the habit* 戒除這種習慣
at the moment 目前　　*EU* 歐盟；歐洲聯盟（= *European Union*）
tobacco〔tə'bæko〕*n.* 煙草
manufacturer〔͵mænjə'fæktʃərɚ〕*n.* 製造商
written〔'rɪtn̩〕*adj.* 寫成的；書面的

22.（**B**）依句意，選 (B) *warnings*〔'wɔrnɪŋz〕*n. pl.* 警告。而 (A) symbol
　　〔'sɪmbl̩〕*n.* 象徵，(C) commercial〔kə'mɝʃəl〕*n.* 商業廣告，
　　(D) decoration〔͵dɛkə'reʃən〕*n.* 裝飾，均不合句意。

23.（**A**）依句意，想戒菸的人數「增加」百分之四十四，選 (A) *increase*〔'ɪnkris〕
　　n. 增加。而 (B) 改變，(C) portion〔'porʃən〕*n.* 部份，(D) drop〔drɑp〕
　　n. 下降，均不合句意。【報紙上公布補習班的答案為 (D)，顯然錯誤。】

24.（**C**）空格本應填入 which highlight，引導形容詞子句，修飾先行詞
　　health warnings，而關代 which 可省略，但須將動詞 highlight 改
　　為現在分詞 highlighting，故選 (C) *highlighting*。
　　highlight〔'haɪ͵laɪt〕*v.* 強調

　　The aim of the campaign is to remind people of the damage the deadly
weed does to their body. It is believed that this would be to the best interest
of all people, <u>especially</u> teens who might be tempted to start smoking. These
　　　　　　　　25
dreadful photos may change the impression among teenagers that smoking
is cool and sexy.

　　這場活動的目的，是要提醒人們，這些致命的香煙會對身體造成傷害。一般認為，這對所有的人而言都有非常大的好處，尤其是青少年，因為他們可能會想開始抽煙。這些可怕的照片，可能會改變青少年認為抽煙很酷而且很性感的印象。

aim〔em〕n. 目的
campaign〔kæm'pen〕n. 運動；宣傳活動
remind〔rɪ'maɪnd〕v. 提醒　　deadly〔'dɛdlɪ〕adj. 致命的
weed〔wid〕n. 香煙；煙草　　*It is believed that*… 一般認為，…
interest〔'ɪntrɪst〕n. 利益
teens〔tinz〕n. pl. 青少年（= *teenagers*）
tempt〔tɛmpt〕v. 誘惑；使（人）想（做）
be tempted to V. 想要～　　dreadful〔'drɛdfəl〕adj. 恐怖的；可怕的
impression〔ɪm'prɛʃən〕n. 印象　　cool〔kul〕adj. 酷的；很棒的
sexy〔'sɛksɪ〕adj. 性感的

25. (**D**) 依句意，選 (D) *especially*〔ə'spɛʃəlɪ〕adv. 尤其；特別是。
而 (A) in fact「事實上」，(B) rather than「而不是」，(C) regarding
〔rɪ'gɑrdɪŋ〕prep. 關於，均不合句意。

Do plants have feelings? There is currently no reason to believe that
plants experience pain, because they are devoid of central nervous systems
and brains. Animals are able to feel pain <u>so that</u> they can use it for self-
　　　　　　　　　　　　　　　　　　　　　　　26
protection. <u>For example</u>, if you touch something hot and feel pain, you will
　　　　　　　27
learn from this <u>discomfort</u> that you should not touch that item in the future.
　　　　　　　　　　　28
　　植物有感覺嗎？目前沒有理由認為植物會覺得痛，因為它們沒有中樞神經
系統以及大腦。動物能感覺到痛，所以牠們能利用這種感覺來保護自己。舉例
來說，如果你碰到熱的東西而且覺得痛，那麼你就會從這種不舒服的感覺中學
到，以後你不該再碰那個東西。

currently〔'kɝəntlɪ〕adv. 目前；現在
experience〔ɪk'spɪrɪəns〕v. 經歷；體驗　　pain〔pen〕n. 痛
devoid〔dɪ'vɔɪd〕adj. 沒有…的；缺乏…的
be devoid of 沒有；缺乏　　nervous〔'nɝvəs〕adj. 神經的
central nervous system 中樞神經系統　　brain〔bren〕n. 腦
self-protection〔,sɛlfprə'tɛkʃən〕n. 自我防護；自我防衛
item〔'aɪtəm〕n. 項目；物品　　*in the future* 將來

26. (**D**) 依句意，選 (D) *so that*「以便於；所以」。而 (A) 雖然，(B) 因為，
(C) 當…時候，均不合句意。

27. (**C**) 依句意，選 (C) *For example*「例如；舉例來說」。而 (A) in contrast
「對比之下；相對地」，(B) before long「不久」，(D) to begin with
「首先」，均不合句意。

28. (**A**) 你會從這種「不舒服」的感覺中學到，以後你不該再碰那個東西，
故選 (A) *discomfort*〔 dɪsˋkʌmfət 〕*n.* 不舒服。而 (B) prescription
〔 prɪˋskrɪpʃən 〕*n.* 藥方；處方，(C) enjoyment〔 ɪnˋdʒɔɪmənt 〕*n.* 快
樂，(D) satisfaction〔ˏsætɪsˋfækʃən 〕*n.* 滿足；滿意，均不合句意。

On the other hand, plants cannot move <u>from place to place</u> and do not need
$\overline{}$
29

to learn to avoid certain things, so this sensation would be unnecessary.
From a physiological standpoint, plants are completely different from
animals. They cannot feel pain. Therefore, <u>unlike</u> animals' body parts,
30

many fruits and vegetables can be harvested over and over again without
dying.

另一方面，植物無法到處移動，也不需要學習避開某些事物，所以這種感覺
是不必要的。從生理學的觀點來看，植物和動物完全不同。它們感覺不到疼
痛。因此，和動物的身體器官不同的是，很多水果和蔬菜都可以一再地被收
割，而不會死。

> *on the other hand* 另一方面　　move〔 muv 〕*v.* 移動
> avoid〔 əˋvɔɪd 〕*v.* 避免　　certain〔ˋsɝtn̩ 〕*adj.* 某些
> sensation〔 sɛnˋseʃən 〕*n.* 感覺
> physiological〔ˏfɪzɪəˋladʒɪkl̩ 〕*adj.* 生理學上的
> standpoint〔ˋstændˏpɔɪnt 〕*n.* 觀點；看法
> completely〔 kəmˋplitlɪ 〕*adv.* 完全地
> part〔 part 〕*n.* 器官；部位　　harvest〔ˋharvɪst 〕*v.* 收割
> *over and over again* 一再地

29. (**B**) 依句意，選 (B) ***from place to place*** 「到處」。而 (A) from door to
door 「挨家挨戶」，(C) top〔tɑp〕 *n.* 頭頂　　toe〔to〕 *n.* 腳趾
from top to toe 「從頭到腳」，(D) case〔kes〕 *n.* 個案；情況
from case to case 「各個情況」，均不合句意。

30. (**C**) 依句意，「和…不同；不像…」選 (C) ***unlike***。

三、文意選填：

　　Falling in love is always magical.　It feels eternal as if love will last
³¹**(F) forever**.　We naively believe that somehow we are ³²**(I) free** from the
problems our parents had.　We are assured that we are destined to live
happily ever after.

　　談戀愛始終是奇妙的。它讓人感覺永恆，就好像愛會持續到永遠一樣。
我們天真地相信，不管怎麼樣，我們不會有父母曾有的問題。我們確信自己
注定從今以後都會過得很幸福。

> ***fall in love*** 戀愛　　　magical〔'mædʒɪkl̩〕*adj.* 神奇的；奇妙的
> feel〔fil〕*v.* 令人覺得　　eternal〔ɪ'tɝnl̩〕*adj.* 永恆的
> ***as if*** 好像　　last〔læst〕*v.* 持續
> naively〔nɑ'ivlɪ〕*adv.* 天真地
> somehow〔'sʌm,hau〕*adv.* 不知何故；不管怎麼樣
> ***be free from*** ~ 沒有~的；免於~的　　assure〔ə'ʃur〕*v.* 使確信
> ***be assured that*** 確信…　　destine〔'dɛstɪn〕*v.* 使注定
> ***be destined to V.*** 注定~　　happily〔'hæpɪlɪ〕*adv.* 幸福地
> ***ever after*** 從今以後

　　But as the magic fades and daily life ³³**(H) takes over**, it happens that
men, forgetting that men and women are supposed to be different, continue
to expect women to think and react the way men do; women, ³⁴**(C) similarly**,
expect men to feel and behave the way women do. ³⁵**(G) Instead of** taking
time to understand and respect each other, we become demanding, resentful,
judgmental, and intolerant.

　　但是當魔法逐漸消失，且被日常生活取代時，男人就會忘記男女應該是不同的，他們繼續期待女人能用男人的方式來思考和反應；而女人，同樣地，也期待男人能以女人的方式來感覺和表現。我們變得苛求、憤怒、愛批判而且心胸狹窄，不再花時間去了解和尊重彼此。

magic (ˈmædʒɪk) n. 魔法　　fade (fed) v. 逐漸消失
daily life 日常生活　　***take over*** 取代　　***be supposed to*** 應該
react (rɪˈækt) v. 反應　　similarly (ˈsɪmələ·lɪ) adv. 同樣地
behave (bɪˈhev) v. 行爲；舉止　　***instead of*** 取代；而不是
take time 花時間　　respect (rɪˈspɛkt) v. 尊重
demanding (dɪˈmændɪŋ) adj. 苛求的
resentful (rɪˈzɛntfḷ) adj. 憤怒的
judgmental (ˌdʒʌdʒˈmɛntḷ) adj. 批判的
intolerant (ɪnˈtɑlərənt) adj. 不能忍受的；心胸狹窄的

[36](B) Consequently, our relationships are filled with unnecessary disagreements and conflicts. Somehow, problems creep in, resentments build, and communication [37](A) breaks down. Mistrust increases and rejection and repression surface. The magic of love is then lost.

　　因此，我們的關係充滿了不必要的意見分歧和衝突。不知何故，問題悄悄來到，憤恨累積，加上溝通失敗。不信任感增加，而且出現了排斥和壓抑的情況。愛的魔法到那時便消失了。

consequently (ˈkɑnsəˌkwɛntlɪ) adv. 因此
relationship (rɪˈleʃənˌʃɪp) n. 關係　　***be filled with*** 充滿
unnecessary (ʌnˈnɛsəˌsɛrɪ) adj. 不必要的
disagreement (ˌdɪsəˈgrimənt) n. 意見的分歧
conflict (ˈkɑnflɪkt) n. 衝突　　creep (krip) v. 悄悄來到
resentment (rɪˈzɛntmənt) n. 憤恨　　build (bɪld) v. 累積
communication (kəˌmjunəˈkeʃən) n. 溝通　　***break down*** 失敗
mistrust (mɪsˈtrʌst) n. 不信任
rejection (rɪˈdʒɛkʃən) n. 排斥　　repression (rɪˈprɛʃən) n. 壓抑
surface (ˈsɝfɪs) v. 表面化；出現　　lost (lɔst) adj. 消失的

Very [38](E) few people are able to grow in love. Yet, it does happen. [39](J) As long as men and women are able to respect and accept their differences, love has a chance to blossom. Love is, [40](D) indeed, magical, and it certainly can last if we remember our differences and respect each other.

很少有人能在愛裡成長。但是，這樣的事眞的會發生。只要男女雙方能夠尊重和接受彼此的差異，愛就有機會發展。愛的確是奇妙的，而且如果我們記得彼此的差異並相互尊重，愛就一定能維持下去。

few (fju) *adj.* 少數的　　grow (gro) *v.* 成長
yet (jɛt) *conj.* 但是；然而　　***as long as*** 只要
accept (ək'sɛpt) *v.* 接受　　difference ('dɪfərəns) *n.* 不同；差異
blossom ('blɑsəm) *v.* 開花；發展　　indeed (ɪn'did) *adv.* 的確
certainly ('sɝtn̩lɪ) *adv.* 一定

四、閱讀測驗：

41-44 爲題組

For many years, I was convinced that my suffering was due to my size. I believed that when the weight disappeared, it would take old wounds, hurts, and rejections with it.

多年來，我深信我所受的苦都是因爲我的身材。我相信當這些體重消失時，它也會帶走從前的傷害、痛苦和排斥。

convinced (kən'vɪnst) *adj.* 確信的　　suffering ('sʌfərɪŋ) *n.* 痛苦
due to 由於　　size (saɪz) *n.* 身材　　weight (wet) *n.* 體重
wound (wund) *n.* 傷害　　hurt (hɝt) *n.* 傷害；痛苦
rejection (rɪ'dʒɛkʃən) *n.* 拒絕；排斥

Many weight-conscious people also mistakenly believe that changing our bodies will fix *everything*. Perhaps our worst mistake is believing that being thin equals being loved, being special, and being cherished. We fantasize about what it will be like when we reach the long-awaited goal. We work very hard to realize this dream. Then, at last, we find ourselves there.

　　許多注重體重的人，也都會誤認爲改變自己的體型，就能解決一切。也許我們最大的錯，就是認爲苗條等於被喜歡、特別而且會被疼愛。我們幻想著，當自己達到這個期待已久的目標時，會是什麼樣子。我們很努力地實現這個夢想。到最後，我們發現自己已經達成目標了。

conscious ('kɑnʃəs) adj. 注重…的
mistakenly (mə'stekənlɪ) adv. 錯誤地；誤解地
fix (fɪks) v. 解決　　worst (wɜst) adj. 最糟的
thin (θɪn) adj. 苗條的；瘦的　　equal ('ikwəl) v. 等於
cherish ('tʃɛrɪʃ) v. 珍惜；疼愛　　fantasize ('fæntə,saɪz) v. 幻想
long-awaited ('lɔŋə,wetɪd) adj. 期待已久的　　goal (gol) n. 目標
realize ('riə,laɪz) v. 實現；了解　　*at last* 最後；終於
We find ourselves there. 這句話字面的意思是「我們發現自己已經在那裡了。」引申爲「我們發現自己已經達成目標了。」there 在這裡指的是「達成目標」，這句話也可以說成：We find ourselves at our goal.

　　But we often gain back what we have lost. Even so, we continue to believe that next time it will be different. Next time, we will keep it off. Next time, being thin will finally fulfill its promise of everlasting happiness, self-worth, and, of course, love.

　　但是我們已經減掉的體重常常會再胖回來。即使如此，我們依然相信，下一次情況就會有所不同。下一次，我們就不會復胖。下一次，變瘦最後就會履行它的承諾，給我們永遠的幸福、自尊，當然還有愛。

continue (kən'tɪnju) v. 繼續；依然
keep off 使避開；不讓接近
keep it off 在這裡 it 是指「體重」，所以 keep it off 字面意思就是「不讓那些體重接近」引申爲「不會復胖」。
fulfill (fʊl'fɪl) v. 履行；實現　　promise ('prɑmɪs) n. 承諾
everlasting (,ɛvə'læstɪŋ) adj. 永遠的
happiness ('hæpɪnɪs) n. 幸福　　self-worth ('sɛlf'wɜθ) n. 自尊

It took me a long while to realize that there was something more for me to learn about beauty. Beauty standards vary with culture. In Samoa a woman is not considered attractive unless she weighs more than 200 pounds. More importantly, if it's happiness that we want, why not put our energy there rather than on the size of our body? Why not look inside? Many of us strive hard to change our body, but in vain. We have to find a way to live comfortably inside our body and make friends with and cherish ourselves. When we change our attitudes toward ourselves, the whole world changes.

我花了很長一段時間，才了解到對於美麗這件事，我還有更多東西要學。美麗的標準因文化而有所不同。在薩摩亞群島，除非一個女人體重超過兩百磅，才會被認為是很吸引人的。更重要的是，如果我們要的是幸福，那麼為何不多花點精力在那裡，而不是注意自己的身材？為什麼不往裡面看看？我們很多人都努力想要改變自己的體型，但卻徒勞無功。我們必須在自己的身體裡面，找到活得更自在的方式，要和自己做朋友，並珍惜自己。當我們改變對自己的態度之後，整個世界也會跟著改變。

while (hwaɪl) *n.* 時間　　vary ('vɛrɪ) *v.* 不同
vary with 因…而不同
Samoa (sə'moə) *n.* 薩摩亞群島 (*南太平洋中的群島*)
attractive (ə'træktɪv) *adj.* 有吸引力的
unless (ən'lɛs) *conj.* 除非　　weigh (we) *v.* 重…
rather than 而不是　　inside ('ɪn'saɪd) *adv.* 往裡面
strive (straɪv) *v.* 努力　　***in vain*** 徒勞無功
comfortably ('kʌmfətəblɪ) *adv.* 舒服地；自在地
make friends with 與…交朋友　　attitude ('ætə,tjud) *n.* 態度

41. (**B**) 本文是想要強調 ＿＿＿＿＿＿ 的重要性。
(A) 身材　　　　　　　　(B) 生活的態度
(C) 文化差異　　　　　　(D) 不同的審美標準

highlight ('haɪ,laɪt) *v.* 強調

42. (**A**) 第二段中，"*everything*" 這個字是指？
    (A) 所有的問題。 (B) 所有的特性。
    (C) 整個世界。 (D) 全部的事實眞相。

    property (ˈprɑpɚtɪ) *n.* 特性
    absolute (ˈæbsəˌlut) *adj.* 完全的　　truth (truθ) *n.* 事實；眞相

43. (**C**) 我們可以推論出這位作者的什麼事？
    (A) 作者是薩摩亞群島人。 (B) 作者減重成功。
    (C) 作者爲她/他的體重感到煩惱。
    (D) 作者可能在戰爭或意外中受過傷。

    infer (ɪnˈfɝ) *v.* 推論　　trouble (ˈtrʌbl̩) *v.* 使煩惱
    wound (wund) *v.* 傷害

44. (**C**) 根據作者的說法，那些一開始減了一些體重，但後來又胖回來的人，他們的共同看法是什麼？
    (A) 他們對於回復的體重感到生氣。
    (B) 他們不在乎回復的體重。
    (C) 他們對於未來的體重控制計劃感到樂觀。
    (D) 他們認爲自己應該放棄未來的體重控制計劃。

    common (ˈkɑmən) *adj.* 共同的　　view (vju) *n.* 看法
    regained (rɪˈgend) *adj.* 回復的
    indifferent (ɪnˈdɪfərənt) *adj.* 漠不關心的；不在乎的
    optimistic (ˌɑptəˈmɪstɪk) *adj.* 樂觀的　　**give up** 放棄

45-48 爲題組

On December 26, 2003, the worst earthquake in more than a decade devastated Bam, a historic city in Iran. At least 25,000 people died in the quake—nearly a third of the city's population. And thousands more were left homeless, hungry, and grieving.

二〇〇三年十二月二十六日，一場十餘年來最嚴重的地震，破壞了伊朗歷史古城巴姆。至少有二萬五千人死於這次的地震 —— 將近是該城人口的三分之一。另外還有數千人無家可歸，他們飢餓而且悲傷。

earthquake (ˈɝθˌkwek) n. 地震 (= *quake*)

worst (wɝst) adj. 最猛烈的　　decade (ˈdɛked) n. 十年

devastate (ˈdɛvəsˌtet) v. 破壞；蹂躪

Bam 巴姆 (伊朗東南方歷史古城)

historic (hɪsˈtɔrɪk) adj. 具有重大歷史意義的

Iran (aɪˈræn) n. 伊朗 (亞洲西部的共和國，首都德黑蘭)

at least 至少　　　nearly (ˈnɪrlɪ) adv. 將近

a third of ～的三分之一　　population (ˌpɑpjəˈleʃən) n. 人口

more (mor) adj. 另外的　　leave (liv) v. 使處於 (某種狀態)

homeless (ˈhomlɪs) adj. 無家可歸的　　grieve (griv) v. 悲傷

Bam was a city of mud-brick houses, old monuments and an ancient castle. But nearly everything crumbled in the disaster. One reason the earthquake caused such damage was that Bam's buildings were made mostly from baked mud. These buildings collapsed in heaps of dust and sand.

巴姆是個由泥磚屋、古紀念碑，及一座古堡所組成的城市。不過在這場災難中，幾乎所有東西都倒塌了。這場地震造成這麼大損害的原因之一，就是巴姆的建築物，大部分都是用烘土建造的。這些建築物倒塌後，變成大量的塵土和沙子。

mud (mʌd) n. 泥巴　　brick (brɪk) n. 磚頭

mud-brick (ˈmʌdˌbrɪk) adj. 泥磚製的

monument (ˈmɑnjəmənt) n. 紀念碑　　ancient (ˈenʃənt) adj. 古老的

castle (ˈkæsl̩) n. 城堡　　crumble (ˈkrʌmbl̩) v. 崩塌

disaster (dɪzˈæstə) n. 災難　　damage (ˈdæmɪdʒ) n. 損害

be made from 由～所製成　　mostly (ˈmostlɪ) adv. 大部分地

bake (bek) v. 烘培　　***baked mud*** 烘土

collapse (kəˈlæps) v. 倒塌　　heap (hip) n. (一) 堆

heaps of 大量的；許多的　　dust (dʌst) n. 塵土

sand (sænd) n. 沙子

Bam was best known for its 2,000-year-old castle built out of mud, straw, and the trunks of palm trees. The castle was so big that it was once the city of Bam itself. Public dwellings lined its ground level; a marketplace and two mosques also fit comfortably inside.

　　巴姆最著名的是一座有兩千年歷史的城堡，這座城堡是用泥巴、麥稈及棕櫚樹幹所建造的。這座城堡很大，它以前曾經是巴姆城本身。公共住宅排列在城堡的一樓周圍，裡面還有一個市集與兩座清眞寺。

be known for 以～聞名　　　*out of* 用…（材料）
straw〔strɔ〕*n.* 稻草；麥稈　　trunk〔trʌŋk〕*n.* 樹幹
palm tree 棕櫚樹　　once〔wʌns〕*adv.* 曾經
public〔'pʌblɪk〕*adj.* 公用的；公立的
dwelling〔'dwɛlɪŋ〕*n.* 住宅　　line〔laɪn〕*v.* 沿…排列
ground level 一樓　　marketplace〔'mɑrkɪt,ples〕*n.* 市場；市集
mosque〔mɑsk〕*n.* 清眞寺　　fit〔fɪt〕*v.* 符合；被容納
comfortably〔'kʌmfətəblɪ〕*adv.* 寬裕地

Bam once blossomed as a trading post on the Silk Road. In the 16th and 17th centuries, treasures from the Far East were carried along the road into the capital cities of Europe. Fifty years ago, teams of architects began restoring the historic treasures of the city. Ever since, thousands of visitors have come to admire them.

　　巴姆曾經因爲是絲路上的一個貿易站而非常繁榮。十六、七世紀時，來自遠東的寶物，沿著這條路運到歐洲的各個首都。五十年前，建築師所組成的團隊開始修復該城的歷史寶物。從那時起，已經有數千名遊客來這裡欣賞這些寶物。

blossom〔'blɑsəm〕*v.* 繁榮　　*trading post* 貿易站
Silk Road 絲路【古時中亞細亞與中國間的貿易路線，因以絲爲主要
　貿易品，故名】　　treasure〔'trɛʒɚ〕*n.* 寶物
Far East 遠東（西方國家對亞洲最東部地區的稱呼）
capital〔'kæpətl̩〕*adj.* 首都的　*n.* 首都
architect〔'ɑrkə,tɛkt〕*n.* 建築師
restore〔rɪ'stor〕*v.* 將（古建築物等）修復（成原狀）
ever since 從那以後一直　　visitor〔'vɪzɪtɚ〕*n.* 觀光客
admire〔əd'maɪr〕*v.* 欣賞

　　In the face of this tragedy, food and other supplies from around the world landed in the provincial capital of Kerman on Sunday.　With such support, spiritual leader Ayatollah Ali Khamenei vowed, "We will rebuild Bam stronger than before."

　　面臨這場悲劇的發生，來自世界各地的食物與其他補給品，已經在星期天運到克曼省首府。這些援助讓精神領袖阿亞托拉‧阿里‧卡美內誓言：「我們要把巴姆重建得比以前更堅固。」

> *in the face of* 面對　　tragedy〔'trædʒədɪ〕*n.* 悲劇；不幸事件
> supplies〔sə'plaɪz〕*n. pl.* 補給品　　land〔lænd〕*v.* 登陸；到達
> provincial〔prə'vɪnʃəl〕*adj.* 省的　　*Kerman* 克曼省
> support〔sə'port〕*n.* 支持；援助
> spiritual〔'spɪrɪtʃuəl〕*adj.* 精神（上）的；心靈的
> leader〔'lidə〕*n.* 領袖　　vow〔vau〕*v.* 發誓
> rebuild〔ri'bɪld〕*v.* 重建

45.（**A**）本文最有可能取材自 ＿＿＿＿＿＿＿＿。
　　(A) 報紙　　　　　　　　(B) 歷史教科書
　　(C) 書評　　　　　　　　(D) 與國際貿易有關的雜誌

> textbook〔'tɛkst,buk〕*n.* 教科書　　review〔rɪ'vju〕*n.* 評論
> on〔ɑn〕*prep.* 關於　　international〔,ɪntə'næʃən̩〕*adj.* 國際的
> trade〔tred〕*n.* 貿易

46.（**C**）巴姆最有名的是什麼？
　　(A) 漂亮的棕櫚樹。　　　(B) 常有地震。
　　(C) 一座由泥土和麥桿蓋成的古老城堡。
　　(D) 來自遠東地區的寶物。

> frequent〔'frikwənt〕*adj.* 時常發生的；頻繁的

47.（**D**）用烘土興建建築物，說明了 ＿＿＿＿＿＿＿＿。
　　(A) 爲什麼會發生這次的地震
　　(B) 爲什麼巴姆會收集這麼多的寶物
　　(C) 爲什麼巴姆會發展成爲貿易站
　　(D) 爲什麼這次的地震會造成如此巨大的損害

> collect〔kə'lɛkt〕*v.* 收集　　develop〔dɪ'vɛləp〕*v.* 發展

48. (**A**) 關於巴姆所發生的地震，下列何者正確？

　　(A) 大約有五萬人在這次地震中倖存。

　　(B) 送食物和補給品到巴姆的國家不多。

　　(C) 二〇〇三年發生的地震是該地有史以來第一次的地震。

　　(D) 巴姆城在地震發生後就會被遺棄。

　　survive〔sə'vaɪv〕v. 經歷（災難、事故等後）活下來；自…中生還
　　desert〔dɪ'zɜt〕v. 遺棄

49-52 為題組

　　Jet lag, caused by traveling between time zones, is becoming a common problem for frequent travelers: for 49 per cent it is only a nuisance and for 45 percent it is a real problem. It is caused by disruption to the internal biological clock, and may lead to digestive problems, tiredness, and sleep disruption.

　　時差是因為在不同時區間旅行所引起的，對時常旅行的人來說，時差已變成了常見的問題：對百分之四十九的人來說，那只是一件令人討厭的事，而對百分之四十五的人來說，時差則是一個大問題。它是由體內生理時鐘的混亂所引起的，而且可能會導致消化方面的問題，疲倦，以及睡眠時間混亂。

　　jet〔dʒɛt〕n. 噴射機　　　lag〔læg〕n. 落後
　　jet lag 飛機時差症（乘飛機旅行時，因時差過大引起的疲勞、神經過敏等）
　　zone〔zon〕n. 地區　　　***time zone*** 時區
　　common〔'kɑmən〕adj. 常見的　　　frequent〔'frikwənt〕adj. 時常的
　　per cent〔pə'sɛnt〕n. 百分之…（此為英式英語寫法，美式英語則為 percent）
　　nuisance〔'njusn̩s〕n. 令人討厭的事
　　disruption〔dɪs'rʌpʃən〕n. 混亂；中斷
　　internal〔ɪn'tɜnl̩〕adj. 體內的　　　biological〔ˌbaɪə'lɑdʒɪkl̩〕adj. 生物的
　　biological clock 生理時鐘　　　***lead to*** 導致
　　digestive〔daɪ'dʒɛstɪv〕adj. 消化的　　　tiredness〔'taɪrdnɪs〕n. 疲倦

　　Generally speaking, our biological clock is slightly disturbed if we just move into the next time zone, but jet lag becomes a problem once we have passed through three or four time zones. The body takes about one day to get over each hour of time difference.

一般而言，如果我們只是到鄰近的時區去，那麼我們的生理時鐘只會受到輕微地干擾，可是一旦我們通過三個或四個時區時，時差就會變成一個問題。每一個小時的時差，身體大概都要花一天才能加以克服。

> ***generally speaking*** 一般而言　　slightly (ˈslaɪtlɪ) adv. 稍微地
> disturb (dɪˈstɝb) v. 干擾　　next (nɛkst) adj. 鄰近的
> ***pass through*** 通過　　***get over*** 克服

But the seriousness of jet lag problems also depends on our direction of travel. If we go north or south, we won't notice any difference, because there is usually no time zone change. However, if we travel west we will be in advance of ourselves as far as our internal clock is concerned, and problems may arise. A west-to-east journey, on the other hand, makes us late compared to the local time. It often demands even greater effort in adjustment since we are not quick enough to catch up with the new time schedule. Therefore, a trip from New York to Los Angeles often causes fewer problems than a Los Angeles-New York trip.

但是時差問題的嚴重性，也要視我們的旅行方向而定。如果我們是往北方或南方去，那麼就不會注意到任何差別，因為時區通常不會有所改變。然而，如果我們到西方旅行，對我們的生理時鐘而言，我們就會超前自己，那麼可能就會發生問題。反過來說，由西往東的旅行，會使我們的生理時鐘與當地時間相較之下，變得比較晚。我們通常需要更加費力去調適，因為我們跟上新時間表的速度不夠快。因此，從紐約到洛杉磯旅行所引起的問題，常常比從洛杉磯到紐約還要少。

> seriousness (ˈsɪrɪəsnɪs) n. 嚴重性　　***depend on*** 視…而定
> direction (dəˈrɛkʃən) n. 方向　　notice (ˈnotɪs) v. 發覺；注意到
> ***in advance of*** 在…之前；超越　　***as far as…concerned*** 就…而言
> arise (əˈraɪz) v. 發生　　journey (ˈdʒɝnɪ) n. 旅行
> ***on the other hand*** 反過來說　　compare (kəmˈpɛr) v. 比較
> ***compared to*** 與…相比　　local (ˈlokḷ) adj. 當地的
> demand (dɪˈmænd) v. 需要　　effort (ˈɛfɚt) n. 努力
> adjustment (əˈdʒʌstmənt) n. 調整；調適　　***catch up with*** 趕上
> schedule (ˈskɛdʒul) n. 行程表；時間表
> ***New York*** 紐約市 (美國最大的城市，位於美國東岸)
> ***Los Angeles*** 洛杉磯 (美國加利福尼亞州的一城市，位於美國西岸)

49. (**A**) 罹患時差症的旅行者，在 ＿＿＿＿＿＿＿＿ 方面有問題。

    (A) 調整他的生理時鐘

    (B) 知道噴射機的方向

    (C) 了解他飛行的距離

    (D) 逐漸習慣新環境的天氣

    suffer from 罹患　　　adjust〔ə'dʒʌst〕*v.* 調整

    distance〔'dɪstəns〕*n.* 距離　　　flight〔flaɪt〕*n.* 飛行

    get used to 逐漸習慣於

50. (**D**) 如果有人要跨越三個時區旅行，他大約需要 ＿＿＿＿＿＿ 小時來克服
    他的時差問題。

    (A) 二十四　　　　　　　　　(B) 三十六

    (C) 四十八　　　　　　　　　(D) 七十二

51. (**B**) 當一個人 ＿＿＿＿＿＿ 旅行的時候，他可能會罹患最嚴重的時差症。

    (A) 由東向西　　　　　　　　(B) 由西向東

    (C) 由北向南　　　　　　　　(D) 由南向北

    suffer〔'sʌfɚ〕*v.* 遭受　　　case〔kes〕*n.* 病症

52. (**A**) 本文的主旨是 ＿＿＿＿＿＿ 。

    (A) 要解釋造成時差問題的原因

    (B) 要教我們如何避免時差問題

    (C) 要解釋時區間的差異

    (D) 要示範減輕時差問題的程度的方法

    cause〔kɔz〕*n.* 原因　　　avoid〔ə'vɔɪd〕*v.* 避免

    lessen〔'lɛsn̩〕*v.* 減輕　　　degree〔dɪ'gri〕*n.* 程度

53-56 為題組

    Originally from tropical South America, the red fire ant gained entry
to the United States through the port of Mobile, Alabama in the late 1930s
on cargo ships, but the first colony of the red ants was not found until 1942
by a 13-year-old boy in his backyard.

　　紅火蟻原本來自於熱帶地區的南美洲，牠們在 1930 年代後期，跟著貨船從阿拉巴馬的墨比爾港進入美國，但是直到 1942 年，一名十三歲的男孩才在他家後院發現了第一個紅火蟻群。

> originally (əˈrɪdʒənḷɪ) adv. 原本
> tropical (ˈtrɑpɪkḷ) adj. 位於熱帶的　　**red fire ant**　紅火蟻
> gain (gen) v. 得到　　　entry (ˈɛntrɪ) n. 進入
> **gain entry to**　進入 (= enter)　　　port (port) n. 港口
> Alabama (ˌæləˈbæmə) n. 阿拉巴馬州 (位於美國東南部)
> cargo (ˈkɑrgo) n. 貨物　　**cargo ship**　貨船
> colony (ˈkɑlənɪ) n. (生長或生活在一起的) 聚落；群體
> backyard (ˈbækˌjɑrd) n. 後院

　　It immediately began to thrive in the new land and colonies spread quickly throughout the southeastern states. By 1975 the red imported fire ant had colonized over 52 million hectares of the United States. Now, it has infested more than 275 million hectares in the country.

　　紅火蟻很快就開始在新的土地上繁衍，而且蟻群快速蔓延遍布東南部各州。到了 1975 年，美國已經有超過五千兩百萬公頃的土地上，有入侵紅火蟻聚居。現在，紅火蟻已經破壞了美國境內，超過兩億七千五百萬公頃的土地。

> immediately (ɪˈmidɪɪtlɪ) adv. 立刻；馬上
> thrive (θraɪv) v. (動植物) 成長；繁衍
> spread (sprɛd) v. 散播；蔓延　　state (stet) n. 州
> imported (ɪmˈportɪd) adj. 進口的
> **red imported fire ant**　入侵紅火蟻 (= RIFA)
> colonize (ˈkɑləˌnaɪz) v. 聚居　　hectare (ˈhɛktɛr) n. 公頃
> infest (ɪnˈfɛst) v. (害蟲) 破壞 (某地)

　　Red imported fire ants build mounds in any type of soil. They also make mounds indoors. Each nest used to have but one queen, but now many mounds are often found with multiple queens. With multiple queens at work, its population increases rapidly. It's common to find a nest with over 25,000 workers.

入侵紅火蟻在任何一種土壤中，都可以建造蟻丘。牠們也可以在室內建造蟻丘。以前每個蟻丘只有一個蟻后，但是現在在許多蟻丘中，常常都可以發現很多隻蟻后。由於有很多隻蟻后在工作，所以紅火蟻的數量迅速增加。要找到一個超過兩萬五千隻工蟻的蟻窩是很平常的事。

mound〔maʊnd〕*n.* 小丘；蟻丘　　***used to*** 以前

but〔bʌt〕*adv.* 只有　　queen〔kwin〕*n.*（蜂蜜、螞蟻等的）女王

multiple（'mʌltəpl̩）*adj.* 多數的；許多的

at work 在工作

population（ˌpɑpjə'leʃən）*n.* 人口；動植物的總數

increase〔ɪn'kris〕*v.* 增加　　rapidly（'ræpɪdlɪ）*adv.* 迅速地

common（'kɑmən）*adj.* 普通的；常見的

worker（'wɝkə）*n.* 工蟻

Red imported fire ants can cause a number of problems. They construct their colonies on precious farmland, invading crops while searching for insects underground.

入侵紅火蟻會引起很多問題。牠們在珍貴的農地上築巢，當牠們在地底下尋找昆蟲時，也侵害了農作物。

a number of 很多的

construct〔kən'strʌkt〕*v.* 建造　　precious（'prɛʃəs）*adj.* 珍貴的

farmland（'fɑrmˌlænd）*n.* 農地　　invade〔ɪn'ved〕*v.* 入侵；侵害

crop〔krɑp〕*n.* 農作物　　***search for*** 尋找

insect（'ɪnsɛkt）*n.* 昆蟲

underground（'ʌndə'graʊnd）*adv.* 在地下

They also like to make their mounds in sunny areas, heavily infesting lawns and pastures. They can quickly strip fruit trees of their fruit. Small birds such as baby quails are fair game to the expanding colony. They appear to be attracted to electromagnetic fields and attack electrical insulation or wire connections. They can cause electrical shorts, fires, and other damage to electrical equipment. Worst of all, their stings can be fatal to livestock and humans.

牠們還喜歡在有陽光的地方築巢，嚴重破壞草地和牧場。牠們可以很快地吃掉果樹的果實。而像小鵪鶉這類的小鳥，則是牠們擴張聚落時，會攻擊的對象。牠們似乎會受到電磁場的吸引，而攻擊電的絕緣體或電線。牠們會造成電線短路、火災，還有與電器設備相關的其他災害。最糟糕的是，被牠們螫傷的家畜和人類可能會死掉。

sunny〔'sʌnɪ〕adj. 陽光充足的

heavily〔'hɛvɪlɪ〕adv. 猛烈地；大大地　　lawn〔lɔn〕n. 草坪

pasture〔'pæstʃɚ〕n. 牧場　　strip〔strɪp〕v. 剝奪

quail〔kwel〕n. 鵪鶉　　*fair game*（攻擊的）適當對象

expanding〔ɪk'spændɪŋ〕adj. 正在擴張的

appear〔ə'pɪr〕v. 似乎　　attract〔ə'trækt〕v. 吸引

be attracted to 受⋯吸引

electromagnetic〔ɪ,lɛktromæg'nɛtɪk〕adj. 電磁的

electromagnetic field 電磁場　　attack〔ə'tæk〕v. 攻擊

electrical〔ɪ'lɛktrɪkḷ〕adj. 與電有關的

insulation〔,ɪnsə'leʃən〕n. 絕緣體　　wire〔waɪr〕n. 電線

connection〔kən'nɛkʃən〕n. 連接；電路；連結物

short〔ʃɔrt〕n. 短路　　equipment〔ɪ'kwɪpmənt〕n. 設備

worst of all 最糟糕的是　　sting〔stɪŋ〕n. 螫傷

fatal〔'fetḷ〕adj. 致命的　　livestock〔'laɪv,stɑk〕n. 家畜

53.（**B**）美國第一個紅火蟻窩是什麼時候發現的？

(A) 在 1930 年代。　　　　(B) 在 1942 年。

(C) 在 1975 年。　　　　　(D) 在 1975 年之後。

54.（**C**）根據本文，下列哪一個是正確的？

(A) 每一個紅火蟻窩都有一隻蟻后。

(B) 紅火蟻最初是在北美洲被發現的。

(C) 紅火蟻可以很快地繁殖幼蟻。

(D) 紅火蟻不會在房子裡面建造蟻丘。

reproduce〔,riprə'djus〕v. 繁殖

55. (**D**) 紅火蟻會造成哪一類的問題？

　　　(A) 健康、社會，以及農業的問題。
　　　(B) 健康、社會，以及環境的問題。
　　　(C) 社會、環境，以及農業的問題。
　　　(D) 健康、農業，以及環境的問題。

　　　social ('soʃəl) adj. 社會的
　　　environmental (ɪn,vaɪrən'mɛntḷ) adj. 環境的
　　　agricultural (,ægrɪ'kʌltʃərəl) adj. 農業的

56. (**C**) 本文的目的是什麼？

　　　(A) 要尋求協助來消滅紅火蟻。
　　　(B) 要勸導人們保護紅火蟻。
　　　(C) 要提供關於紅火蟻的資訊。
　　　(D) 要尋求政府的協助，來控制紅火蟻。

　　　urge (ɝdʒ) v. 力勸　　protect (prə'tɛkt) v. 保護
　　　provide (prə'vaɪd) v. 提供
　　　information (,ɪnfə'meʃən) n. 資訊　　seek (sik) v. 尋找；尋求
　　　government ('gʌvənmənt) n. 政府
　　　control (kən'trol) v. 控制；抑制

第貳部分：非選擇題

一、翻譯題

1. Human beings $\left\{ \begin{array}{l} \text{have very limited knowledge} \\ \text{have very little knowledge} \\ \text{know very little} \end{array} \right\}$

about outer space, but we've been interested in it for a long time.

2. The fast development of space technology has

$\left\{ \begin{array}{l} \text{enabled us to} \\ \text{made it possible for us to} \end{array} \right\}$ explore the $\left\{ \begin{array}{l} \text{secrets} \\ \text{mysteries} \end{array} \right\}$ of space.

二、英文作文：

In the English class last week, our teacher taught us Lesson 30 "We Are the World." *However*, I became very bored, and started drifting off and daydreaming. Before I knew it, I was sound asleep and having the most unusual dream.

I dreamed that I was teaching up in front of the class. I was trying to explain the fundamentals of English grammar, when much to my surprise all my students fell asleep. They were snoring, breathing loudly and even drooling! *At first*, I was embarrassed and frustrated, but then I started to get very upset. *Therefore*, I yelled "Wake up!" at the top of my lungs to my snoozing students. My scream startled and scared them to death! Suddenly, in fright, I opened my eyes and realized that my teacher was yelling those exact same words at me! Wow! What a shocking surprise! I immediately realized that I had fallen asleep and had dreamed about a situation that was happening to me at that very moment.

drift〔drɪft〕v. 漂流　　***drift off*** 迷迷糊糊地睡去；出神
daydream〔'de.drim〕v. 作白日夢　　***before I know it*** 很快地
be sound asleep 睡得很熟　　fundamental〔.fʌndə'mɛntl〕n. 原理
grammar〔'græmə〕n. 文法
much to one's ***surprise*** 令某人感到非常驚訝的是
snore〔snor〕v. 打呼　　drool〔drul〕v. 流口水
embarrassed〔ɪm'bærəst〕adj. 覺得尷尬的
frustrated〔'frʌstretɪd〕adj. 受挫的　　upset〔ʌp'sɛt〕adj. 不高興的
yell〔jɛl〕v. 大叫　　***at the top of*** one's ***lungs*** 以最大的音量
snoozing〔'snuzɪŋ〕adj. 打瞌睡的　　scream〔skrim〕n. 尖叫
startle〔'startl〕v. 驚嚇　　scare〔skɛr〕v. 使害怕
scare sb. ***to death*** 把某人嚇得半死　　fright〔fraɪt〕n. 驚嚇
exact〔ɪg'zækt〕adj. 確切的；恰好的　　wow〔waʊ〕interj. 哇啊
shocking〔'ʃakɪŋ〕adj. 可怕的；令人震驚的
very〔'vɛrɪ〕adj. 正是那一個的

「94 年大學入學學科能力測驗英文科試題」，經過我們校對後，發現有下列錯誤：

題　　　號	修　　正　　意　　見
第 12 題	*Without* much contact with.... → ***No having had*** much contact with.... 因為句中已經有了 with，不得再用 without，而且依句意，應用完成式分詞，表示先發生，句意才清楚。
第 14 題	... so that they *may* appear.... → ... so that they ***might*** appear.... 主要子句動詞用過去式，根據句意，so that 之後也應該用過去式的 might。
第 16 – 20 題	最後一句：... that *marks* his films with.... 　　　　　→ ... that ***would mark*** his films with....
第 21 – 25 題	第一段：... *At the moment* EU.... 　　　　　→ ... ***At the moment,*** EU.... 第二段：... this would be *to* the best interest of all people.... 　　　　　→ ... this would be ***in*** the best interest of all people.... 因為 in the interest of *one* 對某人有利；為了某人的利益 　　　　　= to *one's* interest
第 45 題	*This passage ... a(n)* → This passage ... ***a***
第 53 題	... *the red ant....* → ... the red ***fire*** ant....
第 54 題	(A) (B) (C) (D) ... *the red ant....* → ... the red ***fire*** ant.... (C)　須將 young ants 去掉 (D)　... *the* house. → ... ***a*** house.
第 55 題	... *the red ant....* → ... the red ***fire*** ant....
第 56 題	(A) (B) (C) (D) ... *the red ant....* → ... the red ***fire*** ant....

九十四年度學科能力測驗（英文考科）大考中心公佈答案

題 號	答 案	題 號	答 案	題 號	答 案
1	A	21	B	41	B
2	C	22	B	42	A
3	B	23	A	43	C
4	B	24	C	44	C
5	A	25	D	45	A
6	D	26	D	46	C
7	D	27	C	47	D
8	A	28	A	48	A
9	C	29	B	49	A
10	D	30	C	50	D
11	B	31	F	51	B
12	C	32	I	52	A
13	D	33	H	53	B
14	A	34	C	54	C
15	B	35	G	55	D
16	B	36	B	56	C
17	A	37	A		
18	D	38	E		
19	A	39	J		
20	D	40	D		

94年學科能力測驗（英文科）各級分人數統計

級 分	人 數	百分比	累計人數	累計百分比
15	4580	2.92	156887	100.00
14	7253	4.62	152307	97.08
13	9003	5.74	145054	92.46
12	10696	6.82	136051	86.72
11	10792	6.88	125355	79.90
10	11670	7.44	114563	73.02
9	12445	7.93	102893	65.58
8	14217	9.06	90448	57.65
7	14242	9.08	76231	48.59
6	14481	9.23	61989	39.51
5	15264	9.73	47508	30.28
4	17518	11.17	32244	20.55
3	12369	7.88	14726	9.39
2	2288	1.46	2357	1.50
1	65	0.04	69	0.04
0	4	0.00	4	0.00

※ 今年英文非選擇題原始總分爲二十八分，平均得分九點七分，與去
年水準差不多。非選擇題的第一題爲翻譯題，有五萬八千多人零分，
比率高達三成六；而拿到滿分八分者，不到三百人。作文部分是看
圖說故事，結果只有兩人拿到滿分二十分，有兩萬多名考生拿零分，
比率高達一成三。（資料來源：聯合報 94.2.24）

心得筆記欄

九十三年大學入學學科能力測驗試題
英文考科

第壹部份：單一選擇題

一、詞彙與慣用語（15％）

說明： 第1至15題，每題選出最適當的一個選項，標示在答案卡之「選擇題答案區」。每題答對得1分，答錯不倒扣。

1. I called the airline to _____ my flight reservation a week before I left for Canada.

   (A) expand　　　(B) attach　　　(C) confirm　　　(D) strengthen

2. In order to write a report on stars, we decided to _____ the stars in the sky every night.

   (A) design　　　(B) seize　　　(C) quote　　　(D) observe

3. Julie wants to buy a _____ computer so that she can carry it around when she travels.

   (A) memorable　(B) portable　(C) predictable　(D) readable

4. My grandmother likes to surprise people. She never calls _____ to inform us of her visits.

   (A) beforehand　(B) anyhow　(C) originally　(D) consequently

5. As the tallest building in the world, Taipei 101 has become a new _____ of Taipei City.

   (A) incident　　(B) geography　(C) skylight　　(D) landmark

6. Many scholars and experts from all over the world will be invited to attend this yearly _____ on drug control.

   (A) reference　　(B) intention　(C) conference　(D) interaction

7. John had failed to pay his phone bills for months, so his telephone was _____ last week.
   (A) interrupted (B) disconnected
   (C) excluded (D) discriminated

8. The organic food products are made of natural ingredients, with no _____ flavors added.
   (A) accurate (B) regular (C) superficial (D) artificial

9. Jessica is a very religious girl; she believes that she is always _____ supported by her god.
   (A) spiritually (B) typically (C) historically (D) officially

10. Jane usually buys things on _____. Her purchases seem to be driven by some sudden force or desire.
    (A) accident (B) compliment (C) justification (D) impulse

11. The week-long rainfall has _____ landslides and flooding in the mountain areas.
    (A) set about (B) brought about
    (C) come about (D) put about

12. In the cross-lake swimming race, a boat will be _____ in case of an emergency.
    (A) standing by (B) turning on
    (C) getting on (D) running down

13. The ground is slippery. Hold onto the rope and don't _____.
    (A) put off (B) turn up (C) let go (D) take apart

14. _____ the weather, the athletic meetings will be held on time.
    (A) Instead of (B) In relation to
    (C) On behalf of (D) Regardless of

15. If people keep polluting the rivers, no fish there will survive _____.
   (A) at all cost　　　　　　(B) for a long while
   (C) in the long run　　　　(D) by no means

二、綜合測驗（15％）

說明：　第16至30題，每題一個空格，請依文意選出最適當的一個選項，標示
　　　　在答案卡之「選擇題答案區」。每題答對得 1 分，答錯不倒扣。

　　Whenever a Dalai Lama died, a search began for his reincarnation.
The ___16___ male child had to have certain qualities. ___17___ was the
ability to identify the belongings of his predecessor, or rather his previous
self. Another requirement was ___18___ he should have large ears, upward-
slanting eyes and eyebrows. Besides, one of his hands should bear a mark
like a conch-shell. The successful candidate, usually ___19___ two or
three, was then removed from his family to Lhasa to begin spiritual
training for his future role. The Panchen Lamas were chosen in a
similar way. The reincarnated leaders were always "discovered" in the
households of lowly families ___20___ noble ones. This was to ensure
that no single and powerful noble family could seize the title and pass it
to the next generation.

16. (A) chosen　　　(B) searching　(C) dead　　　(D) previous
17. (A) It　　　　　(B) All　　　　(C) One　　　　(D) This
18. (A) what　　　　(B) whether　　(C) why　　　　(D) that
19. (A) having aged　(B) aging　　　(C) to age　　　(D) aged
20. (A) relative to　　(B) rather than　(C) as a result of　(D) with regard to

　　The CAMBODIA DAILY is launching a world-wide campaign to
wipe out malaria in Cambodia. You can help save three lives for only
$5 by supporting this effort. Each and every dollar you contribute will
go ___21___ the purchase of family-sized insecticide-treated mosquito

nets costing $5 each. These nets are recognized by medical experts as the best hope for ___22___ the spread of malaria —— Cambodia's most deadly disease. ___23___ the Health Ministry and the Malaria Center, *The* CAMBODIA DAILY will distribute the nets to the most ___24___ areas of the country.

___25___ to this campaign and save three lives for only $5, send your donation to: American Assistance for Cambodia, P.O. Box 2716, GPO, New York, NY 10116. Credit Card donations are also accepted.

21. (A) towards　　(B) against　　(C) down　　(D) over
22. (A) expanding　(B) eliminating　(C) deleting　(D) assisting
23. (A) In view of　(B) In spite of　(C) In case of　(D) In conjunction with
24. (A) affected　　(B) frequent　　(C) effective　　(D) included
25. (A) Contributing　　　　(B) Contribute
　　(C) To contribute　　　　(D) For contributing

　　Learning style means a person's natural, habitual, and preferred way(s) of learning. Research about learning styles has identified ___26___ differences. For example, one study found various differences ___27___ boys and girls in sensory learning styles. Girls were ___28___ more sensitive to sounds and more skillful at fine motor performance than boys. Boys, ___29___, showed an early visual superiority to girls. They were, however, clumsier than girls. They performed poorly at a detailed activity ___30___ arranging a row of beads. But boys excelled at other activities that required total body coordination.

26. (A) cultural　　(B) racial　　(C) age　　(D) gender
27. (A) for　　(B) within　　(C) between　　(D) into
28. (A) very　　(B) both　　(C) still　　(D) thus
29. (A) similarly　(B) moreover　(C) in contrast　(D) in consequence
30. (A) according to　(B) next to　(C) such as　(D) because of

三、文意選填（10％）

說明：第 31 至 40 題，每題一個空格，請依文意在文章後所提供的 (A) 到(J)
　　　選項中分別選出最適當者，並將其英文字母代號標示在答案卡之「選
　　　擇題答案區」。每題答對得 1 分，答錯不倒扣。

　　Although stories about aliens have never been officially confirmed,
their existence has been widely speculated upon.

　　Many people believe that ＿＿31＿＿ from outer space have visited us
for centuries. Some say that life on Earth ＿＿32＿＿ "out there" and was
seeded here. Others say that aliens have ＿＿33＿＿ what happens on Earth,
and are responsible for quite a few legends, and that the ancient Greek
and Roman gods, ＿＿34＿＿ the fairies and dwarfs in many classical tales,
were in fact "space people" living here. Still ＿＿35＿＿ say that aliens
were responsible for the growth of highly evolved civilizations which
have ＿＿36＿＿ perished, including the Incan and Mayan civilizations
and the legendary Atlantis.

　　A lot of ancient civilizations, ＿＿37＿＿ the Egyptians, Hindus,
Greeks, and Mayans, have left writings and ＿＿38＿＿ which indicate
contacts with superior beings "from the stars." Many believe that the
aliens are here to help us, while others hold that the aliens intend us
＿＿39＿＿. Still others think that most aliens visit Earth to study us like
our scientists study primitive natives and animals,and have no interest
in helping us ＿＿40＿＿.

　　It is difficult to comment conclusively on these theories in general,
apart from saying that any and all of them might be possible. Maybe
time will tell.

(A) as well as	(B) beings	(C) drawings	(D) in any way
(E) kept an eye on	(F) like	(G) others	(H) originated
(I) since	(J) harm		

四、閱讀測驗（30％）

說明：第 41 至 55 題，每題請分別根據各篇文章之文意選出最適當的一個
選項，標示在答案卡之「選擇題答案區」。每題答對得 2 分，答錯
不倒扣。

41-44 為題組

　　A sense of humor is just one of the many things shared by Alfred
and Anthony Melillo, 64-year-old twin brothers from East Haven who
made history in February 2002. On Christmas Eve, 1992, Anthony
had a heart transplant from a 21-year-old donor. Two days before
Valentine's Day in 2002, Alfred received a 19-year-old heart, marking
the first time on record that twin adults each received heart transplants.

　　**"I'm 15 minutes older than him, but now I'm younger because
of my heart** and I'm not going to respect him," Alfred said with a grin,
pointing to his brother while talking to a roomful of reporters, who laughed
frequently at their jokes.

　　While the twins knew that genetics might have played a role in their
condition, they recognized that their eating habits might have also
contributed to their heart problems. "We'd put half a pound of butter
on a steak. I overdid it on all the food that tasted good, so I guess I
deserved what I got for not dieting properly."

　　The discussion moved to Anthony's recovery. In the five years
since his heart transplant, he had been on an exercise program where he
regularly rode a bicycle for five miles, swam each day, and walked a
couple of miles. He was still on medication, but not nearly as much as
Alfred, who was just in the early stage of his recovery.

"Right now I feel pretty young and I'm doing very well," Anthony said. "I feel like a new person." Alfred said his goal, of course, was to feel even better than his brother. But, he added, "I love my brother very much. We're very close and I'm sure we'll do just fine."

41. This article is mainly about _____.
    (A) the danger of heart transplant surgery
    (B) becoming young by getting a new heart
    (C) the effect of genetics on the heart
    (D) the twin brothers who received heart transplants

42. What did Alfred and Anthony have in common?
    (A) Lifespan.　　　　　　　　(B) Career goals.
    (C) A sense of humor.　　　　(D) Love for bicycling.

43. What did Alfred and Anthony think caused their heart problems?
    (A) Exercise.　　　　　　　　(B) Diet.
    (C) Surgery.　　　　　　　　 (D) Medicines.

44. Why did Alfred say, "**I'm 15 minutes older than him, but now I'm younger because of my heart**"?
    (A) His heart transplant surgery was more successful than Anthony's.
    (B) His recovery from the heart surgery was faster than Anthony's.
    (C) His exercise program was better than Anthony's.
    (D) His new heart was younger than Anthony's.

45-47 為題組

In 1993, the Metropolitan Museum of Art reluctantly handed over 363 pieces of gold, silver, precious stones, paintings, and sculptures back to Turkey after a court case. Following increasing calls for the return of artistic objects that were removed decades or centuries ago, some of the world's leading museums have signed a declaration that they will not hand back the ancient artifacts to their **countries of origin**. They say people all over the world have only been able to fully appreciate ancient civilizations because these museums have provided access to these artistic objects. The ancient civilizations would not be so deeply admired today if these ancient artifacts were not so widely available to an international public in major museums throughout Europe and America. For example, Egyptian culture would not have become so well-known if the museums had not put Egyptian mummies on show.

The British Museum has not signed the declaration, but says it fully supports it. Over the recent years, it has faced growing pressure to hand back the Elgin Marbles, sculptures taken from the Parthenon in Athens, Greece, in the 19th century. But the British Museum has said that the Museum is the best possible place for them. "They must remain here if the museum is to continue to achieve its aim, which is to **show the world to the world**," said the director of the museum.

45. What reason do the major museums provide for not handing back the ancient objects?
   (A) Only in the leading museums can the objects be fully appreciated by the world.
   (B) It is better for those objects to remain at a certain place than to be moved around.
   (C) They need those well-known ancient objects to attract people from all over the world.
   (D) Ancient civilizations can only be admired if they are removed from their home countries.

46. Which of the following is NOT mentioned as one of the "**countries of origin**" in the article?
    (A) Turkey.　　　(B) Britain.　　　(C) Egypt.　　(D) Greece.

47. What does "**the world**" mean in "**show the world to the world**"?
    (A) The global village.　　　　(B) The leading museums.
    (C) The ancient civilizations.　　(D) The international public.

48-51 為題組

    Some animals have organs in their bodies that produce light. When it is dark, they flash their lights on and off to signal to others of their species, to lure prey toward them, or to escape from predators.

    Some fish are found to produce light in the blackness of the sea. When night falls over the Red Sea, tiny flashlight fish rise to the surface for food, each with a pair of "headlamps," one beneath each eye. With the light produced by bacteria living there, they communicate with other flashlight fish to avoid getting too close to each other, so that the fish may spread out evenly to get enough food. And if a flashlight fish is threatened by a predator, it swims away in a zigzag path, flashing its light on and off very quickly to confuse the animal pursuing it.

    Certain land animals can also produce light. Fireflies, small beetles that live in many warmer parts of the world, use light to attract a mate. After darkness falls in some parts of North America, female fireflies gather on the ground. The males fly overhead, flashing light from the undersides of their bodies. As there are a number of species of firefly, the males of each kind flash their own particular signal. Recognizing the flashing code of her own species, a female signals back to the male, and he lands beside her.

On land as in the sea, living lights can be deceiving. When they are hungry, some female fireflies lure the males of other species to them. They flash a false response when these males signal overhead, but eat them when they land.

48. Which of the following is the best title for the article?
    (A) Mating of Flashlight Fish and Fireflies.
    (B) Darkness and Light.
    (C) Living Lights and Animal Communication.
    (D) Life on Land and in the Sea.

49. Flashlight fish in the Red Sea give out light at night _____.
    (A) when they come out for food
    (B) as they try to look for their companions
    (C) because they want to get rid of the bacteria
    (D) so that they can get close to other flashlight fish

50. According to the passage, NEITHER flashlight fish NOR fireflies send out light to _____.
    (A) attract a mate
    (B) lure their prey
    (C) escape from their enemies
    (D) find their way home

51. Which of the following statements about fireflies is true?
    (A) All kinds of fireflies use the same signals.
    (B) Fireflies use their headlamps to communicate.
    (C) Male fireflies may deceive females with false signals.
    (D) Female fireflies respond from the ground to males' signals.

52-55 為題組

Brooks, Bruce. **Everywhere**. HarperCollins, 1990.
ISBN0060207299. 70 pages.

Peanuts' beloved grandfather has suffered a heart attack.
Peanuts is sad over the possibility of losing his grandfather.
Dooley keeps Peanuts company while the adults in the family
attend to Grandfather. Dooley attempts to save the old man by
a ritual learned from comic books: killing a turtle and trading
his soul for Grandfather's. With the imaginative assistance of
Dooley, Peanuts discovers the healing power of hope and love.

Babbitt, Natalie. **Tuck Everlasting**. Farrar, 1975.
ISBN0374378487. 180 pages.

The Tuck family has discovered a spring whose water brings
eternal life. A man learns their secret and threatens to sell the
water to the highest bidder. Mrs. Tuck kills the man and is jailed
and sentenced to be executed. Though the family knows she
cannot be killed, they worry that their secret will be revealed
when they try to kill her.

Baylor, Byrd. **The Table Where Rich People Sit**. Simon &
Schuster, 1994. ISBN0684196530. 52 pages.

Around an old kitchen table, a young girl calls a family
meeting to show her parents that they should earn more money so
they can have nicer things. As she points out they are not sitting
at a table where rich people would sit, her parents calculate the
value of the desert hills, the blooming cactus, the calls of eagles,
and one another's company. Soon, she realizes that her poor
family is rich in things that matter in life. She concludes that this
is indeed a table where rich people sit.

Goble, Paul. **Beyond the Ridge**. Bradbury, 1989.
ISBN0027365816. 32 pages.

There is no death; only a change of worlds—the author delivers these reassurances to readers in this book, based on the customs of the Plains Indians in America. The book reads like a prayer, expressing specific beliefs about dying. It describes a woman who is called by her long-dead mother to go "beyond the ridge." After a steep climb, she discovers a world that is abundantly beautiful, and there she finds the familiar faces of people who have passed that way before her.

52. Which book is the thickest?
    (A) Everywhere.　　　　　(B) Tuck Everlasting.
    (C) The Table Where Rich People Sit.
    (D) Beyond the Ridge.

53. Which book was published in 1990?
    (A) Everywhere.　　　　　(B) Tuck Everlasting.
    (C) The Table Where Rich People Sit.
    (D) Beyond the Ridge.

    ※ 本題題目原為Which book *is*…? 時態錯誤，我們改為Which book *was*…?

54. Who wrote the book about Native Americans' view of death?
    (A) Bruce Brooks.　　　　(B) Natalie Babbitt.
    (C) Byrd Baylor.　　　　　(D) Paul Goble.

55. Who wrote the book which shows that money is not the only way to measure wealth?
    (A) Bruce Brooks.　　　　(B) Natalie Babbitt.
    (C) Byrd Baylor.　　　　　(D) Paul Goble.

第貳部份：非選擇題

一、翻譯題（10％）

說明：1. 請將以下兩個中文句子譯成正確、通順、達意的英文，並將答案寫
在「答案卷」上。

2. 請依序作答，並標明題號。每題 5 分，共 10 分。

1. 雖然 Lily 生來又瞎又聾，但她從來不氣餒。

2. 她的故事證明了，我們只要努力必能成功。

二、英文作文（20％）

說明：1. 依提示在「答案卷」上寫一篇英文作文。

2. 文長 120 個單詞（words）左右。

提示：請根據以下三張連環圖畫的內容，以 "One evening,…" 開頭，寫
一篇文章，描述圖中主角所經歷的事件，並提供合理的解釋與結局。

93年度學科能力測驗英文科試題詳解

第壹部分：單一選擇題

一、詞彙與慣用語：

1. (**C**) I called the airline to <u>confirm</u> my flight reservation a week before I left for Canada.

   我在動身前往加拿大的前一個禮拜，打電話到航空公司確認我預訂的班機。

   (A) expand〔 ɪk'spænd 〕 v. 擴大
   (B) attach〔 ə'tætʃ 〕 v. 繫上；附上 < *to* >
   (C) *confirm*〔 kən'fɝm 〕 v. 確認
   (D) strengthen〔'strɛŋθən 〕 v. 增強

   airline〔'ɛr͵laɪn 〕 n. 航空公司   flight〔 flaɪt 〕 n. 班機
   reservation〔͵rɛzɚ'veʃən 〕 n. 預訂   *leave for* 動身前往

2. (**D**) In order to write a report on stars, we decided to <u>observe</u> the stars in the sky every night.

   為了要寫關於星星的報告，我們決定每晚觀察天上的星星。

   (A) design〔 dɪ'zaɪn 〕 v. 設計   (B) seize〔 siz 〕 v. 抓住
   (C) quote〔 kwot 〕 v. 引用   (D) *observe*〔 əb'zɝv 〕 v. 觀察

   in order to V. 為了～

3. (**B**) Julie wants to buy a <u>portable</u> computer so that she can carry it around when she travels.

   茱麗想要買一部手提電腦，這樣她就可以在旅行的時候帶著它。

   (A) memorable〔'mɛmərəbl̩ 〕 adj. 難忘的
   (B) *portable*〔'portəbl̩ 〕 adj. 手提式的
   (C) predictable〔 prɪ'dɪktəbl̩ 〕 adj. 可預測的
   (D) readable〔'ridəbl̩ 〕 adj. 易讀的

   carry〔'kærɪ 〕 v. 攜帶   around〔 ə'raʊnd 〕 adv. 到處

4. (**A**) My grandmother likes to surprise people.　She never calls
  <u>beforehand</u> to inform us of her visits.

  我奶奶很喜歡給別人驚喜。她從不<u>事先</u>打電話通知我們她要來
  造訪。

  (A) ***beforehand*** (bɪ'for͵hænd) *adv.* 事先
  (B) anyhow ('ɛnɪ͵hau) *adv.* 無論如何
  (C) originally (ə'rɪdʒənlɪ) *adv.* 獨創性地；原本
  (D) consequently ('kɑnsə͵kwɛntlɪ) *adv.* 因此

  surprise (sə'praɪz) *v.* 使驚訝
  inform (ɪn'fɔrm) *v.* 通知　　visit ('vɪzɪt) *n.* 拜訪

5. (**D**) As the tallest building in the world, Taipei 101 has become a
  new <u>landmark</u> of Taipei City.

  台北 101 大樓是全世界最高的的建築物，現在已經變成了台北市
  的新<u>地標</u>。

  (A) incident ('ɪnsədənt) *n.* 事件
  (B) geography (dʒi'ɑgrəfɪ) *n.* 地理學
  (C) skylight ('skaɪ͵laɪt) *n.* 天窗
  (D) ***landmark*** ('lænd͵mɑrk) *n.* 地標

6. (**C**) Many scholars and experts from all over the world will be invited
  to attend this yearly <u>conference</u> on drug control.

  很多來自世界各地的學者與專家，將被邀請參加這場一年一度的
  毒品管制的<u>會議</u>。

  (A) reference ('rɛfərəns) *n.* 提及；參考
  (B) intention (ɪn'tɛnʃən) *n.* 意圖
  (C) ***conference*** ('kɑnfərəns) *n.* 會議
  (D) interaction (͵ɪntə'ækʃən) *n.* 互相作用

  scholar ('skɑlə) *n.* 學者　　expert ('ɛkspɜt) *n.* 專家
  attend (ə'tɛnd) *v.* 參加　　yearly ('jɪrlɪ) *adj.* 一年一度的
  drug (drʌg) *n.* 藥物；毒品

7. (**B**) John had failed to pay his phone bills for months, so his telephone was <u>disconnected</u> last week.

約翰好幾個月都無法支付他的電話費，所以他的電話上星期被<u>切斷</u>了。

(A) interrupt〔,ɪntə'rʌpt〕 v. 打斷

(B) ***disconnect***〔,dɪskə'nɛkt〕 v. 切斷（某人）的電話

(C) exclude〔ɪk'sklud〕 v. 除外

(D) discriminate〔dɪ'skrɪmə,net〕 v. 歧視；辨別

fail to V. 無法　　bill〔bɪl〕 n. 帳單

8. (**D**) The organic food products are made of natural ingredients, with no <u>artificial</u> flavors added.

有機食品是由天然的材料製成，沒有添加<u>人工</u>調味料。

(A) accurate〔'ækjərɪt〕 adj. 準確的

(B) regular〔'rɛgjələ〕 adj. 規律的

(C) superficial〔,supə'fɪʃəl〕 adj. 表面的

(D) ***artificial***〔,ɑrtə'fɪʃəl〕 adj. 人工的

organic〔ɔr'gænɪk〕 adj. 有機的

ingredient〔ɪn'gridɪənt〕 n. 原料；成份

flavor〔'flevə〕 n. 味道；調味品

9. (**A**) Jessica is a very religious girl; she believes that she is always <u>spiritually</u> supported by her god.

潔西卡是一位虔誠的女孩，她相信她的神總是在<u>精神上</u>支持她。

(A) ***spiritually***〔'spɪrɪtʃuəlɪ〕 adv. 精神上地

(B) typically〔'tɪpɪkḷɪ〕 adv. 典型地

(C) historically〔hɪs'tɔrɪkḷɪ〕 adv. 歷史上地

(D) officially〔ə'fɪʃəlɪ〕 adv. 正式地

religious〔rɪ'lɪdʒəs〕 adj. 虔誠的

support〔sə'port〕 v. 支持　　god〔gɑd〕 n. 神

10. (**D**) Jane usually buys things on <u>impulse</u>. Her purchases seem to be driven by some sudden force or desire.

珍通常會一衝動之下就買了東西。她在採購時似乎是被某種突然的力量或慾望所驅使。

(A) accident ('æksədənt) *n.* 意外

(B) compliment ('kɑmpləmənt) *n.* 稱讚

(C) justification (,dʒʌstəfə'keʃən) *n.* (正當化的) 辯護；理由

(D) *impulse* ('ɪmpʌls) *n.* 衝動

on impulse 一衝動之下

purchase ('pɜtʃəs) *n.* 購買　　drive (draɪv) *v.* 驅使

some (sʌm) *adj.* 某種　　sudden ('sʌdn̩) *adj.* 突然的

desire (dɪ'zaɪr) *n.* 慾望

11. (**B**) The week-long rainfall has <u>brought about</u> landslides and flooding in the mountain areas.

爲期一週的大雨導致山區發生山崩和水災。

(A) set about 著手；開始做；攻擊

(B) *bring about* 導致

(C) come about 發生 (= *happen*)

(D) put about 散布 (謠言)；謠傳

rainfall ('ren,fɔl) *n.* 降雨　　landslide ('lænd,slaɪd) *n.* 山崩

flooding ('flʌdɪŋ) *n.* 氾濫

12. (**A**) In the cross-lake swimming race, a boat will be <u>standing by</u> in case of an emergency.

在跨湖的游泳比賽中，將會有一艘船在一旁待命，以防有緊急狀況發生。

(A) *stand by* 站在旁邊；待命

(B) turn on 打開；使…興奮

(C) get on 搭上 (巴士等大型交通工具)

(D) run down 停止；耗盡

in case of 在 (遇到) …的時候；如果…

emergency (ɪ'mɝdʒənsɪ) *n.* 緊急情況

13. (**C**) The ground is slippery. Hold onto the rope and don't <u>let go</u>.
地上很滑。抓住繩子不要<u>放掉</u>它。

(A) put off 延期 (B) turn up 開大聲
(C) *let go* 放掉 (D) take apart 拆開

slippery〔'slɪpərɪ〕*adj.* 滑的
hold onto 抓住 rope〔rop〕*n.* 繩子

14. (**D**) <u>Regardless of</u> the weather, the athletic meetings will be held
on time. <u>不論天氣如何</u>，運動會將會準時舉行。

(A) instead of 代替；而不是 (B) in relation to 有關…
(C) on behalf of 代表
(D) *regardless of* 不管…如何；不論

athletic〔æθ'lɛtɪk〕*adj.* 運動的
athletic meeting 運動會 (此為英式用法，美國人用 athletic meet)
hold〔hold〕*v.* 舉行 *on time* 準時

15. (**C**) If people keep polluting the rivers, no fish there will survive
<u>in the long run</u>.
如果人類再繼續污染河川，<u>最後</u>將沒有魚能在那裡生存下去。

(A) at all cost 無論如何
(B) for a long while 持續很長一段時間
(C) *in the long run* 最後 (D) by no means 絕不

survive〔sə'vaɪv〕*v.* 生存；存活

二、綜合測驗：

Whenever a Dalai Lama died, a search began for his reincarnation.
The <u>chosen</u> male child had to have certain qualities. <u>One</u> was the ability
16 17
to identify the belongings of his predecessor, or rather his previous self.
Another requirement was <u>that</u> he should have large ears, upward-slanting
18
eyes and eyebrows. Besides, one of his hands should bear a mark like a
conch-shell.

　　每當一位達賴喇嘛過世時，就會開始尋找他的轉世喇嘛。被選上的男童，必須具備某些特質。其中一項便是辨別前任喇嘛所有物的能力，或更確切地說，是辨別他自己前身的能力。另一項必備條件是，男童必須具備大耳朵、上揚的眼型及眉毛。此外，有一隻手上得有海螺殼狀的記號。

Dalai Lama〔 dəˈlaɪ ˈlɑmə 〕n. 達賴喇嘛

search〔 sɜtʃ 〕n. 搜尋

reincarnation〔ˌreɪnkɑrˈneʃən 〕n. 轉世

certain〔ˈsɜtn̩ 〕adj. 某些　　male〔 mel 〕adj. 男性的

quality〔ˈkwɑlətɪ 〕n. 特質　　identify〔 aɪˈdɛntəˌfaɪ 〕v. 辨識

belongings〔 bəˈlɔŋɪŋz 〕n. pl. 所有物

predecessor〔ˌprɛdɪˈsɛsɚ 〕n. 前任（者）

rather〔ˈræðɚ 〕adv. 更確切地說

previous〔ˈpriviəs 〕adj. 之前的　　self〔 sɛlf 〕n. 自己

requirement〔 rɪˈkwaɪrmənt 〕n. 要求的事物；必備條件

upward〔ˈʌpwəd 〕adj. 向上的

slanting〔ˈslæntɪŋ 〕adj. 傾斜的　　eyebrow〔ˈaɪˌbrau 〕n. 眉毛

besides〔 bɪˈsaɪdz 〕adv. 此外　　bear〔 bɛr 〕v. 具有

mark〔 mɑrk 〕n. 痕跡；記號

conch〔 kɑŋk 〕n. 海螺　　shell〔 ʃɛl 〕n. 殼

16.（ **A** ）依句意，選 (A) ***chosen***〔ˈtʃozn̩ 〕adj. 被選上的。而 (B) searching〔ˈsɜtʃɪŋ 〕adj. 正在搜尋的，(C) 死的，(D) 之前的，均不合句意。

17.（ **C** ）文中說明轉世童子必須具備 certain qualities（某些特質），因此當提出第一項時，依句意，選 (C) ***One***「其中一個」。

18.（ **D** ）that 引導名詞子句，即 that he should have…eyebrows，做主詞 Another requirement 的補語。而 (A) what 是複合關代，但是在子句中，已有主詞 he，及受詞 large ears…eyebrows，顯然並不需要關係代名詞，故用法不合；而 (B) whether「是否」，(C) why「為何」，則不合句意。

The successful candidate, usually <u>aged</u> two or three, was then removed
            19
from his family to Lhasa to begin spiritual training for his future role. The
Panchen Lamas were chosen in a similar way. The reincarnated leaders
were always "discovered" in the households of lowly families <u>rather than</u>
                                                                        20
noble ones. This was to ensure that no single and powerful noble family
could seize the title and pass it to the next generation.

檢驗成功的候選人，通常年齡介於二、三歲之間，得離開家人到拉薩去，爲其
未來的角色，接受宗教上的訓練。班禪喇嘛也以類似的方式來遴選。轉世的領
導者一向都是在低下的家庭中被「發掘」，而非貴族家庭。如此做是要確保，沒
有任何單一有權的貴族家庭，能奪去這項頭銜，並傳給下一代。

> candidate (ˈkændəˌdet , -dɪt) n. 候選人
> remove (rɪˈmuv) v. 遷移；拿走；強行遣送
> Lhasa (ˈlɑsə , ˈlæsə) n. 拉薩
> spiritual (ˈspɪrɪtʃuəl) adj. 宗教上的；精神上的
> role (rol) n. 角色   ***Panchen Lama*** 班禪喇嘛
> reincarnated (ˌrɪɪnˈkɑrnetɪd) adj. 轉世的
> discover (dɪˈskʌvɚ) v. 發掘
> household (ˈhausˌhold) n. 家庭   lowly (ˈlolɪ) adj. 地位低的
> noble (ˈnobḷ) adj. 貴族的   ensure (ɪnˈʃur) v. 確保
> seize (siz) v. 抓住；奪去   title (ˈtaɪtḷ) n. 頭銜
> pass (pæs) v. 傳遞   generation (ˌdʒɛnəˈreʃən) n. 世代

19. (**D**) 「人 (who is) aged + 數字」表「某人是～歲」，爲固定用法，故
            選 (D) ***aged***。

20. (**B**) (A) relative to 和～有關連的；和～成比例的
            (B) ***rather than*** 而不是   (C) as a result of 由於
            (D) with regard to 關於

The CAMBODIA DAILY is launching a world-wide campaign to
wipe out malaria in Cambodia. You can help save three lives for only $5
by supporting this effort. Each and every dollar you contribute will go

towards the purchase of family-sized insecticide-treated mosquito nets
　　21

costing $5 each.　These nets are recognized by medical experts as the best

hope for eliminating the spread of malaria—Cambodia's most deadly
　　　　　　22

disease.　In conjunction with the Health Ministry and the Malaria Center,
　　　　　　　　23

The CAMBODIA DAILY will distribute the nets to the most affected areas
　　　　　　　　　　　　　　　　　　　　　　　　　　24

of the country.

　　束埔寨日報正在發起一項全球性的運動，要大家攜手消滅在束埔寨橫行的
瘧疾。如果你想以行動支持這項運動，只要五元，你就可以挽救三個人的生命。
你所捐的每一塊錢，都會拿去購買每個要價五元、並經由殺蟲劑特殊處理過的
家庭號蚊帳。這種蚊帳經過醫學專家的認可，是阻止瘧疾蔓延的最佳武器，而
瘧疾目前是束埔寨的頭號殺手。束埔寨日報將和衛生部，以及抗瘧疾中心共同
合作，把這些蚊帳分送到束埔寨最嚴重的疫區。

> Cambodia〔kæm'bodɪə〕*n.* 束埔寨（中南半島南部的一國，又稱高棉）
> daily〔'delɪ〕*n.* 日報　　launch〔lɔntʃ〕*v.* 展開；發動
> campaign〔kæm'pen〕*n.* 運動　***wipe out*** 消滅
> malaria〔mə'lɛrɪə〕*n.* 瘧疾　　support〔sə'port〕*v.* 支持
> effort〔'ɛfət〕*n.* 努力　　contribute〔kən'trɪbjut〕*v.* 捐（款）
> purchase〔'pɜtʃəs〕*n.* 購買　　insecticide〔ɪn'sɛktə,saɪd〕*n.* 殺蟲劑
> treat〔trit〕*v.*（用化學藥物）處理　　mosquito〔mə'skito〕*n.* 蚊子
> net〔nɛt〕*n.* 網　　***mosquito net*** 蚊帳
> recognize〔'rɛkəg,naɪz〕*v.* 認可
> medical〔'mɛdɪkl̩〕*adj.* 醫學的　　spread〔sprɛd〕*n.* 蔓延
> deadly〔'dɛdlɪ〕*adj.* 致命的　　disease〔dɪ'ziz〕*n.* 疾病
> ministry〔'mɪnɪstrɪ〕*n.*（政府單位）部　　***Health Ministry*** 衛生部
> distribute〔dɪ'strɪbjut〕*v.* 分發；分送

21. (**A**) 依句意，所有的錢都是「用來」購買蚊帳，故選 (A) ***go towards***
　　「被用於；被用來」(= *go to*)。

22. (**B**) 依句意，蚊帳是用來「阻止」瘧疾的蔓延，故選 (B) ***eliminating***。
　　eliminate〔ɪ'lɪmə,net〕*v.* 消除。而 (A) expand〔ɪk'spænd〕*v.* 擴張，
　　(C) delete〔dɪ'lit〕*v.* 刪除，(D) assist〔ə'sɪst〕*v.* 幫助，均不合句意。

23. (**D**) 依句意，柬埔寨日報將會和衛生部，以及抗瘧疾中心「一起」發送
蚊帳，故選 (D) ***in conjunction with*** 「和～一起」。而 (A) in view
of「有鑒於；由於」，(B) in spite of「雖然；儘管」，(C) in case of
「要是；倘若」，均不合句意。

24. (**A**) ***affected areas*** 災區；疫區
(B) frequent〔'frikwənt〕*adj.* 經常的，(C) effective〔ə'fɛktɪv〕*adj.* 有
效的，(D) included〔ɪn'kludɪd〕*adj.* 包含在內的，均不合句意。

<u>To contribute</u> to this campaign and save three lives for only $5, send
                25
your donation to: American Assistance for Cambodia, P.O. Box 2716,
GPO, New York, NY 10116. Credit Card donations are also accepted.

　　若您要捐款贊助這項活動，只要五塊錢，就能拯救三條生命，請將捐款
寄至「美國援助柬埔寨」，紐約州 10116，紐約市郵政信箱 2716 號。我們也
接受信用卡捐款。

　　donation〔do'neʃən〕*n.* 捐款　　assistance〔ə'sɪstəns〕*n.* 援助
　　P.O. Box 郵政信箱　　***GPO*** 郵政總局（ = *General Post Office* ）
　　accept〔ək'sɛpt〕*v.* 接受

25. (**C**) 這裡用不定詞表「目的」，故選 (C) ***To contribute***。對等連接詞 and，
連接兩個不定詞片語，第二個不定詞片語的 to 可省略。

Learning style means a person's natural, habitual, and preferred
way(s) of learning. Research about learning styles has identified <u>gender</u>
                                                                      26
differences. For example, one study found various differences <u>between</u>
                                                                  27
boys and girls in sensory learning styles. Girls were <u>both</u> more sensitive
                                                              28
to sounds and more skillful at fine motor performance than boys.

　　學習風格是指一個人天生的、習慣性的、和偏好的學習方式。關於學習風
格的研究，已經證實性別之間存有差異性。例如，有份研究發現，在感官的學
習風格方面，男孩與女孩之間有各種不同的差異。女孩子對聲音的敏感度比男
孩高，而且在從事細微的肌肉運動方面，女孩子也比男孩子更熟練。

style〔staɪl〕 n. 風格　　natural〔'nætʃərəl〕 adj. 天生的；天賦的
habitual〔hə'bɪtʃʊ(ə)l〕 adj. 習慣性的
preferred〔prɪ'fɜd〕 adj. 被喜好的
research〔rɪ'sɜtʃ, 'risɜtʃ〕 n. 研究（= study）
identify〔aɪ'dɛntə,faɪ〕 v. 確認；證明
various〔'vɛrɪəs〕 adj. 各種不同的
sensory〔'sɛnsərɪ〕 adj. 感官的；知覺的
sensitive〔'sɛnsətɪv〕 adj. 敏感的 < to >
skillful〔'skɪlfəl〕 adj. 熟練的 < at >　　fine〔faɪn〕 adj. 細微的
motor〔'motɚ〕 adj. 肌肉運動的
performance〔pɚ'fɔrməns〕 n. 實行；動作

26. (**D**) 依句意，後面的研究指出，「男孩和女孩」在學習風格的差異，故選
　　(D) **gender**〔'dʒɛndɚ〕 n. 性別。而 (A) cultural〔'kʌltʃərəl〕 adj. 文化的，
　　(B) racial〔'reʃəl〕 adj. 種族的，(C) age「年齡」，均不合句意。

27. (**C**) **the difference between** A **and** B　A 和 B 之間的差異

28. (**B**) **both** A **and** B　A 和 B 兩者

Boys, <u>in contrast</u>, showed an early visual superiority to girls. They were,
　　　　29
however, clumsier than girls. They performed poorly at a detailed activity
<u>such as</u> arranging a row of beads. But boys excelled at other activities that
　　30
required total body coordination.
相較之下，在視覺方面的敏感度，男孩子在早期就表現得比女孩子好。然而他
們的動作卻比女孩子笨拙。他們在做複雜或精細的動作時，像是一串珠子的排
列，就表現得不好。但是男孩子卻擅長做其他需要整個肢體協調的動作。

visual〔'vɪʒʊəl〕 adj. 視覺的
superiority〔sə,pɪrɪ'ɔrətɪ〕 n. 優越 < to >
clumsy〔'klʌmzɪ〕 adj. 笨拙的　　perform〔pɚ'fɔrm〕 v. 表現
detailed〔'diteld, dɪ'teld〕 adj. 精細的；複雜的
arrange〔ə'rendʒ〕 v. 排列　　row〔ro〕 n.（一）排
bead〔bid〕 n. 有孔小珠　　excel〔ɪk'sɛl〕 v. 突出；勝過他人 < at >
require〔rɪ'kwaɪr〕 v. 需要　　total〔'totl〕 adj. 全部的；整體的
coordination〔ko,ɔrdn̩'eʃən〕 n. 協調

29. (**C**) 依句意，前面是說女孩子表現好的方面，後面是說男孩子表現好的
方面，前後有「對照」的意味，故選 (C) *in contrast*「相較之下；
對比之下」。而 (A) similarly〔'sɪmɪləlɪ〕*adv.* 同樣地，(B) moreover
〔mor'ovə〕*adv.* 此外，(D) in consequence「因此」，均不合句意。

30. (**C**) 依句意，舉例說明什麼是複雜精細的行動，故選 (C) *such as*「像
是」。而 (A) according to「根據」，(B) next to「在…隔壁；幾乎」，
(D) because of「因爲」，均不合句意。

三、文意選填：

Although stories about aliens have never been officially confirmed,
their existence has been widely speculated upon.

雖然有關於外星人的故事，從來沒有被正式地證實過，但是它們的存在，
一直被廣泛地猜測。

> alien〔'elɪən〕*n.* 外星人　　officially〔ə'fɪʃəlɪ〕*adv.* 正式地
> confirm〔kən'fɝm〕*v.* 證實；確認　　existence〔ɪg'zɪstəns〕*n.* 存在
> widely〔'waɪdlɪ〕*adv.* 廣泛地　　speculate〔'spɛkjə‚let〕*v.* 猜測；思考

Many people believe that [31](**B**) beings from outer space have visited
us for centuries. Some say that life on Earth [32](**H**) originated "out there"
and was seeded here. Others say that aliens have [33](**E**) kept an eye on
what happens on Earth, and are responsible for quite a few legends, and
that the ancient Greek and Roman gods, [34](**A**) as well as the fairies and
dwarfs in many classical tales, were in fact "space people" living here. Still
[35](**G**) others say that aliens were responsible for the growth of highly evolved
civilizations which have [36](**I**) since perished, including the Incan and
Mayan civilizations and the legendary Atlantis.

許多人認爲，外太空的生物已經來拜訪我們好幾世紀了。有一些人說，在
地球上的生物起源於「外太空」，而在這裡成長。有些人則說，外星人一直密切
在注意地球上所發生的事情，而且是造成相當多傳說的原因，而古希臘、羅馬
的神，和許多經典故事中出現的小仙女及侏儒，事實上就是住在地球上的「外
太空的人」。還有些人說，外星人是造成高度發展的文明國家消失的原因，其中
包括印加文明、馬雅文明，以及傳說中的亞特蘭提斯島。

being〔'biɪŋ〕n. 生物　　***outer space*** 外太空
originate〔ə'rɪdʒə‚net〕v. 起源　　seed〔sid〕v. 在～播種、成長
keep an eye on 密切注意　　***be responsible for*** 是造成～的原因
quite a few 相當多的（= *many*）
legend〔'lɛdʒənd〕n. 傳說；傳奇故事　　ancient〔'enʃənt〕adj. 古代的
Greek〔grik〕adj. 希臘的　　n. 希臘人　　***as well as*** 以及
fairy〔'fɛrɪ〕n. 小仙女　　dwarf〔dwɔrf〕n. 侏儒
classical〔'klæsɪkḷ〕adj. 古典的；經典的
some…others…still others… 有些…，有些…，還有一些…
tale〔tel〕n. 故事　　evolve〔ɪ'vɑlv〕v. 發展
civilization〔‚sɪvḷə'zeʃən〕n. 文明；文明國家
since〔sɪns〕adv. 從那時起　　perish〔'pɛrɪʃ〕v. 消失；毀滅
Incan〔'ɪŋkən〕adj. 印加人的　　Mayan〔'mɑjən〕adj. 馬雅人的
legendary〔'lɛdʒənd‚ɛrɪ〕adj. 傳說的
Atlantis〔ət'læntɪs〕n. 亞特蘭提斯島（據說在直布羅陀海峽的西方，
但因受神處罰，而沉沒海底的神秘島嶼）

A lot of ancient civilizations, [37](F) like the Egyptians, Hindus,
Greeks, and Mayans, have left writings and [38](C) drawings which indicate
contacts with superior beings "from the stars." Many believe that the aliens
are here to help us, while others hold that the aliens intend us [39](J) harm.
Still others think that most aliens visit Earth to study us like our scientists
study primitive natives and animals, and have no interest in helping us
[40](D) in any way.

　　很多古代的文明，像埃及人、印度人、希臘人及馬雅人，都留下了著作和
圖畫，顯示他們有和「來自星星」的優秀生物接觸過。許多人認為，外星人是
到這裡來幫助我們的，而有些人卻認為，外星人是打算要傷害我們。還有些人
認為，大多數的外星人拜訪地球是想來研究我們，就像我們的科學家研究原始
的土著和動物一樣，而且根本沒有興趣幫助我們。

like〔laɪk〕prep. 像是　　Egyptian〔ɪ'dʒɪpʃən〕n. 埃及人
Hindu〔'hɪndu〕n. 印度人　　writing〔'raɪtɪŋ〕n. 著作
drawing〔'drɔ·ɪŋ〕n. 圖畫　　indicate〔'ɪndə‚ket〕v. 顯示
contact〔'kɑntækt〕n. 接觸　　superior〔sə'pɪrɪɚ〕adj. 較優秀的
while〔hwaɪl〕conj. 然而　　hold〔hold〕v. 認為

intend〔ɪnˈtɛnd〕v. 打算將（某物）給（某人）
intend us harm 打算傷害我們　　study〔ˈstʌdɪ〕v. 研究
primitive〔ˈprɪmətɪv〕adj. 原始的　　native〔ˈnetɪv〕n. 土著
not…in any way 絕不；一點也不（ = *in no way*）

It is difficult to comment conclusively on these theories in general, apart from saying that any and all of them might be possible.　Maybe time will tell.

我們除了說這些理論都有可能之外，一般說來，很難對這些理論斷然地作評論。也許時間可以證明一切。

comment〔ˈkɑmɛnt〕v. 評論
conclusively〔kənˈklusɪvlɪ〕adv. 斷然地　　***in general*** 一般而言
apart from 除了～之外　　tell〔tɛl〕v. 顯示；證明

四、閱讀測驗：

41-44 為題組

A sense of humor is just one of the many things shared by Alfred and Anthony Melillo, 64-year-old twin brothers from East Haven who made history in February 2002.　On Christmas Eve, 1992, Anthony had a heart transplant from a 21-year-old donor.　Two days before Valentine's Day in 2002, Alfred received a 19-year-old heart, marking the first time on record that twin adults each received heart transplants.

幽默感是阿爾弗烈德・米利洛與安東尼・米利洛這一對現年六十四歲的雙胞胎兄弟，所共有的許多事物之一，來自東漢文的這對雙胞胎兄弟，在二〇〇二年的二月寫下了歷史性的一頁。一九九二年聖誕夜，安東尼接受一位二十一歲的人士捐贈，進行了心臟移植手術。而在二〇〇二年的情人節前兩天，阿爾弗烈德也從一位十九歲的捐贈者獲得了心臟，這在歷史上寫下了第一次有成年的雙胞胎，雙雙進行心臟移植手術的紀錄。

sense of humor 幽默感　　share〔ʃɛr〕v. 共有
twin〔twɪn〕adj. 雙胞胎的　n. 雙胞胎之一
make history 創造歷史
transplant〔ˈtrænsplænt〕n. 移植（手術）
donor〔ˈdonɚ〕n. 捐贈人　***Valentine's Day*** 情人節（每年二月十四日）
mark〔mɑrk〕v. 作記號；留下痕跡

"**I'm 15 minutes older than him, but now I'm younger because of my heart** and I'm not going to respect him," Alfred said with a grin, pointing to his brother while talking to a roomful of reporters, who laughed frequently at their jokes.

「我雖然比他大十五分鐘，不過我現在因為心臟的關係，比他還年輕，而且我也不打算要尊敬他，」阿爾弗烈德邊指著他弟弟，邊露齒笑著，說給當時滿屋子的記者聽，而這些記者不時因為他們的笑話而大笑。

grin〔grɪn〕*n.* 露齒而笑　　***point to*** 指著
roomful〔'rumfəl〕*n.* 滿房間（的人）
frequently〔'frikwəntlɪ〕*adv.* 經常

While the twins knew that genetics might have played a role in their condition, they recognized that their eating habits might have also contributed to their heart problems. "We'd put half a pound of butter on a steak. I overdid it on all the food that tasted good, so I guess I deserved what I got for not dieting properly."

這對雙胞胎雖然知道，遺傳基因可能在他們的健康狀況，扮演了重要的角色，但他們也承認，飲食習慣也可能是造成他們心臟疾病的原因。「我們之前都會在牛排上塗半磅的奶油。我在享用所有好吃的食物時，都會不知節制，所以我想我是因為飲食不當，而活該受罪的。」

genetics〔dʒə'nɛtɪks〕*n.* 遺傳學
play a role in 在…方面扮演角色；在…方面有影響力
condition〔kən'dɪʃən〕*n.*（健康等）狀態
recognize〔'rɛkəɡ,naɪz〕*v.* 承認
contribute〔kən'trɪbjut〕*v.* 促成 < *to* >
steak〔stek〕*n.* 牛排　　overdo〔'ovɚ'du〕*v.* 做得過火
deserve〔dɪ'zɝv〕*v.* 應得　　diet〔'daɪət〕*v.* 進食
properly〔'prɑpəlɪ〕*adv.* 適當地

The discussion moved to Anthony's recovery. In the five years since his heart transplant, he had been on an exercise program where he regularly rode a bicycle for five miles, swam each day, and walked a couple of miles. He was still on medication, but not nearly as much as Alfred, who was just in the early stage of his recovery.

討論的主題轉到安東尼的復原狀況。自從他接受移植手術之後的這五年間，他就持續在進行運動計畫，他定期騎五英哩的腳踏車、每天游泳，而且還步行好幾英哩。他仍在進行藥物治療中，不過沒有阿爾弗德那麼嚴重，阿爾弗烈德還在康復的早期階段而已。

recovery〔rɪˋkʌvərɪ〕n. 康復　　program〔ˋprogræm〕n. 計劃
regularly〔ˋrɛgjələlɪ〕adv. 定期地　　*a couple of* 好幾個的
medication〔ˏmɛdɪˋkeʃən〕n. 藥物治療
stage〔stedʒ〕n. 階段

"Right now I feel pretty young and I'm doing very well," Anthony said. "I feel like a new person." Alfred said his goal, of course, was to feel even better than his brother. But, he added, "I love my brother very much. We're very close and I'm sure we'll do just fine."

「我現在覺得自己相當年輕，而且進展得很順利，」安東尼說。「我覺得我真是煥然一新。」阿爾弗烈德說，他的目標當然就是要覺得比他弟弟更健康。不過他還說：「我深愛我弟弟。我們非常親密，我確信我們都會很順利。」

pretty〔ˋprɪtɪ〕adv. 相當　　*do well* 進展順利
goal〔gol〕n. 目標　　add〔æd〕v. 又說
close〔klos〕adj. 親密的　　fine〔faɪn〕adv. 很好地

41. (**D**) 本文主要是關於 _____。
　　(A) 心臟移植手術的危險　　(B) 藉由換顆新的心臟而變年輕
　　(C) 基因遺傳對心臟的影響　　(D) 接受心臟移植手術的雙胞胎兄弟
mainly〔ˋmenlɪ〕adv. 主要地　　surgery〔ˋsɝdʒərɪ〕n. 手術
effect〔ɪˋfɛkt〕n. 影響 < on >

42. (**C**) 阿爾弗烈德和安東尼和有何共同之處？
　　(A) 壽命。　　　　　　　(B) 生涯目標。
　　(C) 幽默感。　　　　　　(D) 喜歡騎腳踏車。
in common 共同的　　lifespan〔ˋlaɪfˏspæn〕n. 壽命
career〔kəˋrɪr〕n. 生涯　　bicycle〔ˋbaɪsɪkl̩〕v. 騎腳踏車

43. (**B**) 阿爾弗烈德和安東尼認為，是什麼造成他們的心臟方面有問題？
　　(A) 運動。　　(B) 飲食。　　(C) 手術。　　(D) 藥物。

44. (**D**) 為什麼阿爾弗烈德說：「我雖然比他大十五分鐘，不過我現在因為心臟的關係，比他還年輕」？
　　(A) 他的心臟移植手術比安東尼的心臟移植手術成功。
　　(B) 他心臟開完刀之後，復原的速度比安東尼的復原速度快。
　　(C) 他的運動計劃比安東尼的運動計劃好。
　　(D) 他新移植的心臟比安東尼所換的心臟年輕。

45-47 為題組

　　In 1993, the Metropolitan Museum of Art reluctantly handed over 363 pieces of gold, silver, precious stones, paintings, and sculptures back to Turkey after a court case. Following increasing calls for the return of artistic objects that were removed decades or centuries ago, some of the world's leading museums have signed a declaration that they will not hand back the ancient artifacts to their **countries of origin**.

　　在一九九三年，大都會博物館，在經過法院訴訟之後，很不情願地將三百六十三項金、銀、寶石製品、繪畫及雕刻品，交還給土耳其。在退還數十年前，甚至數世紀前奪取的藝術品的呼籲聲浪日益增多的情況下，全世界一些重量級的博物館，已簽下一項聲明，它們不再把古代藝術品，退還給原屬的國家。

metropolitan (ˌmɛtrəˈpɑlətn̩) adj. 大都會的
reluctantly (rɪˈlʌktəntlɪ) adv. 不情願地
hand over 轉交　　**precious stone** 寶石
sculpture (ˈskʌlptʃɚ) n. 雕刻品　　Turkey (ˈtɝkɪ) n. 土耳其
court (kort , kɔrt) n. 法院　　case (kes) n. 訴訟
following (ˈfɑloɪŋ) prep. 在～之後　　call (kɔl) n. 請求；呼籲
artistic (arˈtɪstɪk) adj. 藝術的　　object (ˈɑbdʒɪkt) n. 物品
remove (rɪˈmuv) v. 拿去；奪走　　decade (ˈdɛked) n. 十年
century (ˈsɛntʃərɪ) n. 世紀
leading (ˈlidɪŋ) adj. 主要的；重量級的
sign (saɪn) v. 簽署　　declaration (ˌdɛkləˈreʃən) n. 聲明
hand back 退還　　artifact (ˈɑrtɪˌfækt) n. 藝術品
origin (ˈɔrədʒɪn) n. 起源

They say people all over the world have only been able to fully appreciate ancient civilizations because these museums have provided access to these artistic objects. The ancient civilizations would not be so deeply admired today if these ancient artifacts were not so widely available to an international public in major museums throughout Europe and America. For example, Egyptian culture would not have become so well-known if the museums had not put Egyptian mummies on show.

他們說全世界的人們能充份地欣賞這些古代文明，那是因爲博物館提供途徑，讓大家來觀賞這些藝術品。若非這些古代藝品陳列在歐、美兩洲的大博物館中，使國際大衆皆能廣泛地欣賞到它們，那麼古文明也無法像現今這般深受讚賞。舉例來說，若非博物館陳列木乃伊，埃及文化就無法變得如此有名。

> appreciate〔əˋpriʃɪ͵et〕v. 欣賞
> access〔ˋækses〕n. 方法；途徑＜to＞
> admire〔ədˋmaɪr〕v. 欣賞
> available〔əˋveləbḷ〕adj. 可獲得的
> international〔͵ɪntəˋnæʃənḷ〕adj. 國際的
> public〔ˋpʌblɪk〕n. 一般民衆　　major〔ˋmedʒə〕adj. 主要的
> throughout〔θruˋaʊt〕prep. 遍及
> Egyptian〔ɪˋdʒɪpʃən, i-〕adj. 埃及的
> well-known〔ˋwɛlˋnon〕adj. 著名的
> mummy〔ˋmʌmɪ〕n. 木乃伊　　*put～on show* 展示

The British Museum has not signed the declaration, but says it fully supports it. Over the recent years, it has faced growing pressure to hand back the Elgin Marbles, sculptures taken from the Parthenon in Athens, Greece, in the 19th century. But the British Museum has said that the Museum is the best possible place for them. "They must remain here if the museum is to continue to achieve its aim, which is to **show the world to the world**," said the director of the museum.

　　大英博物館並未簽署這項聲明，但卻言明它完全支持。在近年來，它也面對與日俱增的壓力，要歸還亞爾金大理石像，那是在十九世紀從希臘雅典巴特農神廟中拿走的雕刻品。但大英博物館也指出，該博物館是陳列這些雕像的最佳場所。「如果博物館要繼續達成其目的，即把全世界展示給世人觀賞，這些雕像就得繼續留在這裡，」博物館館長說。

British〔'brɪtɪʃ〕*adj.* 英國的　　growing〔'groɪŋ〕*adj.* 漸增的
pressure〔'prɛʃɚ〕*n.* 壓力　　marble〔'marbl̩〕*n.* 大理石像
Parthenon〔'parθə,nan〕*n.* 巴特農神廟
Athens〔'æθənz〕*n.* 雅典　　Greece〔gris〕*n.* 希臘
aim〔em〕*n.* 目標　　show〔ʃo〕*v.* 給～看
the world 全世界；全世界的人　　director〔də'rɛktɚ〕*n.* 館長

45. (**A**) 大博物館對不歸還古代物品提出了什麼理由？
　　(A) 這些物品只有放在大博物館中，世人才能充份欣賞到它們。
　　(B) 這些物品最好放在某一地點，不要到處移動。
　　(C) 他們需要那些有名的古代文物，以吸引全世界的人。
　　(D) 古文明只有由祖國外移，才能被欣賞。

46. (**B**) 在本文中，以下何者未被提及是「原屬國」之一？
　　(A) 土耳其。　　　　　(B) 英國。
　　(C) 埃及。　　　　　(D) 希臘。

Britain〔'brɪtn̩〕*n.* 英國

47. (**C**) 在 "show the world to the world" 中，"the world" 的意思是什麼？
　　(A) 地球村。　　　　　(B) 重量級的博物館。
　　(C) 古文明。　　　　　(D) 國際大眾。

global〔'globl̩〕*adj.* 全球的　　village〔'vɪlɪdʒ〕*n.* 村莊

48-51 為題組

Some animals have organs in their bodies that produce light. When it is dark, they flash their lights on and off to signal to others of their species, to lure prey toward them, or to escape from predators.

某些動物的身上有會發光的器官。在黑暗中，牠們會斷斷續續地發光，好向其他同類發出信號、引誘獵物接近，或是逃離捕食者。

organ (ˈɔrgən) *n.* 器官　　flash (flæʃ) *v.* 使閃光；閃現
on and off 斷斷續續地　　signal (ˈsɪgnḷ) *v.* 向…發信號
species (ˈspiʃɪz) *n.* 種　　lure (lur) *v.* 引誘
prey (pre) *n.* 獵物　　predator (ˈprɛdətɚ) *n.* 捕食者

Some fish are found to produce light in the blackness of the sea. When night falls over the Red Sea, tiny flashlight fish rise to the surface for food, each with a pair of "headlamps," one beneath each eye. With the light produced by bacteria living there, they communicate with other flashlight fish to avoid getting too close to each other, so that the fish may spread out evenly to get enough food. And if a flashlight fish is threatened by a predator, it swims away in a zigzag path, flashing its light on and off very quickly to confuse the animal pursuing it.

有些魚會在黑暗的海裡發光。當黑夜降臨紅海，微小的閃光魚就會浮到水面上覓食，每條魚都有一對「頭燈」，每隻眼睛下面都有一個。牠們靠著生活在那裡的細菌所發出的光，和其他閃光魚交談，以避免太接近對方，這樣一來，這些魚就能平均地散佈，以獲得足夠的食物。而且如果有一隻閃光魚受到捕食者的威脅，牠就會以Z字型的路線游開，並以非常快的速度斷斷續續地發光，讓追捕牠的動物分不清牠的位置。

blackness (ˈblæknɪs) *n.* 黑暗　　fall (fɔl) *v.* 降臨；來臨
the Red Sea 紅海　　tiny (ˈtaɪnɪ) *adj.* 微小的
rise (raɪz) *v.* 上升　　flashlight (ˈflæʃ͵laɪt) *n.* 閃光
flashlight fish 閃光魚　　surface (ˈsɝfɪs) *n.* 水面；表面
headlamp (ˈhɛd͵læmp) *n.* 前照燈；頭燈 (= *headlight*)
beneath (bɪˈniθ) *prep.* 在…之下
bacteria (bækˈtɪrɪə) *n. pl.* 細菌　　spread (sprɛd) *v.* 分散；散佈
evenly (ˈivənlɪ) *adv.* 平均地　　threaten (ˈθrɛtṇ) *v.* 威脅
zigzag (ˈzɪgzæg) *adj.* Z字型的；鋸齒形的；彎彎曲曲的
path (pæθ) *n.* 路線　　confuse (kənˈfjuz) *v.* 使混淆
pursue (pɚˈsu) *v.* 追捕

Certain land animals can also produce light. Fireflies, small beetles that live in many warmer parts of the world, use light to attract a mate. After darkness falls in some parts of North America, female fireflies gather on the ground. The males fly overhead, flashing light from the undersides of their bodies. As there are a number of species of firefly, the males of each kind flash their own particular signal. Recognizing the flashing code of her own species, a female signals back to the male, and he lands beside her.

有些陸地上的動物也會發光。螢火蟲是一種小型甲蟲，牠們住在地球上許多較為溫暖的地區，牠們就是利用光線來吸引配偶。在黑暗降臨北美洲的部分地區之後，雌性的螢火蟲會聚集在地面上。雄性螢火蟲則會在上頭盤旋，並從身體的下方發出亮光。因為有許多種類的螢火蟲，所以每一個種類的雄性螢火蟲都會發出牠們自己特有的信號。雌性螢火蟲在認出與她同種類的閃光暗號之後，就會發出信號回應雄性螢火蟲，然後牠就會降落在她身旁。

> firefly (ˈfaɪrˌflaɪ) n. 螢火蟲　　beetle (ˈbitḷ) n. 甲蟲
> mate (met) n. 配偶　　female (ˈfimel) adj. 雌性的
> gather (ˈgæðɚ) v. 聚集　　male (mel) n. 雄性動物
> overhead (ˈovɚˈhɛd) adv. 在上頭　　underside (ˈʌndɚˌsaɪd) n. 下側
> signal (ˈsɪgnḷ) n. 信號　　recognize (ˈrɛkəgˌnaɪz) v. 認出
> flashing (ˈflæʃɪŋ) adj. 閃爍的　　code (kod) n. 暗號
> land (lænd) v. 降落　　n. 陸地

On land as in the sea, living lights can be deceiving. When they are hungry, some female fireflies lure the males of other species to them. They flash a false response when these males signal overhead, but eat them when they land.

在陸上地就和在海裡一樣，生物發出來的光可以用來欺騙別人。當牠們肚子餓的時候，有些雌性螢火蟲會引誘其他種類的雄性螢火蟲過來。牠們會發出假的回應給在上頭發信號的雄性螢火蟲，然後卻趁牠們降落時，把牠們吃掉。

> living (ˈlɪvɪŋ) adj. 活的　　deceiving (dɪˈsivɪŋ) adj. 欺騙的
> false (fɔls) adj. 假的　　response (rɪˈspɑns) n. 回應

48. (**C**) 下列何者是本文最適合的標題？
　　(A) 閃光魚和螢火蟲的交配。
　　(B) 黑暗與光明。
　　(C) 生物發出來的光和動物的溝通。
　　(D) 在陸上和海裡的生物。

> mating (ˈmetɪŋ) n. 交配　　life (laɪf) n. 生物（集合名詞）

49. (**A**) 紅海裡的閃光魚，＿＿＿＿＿＿＿ 會在晚上發光。

    (A) 當牠們出來覓食時　　　(B) 當牠們試圖尋找同伴時

    (C) 因爲牠們想要擺脫細菌

    (D) 爲了接近其他的閃光魚

    companion〔kəm'pænjən〕*n.* 同伴　　***get rid of*** 擺脫

50. (**D**) 根據本文，閃光魚和螢火蟲都不會發光來＿＿＿＿＿＿＿。

    (A) 吸引配偶　　　　　　(B) 引誘牠們的獵物

    (C) 逃離敵人　　　　　　(D) 找到回家的路

51. (**D**) 下列有關螢火蟲的敘述，何者爲眞？

    (A) 所有種類的螢火蟲都使用相同的信號。

    (B) 螢火蟲用牠們的頭燈來溝通。

    (C) 雄性螢火蟲可能會以假的信號來欺騙雌性螢火蟲。

    (D) 雌性螢火蟲會從地面回應雄性螢火蟲的信號。

52-55 爲題組

Brooks, Bruce. **Everywhere.** HarperCollins, 1990. ISBN0060207299. 70 pages.

    Peanuts' beloved grandfather has suffered a heart attack. Peanuts is sad over the possibility of losing his grandfather. Dooley keeps Peanuts company while the adults in the family attend to Grandfather. Dooley attempts to save the old man by a ritual learned from comic books: killing a turtle and trading his soul for Grandfather's. With the imaginative assistance of Dooley, Peanuts discovers the healing power of hope and love.

布魯克‧布魯斯。無所不在。哈博克林出版，1990 年。ISBN0060207299。共 70 頁。

    小畢最愛的爺爺心臟病發作了。小畢因爲可能會失去爺爺而感到難過。在大人們忙著照顧爺爺的同時，杜立陪伴了小畢一起度過這一切。杜立試圖使用從漫畫中學到的祭典拯救爺爺：也就是殺死一隻烏龜，並將牠的靈魂和爺爺的靈魂互相交換。小畢透過杜立富有想像力的協助，發現了愛與希望的醫治能力。

ISBN 國際標準圖書編號 (= *International Standard Book Number*)

beloved〔bɪˈlʌvɪd〕*adj.* 深愛的；鍾愛的

suffer〔ˈsʌfə〕*v.* 遭受　　***heart attack*** 心臟病發作

possibility〔ˌpɑsəˈbɪlətɪ〕*n.* 可能性 (= *probability*)

attend to 照料　　attempt〔əˈtɛmpt〕*v.* 嘗試；企圖

ritual〔ˈrɪtʃuəl〕*n.* 儀式　　trade〔tred〕*v.* 交換

soul〔sol〕*n.* 靈魂

imaginative〔ɪˈmædʒəˌnetɪv〕*adj.* 富於想像力的

assistance〔əˈsɪstəns〕*n.* 協助　　healing〔ˈhilɪŋ〕*adj.* 治療的

Babbitt, Natalie. **Tuck Everlasting.** Farrar, 1975. ISBN0374378487. 180 pages.

　　The Tuck family has discovered a spring whose water brings eternal life. A man learns their secret and threatens to sell the water to the highest bidder. Mrs. Tuck kills the man and is jailed and sentenced to be executed. Though the family knows she cannot be killed, they worry that their secret will be revealed when they try to kill her.

白璧德・娜塔莉。永垂不朽的塔克。法樂出版，1975 年。ISBN0374378487。共 180 頁。

　　塔克一家人發現了能使人長生不老的泉水。有一位男士得知了他們的秘密，並且威脅要將泉水賣給出價最高的競標者。塔克太太殺了那名男士，而被囚禁，並且被判處死刑。雖然全家都知道她不可能會死，但他們卻擔心，秘密會因此而被揭發。

spring〔sprɪŋ〕*n.* 泉水

everlasting〔ˌɛvəˈlæstɪŋ〕*adj.* 永遠的；不朽的

eternal〔ɪˈtɜnḷ〕*adj.* 永久的；永恆的　　learn〔lɜn〕*v.* 知道

threaten〔ˈθrɛtṇ〕*v.* 威脅　　bidder〔ˈbɪdə〕*n.* 出價者；競標者

jail〔dʒel〕*v.* 囚禁　　sentence〔ˈsɛntəns〕*v.* 判處

execute〔ˈɛksɪˌkjut〕*v.* 處死　　reveal〔rɪˈvil〕*v.* 揭發

Baylor, Byrd. **The Table Where Rich People Sit.** Simon & Schuster, 1994. ISBN0684196530. 52 pages.

Around an old kitchen table, a young girl calls a family meeting to show her parents that they should earn more money so they can have nicer things. As she points out they are not sitting at a table where rich people would sit, her parents calculate the value of the desert hills, the blooming cactus, the calls of eagles, and one another's company. Soon, she realizes that her poor family is rich in things that matter in life. She concludes that this is indeed a table where rich people sit.

貝勒·伯德。有錢人的餐桌。賽門休斯特出版，1994年。ISBN0684196530。 共52頁。

有一次小女孩召集了家人，圍繞著破舊的餐桌，召開家庭會議，告訴她的 父母，該多賺些錢，這樣他們才能擁有更好的東西。當她指出，有錢人是不可 能會使用像面前這麼破舊的桌子時，她的父母就估計出附近沙漠小丘、盛開的 仙人掌、老鷹的叫聲，及有家人陪伴的價值。不久，她終於了解，自己貧窮的 家庭其實是充滿了生命中最重要的事物。她的結論就是，面前的餐桌的確是富 裕的人所使用的桌子。

```
call ( kɔl ) v. 召開（會議）
show ( ʃo ) v. 告知；向（某人）指出
point out 指出     sit at a table 坐在桌子旁邊
calculate ('kælkjə,let ) v. 計算；估計     value ('vælju ) n. 價值
desert ('dɛzət ) n. 沙漠     hill ( hɪl ) n. 小丘
blooming ('blumɪŋ ) adj. 盛開的
cactus ('kæktəs ) n. 仙人掌
call ( kɔl ) n. 叫聲     company ('kʌmpənɪ ) n. 陪伴
rich ( rɪtʃ ) adj. 富裕的；豐富的 < in >
matter ('mætə ) v. 重要
conclude ( kən'klud ) v. 斷定；下結論
indeed ( ɪn'did ) adv. 的確
```

Goble, Paul. **Beyond the Ridge.** Bradbury, 1989. ISBN0027365816. 32 pages.

There is no death; only a change of worlds—the author delivers these reassurances to readers in this book, based on the customs of the Plains Indians in America. The book reads like a prayer, expressing specific beliefs about dying. It describes a woman who is called by her long-dead mother to go "beyond the ridge." After a steep climb, she discovers a world that is abundantly beautiful, and there she finds the familiar faces of people who have passed that way before her.

哥比·保羅。在山的另一邊。布來德布里出版。1989年。ISBN0027365816。共32頁。

其實並沒有死亡；我們只會到不同的世界——作者根據平原印地安人的習俗，說這些使讀者安心的話。這本書唸起來像是個祈禱文，表達作者對死亡的特定的看法。書中描述一位女士被早已去世的母親叫到「山的另一邊」。經過了險峻的攀登，她發現了一個非常美妙的世界，也在那裡找到比她先走過那條路的熟悉面孔。

beyond〔bɪ'jɑnd〕*prep.* 在～的那一邊；越過
ridge〔rɪdʒ〕*n.* 山脊　　deliver〔dɪ'lɪvɚ〕*v.* 發表；說
reassurance〔,riə'ʃʊrəns〕*n.* 再三保證；勉勵
based on 根據　　custom〔'kʌstəm〕*n.* 習俗
Plains Indians 平原印地安人　　specific〔spɪ'sɪfɪk〕*adj.* 特定的
belief〔bɪ'lif〕*n.* 信念；意見　　prayer〔'prɛɚ〕*n.* 祈禱
long-dead *adj.* 早已去世的
ridge〔rɪdʒ〕*n.* 山背；山脊；分水嶺
steep〔stip〕*adj.* 陡峭的；險峻的　　climb〔klaɪmb〕*n.* 攀登
abundantly〔ə'bʌndəntlɪ〕*adv.* 豐富地；大量地
familiar〔fə'mɪljɚ〕*adj.* 熟悉的

52. (**B**) 哪一本書最厚？
　　(A) 無所不在。　　　　　(B) 永垂不朽的塔克。
　　(C) 有錢人的餐桌。　　　(D) 山的另一邊。
　　thick〔θɪk〕*adj.* 厚的

53. (**A**) 哪一本書是 1990 年發行的？

    (A) <u>無所不在。</u>   (B) 永垂不朽的塔克。

    (C) 有錢人的餐桌。   (D) 山的另一邊。

    publish〔'pʌblɪʃ〕v. 出版；發行

54. (**D**) 哪一位作者說明了美國原住民對死亡的想法？

    (A) 布魯斯・布魯克。   (B) 娜塔莉・白璧德。

    (C) 伯德・貝勒。   (D) <u>保羅・哥比。</u>

    native〔'netɪv〕adj. 土著的   view〔vju〕n. 看法

55. (**C**) 哪一位作者說明了金錢並不是唯一衡量財富的方式？

    (A) 布魯斯・布魯克。   (B) 娜塔莉・白璧德。

    (C) <u>伯德・貝勒。</u>   (D) 保羅・哥比。

    show〔ʃo〕v. 說明   measure〔'mɛʒɚ〕v. 測量

    wealth〔wɛlθ〕n. 財富

第貳部分：非選擇題

一、翻譯題

1. $\left\{\begin{array}{l}\text{Though} \\ \text{Although}\end{array}\right\}$ Lily was born both blind and deaf,

   she $\left\{\begin{array}{l}\text{was never discouraged.} \\ \text{never lost heart.}\end{array}\right.$

2. Her story proves that we can $\left\{\begin{array}{l}\text{succeed} \\ \text{make it} \\ \text{achieve success}\end{array}\right\}$ as long as

   we $\left\{\begin{array}{l}\text{strive.} \\ \text{work hard.} \\ \text{make an effort.}\end{array}\right.$

   或 Her story proved that we could....

二、英文作文：

The Wrong Taxi

One evening Mr. Chang attended a wedding banquet. The food was wonderful and so was the wine. He had a very good time, but unfortunately he drank too much. When Mr. Chang left the party he wondered how he could get home. He knew that he should not drive his car. If he drove his car while drunk, he might cause an accident. Then he would be in trouble with the police.

Luckily, as Mr. Chang was thinking about what to do, a taxi passed by. He quickly called the taxi and climbed into the car. The driver said he knew where to go and the car started to move. "What a good taxi driver," Mr. Chang thought. He soon fell asleep.

When Mr. Chang woke up it was morning. But he was not at home. To his surprise, he was at a police station. The taxi he had taken the night before was not a taxi at all. It was a police car! And the driver was a police officer, who had taken him directly to the police station.

wedding ('wɛdɪŋ) *n.* 結婚典禮
banquet ('bæŋkwɪt, 'bænkwɪt) *n.* 宴會
wedding banquet 結婚喜宴
unfortunately (ʌn'fɔrtʃənɪtlɪ) *adv.* 不幸地
be in trouble with 被…責罵；處罰　　**pass by** 經過
climb (klaɪm) *v.* 登上（交通工具）
directly (də'rɛktlɪ) *adv.* 直接地
police station 警察局

九十三年度學科能力測驗（英文考科）大考中心公佈答案

題 號	答 案	題 號	答 案	題 號	答 案
1	C	21	A	41	D
2	D	22	B	42	C
3	D	23	D	43	B
4	A	24	A	44	D
5	D	25	C	45	A
6	C	26	D	46	B
7	B	27	C	47	C
8	D	28	B	48	C
9	A	29	C	49	A
10	D	30	C	50	D
11	B	31	B	51	D
12	A	32	H	52	B
13	C	33	E	53	A
14	D	34	A	54	D
15	C	35	G	55	C
16	A	36	I		
17	C	37	F		
18	D	38	C		
19	D	39	J		
20	B	40	D		

九十三學年度學科能力測驗

各科各級分人數累計表

	級分	人　數	百分比 (%)	累計人數	累計百分比 (%)
	15	3986	2.59	154042	100.00
	14	6327	4.11	150056	97.41
	13	7697	5.00	143729	93.31
	12	9091	5.90	136032	88.31
	11	11500	7.47	126941	82.41
英	10	12260	7.96	115441	74.94
	9	13545	8.79	103181	66.98
	8	15949	10.35	89636	58.19
	7	15246	9.90	73687	47.84
	6	16506	10.72	58441	37.94
文	5	14083	9.14	41935	27.22
	4	13980	9.08	27852	18.08
	3	11572	7.51	13872	9.01
	2	2228	1.45	2300	1.49
	1	67	0.04	72	0.05
	0	5	0.00	5	0.00

九十三學年度學科能力測驗
總級分與各科成績標準一覽表

考　科	頂標	前標	均標	後標	底標
國　文	13	12	11	9	8
英　文	12	11	8	5	4
數　學	11	9	6	4	3
社　會	13	12	11	9	8
自　然	13	12	10	8	7
總級分	59	53	45	38	31

※ 各科成績五項標準以到考考生成績計算，總級分五項標準之計算不
　含五科均缺考之考生，各標準計算方式如下：

　　　頂標：成績位於第 88 百分位數之考生成績
　　　前標：成績位於第 75 百分位數之考生成績
　　　均標：成績位於第 50 百分位數之考生成績
　　　後標：成績位於第 25 百分位數之考生成績
　　　底標：成績位於第 12 百分位數之考生成績

九十二年大學入學學科能力測驗試題
英文考科①

第壹部份：單一選擇題

一、詞彙與慣用語（15％）

說明： 第 1 至 15 題，每題選出最適當的一個選項，標示在答案卡之「選擇題答案區」。每題答對得 1 分，答錯不倒扣。

1. All the flights to and from Kaohsiung were ＿＿＿＿＿ because of the heavy thunderstorm.

   (A) advised   (B) disclosed   (C) cancelled   (D) benefited

2. The woman told the truth to her lawyer without ＿＿＿＿＿ because he was the only person she could rely on.

   (A) reservation   (B) combination   (C) impression   (D) foundation

3. The man was severely injured in last weekend's tragic car accident and died ＿＿＿＿＿ afterwards.

   (A) mostly   (B) shortly   (C) easily   (D) hardly

4. Mr. Smith's work in Taiwan is just ＿＿＿＿＿. He will go back to the U.S. next month.

   (A) liberal   (B) rural   (C) conscious   (D) temporary

5. Helen ＿＿＿＿＿ with anger when she saw her boyfriend kissing an attractive girl.

   (A) collided   (B) exploded   (C) relaxed   (D) defeated

6. Dr. Liu's new book is a collection of his ＿＿＿＿＿ of the daily life of tribal people in Africa.

   (A) observations   (B) interferences   (C) preventions   (D) substitutions

7. The young couple decided to _____ their wedding until all the details were well taken care of.
   (A) announce (B) maintain (C) postpone (D) simplify

8. The conflicts between John and his teacher made it difficult for the teacher to judge his performance _____.
   (A) objectively (B) painfully (C) excitedly (D) intimately

9. Living in a highly _____ society, you definitely have to arm yourself with as much knowledge as possible.
   (A) tolerant (B) permanent (C) favorable (D) competitive

10. The 70-year-old professor sued the university for age _____, because his teaching contract had not been renewed.
    (A) possession (B) commitment (C) discrimination (D) employment

11. Kevin burst into tears _____ because his teacher punished him in front of the whole class.
    (A) on the side   (B) on the spot
    (C) on any account   (D) on the mark

12. As soon as the couple realized that they didn't love each other anymore, they _____.
    (A) fell off (B) cut in (C) broke up (D) stood by

13. The power workers had to work _____ to repair the power lines since the whole city was in the dark.
    (A) around the clock   (B) in the extreme
    (C) on the house   (D) in the majority

14. After retirement, Mr. Wang _____ ice skating, which he had always loved but had not had time for.
    (A) appealed to (B) took to (C) related to (D) saw to

15. Why do we have to _____ Sue's selfish behavior? We have to
teach her to care for others.
  (A) get over with
  (B) hang out with
  (C) make up with
  (D) put up with

二、句子配合題（5％）

說明：1. 第 16 至 20 題，每題皆為未完成的句子。請逐題依文意與語法，從
右欄 (A) 到 (J) 的選項中選出最適當者，合併成一個意思通順、用
法正確的句子。

2. 請將每題所選答案之英文字母代號標示在答案卡之「選擇題答案
區」。每題答對得 1 分，答錯不倒扣。

16. Since it was a holiday,	(A) … so he went abroad to study.
17. Unless he prepares well,	(B) … I stayed in bed an extra hour.
18. If I had known the fact,	(C) … or she might miss the class.
19. Belle was the person	(D) … he will fail the exam.
20. A person who exercises regularly	(E) … who changed him into a gentleman.
	(F) … she had gone bankrupt.
	(G) … is more likely to look young.
	(H) … and is sure to have a healthy body.
	(I) … I admired her most in the world.
	(J) … I would have taken action right away.

三、綜合測驗（10％）

說明：第 21 至 30 題，每題一個空格，請依文意選出最適當的一個選項，標示
在答案卡之「選擇題答案區」。每題答對得 1 分，答錯不倒扣。

The first American space toilet was Alan Shepard's space suit. His
flight was supposed to last only 15 minutes, so there was no provision
made for him to relieve himself in the capsule. His flight, ___21___, was

delayed for hours. It was then decided that Alan Shepard should relieve himself in his space suit, and continue with the mission as scheduled. ___22___ problem urged NASA to develop the first space toilet, a modified diaper. Diapers are ___23___ used by astronauts when they are outside the space shuttle, wearing a spacesuit. As the flights grew longer, a new set of two collection bags was devised, ___24___ for liquid wastes and the other for solid wastes. Once used, the bags are sealed and stored for the flight back to the earth, ___25___ they are disposed of.

21. (A) therefore   (B) similarly   (C) however   (D) otherwise

22. (A) Each   (B) This   (C) Their   (D) Another

23. (A) rather   (B) almost   (C) ever   (D) still

24. (A) the one   (B) someone   (C) no one   (D) one

25. (A) where   (B) what   (C) which   (D) whether

Up to about 250 million years ago the world had just one huge super-continent called Pangaea. Animals were able to move and intermix with ___26___. About 200 million years ago this super-continent broke up into two continents: Laurasia and Gondwana. About 60 million years ago Gondwana broke up into ___27___ later became South America, Africa, Antarctica, India and Australia. Since then Australia ___28___ from the rest of the world by vast oceans. The animals there no longer had ___29___ with animals from other parts of the world. They evolved separately. As a result, about 95 % of Australia's mammals and 94 % of its frogs are found ___30___ else in the world. Australia has lots of very unusual animals.

26. (A) another   (B) one another   (C) other   (D) the other

27. (A) which   (B) where   (C) what   (D) that

28. (A) is isolated   (B) had isolated
    (C) has isolated   (D) has been isolated

29. (A) confusion   (B) marriage   (C) contact   (D) transaction

30. (A) nowhere   (B) somewhere   (C) everywhere   (D) anywhere

四、文意選填 (10 %)

說明： 第 31 至 40 題，每題一個空格，請依文意在文章後所提供的(A) 到 (J)
選項中分別選出最適當者，並將其英文字母代號標示在答案卡之「選
擇題答案區」。每題答對得 1 分，答錯不倒扣。

Stress has become a favorite subject of everyday conversation. It is
not ___31___ to hear friends and family members talk about the difficulty
they have in ___32___ the stress of everyday life and the efforts they
make to control the events ___33___ cause stress.

Most of us understand the results of not controlling our reactions
___34___ stress. Forty-three percent of all adults suffer terrible health
effects ___35___ stress. Most physician office visits are for stress-related
illnesses and complaints. Stress is linked to the six ___36___ causes of
death— heart disease, cancer, lung disease, accidents, liver disease, and
suicide. Currently, health care costs account for ___37___ twelve percent
of the gross domestic product.

Yet, while stress may damage our health, it is sometimes necessary,
___38___ desirable. Exciting or challenging events ___39___ the birth of
a child, completion of a major project at work, or moving to a new city
generate ___40___ much stress as does tragedy or disaster. And without
stress, life would be dull.

(A) about   (B) from   (C) even   (D) as   (E) managing
(F) like   (G) to   (H) that   (I) unusual   (J) leading

五、閱讀測驗（30％）

說明： 第 41 至 55 題，每題請分別根據各篇文章之文意選出最適當的一個選
項，標示在答案卡之「選擇題答案區」。每題答對得 2 分，答錯不倒扣。

41-43 為題組

I usually go to work by subway, and I get to work by 8:00 A.M.
Before I start my job, I put on my uniform and look at myself in the
mirror to make sure that I look neat. At 8:30 in the morning, I go on
duty. I usually eat lunch from twelve to one and generally take a
fifteen-minute break in the morning and in the afternoon. At 4:30 in the
afternoon, I go off duty.

I enjoy my job very much. I meet all kinds of people and talk to
everyone. Many people ask me questions, and I give them the necessary
information. I try to be very helpful. I always call out floors very
clearly, and I am constantly on the move. Most men take off their hats
in my car, and sometimes I have to tell passengers to put out their
cigarettes. Some people smile at me, but others just ignore me. In fact,
my life can be described as consisting of a series of "ups" and "downs."

41. The passage is written mainly to describe _____.
    (A) what the author looks like
    (B) what "life" means to the author
    (C) what a typical day is like for the author
    (D) what kinds of people the author works with

42. We may infer from the passage that the author is a(n) _____.
    (A) policeman   (B) driver
    (C) floor cleaner   (D) elevator operator

43. The expression "constantly on the move" in the passage refers to
the fact that _____.
(A) the author always calls out floors very clearly
(B) the author seldom stays in one place for a long while
(C) the author meets all kinds of people and talks to everyone
(D) the author frequently helps passengers move their baggage

44-47 為題組

Magic is believed to have begun with the Egyptians, in 1700 BC.
A magician named Dedi of Dedsnefu was reported to have performed
for the pharaoh, or the king. He was also known to have entertained
the slaves who built the pyramids. The "Cups and Balls" trick which
he was particularly good at is still performed by magicians all over the
world today.

The ancient Greeks and Romans were also fascinated by the idea
of magic. Actually, one of their main interests was the art of deception.
This explains why at that time the priests even built magic devices into
their temples. These devices made it possible for doors to open by
themselves and wine to flow magically out of statues' mouths. This was
done mainly to convince people that the priests were powerful.

Magic, however, was not well accepted before the 1800s. Magicians
were thought of as freaks and were only allowed to perform in a circus.
It was in the 19th century that the magician Robert Houdin came along
and changed people's views and attitudes about magic. It was also
because of Robert Houdin that many magicians were able to add Dr. or
MD to their names. Today magicians try hard to find new ways to
show their practiced skills. Magic is now entertainment for families
all over the world.

44. What is the best title for the passage?
    (A) Magical Tricks
    (B) A Great Magician
    (C) Magic as Entertainment
    (D) The History of Magic

45. In ancient Greece, what did the priests do to show people they had unusual power?
    (A) They performed magical tricks to entertain people.
    (B) They made the statues in the temples drink wine as they wished.
    (C) They treated the people with wine flowing down from statues' mouths.
    (D) They built magic devices in the temples to make doors open by themselves.

46. What did people think of magic before 1800?
    (A) Magic should be used only in temples.
    (B) Magic could only be performed in a circus.
    (C) Magic was performed by freaks and doctors.
    (D) Magic was the major daily activity for the pharaohs.

47. Which of the following statements is true?
    (A) Magic began about 3,700 years ago.
    (B) Dedi of Dedsnefu performed magic for kings only.
    (C) Robert Houdin was the first magician to perform magic.
    (D) The "Cups and Balls" trick has been performed for about 1,700 years.

48-51 為題組

There are three branches of medicine. One is called "doctor medicine," or "scientific medicine." Scientific doctors try to observe sicknesses, look for logical patterns, and then find out how the human body works. From there they figure out what treatments may work.

This kind of medicine is believed to date from the 4th century BC. Although nowadays it is successful, in the ancient world this approach probably did not cure many patients.

A second kind of medicine is called "natural cures," or "folk medicine," in which less educated people try to cure sicknesses with various herbs. These folk healers also use observation and logic, but they are not so aware of it. They try things until they find something that seems to work, and then they keep doing that. Folk medicine flourished long before the development of scientific medicine and was more successful in ancient times than doctor medicine.

The third kind is called "health spas," or "faith healing." Sometimes this may be as simple as touching the holy man and being immediately healed. Other times, a magician may make you a magic charm, or say a spell, to cure you. Some religious groups organize special healing shrines for the sick. In these places people rest, get plenty of sleep, eat healthy food, drink water instead of wine, and exercise in various ways. They also talk to the priests and pray to the gods. If you are feeling depressed or you have been working too hard, going to these places may be just the right thing to make you feel better.

48. Doctor medicine _____.
   (A) has a longer history than folk medicine
   (B) has been practiced for around 1,600 years
   (C) bases its treatments on observation and logic
   (D) was very successful in curing sicknesses in ancient times

49. According to the passage, which of the following is **NOT** used in health spas?
   (A) Magic power.   (B) Various herbs.
   (C) Religious faith.   (D) A healthy life style.

50. According to the passage, which of the following statements is true?
   (A) Folk healers choose different herbs to cure diseases without any sound basis.
   (B) People who practice folk medicine need lots of formal education on herbs.
   (C) The success of folk medicine led to the development of doctor medicine.
   (D) Natural cures worked better than scientific medicine in ancient times.

51. The author's primary purpose in this passage is to _____.
   (A) describe different types of medicine
   (B) argue for the importance of medicine in health care
   (C) show the crucial role religion plays in medical treatments
   (D) compare the educational background of three different types of patients

52-55 為題組

   Today's teen consumer market is the most profitable it has ever been. Even though 65% of teens claim that they rely on themselves for their fashion ideas, it is estimated that less than 20% of the teen population is innovative enough to drive fashion trends, according to a recent study by a marketing firm. Marketers recognize this fact and often use elements of youth culture to promote their products. Perhaps one of the best examples is their use of hip-hop culture. It is reported that hip-hop fashion alone generates $750 million to $1 billion annually. Sales of rap music and videos each exceed that amount.

   Rap's rise and sustained global popularity is a good illustration of how influential youth culture is on youth attitudes and behavior. Remember when Madonna hit the charts with her bra in full view while singing about "virginity"? Soon after that, adolescent girls around the world began wearing their underwear outside their clothes.

Fashion designer Tommy Hilfiger was fully aware of the power of youth culture. He marketed his brand by giving clothes to famous MTV stars and featuring teen stars in his print ads. Picking up on teens' interest in computer games, Hilfiger sponsored a Nintendo competition and installed Nintendo terminals in his stores. The payoff? Teens rated Hilfiger jeans as their number one brand in a survey in 2000.

52. What is the best title for this passage?
    (A) The Importance of Marketing
    (B) The Power of Youth Culture
    (C) The Popularity of Hip-hop Fashion
    (D) The Success of Tommy Hilfiger

53. How much money do sales of rap music and videos together make each year?
    (A) More than $1 billion.
    (B) Between $750 million and $1 billion.
    (C) Between $500 million and $750 million.
    (D) Less than $500 million.

54. According to the passage, which of the following statements is true?
    (A) The purchasing power of teenagers has been decreasing over the years.
    (B) Many teenagers make a lot of profits in the fashion market today.
    (C) Madonna led the fashion of wearing underwear outside clothes.
    (D) Marketers recognize youth culture as a part of hip-hop culture.

55. It can be inferred from the passage that Hilfiger _____.
    (A) believed that MTV stars could drive fashion trends among teens
    (B) sold Nintendo terminals together with teens' clothes in his stores
    (C) sponsored a Nintendo competition out of his own interest in computer games
    (D) was rated by teens and adults as the best designer of jeans around the world in 2000

第貳部份：非選擇題

一、簡答題（10％）

說明：1. 閱讀下面這篇文章，然後簡答下列問題。答案必須寫在「答案卷」
上。

2. 請依序作答，並標明題號。答案應簡明扼要，只寫重要詞彙（key
words），請勿超過五個英文單詞（words）。每題 2 分，共 10 分。
注意：請勿抄下整句或整行，否則不予記分。

The guitar is one of the oldest instruments known to man. It
probably originated in the vicinity of China. There were guitars in
ancient Egypt and Greece as well, but the written history of the guitar
starts in Spain in the 13th century. By 1500 the guitar was popular in
Italy, France, and Spain. A French document of that time concludes
that many people were playing the guitar. Stradivarius, the undeniable
king of violin makers, could not resist creating a variety of guitars. Also,
there was no lack of music written for the instrument. Haydn, Schubert,
and others wrote guitar music. When the great Beethoven was asked to
compose music for the guitar, he went into a rage and refused, but
eventually even Beethoven could not ignore the challenge. Legend tells
us he finally called the guitar a miniature orchestra. Indeed the guitar
does sound like a little orchestra! Perhaps that is why in rural areas
around the world the guitar has been a source of music for **millions** to
enjoy.

1. Where is the earliest written record of the guitar found?

2. What musical instrument was Stradivarius most famous for making?

3. What was Beethoven's first reaction when he was asked to write
music for the guitar?

4. What was the challenge that Beethoven could not ignore?

5. What does "**millions**" in the last line refer to?

二、英文作文（20％）

說明： 1. 依提示在「答案卷」上寫一篇英文作文。

2. 文長 120 個單詞（words）左右。

提示： 請以 "Music Is An Important Part of Our Life" 為題，說明音樂（例如古典音樂、流行歌曲、搖滾音樂等）在生活中的重要性，並以你或他人的經驗為例，敘述音樂所帶來的好處。

92年度學科能力測驗英文科試題①詳解

第壹部分：單一選擇題

一、詞彙與慣用語：

1. (**C**) All the flights to and from Kaohsiung were <u>cancelled</u> because of the heavy thunderstorm.
   因為有強烈的雷雨，所以所有往返高雄的班機都被<u>取消</u>了。

   (A) advise ﹝əd'vaɪz﹞ v. 勸告
   (B) disclose ﹝dɪs'kloz﹞ v. 透露
   (C) **cancel** ﹝'kænsḷ﹞ v. 取消
   (D) benefit ﹝'bɛnəfɪt﹞ v. 使獲益

   flight ﹝flaɪt﹞ n. 班機　　thunderstorm ﹝'θʌndɚ,stɔrm﹞ n. 雷雨

2. (**A**) The woman told the truth to her lawyer without <u>reservation</u> because he was the only person she could rely on. 那個女人毫無<u>保留</u>地把眞相告訴她的律師，因為他是她唯一可以信賴的人。

   (A) **reservation** ﹝,rɛzɚ'veʃən﹞ n. 保留
   (B) combination ﹝,kɑmbə'neʃən﹞ n. 組合
   (C) impression ﹝ɪm'prɛʃən﹞ n. 印象
   (D) foundation ﹝faʊn'deʃən﹞ n. 基礎

   lawyer ﹝'lɔjɚ﹞ n. 律師　　**rely on** 信賴

3. (**B**) The man was severely injured in last weekend's tragic car accident and died <u>shortly</u> afterwards.
   那名男子在上週末悲慘的車禍中受重傷，並在<u>不久後</u>死亡。

   (A) mostly ﹝'mostlɪ﹞ adv. 大多　　(B) **shortly** ﹝'ʃɔrtlɪ﹞ adv. 不久
   (C) easily ﹝'izɪlɪ﹞ adv. 容易地　　(D) hardly ﹝'hɑrdlɪ﹞ adv. 幾乎不
   severely ﹝sə'vɪrlɪ﹞ adv. 嚴重地　　injure ﹝'ɪndʒɚ﹞ v. 使受傷
   tragic ﹝'trædʒɪk﹞ adj. 悲慘的　　afterwards ﹝'æftɚwɚdz﹞ adv. 之後

4. (**D**) Mr. Smith's work in Taiwan is just <u>temporary</u>. He will go back to the U.S. next month.

史密斯先生在台灣的工作只是<u>暫時的</u>。他下個月就會回美國了。

(A) liberal ('lɪbərəl) adj. 自由的；寬大的

(B) rural ('rʊrəl) adj. 鄉村的；田園的

(C) conscious ('kɑnʃəs) adj. 知道的

(D) ***temporary*** ('tɛmpə,rɛrɪ) adj. 暫時的

5. (**B**) Helen <u>exploded</u> with anger when she saw her boyfriend kissing an attractive girl.

當海倫看見她男朋友親吻一個迷人的女孩時，她<u>大發脾氣</u>。

(A) collide (kə'laɪd) v. 相撞

(B) ***explode*** (ɪk'splod) v. (感情) 激發；發作

(C) relax (rɪ'læks) v. 放鬆　　(D) defeat (dɪ'fit) v. 打敗

attractive (ə'træktɪv) adj. 吸引人的；迷人的

6. (**A**) Dr. Liu's new book is a collection of his <u>observations</u> of the daily life of tribal people in Africa.

劉博士的新書，集結了他對非洲部落居民的日常生活所做的<u>觀察</u>。

(A) ***observation*** (,ɑbzɚ'veʃən) n. 觀察

(B) interference (,ɪntɚ'fɪrəns) n. 妨礙

(C) prevention (prɪ'vɛnʃən) n. 預防

(D) substitution (,sʌbstə'tjuʃən) n. 代替

collection (kə'lɛkʃən) n. 收集　　***daily life*** 日常生活

tribal ('traɪbḷ) adj. 部落的　　Africa ('æfrɪkə) n. 非洲

7. (**C**) The young couple decided to <u>postpone</u> their wedding until all the details were well taken care of.

那對年輕的情侶決定要將婚期<u>延後</u>，直到處理好所有的細節為止。

(A) announce (ə'naʊns) v. 宣佈　　(B) maintain (men'ten) v. 維持

(C) ***postpone*** (post'pon) v. 延期　　(D) simplify ('sɪmplə,faɪ) v. 簡化

couple ('kʌpḷ) n. 一對　　wedding ('wɛdɪŋ) n. 婚禮

detail ('ditel) n. 細節　　***take care of*** 處理

8. (**A**) The conflicts between John and his teacher made it difficult for the teacher to judge his performance <u>objectively</u>.
約翰和他的老師之間的衝突，讓老師很難客觀地評斷他的表現。

(A) *objectively* (əb'dʒɛktɪvlɪ) *adv.* 客觀地
(B) painfully ('penfəlɪ) *adv.* 痛苦地
(C) excitedly (ɛk'saɪtɪdlɪ) *adv.* 興奮地
(D) intimately ('ɪntəmɪtlɪ) *adv.* 親密地

conflict ('kɑnflɪkt) *n.* 衝突　　judge (dʒʌdʒ) *v.* 評斷
performance (pɚ'fɔrməns) *n.* 表現

9. (**D**) Living in a highly <u>competitive</u> society, you definitely have to arm yourself with as much knowledge as possible.
生活在一個高度競爭的社會裡，你一定要儘可能地以知識充實自己。

(A) tolerant ('tɑlərənt) *adj.* 寬容的
(B) permanent ('pɜmənənt) *adj.* 永久的
(C) favorable ('fevərəbḷ) *adj.* 有利的
(D) *competitive* (kəm'pɛtətɪv) *adj.* 競爭的

highly ('haɪlɪ) *adv.* 高度地；非常地
definitely ('dɛfənɪtlɪ) *adv.* 一定　　arm (ɑrm) *v.* 供給；配備；加強
arm oneself with knowledge 以知識充實自己
as…as possible 儘可能

10. (**C**) The 70-year-old professor sued the university for age <u>discrimination</u>, because his teaching contract had not been renewed.
那位七十歲的教授，控告該所大學年齡歧視，因為他的教學聘約沒有被續約。

(A) possession (pə'zɛʃən) *n.* 擁有
(B) commitment (kə'mɪtmənt) *n.* 承諾
(C) *discrimination* (dɪ,skrɪmə'neʃən) *n.* 歧視
(D) employment (ɪm'plɔɪmənt) *n.* 雇用；工作

professor (prə'fɛsɚ) *n.* 教授　　sue (su) *v.* 控告
contract ('kɑntrækt) *n.* 合約　　renew (rɪ'nju) *v.* 重訂 (合約)

11. (**B**) Kevin burst into tears <u>on the spot</u> because his teacher punished him in front of the whole class.
凱文當場大哭，因為老師在全班同學的面前處罰他。

    (A) on the side　作為兼職；作為副業

    (B) *on the spot*　當場

    (C) on any account　無論如何

    (D) on the mark　中肯的

    burst into tears　突然大哭　　punish〔ˋpʌnɪʃ〕*v.* 處罰

12. (**C**) As soon as the couple realized that they didn't love each other anymore, they <u>broke up</u>.
當那對情侶一了解到他們彼此已經不再相愛時，就分手了。

    (A) fall off　脫落   (B) cut in　插嘴

    (C) *break up*　分手   (D) stand by　站在旁邊；作好準備

    not…anymore　不再

13. (**A**) The power workers had to work <u>around the clock</u> to repair the power lines since the whole city was in the dark.
發電廠工人必須日夜不停地搶修電線，因為整個城市都陷入黑暗中。

    (A) *around the clock*　二十四小時地；日夜不停地

    (B) in the extreme　極端地

    (C) on the house　免費

    (D) in the majority　佔大多數

    power worker 發電廠工人　　repair〔rɪˋpɛr〕*v.* 修理
    power line 電線　　*in the dark* 在黑暗中

14. (**B**) After retirement, Mr. Wang <u>took to</u> ice skating, which he had always loved but had not had time for.
退休之後，王先生開始從事他一直很喜歡，但卻沒有時間去玩的溜冰。

    (A) appeal to　吸引；呼籲   (B) *take to*　開始從事

    (C) relate to　有關   (D) see to　照料；留意

    retirement〔rɪˋtaɪrmənt〕*n.* 退休　　*ice skating* 溜冰

15. (**D**) Why do we have to <u>put up with</u> Sue's selfish behavior? We have to teach her to care for others.

為什麼我們必須<u>忍受</u>蘇自私的行為？我們必須教導她要尊重別人。

(A) get over with　做完　　　　　(B) hang out with　和～鬼混
(C) make up with　和～和好　　　(D) ***put up with***　忍受

selfish〔'sɛlfɪʃ〕*adj.* 自私的　　behavior〔bɪ'hevjɚ〕*n.* 行為
care for 尊重

二、句子配合題：

16. (**B**) Since it was a holiday, <u>I stayed in bed an extra hour.</u>

因為那天是假日，所以我在床上多睡了一個小時。

in bed 在床上　　extra〔'ɛkstrə〕*adj.* 額外的

17. (**D**) Unless he prepares well, <u>he will fail the exam.</u>

除非他有充份的準備，否則考試就會不及格。

fail〔fel〕*v.* 不及格

18. (**J**) If I had known the fact, <u>I would have taken action right away.</u>

如果我當時知道這個事實，我就會立刻採取行動。

take action 採取行動　　***right away*** 立刻

19. (**E**) Belle was the person <u>who changed him into a gentleman.</u>

貝兒就是那個將他變成一個紳士的人。

20. (**G**) A person who exercises regularly <u>is more likely to look young.</u>

有規律運動的人，比較可能看起來年輕一點。

regularly〔'rɛgjələˑlɪ〕*adv.* 規律地　　***be likely to*** 可能

三、綜合測驗：

<u>第 21 至 25 題為題組</u>

　　The first American space toilet was Alan Shepard's space suit. His flight was supposed to last only 15 minutes, so there was no provision made for him to relieve himself in the capsule. His flight, <u>however</u>, was

delayed for hours. It was then decided that Alan Shepard should relieve
himself in his space suit, and continue with the mission as scheduled. This
₂₂
problem urged NASA to develop the first space toilet, a modified diaper.

　　第一個美國的太空廁所，就是艾倫・薛帕德的太空衣。他的飛行任務，原
本應該只有十五分鐘，所以太空艙內，並沒有準備讓他上廁所的地方。然而，
他的飛行任務卻耽擱了好幾個鐘頭。後來大家就決定，要艾倫・薛帕德直接在
他的太空衣裡面上廁所，然後再繼續原定的任務。這個問題促使美國國家航空
太空總署，研發了第一個太空廁所，也就是一種改良型的尿布。

> ***space toilet*** 太空廁所　　***space suit*** 太空衣
> flight〔flaɪt〕*n.* 飛行　　***be supposed to* + *V.*** 應該
> last〔læst〕*v.* 持續　　provision〔prə'vɪʒən〕*n.* 準備
> ***relieve* oneself** 上廁所　　capsule〔'kæpsḷ〕*n.* 太空艙
> delay〔dɪ'le〕*v.* 使耽擱　　mission〔'mɪʃən〕*n.* 任務
> ***as scheduled*** 按照原定計劃的　　urge〔ɝdʒ〕*v.* 促使
> ***NASA*** 美國國家航空太空總署（= *National Aeronautics and Space Administration*）　　modified〔'mɑdə,faɪd〕*adj.* 改良的
> diaper〔'daɪəpɚ〕*n.* 尿布

21. (**C**) 本來太空任務只有十五分鐘，「然而」，後來耽擱了好幾個鐘頭，故選
　　　(C) ***however***。而 (A) therefore「因此」，(B) similarly「同樣地」，(D)
　　　otherwise〔'ʌðɚ,waɪz〕*adv.* 否則，均不合句意。

22. (**B**) 「這個」問題促使太空總署發明了第一個太空廁所，故選 (B) ***This***。

Diapers are <u>still</u> used by astronauts when they are outside the space shuttle,
₂₃
wearing a space suit. As the flights grew longer, a new set of two collection
bags was devised, <u>one</u> for liquid wastes and the other for solid wastes. Once
₂₄
used, the bags are sealed and stored for the flight back to the earth, <u>where</u>
₂₅
they are disposed of.

直到現在,當太空人身穿太空衣,在太空梭外執行任務時,他們仍然會使用這種尿布。隨著太空任務時間變得愈來愈長,所以後來就發明了一套內含兩個收集袋的新裝置,其中一個是用來裝液態排泄物,另一個則是裝固態排泄物。這些袋子一旦使用過後,就會被密封保存,直到任務結束,回到地球後再丟棄。

> astronaut〔'æstrə,nɔt〕n. 太空人　　***space shuttle*** 太空梭
> grow〔gro〕v. 變得　　***a set of*** 一套
> devise〔dɪ'vaɪz〕v. 設計　　***liquid wastes*** 液態排泄物
> ***solid wastes*** 固態排泄物　　seal〔sil〕v. 密封
> store〔stor〕v. 儲存　　***the earth*** 地球　　***dispose of*** 丟掉

23.(**D**) 依句意,這種改良型尿布,直到現在「仍然」被太空人使用,故選
(D) ***still***。

24.(**D**) 表特定的兩者,其中一個用 *one*,另一個則用 the other,選 (D)。

25.(**A**) 表地點的關係副詞 *where*,引導形容詞子句,修飾先行詞 the earth。

第 26 至 30 題為題組

　　Up to about 250 million years ago the world had just one huge super-continent called Pangaea. Animals were able to move and intermix with <u>one another</u>. About 200 million years ago this super-continent broke up into two
₂₆
continents: Laurasia and Gondwana. About 60 million years ago Gondwana broke up into <u>what</u> later became South America, Africa, Antarctica, India
₂₇
and Australia.

　　一直到兩億五千萬年前,世界還只是一個巨大的超大陸,稱為「盤古大陸」。當時的動物可以自由遷徙,相互混種。大約兩億年前,這個超大陸就分裂成兩塊:即勞亞古大陸和岡瓦納古大陸。大約到六千萬年前,岡瓦納古大陸再度分裂,成為後來的南美洲、非洲、南極洲、印度、和澳洲。

> ***up to*** 直到　　huge〔hjudʒ〕adj. 巨大的
> continent〔'kɑntənənt〕n. 大陸　　***super-continent*** 超大陸
> ***Pangaea*** 盤古大陸　　move〔muv〕v. 遷移
> intermix〔,ɪntɚ'mɪks〕v. 混合　　***break up into*** 分裂成
> ***Laurasia*** 勞亞古大陸　　***Gondwana*** 岡瓦納古大陸
> later〔'letɚ〕adv. 後來　　Antarctica〔ænt'ɑrktɪkə〕n. 南極洲

26. (**B**) 依句意，這些動物「互相」混種，選 (B) *one another*。

27. (**C**) 空格應填兼具先行詞作用的複合關代，引導名詞子句，做介系詞 into
    的受詞，及動詞 became 的主詞，故選 (C) *what* (= *the things that*)。

Since then Australia <u>has been isolated</u> from the rest of the world by vast
                              28
oceans. The animals there no longer had <u>contact</u> with animals from other
                                              29
parts of the world. They evolved separately. As a result, about 95 % of
Australia's mammals and 94 % of its frogs are found <u>nowhere</u> else in the
                                                        30
world. Australia has lots of very unusual animals.

從那時起，廣大的海洋就將澳洲和世界上的其他地區隔離。生長在澳洲的動物，
再也無法接觸世界其他地方的動物。牠們獨自進化。因此，在澳洲，大約有百
分之九十五的哺乳類動物，和百分之九十四的青蛙，是在世界上的其他地方都
找不到的。澳洲有很多非常罕見的動物。

> ***the rest*** 其餘的部份　　vast〔væst〕*adj.* 廣大的
> ocean〔'oʃən〕*n.* 海洋　　***no longer*** 不再　　evolve〔ɪ'vɑlv〕*v.* 進化
> separately〔'sɛpərɪtlɪ〕*adv.* 獨自地　　***as a result*** 因此
> mammal〔'mæml〕*n.* 哺乳類動物　　frog〔frɑg〕*n.* 青蛙
> else〔ɛls〕*adj.* 其他的　　unusual〔ʌn'juʒuəl〕*adj.* 不尋常的；罕見的

28. (**D**) 由後面的 by vast oceans 可知，澳洲是「被廣大的海洋所阻隔」，應用
    被動；又由前面的 since then「從那時起」可知，此表由過去持續到
    現在的狀態，應用現在完成式，故選 (D) *has been isolated*。
    isolate〔'aɪsə,let〕*v.* 隔離

29. (**C**) 依句意，由於海洋的阻隔，澳洲的動物不再和世界上其他地方的動物
    有所「接觸」，故選 (C) *contact*〔'kɑntækt〕*n.* 接觸。而 (A) confusion
    〔kən'fjuʒən〕*n.* 混淆，(B) marriage〔'mærɪdʒ〕*n.* 婚姻，(D) transaction
    〔træns'ækʃən〕*n.* 交易，均不合句意。

30. (**A**) 依句意，澳洲的生物獨自進化，因此大部分的動物在「其他地方都找
    不到」，故選 (A) *nowhere*。

四、文意選填：

第 31 至 40 題為題組

Stress has become a favorite subject of everyday conversation. It is not ³¹(I) unusual to hear friends and family members talk about the difficulty they have in ³²(E) managing the stress of everyday life and the efforts they make to control the events ³³(H) that cause stress.

壓力已經成為日常對話中，人們最喜歡的話題。我們常會聽到朋友和家人談論，他們在處理日常生活中的壓力時，所面臨的困難，以及在掌控會帶來壓力的事件時，所做的努力。

  stress (strɛs) n. 壓力 subject ('sʌbdʒɪkt) n. 主題
  everyday ('ɛvrɪ,de) adj. 日常的 member ('mɛmbɚ) n. 成員
  manage ('mænɪdʒ) v. 管理；處理 effort ('ɛfɚt) n. 努力
  event (ɪ'vɛnt) n. 事件 cause (kɔz) v. 導致；造成

Most of us understand the results of not controlling our reactions ³⁴(G) to stress. Forty-three percent of all adults suffer terrible health effects ³⁵(B) from stress. Most physician office visits are for stress-related illnesses and complaints. Stress is linked to the six ³⁶(J) leading causes of death—heart disease, cancer, lung disease, accidents, liver disease, and suicide. Currently, health care costs account for ³⁷(A) about twelve percent of the gross domestic product.

我們大部份的人都知道，沒有好好掌控對壓力的反應，所造成的結果會是如何。有百分之四十三的成人因為壓力，而使得健康受到嚴重的影響。大部份醫生的門診病患，都是罹患和壓力有關的疾病，或因壓力而導致的身體不適。壓力和六個主要的死亡原因有關—心臟病、癌症、肺部疾病、意外事故、肝臟疾病，以及自殺。目前，醫療保健的費用大約佔國內生產毛額的百分之十二。

  reaction (rɪ'ækʃən) n. 反應 < to > suffer ('sʌfɚ) v. 遭受
  terrible ('tɛrəbl̩) adj. 可怕的；嚴重的 effect (ɪ'fɛkt) n. 影響
  physician (fə'zɪʃən) n. 醫師 office ('ɔfɪs) n. 診所
  visit ('vɪzɪt) n. 就診 related (rɪ'letɪd) adj. 與⋯有關的

complaint〔kəm'plent〕*n.* 疾病；身體不適　　link〔lɪŋk〕*v.* 連結
be linked to 與～有關　　leading〔'lidɪŋ〕*adj.* 主要的；最重要的
cause〔kɔz〕*n.* 原因　　cancer〔'kænsɚ〕*n.* 癌症
lung〔lʌŋ〕*n.* 肺　　liver〔'lɪvɚ〕*n.* 肝臟
suicide〔'suə,saɪd〕*n.* 自殺　　currently〔'kɝəntlɪ〕*adv.* 目前
health care 保健　　***account for*** （在數量、比例方面）佔～
gross〔gros〕*adj.* 總共的　　domestic〔də'mɛstɪk〕*adj.* 國內的
gross domestic product 國內生產毛額

　　Yet, while stress may damage our health, it is sometimes necessary,
[38](C) even desirable. Exciting or challenging events [39](F) like the birth of a
child, completion of a major project at work, or moving to a new city
generate [40](D) as much stress as does tragedy or disaster. And without
stress, life would be dull.

　　然而，雖然壓力可能會造成健康上的傷害，但有時候卻是必要的，甚至是
值得擁有的。刺激的或具挑戰性的事件，例如生小孩、完成工作上的重要計劃，
或是搬遷到新的城市時，所產生的壓力，和不幸的事件或災難所造成的壓力一
樣大。而且如果沒有壓力，生活將會變得很無趣。

desirable〔dɪ'zaɪrəbḷ〕*adj.* 理想的；值得擁有的
challenging〔'tʃælɪndʒɪŋ〕*adj.* 有挑戰性的
completion〔kəm'pliʃən〕*n.* 完成　　major〔'medʒɚ〕*adj.* 重大的
project〔'prɑdʒɛkt〕*n.* 計劃　　generate〔'dʒɛnə,ret〕*v.* 產生
tragedy〔'trædʒədɪ〕*n.* 悲劇；不幸的事
disaster〔dɪz'æstɚ〕*n.* 災難　　dull〔dʌl〕*adj.* 乏味的；單調的

五、閱讀測驗：

41-43 為題組

　　I usually go to work by subway, and I get to work by 8:00 A.M. Before
I start my job, I put on my uniform and look at myself in the mirror to make
sure that I look neat. At 8:30 in the morning, I go on duty. I usually eat
lunch from twelve to one and generally take a fifteen-minute break in the
morning and in the afternoon. At 4:30 in the afternoon, I go off duty.

我通常搭地鐵上班,然後在早上八點,到達工作地點。開始工作以前,我會穿上我的制服,照照鏡子,確定自己看起來很整潔。早上八點半,我開始上班。我通常會在十二點到一點之間吃午餐,在早上和下午,各休息十五分鐘。下午四點半,我就下班了。

subway ('sʌb,we) n. 地鐵　　　 get to 到達
work (wɜk) n. 工作地點　　　 by (baɪ) prep. 在~之前
put on 穿上　　 uniform ('junə,fɔrm) n. 制服
mirror ('mɪrə) n. 鏡子　　 make sure 確定
neat (nit) adj. 整潔的　　 go on duty 上班
take a break 休息一下　　 go off duty 下班

I enjoy my job very much. I meet all kinds of people and talk to everyone. Many people ask me questions, and I give them the necessary information. I try to be very helpful. I always call out floors very clearly, and I am constantly on the move. Most men take off their hats in my car, and sometimes I have to tell passengers to put out their cigarettes. Some people smile at me, but others just ignore me. In fact, my life can be described as consisting of a series of "ups" and "downs."

我很喜歡我的工作。我會遇見各式各樣的人,並且和每個人說話。很多人會問我問題,然後我也告訴他們必要的資訊。我會儘量去幫助別人。我總是清楚地喊出每個樓層,而且不斷地在移動中。大部分的男人,會在我的電梯裡脫下帽子,而有的時候,我得告訴搭乘電梯的人,要把煙熄掉。有些人會對我微笑,也有些人會忽視我的存在。事實上,我的生活可以說是由不斷的「上升」和「下降」所組成的。

information (,ɪnfə'meʃən) n. 資訊　　 call out 叫喊
floor (flor) n. 樓層　　 take off 脫掉
car (kar) n. (電梯的) 升降室;梯廂
constantly ('kanstəntlɪ) adv. 不斷地　　 on the move 在移動中
passenger ('pæsṇdʒə) n. 乘客　　 put out 熄滅
cigarette ('sɪgə,rɛt) n. 香煙　　 some…others 有些…有些
ignore (ɪg'nor) v. 忽視　　 be described as 被說成
consist of 由~組成　　 a series of 一連串的

41. (**C**) 本文主要是在描述 _____。

 (A) 作者看起來如何   (B) 「生命」對作者的意義

 (C) 作者的典型的一天   (D) 作者和什麼樣的人一起工作

 mainly〔ˋmenlɪ〕 *adv.* 主要地   author〔ˋɔθɚ〕 *n.* 作者

 typical〔ˋtɪpɪkl〕 *adj.* 典型的

42. (**D**) 我們可從本文推知，作者是一位 _____。

 (A) 警察   (B) 司機

 (C) 地板的清理工   (D) 電梯操作員

 infer〔ɪnˋfɝ〕 *v.* 推論   cleaner〔ˋklinɚ〕 *n.* 清潔工

 elevator〔ˋɛləˏvetɚ〕 *n.* 電梯   operator〔ˋɑpəˏretɚ〕 *n.* 操作者

43. (**B**) 本文中的"constantly on the move"這個片語指的事實是 _____。

 (A) 作者總是很清楚地喊出每個樓層

 (B) 作者很少停留在一個地方很久

 (C) 作者會遇見各式各樣的人，並和每個人說話

 (D) 作者常常幫乘客搬行李

 expression〔ɪkˋsprɛʃən〕 *n.* 辭句；說法   ***refer to*** 是指

 for a long while 很久   move〔muv〕 *v.* 搬動

 baggage〔ˋbægɪdʒ〕 *n.* 行李

44-47 為題組

 Magic is believed to have begun with the Egyptians, in 1700 BC. A magician named Dedi of Dedsnefu was reported to have performed for the pharaoh, or the king. He was also known to have entertained the slaves who built the pyramids. The "Cups and Balls" trick which he was particularly good at is still performed by magicians all over the world today.

 一般認為，魔術是由西元前 1700 年的埃及人發明的。據說有位來自德茲耐夫，名叫德地的魔術師，曾為法老，也就是國王，做過表演。大家都知道，他也曾提供娛樂給那些建造金字塔的奴隸。他特別擅長的「杯子和球」的戲法，現在全世界的魔術師仍然會表演。

magic ('mædʒɪk) *n.* 魔術　　***begin with*** 始於
Egyptian (ɪ'dʒɪpʃən) *n.* 埃及人　　magician (mə'dʒɪʃən) *n.* 魔術師
report (rɪ'port) *v.* 傳說　　perform (pə'fɔrm) *v.* 表演
pharaoh ('fɛro) *n.* 法老 (古埃及王的尊稱)　　or (ɔr) *conj.* 也就是
entertain (,ɛntə'ten) *v.* 娛樂　　slave (slev) *n.* 奴隸
pyramid ('pɪrəmɪd) *n.* 金字塔　　trick (trɪk) *n.* 戲法;把戲
be good at 擅長　　***all over the world*** 在全世界

　　The ancient Greeks and Romans were also fascinated by the idea of magic. Actually, one of their main interests was the art of deception. This explains why at that time the priests even built magic devices into their temples. These devices made it possible for doors to open by themselves and wine to flow magically out of statues' mouths. This was done mainly to convince people that the priests were powerful.

　　古希臘人和羅馬人,也對魔術這個觀念非常著迷。事實上,他們主要感興趣的部份,是幻術的技巧。這就解釋了為什麼那時候的祭師,甚至會在他們的神殿裡,建造魔術的機關。這些裝置讓門可以自動打開,也讓酒可以神奇地從雕像的嘴裡流出來。這樣做主要是為了讓人民相信,祭師是很有力量的。

ancient ('enʃənt) *adj.* 古代的　　Greek (grik) *n.* 希臘人
Roman ('romən) *n.* 羅馬人　　fascinate ('fæsn̩,et) *v.* 使著迷
art (ɑrt) *n.* 技巧　　deception (dɪ'sɛpʃən) *n.* 幻術
priest (prist) *n.* 祭師　　device (dɪ'vaɪs) *n.* 裝置
temple ('tɛmpl̩) *n.* 神殿　　***by oneself*** 自己
wine (waɪn) *n.* 酒　　magically ('mædʒɪklɪ) *adv.* 神奇地
statue ('stætʃu) *n.* 雕像　　convince (kən'vɪns) *v.* 說服;使相信

　　Magic, however, was not well accepted before the 1800s. Magicians were thought of as freaks and were only allowed to perform in a circus. It was in the 19th century that the magician Robert Houdin came along and changed people's views and attitudes about magic. It was also because of Robert Houdin that many magicians were able to add Dr. or MD to their names. Today magicians try hard to find new ways to show their practiced skills. Magic is now entertainment for families all over the world.

　　然而，魔術在十九世紀之前，並未完全被人們所接受。魔術師被當作怪胎，並且只准在馬戲團裡表演。一直要到十九世紀，羅勃特•哈丁出現後，人們對魔術的觀念和態度才有所改變。而且也是由於羅勃特•哈丁的緣故，許多的魔術師才能在自己名字前，加上博士或醫學博士的頭銜。現在的魔術師，非常努力想找到新方法，來展現他們熟練的技巧。現在在全世界，魔術已經成爲供全家人觀賞的一種娛樂。

accept (ək'sɛpt) v. 接受　　**the 1800s** 十九世紀
be thought of as 被認爲是　　freak (frik) n. 怪胎
allow (ə'laʊ) v. 准許　　circus ('sɝkəs) n. 馬戲團
century ('sɛntʃərɪ) n. 世紀　　**come along** 出現
view (vju) n. 看法　　attitude ('ætə,tjud) n. 態度
add…to~ 把…加在~　　**Dr.** 博士 (= *Doctor*)
MD 醫學博士 (= *Doctor of Medicine*)
practiced ('præktɪst) adj. 熟練的
entertainment (,ɛntə'tenmənt) n. 娛樂

44. (**D**) 何者是本文最好的標題？
　　(A) 魔術戲法　　　　　　(B) 一位偉大的魔術師
　　(C) 供娛樂的魔術　　　　(D) 魔術的歷史
　　title ('taɪtḷ) n. 標題　　history ('hɪstrɪ) n. 歷史

45. (**D**) 在古希臘，祭師會做什麼，來向人民顯示自己有不尋常的能力？
　　(A) 他們會表演魔術戲法，來娛樂民衆。
　　(B) 他們能隨意讓神殿裡的雕像喝酒。
　　(C) 他們用從雕像嘴裡流出來的酒，替民衆治病。
　　(D) 他們在神殿裡建造魔術的機關，讓門自動打開。
　　treat (trit) v. 治療

46. (**B**) 在西元 1800 年以前，人們認爲魔術是什麼？
　　(A) 魔術應該只在神殿裡使用。
　　(B) 魔術只能在馬戲團裡表演。
　　(C) 魔術是由怪胎和醫生表演的。
　　(D) 魔術是法老每天主要的活動。
　　major ('medʒɚ) adj. 主要的　　daily ('delɪ) adj. 每天的
　　activity (æk'tɪvətɪ) n. 活動

47. (**A**) 下列敘述何者爲眞？

 (A) <u>魔術創始於大約三千七百年前。</u>

 (B) 來自德茲耐夫的德地，只爲國王表演魔術。

 (C) 羅勃特・哈丁是第一個表演魔術的魔術師。

 (D) 「杯子和球」的戲法，已經被表演了大約一千七百年。

<u>48-51 爲題組</u>

 There are three branches of medicine. One is called "doctor medicine," or "scientific medicine." Scientific doctors try to observe sicknesses, look for logical patterns, and then find out how the human body works. From there they figure out what treatments may work. This kind of medicine is believed to date from the 4th century BC. Although nowadays it is successful, in the ancient world this approach probably did not cure many patients.

 醫學有三個分支。其中一支稱爲「醫師醫學」，或「科學醫學」。科學醫師會嘗試去觀察疾病，找出合邏輯的模式，然後查明人體是如何運作的。由此，他們就能知道，什麼治療方法可能會有效。一般認爲，這樣的醫學起源於西元前四世紀。儘管現在這種醫學十分成功，但在古代，這種方法卻不見得能夠治好很多病人。

 branch〔bræntʃ〕*n.* 分支；分科 observe〔əbˋzɝv〕*v.* 觀察

 logical〔ˋlɑdʒɪkl〕*adj.* 合邏輯的；合理的 pattern〔ˋpætən〕*n.* 模式

 find out 找出；查明 work〔wɝk〕*v.* 運作；有效

 figure out 知道 treatment〔ˋtritmənt〕*n.* 治療

 date from 追溯自；源自 (= *date back to* = *trace back to*)

 nowadays〔ˋnaʊəˏdez〕*adv.* 現在 approach〔əˋprotʃ〕*n.* 方法

 cure〔kjʊr〕*v.* 治好；治療

 A second kind of medicine is called "natural cures," or "folk medicine," in which less educated people try to cure sicknesses with various herbs. These folk healers also use observation and logic, but they are not so aware of it. They try things until they find something that seems to work, and then they keep doing that. Folk medicine flourished long before the development of scientific medicine and was more successful in ancient times than doctor medicine.

　　第二種醫學稱為「自然療法」，或「民俗療法」，這種療法就是受過較少教育的人，會試著利用各種不同的藥草治療疾病。這些民俗醫療者，也會使用觀察法與邏輯，但他們卻沒有意識到這一點。他們會一直嘗試各種東西，直到找到好像有用的東西為止，然後就一直沿用。民俗醫學，早在科學醫學開始發展之前就很盛行，而且在古代的療效，比醫師醫學來得更好。

cure〔kjʊr〕n. 治療法　　　folk〔fok〕adj. 民間的；通俗的
educated〔'ɛdʒʊ͵ketɪd〕adj. 受過教育的
various〔'vɛrɪəs〕adj. 各種不同的　　herb〔hɜb〕n. 藥草
healer〔'hilə〕n. 醫治者　　observation〔͵abzə'veʃən〕n. 觀察
logic〔'lɑdʒɪk〕n. 邏輯；推理　　**be aware of** 知道；意識到
flourish〔'flɜɪʃ〕v. 興盛；繁榮　　**in ancient times** 在古代

The third kind is called "health spas," or "faith healing." Sometimes this may be as simple as touching the holy man and being immediately healed. Other times, a magician may make you a magic charm, or say a spell, to cure you. Some religious groups organize special healing shrines for the sick. In these places people rest, get plenty of sleep, eat healthy food, drink water instead of wine, and exercise in various ways. They also talk to the priests and pray to the gods. If you are feeling depressed or you have been working too hard, going to these places may be just the right thing to make you feel better.

　　第三種稱為「健康水療」，或「信仰療法」。有時候，可能只是簡單到摸摸神職人員，就會立刻痊癒了。有時候，術士可能會為了治療你，而施展法術，或下咒語。有些宗教團體，會為病人安排特別的治療殿堂。人們會在這些地方休息，有充足的睡眠，吃健康食品，不喝酒而喝水，以及做各種不同的運動。他們也會與神職人員談話，並向神明祈禱。如果你覺得沮喪，或是工作過度，去這些地方，也許是正確的做法，會讓你覺得好一點。

spa〔spɑ〕n. 溫泉浴場；水療　　faith〔feθ〕n. 信仰
faith healing 信仰療法　　holy〔'holɪ〕adj. 神聖的
holy man 神職人員　　heal〔hil〕v. 治好
sometimes…other times~ 有時…有時~
magician〔mə'dʒɪʃən〕n. 術士；巫師
charm〔tʃɑrm〕n. 符咒；咒語（= spell）

religious〔rɪ'lɪdʒəs〕*adj.* 宗教的

organize〔'ɔrgən,aɪz〕*v.* 組織；安排

shrine〔ʃraɪn〕*n.* 寺廟；殿堂　　***the sick*** 病人（= *sick people*）

plenty of 許多的　　***instead of*** 而不是

priest〔prist〕*n.* 神職人員；牧師；神父　　pray〔pre〕*v.* 祈禱

depressed〔dɪ'prɛst〕*adj.* 沮喪的

48.（**C**）醫師醫學 _____ 。

(A) 的歷史比民俗醫療更久

(B) 被採用的時間大約有一千六百年之久

(C) 是根據觀察和邏輯思考來進行治療

(D) 在古代治療疾病非常成功

practice〔'præktɪs〕*v.* 實行　　***base~on…*** ～以…爲基礎

49.（**B**）根據本文，健康水療沒有使用下列何者？

(A) 魔力。　　　　　　　　　　(B) 各種不同的藥草。

(C) 宗教信仰。　　　　　　　　(D) 健康的生活方式。

50.（**D**）根據本文，下列敘述何者正確？

(A) 民俗醫療者選擇不同的草藥治療疾病，毫無確實的根據。

(B) 進行民俗療法的人，需要接受很多關於藥草的正式教育。

(C) 民俗療法的成功導致醫師醫學的發展。

(D) 在古代，自然療法比科學醫療更有效。

sound〔saʊnd〕*adj.* 有確實根據的　　basis〔'besɪs〕*n.* 基礎；根據

formal〔'fɔrml̩〕*adj.* 正式的　　***lead to*** 導致

51.（**A**）本文作者的主要目的是 _____ 。

(A) 描述不同類型的醫療

(B) 提倡保健醫學的重要性

(C) 顯示宗教在醫療中所扮演的重要角色

(D) 比較三種不同類型病人的學歷

primary〔'praɪ,mɛrɪ〕*adj.* 主要的　　argue〔'ɑrgju〕*v.* 爲…辯護< *for* >

crucial〔'kruʃəl〕*adj.* 非常重要的　　compare〔kəm'pɛr〕*v.* 比較

educational background 學歷　　patient〔'peʃənt〕*n.* 病人

52-55 為題組

　　Today's teen consumer market is the most profitable it has ever been. Even though 65% of teens claim that they rely on themselves for their fashion ideas, it is estimated that less than 20% of the teen population is innovative enough to drive fashion trends, according to a recent study by a marketing firm. Marketers recognize this fact and often use elements of youth culture to promote their products. Perhaps one of the best examples is their use of hip-hop culture. It is reported that hip-hop fashion alone generates $750 million to $1 billion annually. Sales of rap music and videos each exceed that amount.

　　現在的年輕族群消費市場，是有史以來最有利可圖的。即使百分之六十五的青少年宣稱，他們的時髦想法是自我的主張，但是根據行銷公司最近的研究，估計只有不到百分之二十的年輕族群，有足夠的創新能力，來帶動流行趨勢。行銷者了解這個事實，並經常使用年輕人文化中的元素，來促銷他們的產品。或許其中最好的例子，就是他們運用了嘻哈文化。據報導，光是嘻哈流行商品，每年就能帶來七億五千萬到十億元的收益。饒舌音樂和錄影帶的銷售，分別都超過這個金額。

teen〔tin〕*adj.* 十幾歲的　　consumer〔kənˈsumɚ〕*n.* 消費者
profitable〔ˈprɑfɪtəbḷ〕*adj.* 有利潤的
teens〔tinz〕*n.pl.* 十幾歲的青少年（= *teenagers*）
claim〔klem〕*v.* 宣稱　　estimate〔ˈɛstəˌmet〕*v.* 估計
innovative〔ˈɪnoˌvetɪv〕*adj.* 創新的　　drive〔draɪv〕*v.* 帶動
trend〔trɛnd〕*n.* 趨勢　　recent〔ˈrisṇt〕*adj.* 最近的
study〔ˈstʌdɪ〕*n.* 研究　　***marketing firm*** 行銷公司
marketer〔ˈmɑrkɪtɚ〕*n.* 出售商品的人或公司
recognize〔ˈrɛkəgˌnaɪz〕*v.* 認清；確認　　element〔ˈɛləmənt〕*n.* 元素
promote〔prəˈmot〕*v.* 促銷　　***hip-hop*** 嘻哈
alone〔əˈlon〕*adv.* 單單；僅僅　　generate〔ˈdʒɛnəˌret〕*v.* 產生
billion〔ˈbɪljən〕*n.* 十億　　annually〔ˈænjʊəlɪ〕*adv.* 每年
rap〔ræp〕*n.* 饒舌　　video〔ˈvɪdɪˌo〕*n.* 錄影帶
exceed〔ɪkˈsid〕*v.* 超過　　amount〔əˈmaʊnt〕*n.* 金額

Rap's rise and sustained global popularity is a good illustration of how influential youth culture is on youth attitudes and behavior. Remember when Madonna hit the charts with her bra in full view while singing about "virginity"? Soon after that, adolescent girls around the world began wearing their underwear outside their clothes.

饒舌音樂的興起,和持續在全球的流行,是一個很好的例證,說明年輕人文化,對於年輕人的態度和行為,是多麼具有影響力。還記得當瑪丹娜在眾目睽睽之下,穿著她的胸罩,打進熱門歌曲排行榜,但卻高唱著宛如「處女」嗎?在那之後不久,全世界的少女,都開始內衣外穿。

rise (raɪz) n. 興起　　sustain (sə'sten) v. 持續
global ('globl) adj. 全球的　　popularity (ˌpɑpjə'lærətɪ) n. 流行
illustration (ˌɪləs'treʃən) n. 例證
influential (ˌɪnflu'ɛnʃəl) adj. 有影響力的
the charts 熱門音樂歌曲排行榜
hit the charts 登上了排行榜 (= *make the charts*)
bra (brɑ) n. 胸罩　　*in full view* 一覽無遺
virginity (və'dʒɪnətɪ) n. 處女身份;童貞
adolescent (ˌædl'ɛsnt) adj. 青春期的　　*around the world* 全世界
underwear ('ʌndəˌwɛr) n. 內衣

Fashion designer Tommy Hilfiger was fully aware of the power of youth culture. He marketed his brand by giving clothes to famous MTV stars and featuring teen stars in his print ads. Picking up on teens' interest in computer games, Hilfiger sponsored a Nintendo competition and installed Nintendo terminals in his stores. The payoff? Teens rated Hilfiger jeans as their number one brand in a survey in 2000.

時裝設計師 Tommy Hilfiger 完全察覺到年輕文化的力量。他藉由提供服裝給著名的音樂錄影帶明星,並且利用以年輕明星為特色所印製的廣告,來銷售其品牌服裝。他了解年輕人對於電玩遊戲的興趣,所以就贊助任天堂的比賽,並且在店裡設置任天堂的終端機。那收益如何呢?在 2000 年的一份調查中,年輕人評定 Tommy Hilfiger 的牛仔褲,是他們心目中的的頭號品牌。

fashion〔'fæʃən〕*n.* 時裝;流行　　designer〔dɪ'zaɪnə〕*n.* 設計師

be aware of 知道　　market〔'mɑrkɪt〕*v.* 銷售

brand〔brænd〕*n.* 品牌　　feature〔'fitʃə〕*v.* 以~為特色

print〔prɪnt〕*adj.* 印刷的　　***ad*** 廣告(= *advertisement*)

pick up on 了解　　sponsor〔'spɑnsə〕*v.* 贊助

install〔ɪn'stɔl〕*v.* 安裝　　terminal〔'tɜmənḷ〕*n.* 終端機

payoff〔'pe,ɔf〕*n.* 收益;報酬　　rate〔ret〕*v.* 評價為 < *as* >

jeans〔dʒinz〕*n. pl.* 牛仔褲　　survey〔sə've〕*n.* 調查

52. (**B**) 什麼是最適合本文的標題?

(A) 行銷的重要性

(B) 年輕人文化的威力

(C) 嘻哈文化的流行

(D) Tommy Hilfiger 的成功

53. (**A**) 饒舌音樂和錄影帶,每一年的銷售金額有多少?

(A) 超過十億。　　　　　　(B) 七億五千萬到十億。

(C) 五億到七億五千萬。　　　(D) 不到五億。

54. (**C**) 根據本文,下列敘述何者正確?

(A) 青少年的購買力逐年下降。

(B) 現今許多青少年在時尚市場中,賺進了許多利潤。

(C) 瑪丹娜帶起了內衣外穿的流行。

(D) 行銷者視年輕人文化為嘻哈文化的一部分

purchase〔'pɜtʃəs〕*v.* 購買　　decrease〔dɪ'kris〕*v.* 減少

profit〔'prɑfɪt〕*n.* 利潤　　lead〔lid〕*v.* 領導

55. (**A**) 從本文可以推論,Tommy Hilfiger ＿＿＿＿＿＿。

(A) 相信音樂錄影帶的明星,可以帶動年輕人的流行趨勢

(B) 在他的店裡賣年輕人的衣服,也賣任天堂終端機

(C) 贊助任天堂的比賽,是出自於自己對電玩遊戲的興趣

(D) 被年輕人及成人評選為 2000 年全球最佳的牛仔褲設計師

第貳部分：非選擇題

一、簡答題：【本篇文章曾經出現在「劉毅英文」91 年 9 月 11 日的模考題中】

The guitar is one of the oldest instruments known to man. It probably originated in the vicinity of China. There were guitars in ancient Egypt and Greece as well, but the written history of the guitar starts in Spain in the 13th century. By 1500 the guitar was popular in Italy, France, and Spain. A French document of that time concludes that many people were playing the guitar. Stradivarius, the undeniable king of violin makers, could not resist creating a variety of guitars.

　　吉他是最古老的樂器中，爲人們所熟知的一種樂器。它可能起源於中國附近。古埃及和希臘也有吉他，但是根據歷史記載，吉他始於十三世紀的西班牙。直到西元 1500 年，吉他在義大利、法國、和西班牙，都很受歡迎。有一份那時候的法國文獻資料斷定，當時有許多人演奏吉他。連史特拉第瓦里，被公認是最優秀的小提琴製造家，都無法抗拒製造各式各樣的吉他。

> guitar〔gɪˋtɑr〕 *n.* 吉他　　instrument〔ˋɪnstrəmənt〕 *n.* 樂器
> **be known to** 爲…熟知　　man〔mæn〕 *n.* 人類
> originate〔əˋrɪdʒə͵net〕 *v.* 發源　　vicinity〔vəˋsɪnətɪ〕 *n.* 鄰近地區
> Egypt〔ˋidʒəpt〕 *n.* 埃及　　Greece〔gris〕 *n.* 希臘
> Italy〔ˋɪtlɪ〕 *n.* 義大利　　France〔fræns〕 *n.* 法國
> Spain〔spen〕 *n.* 西班牙　　document〔ˋdɑkjəmənt〕 *n.* 文件
> conclude〔kənˋklud〕 *v.* 斷定
> Stradivarius〔͵strædəˋvɛrɪəs〕 *n.* 史特拉第瓦里
> undeniable〔͵ʌndɪˋnaɪəbl̩〕 *adj.* 無可否認的；公認優秀的
> king〔kɪŋ〕 *n.* 首屈一指者；聲望最高者
> violin〔͵vaɪəˋlɪn〕 *n.* 小提琴　　resist〔rɪˋzɪst〕 *v.* 抗拒
> create〔krɪˋet〕 *v.* 製造　　**a variety of** 各種的

Also, there was no lack of music written for the instrument. Haydn, Schubert, and others wrote guitar music. When the great Beethoven was asked to compose music for the guitar, he went into a rage and refused, but eventually even Beethoven could not ignore the challenge. Legend tells us he finally called the guitar a miniature orchestra. Indeed the guitar does sound like a little orchestra! Perhaps that is why in rural areas around the world the guitar has been a source of music for **millions** to enjoy.

此外，為這個樂器所編寫的曲目也不少。海頓、舒伯特和其他音樂家，都有編寫過吉他的樂曲。當偉大的貝多芬被要求為吉他編曲時，他勃然大怒，並且拒絕，但到最後，即使是貝多芬，都不能忽視這項挑戰。傳說告訴我們，他最後稱吉他為一個小型的管絃樂隊。吉他的確聽起來就像是一個小型管絃樂隊！或許這就是為什麼在世界各地的鄉村地區，吉他一直是一種，供衆人欣賞的音樂的來源。

Haydn〔'haɪdn̩〕*n.* 海頓（奧地利作曲家）
Schubert〔'ʃubət〕*n.* 舒伯特（奧地利作曲家）
Beethoven〔'betovən〕*n.* 貝多芬（德國作曲家）
compose〔kəm'poz〕*v.* 作（曲）　　rage〔redʒ〕*n.* 狂怒
go into a rage 勃然大怒　　refuse〔rɪ'fjuz〕*v.* 拒絕
eventually〔ɪ'vɛntʃuəlɪ〕*adv.* 最後
challenge〔'tʃælɪndʒ〕*n.* 挑戰　　legend〔'lɛdʒənd〕*n.* 傳說
miniature〔'mɪnɪətʃə〕*adj.* 縮小的
orchestra〔'ɔrkɪstrə〕*n.* 管絃樂隊　　indeed〔ɪn'did〕*adv.* 的確
rural〔'rurəl〕*adj.* 鄉村的　　source〔sors〕*n.* 來源
millions〔'mɪljənz〕*n. pl.* 大衆；群衆

1. 最早記載吉他的文獻，是在何處被發現？
　　答：Spain. 西班牙。

2. 史特拉第瓦里以製作什麼樂器最有名？
　　答：Violins. 小提琴。

3. 當貝多芬被要求為吉他作曲時，他的第一個反應是什麼？
　　答：He went into a rage. / He was enraged. / He was angry. 他很生氣。

4. 貝多芬所無法忽視的挑戰是什麼？
　　答：compose music for the guitar 為吉他作曲

5. 最後一行的"**millions**"是指什麼？
　　答：People. 人。

二、英文作文：

Music Is an Important Part of Our Life

　　There is no denying that music plays an important role in everyone's life. It is not only an important art form, but also something that affects our feelings. Attending a concert by professional musicians can help us see and appreciate the beauty of life, while humming a simple tune can help us forget our cares. *In addition*, music always plays a symbolic role at important events such as weddings and graduations. It can put us in the proper mood to enjoy the events.

　　Music affects my own life in many ways. *First of all*, I play a musical instrument, the piano. I try to spend some time practicing the piano every day. Playing it helps me relax and also gives me a feeling of accomplishment. *Second*, I enjoy listening to music, especially when I feel sad or discouraged. Listening to music can always help me forget my troubles and improve my mood. *Finally*, I like to sing with my friends or family at a KTV. It is a wonderful way to spend free time and it brings us all closer together.

　　In conclusion, music is important in my life because it relaxes me and makes me happy. *Furthermore*, I believe that music can bring joy to everyone's life. That is why I cannot imagine a world without music.

there's no denying that~　不可否認　　form〔fɔrm〕 n. 型式
affect〔əˈfɛkt〕 v. 影響　　attend〔əˈtɛnd〕 v. 參加
concert〔ˈkɑnsɝt〕 n. 音樂會　　professional〔prəˈfɛʃənḷ〕 adj. 專業的
appreciate〔əˈpriʃɪ͵et〕 v. 欣賞；了解　　hum〔hʌm〕 v. 低聲哼唱
tune〔tjun〕 n. 曲調；旋律　　care〔kɛr〕 n. 擔憂的事
in addition 此外　　symbolic〔sɪmˈbɑlɪk〕 adj. 象徵性的
event〔ɪˈvɛnt〕 n. 重大事件；活動
graduation〔͵grædʒʊˈeʃən〕 n. 畢業　　proper〔ˈprɑpɚ〕 adj. 適當的
mood〔mud〕 n. 心情　　*musical instrument* 樂器
accomplishment〔əˈkɑmplɪʃmənt〕 n. 成就
discouraged〔dɪsˈkɝɪdʒd〕 adj. 沮喪的　　troubles〔ˈtrʌblz〕 n.pl. 煩惱
improve〔ɪmˈpruv〕 v. 改善；使好轉　　*in conclusion* 總之
furthermore〔ˈfɝðɚ͵mɔr〕 adv. 此外　　imagine〔ɪˈmædʒɪn〕 v. 想像

九十二年大學入學學科能力測驗試題
英文考科②

第壹部份：單一選擇題

一、詞彙與慣用語（15％）

說明： 第 1 至 15 題，每題選出最適當的一個選項，標示在答案卡之「選擇題答案區」。每題答對得 1 分，答錯不倒扣。

1. Jane felt _____ speaking in front of the class but was quite relaxed talking with her good friends.

   (A) considerate　　(B) awkward　　　(C) behaved　　　(D) intensive

2. Jack made a(n) _____ payment on the new computer because he did not have enough money for it.

   (A) partial　　　　(B) original　　　(C) effective　　　(D) courteous

3. Joseph's behavior is so unpredictable that no one can _____ exactly what he will do.

   (A) persuade　　　(B) interact　　　(C) anticipate　　　(D) request

4. Strict _____ measures are a must when President Chen travels around the island.

   (A) security　　　(B) motion　　　　(C) reward　　　　(D) extension

5. It is impolite to _____ when someone else is speaking. We should wait until the person finishes his turn.

   (A) shrink　　　　(B) transfer　　　(C) interrupt　　　(D) eliminate

6. Sue would _____ have followed the majority if she didn't want to get into an argument.

   (A) furiously　　　(B) undoubtedly　　(C) invisibly　　　(D) spaciously

7. As the rumor of his scandal _____ quickly during the election campaign, more and more people began to question the honesty of the candidate.

   (A) explored   (B) departed   (C) breezed   (D) spread

8. The many awards that Professor Wang has won over the years are clear _____ that he is a distinguished scholar.

   (A) evidence   (B) convenience   (C) influence   (D) obedience

9. Since we are short of manpower in the factory, it is very _____ we will hire some people next month.

   (A) badly   (B) nearly   (C) mostly   (D) likely

10. The teacher showed _____ for the noise in the classroom and continued with his lecture as if he had not heard anything.

    (A) connection   (B) rejection   (C) tolerance   (D) involvement

11. I will only be away for a week _____ --probably only four or five days.

    (A) at all   (B) at last   (C) at most   (D) at large

12. During the discussion, all the students presented their ideas _____.

    (A) in season   (B) in turn

    (C) in charge   (D) in case

13. The proposal Mr. Lin _____ last week has very little chance of being accepted by the committee.

    (A) put forward   (B) got over   (C) stood out   (D) threw up

14. The foreigner was speaking so fast that nobody was able to _____ what he was saying.

    (A) put through   (B) make out   (C) come down   (D) get about

15. Don't worry. It's not the first time we've _____ this sort of
    problem. We'll soon find a way out.
    (A) come along   (B) come about
    (C) come over   (D) come across

二、句子配合題（5%）

說明：1. 第16至20題，每題皆為未完成的句子。請逐題依文意與語法，從
      右欄 (A) 到 (J) 的選項中選出最適當者，合併成一個意思通順、用
      法正確的句子。

   2. 請將每題所選答案之英文字母代號標示在答案卡之「選擇題答案
      區」。每題答對得1分，答錯不倒扣。

16. We didn't have the chance to talk to the man	(A) or you'll be in big trouble.
17. Under no circumstances	(B) I would have gone with you.
18. When Mike enters the living room,	(C) the traffic and the noise bothered him greatly.
19. Tell me the truth,	(D) I could not help you solve the problem.
20. If you had told me the situation earlier,	(E) until he sees Mary immediately.
	(F) he'll see John sitting by the fire.
	(G) should John be allowed to do it alone.
	(H) then John knew he had passed it.
	(I) did John realize how easy it was.
	(J) whose car was stolen.

三、綜合測驗（10％）

說明：第 21 至 30 題，每題一個空格，請依文意選出最適當的一個選項，標示在答案卡之「選擇題答案區」。每題答對得 1 分，答錯不倒扣。

Are you too busy or tired to cook? Is eating out too expensive for you? Do you feel TV dinners too unhealthy? If your answer is "Yes!" to these questions, then you have good ___21___ to take the course we have designed especially for people like you. In this course, you will learn ___22___ to cook two weeks of healthy, inexpensive meals in just one day. Specifically, you will learn to prepare ___23___ delicious items as roasted chicken, chili, turkey loaf, meatballs, and pasta, among others. You will also learn important information about ___24___ for fresh and inexpensive foods, the use of herbs and spices, and the proper ways of storing different kinds of food.

At the end of the class, you ___25___ with your classmates the meals you have created, and you will leave with recipe handouts and, more importantly, the ability to cook two weeks of fantastic, low-cost meals.

21. (A) answer   (B) reason   (C) health   (D) food
22. (A) what   (B) where   (C) when   (D) how
23. (A) many   (B) much   (C) such   (D) so
24. (A) shopping   (B) buying   (C) marketing   (D) growing
25. (A) share   (B) are shared   (C) are sharing   (D) will share

Some species of ants keep slaves. Probably the best known for the practice is the large brownish-red Amazon ant. A slave raid starts with an assembly of the Amazon warriors outside their own nest. Then, almost ___26___ at a given signal, the group begins to march toward the colony ___27___. When the Amazons reach the nest of their intended victims, a fierce battle may take place. The Amazons fight on ___28___ they seize the pupae of the raided nest. They carry these back home. In time the pupae develop into adults and spend their lives working for the Amazons. The Amazons are completely dependent on their slaves ___29___ their sharp jaws, so well suited for fighting, are useless in taking care of larvae or for digging. Also, the masters become so lazy that, after a while, they lose their muscles, and they become too weak ___30___ to feed themselves. Finally, they become so unhealthy that they die.

26. (A) as if   (B) even though (C) in case   (D) such as
27. (A) raided   (B) raiding   (C) to be raided (D) to be raiding
28. (A) and   (B) but   (C) after   (D) until
29. (A) unless   (B) that   (C) if   (D) because
30. (A) only   (B) also   (C) even   (D) neither

四、文意選填（10％）

說明：　第 31 至 40 題，每題一個空格，請依文意在文章後所提供的(A) 到 (J) 選項中分別選出最適當者，並將其英文字母代號標示在答案卡之「選擇題答案區」。每題答對得 1 分，答錯不倒扣。

　　The term "standard of living" usually refers to the economic well-being enjoyed by a person, family, community, or nation. A standard of living is considered high when it includes ___31___ necessities but also certain comforts and luxuries; it is considered low when food, clean water, housing, and ___32___ necessities are limited or lacking.

　　Different ___33___ have been employed by economists to measure standard of living. One of ___34___ measures is to calculate the percentage of income that people spend on certain necessities. The higher this percentage is, the ___35___ is the standard of living of these people.

The U.S. has one of the world's highest standards of living. But income is not distributed ___36___ throughout its population. Some Americans enjoy great wealth, ___37___ others suffer in extreme poverty. Americans ___38___ different racial and educational backgrounds may vary in their standards of living. People living in different parts of the U.S. ___39___ show different standards of living. Of course, in determining the overall standard of living of Americans, factors ___40___ household composition and family size need also to be taken into consideration.

(A) these   (B) lower   (C) evenly   (D) other   (E) while

(F) not only   (G) methods   (H) with   (I) such as   (J) also

五、閱讀測驗（30％）

說明： 第 41 至 55 題，每題請分別根據各篇文章之文意選出最適當的一個選項，標示在答案卡之「選擇題答案區」。每題答對得 2 分，答錯不倒扣。

41-43 為題組

Laura was at the door, thrusting a bracelet at Amy. It was a thin gold chain with a heart dangling on it and Amy loved it the minute she saw it. Amy gave Laura a big hug and promised that she would come back to see her. But she really didn't know if she would ever come back to the little town. She watched as Laura walked down the block, turning and waving and walking backwards until she got to the corner.

Mama was hurrying her. Amy made sure her gold bracelet was secure on her wrist. Then she put on both her sweater and her coat so that she wouldn't have to carry them. They could take only what they could carry, and her two suitcases were already full.

Mama took a last look around the house, going from room to room. Amy followed her, trying to recall how each one had looked when they were filled with furniture and rugs and pictures and books. They went out for a last look at the garden Papa loved. If he were here now, Amy knew he would pick one of the prettiest carnations and gave it to Mama. She would beam and put it in her best crystal vase. But now the garden looked shabby and bare. It looked the way Amy felt—lonely and abandoned.

41. The passage is mainly about _____.
    (A) a beautiful gift   (B) an empty house
    (C) a sad goodbye   (D) a sweet memory

42. Which of the following statements is explicitly mentioned in the passage?
    (A) Amy's father planted carnations in the garden.
    (B) All of Amy's friends knew that she was leaving.
    (C) Amy's mother sold all the furniture before they left.
    (D) Amy and her mother carried only a few suitcases with them.

43. Which of the following is **NOT** true according to the passage?
    (A) Amy treasured the gold bracelet Laura gave her.
    (B) Amy turned and walked backwards as she left.
    (C) Amy's father was not around when they were leaving.
    (D) Amy did not know if she could keep her promise to Laura.

44-47 為題組

In the last several decades, the western world has been rediscovering the soybean, a plant whose use dates back to before recorded history in Asia. For thousands of years, the Chinese have valued highly the soybean, considering it one of the five important grains (along with rice, millet, barley, and wheat). Since it is cheap to produce and rich in protein, and has many uses, the soybean could provide food to the world's growing population. Besides, soybeans can be fed to a variety of other animals ranging from livestock to silk worms.

The soybean is an almost perfect source of protein. If you are a vegetarian, or if your diet includes little meat, soy protein is a good alternative, and may even be essential to maintaining your health. The soybean's high fiber content is beneficial in preventing digestive disorders. The soybean is free of cholesterol, and more importantly, the soy oil contains some special substances, called Omega 3 fatty acids, which reduce cholesterol and prevent blood from clotting in the human body. Research shows that consuming a minimum of 25 grams of soy protein a day can lower blood cholesterol levels in people with high cholesterol problems.

In view of all these strengths, in the 1930s the United States and Canada undertook a research project in which they managed to breed an especially nutritious soybean with a high oil content. Since then, the United States has become the world's largest producer of soybeans and has exported much of its soybean produce. In recent years, the soybean has been used in making many different foods and has become the atom of health food. Health-conscious Americans are adding tofu, the most popular soybean product, to salads and using it as a meat substitute. In the health food stores of major cities, it is now possible to buy tofu burgers and even tofu hot dogs.

44. What is the main idea of the passage?
    (A) Asians have used soybean produce for thousands of years.
    (B) Health-conscious Americans are eating more tofu in their diet.
    (C) The soybean provides food for the world's growing population.
    (D) The soybean is healthful and has become popular in the western world.

45. One major advantage of the soybean as a food source is that _____.
    (A) it is free of oil (B) it is cheap to produce
    (C) it is low in protein (D) it is high in cholesterol

46. The soybean helps to keep cholesterol down mainly because it contains _____.
    (A) rich protein (B) rich vitamin
    (C) some fatty acids (D) high fiber content

47. According to the passage, which of the following statements is true?
    (A) Tofu is a rich protein source.
    (B) Soybean protein prevents digestive problems.
    (C) The United States exports most of its soybean produce to Canada.
    (D) Vegetarians should eat less than 25 grams of soy protein every day.

48-51 為題組

Big brothers and sisters usually develop leadership tendencies early in life, mainly because of the responsibilities for younger children given to them by their parents. Firstborns, under normal circumstances, are usually the most strongly motivated toward achievement. This is mainly a result of parental expectations. Research also suggests that firstborn children generally become more conservative than other children because they receive most of the parental discipline. Used to caring for others, they are more likely to move toward such leadership professions as teaching and politics. Less social and flexible because they become accustomed in the very early years to acting alone, they may have difficulty making close friends.

By contrast, later children are more likely to be more relaxed and sociable because their parents are more relaxed. However, later children are often less ambitious and may be uncomfortable making decisions for others. This may help explain why younger children tend to favor the creative fields such as music, art, and writing. Later children may make good salespersons because persuasion may have been the only tool they had to deal with older siblings. Youngest children tend to remain forever "the baby," enjoyable to be around, but at times over-dependent on others.

48. The passage is mainly about _____.
    (A) the personality tendencies of older children
    (B) the personality tendencies of younger children
    (C) the relation between birth rank and job success
    (D) the relation between birth rank and personality

49. According to the passage, the first child tends to be _____.
    (A) creative   (B) sociable
    (C) persuasive   (D) conservative

50. It can be inferred from the passage that a younger child is more likely to be a good _____.
    (A) librarian   (B) doctor
    (C) writer   (D) teacher

51. From the passage, we learn that _____.
    (A) children's personalities depend entirely on parental attitudes
    (B) artists do not usually like to make decisions for other people
    (C) older children are used to taking care of people and are fun to be with
    (D) younger children are particularly weak in delivering a speech in public

52-55 為題組

According to the U.S. Environmental Protection Agency (EPA), medical waste is a major source of dioxin pollution in the country. Linked to the dioxin issue is the use of PVC plastic, which is widely used in the production of blood bags, plastic tubing, and other products in hospitals and health clinics. Dioxin is an unwanted byproduct that is created when PVC is burned. Dioxin travels by air currents and settles onto grass, which is then eaten by cows and chickens in their feed. We eat polluted dairy products and meat and take the dioxin into our bodies, where it is stored in our fat for years and builds up over time. In this way, dioxin is globally distributed, and as a consequence, every member of the human population is constantly exposed to this poisonous substance. This poses special problems for childbearing women, who pass dioxin to an unborn baby or to a breastfeeding baby. In fact, the infant is the most vulnerable member of society to this chemical.

Plastics used to account for as little as 10% of medical waste in the late 1970s, before disposables began rapidly replacing reusables. They now make up as much as 30%. The EPA estimates that the average levels of dioxin in all Americans are so high that we can expect to see a variety of health effects, including cancer. Given the harm caused by the burning of medical waste, physicians and nurses have the responsibility to take a lead in reducing the use of plastics in the hospitals. After all, they can't be treating cancer on the inside of hospitals and contributing to **it** on the outside.

52. What is the major message the author is trying to convey to readers?
    (A) All people, especially those working in the hospitals, should reduce the use of plastics.
    (B) Americans should lead the world to fight dioxin pollution, or mankind will die out soon.
    (C) We had better eat more vegetables than meat in order to reduce the risk of dioxin pollution.
    (D) We had better not breastfeed our babies, since babies are most likely to be poisoned by dioxin.

53. Dioxin is produced _____.
    (A) when plastics are burned
    (B) in the making of hospital blood bags
    (C) when reusables are disposed of
    (D) in the handling of all kinds of medical waste

54. What does **it** in the last line refer to?
    (A) Dioxin.   (B) Cancer.
    (C) Medical waste.   (D) Use of plastics.

55. Which of the following statements can be inferred from the article?
    (A) Living in the countryside will keep one safe from dioxin
        poisoning.
    (B) Dioxin can be released from our bodies, if we drink a lot of
        clean, pure water.
    (C) Using reusables as people did in the old days will help lessen
        dioxin pollution.
    (D) You have to lose weight, or the amount of dioxin in your body
        fat will kill you.

第貳部份：非選擇題

一、簡答題（10％）

說明：1. 閱讀下面這篇文章，然後簡答下列問題。答案必須寫在「答案卷」上。
　　　2. 請依序作答，並標明題號。答案應簡明扼要，只寫重要詞彙（key
　　　　　words），請勿超過五個英文單詞（words）。每題2分，共10分。
　　　　　注意：請勿抄下整句或整行，否則不予記分。

　　It's easier for the human face to smile than frown. It takes twice as
many muscles to frown as it does to smile. Moreover, we do not have to
"learn" to do it. Although babies imitate the facial expressions they see,
smiling isn't just learned by imitation. Children born blind never see
anybody smile, but they show the same kinds of smiles under the same
situations as sighted people.

Smiling is of great help to us. Some studies suggest that the act of shaping our mouths into a smile (creating a "physical smile") can help us see the brighter, funnier side of things. People wearing the physical smile tend to feel happier. In addition, smiles signal to others that we are people who might be nice to talk to and work with—and that can help us make friends.

Unfortunately, sometimes you may find it difficult to smile. Anything from getting a bad grade on a test to losing an important game can make you feel sad. In such **hard times**, there seems to be no reason to smile. But there is some good part to almost every bad thing. Turning something that seems all bad into something good is one way to help you smile. Hanging around people who are positive and in good moods is another way to help you find your smile again.

1. Why is smiling physically easier than frowning?

2. What kind of feeling can a physical smile help to create?

3. In what aspect can smiling help a person in his social life?

4. Give one example of "hard times" mentioned in the passage.

5. What particular group of people are cited in the passage to show that smiling is not learned?

二、英文作文（20％）

說明： 1. 依提示在「答案卷」上寫一篇英文作文。
　　　 2. 文長 120 個單詞（words）左右。

提示： 請以自己的經驗為例，敘述當你感到不快樂或情緒低落時，（除了簡答題選文中所提及的方法外，）你最常用哪一種方法幫自己渡過低潮，並舉實例說明這個方法何以有效。

✵ 92年度學科能力測驗英文科試題②詳解 ✵

第壹部分：單一選擇題

一、詞彙與慣用語：

1. (**B**) Jane felt <u>awkward</u> speaking in front of the class but was quite relaxed talking with her good friends.

   珍覺得在全班同學面前演講很<u>不自在</u>，但和自己的好友聊天就很輕鬆。

   (A) considerate〔kən'sɪdərɪt〕adj. 體貼的
   (B) **awkward**〔'ɔkwəd〕adj. 笨拙的；不自在的
   (C) behave〔bɪ'hev〕v. 行為舉止
   (D) intensive〔ɪn'tɛnsɪv〕adj. 密集的

   in front of 在～之前　　relaxed〔rɪ'lækst〕adj. 放鬆的

2. (**A**) Jack made a <u>partial</u> payment on the new computer because he did not have enough money for it.

   傑克只付了<u>一部分</u>新電腦的錢，因為他的錢不夠。

   (A) **partial**〔'parʃəl〕adj. 部分的　(B) original〔ə'rɪdʒənḷ〕adj. 原本的
   (C) effective〔ɪ'fɛktɪv〕adj. 有效的
   (D) courteous〔'kɝtɪəs〕adj. 有禮貌的

   payment〔'pemənt〕n. 付款

3. (**C**) Joseph's behavior is so unpredictable that no one can <u>anticipate</u> exactly what he will do.

   約瑟夫的行為令人無法預測，沒有人能正確地<u>預測</u>，他會做什麼事。

   (A) persuade〔pə'swed〕v. 說服　　(B) interact〔ˌɪntə'ækt〕v. 互動
   (C) **anticipate**〔æn'tɪsəˌpet〕v. 預期；期待
   (D) request〔rɪ'kwɛst〕v. 要求

   behavior〔bɪ'hevjə〕n. 行為
   unpredictable〔ˌʌnprɪ'dɪktəbḷ〕adj. 不可預測的
   exactly〔ɪg'zæktlɪ〕adv. 確切地

4. (**A**) Strict <u>security</u> measures are a must when President Chen travels around the island.

當陳總統到全省各地時，嚴密的<u>安全</u>措施是必要的。

(A) *security* 〔 sɪˈkjʊrətɪ 〕 *adj.* 安全的
(B) motion 〔ˈmoʃən 〕 *n.* 動作
(C) reward 〔 rɪˈwɔrd 〕 *n.* 報酬；獎賞
(D) extension 〔 ɪkˈstɛnʃən 〕 *n.* 延長

strict 〔 strɪkt 〕 *adj.* 嚴格的；嚴密的　　measure 〔ˈmɛʒɚ 〕 *n.* 措施
security measures 安全措施
must 〔 mʌst 〕 *n.* 必備之物；必要條件
around 〔 əˈraʊnd 〕 *prep.* 遍及；在…到處　　island 〔ˈaɪlənd 〕 *n.* 島

5. (**C**) It is impolite to <u>interrupt</u> when someone else is speaking. We should wait until the person finishes his turn.

在別人說話時<u>插嘴</u>是很沒禮貌的。我們應該等那個人說完話。

(A) shrink 〔 ʃrɪŋk 〕 *v.* 縮水
(B) transfer 〔 trænsˈfɝ 〕 *v.* 轉移
(C) *interrupt* 〔ˌɪntəˈrʌpt 〕 *v.* 打斷（談話）；插嘴
(D) eliminate 〔 ɪˈlɪməˌnet 〕 *v.* 除去

impolite 〔ˌɪmpəˈlaɪt 〕 *adj.* 無禮的　　else 〔 ɛls 〕 *adj.* 其他的；別的
turn 〔 tɝn 〕 *n.* 輪流；（輪流的）一次機會

6. (**B**) Sue would <u>undoubtedly</u> have followed the majority if she didn't want to get into an argument.

如果蘇不想和別人爭論，她就會<u>毫無疑問</u>地服從大多數。

(A) furiously 〔ˈfjʊrɪəslɪ 〕 *adv.* 狂怒地；猛烈地
(B) *undoubtedly* 〔 ʌnˈdaʊtɪdlɪ 〕 *adv.* 無疑地
(C) invisibly 〔 ɪnˈvɪzəblɪ 〕 *adv.* 看不見地；無形地
(D) spaciously 〔ˈspeʃəslɪ 〕 *adv.* 寬敞地；廣大地

majority 〔 məˈdʒɔrətɪ 〕 *n.* 大多數
get into 開始（談話、吵架等）
argument 〔ˈɑrgjəmənt 〕 *n.* 爭論

7. (**D**) As the rumor of his scandal <u>spread</u> quickly during the election campaign, more and more people began to question the honesty of the candidate.

在選舉活動期間，由於跟這名候選人的醜聞有關的謠言快速地<u>散播</u>，所以有愈來愈多人開始懷疑他是否誠實。

(A) explore〔ɪkˋsplor〕*v.* 探險；探測

(B) depart〔dɪˋpɑrt〕*v.* 出發；動身

(C) breeze〔briz〕*v.* 微風輕吹　*n.* 微風

(D) *spread*〔sprɛd〕*v.* 散播

rumor〔ˋrumɚ〕*n.* 謠言　　scandal〔ˋskændl〕*n.* 醜聞

election〔ɪˋlɛkʃən〕*n.* 選舉　　campaign〔kæmˋpen〕*n.* 運動；活動

question〔ˋkwɛstʃən〕*v.* 懷疑；詢問

candidate〔ˋkændəˌdet〕*n.* 候選人

8. (**A**) The many awards that Professor Wang has won over the years are clear <u>evidence</u> that he is a distinguished scholar.

王教授這幾年贏得許多獎項，明顯地<u>證明</u>他是一位傑出的學者。

(A) *evidence*〔ˋɛvədəns〕*n.* 證據

(B) convenience〔kənˋvinjəns〕*n.* 方便

(C) influence〔ˋɪnfluəns〕*n.* 影響

(D) obedience〔əˋbidɪəns〕*n.* 服從

award〔əˋwɔrd〕*n.* 獎　　professor〔prəˋfɛsɚ〕*n.* 教授

distinguished〔dɪˋstɪŋgwɪʃt〕*adj.* 傑出的　　scholar〔ˋskɑlɚ〕*n.* 學者

9. (**D**) Since we are short of manpower in the factory, it is very <u>likely</u> we will hire some people next month.

因為工廠人力不足，所以我們下個月很<u>可能</u>會雇用一些人。

(A) badly〔ˋbædlɪ〕*adv.* 拙劣地；惡劣地

(B) nearly〔ˋnɪrlɪ〕*adv.* 將近；幾乎

(C) mostly〔ˋmostlɪ〕*adv.* 大多

(D) *likely*〔ˋlaɪklɪ〕*adj.* 可能的

short〔ʃɔrt〕*adj.* 缺乏的；不足的

manpower〔ˋmænˌpauɚ〕*n.* 人力　　hire〔haɪr〕*v.* 雇用

10. (**C**) The teacher showed <u>tolerance</u> for the noise in the classroom and continued with his lecture as if he had not heard anything.

這位老師<u>容忍</u>教室裡的吵鬧聲，並且就像沒聽到任何聲音一樣，繼續講他的課。

(A) connection〔kə'nɛkʃən〕n. 連接

(B) rejection〔rɪ'dʒɛkʃən〕n. 拒絕

(C) *tolerance*〔'talərəns〕n. 容忍；包容力

(D) involvement〔ɪn'valvmənt〕n. 捲入；涉及

show〔ʃo〕v. 顯示；展現　　noise〔nɔɪz〕n. 噪音

lecture〔'lɛktʃɚ〕n. 講課　　*as if* 就好像

11. (**C**) I will only be away for a week <u>at most</u>--probably only four or five days.

我<u>最多</u>只會離開一個星期—也可能只有四、五天。

(A) not at all　一點也不

(B) at last　最後；終於

(C) *at most*　最多

(D) at large　一般而言；逍遙法外

12. (**B**) During the discussion, all the students presented their ideas <u>in turn</u>.

在討論時，所有的學生<u>依序地</u>提出他們的想法。

(A) in season　正當時令的　　(B) *in turn*　依序地

(C) in charge　負責管理　　(D) in case　以防萬一

present〔prɪ'zɛnt〕v. 提出

13. (**A**) The proposal Mr. Lin <u>put forward</u> last week has very little chance of being accepted by the committee.

林先生上個星期<u>提出</u>的計劃，被委員會接受的可能性很小。

(A) *put forward*　提出　　(B) get over　越過；克服

(C) stand out　突出；卓越　　(D) throw up　投擲；放棄

proposal〔prə'pozḷ〕n. 計劃　　committee〔kə'mɪtɪ〕n. 委員會

14. (**B**) The foreigner was speaking so fast that nobody was able to <u>make out</u> what he was saying.

這個外國人講得太快，以致於沒有人能<u>了解</u>他在說什麼。

(A) put through 接通電話   (B) *make out* 了解
(C) come down 倒塌；下跌   (D) get about 到處走；散播

foreigner (ˈfɔrɪnɚ) *n.* 外國人

15. (**D**) Don't worry. It's not the first time we've <u>come across</u> this sort of problem. We'll soon find a way out.

別擔心。我們不是第一次<u>遇到</u>這種問題。我們很快就能找到解決方法。

(A) come along 過來；一起來   (B) come about 發生
(C) come over 侵襲；籠罩   (D) *come across* 遇到

sort (sɔrt) *n.* 種類   *find a way out* 找到解決方法

二、句子配合題：

16. (**J**) We didn't have the chance to talk to the man whose car was stolen.

我們沒機會和那位車子失竊的人講話。

17. (**G**) Under no circumstances should John be allowed to do it alone.

絕不能約翰單獨做這件事情。

circumstances (ˈsɝkəmˌstænsɪs) *n.pl.* 情況
under no circumstances 在任何情況下絕不
allow (əˈlaʊ) *v.* 允許   alone (əˈlon) *adv.* 單獨地

18. (**F**) When Mike enters the living room, he'll see John sitting by the fire.

當麥克進入房間，他就會看到約翰坐在爐火旁。

living room 客廳   fire (faɪr) *n.* 爐火

19. (**A**) Tell me the truth, or you'll be in big trouble.

告訴我實話，否則你就麻煩大了。

20. (**B**) If you had told me the situation earlier, I would have gone with you.

如果你早一點告訴我情況，我就會跟你一起去了。

三、綜合測驗：

Are you too busy or tired to cook? Is eating out too expensive for you? Do you feel TV dinner too unhealthy? If your answer is "Yes!" to these questions, then you have good <u>reason</u> to take the course we have designed
21
especially for people like you. In this course, you will learn <u>how</u> to cook
22
two weeks of healthy, inexpensive meals in just one day.

你太忙或太累，所以不想煮飯嗎？出去外面吃，對你來說太貴了嗎？你覺得電視餐太不健康了嗎？如果這些問題，你的回答是肯定的，那麼你就很有理由，可以來參加我們特別為像你這樣的人，所設計的課程。在這門課當中，你將會學到，如何在一天之內，做出兩星期份量的健康、便宜的餐點。

too…to 太…以致於不   *eat out* 出去吃飯
unhealthy (ʌnˈhɛlθɪ) adj. 不健康的
course (kors) n. 課程   *take a course* 上一門課
design (dɪˈzaɪn) v. 設計   healthy (ˈhɛlθɪ) adj. 健康的
inexpensive (͵ɪnɪkˈspɛnsɪv) adj. 便宜的
meal (mil) n. 一餐

21. (**B**) 依句意，選 (B) *reason*「理由」。   *have good reason to V.* 很有理由
而 (A) 答案，(C) 健康，(D) 食物，不合句意。

22. (**A**) 依句意，選 (A) *how*「如何」。

Specifically, you will learn to prepare <u>such</u> delicious items as roasted
23
chicken, chili, turkey loaf, meatballs, and pasta, among others. You will also learn important information about <u>shopping</u> for fresh and inexpensive foods,
24
the use of herbs and spices, and the proper ways of storing different kinds of food.

　　明確地說，你將學會做一些好吃的食物，其中包括像是烤雞、紅番椒、火雞肉糕、肉丸子，及義大利麵。你也會學到一些重要資訊，像是如何購買新鮮又便宜的食物，香菜及香料的使用，以及儲存不同種類食物的正確方法。

specifically〔spɪ'sɪfɪkl̩ɪ〕adv. 明確地；說明確些

prepare〔prɪ'pɛr〕v. 製做　　item〔'aɪtəm〕n. 項目；物品

roasted〔'rostɪd〕adj. 烤的　　chili〔'tʃɪlɪ〕n. 紅番椒

loaf〔lof〕n.（用魚肉麵粉等烘製成的）魚糕；肉糕

turkey loaf 火雞肉糕　　meatball〔'mit,bɔl〕n. 肉丸子

pasta〔'pɑstə〕n. 義大利麵（包括通心粉及細麵條等）

among others 其中；尤其　　herb〔hɝb, ɝb〕n. 草；香料植物

spice〔spaɪs〕n. 香料　　proper〔'prɑpɚ〕adj. 適當的；正確的

store〔stor〕v. 儲存

23.（ **C** ）**such…as** 像是～的…

24.（ **A** ）依句意，選 (A) **shop for**「購買」。而 (B) buy「買」，為及物動詞，不須接介系詞，(C) market〔'mɑrkɪt〕v. 銷售，(D) grow〔gro〕v. 種植，則不合句意。

At the end of the class, you <u>will share</u> with your classmates the meals
　　　　　　　　　　　　　　　25
you have created, and you will leave with recipe handouts and, more
importantly, the ability to cook two weeks of fantastic, low-cost meals.

　　課程結束時，你將和你的同班同學分享你所製作的餐點，而且離開時，你可以帶走食譜的講義，而且，更重要的是，你將會有能力，能煮出兩週份量，很棒而且低價的餐點。

create〔krɪ'et〕v. 創造；製造　　recipe〔'rɛsəpɪ〕n. 食譜

handout〔'hænd,aut〕n. 講義　　**more importantly** 更重要的是

fantastic〔fæn'tæstɪk〕adj. 很棒的

low-cost〔'lo'kɔst〕adj. 便宜的；成本低的

25.（ **A** ）依句意為未來式，故選 (A) **will share**。　　share〔ʃɛr〕v. 分享

Some species of ants keep slaves. Probably the best known for the practice is the large brownish-red Amazon ant. A slave raid starts with an assembly of the Amazon warriors outside their own nest. Then, almost <u>as if</u> ₂₆ at a given signal, the group begins to march toward the colony <u>to be raided</u>. ₂₇ When the Amazons reach the nest of their intended victims, a fierce battle may take place. The Amazons fight on <u>until</u> they seize the pupae of the ₂₈ raided nest. They carry these back home. In time the pupae develop into adults and spend their lives working for the Amazons.

有幾種螞蟻會使用奴隸，或許有這種習慣最有名的是，體型很大、身體帶褐色、紅色的亞馬遜螞蟻。襲擊奴隸的行動一開始，亞馬遜戰士會在它們自己的巢穴外集合。然後，幾乎好像在一聲指定的信號之後，大軍即往將被襲擊的蟻群前進。當亞馬遜螞蟻到達預定受害者的巢穴時，可能就會發生一場激烈的戰鬥。亞馬遜螞蟻會一直戰鬥，直到奪取到受襲巢穴中的蟻蛹。他們會把蛹帶回去，一段時間後，這些蛹會長成成蟻，一輩子為亞馬遜螞蟻工作。

ant〔ænt〕*n.* 螞蟻　　slave〔slev〕*n.* 奴隸
practice〔'præktɪs〕*n.* 做法；習慣
brownish〔'braʊnɪʃ〕*adj.* 帶褐色的
Amazon〔'æmə,zɑn〕*n.* 亞馬遜河　　raid〔red〕*n.,v.* 襲擊
assembly〔ə'sɛmblɪ〕*n.* 集合　　warrior〔'wɔrɪɚ〕*n.* 戰士
nest〔nɛst〕*n.* 巢穴　　given〔'gɪvən〕*adj.* 指定的；約定的
signal〔'sɪgnḷ〕*n.* 信號　　march〔mɑrtʃ〕*v.* 行進；行軍
colony〔'kɑlənɪ〕*n.* (動、植物) 群體
intended〔ɪn'tɛndɪd〕*adj.* 預定的；計劃中的
victim〔'vɪktɪm〕*n.* 受害者　　fierce〔fɪrs〕*adj.* 激烈的
battle〔'bætḷ〕*n.* 戰鬥　　seize〔siz〕*v.* 抓住；奪走
pupae〔'pjupi〕*n.,pl.* (昆蟲的) 蛹 (單數為 pupa〔'pjupə〕)
in time 不久；一段時間後 (= *after some time has passed*)

26.(**A**) 依句意，「好像」一聲令下，大軍即前進，選 (A) *as if*。
　　而 (B) even though「即使」, (C) in case「以免」, (D) such as「像是」,
　　均不合句意。

27.(**C**)　此處原爲 toward the colony ***which is*** to be raided，省略關代和 be
　　　　動詞 which is，而成不定詞片語，「be to + V.」可表「預定」之意，
　　　　在此即指「即將被襲擊的」蟻群，故選 (C) ***to be raided***。

28.(**D**)　依句意，它們會一直戰鬥，「直到」奪取到蟻蛹，選 (D) ***until***。

The Amazons are completely dependent on their slaves <u>because</u> their sharp
　　　　　　　　　　　　　　　　　　　　　　　　29
jaws, so well suited for fighting, are useless in taking care of larvae or
for digging. Also, the masters become so lazy that, after a while, they
lose their muscles, and they become too weak <u>even</u> too feed themselves.
　　　　　　　　　　　　　　　　　　　　　30
Finally, they become so unhealthy that they die.
亞馬遜螞蟻完全依賴它們的奴隸，因爲它們尖銳的下顎雖然非常適合戰鬥，但
是在照顧幼蟲和挖掘時，卻無用武之地。此外，這些主人們會變得非常懶惰，
以致於一陣子之後，它們的肌肉都沒了，虛弱到甚至連餵食自己都有問題。最
後，它們會極度不健康而死掉。

　　　　dependent〔dɪˈpɛndənt〕*adj.* 依賴的
　　　　sharp〔ʃɑrp〕*adj.* 尖銳的　　jaw〔dʒɔ〕*n.* 下顎
　　　　suited〔ˈsutɪd〕*adj.* 適合的　　***take care of*** 照顧
　　　　larvae〔ˈlɑrvi〕*n. pl.*（昆蟲的）幼蟲（單數爲 larva〔ˈlɑrvə〕）
　　　　dig〔dɪg〕*v.* 挖掘　　master〔ˈmæstɚ〕*n.* 主人
　　　　muscle〔ˈmʌsl̩〕*n.* 肌肉　　feed〔fid〕*v.* 餵食

29.(**D**)　依句意，它們依賴奴隸，「因爲」自己的能力不足，選 (D) ***because***。

30.(**C**)　依句意，它們會虛弱到「甚至」連餵食自己都有問題，選 (C) ***even***。

四、文意選填：

　　　The term "standard of living" usually refers to the economic well-
being enjoyed by a person, family, community, or nation. A standard of
living is considered high when it includes [31]**(F) not only** necessities but
also certain comforts and luxuries; it is considered low when food, clean
water, housing, and [32]**(D) other** necessities are limited or lacking.

「生活水準」這個名詞，通常是指一個人、一個家庭、一個社區，或一個國家，所享有的經濟幸福水平。當人民不只擁有生活必需品，還擁有某些使生活舒適的用品，以及奢侈品時，生活水準就算很高；當食物、乾淨的用水、住處，及其他必需品都有限或缺乏時，生活水準就被認為很低落。

term〔tɜm〕n. 名詞　　***standard of living*** 生活水準
refer to 是指　　well-being〔'wɛl'biɪŋ〕n. 幸福；福祉
community〔kə'mjunətɪ〕n. 社區　　necessity〔nə'sɛsətɪ〕n. 必需品
not only A ***but also*** B 不只 A 還有 B
certain〔'sɜtn̩〕adj. 某些　　comfort〔'kʌmfət〕n. 使生活舒適的用品
luxury〔'lʌkʃərɪ〕n. 奢侈品　　housing〔'hauzɪŋ〕n. 房屋；住宅

Different [33](G) methods have been employed by economists to measure standards of living. One of [34](A) these measures is to calculate the percentage of income that people spend on certain necessities. The higher this percentage is, the [35](B) lower the standard of living of these people is.

　　經濟學家使用不同的方法，來評估生活水準的高低。這些方法其中之一，就是計算人們將收入，花費在某些生活必需品上的百分比。這個百分比越高，這些人的生活水準就越低。

method〔'mɛθəd〕n. 方法　　employ〔ɪm'plɔɪ〕v. 使用
economist〔ɪ'kɑnəmɪst〕n. 經濟學家
measure〔'mɛʒə〕v. 測量；評估　n. 方法；措施
calculate〔'kælkjə,let〕v. 計算
percentage〔pə'sɛntɪdʒ〕n. 百分比　　income〔'ɪn,kʌm〕n. 收入

The U.S. has one of the world's highest standards of living. But income is not distributed [36](C) evenly throughout its population. Some Americans enjoy great wealth, [37](E) while others suffer in extreme poverty. Americans [38](H) with different racial and educational backgrounds may vary in their standards of living. People living in different parts of the U.S. [39](J) also show different standards of living. Of course, in determining the overall standard of living of Americans, factors [40](I) such as household composition and family size need also to be taken into consideration.

美國是全世界生活水準最高的國家之一，但是全美人口的收入分配並不平均。有些美國人享有大筆財富，而有些人則苦於極度的貧窮。不同種族和不同教育背景的美國人，生活水準程度也可能不相同。住在美國不同地區的人，也顯現出不同程度的生活水準。當然，在判斷美國人整體的生活水準時，像家庭分子的構成、家庭人數的多寡等因素，也必須列入考慮。

distribute〔dɪˋstrɪbjut〕v. 分配　evenly〔ˋivənlɪ〕adv. 平均地
throughout〔θruˋaut〕prep. 遍及　extreme〔ɪkˋstrim〕adj. 極度的
poverty〔ˋpɑvətɪ〕n. 貧窮　racial〔ˋreʃəl〕adj. 種族的
educational〔͵ɛdʒəˋkeʃənḷ〕adj. 教育的
background〔ˋbæk͵graund〕n. 背景　vary〔ˋvɛrɪ〕v. 不同（= differ）
determine〔dɪˋtɝmɪn〕v. 決定；判斷　overall〔͵ovɚˋɔl〕adj. 整體的
factor〔ˋfæktɚ〕n. 因素　household〔ˋhaus͵hold〕adj. 家庭的
composition〔͵kɑmpəˋzɪʃən〕n. 構成
take sth. into consideration 把某事列入考慮

五、閱讀測驗：

41－43 為題組

Laura was at the door, thrusting a bracelet at Amy. It was a thin gold chain with a heart dangling on it and Amy loved it the minute she saw it. Amy gave Laura a big hug and promised that she would come back to see her. But she really didn't know if she would ever come back to the little town. She watched as Laura walked down the block, turning and waving and walking backwards until she got to the corner.

蘿拉站在門口，強行給了艾美一個手鍊。手鍊是一條細的金鍊子，有一顆心懸掛在上頭，艾美第一眼就喜歡上它。艾美熱情地擁抱一下蘿拉，跟她承諾，一定會回來看她。但是艾美真的不知道，自己是否會再回到這個小鎮。她望著蘿拉沿著街道一路走去，轉身、揮手，倒退著走，直到走到街角。

thrust〔θrʌst〕v. 強使接受　bracelet〔ˋbreslɪt〕n. 手鍊；手鐲
chain〔tʃen〕n. 鍊子　dangle〔ˋdæŋgḷ〕v. 懸掛；吊著
the minute 一～就（= as soon as）　hug〔hʌg〕n. 擁抱
block〔blɑk〕n. 街區　wave〔wev〕v. 揮手
backwards〔ˋbækwɚdz〕adv. 向後地

Mama was hurrying her. Amy made sure her gold bracelet was secure on her wrist. Then she put on both her sweater and her coat so that she wouldn't have to carry them. They could take only what they could carry, and her two suitcases were already full.

媽媽在催她了。艾美確定她的金鍊子掛好在手腕上,然後她穿上毛衣、外套,省得拿在手上。她們只能拿拿得動的東西,而艾美的兩個手提箱已經夠滿了。

hurry (ˈhɝɪ) v. 催促　　***make sure*** 確定
secure (sɪˈkjur) adj. (東西) 牢固的;不會掉的
wrist (rɪst) n. 手腕　　***put on*** 穿上
sweater (ˈswɛtɚ) n. 毛衣　　carry (ˈkærɪ) v. 攜帶;拿著
suitcase (ˈsutˌkes) n. 手提箱

Mama took a last look around the house, going from room to room. Amy followed her, trying to recall how each one had looked when they were filled with furniture and rugs and pictures and books. They went out for a last look at the garden Papa loved. If he were here now, Amy knew he would pick one of the prettiest carnations and gave it to Mama. She would beam and put it in her best crystal vase. But now the garden looked shabby and bare. It looked the way Amy felt—lonely and abandoned.

媽媽最後四處看看房子,一個房間走過一個房間。艾美跟在媽媽身後,努力回想每個房間,當初裝滿傢俱、地毯、圖畫和書籍時的模樣。她們走出屋外,對爸爸最愛的花園,做了最後的巡視。如果爸爸現在還在,她知道爸爸一定會摘下一朵最美麗的康乃馨,送給媽媽。媽媽一定會微笑,把花放進她最好的水晶花瓶。但是現在,花園看起來破舊又草木不生,就如同艾美的心情—寂寞又被遺棄。

take a look 看一看　　recall (rɪˈkɔl) v. 回想
furniture (ˈfɝnɪtʃɚ) n. 傢俱　　rug (rʌg) n. 地毯
pick (pɪk) v. 摘下　　pretty (ˈprɪtɪ) adj. 漂亮的
carnation (karˈneʃən) n. 康乃馨　　beam (bim) v. 微笑
crystal (ˈkrɪstl̩) n. 水晶　　vase (ves) n. 花瓶
shabby (ˈʃæbɪ) adj. 破舊的　　bare (bɛr) adj. 草木不生的
abandoned (əˈbændənd) n. 被遺棄的

41. (**C**) 本文的主旨為 _____ 。

    (A) 美麗的禮物   (B) 空空的房子

    (C) <u>悲傷的再見</u>   (D) 甜美的回憶

    mainly (ˈmenlɪ) *adv.* 主要地   memory (ˈmɛmərɪ) *n.* 回憶

42. (**D**) 文中明確地提到以下那一件事？

    (A) 艾美的爸爸在花園裡種康乃馨。

    (B) 艾美的朋友都知道她要走了。

    (C) 艾美的媽媽在她們離開前，賣掉所有的傢俱。

    (D) <u>艾美跟媽媽身上只提著幾個手提箱。</u>

    explicitly (ɪksˈplɪsɪtlɪ) *adv.* 明確地

43. (**B**) 根據本文，以下何者不正確？

    (A) 艾美很珍惜蘿拉給她的金手鍊。

    (B) <u>艾美轉身，並且倒退著走開。</u>

    (C) 當艾美她們要離開，艾美的爸爸並不在身邊。

    (D) 艾美不知道她是否能遵守對蘿拉的承諾。

44－47 為題組

    In the last several decades, the western world has been rediscovering the soybean, a plant whose use dates back to recorded history in Asia. For thousands of years, the Chinese have highly valued the soybean, considering it one of the five important grains (along with rice, millet, barley, and wheat). Since it is cheap to produce and rich in protein, and has many uses, the soybean could provide food to the world's growing population. Besides, soybeans can be fed to a variety of other animals ranging from livestock to silk worms.

    過去數十年來，西方世界重新發現了大豆，這種植物的用途，在亞洲可以追溯至信史時代。數千年來，中國人對大豆非常重視，將它視為五種重要穀類之一（以及稻米、小米、大麥和小麥）。因為大豆種植便宜，富含蛋白質，且有多種用途，大豆可以為全世界逐漸增加的人口提供食物。此外，大豆還可以用來餵養其他各種動物，從家畜到蠶皆可。

decade〔'dɛked〕n. 十年　　rediscover〔ˌridɪ'skʌvɚ〕v. 重新發現
soybean〔'sɔɪˌbin〕n. 大豆；黃豆　　**date back to** 追溯至
recorded history 有紀錄的歷史；信史　　grain〔gren〕n. 穀類
along with 以及　　millet〔'mɪlɪt〕n. 粟；小米
barley〔'barlɪ〕n. 大麥　　wheat〔hwit〕n. 小麥
protein〔'protiɪn〕n. 蛋白質　　growing〔'groɪŋ〕adj. 漸增的
a variety of 各種　　**range from** A **to** B 範圍從 A 到 B 都有
livestock〔'laɪvˌstak〕n. 家畜　　**silk worm** 蠶

The soybean is an almost perfect source of protein. If you are a
vegetarian, or if your diet includes little meat, soy protein is a good
alternative, and may even be essential to maintaining your health. The
soybean's high fiber content is beneficial in preventing digestive disorders.
The soybean is free of cholesterol, and more importantly, the soy oil
contains some special substances, called Omega 3 fatty acids, which
reduce cholesterol and prevent blood from clotting in the human body.
Research shows that consuming a minimum of 25 grams of soy protein a
day can lower blood cholesterol levels in people with high cholesterol
problems.

　　大豆是蛋白質近乎完美的來源之一。如果你吃素，或者你的飲食中很少有
肉，大豆蛋白質是一個很好的選擇，而且對維持你的身體健康而言，可能甚至
是必要的。大豆的高纖含量，也有助於預防消化性疾病。大豆不含膽固醇，而
且更重要的是，大豆油包含某些特殊物質，一般稱爲 Omega 3 脂肪酸，可以降
低膽固醇，預防人體血液凝結。研究顯示，每天攝取至少 25 克的大豆蛋白質，
對於那些有高膽固醇問題的人，可以降低他們血液中膽固醇的含量。

perfect〔'pɝfɪkt〕adj. 完美的　　source〔sors〕n. 來源
vegetarian〔ˌvɛdʒə'tɛrɪən〕n. 素食者　　diet〔'daɪət〕n. 飲食
alternative〔ɔl'tɝnətɪv〕n. 選擇　　essential〔ə'sɛnʃəl〕adj. 必要的
maintain〔men'ten〕v. 維持　　fiber〔'faɪbɚ〕n. 纖維
content〔'kantɛnt〕n. 含量　　beneficial〔ˌbɛnə'fɪʃəl〕adj. 有益的
prevent〔prɪ'vɛnt〕v. 預防　　digestive〔də'dʒɛstɪv〕adj. 消化的
disorder〔dɪs'ɔrdɚ〕n. 疾病　　**be free of** 沒有~的；不含~
cholesterol〔kə'lɛstərəl〕n. 膽固醇　　contain〔kən'ten〕v. 包含

substance (ˈsʌbstəns) *n.* 物質　　fatty (ˈfætɪ) *adj.* 脂肪的
acid (ˈæsɪd) *n.* 酸　　clot (klɑt) *v.* (血液等) 凝結
consume (kənˈsum) *v.* 消耗；吃；喝
minimum (ˈmɪnɪməm) *n.* 最小量；最少量
gram (græm) *n.* 公克　　lower (ˈloə) *v.* 降低
level (ˈlɛvḷ) *n.* 程度；水準；含量

In view of all these strengths, in the 1930s the United States and Canada undertook a research project in which they managed to develop an especially nutritious soybean with a high oil content. Since then, the United States has become the world's largest producer of soybeans and has exported much of its soybean production. In recent years, the soybean has been used in making many different foods and has become the atom of health food. Health-conscious Americans are adding tofu, the most popular soybean product, to salads and using it as a meat substitute. In the health food stores of major cities, it is now possible to buy tofu burgers and even tofu hot dogs.

　　有鑑於所有這些優點，在一九三〇年代，美國和加拿大開始從事一項研究計劃，設法研發出一種特別有營養、且含油量高的大豆。從那時起，美國即成為全世界大豆產量最高的國家，並且出口大量的大豆。在近幾年來，大豆已被用來製成許多不同種類的食物，而且也成為健康食品的基礎。注重健康的美國人，在沙拉中加入了最受歡迎的大豆製品——豆腐，也將豆腐作為肉類替代品。在許多大都市裡的健康食品專賣店，現在也可能買得到豆腐漢堡，甚至還有豆腐熱狗。

in view of 有鑑於　　strength (strɛŋθ) *n.* 優點
undertake (ˌʌndəˈtek) *v.* 開始從事　　project (ˈprɑdʒɛkt) *n.* 計劃
manage to 設法做到　　nutritious (njuˈtrɪʃəs) *adj.* 有營養的
export (ɪksˈport) *v.* 出口　　atom (ˈætəm) *n.* 原子；基礎 (= *basis*)
conscious (ˈkɑnʃəs) *adj.* 有意識的；察覺到的
add (æd) *v.* 添加　　tofu (ˈtofu) *n.* 豆腐
meat (mit) *n.* 肉　　substitute (ˈsʌbstəˌtjut) *n.* 代替品
major (ˈmedʒə) *adj.* 主要的；較大的
burger (ˈbɝgə) *n.* 漢堡　　*hot dog* 熱狗

44.（**D**）本文的主旨為何？

(A) 亞洲人使用大豆產品已有數千年之久。

(B) 注重健康的美國人飲食中包含更多的豆腐。

(C) 大豆為全世界逐漸增加的人口提供食物。

(D) <u>大豆有益健康，而且在西方世界變得很受歡迎。</u>

Asian（ˈeʃən）n. 亞洲人　　healthful（ˈhɛlθfəl）adj. 有益健康的

45.（**B**）大豆作為一種食物來源，其主要優點之一為 ＿＿＿＿＿。

(A) 不含油　　　　　(B) <u>種植便宜</u>

(C) 蛋白質含量低　　(D) 膽固醇含量高

major（ˈmedʒɚ）adj. 主要的　　advantage（ədˈvæntɪdʒ）n. 優點

46.（**C**）大豆有助於預防膽固醇升高，主要是因為它含有 ＿＿＿＿＿。

(A) 豐富的蛋白質　　(B) 豐富的維他命

(C) <u>某些脂肪酸</u>　　(D) 高纖維含量

keep sth. down 抑制

47.（**A**）根據本文，下列敘述何者為真？

(A) <u>豆腐是一種豐富的蛋白質來源。</u>

(B) 大豆蛋白質可以預防消化問題。

(C) 美國所產的大豆大部分都出口到加拿大。

(D) 素食者每天應該攝取 25 克以下的大豆蛋白質。

<u>48～51 為題組</u>

Big brothers and sisters usually develop leadership tendencies early in life, mainly because of the responsibilities for younger children given to them by their parents. Firstborns, under normal circumstances, are usually the most strongly motivated toward achievement. This is mainly a result of parental expectations. .

當哥哥姊姊的人，通常在成長初期，就會培養出具有領導能力的傾向，主要是因為父母會給予他們照顧弟妹的責任。在正常情況下，父母通常會極力地激勵排行老大的小孩，期許他們有成就。這主要是因為父母對她們期望很高。

develop (dɪ'vɛləp) v. 培養；發展
leadership ('lidə˞ˏʃɪp) n. 領導能力
tendency ('tɛndənsɪ) n. 傾向　　mainly ('menlɪ) adv. 主要地
responsibility (rɪˏspɑnsə'bɪlətɪ) n. 責任
firstborn ('fɝstˏbɔrn) n. 長男；長女　adj. 第一胎的
normal ('nɔrml̩) adj. 正常的　　circumstance ('sɝkʌmstəns) n. 情況
strongly ('strɔŋlɪ) adv. 強烈地；極力地
motivate ('moteˏvet) v. 給予（某人）刺激
achievement (ə'tʃivmənt) n. 成就　　result (rɪ'zʌlt) n. 結果
parental (pə'rɛntl̩) adj. 父母的
expectation (ˏɛkspɛk'teʃən) n. 期待

Research also suggests that firstborn children generally become more conservative than other children because they receive most of the parental discipline. Used to caring for others, they are more likely to move toward such leadership professions as teaching and politics. Less social and flexible because they become accustomed in the very early years to acting alone, they may have difficulty making close friends

研究同時也顯示，排行老大的小孩，通常會變得比其他小孩保守，因為他們受到父母最多的訓練。由於他們習慣照顧別人，所以比較有可能從事須具有領導力的工作，如教學或政治。又因為他們從小習慣單獨行動，所以較不善交際，而且不知變通，所以很難交到親密的朋友。

research ('risɝtʃ) n. 研究　　suggest (sə'dʒɛst) v. 暗示；表明
generally ('dʒɛnərəlɪ) adv. 一般地；普遍地
conservative (kən'sɝvətɪv) adj. 保守的
discipline ('dɪsəplɪn) n. 訓練　　*be used to + V-ing* 習慣於
care for 照顧　　move (muv) v. 前進；發展
profession (prə'fɛʃən) n. 職業　　politics ('pɑləˏtɪks) n. 政治
sociable ('soʃəbl̩) adj. 善於交際的
flexible ('flɛksəbl̩) adj. 有彈性的；可變通的
accustomed (ə'kʌstəmd) adj. 習慣的　　act (ækt) v. 行動
alone (ə'lon) adv. 單獨地　　*have difficulty (in) + V-ing* ～有困難
close (klos) adj. 親密的　　*make friends* 交朋友

By contrast, later children are more likely to be more relaxed and sociable because their parents are more relaxed. However, later children are often less ambitious and may be uncomfortable making decisions for others. This may help explain why younger children tend to favor the creative fields such as music, art, and writing. Later children may make good salespersons because persuasion may have been the only tool they had to deal with older siblings. Younget children tend to remain forever "the baby," enjoyable to be around, but at times over-dependent on others.

對比之下，排行較後面的孩子，可能比較輕鬆，而且善於交際，因為他們的父母比較放鬆。然而，排行較後面的孩子，通常比較沒有企圖心，而且對於幫別人做決定，會覺得不自在。這可能有助於解釋，為什麼較年幼的小孩容易偏愛有創意的領域，例如音樂、藝術及寫作。排行較後面的孩子，可能會成為很好的銷售員，因為說服別人一直是他們和年長的兄姊相處的唯一工具。年紀最小的孩子永遠顯得「孩子氣」，喜歡被人包圍，但有時候會過度依賴別人。

by contrast 對比之下　　relaxed〔rɪˈlɛkst〕*adj.* 放鬆的
ambitious〔æmˈbɪʃəs〕*adj.* 有企圖心的　　*make decisions* 做決定
tend to 易於；清係於　　favor〔ˈfevɚ〕*v.* 較喜歡
creative〔krɪˈetɪv〕*adj.* 有創造力的　　field〔fild〕*n.* 領域
make〔mek〕*v.* 成為　　salesperson〔ˈselsˌpɝsn̩〕*n.* 銷售員
persuasion〔pɚˈsweʒən〕*n.* 說服　　tool〔tul〕*n.* 工具
deal with 應付；交往　　sibling〔ˈsɪblɪŋ〕*n.* 兄弟姊妹
remain〔rɪˈmen〕*v.* 仍然　　forever〔fɚˈɛvɚ〕*adv.* 永遠
baby〔ˈbebɪ〕*n.* 孩子氣的人　　enjoyable〔ɪnˈdʒɔɪəbl̩〕*adj.* 愉快的
at times 有時候　　over-dependent〔ˈovɚdɪˈpɛndənt〕*adj.* 過度依賴的

48.(**D**) 這篇文章主要是關於 ＿＿＿＿＿。
　(A) 較年長的孩子的人格傾向
　(B) 較年幼的孩子的人格傾向
　(C) 出生排行和工作成功的關係
　(D) 出生排行和人格之間的關係
　personality〔ˌpɝsn̩ˈæləti〕*n.* 人格　　relation〔rɪˈleʃən〕*n.* 關係
　rank〔ræŋk〕*n.* 排行

49.(**D**) 根據本文，第一個出生的小孩容易 ─────。

    (A) 具有創造力　　　　　　(B) 善於交際。

    (C) 口才好　　　　　　　　(D) 保守

    persuasive〔pɚˋsweSIv〕*adj.* 口才好的；有說服力的

50.(**C**) 從本文可以推論出，較年幼的孩子較有可能當一個好 ─────。

    (A) 圖書館員　　　　　　　(B) 醫生

    (C) 作家　　　　　　　　　(D) 老師

    infer〔ɪnˋfɝ〕*v.* 推論　　librarian〔laɪˋbrɛrɪən〕*n.* 圖書館員

51.(**C**) 從本文我們可知，─────。

    (A) 孩子的人格完全取決於父母的態度

    (B) 藝術家通常不喜歡替別人做決定

    (C) 較年長的孩子習慣照顧別人，而且別人和他相處會很愉快

    (D) 較年幼的孩子特別不擅長公開演講

    depend on 取決於　　　***entirely***〔ɪnˋtaɪrlɪ〕*adv.* 完全地

    attitude〔ˋætə͵tjud〕*n.* 態度　　fun〔fʌn〕*adj.* 有趣的

    particularly〔pɚˋtɪkjələlɪ〕*adv.* 特別地

    weak〔wik〕*adj.* 虛弱的　　***deliver a speech*** 發表演講

    in public 公開地

第 52~55 為題組

    According to the U.S. Environmental Protection Agency (EPA), medical waste is a major source of dioxin pollution in the country. Linked to the dioxin issue is the use of PVC plastic, which is widely used in the production of blood bags, plastic tubing, and other products in hospitals and health clinics. Dioxin is an unwanted byproduct that is created when PVC is burned. Dioxin travels by air currents and settles onto grass, which is then eaten by cows and chickens in their feed. We eat polluted dairy products and meat and take the dioxin into our bodies, where it is stored in our fat for years and builds up over time.

　　根據美國環境保護局的說法，醫療廢棄物是美國境內戴奧辛污染的主要來源。和戴奧辛問題有關聯的是塑膠的使用，它被廣泛地用在製作血袋、塑膠管，以及其他醫院和診所的產品。戴奧辛是燃燒塑膠時製造出來，多餘的副產品。戴奧辛藉氣流而傳播，然後停留在草地上，然後牛和雞會在飼料中吃到。我們吃著被污染的乳製品和肉類，將戴奧辛吸收到體內，儲存在脂肪裡好些年，並且會隨著時間而逐漸增加。

> agency〔ˋedʒənsɪ〕n. 政府機關；局
> **Environmental Protection Agency** 環境保護局（＝EPA）
> medical〔ˋmɛdɪkl̩〕adj. 醫療的　　waste〔west〕n. 廢棄物
> major〔ˋmedʒɚ〕adj. 主要的　　source〔sors〕n. 來源
> dioxin〔daɪˋɑksɪn〕n. 戴奧辛　　pollution〔pəˋluʃən〕n. 污染
> link〔lɪŋk〕v. 連結　　issue〔ˋɪʃjʊ〕n. 問題；爭論點
> **PVC** 塑膠（＝*polyvinyl chloride*）　　plastic〔ˋplæstɪk〕n. 塑膠
> production〔prəˋdʌkʃən〕n. 生產；製造　　blood〔blʌd〕n. 血
> tubing〔ˋtjubɪŋ〕n. 管類　　clinic〔ˋklɪnɪk〕n. 診所
> **health clinic** 衛生診所　　unwanted〔ʌnˋwɑntɪd〕adj. 多餘的
> byproduct〔ˋbaɪˏprɑdəkt〕n. 副產品　　create〔krɪˋet〕v. 產生
> travel〔ˋtrævl̩〕v. 行進　　current〔ˋkɝənt〕n. 氣流；水流
> settle〔ˋsɛtl̩〕v. 降落；停留　　cow〔kaʊ〕n. 母牛
> feed〔fid〕n. 飼料　　dairy〔ˋdɛrɪ〕adj. 乳製品的
> **dairy product** 乳製品　　store〔stor〕v. 儲存
> fat〔fæt〕n. 脂肪　　**build up** 增加；累積
> **over time** 經過一段時間（＝*over a period of time*）

In this way, dioxin is globally distributed, and as a consequence, every member of the human population is constantly exposed to this poisonous substance. This poses special problems for childbearing women, who pass dioxin to an unborn baby or to a breastfeeding baby. In fact, the infant is the most vulnerable member of society to this chemical.

戴奧辛就以這樣的方式，在全球散布，因此，每一個人都會持續地接觸到這種毒的物質。對於懷孕婦女而言，這更會造成一些特別的問題，因為她們把戴奧辛傳給未出世的，或是吃母乳的嬰兒。事實上，嬰兒是社會上最容易受這種化學物質傷害的成員。

in this way 如此一來　　globally (ˈglɑblɪ) *adv.* 全球地

distribute (dɪˈstrɪbjut) *adj.* 分布　　*as a consequence* 因此

member (ˈmɛmbɚ) *n.* 成員　　population (ˌpɑpjəˈleʃən) *n.* 人口

constantly (ˈkɑnstəntlɪ) *adv.* 不斷地

be exposed to 暴露於…之中；接觸到

poisonous (ˈpɔɪznəs) *adj.* 有毒的　　substance (ˈsʌbstəns) *n.* 物質

pose (poz) *v.* 引起 (問題)

childbearing (ˈtʃaɪldˌbɛrɪŋ) *adj.* 生育的

pass (pæs) *v.* 傳遞　　unborn (ʌnˈbɔrn) *adj.* 未出生的

breastfeeding (ˈbrɛstˌfidɪŋ) *adj.* 以母乳養育的

infant (ˈɪnfənt) *n.* 嬰兒　　vulnerable (ˈvʌlnərəbl̩) *adj.* 易受傷害的

member (ˈmɛmbɚ) *n.* 成員　　chemical (ˈkɛmɪkl̩) *n.* 化學物質

Plastics used to account for as little as 10% of medical waste in the late 1970s, before disposables began rapidly replacing reusables. They now make up as much as 30%. The EPA estimates that the average levels of dioxin in all Americans are so high that we can expect to see a variety of health effects, including cancer. Given the harm caused by the burning of medical waste, physicians and nurses have the responsibility to take a lead in reducing the use of plastics in the hospital. After all, they can't be treating cancer on the inside of hospital and contributing to **it** on the outside.

1970 年代末期，在拋棄式用品快速取代可重複使用的物品之前，塑膠在醫療廢棄物上的使用，只佔了百分之十，現在已增加至百分之三十。美國環境保護局估計，所有美國人體內戴奧辛含量很高，所以我們可預期，將會看到各式各樣對健康所造成的影響，其中包括癌症。如果傷害是由燃燒醫療廢棄物所造成，醫生和護士就有責任，率先在醫院裡減少塑膠的使用。畢竟，他們不能一邊在醫院裡治療癌症，一邊又在醫院外頭助長癌症。

used to 以前　　*account for* 說明；是…的原因

in the late 1970s 在 1970 年代末期

disposable (dɪˈspozəbl̩) *n.* 拋棄式用品；用完即丟的用品

rapidly (ˈræpɪdlɪ) *adv.* 快速地　　replace (rɪˈples) *v.* 取代

reusable (riˈjuzəbl̩) *n.* 可重複使用的用品　　*make up* 組成

estimate (ˈɛstəˌmet) *v.* 估計　　average (ˈævərɪdʒ) *adj.* 平均的

level (ˈlɛvl̩) *n.* 含量　　expect (ɪkˈspɛkt) *v.* 預期

a variety of 各種的;各式各樣的   effect (ɪ'fɛkt) *n.* 影響
cancer ('gɪvən) *conj.* 如果   given ('gɪvən) *conj.* 如果
physician (fə'zɪʃən) *n.* 醫生;內科醫生
take a lead 率先   *after all* 畢竟
contribute (kən'trɪbjut) *v.* 促成 <*to*>

52. (**A**) 作者試著要傳達給讀者的最主要訊息是什麼？
     (A) 所有的人，尤其在醫院工作的人，應該要減少使用塑膠。
     (B) 美國人應該帶領全世界，對抗戴奧辛污染，否則人類將會滅絕。
     (C) 我們最好多吃蔬菜少吃肉，以減少戴奧辛污染的風險。
     (D) 我們最好不要用母乳哺育嬰兒，因為嬰兒最有可能被戴奧辛毒害。
     convey (kən've) *v.* 傳達   *die out* 滅絕
     breastfeed ('brɛst,fid) *v.* 以母乳養育   poison ('pɔɪzn) *v.* 毒害

53. (**A**) ──────── 會產生戴奧辛。
     (A) 燃燒塑膠時   (B) 製造醫院的血袋時
     (C) 處理可重複使用的物品時 (D) 處理各式各樣的醫療廢棄物時
     dispose of 處理   handle ('hændl) *v.* 處理

54. (**B**) 最後一行的 it 是指什麼？
     (A) 戴奧辛。   (B) 癌症。
     (C) 醫療廢棄物。   (D) 塑膠的使用。

55. (**C**) 下面哪一項敘述可以從文章中推論出來？
     (A) 住在鄉下可以使人不會有戴奧辛中毒的現象。
     (B) 如果我們喝大量乾淨的純水，戴奧辛就會從體內釋放出來。
     (C) 用像人們早期在用的可重複使用的物品，有助於減少戴奧辛污染。
     (D) 你必須減重，否則你體脂肪內的戴奧辛含量將會害死你。
     infer (ɪn'fɝ) *v.* 推論   article ('ɑrtɪkl) *n.* 文章
     countryside ('kʌntrɪ,saɪd) *n.* 鄉下   poisoning ('pɔɪzn̩ɪŋ) *n.* 中毒
     release (rɪ'lis) *v.* 釋放   pure (pjur) *adj.* 純的
     lessen ('lɛsn̩) *v.* 減少   *lose weight* 減輕體重
     body-fat ('bɑdɪ,fæt) *n.* 體脂肪

第貳部分：非選擇題

一、簡答題

It's easier for the human face to smile than frown. It takes twice as many muscles to frown as it does to smile. Moreover, we do not have to "learn" to do it. Although babies imitate the facial expressions they see, smiling isn't just learned by imitation. Children born blind never see anybody smile, but they show the same kinds of smiles under the same situations as sighted people.

對人的臉部而言，微笑比皺眉頭容易。皺眉頭須動用的肌肉是微笑的兩倍。而且，我們不需要學習就會微笑。雖然嬰兒會模仿他們所看到的臉部表情，但微笑卻不僅僅是從模仿中學到的。天生失明的孩子從未見過任何人微笑，但當他們和看得見的人，處於相同的情況時，卻會露出一樣的微笑。

frown (fraʊn) v. 皺眉頭	twice (twaɪs) adv. 兩倍地
muscle ('mʌsl̩) n. 肌肉	imitate ('ɪmə,tet) v. 模仿
facial ('feʃəl) adj. 臉部的	expression (ɪk'sprɛʃən) n. 表情
born (bɔrn) adj. 天生的	blind (blaɪnd) adj. 瞎的；失明的
situation (,sɪtʃʊ'eʃən) n. 情況	sighted ('saɪtɪd) adj. 眼明的；非盲的

Smiling is of great help to us. Some studies suggest that the act of shaping our mouths into a smile (creating a "physical smile") can help us see the brighter, funnier side of things. People wearing the physical smile tend to feel happier. In addition, smiles signal to others that we are people who might be nice to talk to and work with—and that can help us make friends.

微笑對我們有很大的幫助。有些研究指出，使我們的嘴巴變成微笑形狀的這個動作（製造一個「有形的微笑」），能幫助我們看見事物較光明、較有趣的一面。常常面帶有形微笑的人，就容易覺得比較快樂。此外，微笑可以發出信號，告訴別人我們是好說話、好相處的人——而將那幫助我們結交朋友。

study ('stʌdɪ) n. 研究	suggest (sə'dʒɛst) v. 提議；暗示
shape (ʃep) v. 使成為…的形狀	mouth (maʊθ) n. 嘴巴
physical ('fɪzɪkl̩) adj. 身體的；有形的	bright (braɪt) adj. 光明的
funny ('fʌnɪ) adj. 有趣的	side (saɪd) n. 一面；一邊
wear (wɛr) v. 面帶（微笑）	*in addition* 此外
signal ('sɪgnl̩) v. 發出信號	

Unfortunately, sometimes you may find it difficult to smile. Anything from getting a bad grade on a test to losing an important game can make you feel sad. In such hard times, there seems to be no reason to smile. But there is some good part to almost every bad thing. Turning something that seems all bad into something good is one way to help you smile. Hanging around people who are positive and in good moods is another way to help you find your smile again.

遺憾的是，有時你會發現，要露出微笑是很困難的。從考試考不好，到輸了一場重要的比賽，任何事都可能使你覺得難過。在這種難過的時刻，似乎沒有理由微笑。但幾乎每一件不好的事，都會有某個好的部分。將看起來似乎全然是不好的事，轉變爲好事，是幫助你微笑的一個方法。另一個幫你再次找回自己的微笑的方法，就是和樂觀且心情愉快的人在一起。

> unfortunately〔ʌnˈfɔrtʃənɪtlɪ〕 *adv.* 不幸地；遺憾地
> grade〔gred〕 *n.* 分數；成績　　lose〔luz〕 *v.* 輸掉
> hard〔hɑrd〕 *adj.* 困難的；辛苦的　　***turn* A *into* B** 把 A 變成 B
> seem〔sim〕 *v.* 似乎　　***hang around*** 和…在一起
> positive〔ˈpɑzətɪv〕 *adj.* 樂觀的；積極的　　mood〔mud〕 *n.* 心情

1. 爲什麼有形的微笑比皺眉頭容易？

   答：It takes / requires fewer muscles。（需要用到的肌肉比較少。）

2. 有形的微笑有助於產生什麼樣的感覺？

   答：optimistic / happy（樂觀的 / 快樂的）

3. 微笑對於一個人的社交生活的哪一方面有幫助？

   答：making friends / it can help him make friends

   　　（交朋友 / 它能幫助人們交朋友）

4. 舉一個例子，說明本文中所提到的「難過的時期」。

   答：bad grades / a bad grade on a test / losing an important game

   　　（成績不好 / 考試成績不好 / 輸掉了重要的比賽）

5. 本文中舉哪一群特殊的人爲例，說明微笑不是學來的？

   答：blind people / the blind（盲人）

   　　cite〔saɪt〕 *v.* 引用；舉例

二、英文作文：(作文範例)

　　We must all go through hard times in life. We may fail a test, lose our job or simply get caught in an annoying traffic jam. All of these things can make us feel sad or upset. In times such as these it is important to calm down and recover our good spirits. The following is the way I improve my mood when I feel down.

　　First of all, I tell myself that no matter what happens, it is not the end of the world. Life will go on, and I will overcome the difficulty eventually. *Then* I look for a way to solve my problem. If I can find one, I take action right away. If not, I forget about it for a while. I have found that by putting my troubles and sorrows aside I can have more energy to face challenges. *Therefore*, I will take a break. I will listen to music, watch TV or talk to a friend. *Then*, when I am in a better mood, I can face my problems and solve them.

　　In short, the best way for me to cheer myself up is to forget my problems for a while. That way I can relax and think clearly. *Then* I can find the best solution. Once I have dealt with the problem I will be able to smile again.

---

go through 經歷　　fail〔fel〕*v.* 不及格

get caught in 遇到　　annoying〔əˋnɔɪɪŋ〕*adj.* 討厭的；煩人的

a traffic jam 交通阻塞　　upset〔ʌpˋsɛt〕*adj.* 不高興的

go on 繼續　　overcome〔͵ovɚˋkʌm〕*v.* 克服

eventually〔ɪˋvɛntʃʊəlɪ〕*adv.* 最後　　*take action* 採取行動

right away 立刻　　*for a while* 一會兒；一下子

trouble〔ˋtrʌbl〕*n.* 煩惱　　sorrow〔ˋsɑro〕*n.* 悲傷

energy〔ˋɛnɚdʒɪ〕*n.* 活力　　face〔fes〕*v.* 面對

challenge〔ˋtʃælɪndʒ〕*n.* 挑戰　　*take a break* 休息一下

in short 總之　　*cheer sb. up* 使某人高興起來；激勵某人

that way 那樣一來　　solution〔səˋluʃən〕*n.* 解決之道

deal with 應付；處理

九十二年度學科能力測驗（英文考科）大考中心公佈答案

題 號	答 案	題 號	答 案	題 號	答 案
1	C	21	C	41	C
2	A	22	B	42	D
3	B	23	D	43	B
4	D	24	D	44	D
5	B	25	A	45	D
6	A	26	B	46	B
7	C	27	C	47	A
8	A	28	D	48	C
9	D	29	C	49	B
10	C	30	A	50	D
11	B	31	I	51	A
12	C	32	E	52	B
13	A	33	H	53	A
14	B	34	G	54	C
15	D	35	B	55	A
16	B	36	J		
17	D	37	A		
18	J	38	C		
19	E	39	F		
20	G	40	D		

九十二年度學科能力測驗（英文考科）（補考）
大考中心公佈答案

題　號	答　案	題　號	答　案	題　號	答　案
1	B	21	B	41	C
2	A	22	D	42	D
3	C	23	C	43	B
4	A	24	A	44	D
5	C	25	D	45	B
6	B	26	A	46	C
7	D	27	C	47	A
8	A	28	D	48	D
9	D	29	D	49	D
10	C	30	C	50	C
11	C	31	F	51	B
12	B	32	D	52	A
13	A	33	G	53	A
14	B	34	A	54	B
15	D	35	B	55	C
16	J	36	C		
17	G	37	E		
18	F	38	H		
19	A	39	J		
20	B	40	I		

92年大學入學學科能力測驗（補考）英文試題修正意見

題號	原　　文	修　正　意　見
19	Tell me **all the truth**	應該寫成 **the whole truth**，或 **the truth**。
21-25	…to prepare __(23)__ delicious items as roast chicken, chili, **turkey loaf, turkey loaf,** meatballs, **pasta, among others.**	…to prepare __(23)__ delicious items as roast chicken, chili, **turkey loaf,** meatballs, **and pasta, among others.** 這個錯誤太明顯了。
21-25	At the end of the class, you __(25)__ with **you** classmates the meals you have created, and….	At the end of the class, you __(25)__ with **your** classmates the meals you have created, and…. 這個錯誤太明顯了。
31-40	Different __(33)__ have been employed by economists to **measure standard of living.**	Different __(33)__ have been employed by economists to measure **standards of living.**
31-40	Of course, in determining **overall standards of living** of Americans, factors __(40)__ household composition and family size need….	Of course, in determining **the overall standard of living** of Americans, factors __(40)__ household composition and family size need…. **the overall standard of living** of Americans 所指的是一件東西，所以要用單數。
44-47	…the western world has been rediscovering the soybean, a plant whose use **dates before** recorded history in Asia.	…the western world has been rediscovering the soybean, a plant whose use **dates back to before** recorded history in Asia.
44-47	For thousands of years, the Chinese **have valued highly the soybean,** considering it one of the five most important grains…	For thousands of years, the Chinese **have highly valued the soybean,** considering it one of the five most important grains…或是 For thousands of years, the Chinese **have valued the soybean highly,** considering it one of the five most important grains…
44-47	…which reduce cholesterol and prevent blood from clotting **in human** body.	…which reduce cholesterol and prevent blood from clotting **in the human** body.
44(B)	Health-conscious Americans are **using** more tofu in their diet.	Health-conscious Americans are **eating** more tofu in their diet.
48-51	**Younger** children tend to remain forever "the baby," enjoyable to be around, but at times **overdependent** on others.	**Youngest** children tend to remain forever "the baby," enjoyable to be around, but at times **over-dependent** on others. 這篇文章是在討論兄弟姊妹的排名順序對於他們的個性所帶來的影響。在講到老么時，應該用 **youngest**，而不是用 **younger**，因為前面已經提到老大及老二了。**overdependent** 不是一個字，所以 over 和 dependent 之間要加 hyphen。

九十二學年度學科能力測驗各科各級分人數累計表

	級分	人　　數	百 分 比 (%)	累計人數	累計百分比 (%)
	15	3818	2.32	3818	2.32
	14	6181	3.76	9999	6.08
	13	8987	5.46	18986	11.54
	12	10640	6.47	29626	18.01
英	11	11941	7.26	41567	25.27
	10	12642	7.68	54209	32.95
	9	14302	8.69	68511	41.64
	8	13750	8.36	82261	50.00
	7	14208	8.64	96469	58.64
	6	15137	9.20	111606	67.84
	5	15366	9.34	126972	77.18
	4	16355	9.94	143327	87.12
文	3	14391	8.75	157718	95.86
	2	3752	2.28	161470	98.15
	1	127	0.08	161597	98.22
	0	2	0.00	161599	98.22
	缺考	2922	1.78	164521	100.00

九十二學年度學科能力測驗各科成績標準一覽表

考　科	頂　標	前　標	均　標	後　標	底　標
國　文	13	12	10	8	6
英　文	12	10	7	4	3
數　學	10	8	5	2	1
社　會	13	13	11	9	8
自　然	12	11	9	7	6

※上列標準係依本測驗各該科全體到考考生成績計算均取為整數（小
　數只捨不入）其定義如下：

　　　頂標：該科前百分之二十五考生成績之平均
　　　前標：該科前百分之五十考生成績之平均
　　　均標：該科全體考生成績之平均
　　　後標：該科後百分之五十考生成績之平均
　　　底標：該科後百分之二十五考生成績之平均

九十一年大學入學學科能力測驗試題
英文考科①

第壹部份：單一選擇題

一、詞彙與慣用語（15%）

說明：第1至15題，每題選出最適當的一個選項，標示在答案卡之「選擇題答案區」。每題答對得1分，答錯不倒扣。

1. In the keen competition of this international tennis tournament, she _____ won the championship.
   (A) privately　　(B) distantly　　(C) locally　　(D) narrowly

2. This company, with its serious financial problems, is no longer _____.
   (A) achievable　(B) stretchable　(C) repeatable　(D) manageable

3. Your desk is crowded with too many unnecessary things. You have to _____ some of them.
   (A) remain　　(B) resist　　(C) remove　　(D) renew

4. Most businessmen are more interested in the _____ success of their products than their educational values.
   (A) cultural　(B) commercial　(C) classical　(D) criminal

5. The postal special _____ service is very efficient. A package sent can be received in a couple of hours.
   (A) delivery　　(B) directory　　(C) discovery　　(D) dormitory

6. Children don't learn their native languages _____, but they become fluent in them within a few years.
   (A) previously　(B) variously　(C) consciously　(D) enviously

7. _____ to what you think, our TV program has been enjoyed by a large audience.

 (A) Intensive　　(B) Contrary　　(C) Fortunate　　(D) Objective

8. There is a _____ to one's capacity; one should not make oneself overtired.

 (A) relaxation　　(B) contribution　　(C) hesitation　　(D) limitation

9. It is necessary for you to _____ this point. We simply cannot understand it.

 (A) clarify　　(B) falsify　　(C) purify　　(D) notify

10. Our team will certainly win this baseball game, because all the players are highly _____.

 (A) illustrated　　(B) estimated　　(C) motivated　　(D) dominated

11. This story, _____, is very fascinating: there are many interesting characters in it.

 (A) on the whole　　　　　　　(B) under no circumstances
 (C) in no time　　　　　　　　(D) out of the question

12. Most of our classmates are _____ taking a trip to Kenting National Park.

 (A) in honor of　　(B) in favor of　　(C) in search of　　(D) in place of

13. We haven't seen John for a long time. As a matter of fact, we have _____ him.

 (A) made up for　　　　　　　(B) run out of
 (C) come to pass　　　　　　　(D) lost track of

14. Recently in Taiwan, the manufacturing industry has _____ the information industry.

 (A) found a way of　　　　　　(B) changed the way of
 (C) given way to　　　　　　　(D) had a way of

15. His behavior at the party last night seemed rather _____. Many
of us were quite surprised.
(A) out of practice   (B) out of place
(C) out of politeness   (D) out of pity

二、句子配合題（5%）

說明： 1. 第 16 至 20 題，每題皆爲未完成的句子。請逐題依文意與語法，從
右欄 (A) 到 (J) 的選項中選出最適當者，合併成一個意思通順、用
法正確的句子。
2. 請將每題所選答案之英文字母代號標示在答案卡之「選擇題答案
區」。每題答對得 1 分，答錯不倒扣。

16. There is no doubt that	A.... can you succeed in achieving your goal.
17. What I can never understand	B....moved into a new apartment.
18. Only by working hard	C....more than a copy of the other.
19. The nurse approached the child,	D.... don't lose any opportunity.
20. This painting is nothing	E.... no place is like home.
	F.... after proposing a new plan to the company.
	G.... and it is improper to say so.
	H.... trying to make him relaxed.
	I.... very anxious to carry out the project.
	J.... is why John failed in this exam.

三、綜合測驗（10%）

說明： 第 21 至 30 題，每題一個空格，請依文意選出最適當的一個選項，標示
在答案卡之「選擇題答案區」。每題答對得 1 分，答錯不倒扣。

It is a usual sunny afternoon in the village of Midwich, England. It seems not __21__ any afternoon in the village, but all of a sudden, people and animals lose consciousness. __22__ they awake, all of the women of child-bearing age have become pregnant.

This is an episode from a 1960 science fiction story. The women in the story __23__ birth to children that have the same appearance. They all have blond hair and "strange eyes." __24__ the children grow, they run around the village in a pack, wearing identical clothing and hairstyles, staring at everyone impolitely. __25__ one child learns is also known by the others instantly. Villagers begin to __26__ their belief that the children all have "one mind." In this story, the children are produced by some unexplained force from outer space. But this story written 40 years ago __27__ predicted the arrival of a recent method of genetic engineering—cloning. Cloning is the genetic process of producing copies of an individual. Will the genetic copies of a human really have "one mind" as __28__ in this story? This situation is so strange to us that we do not know what will __29__ of it. Faced with this new situation, people have __30__ to find out how to deal with it.

21. (A) unlike   (B) dislike   (C) like   (D) alike

22. (A) Then   (B) When   (C) Since   (D) And

23. (A) send   (B) make   (C) take   (D) give

24. (A) If   (B) For   (C) As   (D) So

25. (A) Which   (B) While   (C) Where   (D) What

26. (A) express   (B) wonder   (C) select   (D) ignore

27. (A) sometimes   (B) anyway   (C) somehow   (D) anyhow

28. (A) describes   (B) described   (C) describe   (D) describing

29. (A) happen   (B) occur   (C) appear   (D) become

30. (A) not   (B) yet   (C) till   (D) though

四、文意選填（10 ％）

說明： 第 31 至 40 題，每題一個空格，請依文意在文章後所提供的(A) 到 (J)
選項中分別選出最適當者，並將其英文字母代號標示在答案卡之「選
擇題答案區」。每題答對得 1 分，答錯不倒扣。

Amir tied two sacks of salt to the back of his donkey and headed
for the market to sell the salt. On ___31___, Amir and the donkey passed
a stream. The donkey jumped into the stream to cool ___32___. As a
result, much of the salt melted in the water, ruining the salt for Amir but
___33___ the load for the donkey. Amir tried to get to the market on the
following days, but the donkey ___34___ the same trick and ruined the
salt.

Amir was very much ___35___ by the donkey's trick, but did not know
what to do. So he stopped going to the market for three days and tried
to think of a way to ___36___ the donkey a lesson. On the third day, he
___37___ came up with a good idea. The next day, Amir loaded the sacks
___38___ with salt but with sand. When the donkey jumped into the stream
and got the sacks wet, they became much ___39___. The donkey was so
much weighed down by the wet sand that he could hardly get out of the
stream. From then on, the donkey learned the lesson, and ___40___
carried Amir's salt to the market without ruining it.

(A) dutifully   (B) played   (C) heavier   (D) the way   (E) not
(F) lightening   (G) finally   (H) himself   (I) teach   (J) troubled

五、閱讀測驗（30％）

說明：第 41 至 55 題，每題請分別根據各篇文章之文意選出最適當的一個選項，標示在答案卡之「選擇題答案區」。每題答對得 2 分，答錯不倒扣。

41-43 題為題組

　　Tim Welford, aged 33, and Dom Mee, aged 30, both from England, were keen on rowing boats. They made a plan to row across the Pacific Ocean from Japan to San Francisco. The name of their rowboat was "Crackers." It was about 7 meters long.

　　They set out from Japan on May 17, 2001. They had rowed nearly 5,500 miles when their boat was hit by a fishing ship on September 17, 2001. Luckily they both escaped unharmed, but their boat was badly damaged and they had to abandon their journey.

　　In a radio interview, Dom expressed his disappointment and explained how the accident took place.

　　"A fishing ship came towards us with nobody on the bridge and ran us down. It all happened so quickly. I managed to dive into the water. Tim felt it would be safer to stay on board the boat. He was trapped inside as the boat was driven under the water. Finally some people appeared on the ship and saw me in the water. I shouted at them to stop the ship and to get Tim out. When the ship stopped, I eventually saw Tim, and I was very, very relieved that we were still alive. We were very disappointed that we couldn't reach San Francisco. But we are alive. That above everything is the most important."

41. How long had Tim and Dom been at sea when their boat was hit by a fishing boat?
    (A) One month.   (B) Two months.
    (C) Three months.   (D) Four months.

42. According to Dom, the main reason for the accident was that
    _____.
    (A) Tim and Dom were too careless
    (B) nobody on the fishing ship saw them
    (C) the speed of the fishing ship was too fast
    (D) their rowboat was not strong enough

43. Dom said that the most important thing in this accident was
    _____.
    (A) both of them survived
    (B) they enjoyed this journey
    (C) their rowboat was not damaged
    (D) they failed to reach San Francisco

44-46 題為題組

Sometimes the real world can be a confusing place. It is not always fair or kind. And in the real world there are not always happy endings. That is why, every once in a while, we like to escape into the world of fantasy — a place where things always go our way and there is always a happy ending.

We want to believe in fantastic creatures in imaginary lands. We want to believe in magic powers, good friends, and the power of good to overcome evil. We all fantasize about being able to fly and lift buildings off the ground. And how good a magic sword would feel in our hand as we go off to kill a dragon or win the hand of a beautiful princess.

The amazing adventures of Superman, Peter Pan, and Harry Potter have charmed many people, children and adults alike. The main reason is that these stories offer us chances to get away from this real, frustrating world and allow us to find some magical solutions to our problems. For example, Superman always arrives in the nick of time to prevent a disaster from happening, Peter Pan can fly at will to tease the bad guy Captain Hook, and Harry Potter has his magic power to take revenge on his uncle, aunt and cousin, who always ill-treat him.

44. People enter the world of fantasy for the following reasons
    EXCEPT that _____.
    (A) the world of fantasy frightens us
    (B) the real world is often disappointing
    (C) we can find happy endings there
    (D) we can always have our wishes fulfilled

45. Superman, Peter Pan, and Harry Potter have charmed many people,
    because _____.
    (A) the bad guys always have the upper hand
    (B) they end up getting married to beautiful princesses
    (C) their solutions are anything but magical
    (D) they possess powers that ordinary people don't have

46. This article about fantasy literature is intended to _____.
    (A) criticize its unrealistic concepts
    (B) ridicule those people reading it
    (C) explain why people like to read it
    (D) teach people to avoid disasters

47-50 題為題組

In the early part of the twentieth century, racism was widespread in the United States. Many African Americans were not given equal opportunities in education or employment. Marian Anderson (1897-1993) was an African American woman who gained fame as a concert singer in this climate of racism. She was born in Philadelphia and sang in church choirs during her childhood. When she applied for admission to a local music school in 1917, she was turned down because she was black. Unable to attend music school, she began her career as a singer for church gatherings. In 1929, she went to Europe to study voice and spent several years performing there. Her voice was widely praised throughout Europe. Then she returned to the U.S. in 1935 and became a top concert singer after performing at Town Hall in New York City.

Racism again affected Anderson in 1939. When it was arranged for her to sing at Constitution Hall in Washington, D.C., the Daughters of the American Revolution opposed it because of her color. She sang instead at the Lincoln Memorial for over 75,000 people. In 1955, Anderson became the first black soloist to sing with the Metropolitan Opera of New York City. The famous conductor Toscanini praised her voice as "heard only once in a hundred years." She was a U.S. delegate to the United Nations in 1958 and won the UN peace prize in 1977. Anderson eventually triumphed over racism.

47. According to this passage, what did Marian Anderson do between 1917 and 1929?
    (A) She studied at a music school.
    (B) She sang for religious activities.
    (C) She sang at Town Hall in New York.
    (D) She studied voice in Europe.

48. Toscanini thought that Marian Anderson _____.
    (A) had a very rare voice
    (B) sang occasionally in public
    (C) sang only once in many years
    (D) was seldom heard by people

49. Anderson's beautiful voice was first recognized _____.
    (A) at the Lincoln Memorial　　(B) in Washington, D.C.
    (C) in Europe　　　　　　　　(D) at the United Nations

50. This passage shows that Anderson finally defeated racism in the U.S. by _____.
    (A) protesting to the government
    (B) appealing to the United Nations
    (C) demonstrating in the streets
    (D) working hard to perfect her art

51-55 題為題組

　　Five years ago, David Smith wore an expensive suit to work every day. "I was a clothes addict," he jokes. "I used to carry a fresh suit to work with me so I could change if my clothes got wrinkled." Today David wears casual clothes — khaki pants and a sports shirt — to the office. He hardly ever wears a necktie. "I'm working harder than ever," David says, "and I need to feel comfortable."

　　More and more companies are allowing their office workers to wear casual clothes to work. In the United States, the change from formal to casual office wear has been gradual. In the early 1990s, many companies allowed their employees to wear casual clothes on Friday (but only on Friday). This became known as "dress-down Friday" or "casual Friday." "What started out as an extra one-day-a-week benefit for employees has really become an everyday thing," said business consultant Maisly Jones.

Why have so many companies started allowing their employees to wear casual clothes? One reason is that it's easier for a company to attract new employees if it has a casual dress code. "A lot of young people don't want to dress up for work," says the owner of a software company, "so it's hard to hire people if you have a conservative dress code." Another reason is that people seem happier and more productive when they are wearing comfortable clothes. In a study conducted by Levi Strauss and Company, 85 percent of employers said that they believe that casual dress improves employee morale. Only 4 percent of employers said that casual dress has a negative impact on productivity. Supporters of casual office wear also argue that a casual dress code helps them save money. "Suits are expensive, if you have to wear one every day," one person said. "For the same amount of money, you can buy a lot more casual clothes."

51. David Smith refers to himself as having been "a clothes addict," because _____.
   (A) he often wore khaki pants and a sports shirt
   (B) he couldn't stand a clean appearance
   (C) he wanted his clothes to look neat all the time
   (D) he didn't want to spend much money on clothes

52. David Smith wears casual clothes now, because _____.
   (A) they make him feel at ease when working
   (B) he cannot afford to buy expensive clothes
   (C) he looks handsome in casual clothes
   (D) he no longer works for any company

53. According to this passage, which of the following statements is **FALSE**?
   (A) Many employees don't like a conservative dress code.
   (B) Comfortable clothes make employees more productive.
   (C) A casual clothes code is welcomed by young employees.
   (D) All the employers in the U.S. are for casual office wear.

54. According to this passage, which of the following statements is **TRUE**?
    (A) Company workers started to dress down about twenty years ago.
    (B) Dress-down has become an everyday phenomenon since the early 90s.
    (C) "Dress-down Friday" was first given as a favor from employers.
    (D) Many workers want to wear casual clothes to impress people.

55. In this passage, the following advantages of casual office wear are mentioned **EXCEPT** _____.
    (A) saving employees' money
    (B) making employees more attractive
    (C) improving employees' motivation
    (D) making employees happier

第貳部份：非選擇題

一、簡答題（10％）

說明：1. 閱讀下面這篇文章，然後簡答下列問題。答案必須寫在「答案卷」上。

　　　2. 請依序作答，並標明題號。答案應簡明扼要，只寫重要詞彙（key words），約二至三個英文單詞（words）。每題2分，共10分。
　　　　注意：請勿抄下整句或整行，否則不予記分。

　　South America is a place of striking beauty and wonder. The heart of this continent is the Amazon Rainforest, a vast paradise watered by one of the world's greatest rivers. Because of the tremendous amount of oxygen produced in this area, it has been called the "lungs of the earth."

　　A team of scientists, teachers, and students, the AmazonQuest team, recently explored some of the wonders of the Amazon Rainforest. They canoed down rivers, hiked along muddy trails, and climbed into the forest to explore and learn. The following is a report by one of the team members:

"I watched a small piece of the Amazon Rainforest disappear today. This morning, two men from the village of Roaboia led us into the forest. For 20 minutes, we walked along a path past tall weeds, banana trees, and low brush. Our destination was a 150-foot tall capirana tree, by far the biggest tree around. It would take 10 people holding hands to surround the base of its trunk.

The men took out an axe and an electric saw and started cutting into the tree's silky smooth skin. As beautiful as they are, people here chop down capirana trees for their wood. With a loud roar, the saw chewed into the 150-year-old tree. Then, in about 30 minutes after the cutting began, the giant tree crashed down violently and shook the ground under our feet.

This, of course, is just one of the millions of trees that fall in the Amazon each year. Brazil's Environmental Ministry estimates that in 1970, 99 percent of the original Amazon Rainforest remained, but in 2000, only 85 percent. It is estimated that more than 33 million acres of Amazonian Rainforest disappear every year. That means that 64 acres of the rainforest is lost every minute."

1. Which place is called "the lungs of the earth"?

2. What kinds of people are on the AmazonQuest team?

3. How long did it take the two men to cut down the giant capirana tree?

4. Between 1970 and 2000, what percentage of the original Amazon Rainforest was cut down?

5. According to this report, about how many acres of the Amazon Rainforest are lost every second?

二、英文作文（20％）

說明： 1. 依提示在「答案卷」上寫一篇英文作文。

2. 文長 120 個單詞（words）左右。

提示： 以"The Most Precious Thing in My Room"為題寫一篇英文作文，描述你的房間內一件你最珍愛的物品，同時並說明珍愛的理由。（這一件你最珍愛的物品不一定是貴重的，但對你來說卻是最有意義或是最值得紀念的。）

91年度學科能力測驗英文科試題①詳解

第壹部分：單一選擇題

一、詞彙與慣用語：

1. (**D**) *In the keen competition of this international tennis tournament*, she *narrowly* won the championship.

在這場競爭激烈的國際網球錦標賽中，她勉強地贏得冠軍。

(A) privately〔'praɪvɪtlɪ〕*adv.* 私下地
(B) distantly〔'dɪstəntlɪ〕*adv.* 遙遠地
(C) locally〔'lokəlɪ〕*adv.* 地方性地；局部地
(D) *narrowly*〔'nærolɪ〕*adv.* 勉強地

keen〔kin〕*adj.* 激烈的   competition〔͵kɑmpə'tɪʃən〕*n.* 競爭；比賽
tournament〔'tɝnəmənt〕*n.* 比賽；錦標賽
championship〔'tʃæmpɪən͵ʃɪp〕*n.* 冠軍（資格）

2. (**D**) This company, *with its serious financial problems*, is *no longer* manageable. 這家公司財務問題十分嚴重，已經無法管理了。

(A) achievable〔ə'tʃivəbḷ〕*adj.* 可達成的
(B) stretchable〔'strɛtʃəbḷ〕*adj.* 能伸展的
(C) repeatable〔rɪ'pitəbḷ〕*adj.* 可重複的
(D) *manageable*〔'mænɪdʒəbḷ〕*adj.* 可管理的

financial〔faɪ'nænʃəl〕*adj.* 財務的   *no longer* 不再

3. (**C**) Your desk is crowded with *too* many unnecessary things. You have to remove some *of them*.
你的書桌堆滿了太多不必要的東西。你必須把其中的一些移除。

(A) remain〔rɪ'men〕*v.* 仍然   (B) resist〔rɪ'zɪst〕*v.* 抵抗
(C) *remove*〔rɪ'muv〕*v.* 除去   (D) renew〔rɪ'nju〕*v.* 恢復

be crowded with 擠滿了～

4. (**B**) Most businessmen are *more* interested in the commercial

success *of their products* than their educational values.
大部份的商人，比較感興趣的是其產品商業上的成功，而不是教育
方面的價值。

(A) cultural ('kʌltʃərəl) *adj.* 文化的
(B) *commercial* (kə'mɜʃəl) *adj.* 商業的
(C) classical ('klæsɪkḷ) *adj.* 古典的
(D) criminal ('krɪmənḷ) *adj.* 犯罪的

value ('vælju) *n.* 價值

5. (**A**) The postal special delivery service is *very* efficient. A

package sent can be received *in a couple of hours.*
郵局的限時專送服務非常有效率。寄一個包裹，在幾個小時之內
就可以收到。

(A) *delivery* (dɪ'lɪvərɪ) *n.* 遞送　　*special delivery* 限時專送
(B) directory (də'rɛktərɪ) *n.* 指南；電話簿
(C) discovery (dɪ'skʌvərɪ) *n.* 發現
(D) dormitory ('dɔrmə,torɪ) *n.* 宿舍

postal ('postḷ) *adj.* 郵局的　　efficient (ɪ'fɪʃənt) *adj.* 有效率的
a couple of 幾個

6. (**C**) Children don't learn their native languages *consciously*, **but**

they become fluent in them *within a few years.*
孩子們會不自覺地學習本國語言，但是在幾年之內，他們就可以說
得很流利。

(A) previously ('privɪəslɪ) *adv.* 先前
(B) variously ('vɛrɪəslɪ) *adv.* 各式各樣地
(C) *consciously* ('kɑnʃəslɪ) *adv.* 有意識地；有自覺地
(D) enviously ('ɛnvɪəslɪ) *adv.* 嫉妒地

native ('netɪv) *adj.* 本國的　　fluent ('fluənt) *adj.* 流利的

7. (**B**) <u>*Contrary* to *what you think*</u>, our TV program has been enjoyed *by a large audience*.

和你所想的正好<u>相反</u>，我們的電視節目一直深受許多觀眾的喜愛。

(A) intensive〔ɪn'tɛnsɪv〕*adj.* 密集的

(B) *contrary*〔'kɑntrɛrɪ〕*adj.* 相反的　　*be contrary to* 與～相反

(C) fortunate〔'fɔrtʃənɪt〕*adj.* 幸運的

(D) objective〔əb'dʒɛktɪv〕*adj.* 客觀的

a large audience 很多觀眾

8. (**D**) There is a <u>limitation</u> *to one's capacity*; one should not make oneself overtired.

個人的能力有<u>限</u>；不應該讓自己太累。

(A) relaxation〔,rilæks'eʃən〕*n.* 放鬆

(B) contribution〔,kɑntrə'bjuʃən〕*n.* 貢獻

(C) hesitation〔,hɛzə'teʃən〕*n.* 猶豫

(D) *limitation*〔,lɪmə'teʃən〕*n.* 限制

capacity〔kə'pæsətɪ〕*n.* 能力

overtire〔'ovɚ'taɪr〕*v.* 使過度勞累

9. (**A**) It is necessary for you to <u>clarify</u> this point. We *simply* cannot understand it.

你必須把這一點<u>說明清楚</u>。我們實在無法了解。

(A) *clarify*〔'klærə,faɪ〕*v.* 使（意義）清楚；闡明

(B) falsify〔'fɔlsə,faɪ〕*v.* 偽造；欺騙

(C) purify〔'pjʊrə,faɪ〕*v.* 使潔淨

(D) notify〔'notə,faɪ〕*v.* 通知

point〔pɔɪnt〕*n.* 要點　　simply〔'sɪmplɪ〕*adv.* 實在

10. (**C**) Our team will *certainly* win this baseball game, *because all the players are highly motivated.*

這場棒球比賽我們這一隊一定會贏,因為我們所有的球員都士氣高昂。

(A) illustrate (ˈɪləstret) *v.* 說明

(B) estimate (ˈɛstəˌmet) *v.* 估計

(C) ***motivated*** (ˈmotəˌvetɪd) *adj.* 有動機的;積極的

(D) dominate (ˈdɑməˌnet) *v.* 支配

highly (ˈhaɪlɪ) *adv.* 非常地

11. (**A**) This story, on the whole, is *very* fascinating: there are many interesting characters *in it.*

整體而言,這個故事非常吸引人:故事裏有很多有趣的人物。

(A) ***on the whole*** 整體而言

(B) under no circumstances 無論在任何情形下絕不

(C) in no time 立刻

(D) out of the question 不可能

fascinating (ˈfæsnˌetɪŋ) *adj.* 吸引人的

character (ˈkærɪktə) *n.* 人物;角色

12. (**B**) Most *of our classmates* are in favor of taking a trip *to Kenting National Park.*

我們大多數的同學都underlined{贊成}去墾丁國家公園旅行。

(A) in honor of 紀念 (= *in memory of* = *in remembrance of*)

(B) ***in favor of*** 贊成

(C) in search of 尋找

(D) in place of 代替

take a trip 去旅行　　***national park*** 國家公園

13. (**D**) We haven't seen John *for a long time. As a matter of fact,* we have lost track of him.
我們已經很久沒看到約翰了。事實上，我們已經和他失去聯絡。
(A) make up for 彌補
(B) run out of 用完
(C) come to pass 發生；實現
(D) **lose track of** 和～失去聯絡

as a matter of fact 事實上 (= *in fact*)

14. (**C**) *Recently in Taiwan,* the manufacturing industry has given way to the information industry.
最近台灣的製造業，已經被資訊業所取代。
(A) find a way of 找到～的方法
(B) change the way of 改變～的方式
(C) **give way to** 被～取代
(D) have a way of 有～的習慣

recently ('risṇtlɪ) *adv.* 最近
manufacturing (,mænjə'fæktʃərɪŋ) *adj.* 製造業的
industry ('ɪndəstrɪ) *n.* 企業；行業
information (,ɪnfə'meʃən) *n.* 資訊

15. (**B**) His behavior *at the party last night* seemed *rather* out of place. Many *of us* were *quite* surprised.
他昨天晚上在舞會上的行為，似乎非常不適當。我們很多人都覺得非常驚訝。
(A) out of practice （因缺乏練習而）生疏的
(B) **out of place** 不適當的
(C) out of politeness 出於禮貌
(D) out of pity 出自同情心

rather ('ræðæ) *adv.* 相當地

二、句子配合題：

16. (**E**) There is no doubt ***that*** *no place is like home.*
無疑地，沒有一個地方比得上家。

17. (**J**) ***What I can never understand*** is ***why John failed in this exam.***
我無法理解，為什麼這次考試約翰會不及格。
fail〔fel〕*v.* （考試）不及格

18. (**A**) *Only by working hard* can you succeed *in achieving your goal.*
唯有努力工作，你才能成功地達成你的目標。
achieve〔ə'tʃiv〕*v.* 達成   goal〔gol〕*n.* 目標

19. (**H**) The nurse approached the child, *trying to make him relaxed.*
護士走向那個小孩，試著使他放輕鬆。
approach〔ə'protʃ〕*v.* 接近   relaxed〔rɪ'lækst〕*adj.* 放鬆的

20. (**C**) This painting is nothing more than a copy *of the other.*
這幅畫只不過是另一幅畫的複製品。
nothing more than 只不過是   copy〔'kɑpɪ〕*n.* 複製品

三、綜合測驗：

It is a usual sunny afternoon *in the village of Midwich, England.*

It seems not <u>unlike</u> any afternoon *in the village,* ***but*** *all of a sudden,*
21

people and animals lose consciousness. ***When*** *they awake,* all of the
22

women *of child-bearing age* have become pregnant.

　　在英國密得威志村，一個尋常午后，陽光普照。這天的下午感覺與其他日子並無二致，但是就在突然之間，人獸皆失去知覺。在甦醒之後，所有育齡期的女人，都懷孕了。

> **all of a sudden** 突然間
> consciousness〔ˋkɑnʃəsnɪs〕n. 知覺；意識
> awake〔əˋwek〕v. 醒來
> child-bearing〔ˋtʃaɪldˏbɛrɪŋ〕adj. 育齡期的
> pregnant〔ˋprɛgnənt〕adj. 懷孕的

21. (**A**) 第一句強調與其他日子「一樣」，本句以 not unlike「並不會不像」的方式來表達。而 (B) dislike「不喜歡」是動詞，(D) alike「同樣的」，則不合句意。

22. (**B**) 逗點前後兩個子句需要有連接詞連接，依句意，選 (B) **When**「當～時候」。

This is an episode *from a 1960 science fiction story*. The women *in the story* give birth to children *that have the same appearance*. They
23
all have blond hair and "strange eyes." *As the children grow*, they run
24
around the village in a pack, *wearing identical clothing and hairstyles*, *staring at everyone impolitely*.

　　以上是一九六○年代一本科幻小說中的一幕。故事中的女人，生下的小孩，長相都一樣。他們都有金髮和「奇特的眼睛」。小孩長大後，在村子裏成群結隊四處跑，穿相同的衣服，剪一樣的髮型，眼睛還無禮地盯著別人看。

> episode〔ˋɛpəˏsod〕n. 一幕　　*science fiction* 科幻小說（ = *sci-fi*）
> appearance〔əˋpɪrəns〕n. 外貌　　blond〔bland〕adj. 金色頭髮的
> pack〔pæk〕n. 一群　　identical〔aɪˋdɛntɪkl̩〕adj. 相同的
> hairstyle〔ˋhɛrˏstaɪl〕n. 髮型　　stare〔stɛr〕v. 盯著看；瞪著
> impolitely〔ˏɪmpəˋlaɪtlɪ〕adv. 無禮地

23.(**D**) **give birth to** 生（小孩）

24.(**C**) 根據句意，表「時間」，須選 (C) **As**「當～時候」。

What one child learns is also known by the others instantly.
25

Villagers begin to express their belief **that** the children all have
26

"one mind." In this story, the children are produced by some

unexplained force from outer space. **But** this story written 40 years

ago somehow predicted the arrival of a recent method of genetic
27

engineering — cloning. Cloning is the genetic process of producing

copies of an individual. Will the genetic copies of a human really

have "one mind" **as** described in this story? This situation is so
28

strange to us **that** we do not know **what** will become of it. Faced
29

with this new situation, people have yet to find out **how** to deal
30

with it.

某個小孩知道什麼事，其他小孩馬上就知道。村民開始說出他們的看法，這些小孩「思想如出一轍」。故事裏的小孩，都是外太空某種無法解釋的力量，所製造的產物。但是這個四十年前寫的故事，卻也預言了基因工程最近的發展 —— 複製。複製是基因複製人的過程。人在基因複製下的版本，眞的會像故事所描述的「思想如出一轍」嗎？這種情況太不可思議了，以致於沒有人知道以後會如何發展。面對這種新狀況，人類尚未找出因應之道。

instantly (ˈɪnstəntlɪ) adv. 立刻　　villager (ˈvɪlɪdʒɚ) n. 村民

belief (bɪˈlif) n. 看法；相信　　some (sʌm) adj. 某種

unexplained (ˌʌnɪkˈsplend) adj. 無法解釋的

force (fors; fɔrs) n. 力量　　*outer space* 外太空

predict (prɪˈdɪkt) v. 預言　　arrival (əˈraɪvl̩) n. 到達；出現

genetic (dʒəˈnɛtɪk) adj. 遺傳學的；基因的

engineering (ˌɛndʒəˈnɪrɪŋ) n. 工程學

cloning (ˈklonɪŋ) n. 複製

process (ˈprɑsɛs) n. 過程

individual (ˌɪndəˈvɪdʒuəl) n. 個人　　*be faced with* 面對

deal with 處理；應付

25. (**D**) 空格應填一複合關代，故選 (D) *What* (= *The thing which*)。

26. (**A**) (A) *express* (ɪkˈsprɛs) v. 表達；說出

　　　　(B) wonder (ˈwʌndɚ) v. 驚歎；想知道

　　　　(C) select (səˈlɛkt) v. 選擇

　　　　(D) ignore (ɪgˈnor, -ˈnɔr) v. 忽略

27. (**C**) 依句意，選 (C) *somehow*「以某種方法」。而 (A) 有時候，(B) 無論如何，(D) 反正；無論如何 (= *anyway*)，均不合句意。

28. (**B**) 本句是由…as (the one that is) described in this story…轉化而來，故選 (B)。

29. (**D**) A *become of* B 表「B 遇到/遭遇 A」。而 (A)(B)(C) 三動詞之後，皆無加 of 的用法，故不合。

30. (**B**) *yet* 在肯定句中表「到目前尚未」。若選 (A) 一樣有否定含意，但須改成 people have not found out how to deal with it。

四、文意選填：

　　Amir tied two sacks of salt *to the back of his donkey* **and** headed

for the market *to sell the salt*. *On the way*, Amir and the donkey
31

passed a stream. The donkey jumped into the stream *to cool himself*.
32

As a result, much of the salt melted in the water, *ruining the salt for*

Amir **but** lightening *the load for the donkey*. Amir tried to get to
33

the market *on the following days*, **but** the donkey played the same
34

trick **and** ruined the salt.

　　阿米爾綁了二袋鹽在他的驢子背上，然後出發前往市場賣鹽。在途中，阿
米爾和驢子經過了一條小溪。驢子跳下溪去涼快一下，結果，很多鹽都溶在水
裏，毀了阿米爾的鹽，而驢子的負擔卻減輕了。接下來幾天，阿米爾試著想上
市場賣鹽，但驢子都用相同的詭計，把鹽毀了。

　　　　sack〔sæk〕*n.* 袋子　　　donkey〔'dɑŋkɪ〕*n.* 驢子
　　　　head for 出發前往（= *leave for*）
　　　　stream〔strim〕*n.* 小溪　　　***as a result*** 結果
　　　　melt〔mɛlt〕*v.* 溶化　　　ruin〔'ruɪn〕*v.* 毀壞
　　　　load〔lod〕*n.* 負擔

31. (**D**) *on the way* 在途中

32. (**H**) 依句意，驢子跳下溪去「使牠自己」涼快，用 (H) *himself*。

33. (**F**) lighten〔'laɪtn̩〕*v.* 減輕（重量；負擔）

34. (**B**) *play a trick* 玩詭計；惡作劇

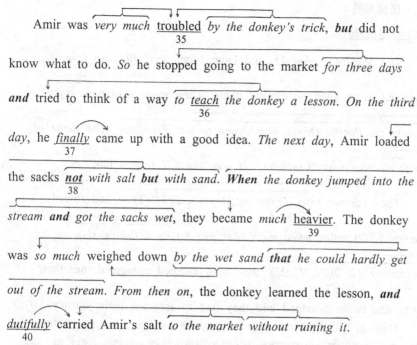

Amir was *very much* troubled *by the donkey's trick*, **but** did not
　　　　　　35

know what to do. *So* he stopped going to the market *for three days*

and tried to think of a way *to teach the donkey a lesson*. *On the third*
　　　　　　　　　　　　　　36

day, he <u>finally</u> came up with a good idea. *The next day*, Amir loaded
　　　　　37

the sacks **not** with salt **but** with sand. *When the donkey jumped into the*
　　　　　38

stream **and** *got the sacks wet*, they became *much* <u>heavier</u>. The donkey
　　　　　　　　　　　　　　　　　　39

was *so much* weighed down *by the wet sand* **that** he could hardly get

out of the stream. *From then on*, the donkey learned the lesson, **and**

<u>dutifully</u> carried Amir's salt *to the market without ruining it.*
40

　　阿米爾對於驢子的詭計十分困擾，但不知如何是好。所以他三天沒到市場
去，試圖想出方法給驢子一個教訓。第三天，他終於想到一個好主意。隔天，
阿米爾袋子裏裝的不是鹽，而是砂。當驢子跳下溪，將袋子弄濕時，袋子變得
更重了。驢子被潮濕的砂壓到幾乎無法從溪裏爬起來。從那時起，驢子學到了
教訓，盡職地將阿米爾的鹽載到市場，而不敢毀壞它。

come up with 想出（主意、計劃等）　　　load〔lod〕*v.* 使裝載
weigh down 以重量壓下

35. (**J**) troubled〔'trʌbḷd〕*adj.* 困擾的

36. (**I**) *teach sb. a lesson* 給某人一個教訓

37. (**G**) 依句意，他「終於」想到一個好主意，選 (G) *finally*。

38. (**E**) *not* A *but* B 不是 A 而是 B

39. (**C**) 潮濕的砂會變得「更重」，選 (C) *heavier*。

40. (**A**) dutifully〔'djutɪfəlɪ〕*adv.* 盡職地

五、閱讀測驗：

41-43 題為題組

Tim Welford, *aged 33*, and Dom Mee, *aged 30, both from England*, were keen on rowing boats. They made a plan *to row across the Pacific Ocean from Japan to San Francisco*. The name *of their rowboat* was "Crackers." It was *about* 7 meters long.

They set out *from Japan on May 17, 2001*. They had rowed nearly 5,500 miles **when** *their boat was hit by a fishing ship on September 17, 2001*. *Luckily* they both escaped unharmed, **but** their boat was *badly* damaged **and** they had to abandon their journey.

提姆・偉福，三十三歲，唐姆・米，三十歲，二人均來自英國，對划船非常熱衷。他們計劃從日本到舊金山，划船橫越太平洋。他們的小船名叫「瘋狂號」，約有七公尺長。

他們在西元二〇〇一年五月十七日，由日本出發。二〇〇一年九月十七日，在划了將近五千五百哩時，他們的小船被一艘漁船撞上。幸好，二人都安然逃脫，不過他們的船已經嚴重受損，他們只好放棄這趟旅程。

> keen〔kin〕*adj.* 熱衷的＜on＞   row〔ro〕*v.* 划（船）
> rowboat〔'ro,bot〕*n.* 小船
> crackers〔'krækəz〕*adj.* 瘋狂的（＝*nuts*）
> **set out** 出發   nearly〔'nırlı〕*adv.* 將近
> escape〔ə'skep〕*v.* 逃脫   unharmed〔ʌn'hɑrmd〕*adj.* 沒有受傷的
> abandon〔ə'bændən〕*v.* 放棄

In a radio interview, Dom expressed his disappointment **and** explained **how** *the accident took place*.

"A fishing ship came towards us *with nobody on the bridge* ***and***
ran us down. It all happened *so quickly*. I managed to dive into the
water. Tim felt it would be safer to stay *on board the boat*. He was
trapped inside ***as the boat was driven under the water***. *Finally* some
people appeared *on the ship* ***and*** saw me *in the water*. I shouted at
them *to stop the ship* ***and*** *to get Tim out*. ***When*** *the ship stopped*, I
eventually saw Tim, ***and*** I was *very, very* relieved ***that*** *we were*
still alive. We were *very* disappointed ***that*** *we couldn't reach San*
Francisco. ***But*** we are alive. That *above everything* is the most
important."

　　在電台訪問中，唐姆表達了他的失望之意，並說明了意外發生的經過。
　　「一艘漁船朝向我們而來，艦橋上沒有人，直接撞上我們。一切發生得如
此之快。我設法潛入水中，而提姆認為待在船上可能比較安全。當小船沈入水
中時，他被困在裏面。最後，有一些人出現在漁船上，他們看見我在水裏。我
對他們大叫停船，把提姆救出來。當漁船停下來，我終於看到提姆，我感到非
常、非常欣慰，我們二人還活著。我們很失望無法到達舊金山，但是我們都活
著。那是最重要的事了。」

interview〔ˋɪntɚˏvju〕*n.* 訪問
disappointment〔ˏdɪsəˋpɔɪntmənt〕*n.* 失望
explain〔ɪkˋsplen〕*v.* 說明；解釋
bridge〔brɪdʒ〕*n.* 艦橋；船橋
run down 撞上　　***manage to*** + *V.* 設法　　dive〔daɪv〕*v.* 潛水
on board 在～（交通工具）上　　trap〔træp〕*v.* 困住
drive〔draɪv〕*v.* 推動；迫使
eventually〔ɪˋvɛntʃʊəlɪ〕*adv.* 終於
relieved〔rɪˋlivd〕*adj.* 欣慰的；鬆了一口氣的

41. (**D**) 提姆和唐姆的小船被漁船撞上時，他們在海上待多久了？
　　　(A) 一個月。　　　　　　　　(B) 二個月。
　　　(C) 三個月。　　　　　　　　(D) 四個月。

42. (**B**) 根據唐姆的說法，這場意外的主因是
　　　(A) 提姆和唐姆太不小心了。　　(B) 漁船上沒有人看見他們。
　　　(C) 漁船的速度太快。　　　　　(D) 他們的小船不夠堅固。
　　　careless ('kɛrlɪs) *adj.* 不小心的

43. (**A**) 唐姆說，這次意外中最重要的是
　　　(A) 他們二人都生還。　　　　　(B) 他們旅途愉快。
　　　(C) 他們的小船沒有受損。　　　(D) 他們未能到達舊金山。
　　　survive (sə'vaɪv) *v.* (從災難中) 生還

44~46 題為題組

Sometimes the real world can be a confusing place. It is *not always* fair or kind. And *in the real world* there are *not always* happy endings. That is **why**, *every once in a while, we like to escape into the world of fantasy* — *a place* **where** things always go our way **and** there is always a happy ending.

有時候現實世界可能是個令人感到困惑的地方。它不一定是公平或是令人愉快的。而且在現實世界中，不一定會有快樂的結局。那就是為什麼，我們偶爾會想逃避，想要進入幻想中的世界 —— 一個凡事總會依照我們想要的方式進行，而且總會有快樂結局的地方。

　　　fair (fɛr) *adj.* 公平的　　　kind (kaɪnd) *adj.* 令人愉快的
　　　not always 未必　　　ending ('ɛndɪŋ) *n.* 結局
　　　once in a while 偶爾 (= *every now and then*)
　　　escape (ə'skep) *v.* 逃避　　　fantasy ('fæntəsɪ) *n.* 幻想
　　　go (go) *v.* (事情) 進行

We want to believe in fantastic creatures *in imaginary lands*. We want to believe in magic powers, good friends, **and** the power *of good to overcome evil*. We all fantasize about being able to fly **and** lift buildings *off the ground*. **And** *how* good a magic sword would feel *in our hand* **as** *we go off to kill a dragon* **or** *win the hand of a beautiful princess*.

我們想要相信，在幻想的世界中，有奇妙的生物存在。我們想要相信，有魔力和好朋友的存在，以及正義終將戰勝邪惡。我們都會幻想自己可以飛行，並且可以將建築物自地面舉起。我們還會想像，當我們手中握著魔劍動身去殺一隻龍，或是贏得美麗公主的結婚承諾時，那種感覺有多棒。

believe in 相信～的存在
fantastic〔fæn'tæstɪk〕*adj.* 幻想的；奇特的
creature〔'kritʃɚ〕*n.* 生物
imaginary〔ɪ'mædʒəˏnɛrɪ〕*adj.* 想像的；幻想的
land〔lænd〕*n.* 國家；地帶　　magic〔'mædʒɪk〕*adj.* 有魔力的
good〔gʊd〕*n.* 善　　overcome〔ˏovɚ'kʌm〕*v.* 戰勝；克服
evil〔'ivl̩〕*n.* 邪惡　　fantasize〔'fæntəˏsaɪz〕*v.* 幻想
lift〔lɪft〕*v.* 舉起　　sword〔sord〕*n.* 劍　　**go off** 離開；出發
dragon〔'dʒægən〕*n.* 龍　　hand〔hænd〕*n.* 結婚承諾
princess〔'prɪnsɪs〕*n.* 公主

The amazing adventures *of Superman, Peter Pan,* **and** *Harry Potter* have charmed many people, *children and adults alike*. The main reason is **that** *these stories offer us chances to get away from this real, frustrating world* **and** *allow us to find some magical solutions to* *our problems. For example,* Superman *always* arrives *in the nick of time* to prevent a disaster *from happening,* Peter Pan can fly *at will to tease the bad guy Captain Hook,* **and** Harry Potter has his magic power *to take revenge on his uncle, aunt and cousin,* **who** always ill-treat him.

　　超人、彼得潘，和哈利波特，他們令人驚奇的冒險故事，已經使許多人為之著迷，其中包括大人和小孩。其主要原因就是，這些故事提供我們機會，逃離這個真實而且令人沮喪的世界，讓我們找到一些魔法般的解決之道，來解決問題。舉例來說，超人總是在緊要關頭時到達，防止災難的發生，彼得潘可以任意飛行，作弄壞人虎克船長，還有哈利波特，可以用他的魔力，來報復虐待他的姨丈、阿姨和表哥。

amazing〔ə'mezɪŋ〕 *adj.* 令人驚奇的
adventure〔əd'vɛntʃɚ〕 *n.* 冒險　　charm〔tʃɑrm〕 *v.* 吸引；使著迷
main〔men〕 *adj.* 主要的　　***get away from*** 遠離
frustrating〔'frʌs,tretɪŋ〕 *adj.* 令人沮喪的
magical〔'mædʒɪkl̩〕 *adj.* 魔法的；不可思議的
solution〔sə'luʃən〕 *n.* 解決之道　　***in the nick of time*** 在緊要關頭
prevent〔prɪ'vɛnt〕 *v.* 防止 <*from*>　　disaster〔dɪ'zæstɚ〕 *n.* 災難
at will 任意地　　tease〔tiz〕 *v.* 作弄　　captain〔'kæptɪn〕 *n.* 船長
take revenge on sb. 報復某人
cousin〔'kʌzn̩〕 *n.*（表）堂兄弟姊妹　　ill-treat〔,ɪl'trit〕 *v.* 虐待

44.(**A**) 人們因為下列的原因而進入幻想世界，除了 ＿＿＿＿＿ 之外。

(A) <u>幻想世界使我們受到驚嚇</u>
(B) 現實世界常常令人失望
(C) 我們可以在那裏找到快樂的結局
(D) 我們總是可以讓我們的願望實現

frighten〔'fraɪtn̩〕 *v.* 使驚嚇
fulfill〔fʊl'fɪl〕 *v.* 實現

45.(**D**) 超人、彼得潘,和哈利波特令很多人著迷,因為 —————— 。
     (A) 壞人總是佔上風
     (B) 他們結果都和美麗的公主結婚
     (C) 他們的解決方法根本不具有魔力
     (D) 他們擁有一般人所沒有的力量
     have the upper hand 佔上風   ***get married to*** 和~結婚
     anything but 絕非   possess〔 pə'zɛs 〕*v.* 擁有
     ordinary〔'ɔrdṇˌɛrɪ 〕*adj.* 一般的;普通的

46.(**C**) 這篇關於奇幻文學的文章是想要 —————— 。
     (A) 批評它不切實際的觀念   (B) 嘲笑閱讀它的人
     (C) 解釋為什麼人們喜歡閱讀它
     (D) 教導人們如何避免災難
     literature〔'lɪtərətʃə 〕*n.* 文學   intend〔 ɪn'tɛnd 〕*v.* 打算
     criticize〔'krɪtəˌsaɪz 〕*v.* 批評
     unrealistic〔ˌʌnrɪə'lɪstɪk 〕*adj.* 不切實際的
     concept〔'kɑnsɛpt 〕*n.* 觀念   ridicule〔'rɪdɪkjul 〕*v.* 嘲笑

47–50 題為題組

In the early part of the twentieth century, racism was widespread *in the United States*. Many African Americans were not given equal opportunities *in education or employment*. Marian Anderson (1897-1993) was an African American woman *who gained fame as a concert singer in this climate of racism*. She was born *in Philadelphia* *and* sang *in church choirs during her childhood*. *When* she applied for admission to *a local music school in 1917*, she was turned down *because* she was black.

Unable to attend music school, she began her career *as a singer for church gatherings. In 1929*, she went to Europe *to study voice* **and** spent several years performing *there*. Her voice was *widely* praised *throughout Europe. Then* she returned *to the U.S. in 1935* **and** became a top concert singer *after performing at Town Hall in New York City.*

在二十世紀初，美國種族歧視的現象很普遍。很多非洲裔美國人在教育或就業機會方面，未受到平等的待遇。有一位非洲裔美國人，名叫瑪麗安・安德生（1897－1993），在這種充滿種族歧視的社會氣氛下，成為一位能在音樂會上演唱的知名歌手。她出生於費城，童年時期是教堂唱詩班的一員。一九一七年，她申請就讀當地的音樂學校，但因為她是黑人而被拒絕。由於未能進入音樂學校就讀，她就此展開她在教堂集會的歌唱生涯。一九二九年，她前往歐洲學習發聲技巧，在那裡從事好幾年的表演工作。她的聲音在全歐洲廣受好評。之後在一九三五年，她返回美國，在紐約市政廳表演後，成為頂尖的音樂會歌手。

racism (ˈresɪzəm) *n.* 種族歧視
widespread (ˈwaɪd,sprɛd) *adj.* 普遍的
African American 非洲裔美國人；黑人
equal (ˈikwəl) *adj.* 平等的
employment (ɪmˈplɔɪmənt) *n.* 雇用；就業　　fame (fem) *n.* 名聲
concert (ˈkɑnsət) *adj.* 音樂會的
climate (ˈklaɪmɪt) *n.* (某一時期社會上的) 風氣；趨勢
Philadelphia (ˌfɪləˈdɛlfjə) *n.* 費城
choir (kwaɪr) *n.* (教堂的) 唱詩班
apply for 申請　　admission (ədˈmɪʃən) *n.* 入學許可 < to >
local (ˈlokl̩) *adj.* 當地的　　***turn down*** 拒絕
career (kəˈrɪr) *n.* 職業；生涯
gathering (ˈgæðərɪŋ) *n.* 集會　　voice (vɔɪs) *n.* 發聲法
throughout (θruˈaʊt) *prep.* 遍及　　***town hall*** 市政廳
top (tɑp) *adj.* 頂尖的

Racism *again* affected Anderson *in 1939*. ***When it was arranged***
for her to sing at Constitution Hall in Washington, D.C., the Daughters
of the American Revolution opposed it *because of her color*. She
sang *instead at the Lincoln Memorial for over 75,000 people*. *In 1955*,
Anderson became the first black soloist *to sing with the Metropolitan*
Opera of New York City. The famous conductor Toscanini praised her
voice *as "heard only once in a hundred years."* She was a U.S. delegate
to the United Nations in 1958 ***and*** won the UN peace prize *in 1977*.
Anderson *eventually* triumphed over racism.

在一九三九年，種族歧視的偏見又再度影響到安德生。有人安排她在華盛頓特區的憲法大廳表演歌唱，但「美國革命之女」卻因其膚色而加以反對。她改到林肯紀念堂表演，觀眾超過七萬五千人。一九五五年，安德生成為第一個與紐約市立大都會歌劇團合唱的黑人獨唱歌手。知名的指揮家托斯卡尼尼，稱讚她的聲音是「百年難得一見的」。一九五八年，她成為派到聯合國的美國代表，在一九七七年，她獲頒聯合國和平獎。最後，安德生終於戰勝種族歧視。

affect〔ə'fɛkt〕*v.* 影響　　arrange〔ə'rendʒ〕*v.* 安排
constitution〔,kɑnstə'tjuʃən〕*n.* 憲法
oppose〔ə'poz〕*v.* 反對　　color〔'kʌlɚ〕*n.* 膚色
instead〔ɪn'stɛd〕*adv.* 作為代替；改換
memorial〔mə'morɪəl〕*n.* 紀念館　　soloist〔'soloɪst〕*n.* 獨唱者
metropolitan〔,mɛtrə'polətn̩〕*adj.* 大都會的
conductor〔kən'dʌktɚ〕*n.* 指揮家
delegate〔'dɛlə,get〕*n.*（會議、組織的）代表
Union Nations 聯合國　　eventually〔ɪ'vɛntʃʊəlɪ〕*adv.* 最後
triumph〔'traɪəmf〕*v.* 戰勝＜*over*＞

47. (**B**) 根據本文，瑪麗安・安德生在一九一七至一九二九年間做了什麼？

　　(A) 她在一所音樂學校讀書。　　(B) <u>她為宗教活動唱歌。</u>

　　(C) 她在紐約市政廳唱歌。　　(D) 她在歐洲學習發聲技巧。

48. (**A**) 托斯卡尼尼認為瑪麗安・安德生 ＿＿＿＿＿＿＿＿。

　　(A) <u>有極好的嗓音</u>　　(B) 偶爾會公開表演唱歌

　　(C) 很多年才唱一次　　(D) 鮮少為人所知

　　rare 〔 rɛr 〕 *adj.* 罕見的；極好的

　　occasionally 〔 ə'keʒənlɪ 〕 *adv.* 偶爾　　***in public*** 公開地

49. (**C**) 安德生美妙的聲音最早是在 ＿＿＿＿＿＿＿＿ 得到認可。

　　(A) 林肯紀念堂　　(B) 華盛頓特區

　　(C) <u>歐洲</u>　　(D) 聯合國

　　recognize 〔'rɛkəg,naɪz 〕 *v.* 承認；認可

50. (**D**) 本文顯示，安德生在美國最後戰勝了種族歧視，是藉由 ＿＿＿＿＿＿＿＿。

　　(A) 向政府抗議　　(B) 向聯合國申訴

　　(C) 走上街頭示威遊行　　(D) <u>努力使她的藝術技巧趨於完美</u>

　　defeat 〔 dɪ'fit 〕 *v.* 戰勝；打敗　　protest 〔 prə'tɛst 〕 *v.* 抗議

　　appeal 〔 ə'pil 〕 *v.* 申訴 < *to* >

　　demonstrate 〔'dɛmən,stret 〕 *v.* 示威遊行

　　perfect 〔'pɝfɪkt 〕 *v.* 使完美

<u>51～55 題為題組</u>

Five years ago, David Smith wore an expensive suit to work

every day. "I was a clothes addict," he jokes. "I used to carry a fresh

suit to work *with me so I could change if my clothes got wrinkled*."

Today David wears casual clothes — *khaki pants and a sports shirt* —

to the office. He *hardly ever* wears a necktie. "I'm working *harder*

than ever," David says, "*and* I need to feel comfortable."

五年前，大衛‧史密斯每天穿昂貴的西裝上班。「我以前是個衣癡，」他開玩笑地說。「我以前會另外帶一套乾淨的西裝上班，這樣衣服皺掉的話就可以換下來。」現在，大衛上班都穿得很休閒——卡其褲配運動衫。他很少打領帶。「我比以前工作得更賣力，」大衛說，「而且我需要感到很舒適。」

suit〔sjut〕*n.* 西裝；套裝　　addict〔'ædɪkt〕*n.* 沉迷者；上癮者
fresh〔frɛʃ〕*adj.* 新鮮的；乾淨的　　wrinkle〔'rɪŋkl〕*v.* 起皺紋
casual〔'kæʒʊəl〕*adj.* 非正式的；休閒的　　khaki〔'kɑkɪ〕*n.* 卡其布
pants〔pænts〕*n. pl.* 褲子　　***sports shirt*** 運動衫

More and more companies are allowing their office workers to wear casual clothes to work. *In the United States*, the change *from formal to casual office wear* has been gradual. *In the early 1990s*, many companies allowed their employees to wear casual clothes *on Friday* (***but** only on Friday*). This became known as "dress-down Friday" or "casual Friday." "***What** started out as an extra one-day-a-week benefit for employees* has *really* become an everyday thing," said business consultant Maisly Jones.

愈來愈多公司，允許員工穿著非正式的服裝來上班。在美國，上班服裝由正式轉變為非正式，這個趨勢是逐漸形成的。在九〇年代初期，許多公司准許他們的員工，在星期五穿著非正式的服裝（不過只有星期五）。這就是衆所皆知的「星期五穿便服」，或稱「休閒星期五」。商業顧問梅斯里‧瓊斯說：「這原本是給員工一個禮拜一天的額外福利，現在每天都有了。」

formal〔'fɔrml〕*adj.* 正式的　　***office wear*** 辦公服裝
gradual〔'grædʒʊəl〕*adj.* 逐漸的　　***become known as*** 以～爲人所知
dress-down〔'drɛs'daʊn〕*n.* 穿便服；作休閒打扮
start out 開始　　benefit〔'bɛnəfɪt〕*n.* 利益；福利
consultant〔kən'sʌltənt〕*n.* 顧問

Why have so many companies started allowing their employees to wear casual clothes? One reason is ***that*** *it's easier for a company to attract new employees* ***if*** *it has a casual dress code.* "A lot of young people don't want to dress up for work," says the owner *of a software company,* "***so*** *it's hard to hire people* ***if*** *you have a conservative dress code.*"

爲什麼有這麼多公司開始允許員工穿著休閒的服裝？理由之一是因爲，公司如果規定穿著非正式的服裝，比較容易吸引新員工。「很多年輕人不想爲上班盛裝打扮，」一位軟體公司的老闆說，「如果公司的服裝規定保守，就很難請到員工。」

> ***dress code*** 服裝規定　　***dress up*** 盛裝打扮
> conservative〔kən'sɜvətɪv〕*adj.* 保守的

Another reason is ***that*** *people seem happier and more productive* ***when*** *they are wearing comfortable clothes.* ***In a study conducted by*** *Levi Strauss and Company,* 85 percent of employers said ***that*** *they believe* ***that*** *casual dress improves employee morale.* Only 4 percent of employers said ***that*** *casual dress has a negative impact on productivity.*

另一個理由是，當員工穿著舒適的服裝，似乎心情較好、生產力較高。在一個由李維・史特勞斯公司所做的研究中，百分之八十五的雇主說，他們相信休閒的打扮能夠提升員工的士氣。只有百分之四的雇主，認爲休閒的打扮對生產力有負面的影響。

productive〔prə'dʌktɪv〕*adj.* 有生產力的
conduct〔kən'dʌkt〕*v.* 進行
Levi Strauss〔'livaɪ'straʊs〕*n.* 李維‧史特勞斯（德裔美國人，以創造
　　Levi's 牛仔褲聞名於世）
morale〔mo'ræl〕*n.* 士氣　　negative〔'nɛgətɪv〕*adj.* 負面的
impact〔'ɪmpækt〕*n.* 影響 < on >
productivity〔,prodʌk'tɪvətɪ〕*n.* 生產力

Supporters *of casual office wear also* argue *that a casual dress code*

helps them save money. "Suits are expensive, *if you have to wear*

one every day," one person said. "*For the same amount of money,*

you can buy a lot more casual clothes."

支持穿著非正式服裝上班的人同時也認為，休閒服裝有助於省錢。「如果你每天
都穿套裝，要花很多錢的，」有個人這麼說，「同樣的錢，你可以買更多的休閒
服飾。」

　　　　argue〔'ɑrgju〕*v.* 認為；主張　　amount〔ə'maʊnt〕*n.* 量

51.(**C**) 大衛‧史密斯說他自己曾是個「衣癡」，因為 _____。
　　(A) 他以前經常穿卡其褲和運動衫
　　(B) 他無法忍受整潔的外觀
　　(C) 他希望他的衣服看起來一直很整潔
　　(D) 他不希望花太多錢在衣服上
　　refer to A ***as*** B 稱呼 A 為 B
　　neat〔nit〕*adj.* 整潔的　　***all the time*** 一直

52.(**A**) 大衛‧史密斯現在穿得很休閒，因為 _____。
　　(A) 這讓他在工作時感到很舒適　　(B) 他買不起昂貴的衣服
　　(C) 他穿休閒的服裝看起來英俊瀟灑
　　(D) 他不再替這家公司工作了
　　at ease 舒適的　　afford〔ə'ford〕*v.* 負擔得起
　　no longer 不再

53.(**D**) 根據本文,下列何者為非?

(A) 多數員工不喜歡保守的服裝規定。

(B) 舒適的服裝讓員工更有生產力。

(C) 年輕員工喜歡穿得很休閒。

(D) 美國所有的雇主都贊成休閒的上班打扮。

for〔fɔr〕*prep.* 贊成(↔ *against* 反對)

54.(**C**) 根據本文,下列何者為真?

(A) 公司員工約在二十年前開始穿著便服來上班。

(B) 從九〇年代初期開始,穿便服變成日常現象。

(C) 「星期五穿便服」起初是雇主給員工的一項福利。

(D) 許多員工想藉由休閒的打扮,讓別人印象深刻。

dress down 穿便服　　phenomenon〔fə'namə,nɑn〕*n.* 現象

favor〔'fevɚ〕*n.* 恩惠;福利　　impress〔ɪm'prɛs〕*v.* 使印象深刻

55.(**B**) 根據本文,穿著非正式的服裝上班有下列優點,除了 _____。

(A) 替員工省錢　　　　　　(B) 使員工更迷人

(C) 更加激勵員工　　　　　(D) 讓員工心情更好

advantage〔əd'væntɪdʒ〕*n.* 優點;好處

motivation〔,motə'veʃən,〕*n.* 激勵

第貳部分:非選擇題

一、簡答題

South America is a place *of striking beauty and wonder*. The heart *of this continent* is the Amazon Rainforest, *a vast paradise watered by one of the world's greatest rivers. Because of the tremendous amount of oxygen produced in this area*, it has been called the "lungs of the earth."

南美洲充滿了懾人的美和奇景。這塊大陸的心臟地帶是亞馬遜雨林區,這是一片廣大的樂土,水源來自全世界最大的河流之一。由於這個地區所製造的氧氣量龐大,此地被稱為「地球之肺」。

striking (ˈstraɪkɪŋ) adj. 顯著的   wonder (ˈwʌndɚ) n. 奇景
continent (ˈkɑntənənt) n. 洲；大陸
Amazon (ˈæməˌzɑn) n. 亞馬遜河
rainforest (ˈrenˌfɔrɪst) n. 熱帶雨林
vast (væst) adj. 廣大的   paradise (ˈpærəˌdaɪs) n. 天堂；樂土
water (ˈwɔtɚ) v. 供給水源   tremendous (trɪˈmɛndəs) adj. 極大的
oxygen (ˈɑksədʒən) n. 氧

A team of scientists, teachers, and students, *the AmazonQuest team, recently* explored some of the wonders *of the Amazon Rainforest*. They canoed *down rivers*, hiked *along muddy trails*, **and** climbed *into the forest to explore and learn*. The following is a report *by one of the team members*:

　一組由科學家、老師和學生組成的「亞馬遜探險隊」，最近去探索亞馬遜雨林區的部分奇景。他們划獨木舟順流而下，徒步走過泥濘的小徑，並爬入森林地區探索學習。以下是探險隊成員之一所寫下的報告：

quest (kwɛst) n. 探索   explore (ɪkˈsplor) v. 探索
canoe (kəˈnu) v. 划獨木舟   hike (haɪk) v. 徒步旅行
muddy (ˈmʌdɪ) adj. 泥濘的   trail (trel) n. 小徑

"I watched a small piece *of the Amazon Rainforest* disappear today. *This morning*, two men *from the village of Roaboia* led us *into the forest. For 20 minutes*, we walked *along a path past tall weeds, banana trees, and low brush*. Our destination was a 150-foot tall capirana tree, *by far the biggest tree around*. It would take 10 people holding hands to surround the base *of its trunk*.

「我今天看到亞馬遜雨林區的一小部分消失了。今天早上,兩個來自羅伯伊亞村的人,帶領我們進入森林。我們沿著一條小徑,走了約二十分鐘,經過了很高的草、香蕉樹和矮樹叢。我們的目的地是一棵一百五十呎高的卡皮蘭那樹,它顯然是附近最高的樹,而且要十個人手牽手,才能圍住它的樹幹底部。

The men took out an axe and an electric saw *and* started cutting into the tree's silky smooth skin. *As beautiful as they are*, people *here* chop down capirana trees *for their wood*. *With a loud roar*, the saw chewed into the 150-year-old tree. *Then, in about 30 minutes after the cutting began*, the giant tree crashed down *violently and* shook the ground *under our feet*.

那二人拿出一把斧頭和一支電鋸,開始往大樹光滑的樹皮上砍下去。雖然卡皮蘭那樹很美,但這裡的人都把它們砍下來當柴薪。轟然一聲巨響,電鋸鋸進了這棵樹齡一百五十歲的樹。然後,從開始砍經過了大約三十分鐘,大樹猛然倒了下來,撼動了我們腳下的土地。

axe〔æks〕*n.* 斧頭　　saw〔sɔ〕*n.* 鋸子

silky〔'sɪlkɪ〕*adj.* 光滑的　　chop〔tʃɑp〕*v.* 砍;劈

roar〔ror〕*n.* 轟鳴聲　　chew〔tʃu〕*v.* 咀嚼;咬碎

giant〔'dʒaɪənt〕*adj.* 巨大的　　crash〔kræʃ〕*v.* 墜毀

violently〔'vaɪələntlɪ〕*adv.* 猛烈地　　shake〔ʃek〕*v.* 搖晃

This, *of course*, is *just* one of the millions of trees *that fall in the Amazon each year*. Brazil's Environmental Ministry estimates *that in 1970, 99 percent of the original Amazon Rainforest remained, but in 2000, only 85 percent.* It is estimated ***that*** *more than 33 million*

acres of Amazonian Rainforest disappear every year. That means ***that***

64 acres of the rainforest is lost every minute."

　　這當然只是亞馬遜地區，每年倒下的數百萬棵樹之一。巴西環境部估計，在一九七〇年，亞馬遜雨林區的原始森林，百分之九十九還存在，但是到了公元二千年，只剩下百分之八十五。根據估計，每年亞馬遜雨林區，有超過三千三百萬英畝的土地消失，意思就是，每分鐘有六十四英畝的雨林地消失了。」

> Brazil〔brə'zɪl〕*n.* 巴西　　ministry〔'mɪnɪstrɪ〕*n.* 部
> estimate〔'ɛstə,met〕*v.* 估計
> original〔ə'rɪdʒənḷ〕*adj.* 原始的
> remain〔rɪ'men〕*v.* 保持；仍然存在　　acre〔'ekɚ〕*n.* 英畝

1. 什麼地方被稱爲「地球之肺」？
   答：the Amazon Rainforest

2. 參加「亞馬遜探險隊」的是哪種人？
   答：scientists, teachers, students

3. 那二個人花了多久的時間把那棵巨大的卡皮蘭那樹砍倒？
   答：about 30 minutes

4. 在一九七〇年到二千年之間，亞馬遜雨林區有多少百分比的原始森林被砍伐？
   答：14%
   percentage〔pɚ'sɛntɪdʒ〕*n.* 百分比

5. 根據這篇報告，每秒鐘大約有多少英畝的亞馬遜雨林區消失？
   答：1.06 acres 或 a little more than one

二、英文作文：（作文範例）

The Most Precious Thing in My Room

My room is a special and important place to me. I spend a lot of time there studying, and I also like to relax in my room by listening to music or reading a novel. *Therefore*, I have taken care to make my room an attractive and comfortable place. I have decorated it with posters of my favorite singers and sports stars. I have also equipped it with a comfortable desk and a good computer on which to do my homework. *However*, the one thing in my room that is most precious to me is a photograph.

This photograph is of my junior high school basketball team. It is precious to me for several reasons. *First*, it reminds me of the good times I had in junior high and the good friendships I had there. I still keep in touch with some of my teammates and we continue to challenge and encourage each other. *Second*, because the photo was taken after our team had won the championship game, it is a symbol of achievement. We were the underdogs that year, and so the photograph reminds me that it is possible to achieve anything with determination and hard work. *Finally*, the photo reminds me that there is more to life than study. Although I have to work hard now, I still make time to relax by playing a game of basketball with good friends.

> ***take care*** 當心；注意   decorate（'dɛkə,ret）*v.* 裝飾；佈置
> poster（'postɚ）*n.* 海報   sports（sports）*adj.* 運動的
> equip（ɪ'kwɪp）*v.* 裝備；配備＜*with*＞
> remind（rɪ'maɪnd）*v.* 使想起＜*of*＞
> ***keep in touch with*** *sb.* 與某人保持連絡
> teammate（'tim,met）*n.* 隊友   challenge（'tʃælɪndʒ）*v.* 向～挑戰
> symbol（'sɪmbḷ）*n.* 象徵   achievement（ə'tʃivmənt）*n.* 成就
> underdog（'ʌndɚ'dɔg）*n.* 處於劣勢的一方
> determination（dɪ,tɜmə'neʃən）*n.* 決心   ***make time*** 騰出時間

九十一年大學入學學科能力測驗試題
英文考科②

第壹部份：單一選擇題

一、詞彙與慣用語（15％）

說明：第 1 至 15 題，每題選出最適當的一個選項，標示在答案卡之「選擇題答案區」。每題答對得 1 分，答錯不倒扣。

1. The teacher loved to teach young students, _____ those who were smart.
   (A) officially   (B) especially   (C) popularly   (D) similarly

2. Eating dessert before meals may kill your _____.
   (A) energy   (B) character   (C) quality   (D) appetite

3. In Taiwan, some cable TV companies have up to 70 or 80 _____.
   (A) channels   (B) events   (C) items   (D) patterns

4. It was fortunate that John _____ escaped being killed in a traffic accident.
   (A) privately   (B) locally   (C) narrowly   (D) distantly

5. Since the typhoon, the basement has been filled with water. We have to _____ the water as soon as possible.
   (A) reserve   (B) repair   (C) retire   (D) remove

6. Some waste from nuclear power plants is buried in _____ containers.
   (A) crashed   (B) paved   (C) risked   (D) sealed

7. A human body usually has a _____ temperature of about 37 degrees C.
   (A) steady   (B) various   (C) gradual   (D) precious

8. If you expect to have quick _____ of the goods, it is better to have them airmailed.

(A) discovery   (B) directory   (C) delivery   (D) dormitory

9. This project is mainly for scientific research. It doesn't have any _____ value at all.

(A) commercial   (B) reluctant   (C) opposite   (D) inferior

10. These two countries are trying to _____ trade and cultural exchanges between them.

(A) notify   (B) intensify   (C) personify   (D) signify

11. The manager must try to find out who is really _____ for this serious sales problem.

(A) on line   (B) in service   (C) at fault   (D) by law

12. This talk show, _____, is quite popular with the audience.

(A) on the whole   (B) by no means

(C) out of the question   (D) in no sense

13. Mr. Brown suggested that Mary stay with the company, _____, because the company needed her.

(A) back and forth   (B) for better or worse

(C) off and on   (D) up and down

14. How did you talk your sister _____ the chores for you? She normally avoids them.

(A) for going   (B) against getting

(C) without taking   (D) into doing

15. In modern times, many traditional concepts have _____ new ideas.

(A) found a way of   (B) changed the way of

(C) given way to   (D) had a way of

二、句子配合題（5％）

說明： 1. 第 16 至 20 題，每題皆為未完成的句子。請逐題依文意與語法，從右欄 (A) 到 (J) 的選項中選出最適當者，合併成一個意思通順、用法正確的句子。

2. 請將每題所選答案之英文字母代號標示在「答案卡」之「選擇題答案區」。每題答對得 1 分，答錯不倒扣。

16. Losing weight requires	A.... broken into pieces before being eaten.
17. Pets are wonderful,	B.... with the freshest ingredients.
18. When you reach the voice mailbox,	C.... for the popularity of her novels.
19. Delicious dishes can be prepared only	D.... to throw away their toy guns and knives.
20. When you begin a new job in an office,	E.... make your message brief.
	F.... you should learn how to do it well.
	G.... but their owners should be responsible.
	H.... discipline and a good plan.
	I.... keep in mind the direction of the street.
	J.... better than studying alone at home.

三、綜合測驗（10％）

說明： 第 21 至 30 題，每題一個空格，請依文意選出最適當的一個選項，標示在答案卡之「選擇題答案區」。每題答對得 1 分，答錯不倒扣。

　　Now that you are planning to go to college, how can you select an ideal college for yourself? ___21___ its reputation or the test scores it requires for admission? In fact, it is not ___22___ simple as that.

College education is far more complicated than ___23___ the reputation of a college or the test scores it requires. In addition to these two factors, you should also have ___24___ important information. Finding out which college suits you involves time and energy, but ___25___ more than those you might spend on buying a motorcycle or a computer.

Here are some tips ___26___ choosing an ideal one from a number of colleges.

1. Visit the websites of these colleges and find out which college has departments ___27___ courses that interest you or will help you prepare for your future career.

2. Are the professors in the departments you plan to ___28___ into experts in their own fields?

3. Do the colleges allow you to participate in activities ___29___ will help you develop yourself intellectually and emotionally?

I hope the ___30___ advice is helpful to you in selecting the right college.

21. (A) In	(B) By	(C) With	(D) At
22. (A) as	(B) too	(C) still	(D) quite
23. (A) thus	(B) just	(C) so	(D) yet
24. (A) many	(B) even	(C) other	(D) few
25. (A) no	(B) all	(C) some	(D) any
26. (A) of	(B) on	(C) to	(D) from
27. (A) offer	(B) offers	(C) offered	(D) offering
28. (A) get	(B) join	(C) learn	(D) try
29. (A) what	(B) they	(C) that	(D) those
30. (A) upper	(B) over	(C) upward	(D) above

四、文意選填（10％）

說明： 第 31 至 40 題，每題一個空格，請依文意在文章後所提供的(A) 到 (J)
選項中分別選出最適當者，並將其英文字母代號標示在答案卡之「選
擇題答案區」。每題答對得 1 分，答錯不倒扣。

Can young people really improve the world by influencing their
elders to change a policy? Read this story and decide for ___31___.
Dolphins, like most of us, love to eat tuna. So in many parts of the
world dolphins and fishermen are in ___32___ for tuna. In the past,
there wasn't much conflict ___33___ dolphins and fishermen, because
the numbers of tuna in the ocean were enormous. Now, however, men
have developed huge fishing nets that form underwater "walls" that
___34___ for miles. They can catch thousands of tuna at one time.
Unfortunately, they ___35___ catch many dolphins at the same time.
Dolphins, like us, have to breathe air. When they are ___36___ in the
nets too long, they cannot breathe. By the time they are brought
___37___ the ship, they will be dead. Many children were upset to hear
about the ___38___ death of these wonderful sea creatures and decided
to help ___39___ them. They wrote letters to the tuna companies
and supermarkets asking them to find a way to spare dolphins.
Eventually their hard work paid ___40___. Now you can buy tuna with
the label "dolphin-free tuna." So you see, everyone can make a
difference.

(A) also   (B) trapped   (C) between   (D) stretch   (E) save

(F) senseless   (G) competition   (H) aboard   (I) yourself   (J) off

五、閱讀測驗（30％）

說明：第 41 至 55 題，每題請分別根據各篇文章之文意選出最適當的一個選項，標示在答案卡之「選擇題答案區」。每題答對得 2 分，答錯不倒扣。

41-43 為題組

　　Folk tales are stories passed down by word of mouth generation after generation. They often concern very strong or clever people who come from humble backgrounds. These people usually triumph over their enemies because of their wit and their great energy. Folk tales are both down-to-earth and highly imaginative.

　　Many folk tales originally had some basis in fact and grew out of the lives of real people. They changed, however, as they were told and retold. A man might once have fought a bear, for example, and the tales told about him might make him into the greatest bear fighter who ever lived. Through the power of imagination, folk tales can turn humble people into heroes. Many folk tales are also tall tales—stories of unbelievable events told with perfect seriousness. A tall tale, in other words, is a story in which the truth has been exaggerated.

　　A culture's folk tales, fables, songs, and proverbs are an important part of its literature. By reading and listening to folk tales, we may gain a better understanding of the true values, beliefs, and goals of a people.

41. Folk tales are usually the stories of _____.
　　(A) wise scholars　　　　　　　(B) brave princes
　　(C) greedy folk　　　　　　　　(D) ordinary people

42. Which of the following statements about tall tales is NOT TRUE?
　　(A) Tall tales are factual stories.
　　(B) It takes imagination to create tall tales.
　　(C) Tall tales overstate the power of humans.
　　(D) People are serious when telling tall tales.

43. According to this passage, folk tales _____.
   (A) are written by native writers
   (B) explain the origin of world literature
   (C) reveal people's ideas about life
   (D) teach people how to survive

44-46 為題組

It used to be that athletes and VIPs gave away their signatures for free, and a signed baseball or photograph would just sit on a shelf and collect dust. But nowadays, autographs (signatures) are big business.

Many athletes and VIPs demand payment for their signatures, and many people are willing to pay. Autograph dealers can be found in almost any sizable city, and collectors may get hundreds, even thousands, of dollars for things signed by anyone from Mozart to Madonna, Thomas Jefferson to JFK.

A 54-page manuscript written by Albert Einstein recently was sold for $398,500 at Christie's in New York. And in 1994, Microsoft CEO (chief executive officer) Bill Gates paid $30.8 million for a handwritten notebook penned by Leonardo da Vinci. Meanwhile, fans across the U.S. are flocking to sports shows to have their heroes sign anything from a bat to a box of cereal.

What is the real reason many collectors want autographs? To connect with someone famous, or maybe even to imagine themselves as the hero they admire.

44. In the past, the signatures of athletes and VIPs _____.
   (A) were highly priced   (B) cost nothing at all
   (C) attracted great attention   (D) were for sale to the public

45. According to this passage, many people now collect athletes' and VIPs' signatures _____.
   (A) for their artistic value
   (B) to show them off to their friends
   (C) as historical documents
   (D) to be associated with famous people

46. The overall tone (attitude) of this passage is _____.
   (A) factual   (B) ironic
   (C) negative   (D) enthusiastic

47-50 為題組

   In Taiwan much time and energy are spent on getting a proper education and finding a good job. As a result, health concerns have been neglected. A new study by the Department of Health in Taiwan shows that more than half of the adult population in Taiwan lacks an understanding of important health problems. More than 2,000 adults took part in the survey to find out about their knowledge of diet, health care, disease control, and medication. Surprisingly, only 51 percent of the people surveyed understand that the common cold has no cure. Colds are caused by viruses, not bacteria, so taking medicine is absolutely no use at all. The problem is made worse by doctors who give their patients large doses of useless drugs. More than two-thirds believe that it is only the nicotine in cigarettes rather than the other chemicals that cause cancer. These people believe that if they smoke "light" cigarettes with less nicotine, they will not get cancer. Since 26 percent of Taiwanese adults smoke, such a misunderstanding will lead to more illness, suffering, and early death. But the outlook for health education in Taiwan is not all negative. The survey concludes that younger Taiwanese have a better understanding of health concerns than their parents, while senior citizens have the least understanding among the three age groups.

47. Recently a health survey was carried out in Taiwan to determine
   _____.
   (A) why people ignore their health
   (B) when to teach health education
   (C) what people know about health
   (D) who is more likely to become ill

48. According to the article, which of the following is TRUE about
   medicines for colds?
   (A) They can cure the common cold.
   (B) Many Taiwanese take too many of them.
   (C) Doctors often refuse to sell them.
   (D) About 51 percent of patients use them.

49. According to the survey, most Taiwanese believe that _____.
   (A) nicotine alone makes people fall victim to cancer
   (B) only a small percentage of smokers will develop cancer
   (C) smoking fewer cigarettes decreases the risk of cancer
   (D) other chemicals besides nicotine cause lung diseases

50. The results of the survey show that _____.
   (A) the health statistics in Taiwan are neglected
   (B) there is hope for improvement in the younger generation
   (C) the older generation depends on the healthcare system
   (D) many people value a career over their health

51-55 為題組

   "I have a regular film camera but I just don't use it much," said Ms.
Lowery, 23, a computer programmer. "When I got married last year, I
had all these pictures that didn't come out right. With digital cameras,
you aren't spending money on film for wasted pictures," she said.

And there are plenty of models from which to choose: from simple $200 point-and-shoot snappers to $1,000 wonders with all the features that any advanced amateur could want. The wide selection is a sure sign that in many consumers' minds, digital cameras have risen from mere gadgets to must-have items.

Digital cameras offer more than just the instant previewing of pictures on small color screens. They can store dozens, sometimes hundreds, of images that can be printed easily at home or sent by e-mail. Although there are extra costs involved in going digital — the cost of memory cards for storage and the special paper for printing — many buyers have been willing to make the switch.

Although about 90 percent of American households still use film cameras, digital cameras are capturing a growing share of the consumer market. And the number of digital-camera households, now at about 10 percent, is certain to grow, as manufacturers introduce more and more cameras whose quality is as good as film cameras. Soon, even professionals will use them.

Salesmen expect digital cameras to be popular gifts this holiday season. "They are very hot this year," said Yossi Fogel at B&H Photo in New York. "The prices have come down and the quality has gone up. Who wants to travel with 30 rolls of film? With a large memory card to store pictures, you can shoot and shoot and never have to worry about changing a roll. How many times have you missed a picture because you failed to reload the film?"

51. Which of the following is **NOT** an advantage of the digital camera over the film camera?
    (A) The user has to spend additional money for it.
    (B) It comes in many models for the customer.
    (C) It saves money from unwanted pictures.
    (D) Its pictures can be sent by e-mail.

52. According to this passage, the American households using digital cameras will increase if _____.
   (A) their producers invest more money
   (B) their operation becomes simpler
   (C) their salesmen are more friendly
   (D) their quality keeps improving

53. Which of the following is **NOT TRUE** about film cameras?
   (A) Their pictures can be printed at a photo shop.
   (B) Their pictures can be enlarged as desired.
   (C) Their pictures can be seen before they are printed.
   (D) Their pictures can be stored for a long time.

54. According to this article, digital cameras nowadays are used mainly by _____.
   (A) professionals   (B) amateurs
   (C) housewives   (D) students

55. With a digital camera, it is necessary to _____.
   (A) carry a lot of film
   (B) print pictures at a photo shop
   (C) have a memory card
   (D) spend more time in using it

第貳部份：非選擇題

一、簡答題（10％）

說明： 1. 閱讀下面這篇文章，然後簡答下列問題。答案必須寫在「答案卷」上。

2. 請依序作答，並標明題號。答案應簡明扼要，只寫重要詞彙（key words），約二至三個英文單詞（words）。每題2分，共10分。
注意：請勿抄下整句或整行，否則不予記分。

Do women really use language differently from men? Over the years, researchers have given different answers to this question. In the legends of some cultures, it is even claimed that men and women speak different languages. If this were true, how could boys communicate with their mothers? One research report shows men and women use much the same grammar and vocabulary in English, although each sex uses certain kinds of words and structures more frequently than the other. Most men use more swear words, while far more women use adjectives such as "super" and "lovely," and exclamations such as "Goodness me!" and "Oh dear!" Women have been found to ask more questions, make more use of positive and encouraging "noises," use a wider range of intonation patterns, and make greater use of the pronouns "you" and "we." By contrast, men are much more likely to interrupt (about three times as often in some studies), to argue about what has been said, to ignore or respond poorly to what has been said, to introduce more new topics into the conversation, and to make more assertions.

1. What stories in some cultures state that men and women speak differently?

2. According to one research report, which two parts of English are generally shared by men and women?

3. What adjectives do women use more often than men?

4. What kind of words do men use more frequently than women?

5. According to some studies, how often do men interrupt as compared with women?

二、英文作文（20％）

說明： 1. 依提示在「答案卷」上寫一篇英文作文。

2. 文長 120 個單詞（words）左右。

提示： 以 "Growing up is a/an ＿＿＿＿＿ experience" 為題寫一篇英文
作文，描述你成長的經驗是令人興奮的（exciting），令人困惑的
（confusing），快樂的（happy）或是痛苦的（painful）。除了這
些形容詞之外，你也可以用其他的形容詞來描述你成長的經驗。請務
必提出具體的例子以描述你成長的經驗。（注意：如果你用的形容詞
以子音起始，請選擇冠詞 "a"，如 "a confusing experience"；如果
你用的形容詞以母音起始，請選擇冠詞 "an"，如 "an exciting
experience"。）

❈ 91年度學科能力測驗英文科試題②詳解 ❈

第壹部分：單一選擇題

一、詞彙與慣用語：

1. (**B**) The teacher loved to teach young students, *especially those who were smart*.

   老師喜歡教年輕的學生，<u>特別是</u>聰明的學生。
   (A) officially (ə'fɪʃəlɪ) *adv.* 正式地
   (B) *especially* (ə'spɛʃəlɪ) *adv.* 特別是
   (C) popularly ('pɑpjələlɪ) *adv.* 通俗地；普遍地
   (D) similarly ('sɪmələlɪ) *adv.* 同樣地
   smart (smɑrt) *adj.* 聰明的

2. (**D**) Eating dessert *before meals* may kill your <u>appetite</u>.
   吃正餐之前吃點心，會降低你的<u>食慾</u>。
   (A) energy ('ɛnədʒɪ) *n.* 精力　　(B) character ('kærɪktə) *n.* 性格
   (C) quality ('kwɑlətɪ) *n.* 品質
   (D) *appetite* ('æpə,taɪt) *n.* 食慾
   dessert (dɪ'zɜt) *n.* 點心　　meal (mil) *n.* 一餐
   kill (kɪl) *v.* 破壞

3. (**A**) *In Taiwan*, some cable TV companies have *up to* 70 or 80 <u>channels</u>.
   在台灣，有些有線電視公司擁有多達七十或八十個<u>頻道</u>。
   (A) *channel* ('tʃænl) *n.* 頻道
   (B) event (ɪ'vɛnt) *n.* 事件　　(C) item ('aɪtəm) *n.* 項目
   (D) pattern ('pætən) *n.* 模式
   cable ('kebl) *n.* 電纜　　*cable TV* 有線電視
   up to 高達

4. (**C**) It was fortunate *that John narrowly escaped being killed in a traffic accident*.

約翰勉強在車禍中逃過一劫,大難不死,真是幸運。

(A) privately (ˈpraɪvɪtlɪ) adv. 私下地
(B) locally (ˈlokəlɪ) adv. 局部地
(C) **narrowly** (ˈnærolɪ) adv. 勉強地;間不容髮地
(D) distantly (ˈdɪstəntlɪ) adv. 遙遠地

escape (əˈskep) v. 逃脫

5. (**D**) *Since the typhoon*, the basement has been filled with water. We have to remove the water *as soon as possible*.

從颱風以後,地下室充滿了水。我們必須儘快把水排乾。

(A) reserve (rɪˈzɜv) v. 預約 (B) repair (rɪˈpɛr) v. 修理
(C) retire (rɪˈtaɪr) v. 退休 (D) **remove** (rɪˈmuv) v. 排除

basement (ˈbesmənt) n. 地下室 **be filled with** 充滿了

6. (**D**) Some waste *from nuclear power plants* is buried *in sealed containers*.

有些核能發電廠產生的廢料,被埋在密封的容器中。

(A) crash (kræʃ) v. 粉碎 (B) pave (pev) v. 鋪 (路)
(C) risk (rɪsk) v. 冒險 (D) **sealed** (sild) adj. 密封的

waste (west) n. 廢料 **nuclear power plant** 核能發電廠
bury (ˈbɛrɪ) v. 埋 container (kənˈtenə) n. 容器

7. (**A**) A human body *usually* has a steady temperature *of about 37 degrees C*.

人體通常體溫穩定,大約三十七度 C。

(A) **steady** (ˈstɛdɪ) adj. 穩定的 (B) various (ˈvɛrɪəs) adj. 各式各樣的
(C) gradual (ˈgrædʒuəl) adj. 逐漸的
(D) precious (ˈprɛʃəs) adj. 珍貴的

temperature (ˈtɛmprətʃə) n. 溫度 degree (dɪˈgri) n. 度

8. (**C**) **If you expect to have quick _delivery_ of the goods**, it is better

to have them airmailed.

如果你想快速送達貨物，最好用航空郵寄。

(A) discovery (dɪ'skʌvərɪ) *n.* 發現

(B) directory (də'rɛktərɪ) *n.* 電話簿；董事會

(C) **_delivery_** (dɪ'lɪvərɪ) *n.* 遞送

(D) dormitory ('dɔrmə,torɪ) *n.* 宿舍

goods (gudz) *n. pl.* 貨物；商品

airmail ('ɛr,mel) *v.* 用航空郵寄

9. (**A**) This project is _mainly_ for scientific research. It doesn't

have any commercial value _at all_.

這項計劃主要是用作科學研究之用，並不具有任何商業價值。

(A) **_commercial_** (kə'mɝʃəl) *adj.* 商業的

(B) reluctant (rɪ'lʌktənt) *adj.* 不情願的

(C) opposite ('apəzɪt) *adj.* 相對的；相反的

(D) inferior (ɪn'fɪrɪə) *adj.* 較劣的

project ('pradʒɛkt) *n.* 計劃

research ('risɝtʃ) *n.* 研究

10. (**B**) These two countries are trying to intensify trade and cultural

exchanges _between them_.

這兩個國家正試著要加強彼此間貿易和文化上的交流。

(A) notify ('notə,faɪ) *v.* 通知

(B) **_intensify_** (ɪn'tɛnsə,faɪ) *v.* 加強

(C) personify (pɚ'sanə,faɪ) *v.* 擬人化

(D) signify ('sɪgnə,faɪ) *v.* 表示

trade (tred) *adj.* 貿易的　　exchange (ɪks'tʃendʒ) *n.* 交換；交流

11. (**C**) The manager must try to find out *who is really at fault for this serious sales problem.*
經理一定得找出，這次嚴重的銷售問題，究竟是誰該受責備。
(A) on line 在線上；連線中
(B) in service 使用中；服役中
(C) **at fault** 有過失；該受責備
(D) by law 根據法律

12. (**A**) This talk show, *on the whole*, is *quite* popular with the audience. 整體說來，這個脫口秀相當受到觀眾歡迎。
(A) **on the whole** 就整體而言　(B) by no means 絕不
(C) out of the question 不可能 (= *impossible*)
　　cf. out of question 沒問題
(D) in no sense 絕不 (是)
***talk show** 脫口秀　**be popular with**~ 受~歡迎*

13. (**B**) Mr. Brown suggested *that Mary stay with the company, for better or worse, **because** the company needed her.*
布朗先生建議瑪麗無論如何要留在公司裡，因為公司需要她。
(A) back and forth 來回地 (= *to and fro*)
(B) **for better or worse** 不管好壞；無論如何
(C) off and on 斷斷續續地 (= *on and off*)
(D) up and down 上上下下地

14. (**D**) How did you talk your sister <u>into doing</u> the chores *for you*? She *normally* avoids them.
你怎麼說服你姊姊幫你做家事的啊？她通常避之唯恐不及。
(D) ***talk sb. into V-ing** 說服某人做某事*
chores (tʃɔrz) *n. pl.* 雜事　　normally ('nɔrməlɪ) *adv.* 通常
avoid (ə'vɔɪd) *v.* 避開

15. (C) *In modern times*, many traditional concepts have given way
to new ideas.
在現代，很多傳統的觀念都已被新的想法取代。

 (A) find a way of 找到～的方法
 (B) change the way of 改變～的方式
 (C) *give way to* 向～屈服；被～取代
 (D) have a way of 有～的方式

 traditional (trə'dɪʃənḷ) *adj.* 傳統的 concept ('kansɛpt) *n.* 觀念

二、句子配合題：

16. (H) Losing weight requires discipline and a good plan.
減肥需要自制和好的計畫。

 lose weight 減輕體重 require (rɪ'kwaɪr) *v.* 需要
 discipline ('dɪsəplɪn) *n.* 自制

17. (G) Pets are wonderful, *but* their owners should be responsible.
寵物是很棒，但是牠們的主人應該要有責任感。

 pet (pɛt) *n.* 寵物 responsible (rɪ'spansəbḷ) *adj.* 有責任感的

18. (E) *When you reach the voice mailbox*, make your message brief.
當你使用語音信箱時，留言要簡短。

 reach (ritʃ) *v.* 到達 *voice mailbox* 語音信箱
 message ('mɛsɪdʒ) *n.* 訊息；留言 brief (brif) *adj.* 簡短的

19. (B) Delicious dishes can be prepared *only with the freshest*

ingredients. 唯有最新鮮的材料，才能烹煮出美味的菜餚。
 dish (dɪʃ) *n.* 菜餚 fresh (frɛʃ) *adj.* 新鮮的
 ingredient (ɪn'gridɪənt) *n.* 材料

20.(**F**) *When you begin a new job in an office*, you should learn how to do it well.

當你在辦公室開始一個新工作時,應該要學習如何把工作做好。

三、綜合測驗:

*Now **that** you are planning to go to college*, how can you select an ideal college *for yourself*? <u>By</u> its reputation *or* the test
21
scores *it requires for admission*? *In fact*, it is not <u>as</u> simple as that.
22
College education is *far more* complicated *than just* the reputation *of*
23
*a college **or*** the test scores *it requires*. *In addition to these two factors*, you should *also* have <u>other</u> important information. Finding out *which*
24
college suits you involves time and energy, *but* <u>no</u> more than those
25
you might spend on buying a motorcycle or a computer.

由於你正計劃要上大學,該如何為自己選擇一所理想的大學呢?是根據學校的聲望,亦或是錄取分數呢?事實上,沒有那麼簡單。大學教育比僅僅是學校的聲望,或錄取分數要複雜多了。除了這二個因素之外,你應該也要有其他重要的資訊。要找出哪所大學適合你,需要時間和體力,但不會比買機車或買電腦所耗費的多。

now that 既然;由於　　select (sə'lɛkt) *v.* 選擇
reputation (ˌrɛpjə'teʃən) *n.* 聲望
score (skor) *n.* 分數　　require (rɪ'kwaɪr) *v.* 要求;需要
admission (əd'mɪʃən) *n.* 准許入學
complicated ('kɑmpləˌketɪd) *adj.* 複雜的
in addition to 除了~之外 (= *besides*)　　factor ('fæktə) *n.* 因素
suit (sut) *v.* 適合　　involve (ɪn'vɑlv) *v.* 需要
energy ('ɛnədʒɪ) *n.* 體力;精力

21. (**B**) 表示「根據」何種標準，介系詞用 *by*，選 (B)。

22. (**A**) *as~as*… 像…一樣~

23. (**B**) 依句意，大學教育比「僅僅是」學校的聲望更複雜，選 (B) *just*。

24. (**C**) 依句意，你需要「其他」資訊，選 (C) *other*。information 為不可數名詞，而 (A) many，(D) few 均用來修飾可數名詞，用法不合。

25. (**A**) 依句意，「不會比~更多」，選 (A) *no more than~*。

Here are some tips *on* choosing an ideal one *from a number of*
                                 26
colleges.

1. Visit the websites *of these colleges* **and** find out **which college**

has departments [*offering* courses **that** interest you **or** will help
                 27

you prepare for your future career.]

2. Are the professors *in the departments you plan to get into*
                                     28

experts *in their own fields*?

3. Do the colleges allow you to participate in activities *that* will
                                         29

help you develop yourself intellectually and emotionally?

I hope the above advice is helpful to you *in selecting the right*
              30
college.

以下是有關如何從多所大學中，選出最理想學校的一些小祕訣。

1. 到這些大學的網站上看看，查出哪一所大學的科系所提供的科目，是你有興趣的，或是能幫助你為未來的事業做準備。

2. 你計劃要就讀的那些科系的教授，是否為該領域的佼佼者呢？

3. 這些大學是否允許你參加，有助於你智力和情緒發展的活動？

我希望以上的建議，對你在選擇適合的大學時，能有所助益。

tip〔 tɪp 〕 *n.* 祕訣　　***a number of*** 許多的（= *many*）
website〔'wɛb,saɪt〕 *n.* 網站　　department〔 dɪ'pɑrtmənt 〕 *n.* 科系
professor〔 prə'fɛsə 〕 *n.* 教授　　expert〔'ɛkspɝt〕 *n.* 專家
field〔 fild 〕 *n.* 領域　　participate〔 pə'tɪsə,pet 〕 *v.* 參加＜ *in* ＞
intellectually〔,ɪntl'ɛktʃuəlɪ 〕 *adv.* 智力上
emotionally〔 ɪ'moʃənlɪ 〕 *adv.* 情緒上

26.（ **B** ）表示「有關～」的祕訣，介系詞用 ***on***，選 (B)。

27.（ **D** ）此處原為 which college has departments ***that offer*** courses…省略關代 which，動詞 offer 應改為 offering，選 (D)。

28.（ **A** ）依句意，「就讀」某個科系，用 ***get into***，選 (A)。

29.（ **C** ）此處需要關代引導形容詞子句，修飾先行詞 activities，選 (C) ***that***。

30.（ **D** ）表「以上的」建議，選 (D) ***above***。而 (A) upper〔'ʌpə 〕 *adj.*（地點、位置）在上方的，(B) over「在～上」，為介系詞，(C) upward〔'ʌpwəd 〕 *adj.* 往上的；向上的，均不合。

四、文意選填：

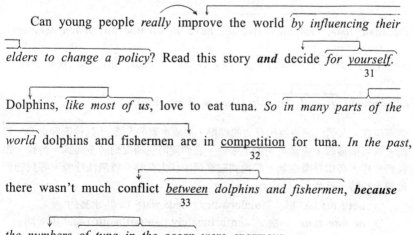

Can young people *really* improve the world *by influencing their elders to change a policy*? Read this story *and* decide *for yourself*.
<u>　　　31　　</u>

Dolphins, *like most of us*, love to eat tuna. *So in many parts of the world* dolphins and fishermen are in <u>competition</u> for tuna. *In the past*,
<u>　　32　　</u>

there wasn't much conflict <u>*between* dolphins and fishermen</u>, ***because***
<u>　　33　　</u>

the numbers of tuna in the ocean were enormous.

年輕人是否眞能影響他們的長輩，改變策略因而改善世界呢？請你讀以下這則故事，自己決定是否如此。海豚，跟我們大多數人一樣，喜歡吃鮪魚。所以在世界上許多地區，海豚跟漁夫爲了搶鮪魚而競爭。在過去，海豚與漁夫之間的衝突並不多，因爲海裏的鮪魚數量十分龐大。

improve〔ɪmˈpruv〕v. 改善　　influence〔ˈɪnfluəns〕v. 影響
elder〔ˈɛldɚ〕n. 年長者；長輩　　policy〔ˈpɑləsɪ〕n. 政策
dolphin〔ˈdɑlfɪn〕n. 海豚　　tuna〔ˈtunə〕n. 鮪魚
fishermen〔ˈfɪʃəmən〕n. pl. 漁夫　　conflict〔ˈkɑnflɪkt〕n. 衝突
enormous〔ɪˈnɔrməs〕adj. 龐大的

31.(**I**) *for oneself* 自己；自行
　　本句爲祈使句，主詞應爲「你」，故空格用 *yourself*，選 (I)。

32.(**G**) *in competition for sth.* 彼此競爭角逐某物

33.(**C**) *between* A *and* B 在 A 與 B 之間

Now, however, men have developed huge fishing nets *that form*
underwater "walls" *that stretch for miles.* They can catch thousands
　　　　　　　　　　　　　　　　　34
of tuna *at one time. Unfortunately,* they *also* catch many dolphins *at*
　　　　　　　　　　　　　　　　　　　35
the same time. Dolphins, *like us,* have to breathe air. *When* they are
trapped in the nets *too long,* they cannot breathe. *By the time* they
36
are brought *aboard the ship,* they will be dead.
　　　　　37

然而現在，人們已經發展出巨大的漁網，形成水裏的「牆」，延伸數哩之長。它們一次可捕獲數千隻鮪魚。很不幸地，它們同時也捕捉到許多海豚。海豚，跟我們一樣，必須呼吸空氣。當牠們被漁網困住太久時，就無法呼吸。等到牠們被帶上船時，就死了。

net〔nɛt〕n. 網　　underwater〔ˈʌndɚˌwɔtɚ〕adj. 水裏的
at one time 一次　　unfortunately〔ʌnˈfɔrtʃənɪtlɪ〕adv. 不幸地
breathe〔brið〕v. 呼吸　　*by the time* 等到~的時候

34. (**D**) stretch〔strɛtʃ〕*v.* 延伸

35. (**A**) 依句意，它們捕獲鮪魚，但「也」捉到海豚，選 (A) *also*。

36. (**B**) trap〔træp〕*v.* 困住

37. (**H**) *aboard the ship* 在船上

Many children were upset to hear about the senseless death *of these*
                                                              38
wonderful sea creatures **and** decided to help save them. They wrote
                                                      39
letters *to the tuna companies and supermarkets asking them to find*
a way to spare dolphins. Eventually their hard work paid off. *Now*
                                                         40
you can buy tuna *with the label "dolphin-free tuna." So* you see,
everyone can make a difference.

許多孩子聽到這些奇妙的海中生物，這樣毫無意義地死亡，感到非常難過，所
以決定要伸出援手來救牠們。他們寫信給鮪魚公司跟超市，要求他們想辦法放
過海豚。最後，他們的努力有了回報。現在你可以買到，貼有這種標籤的鮪魚：
「沒有拖累海豚的鮪魚」。所以，你看，每個人都有能力，可以帶來一些正面的
影響。

> upset〔ʌp'sɛt〕*adj.* 難過的　　creature〔'kritʃɚ〕*n.* 生物
> spare〔spɛr〕*v.* 放過；饒過
> eventually〔ɪ'vɛntʃʊəlɪ〕*adv.* 最後　　label〔'lebl̩〕*n.* 標籤
> **make a difference** 有影響；起作用

38. (**F**) senseless〔'sɛnslɪs〕*adj.* 無意義的

39. (**E**) 依句意，要幫助「解救」牠們，選 (E) *save*。

40. (**J**) *pay off* 順利成功；有回報

五、閱讀測驗：

41－43 為題組

　　Folk tales are stories *passed down by word of mouth generation after generation*. They *often* concern *very* strong or clever people *who come from humble backgrounds*. These people *usually* triumph over their enemies *because of their wit and their great energy*. Folk tales are both down-to-earth *and highly* imaginative.

　　民間傳說就是一代一代口耳相傳的故事。它們時常是與出身卑微，但卻非常堅毅或是聰明的人有關。這些人通常會因為他們的睿智及無比的活力，而戰勝敵人。民間傳說可能是實際的，也可能是想像的。

　　folk〔fok〕*adj.* 民間的　　　***folk tale*** 民間傳說
　　pass down 流傳　　***by word of mouth*** 口頭地
　　generation〔͵dʒɛnəˈreʃən〕*n.* 一代
　　concern〔kənˈsɝn〕*v.* 與～有關　　strong〔strɔŋ〕*adj.* 堅毅的
　　clever〔ˈklɛvɚ〕*adj.* 聰明的　　humble〔ˈhʌmbḷ〕*adj.* 卑微的
　　background〔ˈbækͺɡraʊnd〕*n.* 背景
　　triumph〔ˈtraɪəmf〕*v.* 獲得勝利＜*over*＞　　wit〔wɪt〕*n.* 智慧
　　energy〔ˈɛnədʒɪ〕*n.* 活力；精力
　　down-to-earth〔ˈdaʊntəˈɝθ〕*adj.* 實際的
　　highly〔ˈhaɪlɪ〕*adv.* 高度地；非常地
　　imaginative〔ɪˈmædʒəͺnetɪv〕*adj.* 想像的

　　Many folk tales *originally* had some basis *in fact **and*** grew out of the lives *of real people*. They changed, *however*, *as they were told and retold*. A man might *once* have fought a bear, *for example*, ***and*** the tales *told about him* might make him into the greatest bear

fighter **who ever lived.** **Through the power of imagination,** folk tales
can turn humble people into heroes. Many folk tales are **also** tall
tales—**stories of unbelievable events told with perfect seriousness.** A
tall tale, **in other words,** is a story **in which the truth has been**
exaggerated.

　　許多民間傳說原本有一些事實的基礎，而且是源於眞實人們的生活。然而，故事會隨著一再地轉述而改變。舉例來說，有一個人曾經和熊搏鬥，而關於他的故事可能會讓他成爲有史以來最偉大的獵熊者。透過想像力，民間傳說可以使卑微的人變成英雄。許多民間傳說也是荒誕不經的故事——嚴肅地被訴說，卻又令人無法相信的故事，換句話說，所謂荒誕不經的故事，就是誇大事實的故事。

originally〔ə'rɪdʒənḷɪ〕*adv.* 原本　　basis〔'besɪs〕*n.* 基礎
grow out of 產生於　　retell〔ri'tɛl〕*v.* 再講；重述
fight〔faɪt〕*v.* 與～打鬥　　bear〔bɛr〕*n.* 熊
imagination〔ɪˏmædʒə'neʃən〕*n.* 想像力
turn A **into** B 使 A 變成 B　　*a tall tale* 荒誕不經的故事
unbelievable〔ˏʌnbɪ'livəbḷ〕*adj.* 令人難以置信的
with perfect seriousness 非常嚴肅地
exaggerate〔ɪg'zædʒəˏret〕*v.* 誇大

A culture's folk tales, fables, songs, and proverbs are an important
part **of its literature.** **By reading and listening to folk tales,** we may
gain a better understanding **of the true values, beliefs, and goals of a**
people.

　　一個文化的民間傳說、寓言故事、歌曲，以及諺語，都是它文學裏重要的一個部份。藉由閱讀和傾聽民間傳說，我們可能會更了解一個民族眞正的價值觀、信仰，以及目標。

fable (ˈfebl̩) n. 寓言故事　　proverb (ˈprɑvɝb) n. 諺語
literature (ˈlɪtərətʃɚ) n. 文學　　values (ˈvæljuz) n. pl. 價值觀
belief (bɪˈlif) n. 信仰　　goal (gol) n. 目標
people (ˈpipl̩) n. 民族

41. (**D**) 民間傳說通常是 ──────── 的故事。

(A) 聰明學者　　　　　　　　(B) 勇敢的王子
(C) 貪心的人　　　　　　　　(D) 一般人

scholar (ˈskɑlɚ) n. 學者　　brave (brev) adj. 勇敢的
greedy (ˈgridɪ) adj. 貪心的　　folk (fok) n. 一般人；人民
ordinary (ˈɔrdn̩ˌɛrɪ) adj. 普通的

42. (**A**) 下列關於荒誕不經的故事的敘述，何者是錯的？

(A) 荒誕不經的故事是實際的故事。
(B) 要創造荒誕不經的故事需要想像力。
(C) 荒誕不經的故事誇大了人類的力量。
(D) 當人們講荒誕不經的故事時，態度很認真。

factual (ˈfæktʃuəl) adj. 事實的　　overstate (ˈovɚˈstet) v. 誇張

43. (**C**) 根據本文，民間傳說 ──────── 。

(A) 是由當地的作家所寫的　　(B) 解釋了世界文學的起源
(C) 揭露了人們關於生活的想法　(D) 教人們如何生存

native (ˈnetɪv) adj. 當地的　　reveal (rɪˈvil) v. 揭露；顯示
survive (sɚˈvaɪv) v. 生存

44–46 為題組

It used to be *that* athletes and VIPs gave *away their signatures* *for free*, **and** a signed baseball or photograph would *just* sit *on a* *shelf and* collect dust. **But** *nowadays*, autographs (*signatures*) are big business.

從前，運動員及名人經常免費送出他們的簽名，而簽上名的棒球或相片只會被放在架上積灰塵。但現在，親筆簽名可是一種大生意。

athlete（'æθlit）*n.* 運動員　　***VIP*** 大人物（= *very important person*）
give away 贈送　　signature（'sɪgnətʃɚ）*n.* 簽名
for free 免費地　　sign（saɪn）*v.* 簽名　　***sit on*** 擱置
shelf（ʃɛlf）*n.* 架子　　collect（kə'lɛkt）*v.* 收集；累積
autograph（'ɔtə͵græf）*n.* 親筆簽名

Many athletes and VIPs demand payment *for their signatures,*

and many people are willing to pay. Autograph dealers can be found

in almost any sizable city, and collectors may get hundreds, *even*

thousands, of dollars for things *signed by anyone from Mozart to*

Madonna, Thomas Jefferson to JFK.

許多運動員及名人要收錢才願意簽名，而且有許多人願意付這個錢。在許多大城市中，幾乎都能找到買賣名人簽名的經銷商，因為這些簽名收集者，可能把他們擁有的名人所簽名的物件出售，獲得幾百甚至幾千塊錢，這些名人從莫札特到瑪丹娜，湯瑪斯・傑佛遜到約翰・甘迺迪都有。

demand（dɪ'mænd）*v.* 要求　　payment（'pemənt）*n.* 付款
dealer（'dilɚ）*n.* 商人；交易者　　sizable（'saɪzəbḷ）*adj.* 相當大的
Thomas Jefferson 湯瑪斯・傑佛遜（美國第三任總統）
JFK（*John Fitzgerald Kennedy*）約翰・甘迺迪（美國第三十五任總統）

A 54-page manuscript *written by Albert Einstein recently* was sold

for $398,500 at Christie's in New York. And in 1994, Microsoft CEO

(chief executive officer) Bill Gates paid $30.8 million *for a handwritten notebook penned by Leonardo da Vinci. Meanwhile,* fans *across the*

U.S. are flocking to sports shows [*to have their heroes sign anything*

from a bat to a box of cereal.]

最近在紐約的佳士得拍賣會上，一份長達五十四頁的愛因斯坦手稿，以三十九萬八千五百元美金的價格售出。而在一九九四年，微軟總裁比爾‧蓋茲，付了三千零八十萬元美金，買下由達文西親手寫的筆記本。同時，全美的運動迷聚集到運動賽場，為了想讓他們的英雄在任何東西上簽名，從球棒至一盒早餐麥片都有。

manuscript (ˊmænjəˏskrɪpt) *n.* 手稿
Christie's (ˊkrɪstɪz) *n.* 佳士得拍賣會 (發源於倫敦之藝術品及珠寶拍賣會)
CEO 總裁 (= *chief executive officer*)
pen (pɛn) *v.* 寫
Leonardo da Vinci 達文西 (文藝復興時期義大利畫家、雕刻家、建築師)
meanwhile (ˊminˏhwaɪl) *adv.* 同時　　fan (fæn) *n.* 迷
flock (flɑk) *v.* 聚集　　sports (sports) *adj.* 運動的
show (ʃo) *n.* 盛大場面　　bat (bæt) *n.* 球棒
cereal (ˊsɪrɪəl) *n.* 穀類加工食物 (一般指燕麥片、玉米片等早餐食品)

What is the real reason *many collectors want autographs*? To

connect with someone famous, ***or maybe even*** to imagine themselves

as the hero they admire.

簽名收集者要得到簽名的真正原因到底是什麼呢？為了與名人有所接觸，甚至可能幻想他們自己就是他們所崇拜的英雄。

connect with 連結　　imagine (ɪˊmædʒɪn) *v.* 想像
admire (ədˊmaɪr) *v.* 崇拜

44.(**B**) 以前，運動員和名人的簽名 _____。

    (A) 價格很高   (B) <u>完全不用錢</u>

    (C) 吸引很大的注意   (D) 對大眾販售

    price〔praɪs〕*v.* 標價

45.(**D**) 根據本文，現在許多人收集運動員和名人的簽名 _____。

    (A) 爲了它們的藝術價值   (B) 爲了向朋友炫耀

    (C) 當作歷史文獻   (D) <u>爲了跟名人攀關係</u>

    artistic〔ɑr'tɪstɪk〕*adj.* 藝術的   ***show off*** 炫耀

    document〔'dɑkjəmənt〕*n.* 文件；文獻

    associate〔ə'soʃɪ,et〕*v.* 使有關聯 < *with* >

46.(**A**) 本文的整體語調（態度）是 _____。

    (A) <u>寫實的</u>   (B) 諷刺的

    (C) 負面的   (D) 熱心的

    overall〔,ovə'ɔl〕*adj.* 全部的；整體的   tone〔ton〕*n.* 語調

    factual〔'fæktʃuəl〕*adj.* 寫實的   ironic〔aɪ'rɑnɪk〕*adj.* 諷刺的

    negative〔'nɛɡətɪv〕*adj.* 否定的；負面的

    enthusiastic〔ɪn,θjuzɪ'æstɪk〕*adj.* 熱心的

47－50 爲題組

    In Taiwan much time and energy are spent *on getting a proper education and finding a good job. As a result,* health concerns have been neglected. A new study *by the Department of Health in Taiwan* shows ***that** more than half of the adult population in Taiwan lacks an understanding of important health problems*. More than 2,000 adults took part in the survey *to find out about their knowledge of diet,* *health care, disease control, and medication. Surprisingly,* only 51

percent of the people *surveyed* understand *that the common cold has*

no cure.

　　在台灣，人們花了很多時間和精力，想獲得適當的教育，並找到好的工作。因此，健康的問題就受到大家的忽略。台灣衛生署有一項新的研究顯示，台灣有一半以上的成人，對重要的健康問題，都不太了解。有兩千多位成人參加了一項調查，目的是要了解，他們對於飲食、保健、疾病的控制，以及醫藥方面的認識。令人驚訝的是，接受調查的人當中，只有百分之五十一的人知道，並沒有治療普通感冒的方法。

proper (ˈprɑpɚ) *adj.* 適當的　　concern (kənˈsɝn) *n.* 有關的事
neglect (nɪˈɡlɛkt) *v.* 忽略　　**the Department of Health** 衛生署
lack (læk) *v.* 缺乏　　**take part in** 參加
survey (sɚˈve) *n.,v.* 調查
knowledge (ˈnɑlɪdʒ) *n.* 了解；認識
diet (ˈdaɪət) *n.* 飲食　　**health care** 保健
medication (ˌmɛdɪˈkeʃən) *n.* 藥物 (治療)
surprisingly (sɚˈpraɪzɪŋlɪ) *adv.* 令人驚訝的是
common (ˈkɑmən) *adj.* 一般的；普通的
cure (kjʊr) *n.* 治療法

Colds are caused *by viruses, not bacteria, so* taking medicine is

absolutely no use *at all.* The problem is made worse *by doctors*

who give their patients large doses of useless drugs. More than

two-thirds believe *that it is only the nicotine in cigarettes rather than*

the other chemicals that cause cancer. These people believe *that if*

they smoke "light" cigarettes with less nicotine, they will not get cancer. *Since 26 percent of Taiwanese adults smoke*, such a

misunderstanding will lead to more illness, suffering, and early death.

But the outlook *for health education in Taiwan* is not all negative.

The survey concludes *that younger Taiwanese have a better*

*understanding of health concerns *than* their parents, *while* senior*

citizens have the least understanding among the three age groups.

感冒是由病毒所引起而不是細菌,所以吃藥絕對是一點用也沒有。有些醫生給病人大量無用的藥物,使得問題更加嚴重。有三分之二以上的人相信,只有香煙中的尼古丁,而不是其他的化學藥品,會導致癌症。這些人相信,如果他們吸含較少尼古丁的「淡」煙,就不會得癌症。因為有百分之二十六的台灣成人吸煙,所以這樣的誤解會導致更多的疾病、痛苦,以及早死。但是台灣健康教育未來的展望,並不全都是負面的。這項調查得到一個結論,台灣年輕人比他們的父母更了解健康方面的問題,而老年人則是這三個年齡層中,對健康問題最不了解的。

virus (ˈvaɪrəs) *n.* 病毒　bacteria (bækˈtɪrɪə) *n. pl.* 細菌

take medicine 吃藥　absolutely (ˈæbsəˌlutlɪ) *adv.* 絕對

dose (doz) *n.* 劑量　nicotine (ˈnɪkəˌtin) *n.* 尼古丁

chemical (ˈkɛmɪkḷ) *n.* 化學物質

cancer (ˈkænsɚ) *n.* 癌症　light (laɪt) *adj.* 清淡的

misunderstanding (ˌmɪsʌndɚˈstændɪŋ) *n.* 誤解

lead to 導致　suffering (ˈsʌfrɪŋ) *n.* 痛苦

outlook (ˈaʊtˌlʊk) *n.* 前景;展望

negative (ˈnɛgətɪv) *adj.* 負面的

conclude (kənˈklud) *v.* 下結論

senior citizen 老人　*age group* 年齡層

47. (**C**) 最近台灣進行了一項健康方面的調查，目的是要確定 _____ 。

　　(A) 為什麼人們會忽視健康　　　(B) 何時教健康教育

　　(C) 人們對健康的了解程度　　　(D) 誰比較可能會生病

　　recently (ˋrisn̩tlɪ) adv. 最近　　　**carry out** 進行

　　determine (dɪˋtɝmɪn) v. 確定

　　ignore (ɪgˋnor) v. 忽視

48. (**B**) 根據本文，下列有關感冒藥的敘述，何者正確？

　　(A) 它們可以治好普通的感冒。

　　(B) 許多台灣人吃太多這一類的藥。

　　(C) 醫生常常拒絕賣這種藥。

　　(D) 大約有百分之五十一的病人使用這種藥。

49. (**A**) 根據這項調查，大部份的台灣人認為 _____ 。

　　(A) 只有尼古丁會使人們成為癌症病患

　　(B) 只有少數的吸煙者會得癌症

　　(C) 少抽點煙可以減少致癌的危險

　　(D) 除了尼古丁以外，其他的化學物質會導致肺部疾病

　　alone (əˋlon) adv. 單單；僅僅

　　fall victim to 成為～的受害者

　　percentage (pɚˋsɛntɪdʒ) n. 百分比；份量

　　develop (dɪˋvɛləp) v. 獲得；患 (病)　　　lung (lʌŋ) n. 肺

50. (**B**) 調查的結果顯示，_____ 。

　　(A) 在台灣，健康方面的統計數字一直被人們所忽略

　　(B) 年輕的一代有改善的希望

　　(C) 老一輩的人依賴保健制度

　　(D) 許多人重視事業甚於健康

　　statistics (stəˋtɪstɪks) n. pl. 統計數字

　　improvement (ɪmˋpruvmənt) n. 改善

　　depend on 依賴　　　value (ˋvælju) v. 重視

51－55 為題組

"I have a regular film camera *but* I *just* don't use it much," *said* Ms. Lowery, 23, a computer programmer. "*When I got married last year*, I had all these pictures *that didn't come out right.* With digital cameras, you aren't spending money *on film for wasted pictures,*" she said.

「我有一台普通的照相機，但不常用，」洛里女士說道，她今年二十三歲，是一位電腦程式設計師。「我去年結婚時，照了很多照片，卻都不好看。如果用數位相機，所浪費掉的照片所用的底片，就不用花錢了，」她說。

regular〔'rɛgjələ〕adj. 一般的；普通的
film camera （要用底片的）照相機（= *camera*）
programmer〔'progræmə〕n. 程式設計師
come out （照片）顯現 digital〔'dɪdʒətl̩〕adj. 數位式的
digital camera 數位相機 film〔fɪlm〕n. 底片
wasted〔'westɪd〕adj. 浪費掉的

And there are plenty of models *from which to choose: from* simple $200 point-and-shoot snappers to $1,000 wonders *with all the features that any advanced amateur could want.* The wide selection is a sure sign *that in many consumers' minds, digital cameras have risen from mere gadgets to must-have items.*

而且，數位相機有多種款式，可供挑選：從只要二百元的傻瓜相機，到價值一千元的，功能齊全，任何技術很好的業餘攝影師都想要的高檔貨都有。如此多種選擇，明確地顯示出，在許多消費者的心中，數位相機已經從僅僅是小巧精緻的裝置，提升成為一定要擁有的物品了。

plenty of 很多　　model ('mɑdl̩) *n.* 機型；款式
shoot (ʃut) *v.* 拍照　　snap (snæp) *v.* 拍攝 (快照)
snapper ('snæpɚ) *n.* 相機　　wonder ('wʌndɚ) *n.* 很棒的東西
feature ('fitʃɚ) *n.* 特色
advanced (əd'vænst) *adj.* 先進的；技術好的
amateur ('æmə,tʃur) *n.* 業餘愛好者
selection (sə'lɛkʃən) *n.* 選擇　　sign (saɪn) *n.* 跡象
rise (raɪz) *v.* 地位升高
mere (mɪr) *adj.* 僅僅；只是 (= *only*)
gadget ('gædʒɪt) *n.* 小巧的裝置

Digital cameras offer more than just the instant previewing *of
pictures on small color screens*. They can store dozens, *sometimes
hundreds*, of images *that can be printed easily at home **or** sent by
e-mail*. ***Although** there are extra costs involved in going digital—
the cost of memory cards for storage and the special paper for
printing*—many buyers have been willing to make the switch.

　　數位相機的功能，不只是在小小的彩色螢幕上，提供照片的立刻預覽而已。
它們可以儲存數十張，有時數百張圖片，並可在家裏輕鬆列印出來，或用電子
郵件傳送。雖然使用數位相機需要額外的費用 —— 儲存資料的記憶卡的費用，
以及列印時的特殊用紙 —— 許多購買者已經願意做這樣的改變。

instant ('ɪnstənt) *adj.* 立即的　　preview ('pri,vju) *v.* 預覽
screen (skrin) *n.* 螢幕　　store (stor) *v.* 儲存
dozens of 數十個　　image ('ɪmɪdʒ) *n.* 圖片
print (prɪnt) *v.* 列印　　extra ('ɛkstrə) *adj.* 額外的
be involved in 與～有關　　go (go) *v.* 變成
memory ('mɛmərɪ) *n.* 記憶　　storage ('storɪdʒ) *n.* 儲存
willing ('wɪlɪŋ) *adj.* 願意的　　switch (swɪtʃ) *n.* 改變

Although about 90 percent of American households still use film cameras, digital cameras are capturing a growing share *of the consumer market. And* the number *of digital-camera households*, now at about 10 percent, is certain to grow, *as manufacturers introduce more and more cameras* **whose** *quality is as good as film cameras.* Soon, *even* professionals will use them.

雖然大約百分之九十的美國家庭，仍然使用要用底片的相機，但數位相機在消費市場上的佔有率也逐漸在成長。而使用數位相機的家庭，現在約佔百分之十，數量一定會增加，因為製造商生產越來越多機種，品質和普通相機一樣好。不久，就連專業攝影師也會開始使用數位相機。

> household (ˈhaʊsˌhold) *n.* 家庭　　capture (ˈkæptʃɚ) *v.* 捕捉；獲得
> growing (ˈgroɪŋ) *adj.* 成長中的；逐漸增加的
> share (ʃɛr) *n.* 市場佔有率　　***consumer market*** 消費市場
> manufacture (ˌmænjəˈfæktʃərɚ) *n.* 製造商
> introduce (ˌɪntrəˈdjus) *v.* 引進
> professional (prəˈfɛʃənḷ) *n.* 專業人士

Salesmen expect digital cameras to be popular gifts *this holiday season.* "They are *very* hot *this year*," *said Yossi Fogel at B & H Photo in New York.* "The prices have come down **and** the quality has gone up. Who wants to travel *with 30 rolls of film? With a large memory card to store pictures,* you can shoot and shoot **and** *never* have to worry about changing a roll. How many times have you missed a picture ***because*** *you failed to reload the film?*"

　　銷售人員預計，數位相機在今年的假期熱季中，將是很受歡迎的禮物。「數位相機今年會熱賣，」紐約 B&H 攝影公司的尤西・法格說道。「它們的價格下降，品質提升。那誰還要帶著三十捲底片旅行呢？有記憶卡可以大量儲存照片，你可以一照再照，不必擔心要換底片。你曾經有多少次因為沒有換底片，而錯過畫面呢？」

> salesman〔'selzmən〕n. 銷售人員
> **holiday season** 假期熱季（一般商家在每年十一月感恩節後，到一月一日
> 　元旦過完，舉行特賣的期間）　　hot〔hat〕adj. 熱門的
> **come down** 下降　　**go up** 提升　　**a roll of film** 一捲底片
> miss〔mɪs〕v. 錯過　　**fail to + V.** 未能；沒有
> reload〔ri'lod〕v. 重新裝入

51. (**A**) 下列何者不是數位相機勝過普通相機的優點？
　　(A) 使用者必須花費更多的錢。
　　(B) 有很多機型供顧客選擇。
　　(C) 可節省不需要的照片的錢。
　　(D) 照片可以用電子郵件傳送。

> advantage〔əd'væntɪdʒ〕n. 優點
> additional〔ə'dɪʃənḷ〕adj. 額外的（= extra）
> **come in** 有～　　unwanted〔ʌn'wɑntɪd〕adj. 不需要的

52. (**D**) 根據本文，使用數位相機的美國家庭會增加，如果 ＿＿＿＿＿＿。
　　(A) 製造商投資更多錢　　(B) 相機的操作變得更簡單
　　(C) 銷售人員更友善一點　　(D) 相機品質繼續改善

> invest〔ɪn'vɛst〕v. 投資　　operation〔ˌɑpə'reʃən〕n. 操作

53. (**C**) 下列有關普通要用底片的相機的說法何者為非？
　　(A) 它們的照片可在照相館印出。
　　(B) 它們的照片可依需要放大。
　　(C) 它們的照片可在印出之前先看到。
　　(D) 它們的照片可以保存很久。

> **photo shop** 照相館　　enlarge〔ɪn'lɑrdʒ〕v. 放大
> desire〔dɪ'zaɪr〕v. 要求

54. (**B**) 根據本文，數位相機現在的使用者主要是 _____。
　　(A) 專業攝影師　　　　　　　　(B) 業餘攝影師
　　(C) 家庭主婦　　　　　　　　　(D) 學生

55. (**C**) 擁有一台數位相機，必須要 _____。
　　(A) 攜帶很多底片　　　　　　　(B) 到照相館列印照片
　　(C) 有記憶卡　　　　　　　　　(D) 花更多時間使用

第貳部分：非選擇題

一、簡答題

Do women *really* use language *differently* from men? *Over the years*, researchers have given different answers *to this question. In the legends of some cultures*, it is *even* claimed ***that*** men and women speak different languages. *If this were true*, how could boys communicate *with their mothers*? One research report shows men and women use much the same grammar and vocabulary in English, ***although*** each sex uses certain kinds of words and structures more frequently ***than*** the other.

　　女人真的和男人在語言的使用上有所不同嗎？多年來，研究者針對這個問題一直提供不同的答案。在某些文化的傳說中，甚至主張女人和男人說的是不同的語言。如果這是真的，那小男孩們要如何和他們的母親溝通呢？有一份研究報告顯示，男人和女人會使用十分相似的英文文法與字彙，雖然男女雙方會比對方更常使用某一種類型的字詞與語句結構。

　　researcher (ˈrisɝtʃɚ) n. 研究人員　　legend (ˈlɛdʒənd) n. 傳說
　　claim (klem) v. 宣稱；主張　　grammar (ˈɡræmɚ) n. 文法
　　vocabulary (vəˈkæbjəˌlɛrɪ) n. 字彙　　sex (sɛks) n. 性別
　　structure (ˈstrʌktʃɚ) n. 結構

Most men use more swear words, **while** *far* more women use
adjectives *such as "super" and "lovely,"* **and** exclamations *such as*
"Goodness me!" and "Oh dear!" Women have been found to ask
more questions, make more use of positive and encouraging "noises,"
use a wider range *of intonation patterns*, **and** make greater use of the
pronouns *"you" and "we."* *By contrast*, men are *much more* likely to
interrupt (*about three times as often in some studies*), to argue about
what *has been said*, to ignore or respond *poorly* to **what** *has been*
said, to introduce more new topics *into the conversation*, **and** to
make more assertions.

大部分的男人會用比較多罵人的字眼,然而有更多女人,會使用形容詞,例如,
「真了不起」和「可愛的」,以及感嘆詞,像是「天啊!」和「唉呀!」女人會
問比較多的問題,常會使用積極與鼓勵性的「聲音」,使用各種的語調,以及較
多的代名詞,如「你們」和「我們」。相反地,男人就比較可能會打岔(有些研
究指出通常是女人的三倍),爭論剛才的談話內容,忽視或拙劣地回應剛才的對
話,並加入更多新話題在對話中,而且發表更多的主觀意見。

swear〔swɛr〕*v.* 咒罵   ***swear words*** 罵人的字眼

adjective〔ˈædʒɪktɪv〕*n.* 形容詞   super〔ˈsupɚ〕*adj.* 了不起的

lovely〔ˈlʌvlɪ〕*adj.* 可愛的

exclamation〔ˌɛkskləˈmeʃən〕*n.* 感嘆詞

Goodness me! 天啊!(= *My goodness!* = *My God!*)

Oh, dear! 哎呀;天呀   positive〔ˈpɑzətɪv〕*adj.* 正面的

encouraging〔ɪnˈkɝɪdʒɪŋ〕*adj.* 鼓勵的   range〔rendʒ〕*n.* 範圍

intonation〔ˌɪntoˈneʃən〕*n.* 語調   pronoun〔ˈpronaʊn〕*n.* 代名詞

by contrast 相反地   interrupt〔ˌɪntəˈrʌpt〕*v.* 打斷

time〔taɪm〕n. 倍　　study〔'stʌdɪ〕n. 研究
argue〔'argju〕v. 爭論　　ignore〔ɪg'nor〕v. 忽視
respond〔rɪ'spand〕v. 回應　　poorly〔'purlɪ〕adv. 拙劣地
introduce〔ˌɪntrə'djus〕v. 引進；採用
assertion〔ə'sɝʃən〕n. 斷言；主見

1. 在某些文化中的什麼故事，說明了男人和女人說話方式的不同？
   答：legends（傳說）

2. 根據一份研究報告的說法，英文裏的哪兩個部份通常會被男人和女人共同使用？
   答：grammar and vocabulary

3. 女人比男人更常使用那些形容詞？
   答：super and lovely（眞了不起和可愛的）

4. 男人比女人更常使用那種類型的字詞？
   答：swear words（罵人的字眼）

5. 根據一些研究，和女人相比，男人打岔的頻率有多高？
   答：three times as often（三倍）
   as compared with 和～相比

二、英文作文：（作文範例）

Growing Up Is a Rewarding Experience

There is a great difference between children and adults, and all of us will change significantly as we move from childhood to adulthood. This process is called growing up. It may be happy at some times and painful at others. It may be exciting, confusing or frustrating. Most likely, it will be all of these things. But for me, the process has been, over all, rewarding, because as I have matured I have developed physically, mentally and emotionally. Now when I look back on my childhood and see how much I have advanced, I feel a great sense of achievement.

One way in which growing up has been rewarding is that it has made me more independent and confident. When I was younger, I would not have been capable of, and never would have dared to, take on a lot of responsibility. But recently I have done just that. Last month, my grandmother fell ill and my mother went back to her hometown to care for her. At the time, my father was overseas on business. I was left in charge of the house and my younger brother and sister. At first I was afraid I was not up to the challenge, but I soon found that I could handle the responsibility well. I felt proud of myself but, best of all, my parents said they were proud of me, too. Now they see me as a young adult instead of a child, and that is very rewarding to me.

rewarding (rɪ'wɔrdɪŋ) *adj.* 有益的；值得的
significantly (sɪg'nɪfəkəntlɪ) *adv.* 相當大地
move (muv) *v.* 進展；發展　　adulthood (ə'dʌlt,hud) *n.* 成年期
process ('prɑsɛs) *n.* 過程　　painful ('penfəl) *adj.* 痛苦的
frustrating ('frʌs,tretɪŋ) *adj.* 令人沮喪的
over all 整體而言　　mature (mə'tʃur) *v.* 成熟
physically ('fɪzɪklɪ) *adv.* 身體上
mentally ('mɛntlɪ) *adj.* 智力上；心理上
emotionally (ɪ'moʃənlɪ) *adv.* 情緒上
look back on 回顧　　advance (əd'væns) *v.* 提升；進步
achievement (ə'tʃivmənt) *n.* 成就
a sense of achievement 成就感　　**be capable of** 能夠
dare to V. 敢～　　**take on** 承擔
hometown ('hom'taun) *n.* 故鄉　　**care for** 照顧
overseas ('ovə'siz) *adv.* 在國外　　**on business** 因公；出差
in charge of 負責照料　　**be up to** 能勝任
challenge ('tʃælɪndʒ) *n.* 挑戰　　handle ('hændl) *v.* 處理
see A **as** B 把 A 看作是 B　　**instead of** 而不是

九十一年度學科能力測驗（英文考科）大考中心公佈答案

題 號	答 案	題 號	答 案	題 號	答 案
1	D	21	A	41	D
2	D	22	B	42	B
3	C	23	D	43	A
4	B	24	C	44	A
5	A	25	D	45	D
6	C	26	A	46	C
7	B	27	C	47	B
8	D	28	B	48	A
9	A	29	D	49	C
10	C	30	B	50	D
11	A	31	D	51	C
12	B	32	H	52	A
13	D	33	F	53	D
14	C	34	B	54	C
15	B	35	J	55	B
16	E	36	I		
17	J	37	G		
18	A	38	E		
19	H	39	C		
20	C	40	A		

九十一年度學科能力測驗（英文考科）（補考）
大考中心公佈答案

題 號	答 案	題 號	答 案	題 號	答 案
1	B	21	B	41	D
2	D	22	A	42	A
3	A	23	B	43	C
4	C	24	C	44	B
5	D	25	A	45	D
6	D	26	B	46	A
7	A	27	D	47	C
8	C	28	A	48	B
9	A	29	C	49	A
10	B	30	D	50	B
11	C	31	I	51	A
12	A	32	G	52	D
13	B	33	C	53	C
14	D	34	D	54	B
15	C	35	A	55	C
16	H	36	B		
17	G	37	H		
18	E	38	F		
19	B	39	E		
20	F	40	J		

九十年大學入學學科能力測驗試題
英文考科

第壹部份：單一選擇題

一、詞彙與慣用語（15％）

說明： 第 1 至 15 題，每題選出最適當的一個選項，標示在答案卡之「選擇題答案區」。每題答對得 1 分，答錯不倒扣。

1. The ballet dancers' _____ movements delighted all the audience.
   (A) truthful　　　(B) doubtful　　　(C) graceful　　　(D) helpful

2. At the closing ceremony of the Olympic Games, all the athletes _____ good-bye to the audience.
   (A) charmed　　　(B) waved　　　(C) dared　　　(D) gazed

3. The drug problem is universal. It is not _____ to one country.
   (A) protected　　　(B) detected　　　(C) admitted　　　(D) restricted

4. I think that this new program will be _____ of your effort.
   (A) cautious　　　(B) fruitful　　　(C) worthy　　　(D) patient

5. This textbook is _____ more difficult to read than the other one.
   (A) considerably　(B) favorably　(C) desirably　(D) respectably

6. The _____ of Linda's love for music made her fly to Vienna to enter a music school.
   (A) quantity　　　(B) intensity　　　(C) creativity　　　(D) formality

7. E-mail plays a _____ role in modern communication.
   (A) vital　　　(B) violent　　　(C) vivid　　　(D) various

8. I _____ accept your plan, but I think it should be somewhat reworded.
   (A) basically　　　(B) leisurely　　　(C) modestly　　　(D) properly

9. This poem may be _____ in several different ways and each of them makes sense.

(A) negotiated   (B) designated   (C) interpreted   (D) substituted

10. The _____ of this piece of cloth is too coarse. Do you have a finer one?

(A) content   (B) display   (C) extent   (D) texture

11. His plan _____ in failure though it had been supported by many people.

(A) held on   (B) ended up   (C) put away   (D) brought about

12. Sara enjoys amusing her friends by _____ stories.

(A) speaking out   (B) setting off   (C) making up   (D) giving away

13. As the applause _____, the curtain on the stage dropped slowly.

(A) took off   (B) died down   (C) passed out   (D) stayed up

14. No one can possibly know _____ when an earthquake will strike.

(A) in advance   (B) in particular   (C) in vain   (D) in case

15. The scientist's project to build a modern laboratory was _____ on account of its huge budget.

(A) taken for granted   (B) started out

(C) got into difficulty   (D) called into question

二、綜合測驗（10％）

說明：第 16 至 25 題，每題一個空格，請依文意選出最適當的一個選項，標示在答案卡之「選擇題答案區」。每題答對得 1 分，答錯不倒扣。

At times, it seems like there are not many things that we can give a student who has everything. But ___16___ that Christmas is just a few weeks away, ___17___ is a gift idea. Those who have an inclination for crazy technological advances aren't hard ___18___. One simple way is a few new items that might ____19____ life more enjoyable. They don't look too revolutionary, but you'd be surprised ____20____ they are capable of. The following is one of the items.

____21____ a student who is never on time, there is the new Projection Alarm Clock. Many ordinary clocks are hard to read early in the morning, deceiving students of the correct time, ____22____ causing them to be late for school. Through a projector, this attractive radio-alarm-clock is able to display the time onto a wall, ceiling, or anywhere ____23____. The benefits include an easier visibility of the time, and an alarm that gets increasingly louder ____24____ turned off. It won't magically transport a student to school on time every day, but it just might make ____25____ a little easier.

16. (A) given   (B) give   (C) giving   (D) to give
17. (A) it   (B) here   (C) that   (D) where
18. (A) to be pleased   (B) to please
    (C) to be pleasing   (D) to have pleased
19. (A) do   (B) take   (C) make   (D) find
20. (A) how much   (B) at that   (C) what if   (D) such as
21. (A) Once   (B) Like   (C) Just   (D) For
22. (A) though   (B) therefore   (C) otherwise   (D) however
23. (A) else   (B) too   (C) also   (D) then
24. (A) when   (B) as   (C) until   (D) since
25. (A) to wake up   (B) wake up   (C) woke up   (D) waking up

三、配合題（5％）

說明： 1. 第26至30題，每題皆為未完成的句子。請逐題依文意與語法，從右
      欄(A)到(J)的選項中選出最適當者，合併成一個意思通順、用法正
      確的句子。
     2. 請將所選答案之英文字母代號標示在答案卡之「選擇題答案區」。
      每題答對得1分，答錯不倒扣。

26. People in this village…	A….unlikely that he would succeed.
27. After his graduation from college, …	B…. in that someone will take care of it.
	C….when I met an old friend of mine.
28. Ruth is attracted…	D….whether Mary would come or not.
29. It has been many years…	E…. have carried out many welfare programs.
30. I was taking a walk in the park…	F…. still nobody accepted Mary.
	G….since I last saw him.
	H…. to this new form of art.
	I…. and it certainly hurts.
	J…. he found a job in a computer company.

四、文意選填（10％）

說明：第 31 至 40 題，每題一個空格，請依文意在文章後所提供的(A) 到 (J) 選項中分別選出最適當者，並將其英文字母代號標示在答案卡之「選擇題答案區」。每題答對得 1 分，答錯不倒扣。

I had an extraordinary dream last night. In the dream the cloakroom attendant at a theater stopped me in the lobby and insisted on my __31__ my legs behind. I was not surprised, but I was __32__ annoyed. I said I had never heard of such a rule at a theater before. The man replied that he was very __33__ about it, but people often complained that other people's legs were always in the __34__. Therefore, it had been decided that people should leave their legs __35__. It seemed to me that the management had gone beyond their legal right in making this order. Under __36__ circumstances, I should have disputed it. However, I didn't want to __37__ a disturbance, so I sat down and prepared to obey the rule. I had never before known that the human leg could be taken off. I had always thought it was more __38__ fixed. But the man showed me how to undo them, and I found that they ___39___ off quite easily. The discovery did not surprise me ___40___ more than the original request that I should take them off. Nothing does surprise one in a dream.

(A) sorry　　(B) outside　　(C) leaving　　(D) securely　　(E) any

(F) normal　(G) quite　　(H) came　　(I) make　　(J) way

五、閱讀測驗（30％）

說明：　第41至55題，每題請分別根據各篇文章選出最適當的一個選項，標示
　　　　在答案卡之「選擇題答案區」。每題答對得2分，答錯不倒扣。

41-43題為題組

　　Believe it or not, America's favorite snack food is the potato chip. There is a story behind how it was first made. One might think that somewhere a genius thought up the first potato chips, but it didn't happen that way. Picture an elegant restaurant in Saratoga Springs, New York, in 1853. The Moon Lake Restaurant's menu included French-fried potatoes, a popular food recipe brought back from France by Thomas Jefferson. These were thickly cut potatoes, fried until golden brown and crisp on the outside. One evening a guest in the dining hall felt that his potatoes were too thick and sent them back to the kitchen. The cook sliced some potatoes thinner than before and prepared them for the complaining guest. He was still not satisfied and sent them back again! By this time the cook was angry and decided to do exactly what the dinner guest wanted: slice the potatoes as thin as possible. Then they would be so crisp that the diner wouldn't be able to use his fork to eat them. When the paper-thin browned potatoes arrived, the diner was pleased. He was so happy with them that other guests started ordering the new potatoes. The cook's plan to stop the dinner guest from complaining did not turn out as he had planned. Soon Saratoga Chips appeared on the menu and became so popular that people wanted to take some home. The restaurant started selling small packages of the potato chips. A few years later, they were selling all over the United States. But because the potatoes had to be peeled by hand, it was a time-consuming chore and potato chips were often out of stock. In the 1920s a mechanical potato peeler was invented and soon there were potato chips in abundance. They gradually spread all over the world, and have remained popular ever since.

41. According to this passage, mass production of potato chips was made possible when _____.
   (A) potatoes could be peeled by machines
   (B) potatoes were peeled by a large number of cooks
   (C) there was a growing demand for them
   (D) they first appeared in a Saratoga restaurant

42. According to this passage, the cook of the Moon Lake Restaurant _____.
   (A) enjoyed making potato chips very much
   (B) planned to sell potato chips everywhere
   (C) wanted to silence a complaining diner
   (D) was pleased that other guests liked the chips

43. Potato chips have been popular in the U.S. _____.
   (A) for more than 200 years   (B) ever since 1920
   (C) for less than 100 years   (D) since the 19ᵗʰ century

44-46 題爲題組

Even though they were written 150 years ago, Alexander Dumas' action novels still excite millions of readers around the world, in close to a hundred languages.

Dumas's two most famous stories, *The Three Musketeers* and *The Count of Monte Cristo*, have inspired more than 100 films. His 1848 novel, *The Man in the Iron Mask*, was recently made into a movie. In this movie, Leonardo DiCaprio played both King Louis XIV and his twin brother Philippe.

Few people know, however, that the author was the grandson of a Haitian slave. Even fewer people know that Dumas' father rose rapidly from a soldier to a general in the French Army before he was 31. The general died young, leaving Alexander penniless. But Dumas overcame poverty, the lack of formal education, and the hardship of racism to become one of the world's most popular writers.

Dumas's life sometimes was just like his action novels. He participated in three revolutions and fought with people when he was insulted. After making a fortune by writing novels, he built a mansion outside Paris and kept it open to starving artists, friends, and even strangers. Luckily for his fans, the mansion has recently been restored and opened to the public.

44. Which of the following statements about Alexander Dumas is **FALSE**?
   (A) He was a victim of racism.
   (B) He was well-educated.
   (C) He was the son of a general.
   (D) He was the grandson of a slave.

45. Alexander Dumas's novels _____.
   (A) have lasted for less than 100 years
   (B) have been translated into more than 100 languages
   (C) have not been well received until recently
   (D) have fascinated readers for many years

46. We may infer from the article that Dumas _____.
    (A) did not lead a colorful life
    (B) was a man who kept money to himself
    (C) was a generous and kind-hearted man
    (D) was a peace-loving writer

47-50題為題組

　　Zoe was just 2 weeks old when she was spotted wandering in a village market near Kenya's Tsavo National Park in December 1995. Zoe's mother had died and the baby was left alone. She was no ordinary orphan: she was an elephant. So she was trucked to a most unusual orphanage in Nairobi, run by a woman named Daphne Sheldrick.

　　Daphne's husband, David Sheldrick, founded Tsavo National Park. Daphne has been working with wild animals for some 60 years, and in 1977 she opened the elephant orphanage at her home in Nairobi. As of 1997, the orphanage, which depends on private contributions, has saved more than 100 infants.

　　Zoe was rather healthy when she was found, and once under the care of the orphanage she was very happy, consuming six gallons of vitamin-rich milk a day and earning a reputation as a confident, naughty and mischievous youngster. After a year in the orphanage with the constant companionship of her human family, Zoe was taken to a refuge at Tsavo National Park. There her keepers have gradually introduced her to the ways of the wild, helping her to find food and water. Zoe lives together with other elephant youngsters in a protected area. It may take some years, but the final aim is to release all of them to a wild herd.

　　Daphne said that her dream for the future is to see ivory banned, all stored ivory destroyed and no one wearing an ivory ornament ever again. "There will always be competition for land," she explained, "but we can protect elephants in the parks and give the young a chance."

47. Zoe was trucked to an elephant orphanage because _____.
    (A) Tsavo National park needed a baby elephant
    (B) she could not find her way home
    (C) she was very young when she lost her mother
    (D) Daphne wanted to keep her as a pet

48. The elephant orphanage is _____.
    (A) supported by the government
    (B) located inside Tsavo National Park
    (C) home to many kinds of animals
    (D) operated with personal funds

49. At Tsavo National Park, Zoe has been _____.
    (A) released to a wild herd to be protected
    (B) taught to adjust to life in the wild
    (C) allowed to wander in the village market
    (D) accompanied all the time by her keepers

50. According to this passage, Daphne would like to _____.
    (A) make elephants live in their own groups
    (B) set up as many orphanages as possible
    (C) sell ivory for maintaining the orphanage
    (D) send Zoe to a zoo in Europe or America

51-55 題為題組

　　Every object tells a story. Even the most ordinary objects can present to us powerful images. Sometimes it is the ordinary nature of these objects that actually makes them so extraordinary. Such is the case with an old leather shoe in a museum in Alaska. At first glance it does not look like much. It is a woman's shoe of a style popular in the 1890s. But what is unique about this shoe is where it was found. It was discovered on the Chilkoot Pass, the famous trail used by the people seeking gold in Alaska.

Who it belonged to or why it was left there is not known. Was it perhaps dropped by accident as the woman climbed up the 1,500 stairs carved out of ice? Or did she throw away goods that she didn't need in order to travel lighter?

Over 100,000 people with "gold fever" made this trip hoping to become millionaires. Few of them understood that on their way they would have to cross a harsh wilderness. Unprepared for such a dangerous journey, many died of starvation and exposure to the cold weather. The Canadian government finally started requiring the gold seekers to bring one ton of supplies with them. This was thought to be enough for a person to survive for one year. They would carry their supplies in backpacks each weighing up to fifty pounds; it usually took at least 40 trips to get everything to the top and over the pass. Whoever dropped the shoe must have been a brave and determined woman. Perhaps she was successful and made it to Alaska. Perhaps she had to turn back in defeat. No one will ever know for sure, but what we do know is that she took part in one of the greatest adventures in the 19th century.

51. The ordinary woman's leather shoe is considered unusual because _____.
   (A) it was an important clue to life in the past
   (B) it was found near a famous trail
   (C) it at one time belonged to a VIP
   (D) it was a fashionable shoe at that time

52. According to this passage, many people who went to Alaska _____.
   (A) eventually became millionaires
   (B) brought with them many shoes
   (C) had conflicts with the Eskimos
   (D) were not properly equipped

53. The Canadian government made gold seekers bring one year's supplies with them so that _____.
    (A) they would not die of hunger and cold
    (B) the army would have enough food for fighting a war
    (C) they could trade these goods with the Eskimos
    (D) the supplies would make Alaska prosperous

54. No matter what happened to the woman who owned the shoe, _____.
    (A) she must have lived a happy life
    (B) she certainly dropped the shoe on purpose
    (C) her adventurous spirit is definitely admirable
    (D) her other shoes were equally fashionable

55. The author of this passage would like us to remember that _____.
    (A) "gold fever" was not worth the lives of many people
    (B) simple objects can stimulate our imagination
    (C) lost shoes should be sent to museums for exhibition
    (D) Alaska was not a place suitable for making a living

第貳部份：非選擇題

一、簡答題（10％）

說明： 1. 閱讀下面這篇文章，然後簡答下列問題。答案必須寫在「答案卷」上。

2. 請依序作答，並標明題號，答案應簡明扼要，不必用完整句，最多三個英文單詞（words）。每題 2 分，共 10 分。注意：請勿抄下整句或整行，否則不予記分。

Every time we watch apes in their cages we are startled by their manlike behavior. The monkey house has a strange fascination. The visitors would be even more startled if they were fully aware of all the existing similarities between them and these animals. These include not only external behavior, but also all the organs, the whole skeleton, every single bone and tooth. The brain of a chimpanzee has the same internal structure and on its surface the same pattern of folds as the human brain, which, however, is three times as large. The way the mother chimpanzee nurses its young is not unlike that of the human mother. These and thousands of other features point to a blood relationship in the truest sense of the word. This can be clearly demonstrated by comparing the genes of chimpanzees and those of humans: the difference between them is just about 2 percent.

1. Write down two physical similarities between humans and apes.

2. Where is the monkey house most probably located?

3. What is the main difference between a chimpanzee's brain and a human's?

4. What is the most precise way to prove a close blood relationship between humans and chimpanzees?

5. What activity shows that a mother chimpanzee and a human mother are very similar to each other?

二、英文作文（20％）

說明： 1. 依提示在「答案卷」上寫一篇英文作文。

2. 文長 120 字左右。

提示： 請以"Something Interesting about a Classmate of Mine"為題，寫出有關你一位同學的一件趣事。這位同學可以是你任何時期的同學，例如中學、小學或幼稚園的同學。

> ※ 今年這份試題只有一個錯字，即 47 題 (A) 中的 park
> 應改為 Park。

90年度學科能力測驗英文科試題詳解

第壹部分：單一選擇題

一、詞彙與慣用語：

1. (**C**) The ballet dancers' <u>graceful</u> movements delighted all the audience.
   芭蕾舞者<u>優雅的</u>動作，使所有的觀眾看得很高興。
   (A) truthful (ˋtruθfəl) *adj.* 誠實的；真實的
   (B) doubtful (ˋdautfəl) *adj.* 懷疑的；可疑的
   (C) ***graceful*** (ˋgresfəl) *adj.* 優雅的
   (D) helpful (ˋhɛlpfəl) *adj.* 有幫助的；有益的
   ballet (bæˋle) *n.* 芭蕾舞　　movement (ˋmuvmənt) *n.* 動作
   delight (dɪˋlaɪt) *v.* 使高興　　audience (ˋɔdɪəns) *n.* 觀眾

2. (**B**) ***At the closing ceremony of the Olympic Games***, all the athletes <u>waved</u> good-bye to the audience.
   在奧運會的閉幕典禮上，所有的運動員向觀眾揮手道別。
   (A) charm (tʃɑrm) *v.* 使陶醉　　(B) ***wave*** (wev) *v.* 揮手表示
   (C) dare (dɛr) *v.* 敢　　　　　　(D) gaze (gez) *v.* 凝視
   closing (ˋklozɪŋ) *adj.* 閉幕的　　ceremony (ˋsɛrə‚monɪ) *n.* 典禮
   the Olympic Games 奧林匹克運動會　　athlete (ˋæθlit) *n.* 運動員

3. (**D**) The drug problem is universal. It is not <u>restricted</u> to one country.
   毒品問題非常普遍，並不僅<u>限</u>於一個國家。
   (A) protect (prəˋtɛkt) *v.* 保護
   (B) detect (dɪˋtɛkt) *v.* 偵測
   (C) admit (ədˋmɪt) *v.* 承認
   (D) ***restrict*** (rɪˋstrɪkt) *v.* 限制；限定
   drug (drʌg) *n.* 毒品　　universal (‚junəˋvɝsḷ) *adj.* 普遍的

4. (**C**) I think *that* this new program will be <u>worthy</u> of your effort.
我認為這個新計劃非常<u>值得</u>你努力。

    (A) cautious（'kɔʃəs）*adj.* 小心的

    (B) fruitful（'frutfəl）*adj.* 成果豐碩的

    (C) *worthy*（'wɝðɪ）*adj.* 值得的＜*of*＞

    (D) patient（'peʃənt）*adj.* 有耐心的

    program（'progræm）*n.* 計劃   effort（'ɛfɚt）*n.* 努力

5. (**A**) This textbook is <u>considerably</u> more difficult to read *than the other one.*

這本教科書讀起來比另一本難<u>很多</u>。

    (A) *considerably*（kən'sɪdərəblɪ）*adv.* 相當地

    (B) favorably（'fevərəblɪ）*adv.* 有利地

    (C) desirably（dɪ'zaɪrəblɪ）*adv.* 合意地

    (D) respectably（rɪ'spɛktəblɪ）*adv.* 高尚地

    textbook（'tɛkst,bʊk）*n.* 教科書

6. (**B**) The <u>intensity</u> *of Linda's love for music* made her fly to Vienna *to enter a music school.*

琳達對音樂有<u>強烈</u>的喜愛，所以她搭飛機前往維也納，進入一所音樂學校就讀。

    (A) quantity（'kwɑntətɪ）*n.* 數量

    (B) *intensity*（ɪn'tɛnsətɪ）*n.* 強烈

    (C) creativity（,krie'tɪvətɪ）*n.* 創造力

    (D) formality（fɔr'mælətɪ）*n.* 拘泥形式

    Vienna（vɪ'ɛnə）*n.* 維也納

    fly（flaɪ）*v.* 搭飛機

7. (**A**) E-mail plays a <u>vital</u> role *in modern communication.*
   電子郵件在現代通訊中，扮演<u>非常重要</u>的角色。

   (A) *vital* ('vaɪtl̩) *adj.* 非常重要的
   (B) violent ('vaɪələnt) *adj.* 暴力的
   (C) vivid ('vɪvɪd) *adj.* 生動的
   (D) various ('vɛrɪəs) *adj.* 各式各樣的
   e-mail ('i,mel) *n.* 電子郵件　　role (rol) *n.* 角色
   communication (kə,mjunə'keʃən) *n.* 通訊

8. (**A**) I <u>*basically*</u> accept your plan, *but* I think it should be

   somewhat reworded.
   <u>基本上</u>，我同意你的計畫，但是我認為它應該要稍微改寫一下。

   (A) *basically* ('besɪkl̩ɪ) *adv.* 基本上
   (B) leisurely ('liʒə·lɪ) *adv.* 悠閒地；從容不迫地
   (C) modestly ('mɑdɪstlɪ) *adv.* 謙虛地
   (D) properly ('prɑpə·lɪ) *adv.* 適當地
   accept (ək'sɛpt) *v.* 接受　　somewhat ('sʌm,hwɑt) *adv.* 稍微
   reword (ri'wɝd) *v.* 改寫

9. (**C**) This poem may be <u>interpreted</u> *in several different ways* *and*

   each *of them* makes sense.
   這首詩可以用好幾種不同的方式來<u>解釋</u>，而且每一種方式都說得通。

   (A) negotiate (nɪ'goʃɪ,et) *v.* 談判
   (B) designate ('dɛzɪg,net) *v.* 標明；指派
   (C) *interpret* (ɪn'tɝprɪt) *v.* 解釋
   (D) substitute ('sʌbstə,tjut) *v.* 代替
   make sense 說得通；有道理

10. (**D**) The <u>texture</u> of this piece of cloth is too coarse. Do you have a finer one?

　　這塊布的<u>質地</u>太粗糙了。你有比較細緻的布嗎？

　　(A) content〔'kɑntɛnt〕*n.* 內容　　(B) display〔dɪ'sple〕*n.* 展示

　　(C) extent〔ɪk'stɛnt〕*n.* 程度　　(D) ***texture***〔'tɛkstʃɚ〕*n.* 質地

　　cloth〔klɔθ〕*n.* 布　　coarse〔kors〕*adj.* 粗糙的

　　fine〔faɪn〕*adj.* 細緻的

11. (**B**) His plan <u>ended up</u> in failure ***though it had been supported***

　　by many people.

　　他的計畫雖然有很多人支持，但<u>結果</u>卻失敗了。

　　(A) hold on 堅持下去；(電話) 不掛斷

　　(B) ***end up*** 結果

　　(C) put away 收拾　　(D) bring about 導致

　　support〔sə'port〕*v.* 支持

12. (**C**) Sara enjoys amusing her friends *by* <u>*making up*</u> *stories.*

　　莎拉喜歡<u>編</u>故事，來娛樂朋友。

　　(A) speak out 大聲說出　　(B) set off 出發

　　(C) ***make up*** 編造　　(D) give away 贈送

　　amuse〔ə'mjuz〕*v.* 娛樂；使高興

13. (**B**) ***As the applause*** <u>*died down*</u>, the curtain on the stage dropped

　　slowly. 當掌聲<u>越來越小聲</u>時，舞台上的幕也緩緩地落下。

　　(A) take off 起飛　　(B) ***die down*** 逐漸消失

　　(C) pass out 昏倒　　(D) stay up 熬夜

　　applause〔ə'plɔz〕*n.* 掌聲

　　curtain〔'kɝtṇ〕*n.* (舞台上的) 幕　　stage〔stedʒ〕*n.* 舞台

14. (**A**) No one can possibly know *in advance* **when** an earthquake *will strike.* 沒有人可能事先知道，地震何時會發生。

 (A) *in advance* 事先　　　　(B) in particular 尤其

 (C) in vain 徒勞無功　　　　(D) in case 以防萬一

 earthquake〔'ɝθ,kwek〕*n.* 地震　　strike〔straɪk〕*v.* 侵襲；突然發生

15. (**D**) The scientist's project *to build a modern laboratory* was called into question *on account of its huge budget.*

 科學家打算建一間現代實驗室的計畫受到質疑，因為預算太過龐大。

 (A) take *sth.* for granted 視某事為理所當然

 (B) start out 出發　　　　(C) get into difficulty 陷入困境

 (D) *call sth. into question* 對某事提出疑問

 project〔'prɑdʒɛkt〕*n.* 計劃　　laboratory〔'læbrə,torɪ〕*n.* 實驗室

 on account of 因為　　huge〔hjudʒ〕*adj.* 龐大的

 budget〔'bʌdʒɪt〕*n.* 預算

二、綜合測驗：

 At times, it seems like there are not many things *that we can give a student* **who** *has everything.* **But** *given* **that** *Christmas is just a few weeks away, here* is a gift idea. Those *who have an inclination for crazy technological advances* aren't hard to please. One simple way is a few new items *that might make life more enjoyable.* They don't look *too* revolutionary, **but** you'd be surprised **how much** *they are capable of.* The following is one *of the items.*

　　有時候，要送禮物給一個什麼都不缺的學生，似乎可送的東西並不多。但是，如果耶誕節再過幾個星期就到了，這裏有個送禮的點子。喜歡瘋狂的、科技進步產品的人，並不難取悅。有個簡單的方法，那就是送一些能使生活更愉快的新產品。它們看起來不是什麼革命性的產品，但你會感到很驚訝，它們具有如此的功能。以下就是其中一項產品。

> ***at times*** 有時候；偶爾（＝*sometimes*）
> away〔ə'we〕*adv.* 離～尚有…時間
> inclination〔,ɪnklə'neʃən〕*n.* 喜好＜*for*＞
> technological〔,tɛknə'ladʒɪkḷ〕*adj.* 科技的
> advance〔əd'væns〕*n.* 進步　　item〔'aɪtəm〕*n.* 物品；項目
> enjoyable〔ɪn'dʒɔɪəbḷ〕*adj.* 愉快的
> revolutionary〔,rɛvə'luʃən,ɛrɪ〕*adj.* 革命性的
> ***be capable of*** 有～能力
> following〔'faləwɪŋ〕*n.* 下列的人、事、物

16.（**A**）***given that*** 表「如果；假定」之意，後可接子句，為連接詞用法。而 (B)、(C)、(D)，則無此用法。

17.（**B**）依句意，「這裏」有個點子，選 (B) ***here***。here 為副詞，置於句首，故其後主詞和動詞須倒裝。(A)、(C) 為代名詞，(D) where 為疑問詞，句意均不合。

18.（**B**）***please***〔pliz〕*v.* 取悅，取悅的受詞為全句的主詞 Those who… advances「凡是…的人」，故本題用不定詞 to please 做主詞補語，選 (B)。本句也可改寫成：It is not hard to please those who… advances.

19.（**C**）「使」生活更愉快，應用使役動詞 ***make***，選 (C)。

20.（**A**）how much 引導名詞子句，做 be surprised 的受詞，而在名詞子句中，how much 又做介系詞 of 的受詞。(C)「What if ＋ 子句？」為疑問句用法，表「如果～怎麼辦？」，(D) such as「例如」，句意、文法均不合。

For a student **who is never on time**, there is the new Projection
21

Alpha Clock. Many ordinary clocks are hard to read *early in the*

morning, deceiving students of the correct time, therefore causing them to
22

be late for school. *Through a projector*, this attractive radio-alarm-clock

is able to display the time *onto a wall, ceiling, or anywhere else*.
23

The benefits include an easier visibility *of the time, and* an alarm

that gets increasingly louder until turned off. It won't *magically*
24

transport a student *to school* *on time every day*, **but** it *just* might

make waking up *a little* easier.
25

　　要送給從不準時的學生，有種新的投影式鬧鐘。許多普通的鐘，在一大早都很難看清楚，害學生們搞不清楚正確的時間，因此使得他們上學遲到。透過投影機，這種很迷人的收音機型鬧鐘，能夠將時間投射在牆上、天花板上，或其他任何地方。它的好處包括，時間比較容易看到，而且它的鬧鈴還會越來越大聲，直到被關掉為止。它不會像變魔術一樣，每天準時把學生送到學校，而只是可能會使起床變得容易一點。

on time 準時　　projection〔 prəˋdʒɛkʃən 〕*n.* 投影
alarm clock 鬧鐘　　ordinary〔ˋɔrdn͵ɛrɪ〕*adj.* 普通的
deceive〔 dɪˋsiv 〕*v.* 欺騙　　projector〔 prəˋdʒɛktɚ 〕*n.* 投影機
attractive〔 əˋtræktɪv 〕*adj.* 迷人的
display〔 dɪˋsple 〕*v.* 顯示（= *show*）　　ceiling〔ˋsilɪŋ〕*n.* 天花板
benefit〔ˋbɛnəfɪt 〕*n.* 好處　　visibility〔͵vɪzəˋbɪlətɪ〕*n.* 能見度
alarm〔 əˋlɑrm 〕*n.* 鬧鈴　　increasingly〔 ɪnˋkrisɪŋlɪ〕*adv.* 逐漸地
magically〔ˋmædʒɪklɪ〕*adv.* 魔法似地
transport〔 trænsˋport 〕*v.* 運送

21.(**D**) 送禮物「給」某人，介系詞用 *for*，選 (D)。而 (A) 一旦，(B) 像，(C) 只是，句意均不合。

22.(**B**) 依句意，搞不清楚時間，「因此」上學遲到，選 (B) *therefore*。而 (A) 雖然，(C) 否則，(D) 然而，句意均不合。

23.(**A**) 時間可以投射在牆上、天花板上，或「其他」任何地方，選 (A) *else*。

24.(**C**) 鬧鈴會越來越大聲，「直到」被關掉「爲止」，選 (C) *until*。until 之後省略了 it is。

25.(**D**) wake up 表「醒來；起床」，使「起床」變得較容易，make 爲動詞，其後應接名詞做受詞，故用動名詞 *waking up* 做受詞，a little easier 爲受詞補語。

三、配合題：

26.(**E**) People *in this village* have carried out many welfare programs.
這個村子裏的人已實施了許多福利計劃。
village ('vɪlɪdʒ) *n.* 村莊   *carry out* 實施
welfare ('wɛl,fɛr) *n.* 福利

27.(**J**) *After his graduation from college*, he found a job *in a computer company*. 他大學畢業後，在一家電腦公司找到工作。
graduation (,grædʒʊ'eʃən) *n.* 畢業

28.(**H**) Ruth is attracted to this new form *of art*.
露絲受到這種新藝術的吸引。
be attracted to 受到~的吸引   form (fɔrm) *n.* 形式

29.(**G**) It has been many years *since I last saw him*.
自從我上次見到他，已經很多年了。
last (læst) *adv.* 上次

30. (**C**) I was taking a walk *in the park* **when** *I met an old friend*

of mine. 我在公園裏散步時，遇到了一位老朋友。

take a walk 散步

四、文意選填：

I had an extraordinary dream *last night. In the dream* the

cloakroom attendant *at a theater* stopped me *in the lobby* **and** insisted

on my <u>leaving</u> my legs *behind.* I was not surprised, **but** I was <u>quite</u>
　　　31　　　　　　　　　　　　　　　　　　　　　　32

annoyed. I said *I had never heard of such a rule at a theater before.*

The man replied **that** he was very <u>sorry</u> about it, **but** people often
　　　　　　　　　　　　　33

complained **that** other people's legs were always in the <u>way</u>. *Therefore,*
　　　　　　　　　　　　　　　　　　　　　　　　　　34

it had been decided **that** people should leave their legs <u>outside</u>.
　　　　　　　　　　　　　　　　　　　　　　　　35

　　昨晚我做了一個很不尋常的夢。在夢裏，戲院寄物處的服務員，在大廳把我攔下來，並堅持要我留下我的腿。我並不驚訝，但我相當生氣。我說，我以前從未聽說過，戲院裏有這樣的規定。那人回答說，他很抱歉，但是客人常常抱怨，其他人的腿總是會造成妨礙。因此，戲院就決定了，人們應該將腿留在外面。

　　　　extraordinary (ɪk'strɔrdn̩ˌɛrɪ) *adj.* 不尋常的
　　　　cloakroom ('klokˌrum) *n.* (戲院、旅館的) 寄物處；衣帽間
　　　　attendant (ə'tɛndənt) *n.* 服務員
　　　　lobby ('lɑbɪ) *n.* 大廳
　　　　annoyed (ə'nɔɪd) *adj.* 生氣的

31. (**C**) *insist on*「堅持」，後須接動名詞。 *leave sth. behind* 把某物留下

32. (**G**) *quite*〔kwaɪt〕*adv.* 相當地，在此修飾 annoyed。

33. (**A**) 依句意，服務員應是向客人道歉，選 (A)。

34. (**J**) *in the way* 妨礙

35. (**B**) 依句意，旅館規定客人要把腿留「在外面」，選 (B) *outside*。

It seemed to me *that* the management had gone beyond their legal right in making this order. *However*, I didn't want to make a disturbance, *so I sat down and* prepared to obey the rule.

It seemed to me *that* the management had gone beyond their legal right in making this order. *Under* normal circumstances, I should have disputed it. *However*, I didn't want to make a disturbance, *so I sat down and* prepared to obey the rule.

對我而言，戲院方面下這樣的命令，似乎已超出了他們的法定權利。在正常的
情況下，我早就該為此事爭辯了。然而，我不想起騷動，所以我坐下來，準
備遵守這項規定。

> management〔'mænɪdʒmənt〕*n.* 管理階層　　legal〔'lig!〕*adj.* 法律的
> right〔raɪt〕*n.* 權利　　order〔'ɔrdɚ〕*n.* 命令；規定
> dispute〔dɪ'spjut〕*v.* 爭論

36. (**F**) normal〔'nɔrml̩〕*adj.* 正常的
　　circumstances〔'sɝkəm,stænsɪz〕*n. pl.* 情況
　　under ~ circumstances 在~情況下

37. (**I**) disturbance〔dɪ'stɝbəns〕*n.* 騷動　　*make a disturbance* 引起騷動

I had *never before* known *that* the human leg could be taken off. I had *always* thought *it was* more securely fixed. *But* the man showed me *how* to undo them, *and* I found *that* they came off quite easily.

The discovery did not surprise me *any more* [*than* the original request
40
that I should take them off.] Nothing *does* surprise one *in a dream.*

我以前從來都不知道，人的腿可以被卸下來。我總是以為它是被牢牢固定住的。
不過那個人示範給我看，如何把雙腿卸下來，而我發現，把腿卸下來還挺容易
的。這項發現，和起初請我把腿卸下來的要求，都沒有使我感到驚訝。在夢裡，
沒有一樣事物會使人驚訝。

> *take off* 脫下；取下　　　undo〔ʌn'du〕v. 脫下；解下
> original〔ə'rɪdʒən̩〕adj. 最初的　　　request〔rɪ'kwɛst〕n. 要求

38. (**D**) securely〔sɪ'kjʊrlɪ〕adv. 牢牢地，在此修飾 fixed「被固定住的」。

39. (**H**) *come off* 脫落

40. (**E**) *not~any more than*… 和…一樣不~ (= *no more~than*…)

五、閱讀測驗：

41–43 題為題組

　　Believe it or not, America's favorite snack food is the potato

chip. There is a story *behind how it was first made.* One might

think *that somewhere a genius thought up the first potato chips,* **but**

it didn't happen *that way.*

　　信不信由你，在美國最受喜愛的零食就是洋芋片。洋芋片最初是如何做出
來的，背後有一個故事。也許有人會認為，是某處有個天才發明出最早的洋芋
片，但事情並不是那樣發生的。

> *believe it or not* 信不信由你
> favorite〔'fevərɪt〕adj. 最喜愛的
> snack〔snæk〕n. 點心；零食　　　*potato chips* 洋芋片
> genius〔'dʒinjəs〕n. 天才　　　*think up* 想出；發明

Picture an elegant restaurant *in Saratoga Springs, New York, in 1853.*
The Moon Lake Restaurant's menu included French-fried potatoes, a
popular food recipe *brought back from France by Thomas Jefferson.*
These were *thickly* cut potatoes, *fried **until** golden brown and crisp*
on the outside.

想像一下，在一八五三年，在紐約州的薩拉托加泉，有一家高級餐廳。月湖餐廳的菜單中，有一樣法式炸薯條，這是湯瑪斯‧傑佛遜從法國帶回來的一道很受歡迎的食物。馬鈴薯被切得厚厚的，炸到表面呈金褐色而且很香脆。

picture〔'pɪktʃɚ〕v. 想像　　elegant〔'ɛləgənt〕adj. 精緻的
Saratoga Springs 薩拉托加泉 (美國紐約州東部一城鎮)
spring〔sprɪŋ〕n. 泉水　　***French-fried potatoes*** 法式炸薯條
recipe〔'rɛsəpɪ〕n. 食譜　　thickly〔'θɪklɪ〕adv. 厚厚地
fry〔fraɪ〕v. 油炸　　crisp〔krɪsp〕adj. 脆的

One evening a guest *in the dining hall* felt ***that*** his potatoes were
*too thick **and*** sent them *back to the kitchen.* The cook sliced some
potatoes thinner *than before **and*** prepared them *for the complaining*
guest. He was *still* not satisfied ***and*** sent them back *again*! *By this*
time the cook was angry ***and*** decided to do *exactly **what** the dinner*
guest *wanted:* slice the potatoes *as thin as possible. Then* they would
be *so* crisp ***that** the diner wouldn't be able to use his fork to eat*
them.

有一天晚上，餐廳裏有位客人覺得，他的馬鈴薯切得太厚了，所以把它們退回廚房。廚師就把一些馬鈴薯切得比以前薄，為那位抱怨的客人重新製作馬鈴薯。那位客人仍然不滿意，並且再度把馬鈴薯退回廚房！這一次廚師生氣了，決定完全按照客人的要求：儘可能地將馬鈴薯切得很薄。這樣一來，馬鈴薯就會非常脆，使得那位客人無法用叉子來吃馬鈴薯。

> **dining hall** 餐廳　　slice〔slaɪs〕v. 切成薄片
> complaining〔kəm'plenɪŋ〕adj. 抱怨的
> **by this time** 這時候　　exactly〔ɪg'zæktlɪ〕adv. 完全地
> diner〔'daɪnɚ〕n. 用餐的人　　fork〔fɔrk〕n. 叉子

When the paper-thin browned potatoes arrived, the diner was pleased.

He was *so* happy *with them* **that** other guests started ordering the

new potatoes. The cook's plan *to stop the dinner guest from*

complaining did not turn out **as** he had planned. *Soon* Saratoga

Chips appeared *on the menu* **and** became *so* popular **that** people

wanted to take some home. The restaurant started selling small

packages *of the potato chips.*

當那些像紙一樣薄、炸成褐色的馬鈴薯送到時，客人非常高興。看他那麼高興，其他的客人也開始點這種新的馬鈴薯。那位廚師原本打算要阻止客人抱怨，結果卻出乎他的意料。很快地，薩拉托加洋芋片就出現在菜單上，而且變得非常受歡迎，有些人甚至會想外帶一些回家。這家餐廳就開始出售小包的洋芋片。

> brown〔braʊn〕v. 炸成褐色　　order〔'ɔrdɚ〕v. 點（菜）
> **turn out** 結果是　　package〔'pækɪdʒ〕n. 包裝

A few years later, they were selling *all over the United States*. *But because the potatoes had to be peeled by hand*, it was a time-consuming chore *and* potato chips were *often* out of stock. *In the 1920s* a mechanical potato peeler was invented *and soon* there were potato chips *in abundance*. They *gradually* spread *all over the world*, *and* have remained popular *ever since*.

幾年後，他們便在全美國各地販售。但是因為馬鈴薯必須用手來削皮，是非常浪費時間的工作，所以洋芋片常常缺貨。在一九二○年代，發明了機械式的馬鈴薯削皮器，所以很快地，就有非常多的洋芋片。洋芋片逐漸風行全世界，而且，從那時起就一直非常受歡迎。

peel〔pil〕*v.* 削皮
time-consuming〔'taɪm kən,sjumɪŋ〕*adj.* 費時間的
chore〔tʃor〕*n.* 雜務　　**out of stock** 缺貨
mechanical〔mə'kænɪkḷ〕*adj.* 機械的　　peeler〔'pilɚ〕*n.* 削皮器
abundance〔ə'bʌndəns〕*n.* 豐富；大量　　**in abundance** 大量地
gradually〔'grædʒuəlɪ〕*adv.* 逐漸地
spread〔sprɛd〕*v.* 散布；變得日益常見
remain〔rɪ'men〕*v.* 仍然　　**ever since** 從那時起

41. (**A**) 根據本文，洋芋片能大量生產，是當
　　(A) 可以用機器來削馬鈴薯皮時。
　　(B) 有很多廚師削馬鈴薯皮時。
　　(C) 對馬鈴薯的需求日益增加時。
　　(D) 它們第一次出現在一家薩拉托加的餐廳時。

mass〔mæs〕*adj.* 大量的　　production〔prə'dʌkʃən〕*n.* 生產
a large number of 很多　　growing〔'groɪŋ〕*adj.* 日益增加的
demand〔dɪ'mænd〕*n.* 需求

42.(**C**) 根據本文，月湖餐廳的廚師
　　(A) 非常喜歡製作洋芋片。
　　(B) 打算在各地出售洋芋片。
　　(C) 想要讓一位正在抱怨的客人停止抱怨。
　　(D) 很高興其他客人喜歡洋芋片。

　　silence〔'saıləns〕v. 使沉默　　pleased〔plizd〕adj. 高興的

43.(**D**) 洋芋片在美國很受歡迎，
　　(A) 已超過兩百年。　　　　　　(B) 是從一九二○年以來。
　　(C) 不超過一百年。　　　　　　(D) 是從十九世紀起。

44-46題為題組

Even though they were written 150 years ago, Alexander Dumas'
action novels *still* excite millions of readers *around the world*, *in
close to a hundred languages.*

　　雖然大仲馬的動作小說是在一百五十年前寫的，但仍然使得全世界數百萬
的讀者感到興奮，這些小說有將近一百種語言的譯本。

　　　　Alexander Dumas 大仲馬（法國小説家及劇作家）
　　　　excite〔ık'saıt〕v. 使興奮　　***close to*** 將近

Dumas's two most famous stories, *The Three Musketeers* **and** *The
Count of Monte Cristo*, have inspired more than 100 films. His 1848
novel, *The Man in the Iron Mask*, was *recently* made into a movie.
In this movie, Leonardo DiCaprio played both King Louis XIV **and**
his twin brother Philippe.

　　大仲馬最有名的兩部小說,「三劍客」和「基督山恩仇記」,是一百多部電影的靈感來源。他一八四八年完成的小說「鐵面人」,最近被拍成電影。在這部電影中,李奧納多·狄卡皮歐一人飾演國王路易十四,和他的孿生弟弟菲利浦,兩個角色。

musketeer〔͵mʌskə'tɪr〕n. 毛瑟槍手　　count〔kaunt〕n. 伯爵
inspire〔ɪn'spaɪr〕v. 給予靈感;促成　　iron〔'aɪən〕n. 鐵
mask〔mæsk〕n. 面具　　twin〔twɪn〕adj. 雙胞胎的

Few people know, *however,* ***that*** *the author was the grandson of a Haitian slave. Even* fewer people know ***that*** *Dumas' father rose rapidly from a soldier to a general in the French Army* ***before*** *he was 31.* The general died young, *leaving Alexander penniless.* ***But*** Dumas overcame poverty, the lack *of formal education,* ***and*** the hardship *of racism to become one of the world's most popular writers.*

　　然而,很少人知道,這位作家是一名海地奴隸的孫子。更少人知道,大仲馬的父親三十一歲前,就在法國軍隊中,從一名士兵,快速晉升爲將軍。這位將軍英年早逝,留下兒子大仲馬,一文不名。但大仲馬克服了貧窮、缺乏正式教育,和種族歧視的艱苦,成爲全世界最受歡迎的作家之一。

Haitian〔'heʃən〕adj. 海地的　　slave〔slev〕n. 奴隸
rise〔raɪz〕v. 升起;晉升　　soldier〔'soldʒə〕n. 士兵
general〔'dʒɛnərəl〕n. 將軍　　army〔'ɑrmɪ〕n. 軍隊
penniless〔'pɛnɪlɪs〕adj. 身無分文的
overcome〔͵ovə'kʌm〕v. 克服
poverty〔'pɑvətɪ〕n. 貧窮　　lack〔læk〕n. 缺乏
hardship〔'hɑrdʃɪp〕n. 艱苦
racism〔'resɪzəm〕n. 種族歧視

Dumas's life *sometimes* was *just* like his action novels. He participated in three revolutions **and** fought *with people* **when** *he was insulted*. *After making a fortune by writing novels*, he built a mansion *outside Paris* **and** kept it open to starving artists, friends, and *even* strangers. *Luckily for his fans*, the mansion has *recently* been restored **and** opened to the public.

  大仲馬的一生，有時就像他的動作小說一樣。他參加過三次革命，當他被人差辱時，也和人打過架。寫小說賺了很多錢後，他在巴黎市郊蓋了一座豪宅，並開放給挨餓的藝術家、朋友，甚至陌生人。對他的書迷來說，很幸運的是，這座豪宅最近已經被修復完成，並開放給大眾參觀。

> participate〔pɑr'tɪsəˌpet〕v. 參加＜ in ＞
> revolution〔ˌrɛvə'luʃən〕n. 革命　　insult〔ɪn'sʌlt〕v. 侮辱；羞辱
> **make a fortune** 發財　　mansion〔'mænʃən〕n. 豪宅
> starving〔'stɑrvɪŋ〕adj. 挨餓的　　luckily〔'lʌkɪlɪ〕adv. 幸運地
> fan〔fæn〕n. 迷　　restore〔rɪ'stor〕v. 修復

44. (**B**) 下列哪一個有關大仲馬的敘述是**錯誤的**？
  (A) 他是種族歧視的受害者。 (B) 他受過良好教育。
  (C) 他是將軍的兒子。   (D) 他是奴隸的孫子。
  victim〔'vɪktɪm〕n. 受害者

45. (**D**) 大仲馬的小說
  (A) 持續不到一百年。   (B) 已被翻譯成一百多種語言。
  (C) 直到最近才廣為大家所接受。 (D) 多年來使讀者非常著迷。
  last〔læst〕v. 持續　　translate〔træns'let〕v. 翻譯
  received〔rɪ'sivd〕adj. 被接受的　　fascinate〔'fæsṇˌet〕v. 使著迷
  ※ 很多考生選 (B)，但文章中第一段 in close to a hundred languages
   是「將近」一百種語言，即「不到」一百種語言。

46. (**C**) 從本文我們可以推論，大仲馬

    (A) 生活過得並不多彩多姿。   (B) 是個用錢很小氣的人。

    (C) <u>是一位慷慨仁慈的人。</u>   (D) 是一位愛好和平的作家。

    infer〔ɪnˋfɝ〕 v. 推論　　***lead a ~ life*** 過~生活

    colorful〔ˋkʌləfəl〕 adj. 多彩多姿的

    keep ~ to oneself 把~留給自己用

    generous〔ˋdʒɛnərəs〕 adj. 慷慨的

    kind-hearted〔ˋkaɪndˋhɑrtɪd〕 adj. 仁慈的

47－50題為題組

Zoe was *just* 2 weeks old *when she was spotted wandering in a village market near Kenya's Tsavo National Park* in December 1995. Zoe's mother had died *and* the baby was left alone. She was no ordinary orphan: she was an elephant. *So* she was trucked to a *most* unusual orphanage *in Nairobi, run by a woman named Daphne Sheldrick.*

    一九九五年十二月，柔依當時只有二個星期大，她在肯亞沙弗國家公園附近村莊的市集裡徘徊時，被人發現。柔依的母親已經死了，留下她孤苦無依。她不是普通的孤兒：她是隻大象。因此，她被用卡車運送到奈洛比一處非常不尋常的孤兒院，那是由一位名叫黛芙妮‧雪菊克的女士所經營的。

    spot〔spɑt〕 v. 發現　　wander〔ˋwɑndə〕 v. 徘徊

    market〔ˋmɑrkɪt〕 n. 市集　　Kenya〔ˋkɛnjə〕 n. 肯亞（東非國家）

    national park 國家公園　　alone〔əˋlon〕 adj. 獨自的

    orphan〔ˋɔrfən〕 n. 孤兒　　truck〔trʌk〕 v. 用卡車運送

    unusual〔ʌnˋjuʒuəl〕 adj. 不尋常的

    orphanage〔ˋɔrfənɪdʒ〕 n. 孤兒院

    Nairobi〔naɪˋrobɪ〕 n. 奈洛比（肯亞的首都）

    run〔rʌn〕 v. 經營；管理

Daphne's husband, *David Sheldrick*, founded Tsavo National Park. Daphne has been working with wild animals *for some 60 years*, **and** *in 1977* she opened the elephant orphanage *at her home in Nairobi.* *As of 1997*, the orphanage, ***which depends on private contributions***, has saved more than 100 infants.

　　黛芙妮的丈夫，大衛·雪菊克，創立了沙弗國家公園。黛芙妮與野生動物在一起，大約已有六十年，在一九七七年，她在故鄉奈洛比，設立了一間大象孤兒院。從一九九七年開始，這家依賴私人捐款的孤兒院，已經拯救了一百多隻小象。

found〔faʊnd〕*v.* 創立　　　wild〔waɪld〕*adj.* 野生的
some〔sʌm〕*adj.* 大約　　　home〔hom〕*n.* 故鄉
as of 從～時候起（*= as from*）
contribution〔͵kɑntrə'bjuʃən〕*n.* 捐款　　　infant〔'ɪnfənt〕*n.* 嬰兒

Zoe was *rather* healthy ***when she was found***, **and** *once under the care of the orphanage* she was *very* happy, *consuming six gallons of vitamin-rich milk a day* **and** *earning a reputation as a confident, naughty and mischievous youngster. After a year in the orphanage with the constant companionship of her human family,* Zoe was taken to a refuge *at Tsavo National Park. There* her keepers have *gradually* introduced her to the ways *of the wild, helping her to find food and water.* Zoe lives *together with other elephant youngsters in a protected area.* It may take some years, ***but*** the final aim is to release all of them *to a wild herd.*

　　柔依被發現時相當健康，並且一受到孤兒院的照顧，便過得很快樂，每天喝六加侖含有豐富維他命的牛奶，成為出了名的有自信、頑皮，而且淘氣的小象。在孤兒院待了一年，得到她的人類家庭持續的陪伴照料後，柔依被帶到沙弗國家公園的一處保護區。在那裡，負責照顧她的人，讓她逐漸熟悉野外的生活方式，幫助她找到食物和水。柔依和其他的小象，一起住在保護區裡。這可能需要幾年的時間，不過最終的目標是，把牠們全部釋放，加入野生的象群中。

rather〔'ræðə〕 *adv.* 相當地　　　consume〔kən'sum〕 *v.* 吃；喝

gallon〔'gælən〕 *n.* 加侖

vitamin-rich〔'vaɪtəmɪn,rɪtʃ〕 *adj.* 含有豐富維他命的

reputation〔,rɛpjə'teʃən〕 *n.* 名聲

confident〔'kɑnfədənt〕 *adj.* 有自信的

naughty〔'nɔtɪ〕 *adj.* 頑皮的　　mischievous〔'mɪstʃɪvəs〕 *adj.* 淘氣的

constant〔'kɑnstənt〕 *adj.* 不斷的

companionship〔kəm'pænjənʃɪp〕 *n.* 同伴之誼

refuge〔'rɛfjudʒ〕 *n.* 動物保護區；避難所

keeper〔'kipə〕 *n.* 飼養者；管理員

introduce〔,ɪntrə'djus〕 *v.* 介紹；使熟悉

together with 和～一起 (= *along with*)

youngster〔'jʌŋstə〕 *n.* 幼小動物

protected area 保護區　　aim〔em〕 *n.* 目標

release〔rɪ'lis〕 *v.* 釋放　　herd〔hɝd〕 *n.* 獸群

Daphne said ***that*** her dream *for the future* is to see ivory banned,

all stored ivory destroyed ***and*** *no one wearing an ivory ornament ever*

again. "There will *always* be competition *for land*," she explained,

"***but*** we can protect elephants *in the parks* ***and*** give the young a

chance."

黛芙妮說，她未來的夢想是看到象牙被禁用，所有貯藏的象牙被銷毀，而且再也沒有人穿戴象牙飾品。「土地的競爭會永遠存在」，她解釋說，「但是我們可以保護公園裡的大象，並給幼象一個機會。」

ivory ('aɪvərɪ) *n.* 象牙　　ban (bæn) *v.* 禁止
stored (stord) *adj.* 貯藏的　　destroy (dɪ'strɔɪ) *v.* 銷毀
ornament ('ɔrnəmənt) *n.* 裝飾品
competition (,kɑmpə'tɪʃən) *n.* 競爭　　***the young*** 幼小動物

47. (**C**) 柔依被用卡車載到大象孤兒院，因爲
　　(A) 沙弗國家公園需要一頭幼象。　　(B) 她找不到回家的路。
　　(C) 她很小就失去了母親。　　(D) 黛芙妮想把她當寵物來飼養。
　　pet (pɛt) *n.* 寵物

48. (**D**) 這間大象孤兒院
　　(A) 是政府資助的。　　(B) 位於沙弗國家公園裡。
　　(C) 是很多種動物的家園。　　(D) 是靠私人的資金經營的。
　　locate (lo'ket) *v.* 使位於　　***be located***~ 位於~
　　operate ('ɑpə,ret) *v.* 經營　　personal ('pɜsn̩l) *adj.* 私人的
　　funds (fʌndz) *n. pl.* 基金；錢

49. (**B**) 在沙弗國家公園，柔依
　　(A) 被放到野生獸群中，接受保護。
　　(B) 被教導適應野外的生活。
　　(C) 被允許在村莊市集遊蕩。　　(D) 一直由她的照顧者陪伴著。
　　adjust (ə'dʒʌst) *v.* 適應 < *to* >　　***in the wild*** 在野外
　　accompany (ə'kʌmpənɪ) *v.* 陪伴

50. (**A**) 根據這篇文章，黛芙妮想要
　　(A) 讓大象在牠們自己的族群裡生活。
　　(B) 儘可能多設立孤兒院。
　　(C) 賣象牙來維持孤兒院。
　　(D) 把柔依送到歐洲或美洲的動物園。
　　set up 設立　　maintain (men'ten) *v.* 維持

51~55題為題組

Every object tells a story. *Even* the *most* ordinary objects can present to us powerful images. *Sometimes* it is the ordinary nature *of these objects that actually* makes them *so* extraordinary. Such is the case with an old leather shoe *in a museum in Alaska.*

　　每一樣東西都訴說著一個故事。即使是最普通的東西，都能給我們強烈的印象。有時候，其實就是這些東西普通的性質，讓它們很特別。在阿拉斯加的一間博物館裏，有一隻舊皮鞋，就是這樣的一個例子。

object ('abdʒɪkt) *n.* 物品；東西
present (prɪ'zɛnt) *v.* 呈現　　powerful ('pauəfəl) *adj.* 強烈的
image ('ɪmɪdʒ) *n.* 形象；印象　　nature ('netʃə) *n.* 性質；本質
actually ('æktʃuəlɪ) *adv.* 事實上　　case (kes) *n.* 情況
***Such is the case with*~**　~的情況就是這樣
leather ('lɛðə) *adj.* 皮製的

At first glance it does not look like much. It is a woman's shoe *of a style popular in the 1890s.* *But what* is unique about this shoe is ***where*** it was found. It was discovered *on the Chilkoot Pass, the famous trail used by the people seeking gold in Alaska.* ***Who*** it *belonged to* **or *why*** it was left there is not known. Was it *perhaps* dropped *by accident* **as the woman climbed up the 1,500 stairs carved out of ice?** ***Or*** did she throw away goods **that she didn't** *need in order to travel lighter?*

第一眼看起來，這隻皮鞋並不怎麼起眼。它是一隻女鞋，是一八九〇年代流行的款式。但是這隻鞋的特色在於它被找到的地方。它是在奇爾庫特山隘被發現的，這是一條著名的小徑，在阿拉斯加，人們走這條路去找尋金礦。這隻鞋是誰的，或為什麼會掉在那裏，都沒有人知道。是不是有位女士在爬上用冰雕刻的一千五百級階梯時，不小心掉下來的呢？或是她為了減輕旅行時的行李，而丟棄不需要的物品呢？

glance〔glæns〕n. 一瞥；看一眼
much〔mʌtʃ〕n. 了不起的東西
style〔staɪl〕n. 款式　　unique〔juˈnik〕adj. 獨特的
pass〔pæs〕n. 山隘　　trail〔trel〕n. 小徑；小路
by accident 意外地　　stair〔stɛr〕n. 階梯
carve〔karv〕v. 雕刻　　goods〔gudz〕n. pl. 物品
light〔laɪt〕adv. 輕快地　　travel light 輕裝旅行

Over 100,000 people *with "gold fever"* made this trip *hoping to become millionaires.* Few of them understood *that* *on their way they* would have to cross a harsh wilderness. *Unprepared for such a dangerous journey,* many died of starvation *and* exposure *to the cold weather.* The Canadian government *finally* started requiring the gold seekers to bring one ton *of supplies with them.* This was thought to be enough *for a person to survive for one year.*

有十萬多個有「淘金熱」的人去了那裏，希望能變成百萬富翁。這些人當中，很少有人了解，途中他們必須通過環境惡劣的荒野。因為沒有為這樣危險的旅程做好準備，很多人因為飢餓，以及暴露於寒冷的天氣中而死亡。加拿大政府最後開始要求這些淘金客，必須隨身攜帶重達一公噸的補給品。一般認為，這樣的份量，足夠一個人存活一年。

fever (ˈfivɚ) n. 狂熱　　***gold fever*** 淘金熱
millionaire (ˌmɪljənˈɛr) n. 百萬富翁
cross (krɔs) v. 越過　　h'arsh (harʃ) adj. (環境、氣候) 惡劣的
wilderness (ˈwɪldɚnɪs) n. 荒野
unprepared (ˌʌnprɪˈpɛrd) adj. 沒有準備的
journey (ˈdʒɜnɪ) n. 旅程　　starvation (starˈveʃən) n. 飢餓
exposure (ɪkˈspoʒɚ) n. 暴露 < to >　　require (rɪˈkwaɪr) v. 要求
seeker (ˈsikɚ) n. 找尋者　　ton (tʌn) n. 公噸
supply (səˈplaɪ) n. 補給品　　survive (səˈvaɪv) v. 存活

They would carry their supplies *in backpacks each weighing up to*
fifty pounds; it *usually* took *at least* 40 trips to get everything *to*
the top and over the pass. ***Whoever*** *dropped the shoe* must have
been a brave and determined woman. *Perhaps* she was successful
and made it *to Alaska*. *Perhaps* she had to turn back *in defeat*. No
one will *ever* know *for sure*, ***but what*** we *do know* is ***that*** *she took*
part in one of the greatest adventures in the 19th century.

他們會把補給品分裝在背包裏帶著，每個背包重達五十磅；通常至少要走四十趟，才能把每樣東西運上山頂，並通過山隘。無論掉落那隻鞋的人是誰，她一定是一位很勇敢，而且很有決心的女士。也許她成功抵達阿拉斯加。也許她失敗了，只好折返。永遠沒有人能確實知道，但我們所知道的是，她曾參加了十九世紀最偉大的冒險之一。

backpack (ˈbækˌpæk) n. 背包　　weigh (we) v. 重～
up to 高達　　pound (paʊnd) n. 磅　　take (tek) v. 需要
trip (trɪp) n. 行程；(一) 趟　　***must have*** + p.p. 當時一定～
brave (brev) adj. 勇敢的　　determined (dɪˈtɜmɪnd) adj. 有決心的
make it 成功；做到　　***turn back*** 折返
defeat (dɪˈfit) n. 失敗　　***for sure*** 確實
take part in 參加　　adventure (ədˈvɛntʃɚ) n. 冒險

51. (**B**) 這隻普通的女用皮鞋被認為很不尋常，是因為
    (A) 它是過去生活的一個重要線索。
    (B) <u>它是在一條有名的小徑附近被發現的。</u>
    (C) 它曾經屬於一位重要人物。
    (D) 它是當時很流行的鞋子。

clue (klu) *n.* 線索　　***at one time*** 一度；曾經
VIP 重要人物 (= *very important person*)
fashionable ('fæʃənəbḷ) *adj.* 流行的

52. (**D**) 根據本文，許多前往阿拉斯加的人
    (A) 最後都變成了百萬富翁。　(B) 隨身攜帶了許多鞋子。
    (C) 和愛斯基摩人起衝突。　(D) <u>沒有適當的裝備。</u>

eventually (ɪ'vɛntʃʊəlɪ) *adv.* 最後　　conflict ('kɑnflɪkt) *n.* 衝突
Eskimo ('ɛskə,mo) *n.* 愛斯基摩人
properly ('prɑpɚlɪ) *adv.* 適當地　　equip (ɪ'kwɪp) *v.* 裝備

53. (**A**) 加拿大政府下令，淘金客必須攜帶一年份的補給品，這樣一來
    (A) <u>他們才不會餓死和冷死。</u>
    (B) 軍隊打仗就有足夠的食物。
    (C) 他們可以用這些商品和愛斯基摩人交易。
    (D) 這些補給品可以讓阿拉斯加繁榮。

trade (tred) *v.* 交易
prosperous ('prɑspərəs) *adj.* 繁榮的

54. (**C**) 無論擁有那隻鞋的女士發生了什麼事，
    (A) 她當時一定過著快樂的生活。
    (B) 她一定是故意使那隻鞋子掉落。
    (C) <u>她愛冒險的精神的確令人欽佩。</u>
    (D) 她其他的鞋子也同樣地流行。

on purpose 故意地　　adventurous (əd'vɛntʃərəs) *adj.* 愛冒險的
spirit ('spɪrɪt) *n.* 精神　　definitely ('dɛfənɪtlɪ) *adv.* 的確
admirable ('ædmərəbḷ) *adj.* 令人欽佩的
equally ('ikwəlɪ) *adv.* 同樣地

55. (**B**) 本文的作者想要我們記住

(A) 「淘金熱」不值得許多人犧牲生命。

(B) 簡單的東西可以激發我們的想像力。

(C) 遺失的鞋子應該被送到博物館展覽。

(D) 阿拉斯加不是一個適合謀生的地方。

worth〔wɝθ〕*adj.* 值得的　　stimulate〔'stɪmjə,let〕*v.* 刺激

exhibition〔,ɛksə'bɪʃən〕*n.* 展覽

suitable〔'sutəbļ〕*adj.* 適合的　　***make a living*** 謀生

第貳部分：非選擇題

一、簡答題

Every time we watch apes in their cages we are startled *by their manlike behavior*. The monkey house has a strange fascination. The visitors would be *even more* startled *if they were fully aware of all the existing similarities between them and these animals*. These include *not only* external behavior, *but also* all the organs, the whole skeleton, every single bone and tooth.

每次看見籠子裏的人猿，我們都會對它們和人類相似的行為感到訝異。猴子展覽館有一種很詭異的吸引力。參觀者如果完全知道，他們自己和這些動物之間，所有的相似之處，會更加驚訝。這些不只包括外在的行為，還包括了所有的器官、整個骨骼架構，以及每一塊骨頭和每一顆牙齒。

ape〔ep〕*n.* 人猿　　cage〔kedʒ〕*n.* 籠子

startle〔'stɑrtļ〕*v.* 使驚訝　　manlike〔'mæn,laɪk〕*adj.* 像人的

monkey house 動物園內的猴子展覽館

fascination〔,fæsn̩'eʃən〕*n.* 魅力　　***be aware of*** 察覺到

existing〔ɪg'zɪstɪŋ〕*adj.* 現存的　　similarity〔,sɪmə'lærətɪ〕*n.* 相似處

external〔ɪk'stɝnļ〕*adj.* 外部的　　organ〔'ɔrgən〕*n.* 器官

skeleton〔'skɛlətn̩〕*n.* 骨骼　　single〔'sɪŋgļ〕*adj.* 單一的

The brain *of a chimpanzee* has the same internal structure **and** *on its surface* the same pattern of folds *as the human brain,* **which,** *however, is three times as large.* The way *the mother chimpanzee nurses its young* is not unlike that *of the human mother.*

黑猩猩的大腦與人腦有相同的內部構造，並且腦部表面的摺層也和人腦一樣，而人腦是黑猩猩腦子的三倍大。母猩猩養育孩子的方式，和人類母親養育孩子的方式並沒有什麼不同。

brain〔bren〕*n.* 腦
chimpanzee〔͵tʃɪmpæn'zi〕*n.* 黑猩猩
internal〔ɪn'tɜnḷ〕*adj.* 內部的
structure〔'strʌktʃɚ〕*n.* 構造　　surface〔'sɝfɪs〕*n.* 表面
pattern〔'pætɚn〕*n.* 型式
fold〔fold〕*n.* 摺層　　nurse〔nɝs〕*v.* 養育

These and thousands of other features point to a blood relationship *in the truest sense of the word.* This can be *clearly* demonstrated *by comparing the genes of chimpanzees* **and** *those of humans:* the difference *between them* is *just about* 2 percent.

　　這些，以及數千個其他的特徵，全都顯示，人類與黑猩猩有真正的血緣關係。藉由比對黑猩猩和人類的基因，這個關係可以明顯地得到證實：兩者的差異大約只有百分之二。

feature〔'fitʃɚ〕*n.* 特徵　　***point to*** 指出；顯示
blood relationship 血緣關係　　sense〔sɛns〕*n.* 意義
in a~sense 從~意義上說　　demonstrate〔'dɛmən͵stret〕*v.* 證明
gene〔dʒin〕*n.* 基因　　compare〔kəm'pɛr〕*v.* 比較

1. 寫出兩種人類與人猿身體上的相似之處。

答：brains and bones

physical〔ˈfɪzɪkḷ〕adj. 身體的

2. 猴子展覽館最可能在哪裏？

答：in the zoo

3. 人腦和黑猩猩的腦，最主要的不同是什麼？

答：the size

4. 要證明人類與黑猩猩之間有相近的血緣關係，最精確的方式是什麼？

答：genetic comparison

precise〔prɪˈsaɪs〕adj. 精確的   close〔klos〕adj. 接近的

genetic〔dʒəˈnɛtɪk〕adj. 基因的

comparison〔kəmˈpærəsn̩〕n. 比較

5. 黑猩猩的母親和人類的母親在哪一方面很相似？

答：nursing of babies / offspring

offspring〔ˈɔf͵sprɪŋ〕n. 後代；子孫

二、英文作文：(參考範例)

Something Interesting about a Classmate of Mine

Something interesting happened to a classmate of mine, Peter, two years ago. This incident was *so* funny and interesting *that* it has left a lasting impression on me. Peter is a normal kid like everyone else, but what had happened to him in class still brings me a good laugh whenever I think about it.

This happened when we were just freshmen. On a sunny afternoon, we were having a lecture on the fine and wonderful history of our great nation. This lesson was important because we needed to know the history of our country, as our teacher said.

However, he had failed to mention that the lesson would be tediously boring. *Needless to say*, all the students were struggling to stay awake. *Halfway through the class*, Peter let out a shriek which scared all of us into wakefulness. With about fifty pairs of eyes on him, Peter tried to look as normal as he could; *however*, it was very hard to conceal his red face. *It turned out that* Peter had dozed off and had fallen onto his pen which he had held inverted.

I was sure that the teachers appreciated the positive aspect which this incident had brought, because after this embarrassing experience, Peter never fell asleep in class again. And I've learned to never hold a pen inverted during a boring class.

incident (ˈɪnsədənt) *n.* 事件　　lasting (ˈlæstɪŋ) *adj.* 持久的
impression (ɪmˈprɛʃən) *n.* 印象
normal (ˈnɔrml̩) *adj.* 普通的；正常的　　lecture (ˈlɛktʃɚ) *n.* 講課
tediously (ˈtidɪəslɪ) *adv.* 令人乏味地　　*needless to say* 不用說
struggle (ˈstrʌgl̩) *v.* 掙扎；努力　　*stay awake* 保持清醒
let out 發出　　shriek (ʃrik) *n.* 尖叫
wakefulness (ˈwekfəlnɪs) *n.* 清醒　　conceal (kənˈsil) *v.* 隱藏
doze off 打瞌睡　　invert (ɪnˈvɝt) *v.* 顛倒
appreciate (əˈpriʃɪˌet) *v.* 感激
aspect (ˈæspɛkt) *n.* 方面　　*positive aspect* 優點

九十年度學科能力測驗（英文考科）大考中心公佈答案

題 號	答 案	題 號	答 案	題 號	答 案
1	C	21	D	41	A
2	B	22	B	42	C
3	D	23	A	43	D
4	C	24	C	44	B
5	A	25	D	45	D
6	B	26	E	46	C
7	A	27	J	47	C
8	A	28	H	48	D
9	C	29	G	49	B
10	D	30	C	50	A
11	B	31	C	51	B
12	C	32	G	52	B
13	B	33	A	53	A
14	A	34	J	54	C
15	D	35	B	55	B
16	A	36	F		
17	B	37	I		
18	B	38	D		
19	C	39	H		
20	A	40	E		

八十九年大學入學學科能力測驗試題
英文考科

第一部份：單一選擇題

一、詞彙與語法：（20%）

說明： 第 1 至 20 題，每題選出最適當的一個選項，標示在答案卡之「選擇題答案區」。每題答對得 1 分，答錯不倒扣。

1. Jack is a ＿＿＿＿ person: he is polite, kind, and always shows respect for others.
   (A) courteous　　(B) handsome　　(C) hateful　　(D) sensitive

2. The traffic in the city was ＿＿＿＿ today, so Jane got home earlier than usual.
   (A) heavy　　(B) weak　　(C) scarce　　(D) light

3. Jonathan had qualified as a doctor but later gave up the ＿＿＿＿ of medicine for full-time writing.
   (A) treatment　　(B) diagnosis　　(C) practice　　(D) consumption

4. Bill was severely punished because he ＿＿＿＿ lied to his mother.
   (A) notoriously　　(B) purposefully　　(C) roughly　　(D) strongly

5. The two security guards will be ＿＿＿＿ from all their duties until further investigation is completed.
   (A) collapsed　　(B) measured　　(C) declared　　(D) suspended

6. He made his instruction ＿＿＿＿ and direct so that everyone could follow easily.
   (A) tentative　　(B) explicit　　(C) plausible　　(D) informal

7. In order for a new product to sell well, manufacturers often invest a large sum of money on its ＿＿＿＿.
   (A) liberation　　(B) promotion　　(C) destruction　　(D) concentration

8. The soldier was put on trial for _____ to obey his commanding officer's order.
   (A) refusing   (B) regretting   (C) resigning   (D) restricting

9. Since Michael was the best candidate, the committee voted _____ for him to take charge of the company's sales department.
   (A) anonymously   (B) drastically
   (C) customarily   (D) unanimously

10. After hiking all day without drinking any water, the students sat down by the stream to quench their _____.
    (A) hunger   (B) energy   (C) thirst   (D) nutrition

11. The more one is _____ the English-speaking environment, the better he or she will learn the language.
    (A) filled in   (B) exposed to   (C) caught on   (D) kept up

12. Peter's sudden death was a great blow to Jane and it took her a long time to _____ the grief.
    (A) put out   (B) come across   (C) go round   (D) get over

13. A person who likes to _____ others is definitely not easy to get along with.
    (A) leave out   (B) let off
    (C) pick on   (D) turn up

14. The old houses will soon be _____ and rebuilt because of the severe damage caused by the earthquake.
    (A) put out   (B) run down
    (C) knocked out   (D) pulled down

15. I'd like to thank you for your hospitality _____ our group.
    (A) on behalf of   (B) instead of
    (C) because of   (D) as a result of

16-20 題為題組

Joe : I see you're busy right now, Sue. As soon as you ___16___, I'd like to talk to you for a few minutes.

Sue : It's O.K. Come on in.

Joe : Oh, no, I don't want to interrupt you. I can wait. I'll come back ___17___.

Sue : I'm afraid it's going to be a long wait!' I'm working ___18___ my history paper.

Joe : History paper? I thought you'd finished it. ___19___ you turn it in on Friday?

Sue : Uh-huh. But the professor just returned it to me. I ___20___ to add 10 more pages.

Joe : Ten more pages! That's a lot. How are you going to do it?

Sue : That's what I'm trying to figure out. Now what can I do for you?

16. (A) finish　　　(B) finished　　(C) are finishing　　(D) will finish
17. (A) later　　　(B) late　　　　(C) latter　　　　　(D) latest
18. (A) by　　　　(B) in　　　　　(C) on　　　　　　(D) along
19. (A) Mustn't　　(B) Needn't　　(C) Couldn't　　　(D) Didn't
20. (A) told　　　(B) was told　　(C) had told　　　(D) had been telling

二、綜合測驗：（20%）

說明： 第 21 至 40 題，每題一個空格。請依文意選出最適當的一個選項，標示在答案卡之「選擇題答案區」。每題答對得 1 分，答錯不倒扣。

21-30 題為題組

　　Basically, there are two kinds of sleep. One is Rapid Eye Movement (REM) sleep. In ___21___, the brain waves of a sleeping person are similar to those of a waking person, and the eyes move about rapidly under the closed lids. ___22___ kind of sleep is Non-Rapid Eye Movement sleep. Scientists have discovered that dreams happen mainly in REM sleep.

Everyone dreams about 20 percent of their sleeping time. __23__ people who say they never dream show about 20 percent of REM sleep. __24__ these "non-dreamers" do their sleeping in a laboratory __25__ researchers can wake them up and ask them whether they were having dreams the moment before, it __26__ that they dream as much as others.

Events in daily life sometimes occur symbolically in dreams. __27__, a boy is having difficulties on the school playground because a bigger boy keeps bullying him. He may dream at night of being alone in the playground, __28__ a lion. At other times the dreaded event from daily life simply occurs in a dream in its real-life form; __29__, the boy dreams of being bullied by the bigger boy.

__30__ scientific research, we have known more about the relationship between sleep and dreams. However, why a dream will take a certain symbolic form is still a mystery.

21. (A) this   (B) each   (C) both   (D) those
22. (A) Other   (B) Another   (C) The other   (D) Others
23. (A) Even   (B) For   (C) Except   (D) Unless
24. (A) If   (B) No matter   (C) No wonder   (D) Although
25. (A) that   (B) where   (C) which   (D) who
26. (A) shows off   (B) crosses out (C) brings up   (D) turns out
27. (A) In general (B) As a result (C) For example (D) In contrast
28. (A) face   (B) faced   (C) facing   (D) to face
29. (A) for instance (B) in addition (C) in a word (D) that is
30. (A) Due to   (B) As far as   (C) In spite of (D) Consisting of

31-35 題為題組

Jane : Hi, Mary. It's been a while. How are you?
Mary : OK, I guess. __31__
Jane : Couldn't be better. By the way, is your house guest still staying with you?
Mary : No. After three weeks, she finally left. __32__

Jane ： So, how did you get rid of her?

Mary ： ___33___ I told her my parents were coming for a visit and I needed the room. I felt bad about it, though. ___34___

Jane ： Oh, I'd have told her to leave after one week. That reminds me. My father-in-law is coming to visit us next week. Can I move in with you for a few days?

Mary ： ___35___

Jane ： Please!

31. (A) It's a small world.　　　　　(B) And you?
　　(C) Thanks a lot.　　　　　　　(D) Where are you going?

32. (A) I look forward to seeing her again.
　　(B) What a shame!
　　(C) We had a great time.
　　(D) Thank goodness!

33. (A) I got no clue.　　　　　　　(B) Well done.
　　(C) Well, I lied to her.　　　　　(D) It's none of your business.

34. (A) What have you done?　　　　(B) What would you have done?
　　(C) What do you think of her?　　(D) What did you do to her?

35. (A) No way.　　　　　　　　　(B) Sure.
　　(C) Big deal!　　　　　　　　(D) Let's check it out.

36-40 題為題組

　　Last Tuesday I took my two nieces, aged three and five, to town in the car. It began to rain heavily so I decided ___36___, while I rushed into a shop. I told the girls I would be back in a few minutes and asked them not to touch anything. Then I locked all the doors and left. I was back at the car in less than five minutes ___37___! I could hardly believe my eyes. The car doors were still locked, the windows tightly shut, and on the back seat were their two jackets. ___38___, I ran to the corner of the street but there was no sign of them. I rushed up to a couple of passers-by and asked in vain whether ___39___. Feeling quite sick with fear, I sat on the driver's seat, trying to stop trembling. Suddenly, behind me I heard a tapping noise and laughter. I jumped out of the car, ran round to open the trunk and there inside ___40___. They had apparently pulled out the back seat, crawled behind it, and then had not been able to push the seat forward again. I almost wept with relief!

36. (A) I would drive them home
    (B) I would take them with me
    (C) I would leave the children in the car
    (D) I would stay in the car with the children

37. (A) and the girls were sitting there
    (B) and the girls had gone home
    (C) but the girls were crying
    (D) but the girls had vanished

38. (A) In a panic
    (B) With delight
    (C) Out of sorrow
    (D) Filled with embarrassment

39. (A) they had seen my car
    (B) there was a shop nearby
    (C) they had seen two small girls
    (D) there was a police station in the neighborhood

40. (A) were two scared and shivering little girls
    (B) were two red-faced and excited children
    (C) was one of the passers-by I had asked
    (D) was nothing at all

三、閱讀測驗：（30%）

說明： 第 41 至 55 題，每題請分別根據各篇文章選出最適當的一個選項，標示
　　　 在答案卡之「選擇題答案區」。每題答對得 2 分，答錯不倒扣。

41-43 題為題組

　　One day Nasreddin borrowed a big pot from his neighbor Ali. The
next day he returned the pot with a small one inside. "That's not mine,"
said Ali. "Yes, it is," said Nasreddin. "While your pot was staying with
me, it had a baby."

　　One week later Nasreddin asked Ali to lend him the pot again. Ali
gladly agreed and waited to see if Nasreddin would again give him back
two pots. One week passed. Then another. In the end, Ali lost patience and
went to demand his pot. "I'm sorry, your pot has died," said Nasreddin.
"Died!" said Ali. "How can a pot die?" "Well, you believed me when I
told you that your pot had a baby, didn't you?"

41. Nasreddin gave Ali an extra small pot in the beginning because ＿＿＿.
　　(A) he and Ali were really good friends
　　(B) he had too many pots at home
　　(C) he wanted to have more baby pots
　　(D) he wanted to trick Ali

42. Why did Ali take Nasreddin's words that his pot had a baby?
　　(A) He had no reason to doubt it.
　　(B) He wanted to keep the small pot.
　　(C) He had seen pots having babies before.
　　(D) He believed in whatever Nasreddin said.

43. It can be inferred that Ali had ＿＿＿ at the end of the story.
　　(A) neither of the pots
　　(B) the big pot
　　(C) the small pot
　　(D) both pots

44-47 題爲題組

Sometimes it is impossible to deliver all the mail that arrives at the post office. Perhaps there is an inadequate or illegible address and there is no return address. The post office cannot just throw the mail away, so it becomes "dead mail." Dead mail is sent to one of the U.S. Postal Service's dead mail offices in Atlanta, New York, Philadelphia, St. Paul, and San Francisco. Seventy-five million pieces of mail can end up in these offices in one year.

The staff of the dead mail offices has a variety of ways to deal with all of these pieces of dead mail. First of all, they look for clues that can help them deliver the mail; they open packages in the hope that something inside will show where the package came from or is going to. Dead mail will also be listed on a computer so that people can call in and check to see if a missing item is there.

However, all of this mail cannot simply be stored forever; there is just too much of it. When a lot of dead mail has piled up, the dead mail offices hold public auctions. Every three months, the public is invited to the offices and bins containing items found in dead mail packages are sold to the highest bidder.

44. Which of the following is NOT mentioned as a way to deal with dead mail?
(A) To search for clues.
(B) To throw dead mail away.
(C) To open dead mail.
(D) To list dead mail on a computer.

45. The staff in a dead mail office may open a package in order to find _____.
(A) some money   (B) some missing objects
(C) an address   (D) a computer

46. The passage indicates that dead mail auctions are held _____.
   (A) once a year   (B) twice a year
   (C) three times a year   (D) four times a year

47. Which is the best title for the passage?
   (A) Dead Mail   (B) Mail Auction
   (C) Unknown Mail   (D) The Dead Mail Office

48-49 題為題組

   I wandered lonely as a cloud
   That floats on high o'er vales and hills,
   When all at once I saw a crowd,
   A host, of golden daffodils,
   Beside the lake, beneath the trees,
   Fluttering and dancing in the breeze.

   Continuous as the stars that shine
   And twinkle on the Milky Way,
   They stretched in never-ending line
   Along the margin of a bay:
   Ten thousand saw I at a glance,
   Tossing their heads in sprightly dance.

48. Where was the poet?
   (A) In a garden.   (B) In a dance hall.
   (C) In the countryside. (D) In a space ship.

49. Which of the following is most likely true about the poet?
   (A) He was a great dancer.
   (B) He liked to be close to Nature.
   (C) He enjoyed the company of people.
   (D) He was a very lonely person.

50-53 題為題組

A linguist is always listening, never off-duty. Once I invited a group of friends round to my house, telling them that I was going to record their speech. I said I was interested in their regional accents, and that it would take only a few minutes. Thus, on one evening, three people turned up at my house and were shown into my front room. When they saw the room they were a bit alarmed, for it was laid out as a studio. In front of each easy chair there was a microphone at head height, with wires leading to a tape-recorder in the middle of the floor. They sat down, rather nervously, and I explained that all I wanted was for them to count from one to twenty. Then we could relax and have a drink.

I turned on the tape-recorder and each in turn solemnly counted from one to twenty in their best accent. When it was over, I turned the tape-recorder off and brought round the drinks. I was sternly criticized for having such an idiotic job, and for the rest of the evening there was general jolly conversation — spoilt only by the fact that I had to take a telephone call in another room, which unfortunately lasted some time.

Or at least that was how it would appear. For, of course, the microphones were not connected to the tape-recorder in the middle of the room at all but to another one, which was turning happily away in the kitchen. The participants, having seen the visible tape-recorder turned off, paid no more attention to the microphones which stayed in front of their chairs, only a few inches from their mouths, thus giving excellent sound quality. And my lengthy absence meant that I was able to obtain as natural a piece of conversation as it would be possible to find.

I should add, perhaps, that I did tell my friends what had happened to them, after the event was over, and gave them the option of destroying the tape. None of them wanted to — though for some years afterwards I was left in no doubt that I was morally obliged to them, in the sense that it always seemed to be my round when it came to the buying of drinks. Linguistic research can be a very expensive business.

50. Why did the author ask his friends to count from one to twenty?

    (A) He wanted them to think that was all he wanted to record.

    (B) He wanted to record how they pronounced numbers.

    (C) He had to check whether his tape-recorder was working.

    (D) He wanted to discover who had the best accent.

51. Why did the author leave the room in the middle of the evening?

    (A) He had to make a phone call to order some drinks.

    (B) He didn't like to be criticized for being idiotic.

    (C) He wanted to turn off a tape-recorder in another room.

    (D) He wanted the others to have a conversation without him.

52. How did the author have the conversation recorded?

    (A) On the tape-recorder in the middle of the floor.

    (B) Through hidden microphones.

    (C) On a tape-recorder in another room.

    (D) In a studio.

53. How did his friends react when the author told them what he had done?

    (A) They wanted him to destroy the recordings he had made.

    (B) They didn't really feel offended.

    (C) They were upset because they felt he had cheated them.

    (D) They made him pay them for the recordings.

54-55 題為題組

    George Bernard Shaw and Winston Churchill apparently disliked each other. It is said that the playwright once sent Churchill two tickets for the opening night of one of his plays, together with a card, which said, "Bring a friend (if you have one)."

    Churchill, however, managed to get the better of this exchange. He returned the tickets, enclosing a note, which said, "I shall be busy that evening. Please send me two tickets for the second night (if there is one)."

    There is no record of whether Shaw ever sent the tickets.

54. What was Shaw trying to say to Churchill on his card?
   (A) Churchill should not go to the play alone.
   (B) Churchill should not bring too many people.
   (C) Churchill may have to waste the two tickets.
   (D) Churchill did not have any friend.

55. Why didn't Churchill want the tickets for the first night?
   (A) He didn't want to take Shaw's insult.
   (B) The theater would not be as crowded the second night.
   (C) He was busy on the first night of the show.
   (D) He couldn't find a friend to go with him the first night.

第二部份：非選擇題

一、簡答題：（10%）

說明： 1. 根據下面這則報導，回答下列問題。答案必須寫在「答案卷」上。
　　　 2. 作答時要標明題號，回答請簡明扼要。每題 2 分，共 10 分。

The Tri Service General Hospital yesterday held a ceremony for 35 children who completed a hospital-sponsored weight-loss program during their summer vacation.

The students lost an average of 2.34 kilograms during the past two months, and the student who lost the most, the nine-year-old Howard Chang, *shed* more than six kilograms.

"My weight dropped to 48.3 from 54.4 kilograms, and my classmates won't be able to call me 'porker' anymore," Chang said happily.

"Howard calculated the calories of everything he ate during his participation in the program," his mother said.

"He would deliberate before eating even a slice of pizza because it has 350 calories," the mother said.

When asked what he most wanted to do following the accomplishment, Chang replied, "Eat at McDonald's."

1. What is the problem common to the children who participated in the program?

2. What do you think the word "shed" means in this passage?

3. Why is Howard Chang specifically mentioned in the passage?

4. Which word in the passage most likely means "to think about something seriously and carefully, especially before making an important decision"?

5. It can be inferred from the passage that Howard will probably gain his weight back again. What is the clue?

二、英文作文：（20%）

說明： 1. 依提示在「答案卷」上寫一篇英文作文。
　　　　2. 文長 120 字左右。

提示： 請寫一篇英文作文，主題為 "Weight Loss"：以你個人或你熟悉的人（朋友、親戚）為例，說明造成這個人體重過重的原因，並提出你認為理想的解決之道。

89年度學科能力測驗英文科試題詳解

第一部分：單一選擇題

一、詞彙與語法：

1. (**A**) Jack is a <u>courteous</u> person: he is polite, kind, **and** *always*
   shows respect *for others*.
   傑克是個<u>有教養的</u>人：他既有禮貌，又親切，而且總是很尊重別人。

   (A) *courteous* (ˈkɝtɪəs) *adj.* 有禮貌的；有教養的（courteous 源自在
   　　宮廷 court 須有禮貌）

   (B) handsome (ˈhænsəm) *adj.* 英俊的

   (C) hateful (ˈhetfəl) *adj.* 憎恨的

   (D) sensitive (ˈsɛnsətɪv) *adj.* 敏感的

   respect (rɪˈspɛkt) *n.* 尊敬

2. (**D**) The traffic *in the city* was <u>light</u> *today*, *so* Jane got home
   earlier than usual.
   今天市區的交通流量<u>不大</u>，所以珍比平常早一點到家。

   (A) heavy (ˈhɛvɪ) *adj.* （交通流量）大的

   (B) weak (wik) *adj.* 虛弱的　　　(C) scarce (skɛrs) *adj.* 稀少的

   (D) *light* (laɪt) *adj.* （交通流量）小的

3. (**C**) Jonathan had qualified as a doctor **but** *later* gave up the
   <u>practice</u> *of medicine for full-time writing*.
   強納森已取得醫生的資格，但後來他為了專心寫作，放棄了開業行醫。

   (A) treatment (ˈtritmənt) *n.* 治療

   (B) diagnosis (ˌdaɪəgˈnosɪs) *n.* 診斷

   (C) *practice* (ˈpræktɪs) *n.* （醫生、律師等的）業務；營業

   (D) consumption (kənˈsʌmpʃən) *n.* 消費

   qualify (ˈkwɑləˌfaɪ) *v.* 取得（專業人員）的資格

   give up 放棄　　full-time (ˈfulˈtaɪm) *adj.* 專任的；全職的

4. (**B**) Bill was *severely* punished ***because*** he *purposefully* *lied to his mother.*

比爾受到嚴厲的處罰，因爲他故意對他母親說謊。

(A) notoriously (no'torɪəslɪ) *adv.* 惡名昭彰地
(B) ***purposefully*** ('pɝpəsfʊlɪ) *adv.* 故意地
(C) roughly ('rʌflɪ) *adv.* 大約；粗暴地
(D) strongly ('strɔŋlɪ) *adv.* 強烈地；極力地

severely (sə'vɪrlɪ) *adv.* 嚴厲地

5. (**D**) The two security guards will be suspended *from all their*

duties ***until*** *further investigation is completed.*

那兩名警衛將被暫時停職，直到更進一步的調查結束爲止。

(A) collapse (kə'læps) *v.* 倒塌
(B) measure ('mɛʒɚ) *v.* 測量
(C) declare (dɪ'klɛr) *v.* 宣布
(D) ***suspend*** (sə'spɛnd) *v.* 使暫停；使停職

security guard 警衛　　duties ('djutɪz) *n. pl.* 職務
further ('fɝðɚ) *adj.* 更進一步的
investigation (ɪn͵vɛstə'geʃən) *n.* 調查

6. (**B**) He made his instruction explicit and direct *so that everyone*

could follow easily.

他讓他的指示非常明確而且直接，使每個人都能很容易地遵循。

(A) tentative ('tɛntətɪv) *adj.* 暫時的
(B) ***explicit*** (ɪk'splɪsɪt) *adj.* 明確的
(C) plausible ('plɔzəbl̩) *adj.* 似眞實的；似合理的
(D) informal (ɪn'fɔrml̩) *adj.* 不正式的

instruction (ɪn'strʌkʃən) *n.* 指示；命令
direct (də'rɛkt) *adj.* 直接的　　follow ('falo) *adj.* 遵從

7. (**B**) *In order for a new product to sell well*, manufacturers *often*
invest a large sum of money *on its promotion*.
為了讓新產品暢銷，製造商常會投資大量的金錢促銷。

(A) liberation (ˌlɪbəˈreʃən) *n.* 解放；釋放
(B) *promotion* (prəˈmoʃən) *n.* 促銷；銷售宣傳
(C) destruction (dɪˈstrʌkʃən) *n.* 破壞
(D) concentration (ˌkɑnsnˈtreʃən) *n.* 集中；專心

manufacturer (ˌmænjəˈfæktʃərə) *n.* 製造業者
invest (ɪnˈvɛst) *v.* 投資

8. (**A**) The soldier was put on trial *for refusing to obey his com-*
manding officer's order.
那名軍人因拒絕服從其指揮官的命令，而被審判。

(A) *refuse* (rɪˈfjuz) *v.* 拒絕　　(B) regret (rɪˈgrɛt) *v.* 後悔
(C) resign (rɪˈzaɪn) *v.* 辭職　　(D) restrict (rɪˈstrɪkt) *v.* 限制

soldier (ˈsoldʒə) *n.* 軍人　　*be put on trial* 被審判
commanding officer （任何自少尉至上校階級之）指揮官

9. (**D**) *Since Michael was the best candidate*, the committee voted
unanimously for him to take charge of the company's sales
department.
因為麥克是最佳人選，所以委員會一致投票贊成他負責管理公司的業
務部。

(A) anonymously (əˈnɑnəməslɪ) *adv.* 匿名地
(B) drastically (ˈdræstɪklɪ) *adv.* 猛烈地；徹底地
(C) customarily (ˈkʌstəmˌɛrəlɪ) *adv.* 習慣上
(D) *unanimously* (juˈnænəməslɪ) *adv.* 全體一致地

candidate (ˈkændəˌdet) *n.* 候選人
committee (kəˈmɪtɪ) *n.* 委員會
vote (vot) *v.* 投票　　*vote for* 投票贊成
take charge of 負責管理　　*sales department* 業務部

10. (**C**) *After hiking all day without drinking any water*, the students sat down *by the stream* to quench their thirst.

學生們徒步旅行了一整天，而且沒喝半滴水，所以就坐在小溪旁解渴。

(A) hunger (ˈhʌŋgɚ) *n.* 餓　　　　(B) energy (ˈɛnɚdʒɪ) *n.* 活力
(C) *thirst* (θɝst) *n.* 渴　　　　(D) nutrition (njuˈtrɪʃən) *n.* 營養
hike (haɪk) *v.* 遠足；徒步旅行　　stream (strim) *n.* 小溪
quench (kwɛntʃ) *v.* 解（渴）

11. (**B**) *The more one is* exposed to *the English-speaking environment*, *the better* he or she will learn the language.

愈常接觸說英文的環境，英文就學得愈好。

(A) fill in 填寫　　　　　(B) *be exposed to* 暴露於；接觸
(C) catch on 了解　　　　(D) keep up 保持

＊the more⋯the better 的用法，詳見文法寶典 p.504。

12. (**D**) Peter's sudden death was a great blow *to Jane* **and** it took her a long time to get over the grief.

彼得的突然去世，對珍而言，是個相當大的打擊，她花了很長的時間，才從悲傷中恢復過來。

(A) put out 熄滅　　　　　(B) come across 偶然遇到
(C) go round 足夠分配　　(D) *get over* 自～中恢復
blow (blo) *n.* 打擊　　　grief (grif) *n.* 悲傷

13. (**C**) A person *who likes to* pick on *others* is *definitely* not easy to get along with. 喜歡批評別人的人，一定很難相處。

(A) leave out 遺漏；刪掉　　(B) let off 放（煙火）
(C) *pick on* 批評　　　　　(D) turn up （把音量）開大聲
definitely (ˈdɛfənɪtlɪ) *adv.* 必定　　*get along with* 相處

14. (**D**) The old houses will *soon* be pulled down and rebuilt *because of the severe damage caused by the earthquake.*

因爲地震造成了嚴重的損害，所以那些舊房子很快就會被拆掉重建。

(A) put out 熄滅

(B) run down （機器）停止；（電池）耗盡

(C) knock out 【拳擊】擊倒

(D) **pull down** 拆除 (= *tear down* = *knock down*)

rebuild (rɪ'bɪld) *v.* 重建　　severe (sə'vɪr) *adj.* 嚴重的

15. (**A**) I'd like to thank you *for your hospitality on behalf of our group.* 我要代表本團感謝您的熱情款待。

(A) **on behalf of** 代表　　(B) instead of 而不是

(C) because of 因爲　　(D) as a result of 由於

hospitality (,hɑspɪ'tælətɪ) *n.* 好客；熱情款待

16~20題

Joe : I see *you're busy right now*, Sue. ***As soon as you finish***, I'd
16
like to talk to you *for a few minutes.*

Sue : It's O.K. Come on in.

Joe : Oh, no, I don't want to interrupt you. I can wait. I'll come
back later.
17

Sue : I'm afraid *it's going to be a long wait*! I'm working on my
18
history paper.

Joe : History paper? I thought *you'd finished it.* Didn't you turn it
        19
      in *on Friday.*

Sue : Uh-huh. **But** the professor *just* returned it to me. I was told
      to add 10 more pages. 20

Joe : Ten more pages! That's a lot. How are you going to do it?

Sue : That's *what I'm trying to figure out. Now* what can I do for you?

喬：蘇，我知道妳現在很忙。妳一忙完我想和妳談幾分鐘。

蘇：沒關係。進來吧。

喬：噢，不用，我不想妨礙妳。我可以等。我待會再來。

蘇：恐怕你會等很久！我正在寫歷史報告。

喬：歷史報告？我還以為妳寫完了。妳不是在星期五就交了嗎？

蘇：嗯，但是教授剛剛把報告退給我。他告訴我要再加十頁。

喬：再加十頁！那麼多啊。妳要怎麼寫？

蘇：我現在正在想。話說回來，你找我有什麼事？

     interrupt〔ˌɪntəˈrʌpt〕 v. 妨礙；打斷　　 ***turn in*** 繳交
     uh-huh〔ˈʌˈhʌ〕 *interj.* 嗯（表示肯定、同意、滿意等的聲音）
     比較 uh-uh〔ˈʌŋˈʌŋ〕 *interj.* 哦（表示否定、不同意等的聲音）
     professor〔prəˈfɛsɚ〕 n. 教授
     add〔æd〕 v. 加　　 ***figure out*** 想出
     now〔naʊ〕 *adv.* （當感嘆詞用）那麼；話說回來

16. (**A**) 表「時間或條件」的副詞子句中，用現在式代替未來式，故選 (A)
      finish。（詳見文法寶典 p.327）

17. (**A**) 依句意，我「待會」再來，選 (A) ***later***〔ˈletɚ〕 *adv.* 稍後；待會。
      而 (B) late〔let〕 *adj.* 遲到的，(C) latter〔ˈlætɚ〕 *n.* 後者，(D) latest
      〔ˈletɪst〕 *adj.* 最新的，則不合句意。

18. (**C**) ***work on*** 從事於

19. (**D**) 全句為過去式，且為疑問否定句，依句意，選 (D) ***Didn't***。

20. (**B**) 依句意，我「被告知」再加寫十頁，故選 (B) ***was told***。

二、綜合測驗：

21-30 題為題組

Basically, there are two kinds *of sleep*. One is Rapid Eye Movement (REM) sleep. *In this*, the brain waves *of a sleeping person*
21
are similar to those *of a waking person*, *and* the eyes move *about rapidly under the closed lids*. The other kind *of sleep* is Non-Rapid
22
Eye Movement sleep. Scientists have discovered *that dreams happen mainly in REM sleep*.

　　基本上，睡眠可分為兩種類型。一種是「眼睛快速移動」（簡稱 REM）型的睡眠。在這種型態的睡眠中，睡著的人的腦波，和清醒的人類似，而且眼睛會在緊閉的眼皮下快速移動。另一種就是「眼睛非快速移動」的睡眠。科學家已經發現，夢主要是發生在 REM 型的睡眠中。

　　　　basically ('besɪkəlɪ) *adv.* 基本上　　rapid ('ræpɪd) *adj.* 快速的
　　　　waking ('wekɪŋ) *adj.* 醒著的　　***move about*** 移動
　　　　closed (klozd) *adj.* 關閉的　　lid (lɪd) *n.* 眼皮 (= *eyelid*)
　　　　mainly ('menlɪ) *adv.* 主要地

21. (**A**) 依句意，在「這種型態的睡眠」中，代名詞用 ***this***，選 (A)。

22. (**C**) 兩者中的一個用 one，另一個則用 ***the other***，選 (C)。而 (A) other
　　　　「其他的」，(B) another「（三者以上）另一個」，(D) others「其他的人或物」，皆不合句意。

Everyone dreams *about 20 percent of their sleeping time*. Even
23
people ***who say they never dream*** show about 20 percent *of REM sleep*.

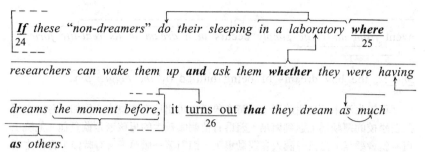

If these "*non-dreamers*" *do their sleeping in a laboratory* *where*
24   25

*researchers can wake them up **and** ask them **whether** they were having*

dreams *the moment before,* it turns out *that* they dream *as* much
26

as others.

　　每個人在睡眠時，有百分之二十的時間是在做夢。即使是聲稱自己從未做過夢的人，也有百分之二十是 REM 的睡眠型態。如果這些所謂「不曾做過夢的人」去實驗室裏睡，在那裏，研究人員可以叫醒他們，問他們剛才是否有做夢，結果就會發現，這些人做的夢，和其他人一樣多。

laboratory (ˈlæbrəˌtorɪ) *n.* 實驗室
researcher (riˈsɝtʃɚ) *n.* 研究人員

23. (**A**) 依句意，選 (A) *Even*「即使」。而 (B) for「爲了」，(C) except「除了～之外」，(D) unless「除非」，均不合句意。

24. (**A**) 依句意，「如果」這些所謂「不曾做過夢的人」能去實驗室裏睡，選 (A) *If*。而 (B) no matter「不論」，(C) no wonder「難怪」，(D) although「雖然」，則不合句意。

25. (**B**) 表地點的關係副詞，用 *where*，引導形容詞子句。其他爲關係代名詞，在形容詞子句中應有位置，須做主詞或受詞等。

26. (**D**) 依句意，選 (D) *turn out*「結果發現」。而 (A) show off「炫耀」，(B) cross out「刪除」，(C) bring up「撫養」，則不合句意。

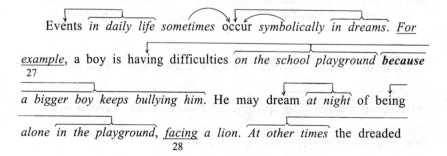

Events *in daily life sometimes* occur *symbolically in dreams.* *For*

example, a boy is having difficulties *on the school playground* *because*
27

a bigger boy keeps bullying him. He may dream *at night* of being

alone *in the playground,* *facing a lion.* *At other times* the dreaded
28

event *from daily life simply* occurs *in a dream in its real-life form*;

that is, the boy dreams of being bullied *by the bigger boy*.
29

　　日常生活中所發生的事，有時會象徵性地出現在夢境中。例如，有個小男孩在學校的運動場上遇到麻煩，因為有位個頭較大的男孩老是欺負他。他晚上可能就會夢見，自己一個人在運動場上，面對著一頭獅子。有時候，日常生活中可怕的事情，會真實地出現在夢境中；也就是說，那男孩會夢到被那個個頭較大的男孩欺負。

> event (ɪ'vɛnt) *n.* 事件
> symbolically (sɪm'bɑlɪkəlɪ) *adv.* 象徵性地
> playground (,ple'graund) *n.* (學校的) 運動場
> bully ('bulɪ) *v.* 欺負
> *at other times* 在別的時候；平常
> dreaded ('drɛdɪd) *adj.* 可怕的
> real-life ('riəl'laɪf) *adj.* 實際生活中發生的；真實的
> *dream of* 夢到

27. (**C**) 依句意，選 (C) *For example*「例如」。而 (A) in general「一般說來」，(B) as a result「因此」，(D) in contrast「對比之下」，則不合句意。

28. (**C**) 兩動詞之間無連接詞，第二個動詞須改為現在分詞，故選選 (C) *facing*「面對」。

29. (**D**) 依句意，選 (D) *that is*「也就是說」。而 (A) for instance「例如」，(B) in addition「此外」，(C) in a word「總之」，則不合句意。

Due to scientific research, we have known more about the
30

relationship *between sleep and dreams. However, **why** a dream will*

take a certain symbolic form is *still* a mystery.

由於科學上的研究，使我們更加了解睡眠和做夢之間的關係。然而，為什麼夢會有某種象徵性的類型，至今仍是個謎。

> **take~form** 有～類型；以～形式
> symbolic〔sɪm'bɑlɪk〕*adj.* 象徵性的　　mystery〔'mɪstrɪ〕*n.* 謎

30.(**A**) 依句意，選 (A) **Due to**「由於」。而(B) as far as「就～而論」，
　　　　(C) in spite of「儘管」，(D) consist of「由～組成」，則不合句意。

<u>31－35題為題組</u>

Jane : Hi, Mary. It's been a while. How are you?

Mary : OK, I guess. <u>And you?</u>
　　　　　　　　　　31

Jane : Couldn't be better. *By the way*, is your house guest *still* staying
　　　　with you?

Mary : No. *After three weeks*, she *finally* left. <u>Thank goodness!</u>
　　　　　　　　　　　　　　　　　　　　　　　　　　　32

Jane : *So*, how did you get rid of her?

Mary : <u>*Well*, I lied to her.</u> I told her *my parents were coming for a*
　　　　　　　　33
　　　　*visit **and*** I needed the room. I felt bad about it, *though*.

　　　　<u>What would you have done?</u>
　　　　　　　　　　34

Jane : Oh, I'd have told her to leave *after one week*. That reminds
　　　　me. My father-in-law is coming to visit us *next week*. Can
　　　　I move in with you *for a few days*?

Mary : <u>No way.</u>
　　　　　35

Jane : Please!

珍　：嗨，瑪麗。好一陣子不見了。妳好嗎？

瑪麗：我想還可以。那妳呢？

珍　：再好也不過了。對了，妳家的那位客人還住在妳家嗎？

瑪麗：沒有。三星期後，她終於走了。感謝老天！

珍　：那妳是怎麼擺脫她的？

瑪麗：嗯，我騙她。我告訴她我父母要來訪，需要房間。不過，我覺得有點
　　　難過。要是妳，妳會怎麼做？

珍　：噢，我一星期就會要她走了。那提醒了我。我公公下星期要來看
　　　我們。我可以搬過去和妳住幾天嗎？

瑪麗：不行。

珍　：拜託！

　　　get rid of 擺脫　　　remind〔rɪ'maɪnd〕v. 提醒
　　　father-in-law〔'faðərɪn‚lɔ〕n. 公公；岳父
　　　（↔ mother-in-law〔'mʌðərɪn‚lɔ〕n. 婆婆；岳母）

31.(**B**)　(A) 世界真小。　　　　　(B) 那妳呢？（= *How about you*?)
　　　　　　(C) 非常感謝。　　　　　(D) 妳要去哪裏？

32.(**D**)　(A) 我期待再次見到她。　(B) 真可惜！（= *What a pity*!)
　　　　　　(C) 我們玩得很愉快。　　(D) 感謝老天！（= *Thank God*!)

33.(**C**)　(A) 我不知道。（= *I don't have a clue.* = *I don't know.*)
　　　　　　(B) 做得好。
　　　　　　(C) 嗯，我騙她。　　　　(D) 少管閒事。

34.(**B**)　(A) 妳做了什麼事？　　　(B) 妳會怎麼做？
　　　　　　(C) 妳認為她如何？　　　(D) 妳對她做了什麼？

　　　　* (B) = What would you have done *if you were me*? (如果妳是
　　　　　　我，妳會怎麼做？)

35.(**A**)　(A) 不行。（= *Nothing doing.*)
　　　　　　(B) 當然可以。
　　　　　　(C) 有什麼了不起！
　　　　　　(D) 我們去看看。

　　　　* ***check out*** 調查；查看

<u>36～40 題為題組</u>

Last Tuesday I took my two nieces, *aged three and five,* *to town* *in the car*. It began to rain *heavily* **so** I decided *I would leave the children in the car*, **while** I rushed into a shop. I told the girls *I*
36
would be back in a few minutes **and** asked them not to touch anything.
Then I locked all the doors and left.

上星期二，我帶著我兩個姪女，一個三歲一個五歲，開車到鎮上。外面開始下大雨，所以我決定把孩子們留車上，而我則衝進一家商店。我告訴小女孩們，我幾分鐘就會回來，要她們不要踫任何東西。然後我把所有的門鎖上，就離開了。

　　aged＋數字　～歲
　　niece〔nis〕*n.* 姪女；外甥女（↔nephew〔'nɛfju〕*n.* 姪子；外甥）
　　rush〔rʌʃ〕*v.* 衝　　lock〔lɑk〕*v.* 鎖

36. (**C**) (A) 我要開車載她們回家　　　　(B) 我要帶她們一起走
　　　　 (C) <u>我要把孩子們留在車上</u>　　(D) 我要和孩子們一起留在車上

I was back at the car *in less than five minutes* **but** the girls had
37
vanished! I could *hardly* believe my eyes. The car doors were *still* locked, the windows *tightly* shut, **and** *on the back seat* were their two jackets. *In a panic*, I ran to the corner *of the street* **but** there was no
38
sign *of them*. I rushed up to a couple of passers-by **and** asked *in vain* **whether** they had seen two small girls. *Feeling quite sick with fear*, I
39
sat *on the driver's seat, trying to stop trembling.*

不到五分鐘,我回到車上,但小女孩們卻消失了!我幾乎不能相信我的眼睛。
車門還是鎖著的,窗戶緊閉,而後座上還有她們的兩件夾克。我驚慌地跑到街
角,但沒有她們的蹤影。我跑去問一些路人,是否看到兩個小女孩,都徒勞無
功。我坐在駕駛座上,覺得非常恐懼,努力想停止顫抖。

tightly (ˈtaɪtlɪ) adv. 緊緊地　　　shut (ʃʌt) v. 關上
sign (saɪn) n. 跡象;足跡　　*a couple of* 幾個
passer-by (ˈpæsɚˌbaɪ) n. 路人　　*in vain* 徒勞無功
sick (sɪk) adj. 心煩意亂的　　tremble (ˈtrɛmbl̩) v. 顫抖

37. (**D**)　(A) 小女孩們還坐在那裏　　　(B) 小女孩們已經回家了
　　　　　　　(C) 但小女孩們正在哭　　　　(D) 但小女孩們卻消失了
　　　vanish (ˈvænɪʃ) v. 消失

38. (**A**)　(A) 驚慌地　　　　　　　　　(B) 高興地
　　　　　　　(C) 由於悲傷　　　　　　　　(D) 非常尷尬
　　　panic (ˈpænɪk) n. 驚慌　　delight (dɪˈlaɪt) n. 高興
　　　sorrow (ˈsɑro) n. 悲傷　　*be filled with* 充滿

39. (**C**)　(A) 他們是否看到我的車　　　　(B) 附近是否有一家商店
　　　　　　　(C) 他們否看到兩個小女孩　　(D) 附近是否有警察局
　　　nearby (ˈnɪrˌbaɪ) adv. 在附近
　　　police station 警察局
　　　neighborhood (ˈnebɚˌhʊd) n. 鄰近地區

Suddenly, ̄*behind me* I heard a tapping noise and laughter. I jumped
out of the car, ran *round to open the trunk* **and** *there inside* were two
red-faced and excited children. They had *apparently* pulled out the
　　　　　　40
back seat, crawled ̄*behind it,* **and then** had not been able to push
the seat *forward again.* I *almost* wept *with relief*!

突然間，在我身後，我聽到一陣輕敲聲和笑聲。我跳下車，跑到車後，打開行李箱，就在那兒，兩個臉紅、興奮的孩子就在裏面。她們顯然是把後座拉開，爬到後面，然後無法把座位再往前推。我幾乎欣慰得哭了出來！

tap〔tæp〕v. 輕敲　　trunk〔trʌŋk〕n.（汽車）行李箱
apparently〔əˈpɛrəntlɪ〕adv. 顯然　　pull〔pʊl〕v. 拉
crawl〔krɔl〕v. 爬　　push〔pʊʃ〕v. 推
forward〔ˈfɔrwəd〕adv. 往前　　weep〔wip〕v. 哭
relief〔rɪˈlif〕n. 欣慰；放心

40. (**B**) (A) 兩個害怕、一直發抖的小女孩
　　　　　 (B) <u>兩個臉紅、興奮的孩子</u>
　　　　　 (C) 一個我曾經問過的路人
　　　　　 (D) 什麼也沒有

scared〔skɛrd〕adj. 害怕的　　shiver〔ˈʃɪvə〕v. 發抖

三、閱讀測驗：

41－43題

One day Nasreddin borrowed a big pot *from his neighbor Ali.*
The next day he returned the pot *with a small one inside.* "That's not mine," said Ali. "Yes, it is," said Nasreddin. "***While your pot was staying with me,*** it had a baby."

有一天，納斯瑞丁向他的鄰居阿里借了一個大鍋子。隔天，他歸還鍋子，裏面還放了一個小鍋子。「那不是我的，」阿里說。「是的，這是你的，」納斯瑞丁說。「你的鍋子在我這裏時，生了一個小鍋子。」

pot〔pɑt〕n. 壺；鍋

One week later Nasreddin asked Ali to lend him the pot *again*.

Ali *gladly* agreed *and* waited to see *if Nasreddin would again give him back two pots*. One week passed. *Then* another. *In the end*, Ali lost patience *and* went to demand his pot. "I'm sorry, your pot has died," said Nasreddin. "Died!" said Ali. "How can a pot die?" "*Well*, you believed me *when I told you that your pot had a baby*, didn't you?"

一個星期之後，納斯瑞丁再次向阿里借鍋子。阿里欣然同意，並等待著，看看納斯瑞丁是否還會再還給他兩個鍋子。一星期過去了。又一個星期。最後，阿里失去耐性，跑去要把鍋子要回來。「很抱歉，你的鍋子死了，」納斯瑞丁說。「死了！鍋子怎麼會死了？」阿里說。「喔，當我告訴你，你的鍋子生了一個小鍋子，你還不是相信了，不是嗎？」。

demand〔dɪˋmænd〕 *v.* 要求

41. (**D**) 納斯瑞丁一開始多給阿里一個小鍋子，是因為
   (A) 他和阿里是非常好的朋友。　(B) 他家裏有太多鍋子。
   (C) 他想要有更多的小鍋子。　(D) 他想要騙阿里。

   trick〔trɪk〕 *v.* 欺騙

42. (**B**) 為什麼阿里會相信納斯瑞丁，說他的鍋子生了一個小鍋子？
   (A) 他沒有理由懷疑。
   (B) 他想要留下那個小鍋子。
   (C) 他以前看過鍋子生小鍋子。
   (D) 他相信納斯瑞丁所說的一切。

43. (**C**) 由此推論，在故事的最後，阿里 ＿＿＿＿＿＿
   (A) 兩個鍋子都沒有。　(B) 有大鍋子。
   (C) 有小鍋子。　(D) 有兩個鍋子。

   infer〔ɪnˋfɝ〕 *v.* 推論

44～47 題為題組

Sometimes it is impossible to deliver all the mail *that arrives at the post office. Perhaps* there is an inadequate or illegible address *and* there is no return address. The post office cannot *just* throw the mail away, *so* it becomes "dead mail." Dead mail is sent to one *of the U.S. Postal Service's dead mail offices in Atlanta, New York, Philadelphia, St. Paul, and San Francisco.* Seventy-five million pieces of mail can end up *in these offices in one year.*

有時候，到達郵局的郵件不可能全部寄得出去。也許是住址寫得不夠詳盡或是難以辨認，而且又沒有寄信人的地址。郵局不能把這種郵件丟掉就算了，所以就變成「無法投遞的郵件」。無法投遞的郵件會被送到美國郵政局，在亞特蘭大、紐約、費城、聖保羅，或舊金山的無法投遞郵件處。每年有七千五百萬份的郵件，最後都來到了這些地方。

deliver〔dɪˈlɪvɚ〕*v.* 遞送　　inadequate〔ɪnˈædəkwɪt〕*adj.* 不足的
illegible〔ɪˈlɛdʒəbļ〕*adj.* 難以辨認的
return address 寄信人的地址　　postal〔ˈpostļ〕*adj.* 郵政的
service〔ˈsɝvɪs〕*n.* 局；處

The staff *of the dead mail offices* has a variety of ways *to deal with all of these pieces of dead mail. First of all*, they look for clues *that can help them deliver the mail*; they open packages *in the hope that* something inside will show *where* the package came from *or is going to.* Dead mail will *also* be listed *on a computer so that* people can call in *and* check to see *if a missing item is there.*

　　無法投遞郵件處裏的工作人員，有各式各樣的方法，來處理所有這些無法投遞的郵件。首先，他們會找尋能幫助他們把郵件寄出去的線索；他們把包裹打開，希望裏面的東西，能透露這個包裹來自哪裏，或要寄往何處。無法投遞的郵件也會被登錄在電腦上，所以人們可以打電話進來，查查是否有他們遺失的物品。

staff〔stæf〕*n*. 全體工作人員
a variety of 各式各樣的（= *various*）
deal with 處理　　　clue〔klu〕*n*. 線索
package〔'pækɪdʒ〕*n*. 包裹　　*in the hope that* 希望～
list〔lɪst〕*v*. 登錄　　missing〔'mɪsɪŋ〕*adj*. 行蹤不明的
item〔'aɪtəm〕*n*. 物品；項目

However, all of this mail cannot *simply* be stored *forever*; there is just too much of it. *When a lot of dead mail has piled up*, the dead mail offices hold public auctions. *Every three months*, the public is invited *to the offices* **and** bins *containing items found in dead mail packages* are sold *to the highest bidder*.

　　然而，這些郵件不能只是永遠存放起來；實在是太多了。當許多無法投遞的郵件堆積如山時，無法投遞郵件處就會舉行公開拍賣。每三個月，民眾會受邀來到這裏，一箱一箱裝著從無法投遞郵件包裹裏取出的物品，就賣給出價最高的人。

store〔stor〕*v*. 儲存　　*pile up* 堆積
auction〔'ɔkʃən〕*n*. 拍賣　　bin〔bɪn〕*n*. 大箱子
bidder〔'bɪdə〕*n*. 出價者

44.(**B**) 下列處理無法投遞的郵件的方法中，何者本文並未提到？
　　(A) 尋找線索。　　　　　　　　(B) 把無法投遞的郵件丟掉。
　　(C) 打開無法投遞的郵件。
　　(D) 把無法投遞的郵件登錄在電腦上。

45. (**C**) 無法投遞郵件處的工作人員可能會打開包裹，以尋找
    (A) 一些錢。　　　　　　(B) 一些失蹤的物品。
    (C) 一個地址。　　　　　(D) 一台電腦。

    object〔ˈɑbdʒɪkt〕n. 物品

46. (**D**) 本文指出，無法投遞郵件的拍賣會
    (A) 一年舉行一次。　　　(B) 一年舉行兩次。
    (C) 一年舉行三次。　　　(D) 一年舉行四次。

47. (**A**) 何者是本文最好的標題？
    (A) 無法投遞的郵件　　　(B) 郵件拍賣
    (C) 未知的郵件　　　　　(D) 無法投遞郵件處

48－49 題為題組

I wandered *lonely as a cloud*	我孤獨地漫步，像一朵
That floats on high o'er vales and hills,	高高飄浮在低谷高山上的雲，
When all at once I saw a crowd,	突然之間我看見一大片，
A host, of golden daffodils,	一大片金色的水仙花，
Beside the lake, beneath the trees,	在湖邊，在樹下，
Fluttering and dancing in the breeze.	在微風中飄動飛舞。

wander〔ˈwɑndɚ〕v. 徘徊；漫步
float〔flot〕v. 飄浮　　　vale〔vel〕n. 山谷（= *valley*）
all at once 突然間（= *suddenly*）
crowd〔kraʊd〕n. 群；堆　　　host〔host〕n. 許多
daffodil〔ˈdæfədɪl〕n. 水仙花
beneath〔bɪˈniθ〕prep. 在～之下
flutter〔ˈflʌtɚ〕v. 飄動　　　breeze〔briz〕n. 微風

Continuous as the stars that shine   持續不斷，像星星閃亮

And twinkle on the Milky Way,   閃爍在銀河上，

They stretched *in never-ending line*   它們延伸永無止境的線

Along the margin of a bay: 沿著海灣邊緣：

Ten thousand saw I at a glance,   我一眼望去有萬朵，

Tossing their heads in sprightly dance.   在快活的舞蹈中搖頭。

continuous ﹝ kənˈtɪnjuəs ﹞ *adj.* 持續的；不斷的
twinkle ﹝ˈtwɪŋkḷ﹞ *v.* 閃爍   *the Milky Way* 銀河
stretch ﹝ strɛtʃ ﹞ *v.* 延伸
never-ending ﹝ˈnɛvəˈɛndɪŋ﹞ *adj.* 永無止境的
margin ﹝ˈmɑrdʒɪn﹞ *n.* 邊緣   bay ﹝ be ﹞ *n.* 海灣
glance ﹝ glæns ﹞ *n.* 看一眼   toss ﹝ tɔs ﹞ *v.* 搖（頭）
sprightly ﹝ˈspraɪtlɪ﹞ *adj.* 快活的

48. (**C**) 作者身在何處？

   (A) 在花園。   (B) 在舞廳。   (C) 在鄉間。   (D) 在太空船。

   dance hall 舞廳   *space ship* 太空船

49. (**B**) 下列關於作者的敘述，何者最可能是真的？

   (A) 他很會跳舞。   (B) 他喜歡親近大自然。
   (C) 他喜歡有人陪伴。   (D) 他是個很寂寞的人。

   company ﹝ˈkʌmpənɪ﹞ *n.* 陪伴

50~53 題為題組

   A linguist is *always* listening, *never* off-duty. *Once* I invited a

group of friends *round to my house, telling them that* I was going to *record their speech.* I said *I was interested in their regional accents,* **and** **that** *it would take only a few minutes. Thus,* on one evening, three people turned up *at my house* **and** were shown into my front room.

語言學家一直都在傾聽，從來不休息。有一次我邀請了一群朋友到我家，並告訴他們我要錄下他們的談話。我說我對他們當地的口音頗感興趣，而整個過程只需要幾分鐘。因此，有一天晚上就有三個人來我家，我便帶他們到客廳去。

linguist〔'lɪŋgwɪst〕 *n.* 語言學家
off-duty〔'ɔf'djutɪ〕 *adj.* 已經下班的　　***invite sb. round*** 請某人過來
regional〔'ridʒənəl〕 *adj.* （特定）地方的　　accent〔'æksɛnt〕 *n.* 口音
turn up 出現　　show〔ʃo〕 *v.* 帶領　　***front room*** 客廳

When *they saw the room* they were *a bit* alarmed, **for** *it was laid out as a studio.* *In front of each easy chair* there was a microphone *at head height,* *with wires leading to a tape-recorder in the middle of the floor.* They sat down, *rather nervously,* **and** I explained **that** *all I wanted was for them to count from one to twenty. Then* we could relax **and** have a drink.

當他們看到客廳時，他們有點不安，因為客廳的擺設，就像一間錄音室。在每張安樂椅前面，都有一個與齊頭的麥克風，而它的電線，是連接到地板中央的錄音機。他們相當緊張地坐下來，接著我向他們說明，我只需要他們從一數到二十。然後我們就能輕鬆地喝一杯。

a bit 有一點　　alarmed〔ə'lɑrmd〕 *adj.* 驚慌的
lay out 佈置；擺設　　studio〔'stjudɪ,o〕 *n.* 錄音室
easy chair 安樂椅　　microphone〔'maɪkrə,fon〕 *n.* 麥克風
wire〔waɪr〕 *n.* 電線　　***lead to*** 通往
rather〔'ræðɚ〕 *adv.* 相當地　　nervously〔'nɝvəslɪ〕 *adv.* 緊張地
count〔kaʊnt〕 *v.* 數　　relax〔rɪ'læks〕 *v.* 放鬆

I turned on the tape-recorder *and* each *in turn solemnly* counted from one to twenty *in their best accent*. *When* it *was over*, I turned the tape-recorder off *and* brought round the drinks. I was *sternly* criticized *for having such an idiotic job, and for the rest of the evening* there was general jolly conversation — spoilt *only by the fact that* I had to take a telephone call *in another room, which* unfortunately *lasted some time*.

我打開錄音機，他們就依序用最好的腔調，非常嚴肅地從一數到二十。當一切都結束之後，我關掉錄音機，並把飲料拿出來。我被嚴厲地批評，說我擁有一個這麼愚蠢的工作，而當晚的其他時間，都是一般愉快的談話 —— 只被一件事破壞，因為我必須去隔壁房間接電話，而不幸的是，那通電話持續了一段時間。

in turn 依序地　　solemnly ('saləmlı) *adv.* 嚴肅地
bring round 拿來　　sternly ('stɜnlı) *adv.* 嚴厲地
criticize ('krɪtə͵saɪz) *v.* 批評　　idiotic (͵ɪdɪ'atɪk) *adj.* 白癡的
jolly ('dʒɑlɪ) *adj.* 愉快的　　spoil (spɔɪl) *v.* 破壞
last (læst) *v.* 持續

Or at least that was *how* it *would appear*. *For*, of course, *the microphones were not connected to the tape-recorder in the middle of the room* at all *but to another one, which was turning happily away in the kitchen*. The participants, *having seen the visible tape-recorder turned off*, paid no more attention to the microphones *which stayed in front of their chairs, only a few inches from their mouths, thus giving*

*excellent sound quality. **And** my lengthy absence meant **that I** was*

*able to obtain as natural a piece of conversation **as it would be***

possible to find.

　或者至少整個情況看起來像是這樣。因為那些麥克風，當然不是連接到房間中央的那台錄音機，而是連接到廚房裏的另外一台，可以很順利地錄音。這幾位參與錄音的人，看到眼前的錄音機被關掉了，就不再留意椅子前面，離他們嘴巴只有幾英吋的麥克風，因此他們就發出絕佳的音質。而我離開這麼久，就意謂著，我能夠取得一段非常自然的談話。

appear〔əˈpɪr〕*v.* 似乎；看起來　　connect〔kəˈnɛkt〕*v.* 連接
turn away（錄音帶）轉動　　happily〔ˈhæpɪlɪ〕*adv.* 順利地
participant〔pɚˈtɪsəpənt〕*n.* 參與者
visible〔ˈvɪzəbl̩〕*adj.* 看得見的　　lengthy〔ˈlɛŋθɪ〕*adj.* 冗長的
absence〔ˈæbsn̩s〕*n.* 缺席　　obtain〔əbˈten〕*v.* 獲得

I should add, *perhaps,* **that I did tell** my friends **what** had happened

to them, **after** the event was over, **and** gave them the option *of*

destroying the tape. None *of them* wanted to — **though** *for some years*

afterwards I was left *in no doubt* **that** I was morally obliged to them,

in the sense **that** it always seemed to be my round **when** it came to the

buying of drinks. Linguistic research can be a *very* expensive business.

　　或許我應該補充說明一下，在整件事結束後，我有告訴朋友們事情的經過，並讓他們選擇是否要銷毀這卷錄音帶。沒有人想要這麼做——雖然之後好幾年，我毫無疑問地覺得，我在道義上對他們有所虧欠，於是就覺得一到了要買飲料的時候，似乎都是我請客。語言學研究也可能是個非常花錢的行業。

add〔æd〕v. 補充說明　　option〔'ɑpʃən〕n. 選擇權
afterwards〔'æftɚwɚdz〕adv. 以後
leave〔liv〕v. 使處於（某種狀態）
in no doubt 無疑地　　　*be obliged to* sb. 感激
morally〔'mɔrəlɪ〕adv. 道德上　　sense〔sɛns〕n. 意義；感覺
round〔raʊnd〕n. 一輪；一回　　*when it comes to* 一提到
linguistic〔lɪŋ'gwɪstɪk〕adj. 語言學的　　research〔'risɝtʃ〕n. 研究

50. (**A**) 為什麼作者要求他的朋友從一數到二十？
    (A) <u>他想讓他們認為那就是他想錄的。</u>
    (B) 他想錄下他們唸數字的發音方式。
    (C) 他必須檢查他的錄音機是否有在運轉。
    (D) 他想要知道誰的口音最好。
    pronounce〔prə'naʊns〕v. 發音

51. (**D**) 為什麼作者在晚上要中途離開房間？
    (A) 他必須打電話叫一些飲料。
    (B) 他不喜歡被人家批評為呆子。
    (C) 他想關掉另一個房間的錄音機。
    (D) <u>他想讓其他人在他不在場時聊天。</u>

52. (**C**) 作者是如何錄下他們的談話？
    (A) 用地板中央的錄音機。　　(B) 用隱藏式麥克風。
    (C) <u>用另外一個房間的錄音機。</u>　(D) 在錄音室裏。
    hidden〔'hɪdn̩〕adj. 隱藏的

53. (**B**) 當作者告訴他的朋友他所做的事，朋友有什麼反應？
    (A) 他們要他銷毀他所錄的音。
    (B) <u>他們其實並不生氣。</u>
    (C) 他們覺得很生氣，因為他欺騙了他們。
    (D) 他們要他為這些錄音付錢。
    recording〔rɪ'kɔrdɪŋ〕n. 錄音　　react〔rɪ'ækt〕v. 反應
    offended〔ə'fɛndɪd〕adj. 生氣的
    upset〔ʌp'sɛt〕adj. 生氣的

54－55 題為題組

George Bernard Shaw and Winston Churchill *apparently* disliked

each other. It is said *that* the playwright once sent Churchill two tickets

for the opening night of one of his plays, together with a card, *which*

said, "*Bring a friend (if you have one).*"

　　喬治‧蕭伯納和溫斯頓‧邱吉爾，兩人顯然互相不喜歡。據說有一次，蕭伯納這位劇作家，送給邱吉爾兩張他的戲劇首演當晚的票，另外還附上一張卡片，上面寫著：「請攜伴參加（如果你有的話）。」

　　　　apparently (əˈpɛrəntlɪ) *adv.* 顯然
　　　　playwright (ˈpleˌraɪt) *n.* 劇作家
　　　　opening (ˈopənɪŋ) *n.* 首演　　　play (ple) *n.* 戲劇

Churchill, *however*, managed to get the better of this exchange.

He returned the tickets, *enclosing a note,* *which* said, "*I shall be*

busy that evening. Please send me two tickets for the second night

(if there is one)."

There is no record *of whether Shaw ever sent the tickets.*

　　不過邱吉爾設法要在這場交鋒中獲勝。他退回這些票，隨函附上一張短箋，上面寫著：「我那晚會很忙。請送我兩張第二天晚上的票（如果有演的話）。」
　　並沒有任何記錄顯示，蕭伯納是否有送出那些票。

　　　　manage (ˈmænɪdʒ) *v.* 設法　　*get the better of* 勝過
　　　　exchange (ɪksˈtʃendʒ) *n.* （言詞激烈、辛辣或詼諧的）交談；交鋒
　　　　enclose (ɪnˈkloz) *v.* 隨函附寄　　note (not) *n.* 短箋

54.(**D**) 蕭伯納在卡片上企圖想對邱吉爾說什麼？

　　　(A) 邱吉爾不該一個人去看戲。

　　　(B) 邱吉爾不該帶太多人來。

　　　(C) 邱吉爾可能會浪費這兩張票。

　　　(D) 邱吉爾沒有朋友。

55.(**A**) 爲什麼邱吉爾不要首演當晚的票？

　　　(A) 他不想接受蕭伯納的侮辱。

　　　(B) 戲院在第二天晚上比較不會那麼擁擠。

　　　(C) 首演那天晚上他很忙。

　　　(D) 首演當晚他找不到朋友陪他去。

　　　insult (ˈɪnsʌlt) n. 侮辱

第二部分：非選擇題

一、簡答題

1－5題

　　The Tri Service General Hospital *yesterday* held a ceremony *for*
35 children **who** *completed a hospital-sponsored weight-loss program*
during their summer vacation.

　　The students lost an average of 2.34 kilograms *during the past*
two months, **and** the student **who** *lost the most, the nine-year-old*
Howard Chang, shed more than six kilograms.

　　"My weight dropped to 48.3 from 54.4 kilograms, **and** my
classmates won't be able to call me 'porker' anymore," Chang
said *happily*.

"Howard calculated the calories *of everything he ate during his participation in the program*," his mother said.

"He would deliberate *before eating even a slice of pizza because it has 350 calories*," the mother said.

When asked what he most wanted to do following the accomplishment, Chang replied, "Eat *at McDonald's*."

　　三軍總醫院昨天為三十五個孩子，舉辦了一場典禮，他們在暑假期間，完成了一項由醫院贊助的減肥課程。

　　在過去的兩個月中，這些學員平均減了 2.34 公斤，九歲的 Howard 張，是瘦最多的學員，他減了六公斤多。

　　「我的體重由 54.4 公斤，降到 48.3 公斤，我的同學再也不能叫我『肥豬』了，」張高興地說。

　　「Howard 參加這個減肥課程期間，他會計算他所吃的每樣東西的卡路里，」他的母親說。

　　「他甚至在吃一片披薩之前，都會考慮再三，因為一片披薩有三百五十卡的熱量，」他的母親說。

　　在被問到達成這項成就後，最想做的事是什麼，張回答：「去吃麥當勞。」

tri- 【字首】表示「三」　　ceremony (ˈsɛrəˌmonɪ) n. 典禮
sponsor (ˈspɑnsɚ) v. 贊助　　average (ˈævərɪdʒ) n. 平均數
shed (ʃɛd) v. 擺脫　　porker (ˈpɔrkɚ) n. 肥豬
calculate (ˈkælkjəˌlet) v. 計算　　calorie (ˈkælərɪ) n. 卡路里
participation (pɑrˌtɪsəˈpeʃən) n. 參與
deliberate (dɪˈlɪbəˌret) v. 慎重考慮　　slice (slaɪs) n. 片
accomplishment (əˈkɑmplɪʃmənt) n. 成就

1. 參與這項課程的小孩，共同的問題是什麼？
　答：The children are all over-weight. (全都體重過重。)

2. 本文中 "shed" 這個字是什麼意思？

答：It means "lose."

3. 爲什麼本文特別提到 Howard 張？

答：Howard lost the most weight.

4. 本文中，那一個字的意思最可能是「仔細愼重地考慮，尤其是在做重要決定時」？

答：deliberate

5. 由本文可以推論，Howard 可能會再次回復之前的體重。線索爲何？

答：He wanted to eat at McDonald's.

二、英文作文：（參考範例）

Weight Loss

Overweight is a common problem for people of all ages and walks of life. *Take* my obese friend Laura *for example*, she eats fast food virtually every day and never fails to include sweets for desserts. *Once* she gets home, she turns into a couch potato. You can hardly get her to move once she sits on her favorite chair and starts devouring a bag of potato chips. *Moreover*, she is too lazy to walk, *not to mention* taking the stairs.

Overweight is not an overnight problem. You cannot simply turn yourself into the likes of Arnold Schwarzenegger or Catherine Zeta Jones *the moment* you decide you want an improved figure. *In other words*, you have to work hard for it. *Although* there are now drugs and clinical methods that claim to help solve the problem of overweight, they are not wonder drugs that promise guaranteed and lasting results. You must have patience, self-discipline and determination if you want to trim down the excess weight. Professionals in this field continue to say that regular exercise, a well-balanced diet, keeping regular hours and avoiding junk food and sweets remain the best way.

overweight（'ovə,wet）*n.* 體重過重　　***walk of life*** 職業

obese（o'bis）*adj.* 極肥胖的　　virtually（'vɝtʃuəlɪ）*adv.* 實際上

fail（fel）*v.* 沒有　　sweets（swits）*n.pl.* 甜食

dessert（dɪ'zɝt）*n.* 甜點　　***turn into*** 變成

couch potato 躺在沙發上看電視的懶人

devour（dɪ'vaur）*v.* 吞食；狼吞虎嚥地吃

potato chips（油炸的）馬鈴薯片　　***not to mention*** 更不用說

take the stairs 爬樓梯　　overnight（'ovə'naɪt）*adj.* 短時間的

the likes of~ 類似~之人或物　　figure（'fɪgə）*n.* 身材

clinical（'klɪnɪkḷ）*adj.* 臨床的　　claim（klem）*v.* 聲稱

wonder drug 仙丹；萬靈藥

guaranteed（,gærən'tid）*adj.* 保證的　　lasting（'læstɪŋ）*adj.* 持久的

self-discipline（'sɛlf'dɪsəplɪn）*n.* 自制

determination（dɪ,tɝmə'neʃən）*n.* 決心

trim（trɪm）*v.* 削減　　excess（ɪk'sɛs）*adj.* 多餘的

field（fild）*n.* 領域　　well-balanced（'wɛl'bælənst）*adj.* 均衡的

diet（'daɪət）*n.* 飲食　　***keep regular hours*** 生活有規律

junk food 垃圾食物

學科能力測驗和大學聯考出題範圍相同，是準
備聯考和中級檢定最佳的資料。因試題不對外
公布重覆出現的比例很高。

心得筆記欄

八十八年大學入學學科能力測驗試題
英文考科

第一部份：單一選擇題

一、字彙與語法：（20%）

說明：　第 1 至 20 題，每題選出最適當的一個選項，標示在答案卡之「選擇題
　　　　第一部份」。每題答對得 1 分，答錯不倒扣。

1. The sentence written on the board is _____. It has more than one meaning.

   (A) ambiguous　　(B) convincing　　(C) elegant　　(D) universal

2. Because Mr. Wang _____ changes his mind, it's very difficult to predict what he will do next.

   (A) additionally　　(B) honorably　　(C) probably　　(D) constantly

3. Many students find it hard to focus on their studies when holidays are _____.

   (A) approaching　　(B) dismissing　　(C) expanding　　(D) presenting

4. During the process of evolution, man has shown remarkable ability to _____ to the environment.

   (A) adorn　　(B) adopt　　(C) adore　　(D) adapt

5. The young scientist showed great _____ for his success. He said that it was as much the result of good luck as his own talent.

   (A) dignity　　(B) modesty　　(C) intensity　　(D) identity

6. Ladies and gentlemen, it is my _____ to speak to you all on this special occasion.

   (A) company　　(B) dignity　　(C) privilege　　(D) eloquence

7. It was a great _____ for his family that he had survived the cold weather in the mountain.

   (A) moral　　(B) promise　　(C) relief　　(D) success

8. The landslide after the typhoon signals that environmental protection _____ our attention.

   (A) accuses   (B) stretches   (C) obtains   (D) deserves

9. Cars in the future will be characterized by their _____ use of gasoline.

   (A) affective   (B) efficient   (C) immediate   (D) traditional

10. Physically, Peter is well-built, yet _____, he is very weak and dependent.

    (A) passionately   (B) relentlessly   (C) emotionally   (D) heartily

11. Kevin is _____, because he broke the living room window this afternoon.

    (A) in control   (B) in trouble   (C) in turn   (D) in vain

12. If all the manufacturers can _____ during this financial crisis, the economy may get better next quarter.

    (A) call up   (B) give in   (C) hang on   (D) let in

13. Don't worry about your grades. Just concentrate on your studies. Hard work often _____ the best in you.

    (A) brings out   (B) gives away

    (C) looks over   (D) splits off

14. The young man owes his success to many people, his parents _____.

    (A) after all   (B) by chance

    (C) on purpose   (D) in particular

15. He was late for the meeting _____ the heavy rain.

    (A) as a result of   (B) in accordance with

    (C) in spite of   (D) apart from

16-20 題為題組

Guest ： My name is Hagen. I'm in room 229. This morning I __(16)__ at 6 o'clock by a telephone call that wasn't for me. Now this is the second time this __(17)__. It's just not good enough! The call was for a Mr. Haugen! Don't you people listen!

Receptionist ： I'm __(18)__ terribly sorry, Mr. Hagen. I will inform the early morning supervisor. She will ensure it doesn't happen again.

Guest ： Well, I hope not! Also, I received this FAX this morning. I've only got the first two pages. __(19)__ should be four more. Didn't anyone check? This is a very important document!

Receptionist ： I __(20)__ apologize, Mr. Hagen. I'll check the FAX office right away. Could I have those two sheets, please?

16. (A) awoke　　(B) woke up　　(C) was woken up　　(D) wakened
17. (A) happens　　　　　　(B) is happening
　　(C) has happened　　　　(D) had happened
18. (A) most　　(B) much　　(C) more　　(D) many
19. (A) They　　(B) These　　(C) Those　　(D) There
20. (A) could　　(B) do　　(C) ought　　(D) may

二、綜合測驗：（20%）

說明： 第 21 至 40 題，每題一個空格。請依文意選出最適當的一個選項，標示在答案卡之「選擇題第一部分」。每題答對得 1 分，答錯不倒扣。

21-30 題為題組

　　Most people like to talk, but few people like to listen. __(21)__ listening well is a rare talent that everyone should treasure. Because they hear more, good listeners __(22)__ to know more and to be more sensitive to what is going on around them than other people. In addition, good listeners are inclined to accept or tolerate __(23)__ to judge and criticize. Therefore, they have __(24)__ enemies than other people. __(25)__, they are probably

the most loved of people. However, there are ___(26)___ to that generality.
For example, John Steinbeck is ___(27)___ to have been an excellent listener,
yet he was hated by some of the people he wrote about. No doubt his
ability to listen contributed ___(28)___ his capacity to write. ___(29)___, the
results of his listening did not make him popular. Thus, ___(30)___ on what
a good listener does, he may become either popular or disliked in his lifetime.

21. (A) Yet   (B) And   (C) Or   (D) So
22. (A) mean   (B) like   (C) tend   (D) act
23. (A) instead of   (B) rather than   (C) in order   (D) in addition
24. (A) little   (B) least   (C) lesser   (D) fewer
25. (A) In contrast   (B) In particular
    (C) In fact   (D) In other words
26. (A) situations   (B) exceptions   (C) perceptions   (D) observations
27. (A) called   (B) named   (C) said   (D) told
28. (A) on   (B) to   (C) for   (D) in
29. (A) Nevertheless   (B) Conversely   (C) Consequently   (D) Moreover
30. (A) depend   (B) depends   (C) depended   (D) depending

31-40 題為題組

It was my first day in this beautiful tropical city. ___(31)___ I was walking
to the beach, a stranger came up to me and tried to shake my hand.

"Don't you remember me, my friend?" he said.

But I couldn't ___(32)___ his face at all. I didn't know a soul in the city.
I had just arrived by plane and still had jetlag.

"I ___(33)___ you at the airport. I work there at the customs. How are
you enjoying our beautiful city?"

I couldn't remember him but I was too ___(34)___ to tell him. He was
so friendly. ___(35)___ he offered to take me to his uncle's seafood restaurant,
just by the beach. I thanked him ___(36)___ but he insisted that we should go
there for dinner.

"You'll love the seafood there," he ___(37)___ me. "And it will be a dinner to remember."

So we went to the restaurant and sat by a window ___(38)___ the bay. The dinner was great indeed, but the coffee they served was quite different. In fact, it tasted very strange…

Anyway, it was not ___(39)___ 10 o'clock the next morning that I finally woke up. But I had no idea where I was. All my money was ___(40)___ and my "friend" had even taken my watch and my shoes!

31. (A) As　　　　　(B) But　　　　(C) Though　　(D) For
32. (A) analyze　　　(B) emphasize　　(C) recognize　　(D) memorize
33. (A) have seen　　(B) saw　　　　(C) had seen　　(D) was seeing
34. (A) exhausted　　(B) interested　　(C) frightened　　(D) embarrassed
35. (A) Even　　　　(B) Then　　　　(C) When　　　(D) While
36. (A) eagerly　　　(B) happily　　　(C) politely　　(D) willingly
37. (A) declared　　　(B) proposed　　(C) responded　　(D) assured
38. (A) overlook　　　(B) overlooking　(C) overlooks　　(D) overlooked
39. (A) before　　　　(B) after　　　　(C) until　　　(D) towards
40. (A) gone　　　　(B) none　　　　(C) no　　　　(D) nothing

三、閱讀測驗：（30%）

說明：　第 41 至 55 題，每題請分別根據各篇文章選出最適當的一個選項，標示在答案卡之「選擇題第一部分」。每題答對得 2 分，答錯不倒扣。

41-44 題為題組

Authors write for many reasons. Often they write about real or make-believe people, places, or events that may be funny, sad, or scary. Sometimes authors write about these things to entertain readers. Authors also write about these things to inform by giving facts or ideas.

The following two paragraphs are examples of these two kinds.

(1) When he finished with unpacking, Nelson carried all the empty boxes down the hallway. On his way to the dump, the bell rang. He needed to hurry. He had no time to go to the dump. Then, he stopped at Adam Joshua's office, which happened to be unlocked, and walked away joyfully. Later in the afternoon, Nelson came to Adam's office with Peter for their biology project. The empty boxes and many other things fell all over them the minute he opened the door. "Adam Joshua!" yelled Nelson, pushing away a basketball and shaking a toy frog off his foot. "This is no way to treat a friend!"

(2) Where the land meets the sea we find seashells. There are many different kinds of shells. They can be round like the moon, long like a jackknife, or shaped like boxes, fans, or tops. The shells we find are usually empty, but once there were soft bodies inside. Animals with hard shells outside and soft bodies inside are called mollusks.

41. What is the best title for this article?
    (A) What's a Friend for
    (B) Seashells and Mollusks
    (C) Appropriate Topics for Writing
    (D) Writing for Different Purposes

42. Regarding the first example, which of the following is FALSE?
    (A) Nelson was not a responsible person.
    (B) Adam and Nelson are military officers.
    (C) Nelson left his empty boxes in Adam's office.
    (D) Adam played a practical joke on Nelson.

43. Which of the following is TRUE according to the first example?
    (A) Nelson and Adam never liked each other.
    (B) Adam didn't know what Nelson put into his office.
    (C) Peter complained to Nelson about the empty boxes.
    (D) Nelson was taught a lesson by Adam.

44. According to the author, the second example is intended to
   (A) express opinions about seashells.
   (B) present facts about seashells.
   (C) show us the beauty of seashells.
   (D) describe the shapes of seashells.

45-48 題為題組

   Kauai, the oldest of the main Hawaiian Islands, has some of the state's most stunning scenery. Rivers and streams flow slowly through jungles of shaded greens. The breathtaking 4,000-foot cliffs of Na Pali Coast rise grandly from the sea. Waimea Canyon, called the "Grand Canyon of the Pacific" by Mark Twain, cuts a deep gash through the rugged central mountains.

   Rising more than 5,000 feet, Mt. Waialeale stands at the center of the nearly round island. This extinct volcano is considered the wettest spot on earth, with almost 500 inches of rainfall each year. Yet this amount of rain is surprisingly localized. Just a few miles west, there's a dry region that receives a mere 6 inches of rain annually.

   The island continues to recover from its 1992 visit from Iniki, the most powerful hurricane to hit Hawaii this century. A few hotels are still being rebuilt, but Kauai remains as beautiful as ever.

   Kauai is not for people who thrive on crowds or nightlife. While it does have its share of resort hotels, shopping centers and good restaurants, and a smattering of museums, art galleries and night spots, its main attractions lie outdoors. Hiking, camping, and scuba diving are excellent on the island.

45. What is the theme of this passage?
   (A) Introduction to a foreign culture.
   (B) Historical background of a region.
   (C) Discussion of environmental problems.
   (D) Geographical information of a place.

46. What is Kauai famous for?
    (A) Cold weather.
    (B) Natural beauty.
    (C) Active volcanoes.
    (D) Amusement parks.

47. What is the rainfall condition of Kauai?
    (A) The rainfall concentrates in some spots.
    (B) It rains a lot except in high mountains.
    (C) There is a lot of rain everywhere most of the year.
    (D) The rainfall changes much with seasons.

48. Which of the following statements is FALSE about the island of Kauai?
    (A) The island of Kauai is almost round in shape.
    (B) The 1992 hurricane caused serious damage to Kauai.
    (C) It is a good place for those who enjoy indoor activities.
    (D) In the center of the island rises a high mountain.

49-50 題為題組

All living things die eventually. In ecological terms, the chemicals of
living things are borrowed from the Earth, and at death they return. All the
material that every animal, from the smallest fly to the largest elephant,
takes in as food also returns to the Earth, as waste matter. The dead
material and waste matter form the diet of a group of living organisms
called decomposers. They include a range of bacteria, fungi, and small
animals that break down nature's wastes into ever smaller pieces until all
the chemicals are released into the air, the soil, and the water, making
them available to other living things. Without the carbon dioxide released
from the process, all plant life would die out. Without the oxygen that
plants give out, and without the food that they supply, life would grind to
a halt and all animals would starve. The decomposers are a vital link in
the natural cycle of life and death.

49. Which of the following statements is NOT true?
   (A) Small living things like bacteria provide food for other living things.
   (B) Carbon dioxide is produced during the process of decomposition.
   (C) Plants are important for supporting the life of animals.
   (D) Decomposers play a minor role in the recycling of nature.

50. According to the passage, death is not the end of life, but rather
   (A) supports many forms of life.
   (B) borrows material from the Earth.
   (C) shows how bacteria become chemicals.
   (D) controls the amounts of soil.

51-55 題爲題組

New York, Nov. 17 — In a swirl of confetti and shredded paper, John Glenn made his second trip through New York's "Canyon of Heroes" in a parade Monday, saluting his return to space 36 years after he became America's first man in orbit.

Glenn's first ticker-tape parade on March 1, 1962, after his Mercury flight, is considered the largest ever in New York. An estimated 3,474 tons of confetti and ticker-tape rained down along a seven-mile route.

For his second parade, despite lunchtime crowds from Wall Street, the turnout Monday was sparse by New York standards and spectators along a route less than a mile long were surprisingly restrained. Police and Glenn's parade was attended by 500,000 — a figure that appeared generously inflated.

The 1962 celebration "was more enthusiastic — a lot more people," said one spectator, who as a young newlywed attended Glenn's first parade and came from her Brooklyn home again for Glenn's second parade.

Another spectator said that too many Americans take the achievements of the space program for granted. "It's become so everyday, so ordinary, nobody cares," he said.

Glenn began the day with decorating the Rockefeller Center Christmas tree. After that event, Glenn recalled the 1962 parade, saying, "It was just so enormous. I remember just a blizzard of paper. You could hardly even look up without getting something in your eye."

Glenn, who retires from the U.S. Senate next month, joins a list of individuals and sports teams honored with more than one ticker-tape parade.

51. This is a report about John Glenn after he
    (A) successfully accomplished his 1962 Mercury flight.
    (B) became the first man to land on the moon.
    (C) was welcomed in New York the second time.
    (D) retired from the U.S. Senate.

52. What impressed Glenn most in the 1962 parade?
    (A) The huge crowd of people around him.
    (B) The huge amount of paper poured over him.
    (C) The Christmas tree in front of the Rockefeller Center.
    (D) The key to the city he received from the mayor.

53. Which of the following statements is TRUE?
    (A) John Glenn is admirable in that he has been to the moon more than once.
    (B) Only John Glenn has received the ticker-tape parade more than once.
    (C) Many Americans are no longer excited about space achievements.
    (D) Glenn's second parade in New York was larger than the first one.

54. According to the passage, how many space flights has Glenn taken?
    (A) One   (B) Two   (C) Three   (D) Four

55. Why does the report say that the figure of Glenn's second parade was "inflated"?
    (A) Because the second parade had a larger crowd than the first parade.
    (B) Because there were many people who attended both parades.
    (C) Because the crowd of the second parade seemed to be far less than 500,000.
    (D) Because the crowd of the second parade was far more enthusiastic.

第二部份：非選擇題

一、簡答題：

說明： 1. 根據下面的求職廣告內容，回答下列問題。注意答案要寫在「答案卷」上。

2. 寫答案時要標明題號，題1與題5的答案用各則廣告的英文字母代號。題2,3,4要寫 job 的名稱。每題2分，共10分。

A

MARKETING PROFESSIONALS

A major US corporation in the health and nutritional industry has announced the opening of its direct selling division in Taiwan.

The company offers the most lucrative compensation plan in the industry and has paid over *$3.5 billion NTD in commissions* in just 6 years in the US. We are a group of top earners.

Applicants should meet the requirements:
(1) Taiwan citizen
(2) Have interest or experience in marketing
(3) Aggressive, energetic, and willing to learn

If you believe you have what it takes to develop this business, please call 2742-6996

B

An international company requires a

Service Technician

To service and maintain electronic medical equipment.

Applicants should possess degree in electronics. The selected candidate will undergo a training program to be conducted by our manufacturer's trained technical personnel.

Interested candidates please apply immediately with resume and mail to P.O. box 594. Or telephone Ms. Chang at 2945-0027 for an immediate interview.

C

Wanted: Reporters & Editors

Qualifications:
% Strong command of English language
% Chinese speaking and reading ability a must
% a university degree
% Journalism education and/or experience a plus

Flexible working hours (30 hours per week)
Good work environment and great co-workers
Medical insurance, etc.

Fax resume and work samples, if any, to
The China Post at (03) 2595-7962.

D

Southeastern Travel Services

OPENINGS ★★★★★★★★★★★★★★★★★★★★★★★★★★★★
TOUR GUIDES

Duties: To conduct escorted tours for foreign visitors; to assist with travel and transportation arrangements.

Qualifications: Good appearance. High school diploma. Good knowledge of English. Outgoing personality.

Call 2703-2172 after 3:00 PM. Ask for Gary.

1. Which advertisements are NOT placed by foreign companies? (Write down the letters representing such advertisements.)

2. Which job has the best benefits in addition to the regular salary?

3. Wendy is good at writing and she doesn't like to work according to a fixed schedule. Which of the four jobs might be more suitable for her?

4. Charles has a strong interest in technology. Which of the four jobs should he apply for?

5. Which advertisement does not need direct contact by making telephone calls? (Write down the letter representing the advertisement.)

二、英文作文：（20%）

說明： 1. 依提示在「答案卷」上寫一篇英文作文。

　　　2. 文長約 120 字。

提示： 根據以上四則求職廣告，寫一篇英文作文。文分兩段：第一段寫出你認為這四種工作中那一種對你而言是最好的工作，並說明理由；第二段則寫出四種工作中你最不可能選擇的工作，也說明理由。假如這四種工作你都不喜歡，則在第一段說明都不喜歡的理由，在第二段寫你喜歡什麼工作，並說明理由。

88年度學科能力測驗英文科試題詳解

第一部分：單一選擇題

一、詞彙與語法：

1. (**A**) The sentence *written on the board* is <u>ambiguous</u>. It has more than one meaning.

   寫在黑板上的句子有點<u>模稜兩可</u>，它不只一個意思。

   (A) ***ambiguous*** 〔 æm'bɪgjuəs 〕 *adj.* 模糊的；模稜兩可的
   (B) convincing 〔 kən'vɪnsɪŋ 〕 *adj.* 有說服力的
   (C) elegant 〔'ɛləgənt 〕 *adj.* 高雅的 (= *graceful* ; *tasteful*)
   (D) universal 〔ˌjunə'vɝsḷ 〕 *adj.* 宇宙的；普遍的

2. (**D**) ***Because Mr. Wang*** <u>constantly</u> ***changes his mind***, it's *very* difficult to predict *what he will do next*.

   因為王先生<u>老是</u>改變主意，所以很難預測他下一步要怎麼做。

   (A) additionally 〔 ə'dɪʃənḷɪ 〕 *adv.* 此外 (= *besides* ; *in addition*)
   (B) honorably 〔'ɑnərəbḷɪ 〕 *adv.* 高尚地；卓越地
   (C) probably 〔'prɑbəblɪ 〕 *adv.* 或許
   (D) ***constantly*** 〔'kɑnstəntlɪ 〕 *adv.* 一直；不斷地

   predict 〔 prɪ'dɪkt 〕 *v.* 預測

3. (**A**) Many students find it hard to focus on their studies *when holidays are* <u>approaching</u>.

   很多學生發現，假期<u>接近</u>時很難專心讀書。

   (A) ***approach*** 〔 ə'protʃ 〕 *v.* 接近
   (B) dismiss 〔 dɪs'mɪs 〕 *v.* 解散；解雇 (= *fire*)
   (C) expand 〔 ɪk'spænd 〕 *v.* 擴張；擴展
   (D) present 〔 prɪ'zɛnt 〕 *v.* 贈送；提出；呈現

   focus on 專心 (= *concentrate on*)

4. (**D**) *During the process of evolution*, man has shown remarkable ability to adapt to the environment.

在演化的過程中，人類展現了適應環境的驚人能力。

(A) adorn〔ə'dɔrn〕*v.* 裝飾（= *decorate*）

(B) adopt〔ə'dɑpt〕*v.* 採用；收養（小孩）

(C) adore〔ə'dor〕*v.* 喜愛；崇拜

(D) ***adapt***〔ə'dæpt〕*v.* 適應；改編

process〔'prɑsɛs〕*n.* 過程　　evolution〔͵ɛvə'luʃən〕*n.* 演化

remarkable〔rɪ'mɑrkəbḷ〕*adj.* 驚人的；了不起的

5. (**B**) The young scientist showed great modesty for his success.

He said *that* it was *as much* the result *of good luck* *as his own talent.*

這位年輕的科學家對他的成功，表現得非常謙虛。他說，除了他自己的天份外，還要靠運氣。

(A) dignity〔'dɪgnətɪ〕*n.* 尊嚴

(B) ***modesty***〔'mɑdəstɪ〕*n.* 謙虛

(C) intensity〔ɪn'tɛnsətɪ〕*n.* 強度；激烈

(D) identity〔aɪ'dɛntətɪ〕*n.* 身分；一致

as much~as… 與…一樣多的~；與…同樣地~

6. (**C**) *Ladies and gentlemen*, it is my privilege to speak to you all *on this special occasion.*

各位先生、各位女士，這是我的榮幸，在這個特殊的場合和你們談談。

(A) company〔'kʌmpənɪ〕*n.* 公司；同伴

(B) dignity〔'dɪgnətɪ〕*n.* 尊嚴

(C) ***privilege***〔'prɪvḷɪdʒ〕*n.* 特權；榮幸

(D) eloquence〔'ɛləkwəns〕*n.* 雄辯；滔滔不絕

occasion〔ə'keʒən〕*n.* 場合

7. (**C**) It was a great <u>relief</u> for his family *that he had survived the cold weather in the mountain.*

得知他從山上的嚴寒天氣中生還，他的家人<u>鬆了一口氣</u>。

(A) moral ('mɔrəl) *n.* 教訓；寓意　*adj.* 道德的

(B) promise ('prɑmɪs) *n.* 承諾；希望

(C) *relief* (rɪ'lif) *n.* 減輕；寬慰

survive (sə'vaɪv) *v.* 從～中生還

8. (**D**) The landslide *after the typhoon* signals *that environmental protection* <u>deserves</u> *our attention.*

颱風後的山崩告訴我們，環境保護<u>值得</u>我們注意。

(A) accuse (ə'kjuz) *v.* 控告；指責

(B) stretch (strɛtʃ) *v.* 伸展；延伸

(C) obtain (əb'ten) *v.* 獲得

(D) *deserve* (dɪ'zɝv) *v.* 應得

landslide ('læn(d),slaɪd) *n.* 山崩　　signal ('sɪgnl̩) *v.* 做信號

9. (**B**) Cars *in the future* will be characterized by their <u>efficient</u> use of gasoline.

未來車的特色將是<u>有效率地</u>使用汽油。

(A) affective (ə'fɛktɪv) *adj.* 感情的

(B) *efficient* (ə'fɪʃənt) *adj.* 有效率的

(C) immediate (ɪ'midɪɪt) *adj.* 立即的

(D) traditional (trə'dɪʃənl̩) *adj.* 傳統的

A *be characterized by* B　A 的特色是 B

10. (**C**) *Physically,* Peter is well-built, *yet* <u>emotionally</u>, he is *very* weak and dependent.

身體上，彼德體格健壯，然而<u>感情上</u>，他很軟弱又依賴人。

(A) passionately ('pæʃənɪtlɪ) *adv.* 熱烈地

(B) relentlessly (rɪ'lɛntlɪslɪ) *adv.* 毫不留情地

(C) *emotionally* (ɪ'moʃənlɪ) *adv.* 感情地

(D) heartily ('hɑrtɪlɪ) *adv.* 誠摯地

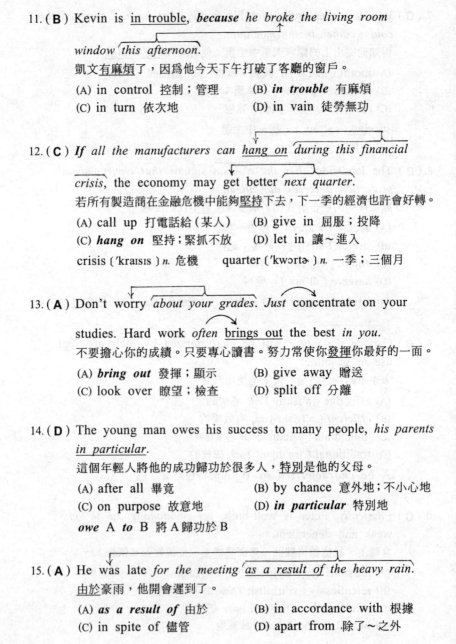

11. (**B**) Kevin is <u>in trouble</u>, ***because*** *he broke the living room window* *this afternoon.*

凱文<u>有麻煩</u>了，因為他今天下午打破了客廳的窗戶。

(A) in control 控制；管理　　(B) ***in trouble*** 有麻煩
(C) in turn 依次地　　(D) in vain 徒勞無功

12. (**C**) ***If*** *all the manufacturers can* <u>hang on</u> *during this financial crisis,* the economy may get better *next quarter.*

若所有製造商在金融危機中能夠<u>堅持</u>下去，下一季的經濟也許會好轉。

(A) call up 打電話給 (某人)　　(B) give in 屈服；投降
(C) ***hang on*** 堅持；緊抓不放　　(D) let in 讓~進入

crisis ('kraɪsɪs) *n.* 危機　　quarter ('kwɔrtɚ) *n.* 一季；三個月

13. (**A**) Don't worry *about your grades.* *Just* concentrate on your studies. Hard work *often* <u>brings out</u> the best *in you.*

不要擔心你的成績。只要專心讀書。努力常使你<u>發揮</u>你最好的一面。

(A) ***bring out*** 發揮；顯示　　(B) give away 贈送
(C) look over 瞭望；檢查　　(D) split off 分離

14. (**D**) The young man owes his success to many people, *his parents in particular.*

這個年輕人將他的成功歸功於很多人，<u>特別</u>是他的父母。

(A) after all 畢竟　　(B) by chance 意外地；不小心地
(C) on purpose 故意地　　(D) ***in particular*** 特別地

owe A ***to*** B 將 A 歸功於 B

15. (**A**) He was late *for the meeting* <u>as a result of</u> *the heavy rain.*

<u>由於</u>豪雨，他開會遲到了。

(A) ***as a result of*** 由於　　(B) in accordance with 根據
(C) in spite of 儘管　　(D) apart from 除了~之外

16－20題

Guest : My name is Hagen. I'm in room 229. This morning I *was woken up* at 6 o'clock by a telephone call *that*
16
wasn't for me. Now this is the second time *this has happened.* It's *just* not good *enough*! The call was for
17
a Mr. Haugen! Don't you people listen!

Receptionist : I'm *most terribly* sorry, Mr. Hagen. I will inform the
18
early morning supervisor. She will ensure *it doesn't happen again.*

客　人：我的名字是哈根，住二二九號房。今天早上六點鐘我就被電話聲吵醒，但不是找我的。到現在已經第二次發生了，實在是不夠好！電話要找一位豪根先生，你們都不會聽話嗎！

接待員：非常抱歉，哈根先生。我會通知早班的值班經理，她會保證這種事不會再發生。

receptionist〔rɪ'sɛpʃənɪst〕n. 接待員
terribly〔'tɛrəblɪ〕adv. 非常地　　inform〔ɪn'fɔrm〕v. 通知
supervisor〔,sjupɚ'vaɪzɚ〕n. 監督者　　ensure〔ɪn'ʃur〕v. 保證

16.（**C**）依句意，我「被電話吵醒」應用被動，選 (C)，wake up 可做不及物動詞，指「（人）醒來」；也可做及物動詞，指「叫醒；吵醒」之意。wake 的三態變化為 wake-woke-woken。(A) awake 的三態變化為 awake-awoke-awoken，(D) waken 的三態為規則變化，(A)(D) 意思、用法均與 wake up 相同，在本題中應改被動才正確。

17.（**C**）依句意，「到現在已經」第二次發生，應用現在完成式，選 (C)。

18.（**A**）I'm terribly sorry. 句中用 most 可加強 terribly 的語氣，等於 very 之意。(B) much 亦可加強語氣，但用於修飾比較級及過去分詞，在此文法不合。

Guest : Well, I hope not! *Also*, I received this FAX *this morning*. I've *only* got the first two pages. There
19
should be four more. Didn't anyone check? This is
a *very* important document!

Receptionist : I *do* apologize, Mr. Hagen. I'll check the FAX office
20
right away. Could I have those two sheets, please?

客　人：嗯，我希望不會。另外，我今天早上收到這份傳眞，可是我只拿到前二頁。應該還有四頁才對。難道沒有人檢查嗎？這是一份很重要的文件！

接待員：眞的很抱歉，哈根先生。我馬上去查傳眞室。請把那兩張給我好嗎？

document〔'dɑkjəmənt〕*n.* 文件　　apologize〔ə'pɑlə,dʒaɪz〕*v.* 道歉
right away 立刻；馬上 (= *at once*)
sheet〔ʃit〕*n.* (紙的) 一張

19. (**D**) 表示「有～」應用 there + be 動詞，選 (D)。

20. (**B**) 助動詞 do, does, did 之後接原形動詞，爲加強語氣用法，譯爲「眞的；的確」。

二、綜合測驗：

21～30題

Most people like to talk, *but* few people like to listen. *Yet*
21
listening *well* is a rare talent *that everyone should treasure.* *Because
they hear more*, good listeners <u>tend</u> to know more *and* to be *more*
22
sensitive to **what is going on around them** *than* other people. *In*

addition, good listeners are inclined to accept or tolerate ***rather than***
　　　　　　　　　　　　　　　　　　　　　　　　　　　　　　23

to judge and criticize. *Therefore*, they have <u>fewer</u> enemies ***than*** other
　　　　　　　　　　　　　　　　　　　24

<u>people</u>. <u>*In other words*</u>, they are *probably* the most loved of people.
　　　　　　　　　　25

　　大部分人都喜歡說話，但很少人喜歡聆聽。然而，聽得好、聽得仔細是個
人人都應珍惜的罕見能力。好的聆聽者因為聽得較多，容易知道較多，也比其
他人對周遭發生的事物更加敏感。此外，好的聆聽者比較容易接受，或容忍別
人的意見，而較不會去判斷，去批評。因此，他們的敵人比其他人少。換句話
說，他們可能是最受人喜愛的人。

　　　talent〔'tæ\lənt〕*n.* 天分；能力　　treasure〔'trɛʒɚ〕*v.* 珍惜
　　　sensitive〔'sɛnsətɪv〕*adj.* 敏感的＜*to*＞　***be going on*** 發生
　　　be inclined to＋原 V　容易～；傾向於～（＝*tend to*）
　　　tolerate〔'tɑlə\ret〕*v.* 容忍　　criticize〔'krɪtə\saɪz〕*v.* 批評

21. (**A**) 依句意，喜歡聆聽的人已經很少，而聽得好的人更罕見，二句話之
　　　　　間語氣有轉折，故選 (A) Yet 然而。

22. (**C**) *tend to*＋原 V　傾向於～；容易～
　　　　　(A) mean to-V　打算

23. (**B**) rather than「而不是～」連接二個文法功能相同的用法，如本句，
　　　　　前句是不定詞，後面也用不定詞。(A) instead of 亦為「而不是～」
　　　　　之意，但為介系詞用法，後接名詞或動名詞。(C) in order to＋V 為
　　　　　了要～，(D) in addition to＋N/V-ing，除了～之外，句意均不合。

24. (**D**) 句中「較少的」敵人，形容詞應用 fewer，因 enemies 為可數名詞。
　　　　　(C) lesser 是 little 的比較級，置於名詞之前，表大小、價值、重要性
　　　　　的「較小」，但不與 than 連用。

25. (**D**) (A) in contrast　對比之下　　(B) in particular　特別地
　　　　　(C) in fact　事實上　　　　　　(D) ***in other words***　換句話說
　　　　　如要選 (C)，則應改成：In fact, *I would say* they are probably....

However, there are <u>exceptions</u> to that generality. *For example*, John
                26

Steinbeck is <u>said</u> to have been an excellent listener, *yet* he was hated
         27

by some of the people he wrote about., *No doubt* his ability *to listen*

contributed <u>to</u> his capacity *to write*. *Nevertheless*, the results *of his*
         28   29

listening did not make him popular. *Thus, <u>depending</u> on **what** a good*
                                              30

listener does, he may become either popular or disliked *in his lifetime*.
然而，那個一般性是有例外的。例如，約翰·史坦貝克，據說就是一個非常優秀
的聆聽者，但是他寫到的人物中，有一些人很討厭他。無疑地，他的聆聽能力
有助於他的寫作能力。然而，他聆聽後的結果並沒有使他受歡迎。因此，一個
好的聆聽者在他的一生中，會受歡迎或是受人厭惡，要視他做什麼事而定。

       generality〔͵dʒɛnəˈrælətɪ〕*n.* 一般性
       John Steinbeck 約翰·史坦貝克（美國小說家，1962 年獲得諾貝爾文學獎）
       no doubt 無疑地（＝*without a doubt*；*undoubtedly*）
       capacity〔kəˈpæsətɪ〕*n.* 能力（＝*ability*）
       dislike〔dɪsˈlaɪk〕*v.* 不喜歡
       lifetime〔ˈlaɪf͵taɪm〕*n.* 一生；終身

26. (**B**) (A) situation〔͵sɪtʃʊˈeʃən〕*n.* 情況
         (B) ***exception***〔ɪkˈsɛpʃən〕*n.* 例外
         (C) perception〔pəˈsɛpʃən〕*n.* 知覺
         (D) observation〔͵ɑbzəˈveʃən〕*n.* 觀察

27. (**C**) 表「據說」的用法有：$\left\{ \begin{array}{l} \text{It is said that} \\ \text{People say that} \end{array} \right\}$＋子句，另外，也可將

        子句中的主詞提出來，變成：S is said to＋原 V 的句型，故本題
        選 (C)。而 said 之後的不定詞若用 to＋原 V，指不定詞與主要子句
        動詞時態相同，若用 to have＋p.p.，則指不定詞的時態比主要子
        句動詞時態發生較早。

28. (**B**) *contribute to~* 促成~；有助於~

29. (**A**) 依句意，前後二句語氣有轉折，選 (A) *nevertheless*〔͵nɛvəðəˈlɛs〕
adv. 然而（= *however*）。(B) conversely〔kənˈvɝslɪ〕*adv.* 相反地
（= *on the contrary*），(C) consequently〔ˈkɑnsə͵kwɛntlɪ〕*adv.*
因此（= *therefore*），和 (D) moreover〔mɔrˈovɚ〕*adv.* 此外
（= *besides*），句意均不合。

30. (**D**) depend on 視~而定，本動詞與後句動詞 may become 之間無連接
詞，應改為分詞，且為主動，故選 (D) *depending*。

31－40題

It was my first day *in this beautiful tropical city*. *As* I was
<u>31</u>
walking to the beach, a stranger came up to me *and* tried to shake
my hand.

"Don't you remember me, my friend?" he said.

But I couldn't <u>recognize</u> his face at all. I didn't know a soul
<u>32</u>
in the city. I had *just* arrived *by plane* *and* *still* had jetlag.

那是我第一天到達這個美麗的熱帶都市。當我朝著海灘走去時，一個陌生
人走向我，試著和我握手。

他說：「你不記得我了嗎，我的朋友？」

但我完全認不得他的臉孔。在這個都市裏我一個人也不認識。我才坐飛機
抵達此地，時差都還沒調整過來。

> tropical〔ˈtrɑpɪkḷ〕*adj.* 熱帶的　　soul〔sol〕*n.* 靈魂；人
> jetlag〔ˈdʒɛt͵læg〕*n.* 時差（= *jet lag*）

31. (**A**) 依句意「當我朝著海灘走去時」，選 (A) *As*，在此即等於 when。

32. (**C**) (A) analyze (ˈænlˌaɪz) v. 分析

        (B) emphasize (ˈɛmfəˌsaɪz) v. 強調

        (C) *recognize* (ˈrɛkəgˌnaɪz) v. 認出

        (D) memorize (ˈmɛməˌraɪz) v. 背誦

"I saw you *at the airport*. I work *there at the customs*. How are
     33

you enjoying our beautiful city?"

I couldn't remember him *but* I was *too* embarrassed to tell him.
                                    34

He was *so* friendly. *Then* he offered to take me to his uncle's
               35

seafood restaurant, *just by the beach*. I thanked him *politely but* he
                                            36

insisted *that we should go there for dinner*.

　「我在機場看到你。我就在海關那兒工作。你喜不喜歡我們這個美麗的都
市啊？」

　我不記得他，但我太不好意思告訴他。他如此地友善。然後，他提議要帶
我去他叔叔的餐廳，就在海灘旁邊。我很客氣地謝謝他，但他堅持我們應該到
那裏吃晚餐。

    customs (ˈkʌstəmz) n.pl. 海關　　offer (ˈɔfə) v. 提議

    insist (ɪnˈsɪst) v. 堅持

33. (**B**) 敘述發生在過去的某個動作，用過去簡單式即可，選 (B) *saw*。

34. (**D**) (A) exhausted (ɪgˈzɔstɪd) adj. 筋疲力盡的

        (B) interested (ˈɪntrɪstɪd) adj. 有興趣的

        (C) frightened (ˈfraɪtn̩d) adj. 害怕的

        (D) *embarrassed* (ɪmˈbærəst) adj. 尷尬的

35. (**B**) 本句是單句，不需要連接詞，而需要承接上下文的轉承語，故選 (B)
    Then，做「然後；後來」解。

36.(C) 依句意是「客氣地」謝謝他，選 (C) *politely* 〔 pəˈlaɪtlɪ 〕 *adv.* 客氣地；有禮貌地。(A) eagerly 〔ˈigəlɪ〕 *adv.* 渴望地，(B) 快樂地，(D) willingly 〔ˈwɪlɪŋlɪ〕 *adv.* 願意地，句意均不合。

"You'll love the seafood *there*," he <u>assured</u> me. "***And*** it will be
37
a dinner *to remember*."

So we went to the restaurant ***and*** sat *by a window overlooking*
38

the bay. The dinner was great *indeed*, ***but*** the coffee *they served*

was *quite* different. *In fact*, it tasted very strange...

Anyway, it was not <u>until</u> 10 o'clock *the next morning* ***that*** I
39
finally woke up. ***But*** I had no idea ***where*** I was. All my money

was <u>gone</u> ***and*** my "friend" had *even* taken my watch and my shoes!
40

「你會喜歡那裏的海鮮的，」他向我保證。「而且，這會是一頓你永遠記得的晚餐。」

所以，我們就去了那家餐廳，並坐在俯視海灣的窗邊。晚餐確實很棒，但是他們供應的咖啡相當地不同。事實上，喝起來味道很奇怪…

反正，直到第二天早上十點，我終於醒過來了。但是我完全不知道自己身在何處。我身上所有的錢都不翼而飛，我那個「朋友」甚至把我的錶和我的鞋都拿走了。

> bay 〔 be 〕 *n.* 海灣
> serve 〔 sɜv 〕 *v.* 供應（食物、餐點）
> anyway 〔ˈɛnɪˌwe〕 *adv.* 反正；無論如何

37.(D) (A) declare 〔 dɪˈklɛr 〕 *v.* 宣布　　(B) propose 〔 prəˈpoz 〕 *v.* 提議
　　　　(C) respond 〔 rɪˈspɑnd 〕 *v.* 反應　(D) ***assure*** 〔 əˈʃur 〕 *v.* 保證

38. (**B**) 本句原爲形容詞子句 *which* overlooked the bay，修飾先行詞
　　　　window，將關代 which 去掉，動詞改成現在分詞 overlooking，
　　　　形成分詞片語，選 (B)。overlook〔͵ovɚ'luk〕*v.* 俯視

39. (**C**) *not～until*… 直到…才～，本句 It is/was not until…that + 子句，
　　　　爲強調句型，做加強語氣之用。

40. (**A**) 依句意，所有的錢都「沒了、不見了」，形容詞用 gone，選 (A)。

三、閱讀測驗:

41－44題

Authors write *for many reasons*. *Often* they write about real or

make-believe people, places, or events *that may be funny*, *sad*, *or*

scary. *Sometimes* authors write about these things *to entertain readers*.

Authors *also* write about these things *to inform by giving facts or ideas*,

　　The following two paragraphs are examples *of these two kinds*.

　　作家寫作有很多種理由。他們常常寫關於眞實的，或虛構的人、地、事，
那可能是好笑的、悲傷的，或嚇人的。有時作家寫這些事物，是爲了要娛樂讀
者。作家也會寫這些事物，想藉由提出事實或想法，來告知讀者一些訊息。
　　以下兩段文章就是此二種類的範例。

　　　　make-believe〔'mekbə͵liv〕*adj.* 假裝的；虛構的
　　　　scary〔'skɛrɪ〕*adj.* 嚇人的　　entertain〔͵ɛntɚ'ten〕*v.* 娛樂
　　　　inform〔ɪn'fɔrm〕*v.* 告知　　paragraph〔'pærə͵græf〕*n.* 段落

(1) *When he finished with unpacking*, Nelson carried all the empty

boxes *down the hallway*. *On his way to the dump*, the bell rang.

He needed to hurry. He had no time to go to the dump. *Then*, he stopped *at Adam Joshua's office, **which** happened to be unlocked,*

and walked away *joyfully. Later in the afternoon,* Nelson came to

Adam's office *with Peter for their biology project.* The empty

boxes and many other things fell *all over them **the minute** he*

opened the door. "Adam Joshua!" yelled Nelson, *pushing away a*

*basketball **and** shaking a toy frog off his foot.* "This is no way

to treat a friend!"

(1) 當尼爾遜把東西都拿出來後，他拿著所有的空盒子沿著走廊走著。在他往垃圾場中途，鈴聲響了。他必須趕快，他沒時間去垃圾場了。後來，他停在亞當・約書亞的辦公室前，門剛好沒鎖，然後就愉快地走開了。下午稍晚，尼爾遜和彼德，為了他們的生物課計劃，來到了亞當的辦公室。他一開門，空盒子和其他許多東西掉的他們滿身。尼爾遜推開一顆籃球，腳上甩開一隻玩具青蛙，大叫：「亞當・約書亞，你怎麼可以這樣對待朋友！」

> ***finish with*** 完成；結束　　unpack (ʌn'pæk) v. 取出（東西）
> hallway ('hɔl,we) n. 走廊　　dump (dʌmp) n. 垃圾場
> ***happen to*** + 原 V. 碰巧～　　unlocked (ʌn'lɑkt) adj. 未上鎖的
> joyfully ('dʒɔɪfəlɪ) adv. 愉快地
> biology (baɪ'ɑlədʒɪ) n. 生物學　　project ('prɑdʒɛkt) n. 計劃
> ***the minute*** 一～就⋯ (= *as soon as*)　　***shake off*** 甩開

(2) *Where the land meets the sea* we find seashells. There are many

different kinds of shells. They can be round *like the moon,* long

like a jackknife, ***or*** shaped like boxes, fans, or tops. The shells *we*

find are *usually* empty, ***but*** *once* there were soft bodies *inside.*

Animals *with hard shells outside and soft bodies inside* are

called mollusks.

(2) 在陸地與海洋交界的地方，我們可以發現貝殼。貝殼有許多不同的種類，有些圓圓的像月亮，有些長的像折疊刀，有些形狀像盒子、扇形或陀螺。我們所找到的貝殼通常是空的，但有一次貝殼裏面還有柔軟的身體。這種外面有堅硬的外殼，裏面是柔軟身體的動物，被稱爲軟體動物。

> seashell〔'si,ʃɛl〕 n. 貝殼（= shell）
> jackknife〔'dʒæk,naɪf〕 n. 大型可折疊式的刀
> **be shaped like~** 形狀像~
> fan〔fæn〕 n. 扇子　　　top〔tɑp〕 n. 陀螺
> mollusk〔'mɑləsk〕 n. 軟體動物（像貝類、蝸牛、章魚、烏賊等）

41. (**D**) 本文最好的標題爲何？
　　　(A) 朋友是做什麼的。　　　　(B) 貝殼與軟體動物。
　　　(C) 寫作的適當主題。　　　　(D) 寫作的不同目的。
　　　appropriate〔ə'propriɪt〕 adj. 適當的　　topic〔'tɑpɪk〕 n. 主題

42. (**B**) 關於第一個範例，以下何者錯誤？
　　　(A) 尼爾遜不是個負責任的人。
　　　(B) 亞當和尼爾遜都是軍官。
　　　(C) 尼爾遜把空盒子留在亞當的辦公室裏。
　　　(D) 亞當對尼爾遜惡作劇。
　　　regarding〔rɪ'gɑrdɪŋ〕 prep. 關於　　**practical joke** 惡作劇

43. (**D**) 根據第一個範例，以下何者正確？
　　　(A) 尼爾遜和亞當從來不喜歡彼此。
　　　(B) 亞當不知道尼爾遜把什麼放在他的辦公室裏。
　　　(C) 彼德向尼爾遜抱怨空盒子的事。
　　　(D) 亞當給了尼爾遜一個教訓。

44. (**B**) 根據作者的說法，第二個範例是爲了
　　　(A) 表達對於貝殼的意見。
　　　(B) 提出有關貝殼的事實。
　　　(C) 讓我們知道貝殼的美麗。
　　　(D) 描述貝殼的形狀。
　　　intend〔ɪn'tɛnd〕 v. 打算；意欲

45－48 題

Kauai, *the oldest of the main Hawaiian Islands*, has some of the state's most stunning scenery. Rivers and streams flow *slowly through jungles of shaded greens.* The breathtaking 4,000-foot cliffs *of Na Pali Coast* rise *grandly* from the sea. Waimea Canyon, *called the "Grand Canyon of the Pacific" by Mark Twain,* cuts a deep gash *through the rugged central mountains.*

卡哇依島，夏威夷群島的主島中最古老的，擁有一些全夏威夷最令人歎為觀止的風景。河流和小溪緩緩流經布滿蔭涼綠地的叢林。納帕里海岸，令人心驚膽跳的四千呎懸崖，雄偉地聳立於海面上。懷美亞峽谷，曾被馬克‧吐溫稱為「太平洋上的大峽谷」，切進崎嶇不平的中央山脈，切割出一條很深的峽谷。

stunning ('stʌnɪŋ) *adj.* 使人嚇呆的；極好的　　stream (strim) *n.* 溪流
jungle ('dʒʌŋgl̩) *n.* 叢林　　　　shade (ʃed) *v.* 使成蔭
breathtaking ('brεθ,tekɪŋ) *adj.* 令人心驚膽跳的
cliff (klɪf) *n.* 懸崖　　　grandly ('grændlɪ) *adv.* 雄偉地
canyon ('kænjən) *n.* 峽谷
the Grand Canyon 大峽谷（位於 Arizona 亞利桑那州）
gash (gæʃ) *n.* 大而深的傷口；缺口　　rugged ('rʌgɪd) *adj.* 崎嶇的

Rising more than 5,000 feet, Mt. Waialeale stands *at the center of the nearly round island.* This extinct volcano is considered the wettest spot *on earth,* with almost 500 inches *of rainfall each year. Yet* this amount *of rain* is *surprisingly* localized. *Just a few miles west,* there's a dry region *that receives a mere 6 inches of rain annually.*

　　聳立五千多呎的懷阿雷阿雷山，位於這個近乎圓形的島嶼中心。這座死火山被認爲是地球上最潮濕的地點，年雨量將近五百吋。然而令人驚訝地，這個雨量非常局部。就在西側幾哩處，就有一個乾燥地區，每年僅有六英吋的雨量。

extinct〔ɪk'stɪŋkt〕*adj.* 絕滅的
extinct volcano 死火山（↔ *active volcano* 活火山）
spot〔spɑt〕*n.* 地點　　rainfall〔'ren,fɔl〕*n.* 雨量
localize〔'lokḷ,aɪz〕*v.* 侷限；局部化
annually〔'ænjʊəlɪ〕*adv.* 每年地（= *each year*）

　　The island continues to recover *from its 1992 visit from Iniki, the most powerful hurricane to hit Hawaii this century,* A few hotels are *still* being rebuilt, ***but*** Kauai remains *as* beautiful *as ever*.

　　Kauai is not for people *who thrive on crowds or nightlife. **While** it does have its share of resort hotels; shopping centers and good restaurants, **and** a smattering of museums, art galleries and night spots,* its main attractions lie *outdoors.* Hiking, camping, and scuba diving are excellent *on the island.*

　　自從一九九二年，本世紀最猛烈的颱風伊尼基侵襲夏威夷，本島持續在復原中。有一些飯店仍在重建，但卡哇伊島還是和從前一樣美。

　　卡哇伊島不適合那些熱愛群衆或夜生活的人。雖然它確實也有一部分的度假飯店、購物中心和好的餐廳，以及少數的博物館、藝廊和夜生活場所，但它主要的吸引力都在戶外。徒步健行、露營和水肺潛水，都是島上很棒的活動。

hurricane〔'hɝɪ,ken〕*n.* 颱風　　*as ~ as ever* 和從前一樣~
thrive〔θraɪv〕*v.* 繁榮；興盛；成功　　share〔ʃɛr〕*n.* 部分
resort〔rɪ'zɔrt〕*n.* 度假勝地　　*a smattering of* 少數的
gallery〔'gælərɪ〕*n.* 藝廊　　lie〔laɪ〕*v.* 在於
scuba〔'skubə〕*n.* 水肺；潛水用的水中呼吸裝備

45. (**D**) 本文的主旨為何？

    (A) 介紹一個外國的文化。   (B) 一個地區的歷史背景。

    (C) 討論環境問題。   (D) 一個地方的地理資料。

    theme〔θim〕 *n.* 主旨　　background〔'bæk,graʊnd〕 *n.* 背景
    geographical〔,dʒiə'græfɪkḷ〕 *adj.* 地理的

46. (**B**) 卡哇依島以什麼聞名？

    (A) 天氣寒冷。   (B) 自然美景。

    (C) 活火山。   (D) 遊樂園。

    amusement〔ə'mjuzmənt〕 *n.* 娛樂
    amusement park 遊樂場；遊樂園

47. (**A**) 卡哇依島的雨量狀況如何？

    (A) 雨量集中在某些地區。   (B) 除了高山外，其他地方常常下雨。

    (C) 全年大部分各地都多雨。   (D) 雨量隨著季節有很大的變動。

    concentrate〔'kɑnsṇ,tret〕 *v.* 集中 ＜*on*＞

48. (**C**) 關於卡哇依島，下列敘述何者錯誤？

    (A) 卡哇依島的形狀幾乎是圓形。

    (B) 一九九二年的颶風造成卡哇依島嚴重損失。

    (C) 對於喜愛室內活動的人而言，這是個很好的地方。

    (D) 島中央聳立一座高山。

49－50題

    All living things die *eventually. In ecological terms,* the chemicals *of living things* are borrowed *from the Earth, **and** at death* they return. All the material *that every animal, from the smallest fly to the largest elephant, takes in as food* also returns to the Earth, *as waste matter.* The dead material and waste matter form the diet *of a group of living organisms called decomposers.*

　　所有的生物最後都會死。以生態學的觀點來看，生物體內的化學物質是借自於大自然，死後即歸還大自然。每一種動物，小至最小的蒼蠅，大至最大的大象，所攝取以為食物的所有物質，也會以廢物的形式回歸大自然。這些死掉的生物和廢物，形成了另一種生物的食物，這種生物稱為分解者。

> eventually (ɪˈvɛntʃʊəlɪ) adv. 最後；終究
> ecological (ˌɛkəˈlɑdʒɪkl̩) adj. 生態 (學) 的
> **in terms of~** 以~的觀點來看
> **take in** 攝取　　diet (ˈdaɪət) n. 飲食
> organism (ˈɔrgənˌɪzem) n. 有機體；生物
> decomposer (ˌdikəmˈpozɚ) n. 分解者

They include a range of bacteria, fungi, and small animals *that*

break down nature's wastes into ever smaller pieces **until** *all the*

chemicals are released into the air, the soil, and the water, making

them available to other living things. Without the carbon dioxide

released from the process, all plant life would die out. Without the

oxygen *that plants give out,* **and** *without the food that they supply,*

life would grind to a halt **and** all animals would starve. The

decomposers are a vital link *in the natural cycle of life and death.*

分解者包括一部分的細菌、黴菌和小型的動物，它們會把自然界的廢物分解成更小的分子，直到所有的化學物質被釋放到空氣、土壤和水中，使這些物質能再次被其他生物所利用。若沒有這個分解過程釋放出二氧化碳，所有的植物都會死光。而若沒有植物放出氧氣，提供食物，生命就會逐漸停止，所有的動物就會餓死。所以分解者在大自然生與死的循環中，是一個非常重要的環節。

range〔rendʒ〕*n.* 範圍　　bacteria〔bæk'tɪrɪə〕*n.pl.* 細菌

fungi〔'fʌndʒaɪ〕*n.pl.* 黴菌　　***break down*** 分解

release〔rɪ'lis〕*v.* 釋放　　soil〔sɔɪl〕*n.* 土壤

carbon dioxide 二氧化碳　　process〔'prɑsɛs〕*n.* 過程

die out 死絕；死光　　oxygen〔'ɑksədʒən〕*n.* 氧氣

give out 放出　　grind〔graɪnd〕*v.* 磨碎；摩擦

halt〔hɔlt〕*n.* 停止　　***grind to a halt*** 逐漸停止

starve〔stɑrv〕*v.* 餓死　　vital〔'vaɪtl̩〕*adj.* 非常重要的

link〔lɪŋk〕*n.* 連結；環節　　cycle〔'saɪkl̩〕*n.* 循環

49.(**D**) 下列敘述何者爲非？

(A) 小型生物如細菌，提供食物給其他生物。

(B) 二氧化碳在分解的過程中被製造出來。

(C) 植物對於維持動物的生命，是很重要的。

(D) <u>分解者在自然循環中所扮演的角色並不重要。</u>

decomposition〔,dikɑmpə'zɪʃən〕*n.* 分解

minor〔'maɪnɚ〕*adj.* 不重要的

50.(**A**) 根據本文，死亡並不是生命的結束，而能夠

(A) <u>維持其他的生命型態。</u>　　　(B) 從大自然中借取物質。

(C) 顯示細菌如何變成化學物質。　(D) 控制土壤的量。

<u>51~55 題</u>

　　New York, Nov. 17 — *In a swirl of confetti and shredded paper,*

John Glenn made his second trip *through New York's "Canyon of*

Heroes" in a parade Monday, saluting his return to space 36 years

***after** he became America's first man in orbit.*

　　Glenn's first ticker-tape parade *on March 1, 1962, after his Mercury*

flight, is considered the largest *ever in New York.* An estimated 3,474

tons of confetti and ticker-tape rained down *along a seven-mile route.*

　　紐約，十一月十七日——在五彩碎紙片的飛舞中，約翰・葛倫在星期一，第二次參加紐約的「英雄峽谷」大遊行，這是為了向他成為美國第一個繞地球軌道飛行的太空人之後三十六年，他重返太空而致敬。

　　葛倫參加的第一場滿天碎紙的大遊行，是在一九六二年三月一日，他的水星號飛行之後舉行。該場遊行被認為是紐約有史以來最盛大的一場。據估計，有三千四百七十四噸的五彩碎紙，沿著七哩長的遊行路線，如雨點般落下。

swirl (swɜl) *n.* 旋轉　　confetti (kən'fɛtɪ) *n.* 五彩碎紙
shred (ʃrɛd) *v.* 撕碎　　salute (sə'lut) *v.* 向～致敬
orbit ('ɔrbɪt) *n.* 軌道
ticker-tape ('tɪkə,tep) *n.* (遊行時由高樓窗子拋下的) 白紙紙帶
Mercury ('mɜkjərɪ) *n.* 水星
estimate ('ɛstə,met) *v.* 估計　　route (rut) *n.* 路線

For his second parade, despite lunchtime crowds from Wall Street, the turnout *Monday* was sparse *by New York standards* **and** spectators *along a route less than a mile long* were *surprisingly* restrained. Police and Glenn's parade was attended *by 500,000 — a figure* **that** *appeared generously inflated.*

The 1962 celebration "was *more* enthusiastic — a lot more people," said one spectator, **who** *as a young newlywed attended Glenn's first parade* **and** *came from her Brooklyn home again for Glenn's second parade.*

Another spectator said **that** *too many Americans take the achievements of the space program for granted.* "It's become *so* everyday, *so* ordinary, nobody cares," he said.

　　而他的第二場遊行，儘管加上了來自華爾街那些外出吃午餐的人潮，星期一參加的人以紐約的標準而言，還是很少，不到一哩長的遊行路線，兩旁的觀眾令人訝異地十分拘謹。警方與葛倫的這場遊行有五十萬人參加，而這個數字似乎有大大地灌水之嫌。

　　有一位觀眾說一九六二年慶祝活動「比較熱烈──人數多很多。」她年輕新婚時就參加過葛倫的第一場遊行，這次再度從她布魯克林的家來此，參加葛倫的第二場遊行。

　　另一位觀眾說，太多的美國人將太空計劃的成就視爲理所當然了。他說：「這變得很平常、很普通，所以，沒有人在乎。」

turnout（＇tɝn‚aʊt）n. 出席人數　　　sparse（spɑrs）adj. 稀少的
spectator（＇spɛktetɚ）n. 觀眾　　　restrain（rɪ＇stren）v. 抑制
figure（＇fɪgɚ）n. 數字　　　generously（＇dʒɛnərəslɪ）adv. 大方地
inflate（ɪn＇flet）v. 膨脹；誇大
enthusiastic（ɪn‚θjuzɪ＇æstɪk）adj. 熱烈的
newlywed（＇njulɪ‚wɛd）n. 新婚的人
take～for granted 把～視爲理所當然
achievement（ə＇tʃivmənt）n. 成就

Glenn began the day *with decorating the Rockefeller Center Christmas tree. After that event,* Glenn recalled the 1962 parade, saying, "It was *just so* enormous. I remember *just* a blizzard of paper. You could *hardly even* look up *without getting something in your eye.*"

Glenn, ***who retires from the U.S. Senate next month,*** joins a list of individuals and sports teams *honored with more than one ticker-tape parade.*

　　葛倫當天以裝飾洛克斐勒中心的耶誕樹，做爲活動的開始。活動結束後，葛倫回想一九六二年的遊行，他說：「那天就是非常盛大。我記得如風雪般的紙片。你幾乎只要一抬頭看，就會有東西跑進眼睛裏面。」

　　葛倫下個月將從美國參議院退休，他成爲少數的個人和體育隊伍中，得到一次以上盛大遊行如此殊榮的成員之一。

> **Rockefeller Center** 洛克斐勒中心（在紐約市 Manhattan 曼哈頓中心區）
> recall〔rɪˋkɔl〕v. 回想　　enormous〔ɪˋnɔrməs〕adj. 巨大的；盛大的
> blizzard〔ˋblɪzəd〕n. 暴風雪
> **hardly～without…**　一～就…　　**look up** 抬頭看
> Senate〔ˋsɛnɪt〕n. 參議院　　honor〔ˋɑnə〕v. 給予榮譽

51. (**C**) 這是一篇關於約翰·葛倫 ＿＿＿＿＿＿＿＿ 之後的報導。

　　(A) 成功地完成一九六二年水星號的飛行

　　(B) 成為第一位登陸月球的人

　　(C) <u>第二次在紐約市受到歡迎</u>　　　(D) 從美國參議院退休

　　accomplish〔əˋkɑmplɪʃ〕v. 完成；達成

52. (**B**) 一九六二年的遊行中，什麼讓葛倫印象最深刻？

　　(A) 包圍著他的大批人群。　　　　　(B) <u>倒了他一身的大量紙片。</u>

　　(C) 洛克斐勒中心前的聖誕樹。　　　(D) 他接受市長頒贈的市鑰。

　　impress〔ɪmˋprɛs〕v. 使印象深刻

　　pour〔por〕v. 傾倒　　mayor〔ˋmeə〕n. 市長

53. (**C**) 下列敘述何者為真？

　　(A) 約翰·葛倫非常令人欽佩，因為他到過月球不只一次。

　　(B) 只有約翰·葛倫接受過不只一次盛大遊行的殊榮。

　　(C) <u>許多美國人對太空成就不再感到興奮。</u>

　　(D) 葛倫在紐約的第二次遊行比第一次盛大。

　　admirable〔ˋædmərəbḷ〕adj. 令人欽佩的

　　in that 因為（＝*because*）

54. (**B**) 根據本文，葛倫做過幾次太空飛行？

　　(A) 一次。　　(B) <u>二次。</u>　　(C) 三次。　　(D) 四次。

55. (**C**) 為什麼這份報導說葛倫的第二場遊行數字被「灌水」？

　　(A) 因為第二場遊行人群比第一場遊行多。

　　(B) 因為有許多人二場遊行都參加。

　　(C) <u>因為第二場遊行的人似乎遠少於五十萬人。</u>

　　(D) 因為第二場遊行的人群更加熱烈。

第二部分：非選擇題

一、簡答題：

Ａ

MARKETING PROFESSIONALS

A major US corporation in the health and nutritional industry has announced the opening of its direct selling division in Taiwan.

The company offers the most lucrative compensation plan in the industry and has paid over $3.5 billion NTD in commissions in just 6 years in the US. We are a group of top earners.

Applicants should meet the requirements:
(1) Taiwan citizen
(2) Have interest or experience in marketing
(3) Aggressive, energetic, and willing to learn

If you believe you have what it takes to develop this business, please call 2742-6996

A.

行銷專員

　　美國一家健康營養業的大公司，已宣布在台灣的直銷部門開張。

　　公司提供同業中利潤最豐厚的薪資計劃，在美國僅僅六年，就已付出新台幣三十五億以上的佣金。我們是一群高薪者。

申請人應要符合以下資格：

(1) 台灣公民　　(2) 對行銷有興趣或經驗　　(3) 積極、有活力，願意學習

如果你相信你具有發展本行的條件，請電 2742-6996。

marketing ('mɑrkɪtɪŋ) n. 行銷

corporation (ˌkɔrpə'reʃən) n. 公司

nutritional (nju'trɪʃən!) adj. 營養的　　announce (ə'nauns) v. 宣布

division (də'vɪʒən) n. 部門　　lucrative ('lukrətɪv) adj. 有利潤的

compensation (ˌkɑmpən'seʃən) n. 薪水；津貼

commission (kə'mɪʃən) n. 佣金　　applicant ('æpləkənt) n. 申請人

requirement (rɪ'kwaɪrmənt) n. 資格；條件

aggressive (ə'grɛsɪv) adj. 積極進取的

B

An international company requires **a**

| Service Technician |

To service and maintain electronic medical equipment.

Applicants should possess degree in electronics. The selected candidate will undergo a training program to be conducted by our manufacturer's trained technical personnel.

Interested candidates please apply immediately with resume and mail to P.O. box 594. Or telephone Ms. Chang at 2945-0027 for an immediate interview.

B.

跨國企業需要一名

維修技師

來維修、保養電子醫療器材

　　申請人應具有電子學的學位。入選者將接受由我們製造商受過訓練的技術人員所指導的訓練課程。

　　有興趣者請立刻備履歷應徵，郵寄至郵政信箱 594 號。或請電 2945-0027，找張小姐，安排立即面試。

service ('sɜvɪs) *n.,v.* 服務；維修
technician (tɛk'nɪʃən) *n.* 技師；技術人員
maintain (men'ten) *v.* 維修；保養
possess (pə'zɛs) *v.* 擁有
electronics (,ɪlɛk'trɑnɪks) *n.* 電子學
candidate ('kændə,det , 'kændədɪt) *n.* 候選人
undergo (,ʌndə'go) *v.* 經歷
conduct (kən'dʌkt) *v.* 指導；領導
technical ('tɛknɪkḷ) *adj.* 技術的　　personnel (,pɜsṇ'ɛl) *n.* 人員
resume (,rɛzu'me ,,rɛzju'me) *n.* 履歷
P.O. box 郵政信箱

C

Wanted: Reporters & Editors

Qualifications:
% Strong command of English language
% Chinese speaking and reading ability a must
% a university degree
% Journalism education and/or experience a plus

Flexible working hours (30 hours per week)
Good work environment and great co-workers
Medical insurance, etc.

Fax resume and work samples, if any, to
The China Post at (03) 2595-7962.

C.

誠徵：記者 & 編輯

資格：

　% 精通英文
　% 中文說與讀的能力必備條件
　% 大學學歷
　% 新聞學教育以及／或經驗附加優點

彈性工時（每週三十小時）
良好的工作環境，優秀的工作同仁
享醫療保險等。

請傳眞履歷及作品範例，如果有的話，至中國英文郵報
(03) 2595-7962。

qualification〔͵kwɑləfəˈkeʃən〕n. 資格
command〔kəˈmænd〕n. 精通　　must〔mʌst〕n. 必要的事
journalism〔ˈdʒɝnḷ͵ɪzəm〕n. 新聞學
plus〔plʌs〕n. 附加的優點　　flexible〔ˈflɛksəbḷ〕adj. 彈性的
insurance〔ɪnˈʃʊrəns〕n. 保險
sample〔ˈsæmpḷ〕n. 範例；樣品

D

| Southeastern Travel Services |

OPENINGS **************************

TOUR GUIDES

Duties: To conduct escorted tours for foreign visitors; to assist with travel and transportation arrangements.

Qualifications: Good appearance. High school diploma. Good knowledge of English. Outgoing personality.

Call 2703-2172 after 3:00 PM. Ask for Gary.

D.

東南旅行社

空缺

導遊

職務：帶領有接送的外國旅行團；協助安排旅遊及交通事宜。

資格：長相清秀。高中文憑。擅長英文。個性外向。電 2703-2172，下午三點後，找 Gary。

escort〔ɪ'skɔrt〕v. 護送　　assist〔ə'sɪst〕v. 協助
transportation〔,trænspə'teʃən〕n. 交通（工具）
arrangement〔ə'rendʒmənt〕n. 安排
diploma〔dɪ'plomə〕n. 文憑
outgoing〔aut'goɪŋ〕adj. 外向的

1. 哪些廣告不是外國公司刊登的？（請寫下代號）

　⇨ B, C, D 或 C, D

2. 哪一個工作除了底薪之外，有最好的福利？

　⇨ 一律給分　　benefit〔'bɛnəfɪt〕n. 福利

3. 溫蒂擅長寫作，而她不喜歡固定工時。這四種工作中哪一個可能最適合她？

　⇨ Reporters & Editors

　　be good at 擅長　　fixed〔fɪkst〕*adj.* 固定的

4. 查爾斯對科技有濃厚的興趣。四個工作他該應徵哪一個？

　⇨ Service Technician　　technology〔tɛk'nɑlədʒɪ〕*n.* 科技

5. 哪一則不需藉由打電話直接連絡？（請寫下代號）

　⇨ B 或 C 或 BC　　contact〔'kɑntækt〕*n.* 連絡

二、作文範例：

　　With my personal qualities and traveling experience, I believe I am well-qualified for the position of tour guide. Being young, bright and energetic, I don't like to work in a cubicle with a fixed schedule. Having the ability to get along with people with different interests and backgrounds, I get used to a new environment quickly. ***Furthermore***, I have traveled throughout Europe and America on my own. A variety of emergencies and problems I've encountered and overcome have taught me how to deal with sickness, criminal incidents, and culture shock. ***Therefore***, I'm sure that my personal background and multi-lingual ability, including English, Spanish and Chinese, will help me handle any hazard which my tour group might face.

　　A service technician will be the last job that I wish to apply for. Besides lacking the relevant academic background, I care nothing about electronics. ***Moreover***, this kind of job cannot provide challenge and freedom where I can use my initiative and creativity. ***To sum up***, in choosing an occupation, one has to consider his/her aptitude above all, or working is a burden, instead of fun.

quality (ˈkwɑlətɪ) *n.* 特質　　position (pəˈzɪʃən) *n.* 職位
bright (braɪt) *adj.* 開朗的；聰明的
cubicle (ˈkjubɪkḷ) *n.* 小房間　　***get along with～*** 與～相處
a variety of 各種　　emergency (ɪˈmɝdʒənsɪ) *n.* 緊急情況
encounter (ɪnˈkaʊntɚ) *v.* 遭遇　　overcome (ˌovɚˈkʌm) *v.* 克服
deal with 處理 (= *handle*)　　criminal (ˈkrɪmənḷ) *adj.* 犯罪的
incident (ˈɪnsədənt) *n.* 事件　　***culture shock*** 文化衝擊
multi-lingual (ˌmʌltəˈlɪŋgwəl) *adj.* 多語的；會說多種語言的
hazard (ˈhæzɚd) *n.* 危險 (= *danger*)
relevant (ˈrɛləvənt) *adj.* 相關的　　academic (ˌækəˈdɛmɪk) *adj.* 學術的
care nothing about 不關心；不在乎
challenge (ˈtʃælɪndʒ) *n.* 挑戰　　initiative (ɪˈnɪʃɪ,etɪv) *n.* 主動；進取
creativity (ˌkrieˈtɪvətɪ) *n.* 創意；創造力
to sum up 總之　　occupation (ˌɑkjəˈpeʃən) *n.* 職業
aptitude (ˈæptə,tjud) *n.* 性向　　burden (ˈbɝdn̩) *n.* 負擔

大考中心發給閱卷老師內部資料
簡答題給分標準

基本原則：

一、第 2 題一律給分。

二、未照題目指示，即題 1 或題 5 未以英文字母代號回答；題 3 或題 4 未以
英文單字寫出答案者，一律扣 1 分。

三、以單字回答，但拼字錯誤者，不論多寡，每題只扣 1 分。

四、大小寫或單複數有錯誤者不扣分。

題號	參 考 答 案	備　　　　註
1	B,C,D 或 C,D	一、四個選項都答者，扣 1 分 二、答案中缺 C 或 D 者，扣 1 分 三、答案中缺 C 及 D 者，扣 2 分
2	一律給分	
3	Reporters & Editors	只答 Reporters 或 Editors 者，扣 1 分
4	Service Technician	只答 Technician 者，扣 1 分； 只答 Service 者，不給分
5	B 或 C 或 B,C	

八十七年大學入學學科能力測驗試題 英文考科

壹：選擇題（第一部份）

一、字彙：片語與語法（20％）

說明：第1至20題，每題依句意選出最適當的一個選項，標示在答案卡之
　　　「選擇題第一部份」。每題答對得1分，答錯不倒扣。

1. Follow the _____ closely, and you will find it easy to assemble the bicycle.
   (A) functions　　(B) diagnoses　　(C) appointments　(D) instructions

2. If I can help you with the project, don't _____ to call me.
   (A) concern　　(B) hesitate　　(C) notify　　(D) submit

3. _____ between good friends should be resolved, not ignored.
   (A) Compliments　　　　　(B) Concerns
   (C) Conflicts　　　　　　(D) Connections

4. Group registrations are not allowed. Each member must register for the conference _____.
   (A) comfortably　(B) individually　(C) intelligently　(D) respectfully

5. Mr. Wang's arguments were very _____, and the committee finally accepted his proposal.
   (A) artificial　　(B) inappropriate　(C) persuasive　　(D) descriptive

6. The woman is so _____ that she cries every time she hears a sad story.
   (A) casual　　(B) harsh　　(C) intimate　　(D) sentimental

7. We _____ believe that with your intelligence and hard work, you will pass the exam without any difficulty.
   (A) firmly　　(B) extremely　　(C) strictly　　(D) inquiringly

8. If we walk at this slow _____, we'll never get to our destination on time.

(A) mood   (B) pace   (C) tide   (D) access

9. The territorial dispute can be _____ back to the year 1917, when the two countries were at war.

(A) held   (B) recalled   (C) traced   (D) switched

10. One key factor to success is to have a definite goal first and then do your best to _____ the goal.

(A) attain   (B) contest   (C) encounter   (D) struggle

11. Jane and Sue are twins, but they seem to have nothing _____.

(A) in common   (B) in comparison   (C) in contact   (D) in contrast

12. How did the traffic accident _____ ?

(A) come about   (B) come around   (C) come off   (D) come over

13. During the lunch hour, Jane _____ her notes so she would remember them for the test.

(A) ran into   (B) ran off   (C) ran out of   (D) ran over

14. We shall expect you at eight o'clock; _____, it's an informal dinner.

(A) by accident   (B) by all means

(C) by the way   (D) by then

15. Stricter measures have been taken to _____ potential dangers concerning cigarette-smoking.

(A) ward off   (B) give in   (C) check out   (D) hang up

16. Henry : Please help me return these books to the library, James.

James : What ?

Henry : I asked you _____ me return these books to the library.

(A) help   (B) to help   (C) helped   (D) would help

17. Mary : Are you ready to go? I can give you a ride.

　　Betty : Thanks, but I think I'll wait until the mail _____.

　　(A) will come　　(B) comes　　　(C) to come　　　(D) come

18. Alice : There's a very good movie on television at eight tonight.

　　John　: Maybe I'll get home _____ to see it.

　　(A) so early　　(B) much early　　(C) early enough　　(D) too early

19. Mr. Lin　: Don't you think our government should build another
　　　　　　　　nuclear power plant in Taiwan?

　　Mr. Liu : Well, I wish I _____ agree with you, but I don't.

　　(A) had to　　　(B) could　　　　(C) do　　　　(D) have to

20. Mary　: Did you ask Tom _____?

　　Helen : No, I didn't, but I will.

　　(A) where had he gone for the summer vacation

　　(B) where was he going for the summer vacation

　　(C) where he goes for the summer vacation

　　(D) where he went for the summer vacation

二、綜合測驗（20％）

說明：　第 21 至 40 題，每題有一個空格。請依文意選出最適當的一個選項，
　　　　標示在答案卡之「選擇題第一部份」。每題答對得 1 分，答錯不倒
　　　　扣。

21-30 題為題組

　　There was once a man in Puerto Rico who had a wonderful parrot.
The parrot was __(21)__, there was no other bird like him in the
whole world. He could learn to say any word--__(22)__ one. He
could not say the name of his native town, Catano.

　　The man __(23)__ everything he could to teach the parrot to say
"Catano," but he never __(24)__. At first he was very gentle with
the bird, but gradually he lost his __(25)__. "You stupid bird!
__(26)__ can't you learn to say that one word? Say 'Catano' or I'll
kill you!" But the parrot would not say it. Many times the man
screamed, "Say 'Catano' or I'll kill you!" But the bird would not
__(27)__ the name.

Finally the man gave up. He picked up the parrot and threw the bird into the chicken house. In the chicken house, there were four old chickens, waiting to be killed ___(28)___ Sunday's dinner. "You are even more stupid than the chickens," the man said as he was leaving.

The next morning, the man went out to the chicken house. When he opened the door, he was ___(29)___ by what he saw. He could not believe his eyes and ears!

On the floor ___(30)___ three dead chickens. The parrot was screaming at the fourth, "Say 'Catano' or I'll kill you!"

21. (A) lonely   (B) unique   (C) sorrowful   (D) personal
22. (A) without   (B) beyond   (C) except   (D) despite
23. (A) did   (B) put   (C) had   (D) made
24. (A) failed   (B) attempted   (C) changed   (D) succeeded
25. (A) pet   (B) thing   (C) temper   (D) possession
26. (A) How   (B) Why   (C) What   (D) When
27. (A) tell   (B) talk   (C) repeat   (D) converse
28. (A) in   (B) on   (C) at   (D) for
29. (A) worried   (B) shocked   (C) delighted   (D) blinded
30. (A) lay   (B) laid   (C) lied   (D) lying

31-40 題為題組

Perhaps most of us are familiar with the saying "Laugh and the world ___(31)___ with you, weep and you weep alone." ___(32)___ did you know that according to recent research, people are losing the art of laughter and it could have a ___(33)___ effect on our health?

In 1930 we laughed on average for 19 minutes each day, but by 1980 it ___(34)___ to six minutes. Children, ___(35)___ , can see the funny side of things more often and may laugh up to 400 times a day.

By exhaling air from the lungs in short ___(36)___ of laughter, breathing is quickened and heartbeats increased, which achieves ___(37)___ good as ten minutes on an exercise bike. Laughter, too, has a beneficial effect on our immune system, ___(38)___ the production of white blood cells and increasing our resistance to infection. ___(39)___ makes a difference to our appearance, too, when we relax our facial muscles!

Laughter ___(40)___ is the best medicine, so why not give yourself a treat? Have a good laugh today--and feel better for it.

31. (A) fights   (B) sings   (C) laughs   (D) cries
32. (A) How   (B) But   (C) So   (D) When
33. (A) good   (B) serious   (C) few   (D) heavy
34. (A) has been decreasing   (B) was decreasing
     (C) should have decreased   (D) had decreased
35. (A) as a result   (B) in addition
     (C) by chance   (D) on the other hand
36. (A) bursts   (B) breaks   (C) circles   (D) pieces
37. (A) as many   (B) as much   (C) so many   (D) so much
38. (A) encourages   (B) encouraged   (C) encouraging   (D) to encourage
39. (A) It   (B) There   (C) What   (D) Where
40. (A) hardly   (B) kindly   (C) rarely   (D) really

三、閱讀測驗（20％）

說明：第 41 至 50 題，請依各篇文章之文意選出最適當的一個選項，標示在答案卡之「選擇題第一部份」。每題答對得 2 分，答錯不倒扣。

<u>41-43 題為題組</u>

One of the most unusual graduation speakers of the 1983 commencement season was not a person at all. The speaker was Robot Redford, a robot who delivered the commencement address at a community college in suburban Maryland.

The speaker, carefully programmed, arrived on the stage under its own power and proceeded to tell the audience of 658 graduates, their families, and friends that they would have to learn to work with robots and technology to solve society's problems. The robot described itself as an extension of a person to help humans increase the workload. Although this particular robot can be programmed to speak, the voice heard wasn't that of the robot, because it was feared that the robot's voice was not loud enough to carry throughout the hall. An amplified voice of a human was used instead, while the listeners watched the robot.

Robot Redford was followed by a person, William Bakaleinikoff, who spoke about the need for cooperation between people and technology. Mr. Bakaleinikoff's experience with his topic included the fact that he had created Robot Redford and had provided the voice for the robot's words to the graduates.

There was quite a bit of controversy over the choice of a robot as a commencement speaker. Some students thought it was insensitive and degrading to use a robot. Others thought the idea was clever and innovative.

"I'll never forget this speech," said one graduate. "You forget a political leader, but you won't forget a robot."

41. Robot Redford's speech was discussed in this article mainly because _____.
(A) it was political
(B) it was psychological
(C) it was controversial
(D) it was insensitive

42. Which of the following statements is NOT true?
(A) Robot Redford was a talking machine.
(B) Robot Redford walked to the stage by itself.
(C) Robot Redford made a graduation speech in 1983.
(D) Robot Redford graduated from a college in Maryland.

43. Which of the following statements can be supported by the passage?
(A) A robot was designed to let humans decrease their productivity.
(B) Robot Redford was the brainchild of William Bakaleinikoff.
(C) Everybody in the commencement was pleased with the arrangement.
(D) Robot Redford's speech was too difficult to understand.

44-46 題為題組

Summers with Father were always enjoyable. Swimming, hiking, boating, fishing--the days were not long enough to contain all of our activities. There never seemed to be enough time to go to church, which disturbed some friends and relatives. Accused of neglecting this part of our education, my father still instituted a summer school for my brother and me. His summer course included ancient history, which Papa felt our schools neglected, and <u>navigation</u>, in which we first had a formal examination in the dining room, part of which consisted of tying several knots in a given time limit. Then we were each separately sent on what was grandly referred to as a cruise in my father's 18-foot boat, spending the night on board, and loaded down, according to my mother, with enough food for a week. I remember that on my cruise I was required to formally plot our course, using the tide table, even though our goal was an island I could see quite clearly across the water in the distance.

44. As used in the passage, "navigation" clearly means _____.
 (A) going to a summer school
 (B) the practice of sailing a boat
 (C) the act of piloting an airplane
 (D) a formal examination in a dinning room

45. Which of the following activities was NOT planned by the father for his children's summer education?
 (A) Going to church.　　　　(B) Going hiking.
 (C) Going swimming.　　　　(D) Studying ancient history.

46. The main reason for holding the summer school was _____.
 (A) to show the children the importance of religion
 (B) to teach the children how to spend a night on board
 (C) to reward the children for completing summer school
 (D) to make up for things missing in a regular classroom

47-50 題為題組

PARIS, Dec. 9--Paris will be given a new Eiffel Tower--but made of wood--for the millennium, city mayor Jean Tiberi said Tuesday, presenting a program of celebration for the year 2,000 which would transform the "city of light" into the "capital of light."

The new structure will be 200 meters high, 100 meters shorter than the cast-iron Eiffel Tower built 100 years ago.

It will be made of timber as an ecological symbol of "the right to a dignified life on a protected Earth," said architects Normier, Henni and Lelievre, who were also responsible for the Europe section at the Seville exhibition.

The tower, of pinewood, will be built on eight pillars and will be topped with a flower of five metal petals of 700 square meters each.

The structure, to be erected in the redeveloped areas of the capital's 13th district, will cost 250 million francs (US$42 million).

Tiberi also said that Paris would be placed under the sign of the lights of "culture and life" and "intelligence."

"If, in 1900, Paris was consecrated the 'city of light', it will become the 'capital of light' for the millennium," Tiberi said.

The mayor said new buildings would be illuminated, notably along the banks of the Seine, which would become a luminous strip, while Notre Dame Cathedral would be lit from the inside to show off its stained glass windows.

A laser clock would be installed on top of the Arc de Triomphe at the top of the Champs Elysees and three laser beams would pick out the hands showing the hours, minutes and seconds in the millennium countdown, Tiberi said.

A giant egg-timer will be set up in the Place de la Concorde and its sand will begin running after a solar eclipse scheduled on April 11, 1999.

47. Why is Paris building a new Eiffel Tower?
   (A) The old Eiffel Tower must be torn down.
   (B) The old iron Eiffel Tower needs to be re-built with wood.
   (C) The tower is built to celebrate the Seville exhibition.
   (D) The tower is built to celebrate the coming of the year 2,000.

48. According to Mayor Tiberi, Paris will be decorated mostly by
　　＿＿＿＿＿＿.
　　(A) flowers　　　(B) lights　　　(C) new buildings　　(D) towers

49. What is "the Seine" mentioned in the passage?
　　(A) A tall monument.　　　　(B) The name of the new tower.
　　(C) A river.　　　　　　　　(D) A crowded street.

50. Why is the new tower made of wood?
　　(A) To serve as a symbol of environmental concerns.
　　(B) To reduce the weight and ensure the safety.
　　(C) Out of the consideration of the limited budget.
　　(D) To form a contrast with the iron structure of the old tower.

（請由 51 題繼續作答）

貳：選擇題（第二部份）（10％）

說明：第 51 至 60 題，每題有一個空格。請依文意選出最適當的一個選項，
　　　標示在答案卡之「選擇題第二部份」。每題答對得 1 分，答錯不倒
　　　扣。

51-60 題爲題組

　　People in the United States ＿(51)＿ tell stories a lot more than they do today. In earlier days, people were ＿(52)＿ by the stories they told and the stories that were told ＿(53)＿ them. Storytelling was a ＿(54)＿ of passing on family history, of giving meaning to experience, of understanding ＿(55)＿ happens in people's lives and of passing that ＿(56)＿ on.

　　＿(57)＿, television, movies, and books have taken over the once personal and ＿(58)＿ activity of storytelling. We have ＿(59)＿ believe that storytelling is just for children. However, recent studies have shown ＿(60)＿ interest in storytelling for adults is returning.

　　　　(A) come to　　　(B) knowledge　　　(C) Today
　　　　(D) Therefore　　(E) that　　　　　(F) about
　　　　(G) interested　　(H) what　　　　　(I) used to
　　　　(J) intimate　　　(K) known　　　　　(L) way

參：非選擇題

一、短詩閱讀（10％）

說明：以下爲一篇短詩，請於閱讀後，以單字或片語簡答詩後所附之問題。
請先標明題號，再將答案寫在「答案卷」上。每題答對得 2 分。

1-5 題爲題組

April Rain Song

by Langston Hughes

Let the rain kiss you.
Let the rain beat upon your head with silver liquid drops.
Let the rain sing you a lullaby.

The rain makes still pools on the sidewalk.
The rain makes running pools in the gutter.
The rain plays a little sleep-song on our roof at night —

And I love the rain.

1. Which season of the year serves as the setting of the poem？

2. Which word in the poem is closest in meaning to *sleep-song*？

3. What does the phrase *silver liquid drops* refer to？

4. Which word in the poem is opposite in meaning to *running*？

5. Which of the following words best describes the rain in this poem: *boring, harsh, depressing, heavy, hopeful, or musical*？

二、英文作文（20％）

說明：1. 請依提示在「答案卷」上寫一篇英文作文。
2. 文長以 120 字左右爲原則。

提示：每個人在不同的情況下對雨可能有不同的感受。請寫一篇短文，敘述你在某一個下雨天的實際經歷或看到的景象，並據此描述你對雨的感覺。

87年度學科能力測驗英文科試題詳解

壹：選擇題（第一部份）

一、字彙：片語與語法

1. (**D**) Follow the <u>instructions</u> *closely*, **and** you will find it easy to assemble the bicycle.

    只要你完全遵照指示，就會發現裝配腳踏車十分容易。

    (A) function〔'fʌŋkʃən〕*n.* 功能
    (B) diagnose〔,daɪəg'noz〕*n.* 診斷
    (C) appointment〔ə'pɔɪntmənt〕*n.* 約會
    (D) *instructions*〔ɪn'strʌkʃənz〕*n., pl.* 命令；指示
    follow〔'falo〕*v.* 遵照　　closely〔'kloslɪ〕*adv.* 密切地
    assemble〔ə'sɛmbḷ〕*v.* 裝配

2. (**B**) *If I can help you with the project*, don't <u>hesitate</u> to call me.

    如果這項計畫需要我幫忙，儘管打電話給我，不要猶豫。

    (A) concern〔kən'sɝn〕*v.* 關心
    (B) *hesitate*〔'hɛzə,tet〕*v.* 猶豫
    (C) notify〔'notə,faɪ〕*v.* 通知
    (D) submit〔səb'mɪt〕*v.* 屈服
    project〔'pradʒɛkt〕*n.* 計畫

3. (**C**) <u>Conflicts</u> *between good friends* should be resolved, not ignored.

    好友之間的衝突，應該要解決，不容忽視。

    (A) compliment〔'kampləmənt〕*n.* 稱讚
    (B) concern〔kən'sɝn〕*n.* 關心
    (C) *conflict*〔'kanflɪkt〕*n.* 衝突
    (D) connection〔kə'nɛkʃən〕*n.* 連接；關係
    resolve〔rɪ'zalv〕*v.* 解決　　ignore〔ɪg'nor〕*v.* 忽視

4. (**B**) Group registrations are not allowed. Each member must

register for the conference *individually*.

團體報名不予受理。每位成員必須個別報名參加這場會議。

(A) comfortably〔'kʌmfətəblɪ〕*adv.* 舒服地

(B) ***individually***〔͵ɪndɪ'vɪdʒʊəlɪ〕*adv.* 個別地；單獨地

(C) intelligently〔ɪn'tɛlədʒəntlɪ〕*adv.* 聰明地

(D) respectfully〔rɪ'spɛktfəlɪ〕*adv.* 有禮貌地

registration〔͵rɛdʒɪ'streʃən〕*n.* 登記　　***register for*** 報名

conference〔'kɑnfərəns〕*n.* 會議

5. (**C**) Mr. Wang's arguments were *very* persuasive, *and* the com-

mittee *finally* accepted his proposal.

王先生的論點十分有說服力，委員會最後接受了他的提議。

(A) artificial〔͵ɑrtə'fɪʃəl〕*adj.* 人造的

(B) inappropriate〔͵ɪnə'proprɪɪt〕*adj.* 不適當的

(C) ***persuasive***〔pə'swesɪv〕*adj.* 有說服力的

(D) descriptive〔dɪ'skrɪptɪv〕*adj.* 描寫的

argument〔'ɑrgjəmənt〕*n.* 論據；理由

committee〔kə'mɪtɪ〕*n.* 委員會

proposal〔prə'pozl〕*n.* 提議

6. (**D**) The woman is *so* sentimental *that she cries every time she*

hears a sad story.

那個女人非常多愁善感，每次聽到悲慘的故事都會哭。

(A) casual〔'kæʒʊəl〕*adj.* 休閒的；非正式的

(B) harsh〔hɑrʃ〕*adj.* 嚴厲的

(C) intimate〔'ɪntəmɪt〕*adj.* 親密的

(D) ***sentimental***〔͵sɛntə'mɛntl̩〕*adj.* 多愁善感的

7. (**A**) We *firmly* believe **that** *with your intelligence and hard work,*

you will pass the exam without any difficulty.

我們堅信，以你的聰明才智與努力，一定會輕易地通過考試。

(A) *firmly*〔'fɜmlɪ〕*adv.* 堅定地

(B) extremely〔ɪk'strimlɪ〕*adv.* 極端地

(C) strictly〔'strɪktlɪ〕*adv.* 嚴格地

(D) inquiringly〔ɪn'kwaɪrɪŋlɪ〕*adv.* 想詢問地；懷疑地

intelligence〔ɪn'tɛlədʒəns〕*n.* 聰明才智

8. (**B**) *If we walk at this slow pace,* we'll *never* get to our des-

tination *on time.*

如果我們走路的步伐這麼慢的話，絕不可能準時到達目的地。

(A) mood〔mud〕*n.* 心情

(B) *pace*〔pes〕*n.* 步調；步伐；速度

(C) tide〔taɪd〕*n.* 潮汐

(D) access〔'æksɛs〕*n.* 接近；使用權

destination〔,dɛstə'neʃən〕*n.* 目的地　　*on time* 準時

9. (**C**) The territorial dispute can be traced *back to the year 1917,*

when the two countries were at war.

這場領土之爭可追溯至一九一七年，兩國交戰的時候。

(A) hold〔hold〕*v.* 掌握；舉行

(B) recall〔rɪ'kɔl〕*v.* 回想起

(C) *trace*〔tres〕*v.* 追溯

(D) switch〔swɪtʃ〕*v.* 轉換

territorial〔,tɛrə'torɪəl〕*adj.* 領土的

dispute〔dɪ'spjut〕*n.* 爭論

10. (**A**) One key factor *to success* is to have a definite goal *first*

    and *then* do your best *to attain the goal.*
    成功最主要的因素之一，就是要先有明確的目標，然後再盡全力
    達成目標。

    (A) *attain* 〔 ə'ten 〕 *v.* 達到
    (B) contest 〔 kən'tɛst 〕 *v.* 競爭；比賽
    (C) encounter 〔 ɪn'kaʊntɚ 〕 *v.* 遭遇（困難）
    (D) struggle 〔'strʌgḷ 〕 *v.* 奮鬥；掙扎
    key 〔 ki 〕 *adj.* 最主要的　　factor 〔'fæktɚ 〕 *n.* 因素
    definite 〔'dɛfənɪt 〕 *adj.* 明確的　　goal 〔 gol 〕 *n.* 目標
    do *one's* *best* 盡全力

11. (**A**) Jane and Sue are twins, *but* they seem to have nothing *in*

    common.
    珍和蘇是雙胞胎，但她們似乎沒有共同點。

    (A) *have nothing in common* 沒有共同點
    　　比較：have a lot in common 有許多共同點
    (B) in comparison with 與～相比
    (C) keep in contact with　與～保持聯繫
    (D) in contrast to　與～對比之下
    twins 〔 twɪnz 〕 *n., pl.* 雙胞胎

12. (**A**) How did the traffic accident come about?
    這場車禍是如何發生的？

    (A) *come about* 發生（＝ *happen*）
    (B) come around 恢復知覺；恢復健康
    (C) come off 舉行；成功；脫落
    (D) come over 從遠處來；順便來訪

13. (**D**) *During the lunch hour*, Jane <u>ran over</u> her notes *so she would remember them for the test*.

珍在午餐時間<u>複習</u>筆記，想牢記筆記，以應付考試。

(A) run into　撞上；偶然遇到　　(B) run off　逃跑；離開

(C) run out of　用完　　(D) ***run over***　複習

14. (**C**) We shall expect you *at eight o'clock*; *by the way*, it's an informal dinner.

我們希望你八點到；順便一提，這是非正式的晚餐。

(A) by accident　意外地 (= *unexpectedly*)

(B) by all means　務必；當然 (= *of course*)

(C) ***by the way***　順便一提 (= *incidentally*)

(D) by then　到了那時候

informal〔ɪn'fɔrml〕*adj.* 非正式的

15. (**A**) Stricter measures have been taken *to* <u>ward off</u> *potential dangers concerning cigarette-smoking*.

我們已採取更嚴厲的措施，來<u>避免</u>抽煙可能導致的危險。

(A) ***ward off***　避免　　(B) give in　屈服

(C) check out　結帳退房　　(D) hang up　掛斷電話

strict〔strɪkt〕*adj.* 嚴格的

measures〔'mɛʒ♂z〕*n., pl.* 步驟；措施

potential〔pə'tɛnʃəl〕*adj.* 可能的；潛在的

concerning〔kən's♂nɪŋ〕*prep.* 關於 (= *about*)

16. (**B**) 亨　利：詹姆斯，請你幫我把這些書還給圖書館。

詹姆斯：什麼？

亨　利：我請你幫我把這些書還給圖書館。

＊ask 為一般動詞，其用法為：ask *sb.* to V.「請求某人～」，

故選 (B)。

17.（**B**）瑪麗：妳準備好要走了嗎？我可以載妳。
　　　　貝蒂：謝謝。但我想等信來了再走。
　　　　＊表時間的副詞子句，要用現在式代替未來式，故選(B)。

18.（**C**）愛麗絲：今晚八點電視有一部很好看的電影。
　　　　約　翰：也許我可以早點回家看。
　　　　＊依句意，應是「及早回家看電視」，故選(C)。

19.（**B**）林先生：你不認為我們政府應該在台灣再蓋另一座核能發電廠嗎？
　　　　劉先生：嗯，真希望我能同意你的看法，但我不這麼認為。
　　　　＊此為表願望的假設用法，依句意與現在事實相反，須用「過去式
　　　　　助動詞＋原形動詞」，故選(B)。

20.（**D**）瑪麗：你問過湯姆他暑假上哪兒去了嗎？
　　　　海倫：沒有，我還沒問，不過我會問他的。
　　　　＊此為間接問句，所以主詞和動詞不須倒裝，依句意為過去式，
　　　　　選(D)。

二、綜合測驗：

There was *once* a man *in Puerto Rico* **who** *had a wonderful*

parrot. The parrot was unique, there was no other bird *like him in*
　　　　　　　　　　　　　21

the whole world. He could learn to say any word — *except* one.
　　　　　　　　　　　　　　　　　　　　　　22

He could not say the name *of his native town*, Catano.

　　　　從前，在波多黎各，有一個人養了一隻神奇的鸚鵡。這隻鸚鵡非常獨
特，全世界沒有其他的鳥像牠一樣。牠可以學會說任何字 —— 除了一個字
之外。牠不會說牠家鄉的名字，卡丹諾。

　　　　parrot〔ˈpærət〕*n.* 鸚鵡　Puerto Rico〔ˌpwɛrtəˈriko〕*n.* 波多黎各
　　　　native〔ˈnetɪv〕*adj.* 出生地的；本國的　***native town*** 出生的城鎮

21. (**B**) 根據後半句「全世界沒有其他的鳥像牠一樣」，可知牠非常「獨特」，
選 (B) ***unique*** 〔 ju′nik 〕*adj.* 獨特的。而 (A) lonely 〔′lonlɪ 〕*adj.* 孤獨
的，(C) sorrowful 〔′sɑrofəl 〕*adj.* 悲傷的，(D) personal 〔′pɜsn̩l 〕*adj.*
私人的，均不合句意。

22. (**C**) 依句意，「除了」一個字之外，其餘的牠都可以學會，選 (C) ***except***
「除了～之外」。而 (A) 沒有，(B) beyond 「遠超過；在～之外」，
(D) 儘管，皆不合句意。

The man <u>did</u> everything *he could* to teach the parrot *to say*
23

"*Catano*," ***but*** he *never* <u>succeeded</u>. *At first* he was *very* gentle with
24

the bird, ***but*** *gradually* he lost his <u>temper</u>. "You stupid bird! <u>Why</u>
25   26

can't you learn to say that one word? Say 'Catano' ***or*** *I'll kill you*!"

But the parrot would not say it. *Many times* the man screamed, "Say

'Catano' ***or*** *I'll kill you*!" ***But*** the bird would not <u>repeat</u> the name.
27

　　這個人竭盡所能去教鸚鵡說「卡丹諾」，但總無法成功。起初他對這
隻鳥還很溫和，但是漸漸地，他生氣了。「你這隻笨鳥！爲什麼你就是學
不會說這一個字？說『卡丹諾』，否則我就宰了你！」可是鸚鵡還是不說。
這個人大叫了好幾次：「說『卡丹諾』，否則我就宰了你！」但鳥兒還是
沒有重覆這個名字。

　　gentle 〔′dʒɛntl̩ 〕*adj.* 溫和的　　　scream 〔 skrim 〕*v.* 尖叫；大叫

23. (**A**) ***do everything one can*** 竭盡所能

24. (**D**) 依句意，沒有「成功」，故選 (D) ***succeeded***。而 (A) 失敗，(B) attempt
〔 ə′tɛmpt 〕*v.* 嘗試，(C) 改變，均不合句意。

25. (**C**) **lose** one's **temper** 生氣；發脾氣

而 (A) pet〔pɛt〕n. 寵物，(B) 東西；事情，(D) possession〔pə'zɛʃən〕n. 擁有；財產，均不合句意。

26. (**B**) 依句意，這個人是問原因，故選 (B) **Why**。

27. (**C**) (A) tell 告訴，句意不合；(B) talk 和 (D) converse〔kən'vɝs〕v. 談話，均爲不及物動詞，不可直接接受詞，文法不合，故選 (C) **repeat**〔rɪ'pit〕v. 重覆。

Finally the man gave up. He picked up the parrot **and** threw the bird *into the chicken house*. *In the chicken house*, there were four old chickens, *waiting to be killed for Sunday's dinner.* "You are
　　　　　　　　　　　　　　　　　　　　　　28
even more stupid *than the chickens*," the man said **as he was leaving.** *The next morning*, the man went out to the chicken house. **When he opened the door**, he was shocked *by* **what** he saw. He could not
　　　　　　　　　　　　　　　　　　29
believe his eyes and ears!

　　最後這個人放棄了。他抓起鸚鵡，把牠丟到雞舍裏。雞舍裏，有四隻老雞，等著被殺來做星期天的晚餐。「你甚至比雞還笨，」這個人要離開時這麼說道。隔天早上，這個人到了雞舍。當他打開門時，他被他眼前所見嚇呆了。他不敢相信自己的眼睛和耳朵！

28. (**D**) 依句意，待宰的雞是爲了做晚餐，表目的、用途，介系詞用 for，選 (D)。

29. (**B**) 依句意，選 (B) **shocked**〔ʃɑkt〕adj. 震驚的。而 (A) worried 擔心的，(C) delighted〔dɪ'laɪtɪd〕adj. 高興的，(D) blinded〔'blaɪndɪd〕adj. 被蒙蔽的；看不見的，句意均不合。

On the floor lay three dead chickens. The parrot was screaming
　　　　　　30

at the fourth, "Say 'Catano' *or I'll kill you!*"

　　地板上躺了三隻死雞。鸚鵡正在對著第四隻雞尖叫著：「說『卡丹諾』，
否則我就宰了你！」

30.(**A**) 本句為倒裝句，原本應是：Three dead chickens *lay on the*
　　　　*floor.*副詞片語置於句首，句子須倒裝，主詞與動詞順序須對調。
　　　　比較選項 (A)、(B)、(C) 三動詞的三態變化：
　　　　　　⎧ lie – lied – lied （說謊）
　　　　　　⎨ lie – lay – lain （躺；在於）
　　　　　　⎩ lay – laid – laid （產卵；放置）

Perhaps most *of us* are familiar with the saying "*Laugh* **and** *the*

world laughs *with you, weep* **and** *you weep alone.*" **But** did you know
　　　　　　31　　　　　　　　　　　　　　　　　　　　　32

that according to recent research, people are losing the art of

laughter **and** it could have a serious effect on our health?
　　　　　　　　　　　　　　　　33

　　或許我們大部分的人都熟悉這句諺語：「笑時萬眾附和，哭時獨自垂
淚。」但是你知道根據最近的研究指出，人們逐漸失去了笑的藝術，而這
對我們的健康可能會有很嚴重的影響嗎？

　　be familiar with ～　熟悉～　　saying ('seɪŋ) *n.* 諺語
　　weep (wip) *v.* 哭泣　　recent ('risṇt) *adj.* 最近的
　　have an effect on ～　對～有影響

31.(**C**) Laugh and the world *laughs* with you, weep and you weep
　　　　alone.這句諺語比喻世態炎涼，錦上添花常常有，雪中送炭無人做。

32.(**B**) 前後句子語氣有轉折，故選 (B) **But**。

33.(**B**) 依句意，選 (B) ***serious*** 嚴重的。而 (A) 好的，(C) 少的，(D) 沉重的，
　　　句意皆不合。

In 1930 we laughed *on average for 19 minutes each day*, ***but*** *by
1980* it <u>had decreased</u> to six minutes. Children, *on the other hand*,
<u>　　　　　34</u>　　　　　　　　　　　　　　　　　　　35
can see the funny side *of things more often* ***and*** may laugh *up to 400
times a day*.

　　一九三○年時，我們平均每天笑十九分鐘，但到了一九八○年時，已
減少到六分鐘。而另一方面，兒童能夠比較常看到事物有趣的一面，一天
可能笑高達四百次。

　　on average 平均　　***up to ~*** 高達~

34.(**D**) 到過去某時已完成的事情，須用「過去完成式」，故選 (D) ***had
　　　decreased***。

35.(**D**) (A) as a result 因此　　　(B) in addition 此外
　　　(C) by chance 偶然地　　　(D) ***on the other hand*** 另一方面

By exhaling air from the lungs in short bursts of laughter,
　　　　　　　　　　　　　　　　　　　36
breathing is quickened ***and*** heartbeats increased, ***which*** *achieves
as much* good *as ten minutes on an exercise bike*. Laughter, *too*,
　37
has a beneficial effect *on our immune system*, <u>encouraging</u> *the pro-
　　　　　　　　　　　　　　　　　　　　　　38
duction of white blood cells* ***and*** *increasing our resistance to infection*. It makes a difference *to our appearance, too*, ***when*** *we
　39
relax our facial muscles*!

在一陣陣短促的笑聲中，藉由從肺部呼出空氣，呼吸加快了，心跳也增加了，如此所得到的好處，和踩運動腳踏車十分鐘一樣。笑對我們的免疫系統也有良效，它能刺激白血球的製造，因而增加我們對傳染病的抵抗力。而當我們放鬆臉部肌肉的同時，它也改變了我們的面容。

exhale 〔ɪksˋhel〕 *v.* 呼出（↔ inhale 〔ɪnˋhel〕 *v.* 吸入）
heartbeat 〔ˋhɑrt͵bit〕 *n.* 心跳　　achieve 〔əˋtʃiv〕 *v.* 達到
beneficial 〔͵bɛnəˋfɪʃəl〕 *adj.* 有益的　　immune 〔ɪˋmjun〕 *adj.* 免疫的
cell 〔sɛl〕 *n.* 細胞　　***white blood cell*** 白血球
resistance 〔rɪˋzɪstəns〕 *n.* 抵抗（力）
infection 〔ɪnˋfɛkʃən〕 *n.* 傳染（病）　　relax 〔rɪˋlæks〕 *v.* 放鬆
facial 〔ˋfeʃəl〕 *adj.* 臉部的　　muscle 〔ˋmʌsl̩〕 *n.* 肌肉

36. (**A**) ***a burst of laughter*** 一陣笑聲
　　　　而 (B) break 〔brek〕 *n.* 休息時間，(C) circle 〔ˋsɝkl̩〕 *n.* 圓圈，
　　　　(D) piece 〔pis〕 *n.* 片，皆不合句意。

37. (**B**) 依句意，二者所得到的好處一樣多，應用「as ~ as …」的句型。
　　　　而句中 good 在此做名詞，表「利益；好處」，爲不可數名詞，要
　　　　用 much 修飾，故選 (B) ***as much*** 。

38. (**C**) 本句是由 Laughter, too, has … system, and encourages …簡化
　　　　連接詞 and 而來的分詞構句，故選 (C) ***encouraging*** 。

39. (**A**) 此處主詞仍然指 Laughter，故代名詞用 It，選 (A)。

Laughter *really* is the best medicine, *so why not give yourself*
　　　　　40
a treat? Have a good laugh *today* — *and* feel better *for it.*
　　笑的確是最佳良藥，所以何不給你自己一件高興的事？今天好好地笑
一場 —— 你會覺得好多了。

　　treat 〔trit〕 *n.* 令人高興的事；樂事

40. (**D**) 爲了加強本句話的語氣，依句意選 (D) ***really*** 「的確」。而 (A) 幾乎
　　　　不，(B) 仁慈地，(C) rarely 〔ˋrɛrlɪ〕 *adv.* 很少，句意均不合。

三、閱讀測驗：

41－43題為題組

One *of the most unusual graduation speakers of the 1983 commencement season* was not a person at all. The speaker was Robot Redford, *a robot* *who delivered the commencement address* at a *community college in suburban Maryland.*

在一九八三年畢業季裏的致詞畢業生中，最特別的其中一個，根本不算個人。這位致詞生是羅勃特‧瑞得弗德。他是個機器人，在馬里蘭市郊的一所社區大學裏，發表畢業演說。

commencement〔kə'mɛnsmənt〕*n.* 畢業典禮
robot〔'robət〕*n.* 機器人　　deliver〔dɪ'lɪvɚ〕*v.* 發表
address〔ə'drɛs , 'ædrɛs〕*n.* 演講
community〔kə'mjunətɪ〕*n.* 社區
suburban〔sə'bɝbən〕*adj.* 市郊的

The speaker, *carefully programmed,* arrived on the stage *under its own power* *and* proceeded to tell the audience *of 658 graduates, their families, and friends* *that* *they would have to learn to work with robots and technology to solve society's problems.* The robot described itself *as an extension of a person* *to help humans increase the workload.* **Although** *this particular robot can be programmed to speak,* the voice *heard* wasn't that *of the robot,* **because it** *was feared **that** the robot's voice was not loud enough to carry*

throughout the hall. An amplified voice *of a human* was used

instead, **while** *the listeners watched the robot.*

這名由程式精心設計出的致詞者，是由自己的力量走到台上，開始對著聽眾，共六百五十八位畢業生及其家人、朋友，說明大家必須學習和機器人以及科技聯手合作，以解決社會問題。這名機器人描述自己是人的延伸，能夠協助提高人類的工作量。雖然這名獨特的機器人能設計用來說話，它的聲音並不是機器人自己發出的。為了怕機器人的聲音不夠宏亮，無法遍及整個會場，所以用擴音器的人聲作為取代，而聽眾眼前看到的卻是機器人。

program〔'progræm〕*v.* 設計程式　　stage〔stedʒ〕*n.* 舞台
proceed〔prə'sid〕*v.* 開始進行
audience〔'ɔdɪəns〕*n.* 觀眾；聽眾
graduate〔'grædʒʊˌet〕*n.* 畢業生
technology〔tɛk'nɑlədʒɪ〕*n.* 科技；技術
extension〔ɪk'stɛnʃən〕*n.* 延伸　　workload〔'wɜkˌlod〕*n.* 工作量
hall〔hɔl〕*n.* 會館　　amplify〔'æmpləˌfaɪ〕*v.* 擴大

Robot Redford was followed *by a person, William Bakaleinikoff,*

who *spoke about the need for cooperation between people and*

technology. Mr. Bakaleinikoff's experience *with his topic* included

the fact **that** *he had created Robot Redford **and** had provided the*

voice for the robot's words to the graduates.

機器人瑞得弗德後面跟著一位名叫威廉‧巴卡萊尼可夫的人，他說明人類與科技合作的必要性。巴卡萊尼可夫自己在這方面的經驗，包括了他創造這名機器人，又提供語音給它，讓它向畢業生致詞。

topic〔'tɑpɪk〕*n.* 主題

There was *quite* a bit of controversy *over the choice of a robot as a commencement speaker*. Some students thought *it was insensitive and degrading to use a robot*. Others thought *the idea was clever and innovative*.

選擇機器人作畢業致詞生這件事，有相當多的爭論。有些學生覺得用機器人是既沒意思又可恥。有些人則認為這個點子很聰明又有創意。

> controversy (ˈkɑntrəˌvɝsɪ) *n.* 爭論
> insensitive (ɪnˈsɛnsətɪv) *adj.* 沒感覺的
> degrading (dɪˈgredɪŋ) *adj.* 可恥的
> innovative (ˈɪnoˌvetɪv) *adj.* 創新的

"I'll *never* forget this speech," said one graduate. "You forget a political leader, **but** you won't forget a robot."

「我永遠忘不了這場演說，」一位畢業生這麼說。「你會忘掉某個政治領袖，但卻不會忘記機器人。」

41. (**C**) 這篇文章討論機器人瑞得弗德的演講，主要是因為 _____。
   (A) 它具有政治性　　　　(B) 它是心理的
   (C) 它具有爭議性　　　　(D) 它沒什麼意思
   psychological (ˌsaɪkəˈlɑdʒɪkḷ) *adj.* 心理的
   controversial (ˌkɑntrəˈvɝʃəl) *adj.* 有爭議性的

42. (**D**) 下列敘述何者為非？
   (A) 機器人瑞得弗德是會說話的機器。
   (B) 機器人瑞得弗德自己走到台上。
   (C) 機器人瑞得弗德在一九八三年發表畢業致詞。
   (D) 機器人瑞得弗德畢業於馬里蘭的一所大學。
   by *oneself* 獨力地

43. (**B**) 本段文章可支持以下的哪個論點？

　　(A) 設計機器人的目的是爲了要降低人類的生產力。

　　(B) 機器人瑞得弗德是由威廉·巴卡萊尼可夫所發明的。

　　(C) 畢業典禮中的每個人都很喜歡這項安排。

　　(D) 機器人瑞得弗德的演講太難以了解。

　　brainchild (ˈbrɛnˌtʃaɪld) *n.* 發明；創作

---

44 － 46 題爲題組

Summers *with Father* were *always* enjoyable. Swimming, hiking, boating, fishing--the days were not long *enough* to contain all *of our activities*. There *never* seemed to be enough time to go to church, *which disturbed some friends and relatives. Accused of neglecting this part of our education,* my father *still* instituted a summer school *for my brother and me.*

　　和父親一起度過的夏天，總是很好玩。游泳、健行、划船、釣魚 —— 要做完我們所有的活動，日子總嫌不夠長。我們似乎永遠都挪不出時間上教堂，而這件事頗讓我們的一些朋友和親戚不安。我父親雖被指責忽略了我們這方面的教育，但他卻仍然爲我和弟弟兩個人設立了一所暑期學校。

　　enjoyable (ɪnˈdʒɔɪəbl̩) *adj.* 愉快的　　hiking (ˈhaɪkɪŋ) *n.* 健行

　　disturb (dɪˈstɝb) *v.* 使不安　　relative (ˈrɛlətɪv) *n.* 親戚

　　accuse sb. of sth. 控告某人；指責某人某事

　　neglect (nɪˈglɛkt) *v.* 忽略　　institute (ˈɪnstəˌtjut) *v.* 設立

His summer course included ancient history, *which Papa felt our schools neglected,* and navigation, *in which* we *first had a formal examination in the dining room, part of which consisted of tying* *several knots in a given time limit. Then we were each separately sent on **what** was grandly referred to as a cruise in my father's 18-foot boat, spending the night on board, **and** loaded down, according to my mother, with enough food for a week. I remember **that** on my cruise I was required to formally plot our course, using the tide table, **even though** our goal was an island I could see quite clearly across the water in the distance.*

父親的暑期課程包括古代史，這是一門父親認爲被學校忽略的課程，以及航海學，這堂課我們首先在餐廳裏舉行了正式的考試，部分內容是包括在規定的時限內要打好幾個繩結。接著我們分別被送上我父親 18 英呎長的小船，進行美其名爲巡航的活動。我們在船上過夜，而根據母親的說法，船上載滿了夠吃一星期的食物。我記得在巡航時，曾被要求用潮汐表畫出正式的航線，即使我們的目標是我遠遠望過水面就可清楚看到的小島。

ancient (ˈenʃənt) *adj.* 古代的
navigation (ˌnævəˈgeʃən) *n.* 航海學
consist of ~ 包含；由~組成　　tie (taɪ) *v.* 綁
knot (nɑt) *n.* 繩結　　grandly (ˈgrændlɪ) *adv.* 堂皇地
refer to A ***as*** B 把 A 稱爲 B
cruise (kruz) *n.* 巡航　　***on board*** 在船上
load (lod) *v.* 裝載　　require (rɪˈkwaɪr) *v.* 要求
plot (plɑt) *v.* 繪製圖表　　course (kors) *n.* 課程；航線
tide table 潮汐表　　***in the distance*** 在遠處

44. (**B**) 就本文的用法，「航海學」顯然是指 ＿＿＿＿＿＿。
　　(A) 上暑期學校　　　　　(B) 駕駛一艘船
　　(C) 駕駛飛機的行爲　　　(D) 餐廳裏的一項正式考試
　　practice (ˈpræktɪs) *n.* 實行；行爲　　pilot (ˈpaɪlət) *v.* 駕駛

45.(**A**) 下列哪項活動不是父親為小孩設計的暑期教育？
　　(A) 上教堂。　　　　　　　(B) 去健行。
　　(C) 去游泳。　　　　　　　(D) 研讀古代史。

46.(**D**) 設立暑期學校的主要理由是 ＿＿＿＿＿＿。
　　(A) 告訴孩子宗教的重要　　(B) 教導孩子如何在船上過夜
　　(C) 獎勵孩子上完暑期學校　(D) 為彌補正規課堂教育的不足
　　reward〔rɪˋwɔrd〕*v.* 獎賞；報酬　　***make up for*** 彌補
　　regular〔ˋrɛgjələ〕*adj.* 正規的；正式的

47 － 50 題為題組

PARIS, Dec. 9--Paris will be given a new Eiffel Tower--*but made of wood--for the millennium*, city mayor *Jean Tiberi* said Tuesday, *presenting a program of celebration for the year 2,000* **which would** transform the "*city of light*" into the "*capital of light.*"

巴黎，十二月九日——巴黎即將有一座新的艾菲爾塔——不過是木造的——以迎接公元二千年的到來，巴黎市長金蒂貝里於週二時宣布了此項消息，他還推出一項慶祝公元兩千年的活動，要將這座「燈火之城」晉升為「燈火之都」。

　　Eiffel Tower 艾菲爾塔
　　millennium〔məˋlɛnɪəm〕*n.* 一千年期間；千禧年
　　mayor〔ˋmeə〕*n.* 市長　　present〔prɪˋzɛnt〕*v.* 提出
　　transform A ***into*** B 把 A 變成 B　　capital〔ˋkæpɪtḷ〕*n.* 首都

The new structure will be 200 meters high, 100 meters shorter *than the cast-iron Eiffel Tower built 100 years ago.*

　　新塔有二百公尺高。比一百年前建造的艾菲爾鐵塔少了一百公尺。

structure〔'strʌktʃɚ〕 n. 建築物
cast-iron〔'kæst'aɪən〕 adj. 鐵製的

It will be made of timber *as an ecological symbol of "the right to a dignified life on a protected Earth,"* said architects *Normier, Henni and Lelievre,* **who** *were also responsible for the Europe section at the Seville exhibition.*

　　在塞維利亞展覽會上，負責歐洲區的建築師諾爾密、亨尼和勒里夫聲稱，這座木造的塔具有生態保護的象徵意義，它代表了「在受保護的地球上，保有生命尊嚴的權利」。

timber〔'tɪmbɚ〕 n. 木材
ecological〔ˌɪkə'ladʒɪkl̩〕 adj. 生態保護的
symbol〔'sɪmbl̩〕 n. 象徵
dignified〔'dɪgnəˌfaɪd〕 adj. 有尊嚴的
architect〔'arkəˌtɛkt〕 n. 建築師
exhibition〔ˌɛksə'bɪʃən〕 n. 展覽會

The tower, *of pinewood,* will be built *on eight pillars* **and** will be topped *with a flower of five metal petals of 700 square meters each.*

　　這座松木塔將由八根柱子所支撐，頂端有一朵由五片金屬花瓣組成的花，每片花瓣面積為七百平方公尺。

pinewood〔'paɪnˌwud〕 n. 松木　　pillar〔'pɪlɚ〕 n. 柱子
top〔tap〕 v. 覆蓋～的頂端　　petal〔'pɛtl̩〕 n. 花瓣

The structure, *to be erected in the redeveloped areas of the capital's 13th district,* will cost 250 million francs (US$42 million).

　　這座塔將矗立在首都第十三區的重建區，所花經費爲二億五千萬法郎（約合美金四千二百萬元）。

　　erect〔ɪˈrɛkt〕v. 豎立　　redevelop〔ˌridɪˈvɛləp〕v. 重建；重新開發
district〔ˈdɪstrɪkt〕n. 行政區；區域

Tiberi *also* said *that Paris would be placed under the sign of the lights of "culture and life" and "intelligence."*

　　帝貝里也提到，寫著「文化與生活」和「智慧」的燈光標示將照耀全巴黎。

"If, in 1900, Paris was consecrated the 'city of light', it will become the 'capital of light' for the millennium," Tiberi said.

　　帝貝里說：「如果一九〇〇年的巴黎被譽爲『燈火之城』，那麼到公元二千年時，它將成爲『燈火之都』。」

　　consecrate〔ˈkɑnsɪˌkret〕v. 奉爲神聖；尊崇

The mayor said *new buildings would be illuminated, notably along the banks of the Seine, which would become a luminous strip, while Notre Dame Cathedral would be lit from the inside to show off its stained glass windows.*

　　市長表示，新的建築物都將被照明，在塞納河畔顯得特別耀眼，形成一條狹長的燈火帶，聖母院則由內部照明，以突顯它的彩繪玻璃。

illuminate〔ɪˈluməˌnet〕v. 照明；照亮
notably〔ˈnotəblɪ〕adv. 顯著地　　　bank〔bæŋk〕n. 河岸
Seine〔sen〕n. 塞納河　　luminous〔ˈlumənəs〕adj. 光亮的；燦爛的
strip〔strɪp〕n. 狹長帶　　*Notre Dame Cathedral* 聖母院
show off 使顯眼　　*stained glass* 彩繪玻璃

A laser clock would be installed *on top of the Arc de Triomphe at the top of the Champs Elysees* **and** three laser beams would pick out the hands *showing the hours, minutes and seconds in the millennium countdown*, Tiberi said.

　　一座雷射時鐘將架設在香舍里榭大道開端的凱旋門上方，三道雷射光束分別代表時針、分針、秒針，可以顯示距離公元二千年倒數計時的時間。

install〔ɪnˈstɔl〕v. 架設　　*Arc de Triomphe* 凱旋門
Champs Elysees 香舍里榭大道　　beam〔bim〕n. 光束
pick out 使明顯　　countdown〔ˈkaʊntˌdaʊn〕n. 倒數計時

A giant egg-timer will be set up *in the Place de la Concorde* **and** its sand will begin running **after** *a solar eclipse scheduled on April 11, 1999.*

　　還有一座大型的煮蛋計時器會放置在協和廣場中，裡面的沙將在一九九九年四月十一日的日蝕過後開始滴漏。

egg-time〔ˈɛgˌtaɪmə〕n. 煮蛋計時器（煮蛋時所使用的三分鐘沙漏）
set up 設置　　*Place de la Concorde* 協和廣場
solar eclipse 日蝕　　schedule〔ˈskɛdʒʊl〕v. 預定

47.(**D**) 爲什麼巴黎要建造一座新艾菲爾塔？
　　(A) 舊艾菲爾塔必須被拆除。
　　(B) 舊艾菲爾鐵塔需要用木材重建。
　　(C) 建造這座塔是爲了慶祝塞維利亞展覽會。
　　(D) 建造這座塔是爲了慶祝公元兩千年的到來。
　　tear down 拆除

48.(**B**) 根據市長帝貝里的說法，巴黎最主要的裝飾是 ＿＿＿＿＿＿。
　　(A) 花　　　　(B) 燈　　　　(C) 新大樓　　　　(D) 塔

49.(**C**) 文中提到的「塞納河」是指什麼？
　　(A) 一座高大的紀念碑。　　(B) 新塔的名稱。
　　(C) 一條河。　　　　　　　(D) 一條擁擠的街道。
　　monument〔'manjəmənt〕*n.* 紀念碑

50.(**A**) 爲什麼新塔是木製的？
　　(A) 作爲環保的象徵。
　　(B) 減少重量並確保安全。
　　(C) 出於預算有限的考量。
　　(D) 作爲和舊鐵塔的對比。
　　serve as 當作；充當
　　ensure〔ɪn'ʃʊr〕*v.* 確保
　　consideration〔kən,sɪdə'reʃən〕*n.* 考慮
　　budget〔'bʌdʒɪt〕*n.* 預算

貳：選擇題（第二部份）

51－60題爲題組

People *in the United States* used to tell stories *a lot more* **than**
　　　　　　　　　　　　　　　　　　　　　51
they *do today.* *In earlier days,* people were known *by the stories*
　　　　　　　　　　　　　　　　　　　52
they told **and** the stories ***that were told about them.*** Storytelling was
　　　　　　　　　　　　　　　53

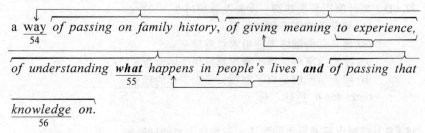

a <u>way</u> *of passing on family history*, *of giving meaning to experience*,
  54

*of understanding **what** happens in people's lives* **and** *of passing that*
            55

<u>knowledge on</u>.
  56

以前美國人說的故事比現在要多出許多。在早期，很多人因為自己所講的故事，或是一些關於他們的故事而為人所熟知。藉由說故事，可以傳遞家族歷史、說明人生經歷、了解人們的生活情形，並將這份知識傳承下去。

storytelling〔'storɪˌtɛlɪŋ〕*n.* 說故事
pass on 傳承

<u>Today</u>, television, movies, and books have taken over the *once*
  57

personal and <u>intimate</u> activity *of storytelling*. We have <u>come to</u> be-
         58   59

lieve ***that** storytelling is just for children. However*, recent studies

have shown ***that** interest in storytelling for adults is returning*.
            60

如今，電視、電影和書籍，已經取代了這種曾經是私人而親密的說故事活動。我們現在會認為說故事只是小孩子的遊戲。但是，最近的研究顯示，大人對說故事的興趣正在回復中。

take over 接管；接收

51.(**I**)	52.(**K**)	53.(**F**)	54.(**L**)	55.(**H**)
56.(**B**)	57.(**C**)	58.(**J**)	59.(**A**)	60.(**E**)

參：非選擇題

一、短詩閱題

1－5題為題組

春 雨 頌

蘭斯頓・休斯

讓雨親吻你。
讓雨用銀色水滴輕拍你的頭。
讓雨為你哼一首搖籃曲。

雨水為人行道添加了平靜的水池。
雨水為排水溝注入了流動的水塘。
夜晚雨水在屋頂上彈奏著催眠曲——

我愛春雨。

beat〔bit〕v. 打　　liquid〔'lɪkwɪd〕adj. 液體的
drop〔drɑp〕n. 滴　　lullaby〔'lʌlə,baɪ〕n. 搖籃曲（= sleep-song）
still〔stɪl〕adj. 靜止的　　sidewalk〔'saɪd,wɔk〕n. 人行道
running〔'rʌnɪŋ〕adj. 流動的　　gutter〔'gʌtɚ〕n. 排水溝
sleep-song〔'slip,sɔŋ〕n. 催眠曲

1. 一年中的哪一個季節可作為這首詩的背景？
   答：spring（春天）
   * setting〔'sɛtɪŋ〕n. 背景

2. 詩中哪一個字的意義最接近 sleep-song（催眠曲）？
   答：lullaby

3. 「銀色水滴」一詞是指何物？
   答：rain
   * *refer to* 是指～

4. 詩中哪一個字的意義和 running（流動的）相反？
   答：still

5. 下列何者最能描述詩中的雨：無聊的、刺耳的、令人沮喪的、沉重的、
   有希望的或悅耳的？
   答：musical
   * depressing〔dɪˋprɛsɪŋ〕adj. 令人沮喪的
   musical〔ˋmjuzɪkl〕adj. 音樂的；悅耳的

二、英文作文：（參考範例）

I have had many rainy day experiences. One such experience happened just recently. It was a sunny day, and I was on my way to my friend's birthday party. Because of the sun, I didn't think an umbrella was necessary. *Unfortunately*, I found out that I had made a big mistake. Dressed in my best clothes, I got caught in a sudden downpour. It was so heavy, and came so fast, that there was no way for me to escape it. I had no time to go back and change, so I continued on. *Consequently*, I arrived soaking wet, and had to stand in a puddle throughout the party.

Despite the inconveniences brought about by rain, it can bring me great joy and happiness. I love flowers very much, and without rain, they wouldn't be possible. The rain also cleans the air and brings coolness on hot summer days, which helps to make life in Taiwan a little more bearable. Like everything, rain has a good side and a bad side. I've learned to live with the bad side, and quite enjoy the good side. *Therefore*, let it rain.

downpour〔ˋdaʊn͵por〕n. 傾盆大雨
soak〔sok〕v. 濕透
puddle〔ˋpʌdl〕n.（雨後）積水處
bearable〔ˋbɛrəbl〕adj. 可忍受的

八十六年大學入學學科能力測驗試題 英文考科

第一部分：單一選擇題

壹、詞彙與語法

說明：第 1 至 15 題，每題選出最適當的一個選項，標示在答案卡之「選擇題第一部分」。每題答對得 1 分，答錯不倒扣。

1. What a small computer! Does it really _____?
   (A) bite   (B) type   (C) work   (D) use

2. For your own _____, please don't open the door until the train fully stops.
   (A) humanity   (B) safety   (C) liberty   (D) vanity

3. Peter told Marie that he couldn't attend her birthday party because he had been _____ engaged.
   (A) necessarily   (B) previously   (C) cautiously   (D) possibly

4. For hours, we have heard nothing but negative criticism. Why can't you say something more _____?
   (A) ambitious   (B) synthetic   (C) determined   (D) constructive

5. This library is famous for its wide _____ of books. You can find books on any topic you are interested in.
   (A) technology   (B) connection   (C) variety   (D) amazement

6. The child was _____. He just sat there and waited for something to happen.
   (A) passive   (B) expressive   (C) extensive   (D) persuasive

7. After dinner, Richard offered to pay the bill, but May insisted that they do it _____.
   (A) generously   (B) separately   (C) completely   (D) extensively

8. This TV program will _____ young viewers' understanding of the changing world.

(A) broaden   (B) soften   (C) tighten   (D) lengthen

9. I like everything about the apartment _____ the rent. It is too expensive.

(A) as for   (B) except for   (C) instead of   (D) in place of

10. _____ all the newspaper and television attention, the problem of child abuse has become well-known.

(A) As a result of   (B) Apart from
(C) In addition to   (D) Regardless of

11. Tim : Someone left a schoolbag on the bus.
     Sam : See if _____ a name inside the bag.

(A) it was   (B) this has   (C) there is   (D) they had

12. Joe : _____ you come to our party tonight?
     Sue: No, but I wish I could.

(A) Must   (B) Shall   (C) Can   (D) May

13. Jack : I wish I were a millionaire. I could buy whatever I want.
     Jane : Well, it may be true. _____ we must bear in mind
            that the love of money is also the root of all evil.

(A) So   (B) Or   (C) For   (D) But

14. Tony : May I have some more coffee, please?
     Anne : I'm sorry, but there doesn't seem to be _____.

(A) left any   (B) any left
(C) leaving any   (D) any leaving

15. Tom : I was looking for John all afternoon. Where was he?
     Pete : I don't know. He _____ to a movie.

(A) would go   (B) might go
(C) would have gone   (D) might have gone

貳、片語

說明：第 16 至 20 題，請選出與劃線部分語意最接近的字詞，標示在答案
卡之「選擇題第一部分」。每題答對得 1 分，答錯不倒扣。

16. Do you think Teresa asked that question on purpose?
   (A) accidentally (B) gradually (C) intentionally (D) permanently

17. Every Taiwanese student should know what 'M.I.T.' stands for.
   (A) holds (B) orders (C) means (D) represents

18. John's reckless behavior gave rise to endless trouble for his parents.
   (A) caused (B) covered (C) lifted (D) saved

19. The idea of becoming famous appeals to many people.
   (A) attracts (B) enjoys (C) claims (D) requires

20. Mike fainted under the hot sun in his rice field. When he came to, he saw a stranger beside him.
   (A) rose (B) discovered (C) entered (D) awoke

參、綜合測驗

說明：第 21 至 40 題，每題一個空格。請依文意選出最適當的一個選項，
標示在答案卡之「選擇題第一部分」。每題答對得 1 分，答錯不倒
扣。

21-25 題為題組

Climbing the most difficult mountains requires a very special mental condition. ___21___ the climber is doing something very difficult, everything that he or she sees, hears, or ___22___ must come together to help in the work of climbing. All of the parts of the body work together smoothly and quietly ___23___ each part feels what is happening in the other parts. There is no room for thinking about what time it is, or about how one looks. ___24___ thinking must focus on what is happening at that moment, and the mind and the body become one. Only by entering this quiet mental state ___25___ a climber really do his or her best.

21. (A) Despite   (B) Because   (C) Unless   (D) Although
22. (A) points   (B) says   (C) walks   (D) feels
23. (A) or   (B) if   (C) as   (D) but
24. (A) One   (B) All   (C) Some   (D) Few
25. (A) can   (B) shall   (C) must   (D) should

26-30 題爲題組

John : What was the weather like while you were camping?

Jack :   26   It rained for a few days towards the end of our holiday, but mostly it was fine. We weren't able to visit the Rainbow Waterfalls as we planned, but...

John :   27

Jack : Well, apart from that, we did everything we wanted to—hiking, fishing and swimming. We even managed to visit an aboriginal village in the forest.

John :   28   did you get so far?

Jack : We rode bicycles there. We also went to the beach several times.

John : Did you take your bikes with you?

Jack : No, we rented some at the nearby village.

John : Where did you stay   29   ?

Jack : Oh, in a lovely valley, about three miles north of the National Park.

John : I remember when we went camping last summer. We forgot to take a can-opener along!

Jack :   30   Do you know what happened to us? A goat came in our tent at night and ate most of our food!

26. (A) It couldn't be better.   (B) Don't mention it.
   (C) Not too bad.   (D) It was terrible.
27. (A) What a pity!   (B) Oh, how wonderful!
   (C) Oh, that was great!   (D) No big deal!
28. (A) How often   (B) How on earth
   (C) How hard   (D) How was that
29. (A) at all   (B) after all   (C) above all   (D) at most
30. (A) That's great.   (B) You deserve it.
   (C) That's nothing.   (D) That's terrible.

<u>31-40 題爲題組</u>

The people in the room were tense. Five young engineers were sitting with their __31__. They were trying to settle details of an important new plant site for a major client.

Suddenly one of the young engineers gave what he thought was a good solution __32__ the problem. What he had to say was __33__ by an uncomfortable silence. The boss then laughingly pointed out that the same proposal had been made and __34__ some minutes before.

The incident seemed funny __35__ the time, but several months later it did not. After the project had been successfully finished, most of the engineers who had worked on it were __36__. But the young man who had made a fool of himself at the meeting was not on the list.

__37__ The young engineer swore that he had never heard the proposal made and rejected. __38__ He was a victim of a bad listening habit that he didn't know he had.

Bad listening habits *can* hurt you a lot in your daily living. Much of your success, both in your work and social life, __39__ *how* you listen. A number of major industries and more than twenty leading colleges __40__. They have set up "listening clinics" and courses to find out what is wrong--and what to do about it.

31. (A) boss　(B) friend　(C) client　(D) doctor
32. (A) of　(B) at　(C) to　(D) in
33. (A) turned　(B) created　(C) greeted　(D) generated
34. (A) agreed to　(B) put up　(C) called upon　(D) turned down
35. (A) in　(B) at　(C) on　(D) for
36. (A) succeeded　(B) promoted　(C) exhausted　(D) aroused
37. (A) What had happened?
　　(B) Why must it be finished?
　　(C) Where did the event take place?
　　(D) When will they have another project?

38. (A) The engineer was too young.　(B) It took a whole month.
　　(C) The boss was satisfied.　　　(D) He was right.

39. (A) is related to　　　　　　　　(B) has an impact on
　　(C) have a lot to do with　　　　(D) are of great importance to

40. (A) are also interested in the rejected proposal
　　(B) have resolved the mystery of listening comprehension
　　(C) are doing extensive research on the young engineer
　　(D) have become very concerned about our bad listening habits

肆、閱讀測驗

說明：第 41 至 55 題，每題請分別根據各篇文章選出最適當的一個選項，
　　　標示在答案卡之「選擇題第一部分」。每題答對得 2 分，答錯不倒
　　　扣。

41-43 題為題組

I wonder how often your family has bought new furniture, curtains or kitchen equipment and then wondered how to dispose of the old items that still have quite a lot of life left in them.

It was in response to this situation that The Carpenters' Shop was opened in the town of Walsall, Staffordshire. Run by a team of church volunteers, the shop will collect any surplus, good-quality items and store them until they can be redistributed to the people who are needing those particular things.

Many have been helped through the scheme, including single parents, disabled people and the elderly, and those who have lost all their household possessions through a disaster such as a house fire.

It's an admirable project, and it is worth finding out if a similar one operates in your hometown. Participation costs the donor nothing and can make such a difference to others.

41. The phrase dispose of in the first paragraph can best be replaced by ＿＿＿＿＿＿.
　　(A) put up with　　　　　　　　(B) get rid of
　　(C) look down upon　　　　　　(D) take notice of

42. The purpose of setting up The Carpenters' Shop was _____.
    (A) to help those who could not afford certain household items
    (B) to open a furniture store run by church volunteers
    (C) to teach people how to destroy disposable furniture
    (D) to sell good-quality furniture to disabled people

43. What is the author's opinion of an item that someone doesn't need any longer?
    (A) It's normally out of style.
    (B) It should be donated to charity.
    (C) It's an admirable project.
    (D) There may be something wrong with it.

44-47 題為題組

What can you do if you "lose" the data from your disks? To find an expert, who would recover the lost information for you, is probably the easiest solution. Jack Olson is one of these experts. Jack and a few of his friends set up a company called "Jack's Disk Doctor Service" in 1984. They work from home and give all the money they earn to charity. The fees are always the same, no matter how precious the data on the disk is. Some people, however, are so grateful that they send extra money to Jack or to the charities his company supports. One oil company offered him $2000 for his help and an architect even sent him a blank check.

It would be difficult to put a value on the things rescued by the Disk Doctor. There have been disks containing medical research, television scripts, manuscripts of whole books, a lawyer's papers for a court case, and even Margaret Thatcher's travel plan for a visit to eastern Europe. For this last case, Jack had to go in person to Thatcher's office "for security reasons"!

Disks are usually sent to the Disk Doctor by post, but sometimes people are in such a hurry that they cannot wait for the mail to come. For example, some radio scripts had to be rushed by taxi to Jack's house because they were needed for broadcasting the next day. When the material has been recovered, the disk is returned to the sender with a diagnosis and a prescription for avoiding the problem in the future. One grateful client, an author, put a "thank you" to Jack in the front of his book. "Jack saved me from a heart attack," he wrote. "But," says Jack, "most people don't take any notice of the doctor's advice!"

44. What does the word rescued in the second paragraph mean?
    (A) recovered   (B) prescribed   (C) examined   (D) discovered

45. Why did the architect send Jack a blank check?
    (A) The architect did not have any money.
    (B) The architect did it for security reasons.
    (C) The architect always followed the doctor's advice.
    (D) The architect thought Jack's service was priceless.

46. Which of the following statements is NOT true?
    (A) Jack's Disk Doctor Service has only one standard fee.
    (B) Jack and his company have made a fortune from their service.
    (C) Margaret Thatcher is a very important person.
    (D) Jack's clients are from all walks of life.

47. From the statement "But... most people don't take any notice of the doctor's advice!" we can infer that _____.
    (A) most people don't take medicine regularly
    (B) many of Jack's patients would probably get sick again
    (C) many of Jack's clients have sought for his help more than once
    (D) most people don't read the instruction when using a computer

48-51 題為題組

Do you know the meaning of the word "relationship"? Here is an easy way of understanding it. Whenever two people come together, even for a brief moment, they exchange looks, feelings, thoughts, ideas, and energy. Their relationship is how they interact with each other. Everything that happens in the world happens through relationships. We human beings need to love and be loved, and this will come from our relationship with others. Accordingly, anyone who wishes to love and be loved will want to establish lasting relationships.

Here are a few <u>tips</u> to help us create enduring relationships. First, know our steps. The relationship between two people is like the art of dancing. Before we can dance with a partner, we need to be able to dance by ourselves. We need to feel the rhythm of the music, hear how it inspires us to move and learn our unique style of movement and expression. Second, trust. As the key building block for enduring relationships, trust is a bond that evolves as two persons get to know each other and experience safety in opening their hearts. Trust develops when we respect each other's needs and develop a history of common experience and caring. Third, be intimate. While intimacy is often limited to the sexual bond, we can be intimate with many people without sexuality. That is, by relating heart to heart. We need to be seen and known by another person. In this way, intimacy enables us to thrive and grow. Lastly, treat relationship as an organism. A new relationship is like an embryo that requires time, care and attention to grow into whatever may evolve. In our proper relationship with others, we will be known and seen for who we are, and love will come out of the seeing and the knowing.

48. The author writes the above passage chiefly to _____.
   (A) encourage readers to build blocks for intimacy
   (B) tell readers that things happen through feelings
   (C) help readers establish sound relationships
   (D) urge readers to become expert dancers

49. The word tips in the second paragraph refers to _____.
   (A) fees　　　　(B) services　　　(C) limitations　　(D) suggestions

50. According to the passage, which of the following is true?
   (A) Intimacy is limited to the sexual bond.
   (B) "Trust" blocks the way to durable relationships.
   (C) If you do not dance, you cannot establish relationships.
   (D) Exposure of one's inner thoughts is essential for enduring relationships.

51. The love we desire will come from all of the following EXCEPT
    _____.

    (A) being fond of the embryo   (B) interacting with people
    (C) trusting our friends   (D) being intimate with others

52-55 題爲題組

Penghu, Nov. 24 — Two Russians, a father and a son, were rescued Saturday near the Penghu Islands off southwestern Taiwan after their sailboat broke down and began drifting.

Medvedev Vladimir, 43, and his son, Maxsine, 14, sailed from an unnamed eastern Russian seaport on August 18, to begin an ambitious around-the-world cruise.

Their voyage, down the coastline of northeastern mainland China, through the East China Sea, then down the Taiwan Strait and into the South China Sea, had been smooth until four days ago when the mainsail of their twin-mast sailboat "Kawasaki" was smashed by strong winds on the high seas.

The father-and-son team started the inboard engine. However, after less than two days, the engine broke down.

Near the "black ditch" of Penghu, battered by winds of up to 70 knots, the rear sail was torn into shreds. The rudder also stopped responding.

Surprised by the father and son's "pale faces" and their battered vessel, the Penghu police and fishers in Paisha rescued them. Speaking only limited English, the Vladimirs spent five hours trying to explain their presence.

It is not immediately known whether the "Kawasaki" can be repaired on the fishing island of Penghu, or when the Vladimirs will be able to set off again and continue their around-the-world voyage.

52. What was the purpose of the voyage of the Vladimirs?
    (A) To go around the world.
    (B) To visit the Penghu Islands.
    (C) To look for their lost family members.
    (D) To start the inboard engine of their vessel.

53. Which course (direction) did the Vladimirs take to get to Penghu?
 (A) East. (B) West. (C) South. (D) North.

54. When did the "Kawasaki" first get into trouble during the voyage?
 (A) Less than two days after departure from Russia.
 (B) About four days before the inboard engine was started.
 (C) After it had sailed from Russia for more than three months.
 (D) Only after it drifted to Paisha County of the Penghu Islands.

55. What did the Vladimirs decide to do after they were rescued?
 (A) To stay in Penghu and do some fishing.
 (B) To sell the boat and return to Russia.
 (C) To repair the boat and sail back to Russia.
 (D) They had not made any decision yet.

第二部分：非選擇題

壹、簡答題

說明：1. 根據以下短文簡答下列五個問題，並將答案寫在「答案卷」上。
　　　2. 不必用完整的句子，大小寫不拘，但需標明題號。每題 2 分，共
　　　　 10 分。

　　Do you know that happy folks recover from illness much more readily than people who are depressed and always complaining?

　　The old sages always used to say that laughter was the best medicine--indeed, better than medicine.

　　Someone else remarked that "a merry heart does good, like medicine"--and infectious laughter is often catching. Don't you find it so? I like the anonymous verse which sums it all up:

　　　When wholesome laughter fills the air,
　　　　Some ills will soon depart;
　　　For laughter is good medicine
　　　　That helps to cheer the heart.

1. According to the passage, what type of people are more likely to get well sooner when they get sick?
2. Which word in the passage means "very wise men"?
3. Which word in the passage is closest in meaning to "infectious"?
4. Who is the author of the poem?
5. In the poem, which word rhymes with "depart"?

貳、英文作文

說明：1. 請依下列提示寫一篇英文作文在「答案卷」上。
　　　2. 文長以 120 字左右為原則，共 20 分。

提示：

你同意 "Laughter is better than medicine" 這種說法嗎？以你自己或親朋好友的經驗或你所知道的故事為例，加以說明。你的論點無論是正面或是反面都不會影響你的得分。

86年度學科能力測驗英文科試題詳解

第一部分：單一選擇題

壹、詞彙與語法：

1. (**C**) What a small computer! Does it *really* work?

   多麼小的一部電腦啊！眞的能用嗎？

   (A) bite〔baɪt〕v. 咬　　　(B) type〔taɪp〕v. 打字
   (C) **work**〔wɜk〕v.（機器）正常運作
   (D) use〔juz〕v. 使用

2. (**B**) *For your own safety,* please don't open the door *until the train fully stops.*

   爲了你自身的安全，火車未完全停下來時，請不要打開車門。

   (A) humanity〔hju'mænətɪ〕n. 人性
   (B) **safety**〔'seftɪ〕n. 安全
   (C) liberty〔'lɪbətɪ〕n. 自由
   (D) vanity〔'vænətɪ〕n. 虛榮

3. (**B**) Peter told Marie *that* he couldn't attend her birthday party *because* he had been *previously* engaged.

   彼得告訴瑪莉，他無法參加她的生日舞會，因爲他之前已經和別人約好了。

   (A) necessarily〔'nɛsə,sɛrəlɪ〕adv. 必然地
   (B) **previously**〔'privɪəslɪ〕adv. 之前
   (C) cautiously〔'kɔʃəslɪ〕adv. 小心地
   (D) possibly〔'pasəblɪ〕adv. 可能地
   engaged〔ɪn'gedʒd〕adj. 有約束的；已被預定的

4. (**D**) *For hours*, we have heard nothing but negative criticism. Why can't you say something *more constructive*?

幾小時以來，我們只聽到負面的批評。你爲什麼不能說點更有建設性的話呢？

(A) ambitious〔æm'bɪʃəs〕 *adj.* 有抱負的
(B) synthetic〔sɪn'θεtɪk〕 *adj.* 合成的
(C) determined〔dɪ'tɜmɪnd〕 *adj.* 堅決的
(D) *constructive*〔kən'strʌktɪv〕 *adj.* 有建設性的
nothing but 只有 (= *only*)　　negative〔'nεɡətɪv〕 *adj.* 負面的

5. (**C**) This library is famous for its wide variety *of books*. You can find books *on any topic you are interested in.*

這個圖書館以其藏書的多樣性而聞名。你可以找到任何你有興趣的主題的書。

(A) technology〔tεk'nɑlədʒɪ〕 *n.* 科技
(B) connection〔kə'nεkʃən〕 *n.* 連接
(C) *variety*〔və'raɪətɪ〕 *n.* 多樣性
(D) amazement〔ə'mezmənt〕 *n.* 驚訝
topic〔'tɑpɪk〕 *n.* 主題

6. (**A**) The child was passive. He *just* sat there *and* waited for something to happen.

這個小孩很被動。他只是坐在那裏等著事情發生。

(A) *passive*〔'pæsɪv〕 *adj.* 被動的
(B) expressive〔ɪk'sprεsɪv〕 *adj.* 表情豐富的
(C) extensive〔ɪk'stεnsɪv〕 *adj.* 廣泛的
(D) persuasive〔pə'swesɪv〕 *adj.* 有說服力的

7. (**B**) *After dinner*, Richard offered to pay the bill, **but** May
insisted **that** they do it separately.
晚餐後，理查提議要付帳，但是梅堅持要各自付帳。
(A) generously ('dʒɛnərəslɪ) adv. 慷慨地
(B) **separately** ('sɛpərɪtlɪ) adv. 各自地
(C) completely (kəm'plitlɪ) adv. 完全地
(D) extensively (ɪk'stɛnsɪvlɪ) adv. 廣泛地
offer ('ɔfə) v. 提議　insist (ɪn'sɪst) v. 堅持

8. (**A**) This TV program will broaden young viewers' understanding
of the changing world.
這個電視節目能擴展年輕觀眾對這個多變世界的了解。
(A) **broaden** ('brɔdn̩) v. 擴展　(B) soften ('sɔfən) v. 使柔軟
(C) tighten ('taɪtn̩) v. 緊縮　(D) lengthen ('lɛŋθən) v. 延長
viewer ('vjuə) n. 觀眾

9. (**B**) I like everything about the apartment except for the rent.
It is too expensive.
這間公寓除了房租之外，我樣樣都喜歡。房租太貴了。
(A) as for 至於
(B) **except for** 除了～之外
(C) instead of 而不是
(D) in place of 代替
rent (rɛnt) n. 房租

10. (**A**) As a result of all the newspaper **and** television attention,
the problem of child abuse has become well-known.
由於所有報紙和電視的注意，虐待兒童的問題變得眾所皆知。
(A) **as a result of** 由於　(B) apart from 除了～之外
(C) in addition to 除了～之外 (D) regardless of 不管
abuse (ə'bjus) n. 虐待　well-known ('wɛl'non) adj. 眾所皆知的

11. (**C**) 提姆：有人把書包忘在公車上。

山姆：看看書包裏有沒有名字。

＊「there＋be 動詞」表「有～」。

schoolbag〔'skul,bæg〕n. 書包

12. (**C**) 喬：你今晚可以來我們的舞會嗎？

蘇：不行，眞希望我可以去。

＊表示「能不能」，助動詞應用 can。

13. (**D**) 傑克： 我希望我是百萬富翁。我可以買任何我想要的東西。

珍　： 嗯，也許你說的沒錯，但是我們必須牢記在心，對於金錢的熱愛也是萬惡之源。

＊前後句意相反，故應選 (D) But。

bear* sth. *in mind 將～牢記在心

root〔rut〕n. 根源　　evil〔'ivḷ〕n. 罪惡

14. (**B**) 東尼： 請問，我可以再來點咖啡嗎？

安　： 抱歉，似乎沒有剩了。

＊形容詞 left 須置於 any 之後，作後位修飾。

15. (**D**) 湯姆： 我整個下午都在找約翰。他上哪兒去了？

皮特： 我不知道。他可能去看電影了。

＊對過去肯定的推測，須用「must have＋p.p.」，表「當時一定～」。

貳、片語：

16. (**C**) Do you think Teresa asked that question *on purpose*?

你想泰瑞莎是故意問那個問題的嗎？

(A) accidentally〔,æksə'dɛntḷɪ〕*adv.* 意外地；附帶地

(B) gradually〔'grædʒʊəlɪ〕*adv.* 逐漸地

(C) ***intentionally***〔ɪn'tɛnʃənḷɪ〕*adv.* 故意地

(D) permanently〔'pɜmənəntlɪ〕*adv.* 永久地

on purpose 故意地

17. (**D**) Every Taiwanese student should know *what* "*M.I.T.*" *stands for*.
　　　每個台灣學生都應該知道 M.I.T.代表什麼。
　　　(A) hold〔hold〕v. 掌握
　　　(B) order〔'ɔrdə〕v. 命令
　　　(C) mean〔min〕v. 意思是～
　　　(D) *represent*〔͵rɛprɪ'zɛnt〕v. 代表
　　　stand for 代表　　*M.I.T.* 台灣製造 (= *Made in Taiwan*)

18. (**A**) John's reckless behavior gave rise to endless trouble *for his parents*.
　　　約翰鹵莽的行為，造成他父母無窮的麻煩。
　　　(A) *cause*〔kɔz〕v. 引起；導致　(B) cover〔'kʌvə〕v. 覆蓋
　　　(C) lift〔lɪft〕v. 提高　　　　　　(D) save〔sev〕v. 節省；拯救
　　　reckless〔'rɛklɪs〕adj. 鹵莽的　　*give rise to* 引起；導致
　　　endless〔'ɛndlɪs〕adj. 無止境的

19. (**A**) The idea *of becoming famous* appeals to many people.
　　　成名的想法吸引許多人。
　　　(A) *attract*〔ə'trækt〕v. 吸引　(B) enjoy〔ɪn'dʒɔɪ〕v. 享受
　　　(C) claim〔klem〕v. 要求　　　　(D) require〔rɪ'kwaɪr〕v. 需要
　　　appeal to 吸引

20. (**D**) Mike fainted *under the hot sun in his rice field. When he came to*, he saw a stranger *beside him*.
　　　麥克大太陽下在稻田裏昏倒。醒來時，他看到身旁有個陌生人。
　　　(A) rise〔raɪz〕v. 升起　　　　　(B) discover〔dɪ'skʌvə〕v. 發現
　　　(C) enter〔'ɛntə〕v. 進入　　　　(D) *awake*〔ə'wek〕v. 醒來
　　　faint〔fent〕v. 昏倒　　*rice field* 稻田　　*come to* 甦醒

參、綜合測驗：

21－25題

Climbing the *most* difficult mountains requires a *very* special mental condition. *Because* the climber is doing something very —21 difficult, everything *that he or she sees, hears, or feels* must 22 come *together to help in the work of climbing.* All *of the parts of the body* work *together smoothly and quietly as* each part 23 feels *what is happening in the other parts.*

攀登最險峻的山，需要非常特殊的精神狀態。因為登山者正從事極為困難的事，所以登山時所看到、聽到或感覺到的各項事物，都必須匯集起來，才能對登山者有所幫助。當身體各部份能感受到其餘部份的反應時，所有部份便能順利而安靜地一起運作。

　　smoothly〔'smuðlɪ〕*adv.* 順利地

21.(**B**) 依句意，選(B)*Because* 因為。而(A) Despite 儘管，(C) Unless 除非，(D) 雖然，皆不合句意。

22.(**D**) 登山時所看到、聽到或「感覺到」的各項事物，都必須匯集起來，選(D)*feels*。而(A) point 指出，(B) 說，(C) 走路，皆不合句意。

23.(**C**) 依句意，選(C)*as* 當～時候。

There is no room *for thinking about what time it is, or about how one looks.* All thinking must focus on *what is happening at that* 24 moment, *and* the mind and the body become one. *Only by entering this quiet mental state* can a climber *really* do his or her best. 25

腦袋中沒有空間去想現在幾點，或一個人外表看起來如何。所有的思緒必須集中於當時所發生的事，而且身心要合而爲一。只有藉著進入這種寧靜的心理狀態，登山者才能眞正盡力而爲。

focus on 集中於～　　*do one's best* 竭盡全力

24. (**B**) 依句意，應選 (B) *All* 全部的。

25. (**A**) 依句意，應選 (A) *can* 能夠。此句爲倒裝句型，Only 引導副詞片語置於句首，後面主詞和助動詞必須倒裝。

26－30題

John：What was the weather like *while you were camping*?

Jack：Not too bad. It rained *for a few days towards the end of our*
　　　　26
　　　holiday, *but* mostly it was fine. We weren't able to visit the
　　　Rainbow Waterfalls *as we planned*, *but*...

John：What a pity!
　　　　27

Jack：Well, *apart from that*, we did everything *we wanted to* —
　　　hiking, fishing and swimming. We *even* managed to visit an
　　　aboriginal village *in the forest*.

約翰：你們去露營的時候天氣怎麼樣？
傑克：不算太壞。在假期最後幾天下了雨，但是大體上天氣很好。我們無
　　　法如預期地去造訪彩虹瀑布，可是……
約翰：眞可惜！
傑克：嗯，除此之外，我們想做的事都做了——健行、釣魚還有游泳。我
　　　們甚至還參觀了森林裏的原住民村落。

rainbow (′ren͵bo) *n.* 彩虹　　waterfall (′wɔtɚ͵fɔl) *n.* 瀑布
apart from 除了～之外　　hiking (′haɪkɪŋ) *n.* 健行
aboriginal (͵æbə′rɪdʒənl) *adj.* 原住民的　　village (′vɪlɪdʒ) *n.* 村莊

26. (**C**) (A) 再好也不過了。 (B) 不客氣。 (C) <u>不算太壞。</u> (D) 很糟糕。

27. (**A**) (A) <u>真可惜！</u>　　　　　　(B) 噢，太棒了！
　　　(C) 噢，太棒了！　　　　　(D) 沒什麼大不了！

John : <u>How *on earth* did you get *so far*?</u>
　　　　　　28

Jack : We rode bicycles *there*. We *also* went to the beach *several times*.

John : Did you take your bikes *with you*?

Jack : No, we rented some *at the nearby village*.

John : Where did you stay *after all*?
　　　　　　　　　　　29

Jack : Oh, in a lovely valley, *about three miles north of the National Park*.

John : I remember *when* we went camping *last summer*. We forgot to take a can-opener *along*!

Jack : That's nothing. Do you know *what happened to us*? A goat
　　　　30
came in our tent *at night* **and** ate most *of our food*!

約翰：你們究竟是如何到達那麼遠的地方？
傑克：我們騎腳踏車去的。我們還去海邊好幾次。
約翰：你們把腳踏車帶去了嗎？
傑克：沒有，我們在附近的村莊租車。
約翰：你們最後住在哪裏？
傑克：哦，在一個美麗的山谷，大約在國家公園北邊三哩左右。
約翰：我想起了去年夏天去露營的事，我們竟忘了帶開罐器！
傑克：那沒什麼。你知道我們發生什麼事嗎？有隻羊晚上跑進我們的帳
　　　篷，吃掉了我們大部分的食物。

rent〔rɛnt〕v. 租　　stay〔ste〕v. 暫住
valley〔'vælɪ〕n. 山谷　　***take ~ along*** 帶著~
can-opener n. 開罐器　　goat〔got〕n. 山羊　　tent〔tɛnt〕n. 帳篷

28. (**B**) (A) 多久一次 (問頻率)　　　　(B) 究竟如何
　　　　(C) 多辛苦　　　　　　　　　　(D) 爲什麼
　　　on earth 究竟

29. (**B**) (A) at all 到底　　　　　　(B) ***after all*** 終究；到最後
　　　　(C) above all 最重要的是　　　(D) at most 最多

30. (**C**) (A) 太棒了。　　(B) 你活該。　　(C) 那沒什麼。　　(D) 眞可怕。
　　　deserve〔dɪˈzɝv〕*v.* 應得

---

31 —40題

　　The people *in the room* were tense. Five young engineers were

sitting *with their boss*. They were trying to settle details *of an*
　　　　　　　　　31

important new plant site for a major client.

　　房裏的人都很緊張。五位年輕的工程師，和他們的老板坐在一起，正
在試著解決一些細部問題，是有關一位大客戶重要的新工廠地點的問題。

　　　tense〔tɛns〕*adj.* 緊張的　　　settle〔ˈsɛtl̩〕*v.* 解決
　　　plant〔plænt〕*n.* 工廠　　　　site〔saɪt〕*n.* 地點
　　　client〔ˈklaɪənt〕*n.* 客戶

31. (**A**) 依句意，選 (A) ***boss***〔bɔs〕*n.* 老板。

　　Suddenly one *of the young engineers* gave ***what** he thought was*

a good solution *to the problem.* ***What** he had to say* was greeted
　　　　　　　32　　　　　　　　　　　　　　　　　　33

by an uncomfortable silence. The boss *then laughingly* pointed out

***that** the same proposal had been made **and** turned down some*
　　　　　　　　　　　　　　　　　　　34
minutes before.

　　突然間，其中一位年輕工程師提出一個他認為很好的解決之道。而他所說的話，卻引起了一陣令人不安的沈默。然後老板笑著指出，同樣的提議在幾分鐘前才被提出且被否決。

laughingly〔'læfɪŋlɪ〕 adv. 笑著　　**point out** 指出
proposal〔prə'pozḷ〕 n. 提議

32. (**C**) a solution **to** a problem　問題的解決之道

33. (**C**) 依句意，選(C) **greet**〔grit〕v. 迎接；遇到。而(A)轉向，(B)create〔krɪ'et〕v. 創造，(D)generate〔'dʒɛnə,ret〕v. 產生，皆不合句意。

34. (**D**) (A) agree to 同意　　　　　(B) put up 提出
　　　　　(C) call upon 拜訪；要求　　(D) **turn down** 拒絕

The incident seemed funny **at the time**, **but** several months later
　　　　　　　　　　　　　　　35
it did not. **After the project had been successfully finished**, most
of the engineers **who had worked on it** were promoted. **But** the
　　　　　　　　　　　　　　　　　　　　　　　　　　36
young man **who had made a fool of himself at the meeting** was
not on the list.

　　這件事當時似乎很好笑，但幾個月之後就不好笑了。在這項計畫成功完成後，大部分參與工作的工程師都升職了。但是那位在會議中當眾出糗的年輕人，卻不在名單上。

incident〔'ɪnsədənt〕 n. 事件　　project〔'pradʒɛkt〕 n. 計畫
work on 從事　　**make a fool of oneself** 出糗；鬧笑話

35. (**B**) **at the time** 當時

36. (**B**) (A) succeed〔sək'sid〕 v. 成功（沒有被動式）
　　　　　(B) **promote**〔prə'mot〕 v. 升職
　　　　　(C) exhausted〔ɪg'zɔstɪd〕 adj. 筋疲力竭的
　　　　　(D) arouse〔ə'rauz〕 v. 喚起

What had happened? The young engineer swore *that he had*
　　　　37
never heard the proposal made and rejected. He was right. He
　　　　　　　　　　　　　　　　　　　　　　　　　　38
was a victim *of a bad listening habit that* he didn't know he had.

　　發生了什麼事呢？那位年輕的工程師發誓，他沒有聽到那個建議被
提出，並且被否決。他說的是真的。他是一個不良聽力習慣的犧牲品，而
他不知道自己有這個習慣。

swear (swɛr) *v.* 發誓　　reject (rɪ'dʒɛkt) *v.* 拒絕
victim ('vɪktɪm) *n.* 犧牲品；受害者

37. (**A**) (A) 發生了什麼事？　　　　(B) 這件事為什麼必須結束？
　　　　(C) 這件事發生在什麼地方？　(D) 他們何時會再有另一個計畫？

38. (**D**) (A) 那位工程師太年輕了。　(B) 這件事花了一整個月的時間。
　　　　(C) 老板很滿意。　　　　　(D) 他說的是真的。

Bad listening habits *can* hurt you *a lot in your daily living.*
Much *of your success, both in your work and social life,* is related
　　　　　　　　　　　　　　　　　　　　　　　　　　　　　39
to *how you listen.* A number of major industries *and* more than
twenty leading colleges have become *very* concerned about our bad
　　　　　　　　　　　　　　　　　　　　　　　　　　　　　40
listening habits. They have set up "listening clinics" and courses *to*
find out what is wrong — and what to do about it.

　　不良聽力習慣在日常生活中，可能對你有很大的傷害。你的大部分成
功，無論在工作或社交生活上，都和你聽力的程度有關。許多大企業和二
十多所主要大學，都很關心人們的不良聽力習慣的問題。他們已經設立了
「聽力診所」和一些課程，來找出什麼地方有錯，以及如何處理這些問題。

social ('soʃəl) *adj.* 社交的　　leading ('lidɪŋ) *adj.* 主要的
set up 設立　　clinic ('klɪnɪk) *n.* 診所

39. (**A**) 主詞 Much of … life 為不可數名詞，視為單數，故須用單數動詞，
    依句意，選 (A)。
    (A) *be related to* 與～有關
    (B) have an impact on 對～有影響
    (C) have a lot to do with 與～關係密切
    (D) be of great importance to 對～很重要

40. (**D**) 依句意，各企業和大學應是「很關心這些問題」，故選 (D)。
    resolve (rɪˈzɑlv) *v.* 解答　　 mystery (ˈmɪstrɪ) *n.* 奧秘
    comprehension (ˌkɑmprɪˈhɛnʃən) *n.* 理解力
    listening comprehension 聽力
    extensive (ɪkˈstɛnsɪv) *adj.* 廣泛的　　 *be concerned about* 關心

肆、閱讀測驗：

41－43 題

I wonder *how* often your family has bought new furniture,
curtains or kitchen equipment *and then* wondered *how* to dispose of
the old items *that* still have quite a lot of life left in them.

It was in response to this situation *that The Carpenters' Shop*
was opened in the town of Walsall, Staffordshire. *Run by a team
of church volunteers*, the shop will collect any surplus, good-quality
items *and* store them *until* they can be redistributed to the people
who are needing those particular things.

　　我想知道你們家每隔多久會購買新的傢俱、窗簾，或是廚具，然後我
也想知道，你們是如何處置那些仍然很有用的舊物品。
　　為因應這種情況，木匠商店就在斯塔福郡的渥梭鎮開幕了。這家店是
由一群教會義工經營，專門收集一些過剩、品質良好的物品，然後貯存著，
直到這些物品可再度被分配給需要那些特別物品的人。

furniture〔'fɜnɪtʃə〕*n.* 傢俱　　curtain〔'kɜtn̩〕*n.* 窗簾
equipment〔ɪ'kwɪpmənt〕*n.* 設備　　***dispose of*** 處理；除去
item〔'aɪtəm〕*n.* 項目；物品　　***in response to*** 響應～；為回答～
carpenter〔'kɑrpəntə〕*n.* 木匠
volunteer〔ˌvɑlən'tɪr〕*n.* 志願者；義工　　surplus〔'sɜplʌs〕*adj.* 過剩的
redistribute〔ˌridɪ'strɪbjut〕*v.* 重新分配

Many have been helped *through the scheme, including single parents, disabled people* **and** *the elderly,* **and** *those* who *have lost all their household possessions through a disaster such as a house fire.*

It's an admirable project, **and** it is worth finding out *if a similar one operates in your hometown.* Participation costs the donor nothing **and** can make such a difference *to others.*

　　許多人都因這個計畫而受惠，包括單親父母、殘障人士、老人，以及那些遭受像家庭大火這樣的災難，而喪失所有家庭用品的人。
　　這是個值得讚許的計畫，也值得你在你的家鄉找找是否有類似的商店。參與並不需要花費捐贈者的錢，但卻對別人的生活能造成如此重大的影響。

scheme〔skim〕*n.* 方案；計畫　　disabled〔dɪs'ebl̩〕*adj.* 殘障的
household〔'haʊsˌhold〕*n.* 家庭
possession〔pə'zɛʃən〕*n.* 所有物　　disaster〔dɪz'æstə〕*n.* 災難
admirable〔'ædmərəbl̩〕*adj.* 值得讚許的　　donor〔'donə〕*n.* 捐贈者
difference〔'dɪfərəns〕*n.* 重要改變；重大的影響

41.(**B**) 第一段的片語 dispose of 可代換成 ＿＿＿＿＿＿＿。
　　(A) 忍受　　　(B) 除去　　　(C) 輕視　　　(D) 注意

42. (**A**) 設立木匠商店的目的是
   (A) 幫助那些無法負擔某些家庭用品的人。
   (B) 開一間由教會義工經營的傢俱店。
   (C) 教導人們如何銷毀用完即丟的傢俱。
   (D) 出售高品質的傢俱給殘障人士。
   disposable〔dɪ'spozəbḷ〕 *adj.* 用完即丟的

43. (**B**) 作者對於人們不再需要的物品的看法爲何？
   (A) 通常都退流行了。　　　　(B) 應該捐給慈善機構。
   (C) 是個值得讚許的計畫。　　(D) 可能有點問題。
   out of style 不流行的　　　donate〔'donet〕 *v.* 捐贈
   charity〔'tʃærətɪ〕 *n.* 慈善機構

44－47題

What can you do *if you 'lose' the data from your disks*? To find an expert, *who would recover the lost information for you*, is *probably* the easiest solution. Jack Olson is one *of these experts.* Jack and a few of his friends set up a company *called "Jack's Disk Doctor Service" in 1984.* They work *from home* **and** give all the money *they earn* to charity. The fees are *always* the same, *no matter how precious the data on the disk is.* Some people, *however,* are *so* grateful *that* they send extra money to Jack **or** to the charities his company supports. One oil company offered him $2000 *for his help* **and** an architect *even* sent him a blank check.

　　如果「遺失」磁片上的資料該怎麼辦？找個專家幫你找回遺失的資料，這大概是最簡單的解決方法。傑克‧歐森就是這方面的專家。傑克和一些朋友，在一九八四年成立了一家名爲「傑克磁片醫生診所」的公司。他們在家裏工作，並且將所賺的錢全部捐給慈善機構。不論磁片上的資料有多貴重，收費一律相同。儘管如此，一些心存感激的人還是會送額外的錢給傑克，或是捐錢給傑克公司所贊助的慈善機構。有家石油公司爲了感謝傑克的幫忙，付給他二千美元，有位建築師甚至寄給他一張空白支票。

data〔'detə〕n. 資料　　disk〔dɪsk〕n. 磁片
expert〔'ɛkspɝt〕n. 專家　　recover〔rɪ'kʌvɚ〕v. 復原
fee〔fi〕n. 費用　　precious〔'prɛʃəs〕adj. 貴重的
grateful〔'gretfəl〕adj. 感激的　　extra〔'ɛkstrə〕adj. 額外的
architect〔'ɑrkəˌtɛkt〕n. 建築師　　blank〔blæŋk〕adj. 空白的

It would be difficult to put a value *on the things rescued by the Disk Doctor*. There have been disks *containing medical research, television scripts, manuscripts of whole books, a lawyer's papers for a court case,* **and** *even Margaret Thatcher's travel plan for a visit to eastern Europe. For this last case,* Jack had to go *in person* to Thatcher's office *'for security reasons'*!

　　磁片醫生所拯救的東西很難以金錢來衡量其價值。這些磁片內有醫學研究、電視劇本、整本書的原稿、律師的訴訟案的文件，甚至還包括柴契爾夫人的東歐訪問行程。爲了最後這件工作，基於「安全理由」，傑克還必須親自到柴契爾夫人的辦公室。

rescue〔'rɛskju〕v. 拯救　　script〔skrɪpt〕n. 劇本
manuscript〔'mænjəˌskrɪpt〕n. 原稿
court〔kort〕n. 法院　　case〔kes〕n. 訴訟案
security〔sɪ'kjurətɪ〕n. 安全

Disks are *usually* sent to the Disk Doctor *by post,* **but** *sometimes* people are in *such* a hurry ***that*** *they cannot wait for the mail to come. For example,* some radio scripts had to be rushed *by taxi to*

Jack's house **because** they were needed for broadcasting the next day. **When** the material has been recovered, the disk is returned to the sender with a diagnosis **and** a prescription for avoiding the problem in the future. One grateful client, an author, put a "thank you" to Jack in the front of his book. "Jack saved me from a heart attack," he wrote. "**But**," says Jack, "most people don't take any notice of the doctor's advice!"

　　磁片通常會以郵寄的方式送到磁片醫生手中,但是有時候情況緊急,無法等待郵件。舉個例子,有些廣播劇本必須以計程車火速送到傑克家,因為隔天就要播出。當資料被找到後,磁片會連同診斷書,以及日後預防問題的處方交還給寄件人。一位心存感激的作家客戶,曾在他的書本前面向傑克致謝。他的書上寫說:「傑克使我免於心臟病。」「可是,」傑克說道:「大部分的人根本不聽醫生的勸告!」

　　post〔post〕n. 郵寄　　　rush〔rʌʃ〕v. 急忙送到
　　broadcasting〔'brɔd,kæstɪŋ〕n. 播出
　　diagnosis〔,daɪəg'nosɪs〕n. 診斷
　　prescription〔prɪ'skrɪpʃən〕n. 處方

44. (**A**) 第二段中的 rescued,意思為何?
　　　(A) 復原　　　　　　　(B) prescribe〔prɪ'skraɪb〕v. 開藥方
　　　(C) 檢查　　　　　　　(D) 發現

45. (**D**) 建築師為何寄給傑克一張空白支票?
　　　(A) 建築師沒錢。
　　　(B) 建築師基於安全理由而這麼做。
　　　(C) 建築師一向聽從醫生的勸告。
　　　(D) 建築師認為傑克的服務是無價的。
　　　priceless〔'praɪslɪs〕adj. 無價的;珍貴的

46. (**B**) 下列敘述何者為非？
　　(A) 傑克磁片醫生診所只有一種收費標準。
　　(B) 傑克和他的公司因其所提供的服務而賺大錢。
　　(C) 柴契爾夫人是個重要人物。
　　(D) 傑克的客戶來自各行各業。
　　standard (ˈstændəd) *adj.* 標準的　　fortune (ˈfɔrtʃən) *n.* 財富
　　all walks of life 各行各業

47. (**C**) 從「可是，……大部分的人根本不聽醫生的勸告！」敘述中，我們
　　可以推斷
　　(A) 大部分的人沒有按時服藥。
　　(B) 許多傑克的客戶大概會再度生病。
　　(C) 許多傑克的客戶都不只一次尋求他的幫助。
　　(D) 大部分的人在使用電腦時都不看指令。
　　infer (ɪnˈfɝ) *v.* 推論　　regularly (ˈrɛgjələlɪ) *adv.* 定期地
　　seek for 尋求　　instruction (ɪnˈstrʌkʃən) *n.* 指令

48－51題

　　Do you know the meaning *of the word "relationship"*? Here is an easy way *of understanding it.* ***Whenever*** two people come together, *even for a brief moment,* they exchange looks, feelings, thoughts, ideas, and energy. Their relationship is ***how they interact*** with each other. Everything ***that*** happens in the world happens through relationships. We *human beings* need to love ***and*** be loved, ***and*** this will come from our relationship *with others. Accordingly,* anyone ***who*** wishes to love ***and*** be loved will want to establish lasting relationships.

　　你知道 relationship（關係）這個字的意思嗎？這兒有個容易了解的方法。每當兩個人聚在一起，即使只是短暫的時間，他們都交換了表情、感覺、思想、意見和能量。他們彼此互相回應的方式，就是他們的關係。世界上所發生的每一件事，都是透過關係而發生的。我們人類需要愛人和被愛，而這來自我們和他人的關係。因此，任何人想要愛人和被愛，都要建立長久的關係。

interact〔͵ɪntɚˋækt〕v. 回應；反應
accordingly〔əˋkɔrdɪŋlɪ〕adv. 因此　　　lasting〔ˋlæstɪŋ〕adj. 長久的

Here are a few tips *to help us create enduring relationships.*

First, know our steps. The relationship *between two people* is like

the art *of dancing.* **Before** *we can dance with a partner*, we need

to be able to dance *by ourselves.* We need to feel the rhythm *of*

the music, hear **how** *it inspires us to move* **and** learn our unique

style *of movement and expression. Second*, trust. *As the key building*

block for enduring relationships, trust is a bond *that evolves* **as** *two*

persons get to know each other **and** *experience safety in opening*

their hearts. Trust develops **when** *we respect each other's needs*

and *develop a history of common experience and caring.*

　　以下是幾個幫助我們發展長久關係的祕訣。第一，要了解步驟。兩個人之間的關係就像舞蹈的藝術。在我們能夠和舞伴共舞之前，我們必須能夠獨自跳舞。我們必須去感覺音樂的節奏、聽出音樂如何鼓舞我們擺動，並學習我們自己獨特的動作及表達方式。第二是信任。信任是長久關係的重要基石，它是在兩個人開始彼此認識，並體驗到敞開心扉的安全感時，發展出來的契合。當我們尊重彼此的需求，並發展一段共同的經驗和關心時，信任感也就慢慢培養出來了。

tip (tɪp) *n.* 訣竅；祕訣　　enduring (ɪn'djʊrɪŋ) *adj.* 長久的

partner ('pɑrtnɚ) *n.* 夥伴　　***by oneself*** 獨自

rhythm ('rɪðəm) *n.* 節奏；旋律　　inspire (ɪn'spaɪr) *v.* 鼓舞；激勵

unique (ju'nik) *adj.* 獨特的　　***building block*** 磚塊；石塊

bond (bɑnd) *n.* 結合　　evolve (ɪ'vɑlv) *v.* 發展

Third, be intimate. ***While intimacy is often limited to the sexual bond***, we can be intimate *with many people without sexuality*. *That is*, by relating heart to heart. We need to be seen and known *by another person*. *In this way*, intimacy enables us to thrive and grow. *Lastly*, treat relationship *as an organism*. A new relationship is like an embryo *that requires time, care and attention to grow into whatever may evolve*. *In our proper relationship with others*, we will be known and seen *for who we are*, *and* love will come out of the seeing *and* the knowing.

第三是親密。雖然親密常常侷限於性關係，但我們和很多人沒有性關係，仍然可以很親密，也就是要交心。我們需要被別人觀察、了解。以這個方式，親密使我們能夠成長。最後，要把關係當作是有生命的東西來對待。新的關係就像胚胎，需要時間、關心和注意，才能繼續發展。在我們與他人的適當關係中，我們會被觀察、被了解到我們是什麼樣的人，而關愛就來自這種觀察和了解。

intimate ('ɪntəmɪt) *adj.* 親密的　　intimacy ('ɪntəməsɪ) *n.* 親密

sexuality (,sɛkʃʊ'ælətɪ) *n.* 性行為　　***that is*** 也就是說

relate A to B 使 A 和 B 有關　　thrive (θraɪv) *v.* 成長；興盛

organism ('ɔrgən,ɪzəm) *n.* 有機體；生物

embryo ('ɛmbrɪ,o) *n.* 胚胎

48. (**C**) 作者寫上面這段文章，主要是為了要 ＿＿＿＿＿＿＿。
　　(A) 鼓勵讀者建立親密的障礙
　　(B) 告訴讀者事情是透過感覺發生的
　　(C) 幫助讀者建立良好的關係
　　(D) 敦促讀者成為舞蹈專家
　　block〔blɑk〕*n.,v.* 阻礙　　　sound〔saʊnd〕*adj.* 良好的
　　urge〔ɝdʒ〕*v.* 催促；激勵　　expert〔ˈɛkspɝt〕*adj.* 熟練的

49. (**D**) 第二段中的 tips 指的是 ＿＿＿＿＿＿＿。
　　(A) 費用　　　(B) 服務　　　(C) 限制　　　(D) 建議

50. (**D**) 根據本文，下列何者為真？
　　(A) 親密只限於性關係。　　　(B) 信任會妨礙建立長久關係。
　　(C) 你若不跳舞，就不能建立關係。
　　(D) 表露個人的內心思想，是建立長久關係所必需的。
　　exposure〔ɪkˈspoʒɚ〕*n.* 暴露
　　essential〔əˈsɛnʃəl〕*adj.* 必要的；不可或缺的

51. (**A**) 我們所希望得到的愛來自下列各項，但何者除外？
　　(A) 喜歡胚胎　　　　　(B) 與人相互回應
　　(C) 信任朋友　　　　　(D) 與他人親密

52 − 55 題

Penghu, Nov. 24 — Two Russians, *a father and a son*, were rescued

Saturday near the Penghu Islands off southwestern Taiwan **after**

their sailboat broke down **and** *began drifting.*

　　Medvedev Vladimir, *43*, **and** his son, *Maxsine*, *14*, sailed *from*

an unnamed eastern Russian seaport on August 18, to begin an

ambitious around-the-world cruise.

　　澎湖，十一月廿四日——有兩名俄國人，他們是一對父子，乘著故障的帆船在海上漂流，星期六在台灣西南外海，靠近澎湖群島的海域獲救。

　　四十三歲的梅德維迪夫·烏拉底米爾和他十四歲的兒子麥可馨，於八月十八日自俄國東方一處不知名的海港出發，開始了他們充滿雄心壯志的環球之旅。

Russian〔ˋrʌʃən〕n. 俄國人　　　sailboat〔ˋselˏbot〕n. 帆船
break down 故障　　　drift〔drɪft〕v. 漂流
unnamed〔ʌnˋnemd〕adj. 未指名的
seaport〔ˋsiˏport〕n. 海港　　　cruise〔kruz〕n. 旅行

Their voyage, *down the coastline of northeastern mainland China, through the East China Sea, then down the Taiwan Strait and into the South China Sea,* had been smooth *until four days ago when the mainsail of their twin-mast sailboat "Kawasaki" was smashed by strong winds on the high seas.*

The father-and-son team started the inboard engine. *However, after less than two days,* the engine broke down.

Near the "black ditch" of Penghu, battered by winds of up to 70 knots, the rear sail was torn into shreds. The rudder *also* stopped responding.

　　他們沿著中國大陸東邊海岸線航行，通過了東海、台灣海峽，進入南海，一直都十分順利。但在四天前，他們那艘雙桅帆船「加外沙基號」，在公海上遭強風吹襲，嚴重受損。

　　於是這對父子便發動了船艙內的引擎。不過，航行不到兩天，引擎就故障了。

　　在靠近澎湖的「黑溝」附近，帆船遭受到時速高達七十海里的強風吹襲，尾帆被風撕裂成碎片，舵也失去了控制。

voyage (ˈvɔɪ·ɪdʒ) n. 航行　　coastline (ˈkostˌlaɪn) n. 海岸線

strait (stret) n. 海峽　　mainsail (ˈmenˌsel) n. 主帆；大帆

twin-mast (ˈtwɪnˌmæst) adj. 雙桅的

smash (smæʃ) v. 使粉碎；重擊　　*the high seas* 公海

inboard (ˈɪnˌbord) adj. 在船艙內的　　ditch (dɪtʃ) n. 水溝

batter (ˈbætɚ) v. 重擊

knot (nɑt) n. 節；浬（一小時行一海里的速度）

rear (rɪr) adj. 後面的　　tear (tɛr) v. 撕裂

shred (ʃrɛd) n. 碎片　　rudder (ˈrʌdɚ) n. 舵

Surprised by the father and son's "pale faces" **and** *their battered vessel,* the Penghu police and fishers *in Paisha* rescued them. *Speaking only limited English,* the Vladimirs spent five hours *trying to explain their presence.*

It is not *immediately* known **whether** the "Kawasaki" can be repaired on the fishing island of Penghu, **or when** the Vladimirs will be able to set off again **and** continue their around-the-world voyage.

　　在白沙的澎湖警方與漁民，看到這對父子「蒼白」的臉，以及他們破爛的船時十分吃驚，就將他們自海中救起。由於梅德維迪夫父子會說的英語十分有限，所以他們花了五個小時的時間來解釋自己為何會在這裏出現。

　　現在我們並不知道「加外沙基號」是否會在澎湖漁島上修理，或是這對父子何時才能再度出發去繼續他們的環球之旅。

pale (pel) adj. 蒼白的

battered (ˈbætɚd) adj. 被打壞了的；敲碎的

vessel (ˈvɛsl̩) n. 船　　presence (ˈprɛzn̩s) n. 存在；在場

set off 出發

52. (**A**) 梅德維迪夫父子航行的目的為何？
 (A) 環遊世界。　　　　　　　(B) 要造訪澎湖群島。
 (C) 尋找失散的家人。　　　　(D) 要發動船艙內的引擎。

53. (**C**) 梅德維迪夫父子是走什麼方向的路線才到了澎湖？
 (A) 東。　　(B) 西。　　(C) 南。　　(D) 北。

54. (**C**) 「加外沙基號」在航程中，何時首度陷入困境？
 (A) 離開俄國不到兩天。
 (B) 在發動船艙內引擎的四天前。
 (C) 自俄國航行三個多月後。
 (D) 在船漂流到澎湖群島的白沙縣時。
 county〔'kaʊntɪ〕n. 縣

55. (**D**) 梅德維迪夫父子獲救後，他們決定要怎麼辦？
 (A) 留在澎湖捕魚。　　　　　(B) 把船賣了再回俄國。
 (C) 先修理船，再開回俄國。　(D) 他們尚未決定。

第二部分：非選擇題
壹、簡答題：

Do you know *that happy folks recover from illness much more readily than people who are depressed and always complaining*?

The old sages *always* used to say *that* laughter was the best medicine— *indeed, better than medicine.*

Someone else remarked *that "a merry heart does good, like medicine"— and* infectious laughter is *often* catching. Don't you find it so? I like the anonymous verse *which sums it all up:*

When wholesome laughter fills the air,
　Some ills will soon depart;
For laughter is good medicine
　That helps to cheer the heart.

　　你知道嗎？愉快的人生病時想恢復健康，要比沮喪或是喜歡抱怨的人容易得多。

　　古聖先賢常說，笑是最佳良藥——的確，笑的功效比藥更好。

　　有人說：「愉快的心十分有益處，就像藥一樣」——而具有感染力的笑聲通常是會傳染的。你不覺得嗎？我很喜歡一首不具名的詩，這首詩就概括地說明了這一切：

　　　　當有益健康的笑聲瀰漫在空氣中，

　　　　　　有些疾病就會遠離；

　　　　因為笑是最佳良藥

　　　　能愉悦我們的心靈。

folks〔foks〕*n. pl.* 人們（ = *people* ）
depressed〔dɪˈprɛst〕*adj.* 沮喪的
sage〔sedʒ〕*n.* 聖賢　　indeed〔ɪnˈdid〕*adv.* 的確
remark〔rɪˈmark〕*v.* 評論；說　　merry〔ˈmɛrɪ〕*adj.* 愉快的
infectious〔ɪnˈfɛkʃəs〕*adj.* 具感染力的
catching〔ˈkætʃɪŋ〕*adj.* 有感染力的
anonymous〔əˈnɑnəməs〕*adj.* 不具名的；作者不詳的
verse〔vɝs〕*n.* 詩　　***sum** sth. **up*** 概括地說～
wholesome〔ˈholsəm〕*adj.* 有益健康的　　cheer〔tʃɪr〕*v.* 使高興

1. 根據本文，哪一種人生病時最容易康復？
   答：happy folks

2. 本文中哪個字是指「非常有智慧的人」？
   答：sages

3. 本文中哪個字與 infectious 意思最接近？
   答：catching

4. 那首詩的作者是誰？
   答：anonymous 或 an unknown author

5. 在那首詩中，哪個字和 depart 押韻？
   答：heart

貳、英文作文：（參考範例）

Laughter Is Better than Medicine

A friend of mine, Julia, was once hospitalized. At first she stayed in a room all by herself. She felt so depressed and had no appetite at all. She looked worse than before, even though she was taking medicine regularly. *Then* her mother moved her to another room which she shared with other patients. One of them always told jokes and made them all laugh. In two days, Julia changed completely. *Not only* did she look happy, *but* her health *also* improved. She checked out of the hospital earlier than the doctor expected.

Medicine is used to cure all kinds of illnesses, but there are some situations where medicine just can't help. When we are nervous, or in low spirits, a good laugh can relieve our tension and put us in a better mood. Laughter sometimes works like a miracle, doing wonders for both physical and mental health. *Therefore*, I truly believe that laughter is really better than any other medicine.

> hospitalize（'hɑspɪtḷ͵aɪz）*v.* 使住院
> appetite（'æpə͵taɪt）*n.* 食慾
> regularly（'rɛgjələlɪ）*adv.* 定期地　　move（muv）*v.* 遷移
> *share with* ~　與~共用　　*check out* 付帳離開
> *be in low spirits* 心情不好　　*relieve one's tension* 消除緊張
> mood（mud）*n.* 心情　　miracle（'mɪrəkḷ）*n.* 奇蹟
> *do wonders* 產生驚人的效果；（藥）有奇效

心得筆記欄

八十五年大學入學學科能力測驗試題
英文考科

第一部分：單一選擇題

I、字彙與片語：

說明：第 1 至 10 題，每題依句意選出最適當的一個選項，標示在答案卡之「選擇題答案區」。每題答對得 1 分，答錯不倒扣。

1. The main _____ of this test is to find out how much you have learned in high school.
   (A) countenance　(B) discipline　　(C) objective　　(D) procedure

2. I hope to live in a student dormitory when I am in college. I am tired of _____ to school in a crowded bus every day.
   (A) commuting　(B) dropping　　(C) swaying　　(D) wandering

3. They were behind schedule and had to apply for _____ manpower to complete their project in time.
   (A) basic　　(B) extra　　(C) introductory　(D) profound

4. Out of _____ and consideration, I always write a thank-you note when someone sends me a gift.
   (A) concentration　(B) convenience　　(C) courtesy　　(D) courtship

5. The boy _____ to the teacher for his improper behavior.
   (A) apologized　(B) appealed　　(C) approached　(D) attached

6. The problem with Jane is that she tends to take criticism too _____ and gets angry easily.
   (A) eventually　(B) positively　　(C) intimately　(D) personally

7. Almost everybody is a _____ of many different "selves"; we show different faces to different people.
   (A) combination　(B) communication　(C) competition　(D) complication

8. John has been working at the computer for twenty-four hours. He _____ needs a good rest.
   (A) accidentally　(B) efficiently　　(C) obviously　(D) previously

9. Nowadays students can _____ information from a variety of sources, such as computers, television, and compact discs.
   (A) press　　(B) express　　(C) oppress　　(D) access

10. Sorry for being late. Someone gave me _____ directions and I got totally lost.
    (A) dreary   (B) faulty   (C) handy   (D) steady

說明：第 11 至 20 題，請選出與劃線部份語意最接近的字詞，標示在答案卡之「選擇題答案區」。每題答對得 1 分，答錯不倒扣。

11. Doctors have repeatedly warned people of the serious <u>effect</u> of noise on their hearing.
    (A) curve   (B) impact   (C) increase   (D) shortcoming

12. People who are <u>determined</u> cannot be easily stopped from doing what they want to do.
    (A) happy-natured   (B) strong-willed
    (C) warm-hearted   (D) well-intentioned

13. The bridge <u>collapsed</u> under the weight of the heavy truck.
    (A) gave up   (B) gave off   (C) gave over   (D) gave in

14. My <u>initial</u> offer was turned down politely. But when I tried again in my most sincere tone, it was gladly accepted.
    (A) numerous   (B) original   (C) responsible   (D) talented

15. The outdoor concert was <u>canceled</u> because of rain.
    (A) called off   (B) cut off   (C) put off   (D) taken off

16. It's <u>next to</u> impossible for me to finish the homework in three days.
    (A) second   (B) never   (C) almost   (D) usually

17. <u>Every now and then</u> they go to a movie together.
    (A) Always   (B) Never   (C) Occasionally   (D) Seldom

18. I was <u>held up</u> by a traffic jam on the freeway for about an hour.
    (A) delayed   (B) maintained   (C) raised   (D) supported

19. I tell you <u>once and for all</u> that you must not do such a stupid thing again.
    (A) at times   (B) for the last time
    (C) more than once   (D) once more

20. I am curious about how John <u>came by</u> such a large sum of money.
    (A) brought   (B) spent   (C) paid   (D) obtained

II、綜合測驗：

說明：第 21 至 40 題，每題有一個空格。請依文意選出最適當的一個選項，標示在答案卡之「選擇題答案區」。每題答對得 1 分，答錯不倒扣。

21-30 題為題組

　　When Levi Strauss arrived in the United States from Bavaria, he was only seventeen, poor, and knew very __21__ English. Like most immigrants, he was __22__ a better life. So, when gold was discovered in the West in 1849, he __23__ thousands of others and rushed to California.

　　__24__ he planned to open a shop in San Francisco, he took many goods with him, __25__ a large quantity of canvas. He hoped to sell __26__ as material for tents or wagon covers. Business, however, was not __27__ he had expected. __28__ , as he sat in a cafe in a small town, he had an idea. He saw a man with a hole in the leg of his trousers and __29__ realized what Californians __30__ for the rough work they were doing--good, strong trousers!

21. (A) easy	(B) some	(C) small	(D) little
22. (A) looking after	(B) looking at	(C) looking for	(D) looking into
23. (A) took	(B) avoided	(C) paid	(D) joined
24. (A) Although	(B) Because	(C) If	(D) Unless
25. (A) including	(B) included	(C) being included	(D) was including
26. (A) much	(B) one	(C) it	(D) others
27. (A) as far as	(B) as good as	(C) as soon as	(D) as well as
28. (A) One day	(B) Another day	(C) Someday	(D) The other day
29. (A) casually	(B) frequently	(C) regularly	(D) suddenly
30. (A) needed	(B) need	(C) needing	(D) have needed

31-40 題為題組

　　All forms of life have an instinctive urge to survive. Nature provides __31__ with the means of survival. We have learned much about survival from __32__ forms of animal life. Lizards, __33__ , can change the color of their skin and __34__ the trees and leaves around them. __35__ , they cannot be detected by other animals that threaten them. Nature provides other forms of protection __36__ environmental dangers. Human beings, too, __37__ special devices to protect __38__ . Their skin is very __39__ to temperature changes. __40__ warm weather, sweating helps humans regulate their body temperature.

31. (A) it   (B) them   (C) this   (D) which
32. (A) better   (B) fewer   (C) less   (D) lower
33. (A) however   (B) for instance   (C) in case   (D) more or less
34. (A) blend with   (B) differ from   (C) gaze upon   (D) migrate to
35. (A) Nevertheless   (B) As a result
     (C) In contrast   (D) On the other hand
36. (A) about   (B) above   (C) against   (D) around
37. (A) give   (B) are going to give
     (C) have given   (D) have been given
38. (A) himself   (B) itself   (C) themselves   (D) yourselves
39. (A) sensational   (B) sensible   (C) sensitive   (D) sentimental
40. (A) During   (B) Instead of   (C) Over   (D) Through

III、閱讀測驗：

說明：第 41 至 50 題，請依各篇文章之文意選出最適當的一個選項，標示在答
案卡之「選擇題答案區」。每題答對得 2 分，答錯不倒扣。

41-43 題為題組

Oct. 6, 1996

Dear Tom,

    It seems only yesterday that Jack and I were helping you learn your ABC's--and now you have finished high school and been accepted at Taipei University.

    We are both very proud of you, Tom. We have followed your high-school career with joy and pleasure and know that your four years at college will be even more rewarding. A word of congratulation just doesn't seem enough, so I am sending you a gift that I'm sure you will find useful--an unabridged dictionary. Jack says you'll not only find it handy in your studies, but a great argument-saver when playing Scrabble with your friends.

    Mom and Dad are coming here for a weekend next month. Please try to take a few days off and come to join us. We are looking forward to seeing you.

Love,
Sally

41. Which of the following is <u>NOT</u> mentioned as a reason for writing the letter?
    (A) To congratulate Tom on his wonderful achievement.
    (B) To tell Tom of his parents' planned visit.
    (C) To invite Tom to join a weekend family get-together.
    (D) To ask Tom to go home for the weekend.

42. "Scrabble" is
    (A) an argument-saver.
    (B) a big dictionary.
    (C) a game.
    (D) a gift.

43. On the basis of the letter, what is the most likely relationship between Sally and Tom?
    (A) Mother and son.
    (B) Sister and brother.
    (C) Grandmother and grandson.
    (D) Niece and nephew.

44-46 題為題組

Generally speaking, all foreigners coming to Taiwan should apply for entry visas through the embassies or consulates of the Republic of China, or agencies authorized by the Ministry of Foreign Affairs.

As of May 1, 1995, all nationals of the following 15 countries are exempted from securing visas for entry into the Republic of China: U.S.A., Japan, Canada, Belgium, Luxembourg, Sweden, Holland, New Zealand, Australia, Austria, Germany, Britain, France, Spain, and Portugal. The maximum duration of stay is 14 days. Requirements for a 14-day non-visa entry are: passport good for at least six months, confirmed onward ticket within 14 days, no violation of law recorded.

If it is necessary to stay more than 14 days and less than 30 days, nationals of the specific countries holding a 14-day non-visa entry should in the meantime apply for a landing-visa with the authorized office in the CKS airport from the Bureau of Consular Affairs of the Ministry of Foreign Affairs. The landing-visa fee is NT$1,500.

44. When an American lady wants to enter Taiwan for a one-week sight-seeing trip, one of the requirements is
    (A) to obtain a landing-visa at the CKS airport.
    (B) to apply for a visa before leaving the U.S.A.
    (C) to make sure her passport was issued before May 1, 1995.
    (D) to make sure her passport is valid for more than six months on the date of arrival.

45. If a British businessman wants to visit some trade partners in Taiwan for about three weeks, what should he do?
    (A) He should obtain a visa for entry into the Republic of China before getting on board the flight to Taiwan.
    (B) He should travel with a friend who is from any of the other 14 countries mentioned.
    (C) He must obtain a landing-visa at the CKS airport.
    (D) He just needs to apply for a non-visa entry when he arrives at the CKS airport.

46. Which of the following is needed for a landing-visa?
    (A) A passport that is valid for more than six months.
    (B) A 14-day non-visa entry.
    (C) An application fee of NT$1,500.
    (D) All of the above.

47-50題爲題組

The brain, which weighs less than 2.2 pounds, is perhaps the most complicated organ in our bodies. Although scientists have not been able to solve all the mysteries of this amazing organ, they have made some progress. They have found that certain parts of the brain are responsible for learning, memory, and language.

Recent studies indicate that the two halves of the brain--the right hemisphere and the left hemisphere--play extremely important roles in learning and communicating. The left hemisphere deals with rules, lists of information, and short-term memory. In contrast, the right hemisphere deals with feelings, colors, and long-term memory. Scientists recognize the importance of both hemispheres in the learning of all sorts, including language learning.

Scientists now relate left and right hemispheres to the way different individuals learn languages. They believe that some learners use one half of their brains more than the other half. Left-brained learners usually concentrate on memorizing rules and lists. They use logic, definition, and repetition to learn. Right-brained learners look for a general picture and concentrate on relating new information to what they already know. They use associations and intuition to learn. Most people fall into one of these types. If teachers know whether their students are left-brained or right-brained, they can help them learn better.

47. Mary is a typical left-brained learner. Which of the following descriptions does NOT fit her?
    (A) She thinks in a very logical way.
    (B) She is very artistic and romantic.
    (C) She often scores A in sentence-combining tests.
    (D) She is very good at math.

48. What is the most significant implication that teachers can draw from the above information? They should
    (A) encourage students to memorize rules.
    (B) show students how to use logic to solve problems.
    (C) urge students to relate new information to what they already know.
    (D) try to find out the best learning styles for individual students.

49. Which of the following statements is TRUE?
    (A) Damage of one hemisphere does not always cause complete loss of speech.
    (B) Remembering one's way home involves short-term memory.
    (C) Language learning takes place only in one hemisphere.
    (D) Scientists have solved all the mysteries of the brain.

50. What is the best title of this passage?
    (A) The Short-term and Long-term Memory
    (B) Discoveries in the Field of Hemispheres
    (C) A Recent Scientific Discovery　　　(D) The Amazing Human Brain

第二部分：非選擇題

I、中譯英：

說明：請將以下短文中劃線的五個中文句子，根據上下文譯成正確、通順、達意的英文，並將答案寫在「答案卷」上。每題4分，共20分。

<u>1-5 題爲題組</u>

　　1. 你有沒有想過未來的旅館會是什麼樣子？ You need not wonder any longer. A hotel in Japan will give you a preview. The name of this hotel is the Capsule Inn; its rooms rent for eleven dollars a night. 2. 每個房間附有一部收音機，一台電視機和一個鬧鐘。 3. 此外，所有房間都有空調。 But here any resemblance to a twentieth-century hotel ends. The rooms are small plastic capsules, and each capsule is about five feet high, by five feet wide, and by seven feet deep. Guests have to crawl into bed through a large porthole entrance. 4. 廁所及洗衣設施位於旅館的共同區域。 5. 信不信由你，這家旅館幾乎經常是客滿， perhaps because the price of the rooms is as small as the rooms themselves.

II、作文：

說明：1. 請依下列提示寫一篇英文作文在「答案卷」上。文長以 120 字爲原則。

　　　2. 評分標準：內容 5 分，組織 5 分，文法 4 分，用字拼字 4 分，體例（格式、標點、大小寫）2 分

背景提示：

　　西元 1939 年紐約世界博覽會前夕，主辦單位在會址的地底下埋了一個時間膠囊(time capsule)，裡面放了許多最能代表當時生活方式的物品，如電話機、開罐器、手錶、香煙、以及一塊煤炭等。這個密封的盒子，要等到西元 6939 年才打開，以便讓五千年後的人知道 1930 年代的生活型態。

　　現在有一個國際性基金會也預備舉辦類似的活動，要將一個真空密閉的時間膠囊埋在地底，膠囊中的東西都不會腐壞，好讓一千年以後的人知道 1996 年世界各地區的生活方式。該基金會公開向各國人士徵求建議。

提示：

　　請你寫一篇英文短文前往應徵，提出最能代表我國人民生活現狀的物品兩件（體積不限），說明你選擇這兩件物品的理由，並以 "The two things I would like to put in the time capsule are..." 作爲短文的開頭。

85年度學科能力測驗英文科試題詳解

第一部分：單一選擇題

I、字彙與片語

1. (**C**) The main objective *of this test* is to find out how much you have learned *in high school*.

這項測驗的主要<u>目標</u>就是要知道，你在中學裏學到了多少。
(A) countenance (ˈkauntənəns) *n.* 表情　(B) discipline (ˈdɪsəplɪn) *n.* 紀律
(C) ***objective*** (əbˈdʒɛktɪv) *n.* 目標　　(D) procedure (prəˈsidʒɚ) *n.* 程序

2. (**A**) I hope to live in a student dormitory *when I am in college*. I am tired of commuting to school *in a crowded bus* *every day*.

我希望我念大學時，能住在學生宿舍裏。我已厭倦了每天坐擁擠的公車<u>通勤</u>上學。
(A) ***commute*** (kəˈmjut) *v.* 通勤　　(B) drop (drɑp) *v.* 掉落
(C) sway (swe) *v.* 搖擺　　(D) wander (ˈwɑndɚ) *v.* 徘徊

3. (**B**) They were behind schedule *and* had to apply for extra manpower *to complete their project in time*.

他們的進度落後，要及時完成計畫，必須申請<u>額外</u>的人力。
(A) basic (ˈbesɪk) *adj.* 基本的　　(B) ***extra*** (ˈɛkstrə) *adj.* 額外的
(C) introductory (ˌɪntrəˈdʌktərɪ) *adj.* 介紹的
(D) profound (prəˈfaund) *adj.* 深的 (= *deep*)
behind schedule 進度落後　　***apply for*** 申請
manpower (ˈmænˌpauɚ) *n.* 人力　　project (ˈprɑdʒɛkt) *n.* 計畫

4. (**C**) *Out of courtesy and consideration*, I *always* write a thank-you note *when someone sends me a gift*.

出於<u>禮貌</u>和體貼，有人送我禮物時，我總會寫張謝卡。
(A) concentration (ˌkɑnsn̩ˈtreʃən, -sɛn-) *n.* 專心
(B) convenience (kənˈvinjəns) *n.* 方便
(C) ***courtesy*** (ˈkɝtəsɪ) *n.* 禮貌　　(D) courtship (ˈkortˌʃɪp) *n.* 求愛
out of 出於　　consideration (kənˌsɪdəˈreʃən) *n.* 體貼

5. (**A**) The boy apologized to the teacher *for his improper behavior*.
這個男孩因行為不當向老師道歉。
(A) *apologize* 〔ə'pɑlə,dʒaɪz〕 v. 道歉　(B) appeal 〔ə'pil〕 v. 吸引
(C) approach 〔ə'protʃ〕 v. 接近　(D) attach 〔ə'tætʃ〕 v. 附著
improper 〔ɪm'prɑpɚ〕 *adj.* 不適當的

6. (**D**) The problem *with Jane* is **that** she tends to take criticism too
personally **and** gets angry easily.
珍的問題就是，她太容易把批評看成是針對個人而發的，而很容易生氣。
(A) eventually 〔ɪ'vɛntʃʊəlɪ〕 *adv.* 最後
(B) positively 〔'pɑzətɪvlɪ〕 *adv.* 積極地
(C) intimately 〔'ɪntəmɪtlɪ〕 *adv.* 親密地
(D) *personally* 〔'pɝsn̩lɪ〕 *adv.* 針對個人地
tend to 傾向於　criticism 〔'krɪtə,sɪzəm〕 *n.* 批評

7. (**A**) *Almost* everybody is a combination *of many different "selves"*;
we show different faces *to different people*.
幾乎每個人都是許多不同自我的結合；我們對不同的人就表現不同的面貌。
(A) *combination* 〔,kɑmbə'neʃən〕 *n.* 結合
(B) communication 〔kə,mjunə'keʃən〕 *n.* 溝通
(C) competition 〔,kɑmpə'tɪʃən〕 *n.* 競爭
(D) complication 〔,kɑmplə'keʃən〕 *n.* 複雜
self 〔sɛlf〕 *n.* 自我（複數為 selves）

8. (**C**) John has been working *at the computer* *for twenty-four hours*.
He *obviously* needs a good rest.
約翰已在電腦前工作了二十四個小時。他顯然需要好好休息。
(A) accidentally 〔,æksə'dɛntl̩ɪ〕 *adv.* 意外地
(B) efficiently 〔ə'fɪʃəntlɪ, ɪ-〕 *adv.* 有效率地
(C) *obviously* 〔'ɑbvɪəslɪ〕 *adv.* 顯然
(D) previously 〔'privɪəslɪ〕 *adv.* 以前地

9. (**D**) *Nowadays* students can acc<u>ess</u> information *from a variety of sources, such as computers, television, and compact discs.*
現在學生可以從各種來源<u>取得</u>資訊，例如電腦、電視和雷射唱片。
(A) press〔prɛs〕*v.* 壓 　　　(B) express〔ɪk'sprɛs〕*v.* 表達
(C) oppress〔ə'prɛs〕*v.* 壓迫 　(D) *access*〔'æksɛs〕*v.* 取得
a variety of 各種 　　source〔sors, sɔrs〕*n.* 來源
compact disc 雷射唱片（簡稱 CD）

10. (**B**) Sorry for being late. Someone gave me <u>faulty</u> directions *and* I got *totally* lost.
抱歉我遲到了。有人給了我<u>錯誤的</u>方向，所以我完全迷路了。
(A) dreary〔'drɪrɪ, 'drirɪ〕*adj.* 陰沈的 　(B) *faulty*〔'fɔltɪ〕*adj.* 錯誤的
(C) handy〔'hændɪ〕*adj.* 方便的 　(D) steady〔'stɛdɪ〕*adj.* 穩定的
totally〔'totl̩ɪ〕*adv.* 完全地

11. (**B**) Doctors have *repeatedly* warned people of the serious <u>effect</u> *of noise on their hearing.*
醫生不斷地警告人們，噪音對人們的聽力有嚴重的<u>影響</u>。
(A) curve〔kɝv〕*n.* 曲線 　　　　(B) *impact*〔'ɪmpækt〕*n.* 影響
(C) increase〔'ɪnkris, 'ɪŋk-〕*n.* 增加
(D) shortcoming〔'ʃɔrt,kʌmɪŋ〕*n.* 缺點
repeatedly〔rɪ'pitɪdlɪ〕*adv.* 不斷地 　　effect〔ə'fɛkt, ɪ-, ɛ-〕*n.* 影響

12. (**B**) People *who are determined* cannot be *easily* stopped *from doing what they want to do.*
<u>堅決的</u>人不容易被阻止，不去做他們想做的事。
(A) happy-natured〔'hæpɪ'netʃəd〕*adj.* 樂天的
(B) *strong-willed*〔'strɔŋ'wɪld〕*adj.* 堅決的
(C) warm-hearted〔'wɔrm'hɑrtɪd〕*adj.* 熱情的
(D) well-intentioned〔'wɛlɪn'tɛnʃənd〕*adj.* 好意的
determined〔dɪ'tɝmɪnd〕*adj.* 堅決的

13. (**D**) The bridge collapsed *under the weight of the heavy truck.*

這座橋不堪卡車的重量而倒塌了。
(A) give up 放棄　　　(B) give off 放出（光、熱、味等）
(C) give over 委託　　(D) ***give in*** 屈服；倒塌
collapse〔kəˋlæps〕v. 倒塌

14. (**B**) My initial offer was turned down *politely.* ***But when I tried again in my most sincere tone,*** it was *gladly* accepted.

我最初的提議被婉拒。但我以非常誠心的語調再試一次時，就很高興地被接受了。
(A) numerous〔ˋnjumərəs〕*adj.* 很多的
(B) ***original***〔əˋrɪdʒənḷ〕*adj.* 最初的
(C) responsible〔rɪˋspɑnsəbḷ〕*adj.* 負責的
(D) talented〔ˋtæləntɪd〕*adj.* 有天分的
initial〔ɪˋnɪʃəl〕*adj.* 最初的　　　offer〔ˋɔfə, ˋɑfə〕*n.* 提議
turn down 拒絕　　sincere〔sɪnˋsɪr〕*adj.* 誠心的
tone〔ton〕*n.* 語調

15. (**A**) The outdoor concert was canceled *because of rain.*
戶外音樂會因雨取消了。
(A) ***call off*** 取消　　　(B) cut off 切斷
(C) put off 拖延；延期　　(D) take off 脫掉；起飛
cancel〔ˋkænsḷ〕*v.* 取消

16. (**C**) It's *next to* impossible for me to finish the homework *in three days.*

三天之內完成作業，對我而言是幾乎不可能的。
(A) second〔ˋsɛkənd〕*adv.* 第二地　(B) never〔ˋnɛvə〕*adv.* 從不
(C) ***almost***〔ˋɔl͵most〕*adv.* 幾乎　(D) usually〔ˋjuʒʊəlɪ〕*adv.* 經常
next to 幾乎（接否定詞）

17. (**C**) *Every now and then* they go to a movie *together*.
他們偶爾會去看場電影。
(A) always（'ɔlwez）*adv.* 總是　　(B) never（'nɛvɚ）*adv.* 從不
(C) *occasionally*（ə'keʒənḷɪ）*adv.* 偶爾
(D) seldom（'sɛldəm）*adv.* 很少
(*every*) *now and then* 偶爾

18. (**A**) I was held up by a traffic jam *on the freeway* *for about an
hour*.
我在高速公路上，因交通阻塞延誤了大約一個小時。
(A) *delay*（dɪ'le）*v.* 延誤　　(B) maintain（men'ten）*v.* 維持
(C) raise（rez）*v.* 舉起　　(D) support（sə'port , -'pɔrt）*v.* 支持
hold up 使延誤　　*traffic jam* 交通阻塞
freeway（'fri,we）*n.* 高速公路

19. (**B**) I tell you *once and for all* *that you must not do such a stupid
thing again*.
我只此一次告訴你，你不可以再做出這麼愚蠢的事了。
(A) at times 偶爾　　　　　(B) *for the last time* 最後一次
(C) more than once 不只一次　(D) once more 再一次
once and for all 只此一次

20. (**D**) I am curious about *how John came by such a large sum of
money*.
我很好奇，約翰是如何得到這麼一大筆錢的。
(A) bring（brɪŋ）*v.* 帶來　　(B) spend（spɛnd）*v.* 花費
(C) pay（pe）*v.* 付錢　　　(D) *obtain*（əb'ten）*v.* 獲得
come by 獲得

II、綜合練習

*When Levi Strauss arrived in the United States *from Bavaria*, he was
only seventeen, poor, *and* knew *very* little English. *Like most immigrants*,
he was looking for a better life. *So*, *when gold was discovered *in the
West in 1849*, he joined thousands of others *and* rushed to California.

　　當李維‧史特勞斯從巴伐利亞來到美國時，他才十七歲，很窮，而且懂的英文很少。他和大部分移民一樣，想尋找一個更好的生活，所以，當美國西部在一八四九年發現黃金時，他加入了數千人的行列，一窩蜂地來到了加州。

Bavaria〔bə'vɛrɪə〕*n.* 巴伐利亞
immigrant〔'ɪməgrənt〕*n.* 移民（移入）　　　rush〔rʌʃ〕*v.* 衝

21.(**D**) 形容英文懂得很少要用 little，選 (D)。

22.(**C**) (A) look after 照顧　　　　(B) look at 看；注視
　　　　　(C) *look for* 尋找　　　　 (D) look into 調查

23.(**D**) 依句意，他「加入」其他人的行列，選 (D) joined。
　　　　　(B) avoid〔ə'vɔɪd〕*v.* 避免

Because he planned to open a shop in San Francisco, he took many
　　24
goods with him, *including a large quantity of canvas*. He hoped to sell
　　　　　　　　　　　　25
it *as material for tents or wagon covers*. Business, *however*, was not
26
as good *as he had expected*. *One day*, *as he sat in a cafe in a small*
　　27　　　　　　　　　　　　　　　28
town, he had an idea. He saw a man *with a hole in the leg of his trou-*
sers **and** *suddenly* realized **what** Californians *needed* for the rough work
　　　　　　　29　　　　　　　　　　　　　　　　30
they were doing--good, strong trousers!

　　因為他計畫在舊金山開一家商店，所以他帶了很多貨物來，其中包括了大量的帆布。他希望把帆布當成帳篷或馬車車篷的材料賣出去，然而生意並不如他所預期的好。有一天，他坐在一個小鎮上的咖啡廳時，他想到了一個主意。他看到一個人長褲褲管上破一個洞，而突然了解到，由於加州人所做的工作十分粗重，他們需要的是質料好而堅固耐穿的褲子。

goods〔gudz〕*n. pl.* 貨物　　　*a large quantity of* 大量的（接不可數名詞）
canvas〔'kænvəs〕*n.* 帆布　　　tent〔tɛnt〕*n.* 帳篷
wagon〔'wægən〕*n.* 馬車　　　cover〔'kʌvɚ〕*n.* 車篷
cafe〔kə'fe , kæ'fe〕*n.* 咖啡廳　　　trousers〔'trauzɚz〕*n. pl.* 褲子
Californian〔ˌkælə'fɔrnɪən〕*n.* 加州人　　　rough〔rʌf〕*adj.* 粗重的

24. (**B**) 依句意，前後二句為因果關係，故連接詞應用 Because，選 (B)。

25. (**A**) 表「包括～」，可用 including ～；～ included；inclusive of ～ 三種用法，故本題選 (A)。

26. (**C**) 此處受詞 canvas 為不可數名詞，視為單數，故用代名詞 it 代替，選 (C)。

27. (**B**) (A) as far as 只要；和～一樣遠
　　　　 (B) *as good as* 和～一樣好 (*adj.*)
　　　　 (C) as soon as 一～就…；和～一樣快
　　　　 (D) as well as 以及；和～一樣好 (*adv.*)

28. (**A**) 依句意，是敘述過去時間的「有一天」，選 (A) one day，此片語可指過去或未來的有一天。(C) someday 指未來的有一天，(D) the other day 前幾天，均不合。

29. (**D**) (A) casually〔'kæʒʊəlɪ〕*adv.* 隨便地
　　　　 (B) frequently〔'frikwəntlɪ〕*adv.* 經常
　　　　 (C) regularly〔'rɛgjələlɪ〕*adv.* 經常
　　　　 (D) *suddenly*〔'sʌdn̩lɪ〕*adv.* 突然地

30. (**A**) 依句意，他終於了解加州人的真正需要，為過去式，故選 (A) needed。

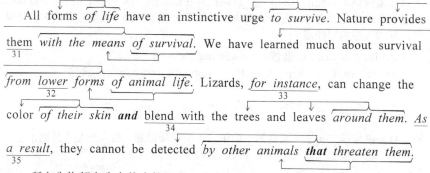

All forms *of life* have an instinctive urge *to survive*. Nature provides them *with the means of survival*. We have learned much about survival
31
from lower forms of animal life. Lizards, *for instance*, can change the
32　　　　　　　　　　　　　　　　　　　33
color *of their skin and* blend with the trees and leaves *around them. As*
34
a result, they cannot be detected *by other animals that threaten them.*
35

　　所有生物都有生存的本能衝動，大自然提供他們生存方法。關於生存，我們已從較低等的動物生活中學到了很多，例如，蜥蜴能改變牠們的膚色，和周圍的樹木及葉子混合在一起，因此就不會被威脅牠們生命的其他動物察覺到。

instinctive〔ɪn'stɪŋktɪv〕*adj.* 本能的　　　urge〔ɝdʒ〕*n.* 衝動
survive〔sə'vaɪv〕*v.* 生存　　*provide sb. with sth.* 提供某人某物
means〔minz〕*n.* 方法 (單複數同形)　　survival〔sə'vaɪvl̩〕*n.* 生存
lizard〔'lɪzəd〕*n.* 蜥蜴　　detect〔dɪ'tɛkt〕*v.* 察覺　　threaten〔'θrɛtn̩〕*v.* 威脅

31. (**B**) 受詞 all forms of life 為複數，故用代名詞 them 來代替，選 (B)。

32. (**D**) 動物是比人類低等的生物，故選 (D) lower 。

33. (**B**) 依句意，此處為舉例說明，故選 (B) for instance 例如。(A) 然而，(C) 以防，(D) 或多或少，均不合。

34. (**A**) (A) **blend with** 與～混合　　(B) differ from 與～不同
　　　　　(C) gaze upon 凝視　　　　(D) migrate ('maɪgret) v. 遷移

35. (**B**) (A) nevertheless (ˌnɛvəðə'lɛs) adv. 然而
　　　　　(B) **as a result** 因此　　　(C) in contrast 成對比
　　　　　(D) on the other hand 另一方面

Nature provides other forms of protection *against environmental dangers*.
　　　　　　　　　　　　　　　　　　　　　　36

Human beings, *too*, have been given special devices *to protect themselves*.
　　　　　　　　　　　　37　　　　　　　　　　　　　38

Their skin is *very* sensitive to temperature changes. *During warm weather*,
　　　　　　　　　39　　　　　　　　　　　　　　　40

sweating helps humans regulate their body temperature.

大自然還提供了其他形式的保護，以對抗外在環境的危險。人們也被賦予特殊的
裝置，來保護他們自己。他們的皮膚對溫度變化非常敏感。天氣暖和時，流汗就
可以幫助人類調節體溫。

　　　device (dɪ'vaɪs) n. 裝置　　sweating ('swɛtɪŋ) n. 流汗
　　　sweat (swɛt) v. 流汗　　n. 汗水　　regulate ('rɛgjə,let) v. 調節

36. (**C**) 依句意，表「對抗」之意，介系詞應用 against ，選 (C)。

37. (**D**) 承接前文句意，大自然「賦予」人類保護措施，故人類是「被賦予」，
　　　　　應用被動，選 (D) have been given 。

38. (**C**) 由於主詞 Human beings 為複數名詞，故反身代名詞亦須用複數，依句
　　　　　意選 (C) themselves 他們自己。

39. (**C**) (A) sensational (sɛn'seʃənḷ) adj. 煽情的
　　　　　(B) sensible ('sɛnsəbḷ) adj. 明智的
　　　　　(C) **sensitive** ('sɛnsətɪv) adj. 敏感的
　　　　　(D) sentimental (ˌsɛntə'mɛntḷ) adj. 多愁善感的

40. (**A**) 依句意，選 (A) During 在～期間。而 (B) 而不是，(C) over 表「在～的
時間內」，(D) 表透過，均不合句意。

III、閱讀測驗

Oct. 6, 1996

Dear Tom,

It seems *only* yesterday ***that** Jack and I were helping you learn your*
ABC's--***and** now* you have finished high school ***and*** been accepted *at*
Taipei University.

親愛的湯姆：

　　傑克和我在教你學 ABC，似乎才只是昨天的事，但如今，你已完成高中學
業，而且考上了台北大學。

　　We are *both very* proud of you, Tom. We have followed your high-
school career *with joy and pleasure **and*** know ***that** your four years at*
college will be even more rewarding. A word *of congratulation just*
doesn't seem enough, ***so*** I am sending you a gift ***that** I'm sure you will*
find useful--an unabridged dictionary. Jack says you'll ***not only*** find it
handy *in your studies,* ***but*** a great argument-saver ***when** playing Scrabble*
with your friends.

　　我們倆個都替你感到驕傲，湯姆。我們很高興地注意著你的高中學業，也知
道你的大學四年生活，一定會更有收穫。一句恭喜似乎還不夠，所以我要送你一
件禮物，我確定你會覺得它很有用—— 一本未刪減的字典。傑克說，你不僅會發
現它在讀書時很方便，在和你的朋友玩 Scrabble 遊戲（一種拼字遊戲）時，它
也可以節省很多爭論。

> follow〔'falo〕*v.* 注意　　rewarding〔rɪ'wɔrdɪŋ〕*adj.* 有收穫的
> ***a word of*** 一句　　unabridged〔ˌʌnə'brɪdʒd〕*adj.* 未刪減的
> argument〔'argjəmənt〕*n.* 爭論

　　Mom and Dad are coming here *for a weekend* *next month*. Please try to take a few days off *and* come to join us. We are looking forward to seeing you.

Love,
Sally

　　爸爸媽媽下個月要來這兒度週末。請休息幾天，來和我們團聚。我們很期待見到你。

愛你的莎莉

41.(**D**) 下列何者<u>沒有</u>被提到爲寫這封信的原因？
　　(A) 恭喜湯姆有如此好的成就。　　(B) 告訴湯姆他的父母計畫來訪。
　　(C) 邀請湯姆參加一個週末的家庭聚會。
　　(D) <u>要湯姆回家度週末。</u>
　　***congratulate** sb. **on** sth.* 恭喜某人某事
　　***tell** sb. **of** (= **about**)* sth. 告訴某人某事
　　get-together〔ˈgɛttʊˌgɛðɚ〕*n.* 聚會

42.(**C**) "Scrabble" 是
　　(A) 節省爭論的工具。　　(B) 一本很大的字典。
　　(C) <u>一種遊戲。</u>　　(D) 一個禮物。

43.(**B**) 根據這封信，莎莉和湯姆之間最可能的關係爲何？
　　(A) 母子。　　　　　　(B) <u>姊弟。</u>
　　(C) 祖母和孫子。　　　(D) 姪女和姪子。
　　on the basis of 根據
　　niece〔nis〕*n.* 姪女；外甥女　　nephew〔ˈnɛfju〕*n.* 姪子；外甥

　　Generally speaking, all foreigners *coming to Taiwan* should apply for entry visas *through the embassies or consulates* *of the Republic of China*, *or agencies authorized by the Ministry of Foreign Affairs.*
　　一般說來，所有要來台灣的外國人，都應該透過中華民國大使館、領事館，或經由外交部授權的辦事處，申請入境簽證。

　　generally speaking 一般說來　　***entry visa*** 入境簽證
　　embassy〔ˈɛmbəsɪ〕*n.* 大使館　　consulate〔ˈkɑnsḷɪt, ˈkɑnsjəlɪt〕*n.* 領事館
　　agency〔ˈedʒənsɪ〕*n.* 辦事處　　authorize〔ˈɔθəˌraɪz〕*v.* 授權
　　the Ministry of Foreign Affairs 外交部

As of May 1, 1995, all nationals of the following 15 countries are exempted from securing visas for entry into the Republic of China: U.S.A., Japan, Canada, Belgium, Luxembourg, Sweden, Holland, New Zealand, Australia, Austria, Germany, Britain, France, Spain, and Portugal. The maximum duration of stay is 14 days. Requirements for a 14-day non-visa entry are: passport good for at least six months, confirmed onward ticket within 14 days, no violation of law recorded.

從一九九五年五月一日起,下列十五個國家的所有國民,可免簽證入境中華民國:美國、日本、加拿大、比利時、盧森堡、瑞典、荷蘭、紐西蘭、澳洲、奧地利、德國、英國、法國、西班牙、葡萄牙。最長的停留時間是十四天。要申請十四天免簽證入境許可的條件為:護照有效期限至少六個月,十四天之內有效、且目的地已確認的機票,以及無違法記錄。

as of 從~起　　national (ˈnæʃənl̩) *n.* 國民
exempt (ɪgˈzɛmpt) *v.* 免除　　secure (sɪˈkjʊr) *v.* 得到
Belgium (ˈbɛldʒɪəm) *n.* 比利時　　Luxembourg (ˈlʌksəm,bɝg) *n.* 盧森堡
Sweden (ˈswidən) *n.* 瑞典　　Holland (ˈhɑlənd) *n.* 荷蘭
Australia (ɔˈstreljə) *n.* 澳洲　　Austria (ˈɔstrɪə) *n.* 奧地利
Germany (ˈdʒɝmənɪ) *n.* 德國　　Britain (ˈbrɪtən) *n.* 英國
Spain (spen) *n.* 西班牙　　Portugal (ˈportʃəgl̩) *n.* 葡萄牙
maximum (ˈmæksəməm) *adj.* 最長的;最大的
duration (djʊˈreʃən) *n.* 持續時間　　requirement (rɪˈkwaɪrmənt) *n.* 條件
passport (ˈpæs,port, -,pɔrt) *n.* 護照
good (gʊd) *adj.* 有效的　　confirm (kənˈfɝm) *v.* 確認
onward (ˈɑnwəd) *adj.* 前進的　　violation (,vaɪəˈleʃən) *n.* 違反

If it is necessary to stay more than 14 days **and** less than 30 days, nationals of the specific countries holding a 14-day non-visa entry should in the meantime apply for a landing-visa with the authorized office in the CKS airport from the Bureau of Consular Affairs of the Ministry of Foreign Affairs. The landing-visa fee is NT$1,500.

如果必須停留十四至三十天之間，以上特定國家之國民除持有十四天免簽證入境許可外，在這段期間應在中正機場，向外交部領事局授權的辦事處，申請落地簽證。落地簽證申請費為台幣一千五百元。

specific〔spɪˈsɪfɪk〕adj. 特定的　　hold〔hold〕v. 持有
in the meantime 在這段期間　　bureau〔ˈbjʊro〕n. 局
consular〔ˈkɑnslə, ˈkɑnsjələ〕adj. 領事的
the Bureau of Consular Affairs 領事局　　fee〔fi〕n. 費用

44.(**D**)　當一位美國小姐想要來台灣做為期一週的觀光旅行時，條件之一是
(A) 在中正機場取得落地簽證。　　(B) 離開美國前先申請簽證。
(C) 確定她的護照是一九九五年五月一日前發給的。
(D) <u>確定她的護照離到達日期還有六個月以上有效期限。</u>
make sure 確定　　issue〔ˈɪʃʊ, ˈɪʃjʊ〕v. 發給
valid〔ˈvælɪd〕adj. 有效的

45.(**C**)　如果一位英國商人要來台灣拜訪一些貿易夥伴，為期大約三週，他該怎麼做？
(A) 他應該在搭乘前往台灣這班飛機之前，取得入境中華民國的簽證。
(B) 他應該和一位來自上述所提其他十四個國家的朋友同行。
(C) <u>他必須在中正機場取得落地簽證。</u>
(D) 他只需在到達中正機場時，申請免簽證入境。
partner〔ˈpɑrtnə〕n. 夥伴　　*on board* 搭乘
flight〔flaɪt〕n. 班機

46.(**D**)　申請落地簽證需要下列哪一項？
(A) 護照有效期限六個月以上。　　(B) 十四天免簽證入境許可。
(C) 申請費一千五百元。　　　　　(D) <u>以上皆是。</u>
application〔ˌæpləˈkeʃən〕n. 申請

The brain, *which weighs less than 2.2 pounds*, is *perhaps* the *most* complicated organ *in our bodies*. *Although* scientists have not been able to solve all the mysteries *of this amazing organ,* they have made some progress. They have found *that* certain parts *of the brain* are responsible *for learning, memory, and language.*

大腦的重量不到 2.2 磅，卻可能是我們體內最複雜的器官。雖然科學家還無法解決這個驚人的器官所有的祕密，但他們已有進步。科學家已發現，大腦的某些部位專門負責學習、記憶，和語言部份。

complicated〔'kɑmplə,ketɪd〕*adj.* 複雜的　　　organ〔'ɔrgən〕*n.* 器官
mystery〔'mɪst(ə)rɪ〕*n.* 神祕；祕密　　　amazing〔ə'mezɪŋ〕*adj.* 驚人的
make progress 有進步　　　***be responsible for*** 負責

Recent studies indicate ***that*** the two halves of the brain--the right hemisphere and the left hemisphere--play extremely important roles in learning and communicating. The left hemisphere deals with rules, lists of information, ***and*** short-term memory. *In contrast*, the right hemisphere deals with feelings, colors, ***and*** long-term memory. Scientists recognize the importance of both hemispheres in the learning of all sorts, including language learning.

最近的研究顯示，大腦的兩半——右腦和左腦，在學習和溝通上扮演極重要的角色。左腦負責處理規則、資料名單和短期記憶。成對比的是，右腦負責處理感情、顏色和長期記憶。科學家承認，在學習所有事物，包括語言學習方面，左右腦都很重要。

recent〔'risn̩t〕*adj.* 最近的　　　indicate〔'ɪndə,ket〕*v.* 顯示
half〔hæf, hɑf〕*n.* 一半（複數為 halves）
hemisphere〔'hɛməs,fɪr〕*n.* 半球　　　***deal with*** 處理　　　list〔lɪst〕*n.* 名單
short-term〔'ʃɔrt'tɝm〕*adj.* 短期的　　　long-term〔'lɔŋ,tɝm〕*adj.* 長期的
recognize〔'rɛkəg,naɪz〕*v.* 承認　　　sort〔sɔrt〕*n.* 種類

Scientists *now* relate left and right hemispheres to the way *different individuals learn languages.* They believe ***that*** some learners use one half of their brains *more than the other half.* Left-brained learners *usually* concentrate on memorizing rules and lists. They use logic, definition, and repetition *to learn.*

　　現在科學家認為左右腦的發展，和不同的個人學習語言的方法有關係。他們相信有些學習者使用一邊的腦多於另外一邊。左腦學習者通常專注於記憶規則和名單，他們使用邏輯、定義和重覆來學習。

> *relate A to B* 把 A 和 B 串連在一起；認為 A 和 B 有關係
> *concentrate on* 專注於；專心於
> memorize〔'mɛmə,raɪz〕 *v.* 記憶；背誦
> logic〔'lɑdʒɪk〕 *n.* 邏輯　　definition〔,dɛfə'nɪʃən〕 *n.* 定義
> repetition〔,rɛpə'tɪʃən〕 *n.* 重覆

Right-brained learners look for a general picture *and* concentrate on relating new information to *what they already know*. They use associations and intuition *to learn*. Most people fall into one *of these types*.

If teachers know whether their students are left-brained or right-brained, they can help them learn *better*.

右腦學習者則會尋找一個大概的意象，專注於將新資訊和他們已知的事物串連在一起，他們使用聯想和直覺來學習。大部分的人都可被歸於其中一類。如果老師們知道他們的學生是左腦學習者，還是右腦學習者，就可以幫助他們學得更好。

> general〔'dʒɛnərəl〕 *adj.* 大概的
> association〔ə,soʃɪ'eʃən, -,sosɪ-〕 *n.* 聯想
> intuition〔,ɪntju'ɪʃən〕 *n.* 直覺　　*fall into* 被歸類；屬於

47. (**B**) 瑪麗是個典型的左腦學習者，下列哪一個描述<u>不適合</u>她？
　　　(A) 他的思考方式很邏輯。　　　　(B) <u>她很有藝術氣質且很浪漫。</u>
　　　(C) 她在合併句子的測驗中常得到 A 的成績。
　　　(D) 她很擅長數學。

> typical〔'tɪpɪkl̩〕 *adj.* 典型的　　description〔dɪ'skrɪpʃən〕 *n.* 描述
> fit〔fɪt〕 *v.* 適合　　logical〔'lɑdʒɪkl̩〕 *adj.* 邏輯的
> artistic〔ɑr'tɪstɪk〕 *adj.* 有藝術氣質的
> score〔skor, skɔr〕 *v.* 得分　　*be good at* 擅長

48. (**D**) 老師從上文得到的最重要暗示為何？他們應該
　　　(A) 鼓勵學生背規則。　　　　(B) 告訴學生如何用邏輯解決問題。
　　　(C) 敦促學生把新資訊和他們已知的事物串連在一起。
　　　(D) <u>試著找出對個別學生最好的學習方法。</u>

> significant〔sɪg'nɪfəkənt〕 *adj.* 重要的
> implication〔,ɪmplə'keʃən〕 *n.* 暗示　　urge〔ɝdʒ〕 *v.* 催促

49.(**A**) 下列敘述何者為眞？
　　　(A) 一邊腦受損傷不一定會導致完全失去語言能力。
　　　(B) 記得回家的路需要短期記憶。
　　　(C) 語言學習只發生在一邊腦。
　　　(D) 科學家已解決了大腦的所有祕密。
　　　involve〔ɪnˈvɑlv〕v. 需要

50.(**D**) 本文最好的標題為何？
　　　(A) 短期與長期記憶。　　　(B) 半球領域的發現。
　　　(C) 最近的一項科學發現。　(D) 驚人的人腦。
　　　field〔fild〕n. 領域

第二部分：非選擇題
I、中譯英

1. Has it *ever* occurred to you ***what** future hotels will be like*? You need not wonder *any longer*. A hotel *in Japan* will give you a preview. The name *of this hotel* is the Capsule Inn; its rooms rent *for eleven dollars a night*. 2. Every room has a radio, a TV set, ***and*** an alarm clock. 3. *Besides*, all rooms have air-conditioning.

　　你有沒有想過未來的旅館會是什麼樣子？你無需再感到疑惑了。日本的一家旅館可以給你一個預覽。這家旅館叫做太空艙旅館；所有的房間都是一個晚上十一元。每個房間附有一部收音機，一台電視機和一個鬧鐘。此外，所有房間都有空調。

　　　sth. ***occur to*** sb. 某人想到某事
　　　wonder〔ˈwʌndɚ〕v. 感到疑惑　　preview〔ˈpriˌvju, priˈvju〕n. 預告
　　　capsule〔ˈkæpsl̩, ˈkæpsjul〕n. 太空艙；膠囊
　　　inn〔ɪn〕n. 旅館；酒館　　rent〔rɛnt〕v. 出租
　　　alarm clock 鬧鐘　　air-conditioning〔ˈɛrkənˈdɪʃənɪŋ〕n. 空調

But *here* any resemblance *to a twentieth-century hotel* ends. The rooms are small plastic capsules, ***and*** each capsule is *about* five feet high, *by* five feet wide, ***and*** *by* seven feet deep. Guests have to crawl into bed *through a large porthole entrance*. 4. The toilets and laundry facilities are located in the common area *of the hotel*. 5. *Believe it or not*, this hotel is *almost always* filled to capacity, *perhaps **because** the price of the rooms is as small **as** the rooms themselves*.

但在此，任何與二十世紀旅館相似之處都沒有了。所有的房間都是小小的、塑膠的太空艙，每個太空艙大約五呎高、五呎寬、七呎深。客人必須由一個很大的艙口爬進去睡覺。廁所及洗衣設施位於旅館的共同區域。信不信由你，這家旅館幾乎經常是客滿，也許是因為房間的價錢和房間本身一樣小吧！

resemblance (rɪ'zɛmbləns) *n.* 相似之處　　plastic ('plæstɪk) *adj.* 塑膠的
crawl (krɔl) *v.* 爬　　porthole ('port,hol , 'pɔrt-) *n.* 艙口
toilet ('tɔɪlɪt) *n.* 廁所　　laundry ('lɔndrɪ , 'lɑn-) *n.* 洗衣服
facility (fə'sɪlətɪ) *n.* 設施（多用複數）　　*be located in* 位於
believe it or not 信不信由你　　*be filled to capacity* 客滿

II、作文（參考範例）

　　The two things I would like to put in the time capsule are a personal computer and an abacus, to indicate where we are going ***as well as*** where we have been. Here in the Far East things are changing at an accelerated pace, and nothing symbolizes this better than the computer, which has, in the opinion of some, even encroached upon our lives. The abacus reminds us of quieter times, with sages sipping tea and chatting, in stark contrast with present-day traffic jams accompanied by the incessant blaring of horns.

　　I hope that the above-mentioned items will help our descendants understand the contradictions so prevalent in modern Chinese society, and give them a better perspective, ***instead of*** referencing the ubiquitous "scorecards" brandished by animal rights activists, environmentalists, sensationalist reporters and whoever else now chooses to look at Chinese in only one aspect, like a racehorse with blinkers put on it. If this can help future historians clarify misunderstanding, it will be worth the effort.

abacus〔'æbəkəs〕n. 算盤　　**Far East** 遠東

accelerate〔æk'sɛlə,ret〕v. 加速　　pace〔pes〕n. 速度；步調

symbolize〔'sɪmbḷ,aɪz〕v. 象徵　　encroach〔ɪn'krotʃ〕v. 侵佔

remind sb. **of** sth. 提醒某人某事；使某人想起某事

sage〔sedʒ〕n. 聖賢　　sip〔sɪp〕v. 啜飲　　stark〔stɑrk〕adj. 完全的

accompany〔ə'kʌmpənɪ〕v. 伴隨　　incessant〔ɪn'sɛsṇt〕adj. 不停的

blaring〔'blɛrɪŋ〕n. 發出聲音　　horn〔hɔrn〕n.（汽車的）喇叭

above-mentioned〔ə'bʌv'mɛnʃənd〕adj. 上述的

item〔'aɪtəm〕n. 項目；物品　　descendant〔dɪ'sɛndənt〕n. 子孫

contradiction〔,kɑntrə'dɪkʃən〕n. 矛盾　　prevalent〔'prɛvələnt〕adj. 普遍的

perspective〔pɚ'spɛktɪv〕n. 對事物整體的看法

instead of 而不是　　reference〔'rɛfərəns〕v. 參考

ubiquitous〔ju'bɪkwətəs〕adj. 遍布的

scorecard〔'skor,kɑrd〕n. 記分卡（比喻爲示威者的旗幟、標語）

brandish〔'brændɪʃ〕v. 揮動

activist〔'æktɪvɪst〕n. 活躍分子；實踐主義者

environmentalist〔ɪn,vaɪrən'mɛntḷɪst〕n. 環保主義者

sensationalist〔sɛn'seʃənḷɪst〕adj. 煽情主義的

aspect〔'æspɛkt〕n. 方面　　racehorse〔'res,hɔrs〕n. 賽馬

blinker〔'blɪŋkɚ〕n. 馬眼罩　　clarify〔'klærə,faɪ〕v. 澄清

心得筆記欄

八十四年大學入學學科能力測驗試題 英文考科

第一部分：單一選擇題

Ｉ、對話

說明：第1至10題，由四則對話組成。每題請根據對話情境選出最適當的一個選項，標示在答案卡之「選擇題答案區」。每題答對得1分，答錯不倒扣。

1－3題為題組

(*Julia and May are sitting on the sofa talking.*)

Julia : Would you excuse me for a moment ? My mom is on the line.

May : _____1_____

(*twenty minutes later*)

Julia : Sorry to keep you waiting. Now, _____2_____

May : We were just talking about going out to a show, _____3_____ we might have to do it some other time.

1. (A) Certainly.　　　　　　　　　(B) Not at all.
　(C) What's the matter ?　　　　　(D) All right.

2. (A) shall we continue our discussion ?　(B) what are you going to say ?
　(C) what did you say ?　　　　　　　　(D) where were we ?

3. (A) but I'm afraid　　　　　　　(B) so I think
　(C) unless it seems　　　　　　　(D) as you know

4－5題為題組

(*John , Bill , and Sue are at a party.*)

John : Where do you work, Bill ?

Bill : I'm in foreign trade. _____4_____

John : I'm an English teacher.

Bill : And you, Sue ? _____5_____

Sue : I'm a flight attendant.

Bill : Really ?

John : Yes, she travels all over the world.

4. (A) Do you speak English ?　　　(B) Are you a worker, too ?
   (C) How do you like it ?　　　　 (D) How about you ?

5. (A) Do you know each other ?　　(B) Where have you been ?
   (C) What do you do ?　　　　　 (D) How are you ?

6－8 題為題組

(*Maria and Jane are talking over the telephone.*)

Maria : Hello. May I speak to Eric Sung ?
Jane　:　_____6_____
Maria : I see. When do you expect him back ?
Jane　:　_____7_____
Maria : Yes. Just tell him Maria Moskovik called.
Jane　: I'm sorry, I didn't catch your last name.
Maria :　_____8_____
Jane　: O.K. I'll give him the message.

6. (A) Hold on. I'll connect you.　(B) Sure. Wait a moment, please.
   (C) I'm sorry, he's not come yet.　(D) I'm sorry, he's out at this moment.

7. (A) I'm not sure. May I leave a message ?
   (B) Any moment. Do you want to talk to him ?
   (C) I'm not sure. Can I take a message ?
   (D) I'm sorry, his line is busy.

8. (A) That's all right.
   (B) Moskovik, M-O-S-K-O-V-I-K.
   (C) It's an unusual name.
   (D) Don't worry. Eric and I are old friends.

9－10 題為題組

(*Tom and Jack are lost on their tour in England.*)

Tom : Well, it looks like we're lost.
Jack :　_____9_____
Tom : Who do you ask in a strange town ?
Jack :　_____10_____
Tom : Where can we find one ?
Jack : See, there is one over there.

9. (A) Don't worry. All we have to do is ask.
   (B) What should we see next ?
   (C) I'm scared. Let's go home.　(D) Yes, we just lost a tire.

10. (A) Who knows !　(B) You ask a policeman.
    (C) There is a police station there.　(D) I don't see any police station.

II、詞彙

說明：第11至20題，每題選出最適當的一個選項，標示在答案卡之「選擇題答案區」。每題答對得1分，答錯不倒扣。

11. I sometimes take John's coat for my own, because the two of them look so _____.
    (A) original　(B) cheerful　(C) curious　(D) similar

12. George at first had difficulty swimming across the pool, but he finally succeeded on his fourth _____.
    (A) attempt　(B) process　(C) instance　(D) display

13. Several motorists were _____ waiting for the light to change.
    (A) impossibly　(B) impracticably　(C) importantly　(D) impatiently

14. Mary wrote a letter of _____ to the manufacturer after her new car broke down three times in the same week.
    (A) complaint　(B) repair　(C) depression　(D) madness

15. John's poor math score must have _____ him a lot, because he is not attending the class any more.
    (A) expelled　(B) discouraged　(C) impressed　(D) finished

16. The issue of environmental protection has not received much attention until very _____ .
    (A) seriously　(B) recently　(C) amazingly　(D) dangerously

17. The old man could _____ swallow because his throat was too dry.
    (A) actually　(B) strictly　(C) exactly　(D) hardly

18. We are more than willing to _____ our ties with those countries that are friendly to us.
    (A) appeal　(B) strengthen　(C) expect　(D) connect

19. The artist is famous for his genius and great_____.
    (A) fragrance   (B) originality   (C) sculptor   (D) therapy

20. Although some things are _____, they nevertheless exist.
    (A) important   (B) intelligible   (C) invisible   (D) interesting

II、綜合測驗

說明：第21至40題，每題一個空格。根據短文選出最適當的一個選項，標示在
　　　答案卡之「選擇題答案區」。每題答對得1分，答錯不倒扣。

21－30題爲題組

America encourages its young people to drink.____21____, our society makes drinking a part of every celebration. Our personal celebrations,____22____ weddings, promotions, graduations, and anniversaries, are____23____ linked with drinking.____24____ children can attend any family affair without seeing the adults enjoying their liquor. Drinking is part of our national celebrations as well. The Fourth of July means beer and New Year's Eve is an entire night dedicated to the proposition that everyone must get____25____. Secondly, the shows young people watch on television encourage them to drink. On____26____ every soap opera, the characters drink casually and often. The rock videos young people watch over and over again feature alcohol, too.____27____ on the videos sit in bars, nightclubs, and road-houses. Drinking, the message goes, is cool. The strongest encouragement to drink that young people receive,____28____, comes from advertisers. Beer companies often sponsor the sports events young people watch. In addition, advertisements for liquor, on TV and in print, show situations that are____29____ to the young. People hoist their glasses ____30____ they are sitting around ski lodges, sailing, dancing, or enjoying a football game. We may say we don't want our children to drink, but our messages say just the opposite.

21. (A) For example
    (C) For one thing
    (B) Afterwards
    (D) On the whole

22. (A) so as   (B) such as   (C) as such   (D) such that

23. (A) simply   (B) clumsily   (C) closely   (D) carefully

24. (A) Few   (B) Little   (C) Small   (D) Many

25. (A) drink   (B) to drink   (C) drinking   (D) drunk

26. (A) almost   (B) mostly   (C) altogether   (D) hardly
27. (A) Stories   (B) Drinks   (C) Characters   (D) Messages
28. (A) furthermore   (B) consequently   (C) moreover   (D) however
29. (A) attentive   (B) attributive   (C) attractive   (D) accustomed
30. (A) where   (B) while   (C) what   (D) why

31-40 題為題組

Although Grants Pass, Oregon, is a fairly small town, it offers much to amuse summer visitors. Water sports are ___31___ the most popular tourist attraction. Visitors can go rafting down the Rogue River ___32___ swimming in the Applegate River. Fishing in the area is another popular activity. Lots of people also go hunting for wild berries that grow along the roadsides. ___33___, there are lovely, clean campgrounds where campers can park their vehicles. ___34___ those who prefer to stay in town, Grants Pass offers several nice hotels. In town, tourists can browse through ___35___ number of interesting shops, such as antique stores and the shop that sells items ___36___ from Oregon's beautiful myrtlewood. Another fun ___37___ is shopping at the open market where local folks sell produce grown in their gardens. And ___38___, Grants Pass has a lot of places to eat, ranging from a low-calorie dessert place to lovely restaurants, some of which offer good food and gorgeous views. ___39___ you can see, Grants Pass offers a lot to do in the summer. ___40___ you want to give your family a nice, wholesome vacation, try visiting this charming town.

31. (A) far from   (B) by far   (C) a bit far   (D) as far
32. (A) also   (B) but   (C) for   (D) or
33. (A) In addition   (B) In due time   (C) For instance   (D) By and large
34. (A) About   (B) For   (C) With   (D) In
35. (A) the   (B) this   (C) a   (D) that
36. (A) to make   (B) make   (C) made   (D) making
37. (A) activity   (B) advice   (C) proposal   (D) sport
38. (A) fairly   (B) happily   (C) gorgeously   (D) finally
39. (A) As   (B) Since   (C) Until   (D) Then
40. (A) Where   (B) What   (C) If   (D) That

Ⅳ、閱讀測驗

說明：第41至50題，每題請分別根據各篇文章選出最適當的一個選項，標示在
　　　答案卡之「選擇題答案區」。每題答對得2分，答錯不倒扣。

41-43題為題組

　　Breaking into the computer codes (known as "hacking") of banks,
large companies or even government departments is the latest game for
super-intelligent teenagers. One young hacker said, "Hacking is just
intellectual. It's your brain against the computer. It's like climbing
Mount Everest — it's something you have to do. You don't even need a
very expensive computer — but you must understand everything about all
kinds of computers."

　　At the moment most of these games are just fun for young people.
But how long will it be before criminal gangs, like the Mafia, start to
use computer experts to help them in their crimes? Future bank robbers will not need explosives to blow open bank safes — all they will need
is someone who can break computer codes. Already in Britain people say
that computer crimes are costing companies between 500 million pounds
and 2.5 billion pounds a year.

41. The preceding passage refers to the word "hacking" in the context of
　　(A) climbing Mount Everest.　　(B) a game for young individuals.
　　(C) breaking into computer codes.　(D) physically dismantling a solid object.

42. According to the passage, breaking into computer codes of banks, large
　　companies, and government departments is
　　(A) a widespread criminal practice.
　　(B) a game for computer literate individuals.
　　(C) being studied by the Mafia for fun.
　　(D) soon to replace coding bank safes.

43. Based on the passage, in order to break into computer codes, one needs
　　(A) an elaborate and expensive multi-media computer.
　　(B) a group of computer science students.
　　(C) the help and financial support from the Mafia.
　　(D) a thorough understanding of a variety of computers.

44—46 題爲題組

There is increasing scientific evidence that large cars cause more highway accidents than small cars. In the news recently was the story of a woman who died of a heart attack while driving her station wagon. The car was moving so fast that it went through the highway-dividing fence, resulting in a collision in which five people died. Those unnecessary deaths are attributable in part to the woman's choice of a large automobile. A lighter and smaller car probably wouldn't have gone through the fence, its remaining energy would have been much less, and this would have reduced the chances of serious injury or death. Because of its small size, it might have missed the other car completely. The present design of the oversized automobile is largely responsible not only for increasing death toll on the highways but also for the rapid depletion of our resources of petroleum, for the pollution of our environment, and for the congestion and inconvenience of our cities.

44. For the five highway deaths, the author blames
　　(A) a large heavy station wagon.　　(B) the lack of more smaller vehicles.
　　(C) the woman's ill-timed heart attack. (D) a weak highway-dividing fence.

45. What is the author's main point in the passage above?
　　(A) Large cars should be banned by the government.
　　(B) Large cars are less safe and less economical than small cars.
　　(C) Small cars are safer for the occupants than large cars.
　　(D) A woman's heart attack caused the death of five people.

46. The author's statement about the highway fence's ability to retain a smaller and lighter car
　　(A) is the author's assumption.　　(B) derives from scientific evidence.
　　(C) rests upon fact.　　(D) can never be verified.

47—50 題爲題組

Three pilot whales are believed to be swimming freely off the Atlantic Coast today. Their names are Tag, Notch, and Baby. These seagoing mammals are among the lucky survivors of a whale-stranding last December at Cape Cod.

As many as 60 pilot whales swam ashore. Scientists are still trying to find out why whales have this self-destructive behavior. Many of the whales died on the beach—crushed by their own weight. Whale experts found Tag, Notch, and Baby alive. The three were believed to be too young to survive on their own if returned to sea.

The three whales were taken in a van to the New England Aquarium in Boston, Mass. They were kept in a 60,000-gallon tank for seven months. Only a few people worked with the whales so that they would not become too accustomed to human beings.

Early this past summer the three whales were pronounced fit enough to be returned to the Atlantic Ocean. A month after their release, the whales were spotted. They were found in a group of 50 whales about 60 miles from where they had been set free.

47. The 60 pilot whales swam ashore as a result of
    (A) a large winter storm off the coast of Cape Cod.
    (B) a behavior currently unknown to scientists.
    (C) a genetic phenomenon currently being studied by whale experts.
    (D) the return to their annual spawning ground near Cape Cod.

48. The pilot whales died on the beaches of Cape Cod due to
    (A) the lack of salt water to facilitate their respiration.
    (B) the lack of nutrition to maintain their enormous body weight.
    (C) their body structure unable to support their body weight out of water.
    (D) a phenomenon yet to be figured out by scientists.

49. The three whales Tag, Notch, and Baby were rescued because
    (A) younger whales have a greater chance of survival than the others.
    (B) amongst the many whales found beached, these three were deemed the healthiest.
    (C) they were alive when the rescue team found them.
    (D) the rescue crew liked them very much.

50. Which of the following is NOT true ?
    (A) Scientists are studying the suicidal behavior of pilot whales.
    (B) Tag, Notch, and Baby were too young to survive by themselves in the sea.
    (C) Pilot whales are mammals that can become used to human beings.
    (D) After their release, Tag, Notch, and Baby were never seen again.

第二部分：非選擇題

Ⅰ、中譯英

說明：試將以下五個中文句子譯成正確、通順、達意的英文，並將答案寫在「答案卷」上。每句4分。

1. 昨天在回家的路上，我看到一個小女孩在路邊哭泣。
2. 我趕緊跑過去，問她到底發生了什麼事。
3. 小女孩說她按了好幾次門鈴，卻沒有人來開門。
4. 看到她哭得那麼傷心，我就陪她等媽媽回來。
5. 雖然晚了半個鐘頭才回到家，我覺得我做了一件有意義的事。

Ⅱ、英文作文

說明：依提示在「答案卷」上寫一封100至150字的信。評分標準：內容5分，組織5分，文法4分，用字拼字4分，體例（格式、標點、大小寫）2分。

提示：

1. 高中生王治平收到美國筆友George的來信，告訴治平他要隨父母到台灣來住兩年左右，並問治平：" Can you give me some advice and suggestions so that I know what I should do and what I should not do when I am in Taiwan?" 現在請你以治平的身份，擬一封適當的回信給George，歡迎他來台灣，並且針對他的問題，提出一些具體的建議。

2. 回信的上下款應依下列方式寫出。

```
                              February 20, 1995
     Dear George:

          ------------------------------
     ------------------------------------
     ------------------------------------
     ------------------------------------
     ------------------------------------
                      ·
                      ·
                      ·
     ------------------------------------
     ------------------------------------
     ------------------------------------
     ------------------------------

                         Your friend,
                         Chih-ping
```

84年度學科能力測驗英文科試題詳解

第一部份：單一選擇題

I、對話

(*Julia and May are sitting on the sofa talking.*)

Julia : Would you excuse me *for a moment*？ My mom is *on the line*.

May : Certainly.

　　　　　　1

(*twenty minutes later*)

Julia : Sorry to keep you waiting. *Now*, where were we？

　　　　　　　　　　　　　　　　　　2

May : We were *just* talking about going out to a show, *but* I'm afraid

　　　　　　　　　　　　　　　　　　　　　　　　　　　　3

　　　 we might have to do it some other time.

（茉莉亞和梅正坐在沙發上聊天。）

茉莉亞：我可以失陪一下嗎？我媽媽打電話找我。

　梅　：當然可以。

（二十分鐘後）

茉莉亞：抱歉讓妳久等了。現在，我們講到哪兒了？

　梅　：我們剛剛正講到要去看秀，不過恐怕我們必須改天了。

> *on the line* = *on the phone* 在講電話中
> *some other time* 改天（= *another day*）

1.（A）(A)當然可以。　　　　　　　(B)一點也不。

　　　　(C)有什麼事？　　　　　　　(D)好。(回答 All right.比較不禮貌)

　　　　What's the matter！＝What's wrong！怎麼回事！

　　　　What's the matter？＝What's up？有什麼事？

2.（D）(A)我們繼續討論，好嗎？　　(B)你想要說什麼？

　　　　(C)你剛剛說什麼？　　　　　(D)我們剛剛講到哪兒？

　　　　Where were we？＝Where did we stop our conversation？

　　　　＝What were we talking about？

3.（A）(A)但我恐怕　　　　　　　　　(B)所以我認為

　　　　(C)除非它似乎　　　　　　　(D)正如你所知

（*John , Bill , and Sue are at a party.* ）

John : Where do you work, Bill?

Bill : I'm in foreign trade.　<u>How about you</u>?

John : I'm an English teacher.　　　4

Bill : And you, Sue?　<u>What do you do</u>?

Sue : I'm a flight attendant.⁵

Bill : Really?

John : Yes, she travels *all over the world.*

（約翰、比爾和蘇在宴會中。）

約翰：你在哪裏工作，比爾？

比爾：我從事外貿工作。你呢？

約翰：我是英文老師。

比爾：蘇，妳呢？妳從事什麼工作？

蘇　：我是空服員。

比爾：眞的嗎？

約翰：眞的，她環遊全世界。

　　　　trade〔tred〕*n.* 貿易　　***flight attendant*** 空服員

4. (**D**) (A)你講英文嗎？　(B)你也是工人嗎？　(C)你覺得怎樣？
　　(D)你呢？ (How about you? = What about you? = And you? 你呢？)

5. (**C**) (A)你們彼此認識嗎？　(B)你去哪裏了？
　　(C)你從事什麼工作？　(D)你好嗎？
　　What do you do? 你從事什麼工作？
　　= What do you do for a living? = What is your job?
　　= What line are you in? = What field are you in?

（*Maria and Jane are talking over the telephone.*）

Maria : Hello.　May I speak to Eric Sung?

Jane　: <u>I'm sorry, he's out</u> *at this moment.*
　　　　　　　　6

Maria : I see.　When do you expect him back?

Jane　: <u>I'm not sure.　Can I take a message</u>?
　　　　　　　　　7

Maria : Yes.　Just tell him Maria Moskovik called.

Jane　: I'm sorry, I didn't catch your last name.

Maria : <u>Moskovik, M-O-S-K-O-V-I-K.</u>
　　　　　　　　8

Jane　: O.K.　I'll give him the message.

（瑪莉亞和珍在講電話。）

瑪莉亞 : 喂，請找艾力克‧宋聽電話。

珍 : 抱歉，他現在不在。

瑪莉亞 : 這樣哦，他什麼時候會回來？

珍 : 我不確定，妳要不要留話？

瑪莉亞 : 好，就告訴他瑪莉亞‧莫斯科維克找他。

珍 : 抱歉，我沒聽清楚妳貴姓。

瑪莉亞 : Moskovik，M-O-S-K-O-V-I-K。

珍 : 好，我會轉告他。

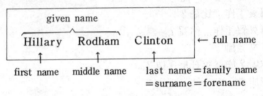

6. (**D**) (A) 稍等，我幫你轉接。　　　(B) 好的，請稍等。
(C) 抱歉，他還沒來。　　　　(D) 抱歉，他現在不在。

hold on （電話）不要掛斷　　connect〔kə'nɛkt〕*v.*（將電話）接通

7. (**C**) (A) 我不確定，我可以留話嗎？　　(B) 隨時（都會回來），你要和他說話嗎？
(C) 我不確定，你要不要留話？　　(D) 抱歉，他的電話佔線。

Can I leave a message ?　　　　Can I take a message ?
= Can I give you a message ?　　= Can you leave a message ?
= Can you take a message ?　　你要不要留話？（接電話者說）
我能留話嗎？（打電話者說）

8. (**B**) (A) 沒關係。　　　　　　(B) Moskovik，M-O-S-K-O-V-I-K。
(C) 這個名字很少見。　　(D) 別擔心，艾力克和我是老朋友。

(*Tom and Jack are lost on their tour in England*.)

Tom : Well, it looks like *we're lost*.

Jack : Don't worry.　All we have to do is ask.
9

Tom : Who do you ask *in a strange town* ?

Jack : You ask a policeman.
10

Tom : Where can we find one ?

Jack : See, there is one *over there*.

（湯姆和傑克在英國旅行時迷路了。）

湯姆：噢，看來我們迷路了。

傑克：別擔心，我們只要問路就可以了。

湯姆：在陌生的小鎮裏你要問誰？

傑克：問警察啊！

湯姆：我們去哪裏找個警察呢？

傑克：你看，那裏就有一個。

　　* All one has to do is（to）+V 某人必須做的是 ～（詳見文法寶典 p. 648）

9.（ A ）(A) 別擔心，我們只要問路就可以了。

　　　　(B) 我們接下來要看什麼？

　　　　(C) 我很害怕，我們回家吧。

　　　　(D) 是的，我們剛才丟了一個輪胎。

10.（ B ）(A) 誰知道！　　　　　　　　(B) 問警察啊！

　　　　(C) 那裏有一個警察局。　　　(D) 我沒看到警察局。

　　* **You** ask a policeman. 一句中，you 是指「任何人」，例如：

　　　You never know when **you** will die.（誰也不知道什麼時候會死。）

Ⅱ、詞彙

11.（ D ） I *sometimes* take John's coat for my own, *because the two of them look so similar.*

我有時會將約翰的外套誤以為是我的，因為它們兩件看起來如此類似。

　　(A) original〔əˋrɪdʒənl̩〕*adj.* 原始的　　(B) cheerful〔ˋtʃɪrfəl〕*adj.* 愉快的

　　(C) curious〔ˋkjʊrɪəs〕*adj.* 好奇的　　(D) *similar*〔ˋsɪmələ〕*adj.* 類似的

　　take for 誤以為

12.（ A ） George *at first* had difficulty *swimming across the pool,* *but* he *finally* succeeded *on his fourth attempt.*

喬治剛開始游過游泳池有困難，不過他終於在第四次嘗試時成功了。

　　(A) *attempt*〔əˋtɛmpt〕*n.* 嘗試　　(B) process〔ˋprɑsɛs〕*n.* 過程

　　(C) instance〔ˋɪnstəns〕*n.* 例子

　　(D) display〔dɪˋsple〕*n.* 展示

　　have difficulty（in）+ V-ing 對～有困難

13. (**D**) Several motorists were *impatiently* waiting for the light to change.
幾位汽車駕駛<u>不耐煩地</u>等著燈號改變。
    (A) impossibly〔ɪmˈpɑsəblɪ〕*adv.* 不可能地
    (B) impracticably〔ɪmˈpræktɪkəblɪ〕*adv.* 不能實行地
    (C) importantly〔ɪmˈpɔrtntlɪ〕*adv.* 重要地
    (D) *impatiently*〔ɪmˈpeʃəntlɪ〕*adv.* 不耐煩地
motorist〔ˈmotərɪst〕*n.* 汽車駕駛人

14. (**A**) Mary wrote a letter *of complaint* to the manufacturer *after her new car broke down three times in the same week.*

瑪麗在新車同一個禮拜拋錨三次後,寫了一封投訴信給廠商。
    (A) *complaint*〔kəmˈplent〕*n.* 訴苦;抱怨 (B) repair〔rɪˈpɛr〕*n.* 修理
    (C) depression〔dɪˈprɛʃən〕*n.* 沮喪 (D) madness〔ˈmædnɪs〕*n.* 瘋狂
manufacturer〔ˌmænjəˈfæktʃərə〕*n.* 製造業者;廠商
break down 故障(= *be out of order*)

15. (**B**) John's poor math score must have <u>discouraged</u> him *a lot, because he is not attending the class any more.*
約翰差勁的數學成績一定使他覺得十分氣餒,因為他再也沒來上課了。
    (A) expel〔ɪkˈspɛl〕*v.* 驅逐
    (B) *discourage*〔dɪsˈkɝɪdʒ〕*v.* 使氣餒
    (C) impress〔ɪmˈprɛs〕*v.* 使印象深刻 (D) finish〔ˈfɪnɪʃ〕*v.* 結束

16. (**B**) The issue *of environmental protection* has not received much attention *until very recently.*
直到<u>最近</u>,環保的問題才受到廣泛的注意。
    (A) seriously〔ˈsɪrɪəslɪ〕*adv.* 嚴重地
    (B) *recently*〔ˈrisntlɪ〕*adv.* 最近地
    (C) amazingly〔əˈmezɪŋlɪ〕*adv.* 驚人地
    (D) dangerously〔ˈdendʒərəslɪ〕*adv.* 危險地

not ~ until … 直到…才~

17. (**D**)　The old man could *hardly* swallow *because his throat was too dry*.
那位老年人幾乎不能吞嚥，因為他的喉嚨太乾了。
　　(A) actually〔'æktʃʊəlɪ〕*adv*. 實際上
　　(B) strictly〔'strɪktlɪ〕*adv*. 嚴厲地
　　(C) exactly〔ɪg'zæktlɪ〕*adv*. 準確地
　　(D) *hardly*〔'hɑrdlɪ〕*adv*. 幾乎不
swallow〔'swɑlo〕*v*. 吞嚥

18. (**B**)　We are *more than* willing to strengthen our ties *with those coun-*
tries that are friendly to us.
我們非常願意與對我們友好的國家加強關係。
　　(A) appeal〔ə'pil〕*v*. 吸引
　　(B) *strengthen*〔'strɛŋθən〕*v*. 加強
　　(C) expect〔ɪk'spɛkt〕*v*. 期待
　　(D) connect〔kə'nɛkt〕*v*. 連接

19. (**B**)　The artist is famous *for his genius and great originality*.
那位藝術家以天才及偉大的創造力聞名。
　　(A) fragrance〔'fregrəns〕*n*. 香味
　　(B) *originality*〔ə,rɪdʒə'nælətɪ〕*n*. 創造力
　　(C) sculptor〔'skʌlptə〕*n*. 雕刻家
　　(D) therapy〔'θɛrəpɪ〕*n*. 治療
be famous for 以～聞名

20. (**C**)　*Although some things are invisible*, they *nevertheless* exist.
雖然有些物體是看不見的，它們依然存在。
　　(A) important〔ɪm'pɔrtn̩t〕*adj*. 重要的
　　(B) intelligible〔ɪn'tɛlɪdʒəbl̩〕*adj*. 清晰的
　　(C) *invisible*〔ɪn'vɪzəbl̩〕*adj*. 看不見的
　　(D) interesting〔'ɪntrɪstɪŋ〕*adj*. 有趣的
nevertheless〔,nɛvəðə'lɛs〕*adv*. 依然

Ⅲ、綜合測驗

America encourages its young people to drink. *__For one thing__*, our
$\overline{}$
21
society makes drinking a part *of every celebration*. Our personal

celebrations, *such as weddings, promotions, graduations, **and** anniver-*
22
saries, are *closely* linked with drinking. Few children can attend any
23   24
family affair *without seeing the adults enjoying their liquor*.

美國鼓勵年輕人喝酒。首先，我們的社會使喝酒成為所有慶祝活動的一部份。
私人的慶祝活動，如婚禮、升職、畢業與週年紀念等，都和喝酒有密切的關係。
幾乎所有的兒童去參加任何的家庭慶祝活動時，都會看到大人們飲酒作樂。

celebration〔͵sɛlə'breʃən〕n. 慶祝活動
wedding〔'wɛdɪŋ〕n. 婚禮   promotion〔prə'moʃən〕n. 升職
anniversary〔͵ænə'vɝsərɪ〕n. 週年紀念   link〔lɪŋk〕v. 關連
affair〔ə'fɛr〕n. 慶典；活動   liquor〔'lɪkɚ〕n. 酒

21.(C) 依句意，選(C) *for one thing*「首先」。因後面有 *secondly*，兩者成對
出現。而(A)例如，(B) afterwards *adv.* 後來，(D) on the whole「大體
而言」，均不合句意。

22.(B) 依句意，選(B) such as「像是…」。而(D) such that 多用於「 such…
that～」的句型，表「如此…，以致於～」，故不合。

23.(C) 依句意，酒是慶祝活動的一部份，各種慶祝活動都和喝酒有「密切」的
關係，故選(C) closely *adv.* 密切地。而(A) simply「只是」，(B) clumsily
〔'klʌmzɪlɪ〕*adv.* 笨拙地，(D) carefully「小心地」，均不合句意。

24.(A) 依前後句意，在慶祝活動中都少不了酒，所以幾乎每個小孩都看過大人
們飲酒作樂，故選(A) Few。few 表「幾乎沒有」，為否定用法的形容
詞，與其後的 without 形成「雙重否定」句型。few…without～「幾
乎沒有…不～；幾乎所有…都～」。(B) little 可表「小的」或「幾乎沒
有」，前者不合句意，而「幾乎沒有」的用法，只能修飾不可數名詞，
故不合。而(C)小的，(D)許多，皆不合句意。

Drinking is part *of our national celebrations as well*. The Fourth of July

means beer **and** New Year's Eve is an entire night *dedicated to the*

proposition **that** *everyone must get drunk*.
                                              25

喝酒也是國家慶典活動的一部份。七月四日就是啤酒的代名詞，而新年前夕，是個
要大家徹夜狂飲，不醉不歸的夜晚。

> ***as well*** 也～   beer〔bɪr〕*n.* 啤酒
> ***be dedicated to*** 奉獻給～；致力於～
> proposition〔͵prɑpə'zɪʃən〕*n.* 主張；提議

25.(**D**) get drunk 喝醉

Secondly, the shows *young people watch on television* encourage them to

drink. *On almost every soap opera*, the characters drink *casually and*
              26

often. The rock videos *young people watch over and over again* feature

alcohol, *too*. Characters *on the videos* sit in bars, nightclubs, and
          27

roadhouses. Drinking, *the message goes*, is cool.

其次，年輕人所觀賞的電視節目也鼓勵他們喝酒。在幾乎每一部連續劇裏，劇中的
人物都會隨便而且經常喝酒。在年輕人百看不厭的MTV中，酒也是其重要的特色
之一。MTV裏的人物，常會坐在酒吧、夜總會和公路旁的酒館裏。這樣的情況所
傳達的訊息是，喝酒很帥。

> * 在Drinking…is cool.一句中，the message goes 爲插入語。(詳見文法寶典p.650)
>
> ***soap opera*** 電視連續劇   character〔'kærɪktɚ〕*n.* 角色；人物
> casually〔'kæʒʊəlɪ〕*adv.* 隨便地
> ***rock video*** 流行音樂錄影帶 (俗稱MTV)
> feature〔'fitʃɚ〕*v.* 以～爲特色   nightclub〔'naɪt͵klʌb〕*n.* 夜總會
> roadhouse〔'rod͵haʊs〕*n.* 路旁酒館   go〔go〕*v.* 表達

26.(**A**) 依句意，選(A) almost *adv.* 幾乎。而(B) mostly〔'mostlɪ〕*adv.* 大部份
地，(C) altogether〔͵ɔltə'gɛðɚ〕*adv.* 完全地，(D) hardly〔'hɑrdlɪ〕*adv.*
幾乎不，則與句意不合。

27. (**C**) 依句意，影片中的「人物」會坐在酒吧、夜總會與路邊酒館裏，故選(C)
characters *n.pl.* 角色；人物。而(A)故事，(B)飲料，(D)訊息，皆不合句意。

The strongest encouragement *to drink* *that* *young people receive*, *however*,
comes from advertisers. Beer companies *often* sponsor the sports events
young people watch. *In addition*, advertisements *for liquor*, *on TV and*
in print, show situations *that are attractive to the young*. People hoist
their glasses *while they are sitting around ski lodges*, *sailing*, *dancing*,
or enjoying a football game. We may say *we don't want our children to*
drink, *but* our messages say just the opposite.

然而，鼓勵年輕人喝酒，最大的來源是廣告商。啤酒公司常會贊助那些年輕人喜歡
觀賞的運動比賽。此外，電視及報章雜誌上酒的廣告內容，對於年輕人而言，十分
具吸引力。在廣告中，人們在滑雪的小屋閒坐、航行、跳舞或觀賞足球賽時，手上
都會握著酒杯。或許我們會說不希望孩子們喝酒，但我們所傳達的訊息卻剛好相反。

advertiser〔'ædvɚˌtaɪzɚ〕*n.* 廣告商
sponsor〔'spɑnsɚ〕*v.* 贊助　　event〔ɪ'vɛnt〕*n.* 比賽
in addition 此外
advertisement〔ˌædvɚ'taɪzmənt〕*n.* 廣告
print〔prɪnt〕*n.* 出版品；報紙　　hoist〔hɔɪst〕*v.* 舉起
lodge〔lɑdʒ〕*n.* 小屋　　opposite〔'ɑpəzɪt〕*n.* 相反的事

28. (**D**) 依句意，選(D)然而。而(A)此外，(B)因此，(C)而且，皆不合句意。

29. (**C**) *attractive*〔ə'træktɪv〕*adj.* 具吸引力的
(A) attentive〔ə'tɛntɪv〕*adj.* 專注的
(B) attributive〔ə'trɪbjətɪv〕*adj.* 附屬的；限定的
(D) accustomed〔ə'kʌstəmd〕*adj.* 習慣的

30. (**B**) 依句意，選(B)while「當～時候」。

Although Grants Pass, Oregon, is a fairly small town, it offers much to amuse summer visitors. Water sports are *by far* the most popular tourist attraction. Visitors can go rafting *down the Rogue River* or swimming *in the Applegate River*. Fishing *in the area* is another popular activity. Lots of people *also* go hunting for wild berries *that grow along the roadsides*. *In addition*, there are lovely, clean campgrounds *where campers can park their vehicles*.

雖然奧勒岡州的葛蘭茲帕斯是個極小的城鎮，它卻提供許多娛樂給夏季的遊客。水上運動顯然是最受歡迎的旅遊焦點。遊客們可從羅格河乘筏而下，或是在蘋果門河裏游泳。釣魚是當地另一項受歡迎的活動。許多人也會去採沿路生長的野莓。此外，還有可愛、整潔的營地可供露營者停車。

　　　attraction〔ə'trækʃən〕*n*. 吸引人的東西　　raft〔ræft〕*v*. 乘筏
　　　hunt for 尋找　　wild〔waɪld〕*adj*. 野生的
　　　berry〔'bɛrɪ〕*n*. 漿果；莓果　　campground〔'kæmp,graʊnd〕*n*. 營地
　　　park〔park〕*v*. 停車　　vehicle〔'viɪkl〕*n*. 車輛

31. (B) 依句意，選(B) by far 顯然地。而(A) far from 絕非，(C) a bit far 有點遠，(D)常用於 as far as～「遠至～」，均不合句意。
　　　　by far the
　　　　far and away the ⎫
　　　　the very ⎬ ＋最高級形容詞 (詳見文法寶典 p.207)
　　　　much the ⎭

32. (D) 依句意，選(D)或者。而(A)也，(B)但是，(C)因為，均不合句意。

33. (A) 依句意，選(A) in addition「此外」。而(B) in due time「在適當的時期」，(C) for instance「例如」，(D) by and large「一般來說」，均不合句意。

For those who prefer to stay in town, Grants Pass offers several nice hotels. *In town*, tourists can browse through a number of interesting shops, *such as antique stores and the shop that sells items made from Oregon's beautiful myrtlewood*. Another fun activity is shopping *at the open market where local folks sell produce grown in their gardens*.

至於喜歡待在市區裏的人，葛蘭玆帕斯也提供一些不錯的旅館。在城裏，遊客可逛逛許多有趣的商店，像是古董店，以及販賣奧勒岡州美麗桃金孃木產品的店。另一項有趣的活動是逛露天市場，在那兒當地居民販售自家花園種植的農產品。

browse〔braʊz〕 v. 瀏覽　　antique〔æn'tik〕 n. 古董
item〔'aɪtəm〕 n. 物品　　myrtle〔'mɝtl̩〕 n. 桃金孃
local〔'lokl̩〕 adj. 當地的　　folk〔fok〕 n. 居民
produce〔'prɑdjus〕 n. 農產品

34. (B) 表「對～而言」用 for，故選(B)。而(A) about「關於」，(C) with「隨著」，(D) in「在…之內」，均不合句意。

35. (C) *a number of*　許多；幾個

36. (C) 依句意，商品是由～「所製成」，表被動，選(C) made。而原句是由 items which are made… 簡化而來。

37. (A) 依句意選(A) activity「活動」。而(B) advice「勸告」，(C) proposal〔prə'pozl̩〕 n. 提議，(D) 運動，均不合句意。

And finally, Grants Pass has a lot of places to eat, *ranging from a low-*
38
calorie dessert place to lovely restaurants, *some of which offer good food*
and gorgeous views. *As you can see*, Grants Pass offers a lot to do *in*
39
the summer. *If you want to give your family a nice*, *wholesome vacation*,
40
try visiting this charming town.

最後，葛蘭玆帕斯也有許多餐飲地點。從低卡路里的點心店到美麗的餐廳都有，有些提供了美食以及華麗的景觀。誠如你所見，葛蘭玆帕斯提供了許多夏日活動。如果你想給家人一個美好、有益身心的假期，試試這個迷人的小鎮吧！

range〔rendʒ〕 v. (範圍)涉及　　calorie〔'kælərɪ〕 n. 卡路里
dessert〔dɪ'zɝt〕 n. 點心　　gorgeous〔'gɔrdʒəs〕 adj. 華麗的
wholesome〔'holsəm〕 adj. 有益身心的　　charming〔'tʃɑrmɪŋ〕 adj. 迷人的

38. (D) 依句意，選(D) finally「最後」。而(A) fairly「相當地」，(B) 快樂地，(C) 華麗地，均不合句意。

39.(**A**)　依句意，選(A) as「正如」。而(B)既然,(C)直到,(D)然後,均不合句意。

40.(**C**)　「如果…」用表條件的從屬連接詞 if，故選(C)。而(A)那裏，(B)什麼，
(D)那個，均不合句意。

Ⅳ、閱讀測驗

Breaking into the computer codes (*known as 'hacking'*) *of banks,*
large companies **or** *even government departments* is the latest game
for super-intelligent teenagers. One young hacker said, "Hacking is
just intellectual. It's your brain against the computer. It's like
climbing Mount Everest — it's something *you have to do*. You don't
even need a *very* expensive computer — **but** you must understand
everything *about all kinds of computers*."

　　侵入銀行、大公司、甚至政府部門的電腦密碼（即破解程式），是天才少年
新興的遊戲。一位年輕的破解族表示：「破解程式純粹靠智力，是人腦對抗電腦。
就像爬上埃弗勒斯峯——這是你必須做的事。你甚至不需要一部很昂貴的電腦—
但你必須要對每一種電腦瞭若指掌。」

> **break into** 闖入；侵入　　　code〔kod〕*n.* 密碼
> hacking〔'hækɪŋ〕*n.* 破解（電腦密碼、程式）
> hacker〔'hækɚ〕*n.* 非法入侵電腦者；駭客
> intellectual〔,ɪntḷ'ɛktʃʊəl〕*adj.* 用智力的

At the moment most *of these games* are *just* fun *for young people*.
But how long will it be **before** *criminal gangs, like the Mafia, start*
to use computer experts to help them in their crimes? Future bank
robbers will not need explosives *to blow open bank safes* — all *they will*
need is someone *who can break computer codes*. *Already in Britain*
people say **that** *computer crimes are costing companies between 500*
million pounds and 2.5 billion pounds a year.

　　目前這些遊戲對年輕人而言，大部分只是好玩而已。但誰知道多久以後，就會有像黑手黨這樣的犯罪集團，開始利用電腦專家幫他們做案呢？以後的銀行搶匪不需要用炸藥來炸開保險箱——他們需要的只是一個能破解電腦密碼的人。在英國，電腦犯罪已使國內公司每年損失五億到二十五億英鎊。

> criminal〔ˊkrɪmənḷ〕*adj.* 犯罪的
> gang〔gæŋ〕*n.* 暴力集團；幫派
> mafia〔ˊmɑfɪ‚ɑ〕*n.* 黑手黨（常用 the Mafia）（西西里島等地出身之義大利人組成的美國犯罪組織）
> explosive〔ɪkˊsplosɪv〕*n.* 炸藥　　safe〔sef〕*n.* 保險箱

41.(**C**) 上述文章所提到的「hacking」是出自哪部份內容？
　　　　(A) 爬上埃弗勒斯峯。　　　　(B) 年輕人的遊戲。
　　　　(C) 侵入電腦密碼。　　　　(D) 有形地拆除一個固體。
preceding〔prɪˊsidɪŋ〕*adj.* 前述的　　　***refer to*** 提及
context〔ˊkɑntɛkst〕*n.* 上下文　　physically〔ˊfɪzɪklɪ〕*adv.* 有形地
dismantle〔dɪsˊmæntḷ〕*v.* 拆除

42.(**B**) 根據本文，侵入銀行、大公司和政府部門的電腦密碼，是
　　　　(A) 一種普遍的犯罪行為。
　　　　(B) 一種熟知電腦的人所玩的遊戲。
　　　　(C) 黑手黨為了好玩而研究它。
　　　　(D) 很快就會取代銀行的密碼保險箱。
widespread〔ˊwaɪd‚sprɛd〕*adj.* 普遍的
practice〔ˊpræktɪs〕*n.* 實行
literate〔ˊlɪtərɪt〕*adj.* 有學問的　　replace〔rɪˊples〕*v.* 取代

43.(**D**) 根據本文，要侵入電腦密碼必須有
　　　　(A) 一台精密、昂貴的多媒體電腦。
　　　　(B) 一群資訊科學的學生。
　　　　(C) 黑手黨的幫忙和財力資助。
　　　　(D) 對各種電腦徹底了解。
elaborate〔ɪˊlæbərɪt〕*adj.* 精密的
multi-media〔ˊmʌltɪ ˊmidɪə〕*adj.* 多媒體的
thorough〔ˊθɝo〕*adj.* 徹底的　　***a variety of*** 各種的

There is increasing scientific evidence *that large cars cause more highway accidents than small cars*. *In the news recently* was the story of a woman *who* died of a heart attack *while* driving her station wagon. The car was moving *so* fast *that it went through the highway-dividing fence*, *resulting in a collision in which five people died*. Those unnecessary deaths are attributable *in part* to the woman's choice *of a large automobile*.

有愈來愈多的科學證據顯示，大車比小車更容易在公路上肇事。最近有一篇新聞，報導了一名女子在開旅行車時，因心臟病發而死亡。她的車子開得很快，衝過了公路分隔欄，引起衝撞，導致五人死亡。這些不必要的死亡，部分原因是這名女子選擇了一輛大車。

> *heart attack* 心臟病發作　*station wagon* 旅行車
> highway-dividing〔ˈhaɪˏwe dəˈvaɪdɪŋ〕*adj.* 公路中央分隔的
> fence〔fɛns〕*n.* 柵欄　　*result in* 導致
> collision〔kəˈlɪʒən〕*n.* 衝撞
> attributable〔əˈtrɪbjutəbl〕*adj.* 起因於～的
> *in part* 部份地（＝*partly*）

A lighter and smaller car *probably* wouldn't have gone through the fence, its remaining energy would have been much less, *and* this would have reduced the chances *of serious injury or death*. *Because of its small size*, it might have missed the other car *completely*. The present design *of the oversized automobile* is *largely* responsible *not only* for increasing death toll *on the highways* *but also* for the rapid depletion *of our resources of petroleum, for the pollution of our environment, and for the congestion and inconvenience of our cities*.

較輕便小巧的車子，就可能不會衝過柵欄，而且它剩餘的馬力也會小得多，這樣就可能降低嚴重死傷的機會。因爲車小，它可能完全撞不到另一部車。現今超大型汽車的設計，不但要爲公路上與日俱增的死亡人數負大部份的責任，也要爲快速消耗石油資源、污染我們的環境、以及造成市區的擁塞和不便負起重責。

injury〔ˈɪndʒərɪ〕n. 傷害　　　remaining〔rɪˈmenɪŋ〕adj. 剩餘的
toll〔tol〕n. 死傷人數　　depletion〔dɪˈpliʃən〕n. 枯竭
petroleum〔pəˈtrolɪəm〕n. 石油　congestion〔kənˈdʒɛstʃən〕n. 擁塞
inconvenience〔ˌɪnkənˈvinjəns〕n. 不便

44.(A) 作者把公路上的五人死亡歸咎於
　　　　(A)大型笨重的旅行車。　　　　　(B)缺乏較小型的車輛。
　　　　(C)那名女子心臟病發得不是時候。(D)脆弱的公路分隔柵欄。
　　ill-timed〔ˈɪl ˈtaɪmd〕adj. 不合時宜的

45.(BC) 上文中，作者的主要論點是什麼？
　　　　(A) 政府應該禁止大車上路。
　　　　(B) 比起小車，大車較不安全也不經濟。
　　　　(C) 小車比大車更能保障乘客安全。
　　　　(D) 一名女子心臟病發引起五人死亡。
　　＊大學入學考試中心公布(B)(C)爲正確答案。
　　ban〔bæn〕v. 禁止　economical〔ˌikəˈnɑmɪkl̩,ˌɛk-〕adj. 經濟的;節省的
　　occupant〔ˈɑkjəpənt〕n. 佔有者

46.(A) 作者提出公路柵欄能擋住小巧輕便的車，這項聲明
　　　　(A) 是作者的假設。　(B) 源自於科學上的證據。
　　　　(C) 有事實根據。　　(D) 永遠無法證明。
　　＊由於文中 A lighter … car **probably wouldn't have gone** … ，以及
　　　Because of … it **might have missed** … . 皆爲假設語氣，故爲作者
　　　本身之假設，選(A)。
　　retain〔rɪˈten〕v. 擋住　assumption〔əˈsʌmpʃən〕n. 假設
　　derive from 源自～　**rest upon** 根據　verify〔ˈvɛrəˌfaɪ〕v. 證明

　　　Three pilot whales are believed to be swimming *freely off the Atlantic Coast today*. Their names are Tag, Notch, **and** Baby. These seagoing mammals are among the lucky survivors *of a whale-stranding* last December *at Cape Cod*.

　　一般相信，目前有三隻**領航鯨**，悠游於美國大西洋岸的外海中，牠們的名字是泰格、諾奇和寶貝。這幾隻生活在大海的哺乳動物，是去年十二月發生於鱈角的鯨魚擱淺事件中，幸運的生還者。

> **the Atlantic Coast** 美國大西洋岸　　**pilot whale** 領航鯨
> seagoing〔'si,go‧ɪŋ〕*adj.* 航行於大洋的
> mammal〔'mæml̩〕*n.* 哺乳動物
> survivor〔sə'vaɪvɚ〕*n.* 生還者
> whale-stranding〔hwel 'strændɪŋ〕*n.* 鯨魚擱淺
> **Cape Cod** 鱈角（美國麻薩諸塞州東端的半島）

As many as 60 pilot whales swam *ashore*. Scientists are *still* trying to find out *why* whales have this *self-destructive behavior*. Many *of the whales* died *on the beach* — crushed *by their own weight*. Whale experts found Tag, Notch, **and** Baby alive. The three were believed to be *too young* to survive *on their own* *if returned to sea*.

　　為數多達六十隻的領航鯨游上岸。科學家仍試圖解釋為什麼鯨魚會有這種自我毀滅的行為。許多鯨魚死在海灘上——被牠們自己的重量壓死。鯨魚專家發現泰格、諾奇和寶貝還活著。他們認為，這三隻鯨魚太小了，如果回到海上，靠自己將無法生存。

> **as many as** 多達～　　ashore〔ə'ʃor〕*adv.* 向岸邊
> self-destructive〔'sɛlf dɪ'strʌktɪv〕*adj.* 自我毀滅的
> crush〔krʌʃ〕*v.* 壓壞；壓碎
> survive〔sə'vaɪv〕*v.* 存活
> **on one's own** 靠自己；獨自

The three whales were taken *in a van to the New England Aquarium in Boston, Mass.* They were kept *in a 60,000-gallon tank for seven months.* *Only* a few people worked *with the whales* so **that** they would not become *too accustomed to human beings.*

這三隻鯨魚被裝在卡車上,載往麻薩諸塞州波士頓的新英格蘭水族館。他們被養在一個可容六萬加侖水的水池中七個月,只有少數人照料這些鯨魚,這樣牠們才不會太習慣於人類。

van〔væn〕n. 有蓋卡車　　aquarium〔ə'kwɛrɪəm〕n. 水族館
gallon〔'gælən〕n. 加侖(容量單位)　　tank〔tæŋk〕n. 水槽
accustomed〔ə'kʌstəmd〕adj. 習慣的

Early this past summer the three whales were pronounced fit *enough to be returned to the Atlantic Ocean. A month after their release*, the whales were spotted. They were found *in a group of 50 whales about 60 miles from where they had been set free.*

去年初夏時,水族館方面宣布,這三隻鯨魚狀況良好,可以送回大西洋了。在牠們被釋放後一個月,這三隻鯨魚被發現了。牠們在距離被釋放的地點六十哩處,與為數五十隻的鯨魚群在一起。

pronounce〔prə'nauns〕v. 宣布
fit〔fɪt〕adj. 健康的　　release〔rɪ'lis〕n. 釋放
spot〔spɑt〕v. 發現　　*set free* 釋放

47. (**B**) 這六十隻領航鯨游上岸,是由於
　　(A) 鱈角外海一個巨大的多季暴風雨。
　　(B) 目前科學家還不明白的一種行為。
　　(C) 目前鯨魚專家正在研究的一種遺傳現象。
　　(D) 要回到鱈角附近,牠們每年一次的產卵地。

genetic〔dʒə'nɛtɪk〕adj. 遺傳學的
phenomenon〔fə'namə,nɑn〕n. 現象　　spawn〔spɔn〕v. 產卵

48. (**C**) 領航鯨死在鱈角的海灘上,是由於
　　(A) 缺乏鹽水來幫助牠們呼吸。
　　(B) 缺乏營養來維持牠們龐大的體重。
　　(C) 出水面後,牠們身體的構造無法支撐牠們的體重。
　　(D) 一種科學家尚未理解的現象。

facilitate〔fə'sɪlə,tet〕v. 使容易
respiration〔,rɛspə'reʃən〕n. 呼吸
nutrition〔nju'trɪʃən〕n. 營養　　*figure out* 理解

49.(**C**) 泰格、諾奇和寶貝這三隻鯨魚獲救，是因為
　　　(A) 年紀較小的鯨魚比其他鯨魚生還的機會大。
　　　(B) 在被發現擱淺的眾多鯨魚中，這三隻被認為是最健康的。
　　　(C) 當救援隊發現牠們時，牠們還活著。
　　　(D) 救援隊員非常喜歡牠們。
　　beach〔bitʃ〕 *v.* 使擱淺　　　deem〔dim〕 *v.* 認為

50.(**D**) 下列何者為非？
　　　(A) 科學家們正在研究領航鯨的自殺行為。
　　　(B) 泰格、諾奇和寶貝太小了，無法獨自在海洋中生存。
　　　(C) 領航鯨是一種可以習慣於人類的哺乳動物。
　　　(D) 泰格、諾奇和寶貝被釋放後，再也沒有人看見牠們。
　　suicidal〔,suəˈsaɪdl̩〕 *adj.* 自殺的

第二部份：非選擇題

Ⅰ、中譯英

1. 昨天在回家的路上，我看到一個小女孩在路邊哭泣。
　On my way home yesterday, I saw a little girl crying on the street.

2. 我趕緊跑過去，問她到底發生了什麼事。
　I rushed to her, and asked her ⎰ what (had) happened to her.
　　　　　　　　　　　　　　　　 ⎨ what was the matter with her.
　　　　　　　　　　　　　　　　 ⎱ what was wrong with her.

3. 小女孩說她按了好幾次門鈴，卻沒有人來開門。
　The little girl said that she had rung the doorbell several times,
　but no one ⎰ answered.
　　　　　　 ⎨ came to open the door.
　　　　　　 ⎱ opened the door.

4. 看到她哭得那麼傷心，我就陪她等媽媽回來。
　Finding her crying sadly, I ⎰ accompanied ⎱ her to wait for her
　　　　　　　　　　　　　　　 ⎱ stayed with　 ⎰
　mother's coming home.

5. 雖然晚了半個鐘頭才回到家，我覺得我做了一件有意義的事。
　Though I arrived home half an hour late, I felt that I had done
　⎰ a meaningful thing.
　⎱ something meaningful.

II、英文作文

February 20, 1995

Dear George,

　　I'm really glad to hear that you're coming to Taiwan. During your stay here, you must make good use of the two years to see Taiwan for yourself. Taiwan, as you already know, is a mountainous island. *Therefore*, the first thing you should do is pay a visit to our scenic mountains, such as Mt. Ali and Mt. Jade. You will be deeply impressed with the grandeur and magnificence of the mountains. After having enough of the gorgeous scenes, try the food at the local night market. The tasty snacks will make you want one more bite.

　　But, beware of the traffic in big cities. You should avoid the rush hours lest you get stuck in the heavy traffic. When you go out to downtown, take the bus if possible. If you drive, you may find it hard to park. When you stroll along the sidewalk, watch out for the blocking motorcycles parked on it. You may bump into one if you are not careful. The traffic in Taiwan is quite different from that in the States. *Finally*, I'm going to say " Welcome to Taiwan." I'm sure you'll find it interesting to live in Taiwan.

Your friend,
Chih-ping

make (*good*) *use of* （好好）利用
mountainous〔'maʊntn̩əs〕*adj.* 多山的
scenic〔'sinɪk,'sɛn-〕*adj.* 風景優美的
grandeur〔'grændʒɚ〕*n.* 壯觀
magnificence〔mæg'nɪfəsn̩s〕*n.* 壯麗
gorgeous〔'gɔrdʒəs〕*adj.* 極好的　　snack〔snæk〕*n.* 小吃
beware of 小心～　　　　*rush hours* 尖峯時間
lest〔lɛst〕*conj.* 以免　　　park *v.* 停車
stroll〔strol〕*v.* 漫步　　blocking〔'blɑkɪŋ〕*adj.* 阻擋的

八十三年大學入學學科能力測驗試題
英文考科

選擇題

第一部分：40 題（※注意：在答案卡第一部分答案區作答）

I、詞彙（10 分）

說明：以下十個題目（1 至 10），每題各有一個空格，並附有四個選項。請選擇一個最適當的，標示在答案卡上。每題答對得 1 分，答錯不倒扣。

1. Because Mr. Chang has been busy these days, it's _____ whether he will come to the party.
   (A) unlikely　　(B) impossible　　(C) doubtful　　(D) inevitable

2. I'm quite _____ to the weather in Taiwan, so I think I'll stay here for another year.
   (A) devoted　　(B) satisfied　　(C) pleased　　(D) accustomed

3. Mr. Smith won't tolerate talking during class; he says it _____ others.
   (A) disturbs　　(B) deserves　　(C) destroys　　(D) dismisses

4. On the basis of the clues, can you predict the _____ of the story?
   (A) outcome　　(B) headline　　(C) cause　　(D) performance

5. A good reader can often figure out what new words mean by using _____.
   (A) contact　　(B) context　　(C) content　　(D) contest

6. I wonder why she _____ turned up the radio when I was studying.
   (A) sympathetically　　(B) primarily　　(C) deliberately　　(D) thoroughly

7. It suddenly _____ me that I had to get to the airport to meet a friend.
   (A) took　　(B) struck　　(C) occurred　　(D) surprised

8. Being a very careful person, he is quite _____ in giving his comments.

   (A) reserved   (B) melancholy   (C) complicated   (D) generous

9. Most viewers agreed that the movie _____ was not as good as the book.

   (A) routine   (B) version   (C) copy   (D) issue

10. The native greeted the travelers in a _____ language which was strange to them.

   (A) contrary   (B) relative   (C) peculiar   (D) spiral

Ⅱ、綜合測驗（20分）

說明：以下兩篇短文共有二十個空格（11至30），每個空格各有四個選項。請仔
　　　細閱讀後，選出一個最適當的，標示在答案卡上。每題答對得1分，答錯不
　　　倒扣。

    The umbrella is not a new invention. The Chinese ___11___ umbrellas in the eleventh century B.C. ___12___ China they traveled to India, Persia, and Egypt. But in Greece and Rome, men ___13___ use them. They believed umbrellas were ___14___ for women.

    When the Spanish explorers went to Mexico, they saw the Aztec kings ___15___ umbrellas. English explorers found out that Indian princes also carried umbrellas on the east coast of North America. It ___16___ that people in different parts of the world invented umbrellas at different times.

    England was probably the first country in Europe ___17___ ordinary people used umbrellas ___18___ the rain. England has a rainy climate, and umbrellas are very useful there.

    The umbrella is now a very ordinary ___19___. Everybody uses it today. It keeps the rain and the sun off people. Some umbrellas fold up, ___20___ it is easy to carry them.

11. (A) have had	(B) had	(C) have	(D) having
12. (A) From	(B) In	(C) For	(D) Around
13. (A) would	(B) could	(C) wouldn't	(D) won't
14. (A) likely	(B) only	(C) nearly	(D) possibly
15. (A) used	(B) to use	(C) used to	(D) using
16. (A) seems	(B) likes	(C) looks	(D) maybe
17. (A) what	(B) when	(C) which	(D) where
18. (A) below	(B) of	(C) against	(D) from
19. (A) subject	(B) object	(C) matter	(D) element
20. (A) so	(B) for	(C) unless	(D) but

　　A person's self-concept is reflected in the way he or she behaves, and the way a person behaves affects other people's reactions. ___21___, the way people think about themselves ___22___ a profound effect on all areas of their lives. For instance, people who have a ___23___ sense of self-esteem usually act with confidence. ___24___ they have self-assurance, they do not need constant praise and encouragement from others to feel ___25___ about themselves. Self-confident people are their own best friends. They participate ___26___ life enthusiastically and spontaneously. They are not affected by ___27___ others think they "should" do. People ___28___ high self-esteem are not hurt by criticism; they do not ___29___ criticism as personal rejection. ___30___, they tend to believe criticism to be suggestion for improvement.

21. (A) By and by	(B) Luckily	(C) In general	(D) Even so
22. (A) have	(B) having	(C) to have	(D) has
23. (A) positive	(B) common	(C) weak	(D) normal
24. (A) Until	(B) Because	(C) Unless	(D) However
25. (A) best	(B) correct	(C) well	(D) good
26. (A) to	(B) at	(C) in	(D) on
27. (A) which	(B) how	(C) why	(D) what
28. (A) losing	(B) by	(C) with	(D) have
29. (A) like	(B) look	(C) watch	(D) regard
30. (A) Instead	(B) In addition	(C) Thus	(D) In case

Ⅲ、閱讀測驗（20分）

說明：以下有三篇短文，共有十個問題（31 至 40）。每題各附有四個選項。請仔
細閱讀後，選出一個最適當的,標示在答案卡上。每題答對得2分,答錯不倒扣。

Most heroes are people like you. But what makes them heroes? They find special courage when they need it. They are brave enough to help in an emergency while others may stand by. A hero sees what needs to be done and does it.

Sometimes heroes are rewarded for their brave acts. One such reward is the Carnegie Medal. It is given to people who act bravely and face danger to save the lives of others.

The medal was named after Andrew Carnegie. In 1886, Carnegie heard about a young man by the name of William Hunter who lost his life trying to save two other boys from drowning. Carnegie became a very rich businessman and set aside money to honor heroes like William. Sometimes these heroes are in need or are hurt. If so, they receive money as well as the Carnegie Medal.

Over 6,000 people have received the Carnegie Medal. Some have saved people from drowning or from burning buildings. Others have pulled people in front of moving trains or saved them from attacks by wild animals. All these heroes have one thing in common, however. They put someone else's safety ahead of their own.

31. The Carnegie Medal is given to those who are
    (A) sick and poor.
    (B) rich and famous.
    (C) young and brave.
    (D) unselfish and courageous.

32. What is the main idea of the passage?
    (A) William Hunter was a very brave boy.
    (B) Hunter saved Carnegie from drowning.
    (C) Some heroes have been rewarded for their bravery.
    (D) Carnegie was a rich businessman and liked to help people.

33. Which of the following statements is NOT true?
    (A) Carnegie knew Hunter in person.
    (B) Brave deeds can take many different forms.
    (C) Over 6,000 people are Carnegie Medal recipients.
    (D) Some heroes have received money as well as the Medal.

On May 26, 1977, George Willig traveled to the top of the 1,350-foot-tall World Trade Center in New York City. He did not take the elevator, however. Instead, like a human fly, George Willig climbed the outside of the immense 110-story building. His climb, which began at 6:30 a.m., took three and a half hours to finish.

At the top, Willig was greeted by both police and reporters. Some of the police officers asked him for his autograph. Then they wanted to put him in jail and charged him with violation of law for climbing the building without a permit. Furthermore, the city also planned to sue him for a quarter of a million dollars. The amount, the police department reported, would pay the costs of rushing special equipment and eighty police officers in order to save him.

By the next day, city officials had reevaluated the situation. At City Hall, Mayor Abraham Beame hosted a news conference that turned into a ceremony in George Willig's honor. Beame announced that the city would not punish "The Human Fly." Instead, he would be fined a penny for each of the 110 floors he had climbed. Instead of punishing Willig, the city treated him as a hero who attempted the impossible and met the challenge.

34. George Willig reached the top of the World Trade Center in New York at
 (A) six thirty in the morning of May 26, 1977.
 (B) six thirty in the evening of May 26, 1977.
 (C) ten o'clock in the morning of May 26, 1977.
 (D) ten o'clock in the evening of May 26, 1977.

35. This passage is a story about
 (A) a man who enjoys dangers and risks.
 (B) a human being who can fly like a fly.
 (C) a man who has escaped from the jail.
 (D) a fly which climbs like a human being.

36. According to the passage, which of the following statements is true?
 (A) Willig was fined $250,000.
 (B) Willig was sent to prison for a year.
 (C) Willig was honored in a party and fined only $1.10.
 (D) Willig climbed the World Trade Center with permission.

Printing is one of the most important means of communication. Without it you would not now be reading this passage. Even the development of radio and television has not diminished the importance of printing.

The first printing was done from wood blocks one letter at a time by hand. This was a slow process, requiring much skill and patience, and every page of every book had to be cut separately.

A great step forward was the use of movable type. The Chinese discovered this in the 11th century, but it was not known in Europe until about 1440. In this method of printing, individual letters were made from separate pieces of metal. If these letters were linked over and pressed on to paper, they would print the words. When the printing was finished, the letters could be taken apart and rearranged to print something else.

One of the first European books to be printed in movable type was Johannes Gutenberg's 42-line Bible. The first book to be printed likewise in English was about the history of Troy. It was printed in Flanders in 1474 by an Englishman, William Caxton. In 1476 he returned to England and established a printing press at Westminster. Altogether he printed nearly 80 books, many being his own translations from the French.

37. Printing is important because
   (A) it is a Chinese invention.
   (B) it has made reading books possible.
   (C) it has helped to develop radio and television.
   (D) William Caxton printed 80 books in English.

38. The use of movable type was first introduced by
   (A) William Caxton.　　　　　(B) the Europeans.
   (C) Johannes Gutenberg.　　　(D) the Chinese.

39. According to the passage, the use of movable type was considered as a "great step forward" because
   (A) it did not need a lot of wood.
   (B) it required less skill and patience.
   (C) the printing letters could be reused.
   (D) every page of every book required individual carving.

40. The first English book printed in movable type was
    (A) done from wood blocks one letter at a time.
    (B) done in a printing press at Westminster.
    (C) Johannes Gutenberg's 42-line Bible.
    (D) about the history of Troy.

第二部分：10題（※注意：在答案卡第二部分答案區作答）

文意閱讀選填（10分）

說明：以下短文共有十個空格（1至10），附有十五個選項（A至O）。請仔細閱
　　　讀後，依據文意選出最適合各空格的選項，並依題號標示在答案卡上。每題
　　　答對得1分，答錯不倒扣。

　　For many years, people thought the ___1___ of smoking were ___2___ to
smokers. But new studies have found that smoke from cigarettes can
be ___3___ to non-smokers too.

　　In December 1987, a U.S. Government report ___4___ that non-
smokers could risk getting lung cancer from ___5___ in other people's
cigarette smoke.

　　Another study looked at non-smoking ___6___ athletes who had smoking
parents or friends. Being ___7___ cigarette smoke hurt the athletes'
lungs, and made them ___8___ more than athletes who did not have smokers
close ___9___ , the study said. Studies like these have promoted the
banning of smoking in ___10___ places.

(A) activated	(B) cough	(C) breathing
(D) adopting	(E) indicated	(F) symptoms
(G) near	(H) harmful	(I) damages
(J) limited	(K) to	(L) by
(M) weak	(N) teenage	(O) public

非選擇題

Ⅰ、中譯英（20分）

說明：請用最適當的句型將下列五個文意連貫的句子譯成通順而達意的英文，每題
　　　4分。答案請寫在答案卷上，務必標示題號，違者不予計分。

1. 對於什麼是最佳的渡假方式，大家都有不同的看法。

2. 有些人喜歡到寧靜的森林中去，在那兒他們可以暫時遠離人群。

3. 有些人卻寧願到大都市去，因為他們可以參觀博物館或購物。

4. 還有一些人喜歡到海邊去，讓海浪沖走他們的煩惱。

5. 有少數人則決定留在家裡，做一些像打掃屋子之類的事。

Ⅱ、英文作文（20分）

說明：1. 請把作文寫在答案卷上，違者不予計分。
　　　2. 文章可以分段，也可以不分段。
　　　3. 評分標準：內容5分，組織5分，文法4分，用字與拼字4分，體例
　　　　 （格式、標點、大小寫）2分。

題目：Things Are Not As Difficult As They Appear

　　在成長過程中，有些事情在開始的時候你可能覺得很難，但經過一番努力後就
不再認為困難了。請寫一篇至少一百二十個單字的英文作文，描述一個親身的經驗。
文章的頭兩句必須是：

Things are not as difficult as they appear. I have a personal
experience to prove this.

83年度學科能力測驗英文科試題詳解

第一部分

I、詞彙

1. (**C**) Because Mr. Chang has been busy these days, it's <u>doubtful</u> whether he will come to the party.

張先生近來很忙，所以他是否能來參加宴會還<u>不確定</u>。

(A) unlikely〔ʌn'laɪklɪ〕adj. 不可能的
(B) impossible〔ɪm'pɑsəbl̩〕adj. 不可能的
(C) **doubtful**〔'daʊtfəl〕adj. 不確定的
(D) inevitable〔ɪn'ɛvətəbl̩〕adj. 無法避免的

2. (**D**) I'm quite <u>accustomed</u> to the weather in Taiwan, so I think I'll stay here for another year.

我相當習慣台灣的天氣，所以我想我會在這兒再待一年。

(A) devoted〔dɪ'votɪd〕adj. 獻身的
(B) satisfied〔'sætɪsˌfaɪd〕adj. 滿意的
(C) pleased〔plizd〕adj. 高興的
(D) **accustomed**〔ə'kʌstəmd〕adj. 習慣的　**be accustomed to** 習慣於

3. (**A**) Mr. Smith won't tolerate talking during class; he says it <u>disturbs</u> others.

史密斯先生不容許上課時講話，他說這樣會妨礙到別人。

(A) **disturb**〔dɪ'stɝb〕v. 妨礙；打擾　(B) deserve〔dɪ'zɝv〕v. 值得
(C) destroy〔dɪ'strɔɪ〕v. 破壞　(D) dismiss〔dɪs'mɪs〕v. 解散
tolerate〔'tɑləˌret〕v. 容忍；容許

4. (**A**) On the basis of the clues, can you predict the <u>outcome</u> of the story?

根據這些線索，你能預測故事的<u>結局</u>嗎？

(A) **outcome**〔'aʊtˌkʌm〕n. 結果　(B) headline〔'hɛdˌlaɪn〕n. 標題
(C) cause〔kɔz〕n. 原因　(D) performance〔pɚ'fɔrməns〕n. 表演
on the basis of 以～爲基礎　clue〔klu〕n. 線索
predict〔prɪ'dɪkt〕v. 預測

5.(**B**) A good reader can *often* figure out ***what*** *new words mean by using context*.

一個好的讀者通常都能利用上下文，推敲出新字的意義。

    (A) contact〔'kɑntækt〕*n*. 接觸

    (B) ***context***〔'kɑntɛkst〕*n*. 上下文

    (C) content〔'kɑntɛnt〕*n*. 內容

    (D) contest〔'kɑntɛst〕*n*. 比賽

figure out 理解

6.(**C**) I wonder ***why*** *she deliberately turned up the radio* ***when*** *I was studying*.

我想知道爲什麼在我讀書時，她故意把收音機的音量開大。

    (A) sympathetically〔,sɪmpə'θɛtəklɪ〕*adv*. 同情地

    (B) primarily〔'praɪ,mɛrəlɪ〕*adv*. 主要地

    (C) ***deliberately***〔dɪ'lɪbərɪtlɪ〕*adv*. 故意地

    (D) thoroughly〔'θɜolɪ〕*adv*. 徹底地

7.(**B**) It *suddenly* struck me ***that*** *I had to get to the airport to meet a friend*.

我突然想到我必須去機場接一個朋友。

    (A) take〔tek〕*v*. 拿

    (B) ***strike***〔straɪk〕*v*. 突然想到 (*sth*. strikes *sb*.)

    (C) occur〔ə'kɜ〕*v*. 想到 (*sth*. occurs to *sb*.)

    (D) surprise〔sə'praɪz〕*v*. 使驚訝

8.(**A**) *Being a very careful person*, he is *quite* reserved *in giving his comments*.

他是一個非常謹慎的人，在發表評論時相當有保留。

    (A) ***reserved***〔rɪ'zɜvd〕*adj*. 謹慎的；有所保留的

    (B) melancholy〔'mɛlən,kɑlɪ〕*adj*. 憂鬱的

    (C) complicated〔'kɑmplə,ketɪd〕*adj*. 複雜的

    (D) generous〔'dʒɛnərəs〕*adj*. 慷慨的

comment〔'kɑmɛnt〕*n*. 評論

9. (B) Most viewers agreed *that the movie version was not as good as*

the book.

大多數觀衆都同意，電影版沒有書那麼好。

(A) routine〔ru'tin〕*n.* 例行工作　(B) *version*〔'vɝʒən〕*n.* ～版

(C) copy〔'kɑpɪ〕*n.* 複本　(D) issue〔'ɪʃʊ〕*n.* (刊物)～期

viewer〔'vjuɚ〕*n.* 觀衆

10. (C) The native greeted the travelers *in a peculiar language which*

was strange to them.

土著以一種遊客們陌生的獨特的語言來歡迎他們。

(A) contrary〔'kɑntrɛrɪ〕*adj.* 相反的　(B) relative〔'rɛlətɪv〕*adj.* 相關的

(C) *peculiar*〔pɪ'kjuljɚ〕*adj.* 獨特的　(D) spiral〔'spaɪrəl〕*adj.* 螺旋形的

native〔'netɪv〕*n.* 土著；原住民

II、綜合測驗

The umbrella is not a new invention. The Chinese had umbrellas *in*

the eleventh century B.C. From China they traveled to India, Persia,

and Egypt. *But in Greece and Rome*, men wouldn't use them. They

believed *umbrellas were only for women.*

傘並不是一項新發明。早在西元前十一世紀中國人就有傘。傘從中國傳入印度、波斯以及埃及。但在希臘與羅馬，男人不用傘。他們認爲傘是女人專用的。

travel〔'trævl〕*v.* 行進；傳導　　India〔'ɪndɪə〕*n.* 印度

Persia〔'pɝʒə, 'pɝʃə〕*n.* 波斯　　Greece〔gris〕*n.* 希臘

11. (B) 依句意，「西元前十一世紀」爲過去的時間，故動詞須爲過去式，選(B) had。

12. (A) 傘是「從」中國傳入印度、波斯與埃及，故選(A) From。

13. (C) 依句意，希臘與羅馬的男人，認爲傘是女人用的，所以「不」用傘，又依句意爲過去式，故選(C)。

14. (B) 依句意，選(B) only *adv.* 僅僅；只是。而(A) likely *adj.* 可能的，(C) nearly *adv.* 幾乎，(D) possibly *adv.* 或許，皆與句意不合。

When the Spanish explorers went to Mexico, they saw the Aztec kings
using umbrellas. English explorers found out *that Indian princes also*
15
carried umbrellas on the east coast of North America. It seems *that*
16
people in different parts of the world invented umbrellas at different times.

當西班牙的探險家到墨西哥時，看見阿茲特克族的國王在用傘。英國的探險家
發現北美東岸的印第安領袖們也會隨身帶傘。似乎世界各地的人，發明傘的時間都
各不相同。

explorer〔ɪk'splorɚ〕*n.* 探險家　Aztec〔'æztɛk〕*adj.* 阿茲特克族的
Indian〔'ɪndɪən〕*adj.* 印第安的　prince〔prɪns〕*n.* 王子；領袖

15.(**D**) 感官動詞 see ＋O. ＋ { 原形 V　表主動
V-ing 表主動進行 ，故選(D) using 。

16.(**A**) It seems that ～　似乎～

England was *probably* the first country *in Europe* **where** *ordinary*
17
people used umbrellas against the rain. England has a rainy climate, ***and***
18
umbrellas are *very* useful *there.*

在歐洲，英國也許是第一個平民會用傘遮雨的國家。英國的氣候多雨，傘在英
國十分有用。

ordinary〔'ɔrdn̩,ɛrɪ,'ɔrdnɛrɪ〕*adj.* 普通的；平凡的

17.(**D**) 空格應填入表地點之關係副詞，引導形容詞子句，修飾先行詞 country ，
故選(D) where 。

18.(**C**) 表「對抗；防備」，介系詞用 against 。

The umbrella is *now* a very ordinary object. Everybody uses it *today.*
19
It keeps the rain ***and*** the sun off people. Some umbrellas fold up, **so** it
20
is easy to carry them.

　　現在傘是非常普遍的東西。每個人都用傘。它使人們免於日曬雨淋。有些傘可摺疊，所以攜帶十分容易。

　　　fold up 摺疊

19.(**B**) 依句意，選(B) object〔ˈɑbdʒɪkt〕*n*.東西。而(A) subject〔ˈsʌbdʒɪkt〕*n*. 科目，
　　　(C) matter〔ˈmætɚ〕*n*.事情，(D) element〔ˈɛləmənt〕*n*. 元素，皆不合句意。

20.(**A**) 依句意，選(A) so *conj*. 所以。而(B) 因為，(C) 除非，(D) 但是，則與句意不合。

　　A person's self-concept is reflected in the way *he or she behaves*,
and the way *a person behaves* affects other people's reactions. *In general*,
the way *people think about themselves* has a profound effect on all areas
of their lives.

　　人的自我意識，會在行為中反映出來。而個人的行為，也會對別人的反應有所影響。一般而言，人們對自己的看法，對他們生活上各方面都有深刻的影響。

　　　self-concept〔ˌsɛlfˈkɑnsɛpt〕*n*.自我意識
　　　profound〔prəˈfaʊnd〕*adj*. 深刻的　　area〔ˈɛrɪə, ˈerɪə〕*n*. 方面

21.(**C**) 依句意，選(C) in general 一般而言。而(A) by and by 不久，(B) luckily *adv*.
　　　幸運地，(D) even so 即使如此，皆不合句意。

22.(**D**) 由於主詞 the way 為單數名詞，故動詞須用單數動詞，選(D) has。

For instance, people *who have a positive sense of self-esteem* usually act
*with confidence. **Because** they have self-assurance*, they do not need constant praise and encouragement *from others* to feel good about themselves.
Self-confident people are their own best friends.

例如，有自尊心的人，通常會很有自信。因為他們很有自信，所以不需要別人不斷的讚美與鼓勵，就會對自己很滿意。自信的人是他們自己最好的朋友。

　　　sense〔sɛns〕*n*. 意識　　self-esteem〔ˌsɛlfəˈstim〕*n*. 自尊心
　　　self-assurance〔ˌsɛlfəˈʃʊrəns〕*n*. 自信
　　　constant〔ˈkɑnstənt〕*adj*. 不斷的

23. (**A**) 依句意 , 選(A) positive 〔'pɑzətɪv 〕 *adj.* 正面的 ; 積極的 。

　　而(B) common sense 常識 , (C) weak 〔 wik 〕 *adj.* 衰弱的 , (D) normal 〔'nɔrml 〕 *adj.* 正常的 , 均不合句意 。

24. (**B**) 空格應填一從屬連接詞 , 引導副詞子句 , 依句意 , 選(B) 因爲 。

　　而(A) 直到 , (C) 除非 , (D) 然而 , 均不合句意 。

25. (**D**) feel good about 對～很滿意

　　而(A) 最好的 , (B) 正確的 , 不合句意 。又 feel 爲不完全不及物動詞 , 須接形容詞爲補語 , 而(C) well 爲一副詞 , 故不選 。

They participate in life *enthusiastically and spontaneously*. They are not
　　　　　　　　　　　26
affected *by __what__ others think they "should" do*. People __with__ high self-
　　　　　　　27　　　　　　　　　　　　　　　　　　　28
esteem are not hurt *by criticism*; they do not <u>regard</u> criticism as
　　　　　　　　　　　　　　　　　　　29
personal rejection. *Instead,* they tend to believe criticism to be sugges-
　　　　　　　　30
tion *for improvement*.

他們會熱忱又自動自發地參與生命。不會因爲別人認爲他們「該」做什麼而受影響。有高度自信心的人不會因別人批評 , 而受到傷害 ; 他們認爲批評並不是對他們個人的否定。相反地 , 他們會認爲批評是希望他們能有所改善的建議。

　　　enthusiastically〔 ɪn,θjuzɪ'æstɪkəlɪ 〕 *adv.* 熱心地
　　　spontaneously〔 spɑn'tenɪəslɪ 〕 *adv.* 自動自發地
　　　criticism〔'krɪtə,sɪzəm 〕 *n.* 批評
　　　rejection〔 rɪ'dʒɛkʃən 〕 *n.* 拒絕 ; 否決　　　*tend to* 傾向於

26. (**C**) *participate in* 參與

27. (**D**) 空格應填兼具先行詞作用的複合關代 , 作介系詞 by 的受詞 , 並引導名詞子句 , 故選(D) what = the thing that 。

28. (**C**) 依句意 , 「有」高度自尊心的人 , 表示「有」介系詞須用 with , 選(C)。

29. (**D**) *regard … as* 認爲…是

30. (**A**) 依句意 , 選(A) instead *adv.* 相反地 。

　　而(B) 此外 , (C) 因此 , (D) 以防萬一 , 皆不合句意 。

II、閱讀測驗

Most heroes are people *like you*. ***But*** what makes them heroes? They find special courage *when they need it*. They are brave *enough* to help *in an emergency* **while** others may stand by. A hero sees **what needs to be done** **and** does it.

Sometimes heroes are rewarded *for their brave acts*. One such reward is the Carnegie Medal. It is given to people **who act bravely and** *face danger to save the lives of others*.

大部份的英雄是像你我一樣的人。但是，是什麼使他們成為英雄？當他們需要特殊勇氣的時候，便自然會有。遇到緊急事件時，別人可能只是袖手旁觀，而他們卻會勇敢地去幫忙。英雄知道自己該做什麼，而且也會去做。

有時候，英雄會因為自己勇敢的行為而受到獎賞。卡內基獎章就是這樣的一種獎賞。它是頒發給勇於冒險，解救他人生命的人。

emergency〔ɪˋmɝdʒənsɪ〕*n.* 緊急事件　　***stand by*** 旁觀
reward〔rɪˋword〕*v.* 獎賞　　medal〔ˋmɛdl̩〕*n.* 獎章

The medal was named *after Andrew Carnegie*. *In 1886*, Carnegie heard about a young man *by the name of William Hunter* **who lost his** *life trying to save two other boys from drowning*. Carnegie became a very rich businessman **and** set aside money *to honor heroes like William*. *Sometimes* these heroes are in need or are hurt. ***If so***, they receive money **as well as** the Carnegie Medal.

這項獎章是以安德魯・卡內基之名而命名。一八八六年，卡內基聽說有位名叫威廉・韓特的年輕人，為了救兩位溺水的男孩而喪生。卡內基為非常富有的商人後，便撥出一筆錢來表揚像威廉這樣的英雄。有時候，這些英雄會遭遇困難或受傷。這樣的話，他們不但會獲頒卡內基獎章，還會得到一筆錢。

name after 以～的名字來命名　　***by the name of*** 名叫～的
set aside 保留；撥出　　***in need*** 在患難中
as well as 而且

Over 6,000 people have received the Carnegie Medal. Some have saved people *from drowning* or *from burning buildings*. Others have pulled people *in front of moving trains* or saved them *from attacks by wild animals*. All these heroes have one thing *in common*, however. They put someone else's safety *ahead of their own*.

有六千多個人曾得到卡內基獎章。有些曾拯救溺水或困在火場中的人。有些曾拉開快被火車撞上的人，或者救了受野獸攻擊的人。然而，這些英雄都有個共同點──他們重視別人的安全甚於自己。

attack〔əˈtæk〕*n.* 攻擊　　***in common*** 共同的

31.(**D**)　卡內基獎章是頒給
　　　　(A) 生病且貧窮的人。　　(B) 有錢又有名的人。
　　　　(C) 年輕又勇敢的人。　　(D) <u>無私又有勇氣的人。</u>

32.(**C**)　本文的主旨為何？
　　　　(A) 威廉‧韓特是個很勇敢的男孩。
　　　　(B) 韓特救了溺水的卡內基。
　　　　(C) <u>有些英雄因其英勇行為而受獎勵。</u>
　　　　(D) 卡內基是富有的商人，他很喜歡幫助別人。

33.(**A**)　下列敘述何者為非？
　　　　(A) <u>卡內基認識韓特本人。</u>
　　　　(B) 英勇的行為有許多不同的表現方式。
　　　　(C) 卡內基獎章的得獎者有六千多人。
　　　　(D) 有些英雄不但得到獎章，也得到獎金。

in person 本人　　recipient〔rɪˈsɪpɪənt〕*n.* 接受者

On May 26, 1977, George Willig traveled to the top *of the 1,350-foot-tall World Trade Center in New York City*. He did not take the elevator, *however*. *Instead*, *like a human fly*, George Willig climbed the outside *of the immense 110-story building*. His climb, ***which began** at 6:30 a.m.*, took three and a half hours *to finish*.

　　一九七七年五月二十六日，喬治・威利格來到紐約市一千三百五十呎高的世界貿易中心大樓的頂端。然而，他並沒有搭電梯。相反地，他像隻蒼蠅一樣，在這棟一百一十層一望無際的大樓外攀爬。他從早上六點半開始爬，花了三個半小時才爬完。

elevator〔'ɛlə,vetɚ〕*n.* 電梯　　immense〔ɪ'mɛns〕*adj.* 一望無際的

At the top, Willig was greeted *by both police and reporters*. Some *of the police officers* asked him for his autograph. *Then* they wanted to put him *in jail and* charged him *with violation of law for climbing the building without a permit. Furthermore*, the city *also* planned to sue him *for a quarter of a million dollars*. The amount, *the police department reported*, would pay the costs *of rushing special equipment and eighty police officers in order to save him*.

　　在大樓頂端，威利格受到警方與記者的歡迎。有些警官向他要親筆簽名。之後，他們想要把他關進牢裏，並控告他未經許可便攀爬這棟大樓。此外，紐約市也計劃要罰他二十五萬美元。警方指出，這筆錢將用來償付那些為了要救他而急速送達的特殊設備與火速趕往現場的八十位警官。

greet〔grit〕*v.* 歡迎　　　　autograph〔'ɔtə,græf〕*n.* 親筆簽名
jail〔dʒel〕*n.* 監牢　　　　charge〔tʃɑrdʒ〕*v.* 控告
violation〔,vaɪə'leʃən〕*n.* 違背　permit〔'pɝmɪt,pɚ'mɪt〕*n.* 許可
sue〔su〕*v.* 控告　　　　　　rush〔rʌʃ〕*v.* 急速行動
equipment〔ɪ'kwɪpmənt〕*n.* 設備

By the next day, city officials had reevaluated the situation. *At City Hall*, Mayor Abraham Beame hosted a news conference *that turned into a ceremony in George Willig's honor*. Beame announced that the city would not punish "The Human Fly." *Instead*, he would be fined a penny *for each of the 110 floors he had climbed. Instead of punishing Willig*, the city treated him *as a hero who attempted the impossible and met the challenge*.

　　隔天，市政府官員重新評估了整個情況。在市政廳中，市長亞伯拉罕・比姆召開了一場記者會，這場記者會變成了表揚喬治・威利格的典禮。比姆宣布，紐約市不會處罰這位「蒼蠅人」。然而，他將被處罰款，每一層樓罰一分錢，而他共爬了一百一十層。威利格非但沒有受到處罰，紐約市還把他視為能嘗試不可能的事，並面對挑戰的英雄。

> reevaluate〔,riɪ'væljʊ,et〕*v.* 再評估　　*City Hall* 市政廳
> mayor〔'meɚ, mɛr〕*n.* 市長　　　host〔host〕*v.* 主辦
> *news conference* 記者招待會　　　*turn into* 變成
> *in one's honor* 對～表示敬意　　ceremony〔'sɛrə,monɪ〕*n.* 典禮
> announce〔ə'naʊns〕*v.* 宣布　　attempt〔ə'tɛmpt〕*v.* 嘗試
> challenge〔'tʃælɪndʒ〕*n.* 挑戰

34.(**C**) 喬治・威利格什麼時候到達世界貿易中心大樓的頂端？
　　(A) 一九七七年五月二十六日早上六點半。
　　(B) 一九七七年五月二十六日晚上六點半。
　　(C) 一九七七年五月二十六日早上十點。
　　(D) 一九七七年五月二十六日晚上十點。

35.(**A**) 這篇文章是一篇關於什麼的故事？
　　(A) 一個喜愛冒險的人。　　(B) 一個能像蒼蠅一樣飛的人。
　　(C) 一個越獄的人。　　　　(D) 一個能像人類一樣爬的蒼蠅。

36.(**C**) 根據本文，下列敘述何者為真？
　　(A) 威利格被罰款二十五萬元。
　　(B) 威利格被監禁一年。
　　(C) 威利格在集會中受到表揚，並且只被處以美金一元十分的罰款。
　　(D) 威利格被准許爬上世界貿易中心大樓。

Printing is one *of the most important means of communication*. *Without* *it* you would not *now* be reading this passage. Even the development *of radio and television* has not diminished the importance *of printing*.

　　印刷術是最重要的傳播方式之一，如果沒有印刷術，你現在就無法讀這段文章。即使發展出收音機和電視，也沒有使印刷術的重要性減低。

> printing〔'prɪntɪŋ〕*n.* 印刷術
> communication〔kə,mjunə'keʃən〕*n.* 傳播
> diminish〔də'mɪnɪʃ〕*v.* 減少

The first printing was done *from wood blocks one letter at a time by hand*. This was a slow process, requiring much skill and patience, ***and*** every page *of every book* had to be cut *separately*.

最初的印刷是用手在木塊上一次刻一個鉛字。這個過程很慢，需要許多技術與耐心，而且每本書的每一頁都必須分別刻版。

　　block〔blɑk〕*n.* 塊　　process〔'prɑsɛs〕*n.* 過程

A great step forward was the use *of movable type*. The Chinese discovered this *in the 11th century,* ***but*** it was not known *in Europe until about 1440. In this method of printing,* individual letters were made *from separate pieces of metal. If these letters were linked over and pressed on to paper,* they would print the words. ***When the printing was finished,*** the letters could be taken *apart and* rearranged to print something else.

活字的使用使印刷術向前邁進一大步。中國人於十一世紀發明了活字印刷，但是直到大約一四四〇年，歐洲才知道這種印刷術。在這種印刷方法中，每個鉛字都是由個別的金屬片製成的。把這些鉛字組合起來，壓在紙上，就能印出字來，印完之後，鉛字可以拆開、重新組合，再印其他東西。

　　type〔taɪp〕*n.* 鉛字

One *of the first European books to be printed in movable type* was Johannes Gutenberg's 42-line Bible. The first book to be printed *likewise in English* was about the history *of Troy.* It was printed *in Flanders in 1474 by an Englishman,* William Caxton. *In 1476* he returned to England ***and*** established a printing press *at Westminster. Altogether* he printed *nearly* 80 books, many being his own translations *from the French.*

歐洲最早以活字印刷的書，其中一本是約翰尼斯‧古騰堡的四十二行聖經。最早以同樣方法印刷的英文書，是有關特洛伊的歷史，這是一四七四年時，由一名英國人威廉‧卡克斯頓，在法蘭德斯印製的。一四七六年，他回到英格蘭，在威斯敏斯特創立一個印刷廠。他總共印了將近八十本書，其中很多是他自己從法文翻譯而成的作品。

likewise〔'laɪk,waɪz〕*adv.* 同樣地　　***printing press*** 印刷廠

37. (**B**)　印刷術很重要，因為
　　　　(A) 它是中國人發明的。　　(B) 它使得讀書成為可能。
　　　　(C) 它有助於收音機和電視的發展。
　　　　(D) 威廉‧卡克斯頓印了八十本英文書。

38. (**D**)　最先引進活字的是
　　　　(A) 威廉‧卡克斯頓。　　(B) 歐洲人。
　　　　(C) 約翰尼斯‧古騰堡。　　(D) 中國人。

39. (**C**)　根據這篇文章，使用活字被認為是「向前邁進一大步」，因為
　　　　(A) 它不需要很多木頭。　　(B) 它比較不需要技術和耐心。
　　　　(C) 印刷鉛字可以再使用。　　(D) 每本書的每一頁都必須個別刻字。

40. (**D**)　第一本用活字印刷的英文書是
　　　　(A) 在木塊上一次刻一個鉛字做成的。
　　　　(B) 在威斯敏斯特的一家印刷廠印製的。
　　　　(C) 約翰尼斯‧古騰堡的四十二行聖經。
　　　　(D) 有關特洛伊的歷史。

第二部分
文意閱讀選填：

For many years, people thought the damages *of smoking* were
₁

limited to smokers. ***But*** new studies have found ***that*** smoke *from*
₂

cigarettes can be harmful to non-smokers too.
₃

In December 1987, a U.S. Government report indicated ***that*** non-
₄

smokers could risk getting lung cancer *from breathing* in other people's
₅

cigarette smoke.

　　多年以來，人們都認為抽煙所導致的**傷害**只有吸煙者才有，但新的研究發現，從香煙中釋放出來的煙，對非吸煙者也會造成傷害。

　　一九八七年十二月，一份美國政府的報告指出，非吸煙者吸入其他人抽煙時的煙，也會有罹患肺癌的危險。

　　symptom〔'sɪmptəm〕*n.* 症狀　　indicate〔'ɪndə,ket〕*v.* 指出
　　risk〔rɪsk〕*v.* 遭受危險　　breathe〔brið〕*v.* 呼吸

　　Another study looked at non-smoking teenage athletes *who had smoking parents or friends*. Being near cigarette smoke hurt the athletes' lungs, **and** made them cough *more **than** athletes who did not have smokers close by*, the study said. Studies *like these* have promoted the banning *of smoking in public places*.

　　另一項研究是針對那些自己不抽煙，但他們的父母或朋友抽煙的十幾歲的運動員。研究指出，接近香煙釋放出來的煙，會傷害到這些運動員的肺部，使他們比那些身旁沒有吸煙者的運動員們，更經常咳嗽。諸如此類的研究，已促使公共場所開始禁煙。

　　teenage〔'tin,edʒ〕*adj.* 十幾歲的　　promote〔prə'mot〕*v.* 促使
　　banning〔'bænɪŋ〕*n.* 禁止

1. (I)　　2. (J)　　3. (H)　　4. (E)　　5. (C)
6. (N)　　7. (G)　　8. (B)　　9. (L)　　10. (O)

非選擇題

I、中譯英：

1. 對於什麼是最佳的渡假方式，大家都有不同的看法。

   People have different views about what the best way is to spend a vacation.

2. 有些人喜歡到寧靜的森林中去，在那兒他們可以暫時遠離人群。

   Some people like to go to a quiet forest, where they can get away from crowds of people { for the time being. / for a bit. / temporarily. }

3. 有些人卻寧願到大都市去，因爲他們可以參觀博物館或購物。

Some people would rather go to a big city because they can visit museums or do some shopping.

4. 還有一些人喜歡到海邊去，讓海浪沖走他們的煩惱。

Still others like to go to the seaside and let the sea waves wash away their worries.

5. 有少數人則決定留在家裡，做一些像打掃屋子之類的事。

And a few people decide to stay at home, and do such things as cleaning their houses.

Ⅱ、英文作文：

Things Are Not As Difficult As They Appear

Things are not as difficult as they appear. I have a personal experience to prove this. *One day* I went hiking in the mountains. Not accustomed to the cold weather and the long trudge, I found it a cruel torment. Disheartened and exhausted, I felt I would never reach the top and I could not keep it up for another minute. Having no chance to return, I climbed up step by step and finally reached the top.

When I went downhill, strangely enough, I found the path short, even though it was still the same path as before. *However*, this time I had in mind that the destination was approaching. Life is like a long path with adversity. We should not be discouraged by tough appearances from trying many things. Once we have experienced them, we will realize things are never as difficult as they appear. *Therefore*, we can reach our goals if we keep going with perseverance.

trudge〔trʌdʒ〕*n.* 跋涉　　torment〔'tɔrmɛnt〕*n.* 痛苦
dishearten〔dɪs'hɑrtn̩〕*v.* 使氣餒
keep it up 照目前情形繼續下去
destination〔͵dɛstə'neʃən〕*n.* 目的地
approach〔ə'protʃ〕*v.* 接近
adversity〔əd'vɝsətɪ〕*n.* 逆境；惡運
perseverance〔͵pɝsə'vɪrəns〕*n.* 堅忍；毅力

★ 電腦統計歷屆學科能力測驗單字 ★

a.m. (83年)

abandon (91①, 92②, 96年)

ability (84, 88, 92②, 93, 96, 97, 98年)

aboard (91年②)

aboriginal (86年)

abroad (92①, 95年)

absence (89年)

absolute (94年)

absolutely (91年②)

abundantly (93年)

accent (89年)

accept (85, 87, 88, 90, 92①②, 93, 94, 96年)

access (85, 87, 93年)

accident (84, 87, 91①②, 92①, 93, 94, 95年)

accidentally (85, 86年)

accompany (90年)

accomplish (88, 97年)

accomplishment (89年, 95)

according (91②, 92②, 95, 97, 98年)

accordingly (86年)

account (90, 92①②年)

accurate (93年)

accuse (88年)

accustomed (83, 84, 92②年)

achievable (91年①)

achieve (87, 91①, 93, 95年)

achievement (85, 88, 92②, 95, 98年)

acid (92②, 96年)

acquaint (95年)

acquire (95年)

acre (91年①)

across (87, 94, 97, 98年)

act (98年)

activate (83, 95年)

active (88, 95, 96, 97年)

activity (84, 87, 90, 91①②, 92①, 93, 95, 96, 98年)

actually (84, 90, 92①, 95, 97年)

ad (92年①)

adapt (88, 96, 98年)

add (89, 92①②, 93, 98年)

addict (91年①)

addition (95年)

additional (91年②)

additionally (88年)

address (87, 89, 98年)

adjective (91年②)

adjust (90, 94, 96年)

adjustment (94年)

admirable (86, 88, 90年)

admire (91②, 92①, 93, 94年)

admission (91①②, 96年)

admit (90, 95年)

adolescent (92①, 96年)

adopt (83, 88, 97年)

adoption (98年)

adore (88年)

adorn (88年)

adult (84, 87, 91①②, 92①②, 93, 95年)

advance (90, 94年)

advanced (91年②)

advancement (98年)

advantage (91①②, 92②年)

adventure (90, 91①年)

adventurous (90年)

advertise (96年)

advertisement (84, 88年)

advertiser (84年)

advertising (96年)

advice (84, 86, 91②, 97, 98年)

advise (92①, 96年)

advocate (98年)

affair (84, 85年)

affect (83, 91①, 93, 95, 97, 98年)

affective (88年)

afford (86, 95, 96年)

afraid (84, 94年)

Africa (96年)

afterwards (84, 89, 92①, 97年)

again (96年)

against (83, 85, 93, 96, 98年)

age group (91年②)

aged (89, 91①, 93年)

agency (85, 92②, 96年)

aggressive (88年)

aging (93, 98年)

ago (96年)

agree (89, 96, 97年)

agreement (95, 98年)

agricultural (94年)

aim (90, 93, 94年)

air (96, 97, 98年)

air conditioner (96年)

air-conditioned (97年)

aircraft (95年)

air current (92年②)

airline (93年)

airmail (91年②)

airplane (87, 98年)

airport (85, 88, 98年)

alarm (97年)

alarm clock (90年)

alarmed (89年)
alcohol (84年)
alien (93年)
alike (91年①)
alive (84, 91①年)
allergic (97年)
allow (87, 91①②, 92①②, 95, 97年)
almost (84, 85, 92①, 95, 96, 97, 98年)
alone (87, 89, 90, 91②, 92①②年)
along (84, 86, 87, 88, 89, 91①, 94, 96, 97, 98年)
already (84, 85, 92②, 96年)
alternative (92年②)
although (84, 85, 86, 87, 89, 91②, 92②, 93, 94, 96, 97年)
altogether (83, 84年)
always (98年)
amateur (91年②)
amaze (96年)
amazement (86年)
amazing (85, 91①, 95年)
amazingly (84年)
Amazon (91年①)
ambiguous (88年)
ambitious (86, 92②, 95年)
America (96, 97, 98年)
American (96年)
among (91②, 92①②, 94年)
amongst (84年)
amount (83, 88, 91①, 92①②, 97年)
amplified (87年)
amuse (84, 90年)
amygdala (96年)
amusement park (88年)
analysis (96年)
analyze (88年)
ancient (87, 92①, 93, 94, 95年)

anger (92年①)
angle (98年)
animal (96, 97, 98年)
anniversary (84年)
announce (83, 88, 92①年)
annoy (90年)
annoying (95年)
annual (84年)
annually (88, 97年)
anonymous (86年)
anonymously (89年)
another (98年)
answer (98年)
ant (92年②)
anticipate (92年②)
antique (84年)
anti-oxidant (97年)
anxious (91①, 95, 98年)
anyhow (91①, 93年)
anymore (89年)
anyway (88, 91①年)
anywhere (90年)
apart (83年)
apartment (91年①)
ape (90年)
apologize (85, 88, 96年)
apparently (89, 97年)
appeal (84, 85, 86年)
appealing (97年)
appear (83, 88, 89, 90, 91①, 94, 96, 98年)
appearance (87, 88, 91①, 97, 98年)
appetite (91年②)
applause (90年)
appliance (97年)
applicant (88, 94年)
application (85年)
apply (88, 91①, 94, 95年)
appointment (87年)

appreciate (93年)
approach (85, 88, 91①, 92①, 98年)
appropriate (88, 97年)
aquarium (84年)
architect (86, 87, 94年)
architecture (97年)
area (83, 87, 93, 94, 95, 96, 97, 98年)
Argentina (98年)
argue (91①②, 92①, 95年)
argument (87, 92②, 95年)
argument-saver (85年)
arise (94年)
arm (96, 97年)
army (90年)
around (88, 93, 94, 97, 98年)
around-the-world (86年)
arouse (86年)
arrange (84, 91①, 93, 94, 98年)
arrangement (87, 88, 95年)
arrest (94, 97年)
arrival (85, 91①年)
arrive (87, 88, 89, 90, 91①, 96年)
article (87, 88, 90, 91①②, 93, 94, 96, 98年)
artifact (93年)
artificial (87, 93年)
artist (84, 90, 92②年)
artistic (85, 91②, 93年)
ashore (84年)
Asia (97年)
Asian (92②, 98年)
asphalt (98年)
assemble (87年)
assembly (92年②)
assertion (91年②)
assign (95年)
assist (88, 93年)
assistance (93年)
associate (97年)

association (85年)

assumption (84年)

assure (88, 94年)

astronaut (92①, 95年)

athlete (83, 90, 91②, 98年)

athletic (93, 98年)

atmosphere (95年)

atom (92年②)

attach (85, 93年)

attack (83, 94, 95年)

attain (87年)

attempt (83, 84, 87, 98年)

attend (84, 86, 88, 91①, 93, 95年)

attendance (95年)

attendant (84, 90年)

attention (84, 86, 88, 89, 91②, 96年)

attentive (84年)

attitude (91②, 92①②, 94, 95年)

attract (86, 90, 91①②, 93, 94, 95, 96年)

attraction (84, 88, 97年)

attractive (84, 90, 91①, 92①, 94, 97年)

attributable (84年)

attributive (84年)

auction (89年)

audience (87,90, 91①②年)

author (84, 86, 88, 89, 90, 92①②, 93, 94, 96, 97, 98年)

authority (94年)

authorize (85年)

autograph (83, 91②年)

automatically (98年)

automobile (84年)

available (88, 93, 94, 96, 97年)

average (89, 92②, 98年)

avoid (85, 86, 91①②, 93, 94, 95, 97, 98年)

awake (86, 88, 91①年)

award (92年②)

aware (90年)

awkward (92年②)

axe (91年①)

B.C. (83, 92①年) (= BC)

back (98年)

background (88, 91②, 92①②年)

backpack (90年)

backwards (92年②)

backyard (94年)

bacteria (88, 91②, 93, 94, 96年)

badly (91①, 92②年)

baggage (92年①)

baked (94年)

balance (95年)

balanced (98年)

ballet (90年)

bamboo (96年)

ban (84, 90年)

band (95年)

banquet (97年)

bank (84, 87, 97, 98年)

bankrupt (92年①)

banning (83年)

bar (84年)

bare (92年②)

bark (98年)

barley (92年②)

Baroque (97年)

base (91年①)

baseball (96年)

based (98年)

basement (91年②)

basic (85年)

basically (89, 90年)

basis (85, 91②年)

bat (91年②)

bath (96年)

batter (86年)

battle (92年②)

bay (88, 89年)

beach (84, 88, 98年)

bead (93年)

beam (87, 92②年)

bear (86, 91②, 93年)

beat (87, 98年)

beautiful (96年)

beauty (88, 94年)

because (98年)

become (97, 98年)

beer (84年)

beetle (93年)

beforehand (93, 97年)

beginning (96年)

behave (83, 94, 95, 96, 98年)

behaved (92年②)

behavior (84, 86, 90, 91①, 92①②年)

behind (89, 90年)

belief (91①②, 93, 96, 97年)

believe (83, 87, 91①, 93, 94, 95, 96年)

Belize (97年)

bell (88年)

belonging (93年)

beloved (93年)

below (83年)

beneath (89, 93年)

beneficial (87, 92②, 97年)

benefit (88, 90, 91①, 92①, 96, 98年)

berry (84年)

beside (89, 93年)

besides (91②, 92②, 93, 95, 96, 98年)

bestseller (96年)

between (97, 98年)

beverage (95年)

beyond (87, 93年)

Bible (83年)

bid (98年)

bidder (89, 93年)

bilingual (95年)

bill (93, 95, 98年)

billion (84, 88, 92①年)

bin (89年)

biological (94, 96年)

biological clock (94年)

biology (88年)

birth (97年)

bit (98年)

bite (86年)

bitter (98年)

bitterly (94年)

blackness (93年)

blame (84年)

blank (86年)

blend (96年)

blessing (98年)

blind (92年②)

blinded (87年)

blizzard (88年)

block (83, 86, 92②, 97年)

blond (91年①)

blood (90, 92②, 95年)

blooming (93年)

blossom (94年)

blow (84年)

board (88, 91①年)

boating (87年)

boiling (98年)

bold (96年)

bomb (95年)

bond (86, 96年)

bone (90年)

bonus (94年)

bookmark (98年)

border (97年)

born (96, 98年)

borrow (88, 89, 94年)

boss (86, 96, 98年)

bother (92②, 98年)

bottom (98年)

bra (92年①)

bracelet (92年②)

brain (84, 85, 89, 90, 94, 95, 96, 97年)

brainchild (87年)

brake (95年)

branch (92年①)

brand (92年①)

brave (83, 90, 91②年)

bravely (83年)

bravery (83年)

Brazil (98年)

break (96, 97年)

breakthrough (98年)

breastfeed (92年②)

breastfeeding (92年②)

breath (87年)

breathe (83, 91②, 95年)

breathtaking (88年)

breed (92②, 96年)

breeze (89, 92②年)

brewed (95年)

bridge (85, 91①年)

brief (86, 91②年)

brilliant (98年)

bring (96, 97, 98年)

broadcast (86, 96年)

broadcasting (96年)

broaden (86年)

broom (94年)

brow (97年)

brown (90年)

browned (90年)

brownish-red (92年②)

browse (84年)

brush (91①, 96年)

brutal (98年)

bubble (97年)

bucket (96年)

bud (95年)

budget (87, 90, 95, 96年)

build (97, 98年)

building (97年)

bulletin (97年)

bully (89年)

bureau (85年)

burger (92年②)

burn (92年②)

burning (83, 92②年)

burst (87年)

bury (91年②)

business (96, 98年)

businessman (83, 85, 91①年)

butter (93年)

byproduct (92年②)

cable (96年)

cable TV (91年②)

cactus (93年)

cafeteria (98年)

caffeine (97年)

cage (90年)

calculate (89, 92②, 93, 98年)

call (97年)

calm (98年)

calorie (89, 95年)

camera (91年②)

camp (86年)

campaign (92②, 93, 94, 98年)

camper (84年)

campground (84年)

camping (88年)

Canada (96, 97年)

Canadian (97年)

cancel (85, 92①年)

cancer (83, 91②, 92①②, 97, 98年)

candidate (88, 92②, 93年)

candy (96年)

canoe (91年①)

can-opener (86年)

canvas (85年)

canyon (88年)

capable (97年)

capacity (88, 91①年)

cape (84年)

capital (87, 94, 97年)

capsule (85, 92①年)

captain (91年①②)

capture (98年)

carbon (98年)

carbon dioxide (88年)

care (86, 96年)

career (85, 91①②, 93年)

careful (98年)

carefully (84, 97年)

careless (91年①)

carelessness (95年)

cargo (94年)

Caribbean (98年)

caring (86年)

carnation (92年②)

carpenter (86年)

carrier (98年)

carry (83, 87, 88, 90, 91①②, 92②, 93, 94, 95, 96, 98年)

carve (90, 97年)

carving (83年)

case (86, 90, 93, 94年)

cash (98年)

cast-iron (87年)

castle (94年)

cattle (98年)

casual (87, 91①年)

casually (84, 85, 97年)

catch (84, 86, 91②, 97年)

cause (83, 84, 85, 86, 88, 91②, 92①②, 93, 94, 95, 96, 97, 98年)

cautious (90年)

cautiously (86年)

cavity (96年)

ceiling (90年)

celebrate (87年)

celebration (84, 87, 88, 96年)

cell (96, 97年)

center (88, 95, 97年)

central (88, 94, 98年)

century (83, 85, 88, 90, 91①, 92①, 93, 94年)

CEO (91年②)

cereal (91年②)

cerebral (96年)

ceremony (83, 89, 90年)

certain (85, 86, 89, 91②, 92②, 93, 94, 95, 96年)

certainly (84, 90, 91①, 94年)

chain (92年②)

challenge (83, 92①, 96, 98年)

challenging (92①, 95年)

championship (91年①)

Champs Elysees (87年)

chance (84, 90, 91①, 92②, 94年)

change (84, 85, 91①②, 92①, 94, 95, 96, 97, 98年)

channel (91②, 97年)

chapter (96年)

character (84, 91①②, 96年)

characteristic (95年)

charcoal (95年)

charge (83, 92②, 95年)

charity (86, 97年)

charm (90, 91①, 92①年)

charming (84年)

chart (92年①)

chatter (98年)

cheat (89, 98年)

check (86, 89, 97年)

cheer (86年)

cheerleader (95年)

cheese (94年)

chef (94年)

chemical (88, 91②, 92②, 97年)

cherish (94年)

chess (95年)

chest (98年)

chew (91年①)

chief (91年②)

chiefly (86年)

childbearing (91①, 92②年)

childhood (91年①)

children (98年)

chili (92年②)

chill (98年)

chimpanzee (90年)

China (97年)

chisel (97年)

chocolate (96, 98年)

choice (84, 87, 96年)

choir (91①, 98年)

cholesterol (92年②)

choose (91②, 92①, 93, 97年)

chop (91年①)

chores (90, 91②年)

chosen (95, 98年)

Christmas (88, 90年)

Christmas Eve (93年)

chronic (95年)

church (86, 87, 98年)

cigarette (83, 91②, 92①, 94年)

cigarette-smoking (87年)

circle (87年)

circulation (96年)

circumstance (90, 92②年)

circus (92年①)

citizen (88, 91②年)

city (98年)

civilization (93, 98年)

claim (86, 91②, 92①, 97年)

clarify (91年①)

clarity (97年)

classical (91①, 93年)

clean (92①, 97年)

clear (95, 97年)

clearly (87, 90, 92①年)

clever (87, 91②年)

client (86年)

cliff (88年)

climate (83, 91①年)

climb (83, 84, 90, 91①, 93, 96年)

climber (86年)

cling (96年)

clinic (86, 92②年)

cloakroom (90年)

cloning (91年①)

close (90, 92②, 93, 96, 97年)

closed (89年)

closely (84, 87, 97, 98年)

closing (90年)

clot (92年②)

cloth (90年)

clothes (91①, 92①, 96年)

clothing (91①, 96年)

cloudy (95年)

clue (83, 89, 90年)

clumsily (84年)

clumsy (93, 97, 98年)

coarse (90年)

coast (83, 84, 88, 96, 98年)

coastline (86年)

coat (98年)

cocaine (94年)

code (84, 91①, 93年)

collapse (85, 89, 94年)

colleague (98年)

collect (86, 91②, 94年)

collection (92年①)

collector (91年②)

college (85, 86, 87, 90, 91②, 94, 95, 96年)

collide (92年①)

collision (84年)

colonize (94年)

colony (92②, 94年)

Colorado (97年)

colorful (90年)

Columbus (98年)

combination (85, 92①, 96年)

comfort (92年②)

comfortable (91①, 96年)

comfortably (87, 94, 96年)

comic book (93年)

command (88, 95, 98年)

commencement (87年)

comment (83, 93, 98年)

commercial (91①②, 94, 98年)

commission (88年)

commitment (92年①)

committee (87, 92②, 98年)

common (83, 89, 91②, 94, 95, 97年)

communicate (85, 91②, 93年)

communication (83, 85, 90, 93, 94, 96年)

communist (97年)

community (87, 92②年)

commute (85, 95年)

companion (93, 96年)

company (96, 97, 98年)

compare (90, 92①, 94年)

compass (98年)

compassion (96年)

compensate (96年)

compensation (88年)

competition (85, 90, 91①②, 92①, 98年)

competitive (92①, 95年)

competitor (97, 98年)

complain (86, 88, 90年)

complaint (84, 92①, 98年)

complete (85, 87, 89, 95, 97, 98年)

completely (84, 86, 94, 95, 96, 98年)

completion (92①, 95年)

complicate (91年②)

complicated (83, 85, 95年)

complication (85年)

compliment (87, 93年)

compose (92①, 97年)

composition (92②, 98年)

compound (97年)

comprehension (86年)

computer (97, 98年)

concentrate (85, 88, 95年)

concentration (85, 89年)

concept (91年①②)

concern (86, 87, 91②, 98年)

concerned (95年)

concerning (96年)

concert (85, 91①年)

conch-shell (93年)

conclude (91②, 92①, 93, 95, 97, 98年)

conclusively (93年)

concrete (98年)

condition (86, 88, 93, 95, 98年)

conditioner (96年)

conduct (88, 91①, 95年)

conductor (91年①)

conference (87, 93年)

confetti (88年)

confidence (83年)

confidential (90年)

confirm (85, 93, 94, 96年)

conflict (87, 90, 91②, 92①, 94, 95, 96年)

confuse (93年)

confusing (91年①②)

congestion (84年)

congratulate (85年)

congratulation (85年)

connect (84, 89, 91②, 97年)

connection (86, 87, 92②, 94, 95, 96年)

conscious (92①②, 94年)

consciously (91①, 94年)

consciousness (91年①)

consecrate (87年)

consequence (98年)

consequently (84, 88, 93, 94年)

conservative (91①, 92②年)

consider (83, 88, 90, 92②, 94, 96, 97年)

considerably (90年)

considerate (92年②)

consideration (87, 92②年)

consist (87, 92①, 94, 95年)

consistent (98年)

constant (83, 95年)

constantly (88, 92①②, 98年)

constitution (91年①)

construct (94, 95年)

construction (96, 97年)

constructive (86年)

consular (85年)

consulate (85年)

consultant (91年①)

consume (90, 92②, 96, 97年)

consumer (92年①)

consumption (89年)

contact (83, 88, 93, 94, 98年)

contain (87, 89, 92②, 96, 97, 98年)

container (91年②)

content (83, 90, 92②, 95年)

contest (83, 87, 95年)

context (83, 84年)

continent (91年①)

continually (95年)

continue (84, 86, 88, 92②, 94, 95, 96, 97, 98年)

continuous (89年)

contract (92①②, 98年)

contrary (83, 91①, 95年)

contrast (85, 87, 91②, 95年)

contribute (88, 92②, 93年)

contribution (90, 91①年)

control (88, 92①, 93, 94, 95, 97年)

controversial (87年)

controversy (87年)

convenience (85, 92②年)

convenient (98年)

conversation (91②, 92①, 97年)

converse (87年)

conversely (88, 95, 96年)

convey (92年②)

convince (88, 92①, 96, 97年)

convinced (94年)

cook (98年)

cooperate (98年)

cooperation (87年)

coordination (93年)

cope (97年)

corner (89, 92②年)

corporation (88年)

correct (83, 90, 94年)

correspondence (98年)

cortex (96年)

cost (98年)

cotton (96年)

cough (83年)

count (89, 96年)

countdown (87年)

countenance (85年)

country (83, 85, 90, 91②, 92②, 93, 94, 96, 97, 98年)

countryside (89, 92②年)

county (86年)

couple (89, 92①, 96, 97年)

courage (83, 94, 98年)

courageous (83年)

courageously (94年)

course (86, 87, 91②, 92②, 96, 97年)

court (86, 93年)

courteous (89, 92②年)

courtesy (85年)

courtship (85年)

cousin (91年①)

cover (85, 86, 96年)

cow (92②, 96, 98年)

co-worker (88年)

cracker (91①, 96年)

crash (91年①②)

crawl (85, 89年)

crazy (90年)

create (86, 87, 91②, 92①②, 95年)

creation (97年)

creative (92②, 94年)

creativity (90, 94年)

creature (91年①②)

credit card (93年)

creep (94年)

crew (84, 95年)

cricket (96年)

crime (84年)

criminal (84, 91 ①年)

crisis (88年)

crisp (90年)

criticism (83, 86, 96年)

criticize (88, 89, 91 ①, 98年)

crop (94年)

cross-lake (93年)

crowd (87, 88, 89, 91 ①年)

crucial (92年①)

cruelty (96年)

cruise (86, 87年)

crumble (94年)

crush (84年)

crust (96年)

cry (97年)

crystal (92年②)

cuisine (97年)

cultivation (95年)

cultural (91 ①②, 93年)

culture (87, 88, 91 ②, 92 ①, 93, 94, 98年)

cure (91②, 92①年)

curious (84, 85年)

currently (84, 92①, 94年)

curriculum (98年)

curtain (86, 90, 97年)

curve (85年)

custom (93年)

customarily (89年)

customer (91年②)

customs (88年)

cycle (88, 98年)

Czech (97年)

daffodil (89年)

daily (86, 92①, 93, 94, 96年)

dairy (92年②)

damage (83, 85, 88, 91①, 92①, 94, 95, 97, 98年)

damaging (96年)

dance hall (89年)

dancer (97年)

danger (83, 85, 93, 94, 95, 96, 98年)

dangerous (90, 95, 98年)

dangerously (84年)

dangling (92年②)

dare (90, 94年)

Darwin (98年)

data (86, 96年)

date (85, 92②, 98年)

daughter (91年①)

daytime (98年)

deadline (98年)

deadly (93, 94年)

dead-mail (89年)

deal (86, 97, 98年)

dealer (91②, 94年)

death (84, 95, 96年)

death toll (84年)

decade (92②, 93, 94, 96年)

deceive (90年)

deceiving (93年)

decent (95年)

deception (92年①)

decide (86, 89, 90, 91②, 92①, 93, 95, 97, 98年)

decision (89, 92②, 94, 96年)

declaration (93年)

declare (88, 89年)

decline (95年)

decomposer (88年)

decomposition (88年)

decorate (87, 88年)

decoration (94, 97年)

decrease (87, 91②, 92①, 96年)

deed (83年)

deem (84年)

deeply (93年)

defeat (91①, 92①, 96年)

defend (97年)

defensive (96年)

define (97年)

definite (87年)

definitely (90, 92①年)

definition (85, 94年)

degrade (87年)

degree (88, 91②, 94年)

delay (85, 92①, 97年)

delegate (91年①)

delegation (95年)

delete (93年)

deliberate (89年)

deliberately (83年)

delicious (91②, 92②年)

delight (89, 90, 96年)

delighted (87年)

deliver (87, 89, 92②, 93年)

delivery (91①②, 98年)

demand (89, 90, 91②, 94, 97年)

demanding (94年)

demonstrate (90, 91①, 94年)

dense (97年)

dentist (96年)

depart (86, 92②, 95年)

department (83, 84, 91②年)

departure (86年)

depend (88, 92②, 94, 96年)

dependent (88, 92②, 95年)

depletion (84年)

deposit (95, 98年)

depress (94年)

depressed (86, 92①年)

depressing (87年)

depression (84, 97年)

describe (87, 88, 91①, 92②, 93, 95年)

describes (98年)

description (85, 98年)

descriptive (87年)

desert (93年)

deserted (94年)

deserve (83, 86, 88, 93, 95, 96年)

design (84, 87, 92②, 93, 94, 97年)

designate (90年)

designer (92①, 96年)

desirable (92年①)

desirably (90年)

desire (86, 91②, 93年)

despite (86, 87, 88, 98年)

dessert (84, 91②年)

destination (87, 91①, 98年)

destine (94年)

destroy (83, 86, 89, 90, 96, 97年)

destruction (89, 97年)

detail (86, 92①, 95年)

detailed (93年)

detect (85, 90, 96年)

determination (95年)

determine (90, 91②, 92②, 96年)

determined (85, 86年)

devastate (94年)

develop (83, 86, 88, 91②, 92①②, 94, 95, 96, 98年)

development (83, 92①, 98年)

device (85, 97年)

devise (92年①)

devoid (94年)

devote (95, 96年)

devoted (83年)

diagnose (87年)

diagnosis (86, 89年)

diaper (92年①)

dictionary (85年)

die (96年)

diet (88, 91②, 92②, 93, 95, 98年)

dieting (98年)

differ (96, 98年)

difference (86, 90, 91②, 93, 94, 95, 96, 97, 98年)

different (83, 88, 92①②, 94, 95, 96, 97, 98年)

differently (91②, 95, 96, 98年)

difficult (83, 86, 87, 90, 92①, 95, 97年)

difficulty (84, 87, 89, 92①②, 97年)

dig (92年②)

digest (96, 97年)

digestive (92②, 94年)

digital (91年②)

digital camera (91年②)

dignify (87, 88年)

diligently (98年)

diminish (83, 96年)

diner (90年)

dinning hall (90年)

dinning room (87年)

dioxin (92年②)

diploma (88年)

direct (88, 96年)

direction (86, 91②, 94, 98年)

director (93, 94, 96年)

directory (91年①②)

disability (98年)

disabled (86年)

disagreement (94年)

disappear (91①, 94, 96年)

disappoint (96年)

disappointed (91①, 95年)

disappointing (91年①)

disappointment (91①, 94年)

disaster (86, 91①, 92①, 94, 97, 98年)

disciple (97年)

discipline (85, 91②, 92②年)

disclose (92年①)

discomfort (94年)

disconnect (93年)

discourage (84, 96年)

discover (83, 85, 86, 89, 90, 93年)

discovery (85, 90, 91①②年)

discriminate (93年)

discrimination (92年①)

discuss (87, 96年)

discussion (84, 88, 92②, 93, 98年)

disease (91②, 92①, 93, 95, 98年)

disguise (94年)

dish (91②, 98年)

dishonest (98年)

disk (86年)

dislike (89, 91①年)

dismantling (84年)

dismiss (83, 88年)

disorder (92②, 98年)

display (84, 90年)

disposable (86, 92②年)

dispose (86, 92①②年)

dispute (87, 90年)

disrupt (95年)

disruption (94年)

dissolve (96年)

distance (94, 96, 97年)

distantly (91年①②)

distinct (94, 95年)

distinguished (92年②)

distribute (92②, 93年)

distribution (96年)

district (87年)

distrust (98年)

disturb (83, 87, 94, 95年)

disturbance (90年)

ditch (86年)

dive (91年①)

division (88, 96年)

document (88, 91②, 92①, 96 年)
dolphin (91 年②)
domestic (92 年①)
dominance (97 年)
dominate (91 年①)
donate (86 年)
donation (93, 96 年)
donkey (91 年①)
donor (86, 93 年)
doodle (98 年)
dormitory (91 年①②)
dose (91 年②)
doubt (89, 91 91 年)
doubtful (83, 90 年)
down-to-earth (91 年②)
downward (96 年)
dozen (91 年②)
Dr. (98 年)
drag (95 年)
dragon (91 年①)
dramatic (96, 97 年)
drastically (89 年)
draw (85 年)
drawback (98 年)
drawing (93 年)
dread (95 年)
dreaded (89 年)
dreadful (94 年)
dreary (85 年)
dress-down (91 年①)
drift (86 年)
drink (98 年)
drive (98 年)
drop (85, 87, 89, 90, 94 年)
drowning (83 年)
drowsiness (94 年)
drug (90, 91②, 93, 94 年)
dry (84, 95, 96, 97 年)
due (95, 97 年)

dull (92 年①)
dump (88 年)
durable (86 年)
duration (85 年)
during (96, 97, 98 年)
dust (91②, 94 年)
dutifully (91 年①)
duty (88 年)
dwarf (93 年)
dwell (95 年)
dwelling (94 年)
eagerly (88 年)
eagle (93 年)
earn (86, 90, 95, 97 年)
earner (88 年)
earth (87, 88, 91 ①, 92 ①, 93, 96, 98 年)
earthquake (90, 96, 98 年)
ease (97, 98 年)
easily (92 年①)
east (83, 86 年)
east-central (96 年)
Easter (98 年)
eastern (86 年)
eat (96 年)
eater (98 年)
eating (98 年)
ecological (87, 88 年)
economic (92②, 98 年)
economical (84 年)
economist (92 年②)
economy (88, 98 年)
editor (88, 96 年)
educate (92①, 96 年)
education (87, 88, 90, 91 ①②, 92 ①, 95, 96 年)
educational (92①②, 96 年)
effect (83, 85, 87, 92 ①②, 95, 97, 98 年)

effective (92②, 93, 96 年)
efficient (88, 91 ①, 94 年)
efficiently (85 年)
effort (90, 92 ①, 93, 94, 98 年)
egg-timer (87 年)
elaborate (84 年)
elder (91 年②)
elderly (86 年)
elect (98 年)
election (92 年②)
electric (91 年①)
electrical (94 年)
electrical short (94 年)
electricity (98 年)
electromagnetic (94 年)
electronic (88 年)
elegant (88, 90 年)
element (83, 92①, 97 年)
elevator (83, 92①年)
eliminate (92②, 93 年)
eloquence (88 年)
else (83, 86, 90, 92②年)
e-mail (98 年)
embarrassed (88 年)
embarrassment (89 年)
embassy (85 年)
embrace (96, 98 年)
embryo (86 年)
emergency (83, 93 年)
emotion (96, 97 年)
emotional (95, 96 年)
emotionally (88, 91 ②, 96 年)
emperor (95 年)
emphasize (88, 97, 98 年)
employ (92 年②)
employee (91 ①, 98 年)
employer (91 年①)
employment (91 ①, 92①年)
empty (88, 92 ②年)

enable (86, 95, 96年)

enclose (89年)

encounter (87年)

encourage (84, 85, 86, 87, 91②, 94年)

encouragement (83, 84年)

encouraging (96年)

end (96, 98年)

endanger (94, 96年)

endless (86年)

enduring (86年)

enemy (88, 91②, 93年)

energetic (88年)

energy (84, 86, 89, 91②, 94, 95, 98年)

engage (86年)

engine (86, 95年)

engineer (86, 97年)

engineering (91①, 95, 97, 98年)

England (97年)

enjoy (96, 97年)

enjoyable (87, 90, 92②, 97年)

enjoyment (94年)

enlarge (91年②)

enormous (84, 88, 91②, 96年)

enough (97, 98年)

ensure (87, 88, 93, 96年)

enter (96, 98年)

entertain (88, 92①年)

entertainment (92①, 94, 96年)

enthusiastic (88, 91②年)

enthusiastically (83年)

entire (84, 97年)

entirely (92年②)

entrance (85, 95年)

entry (85, 94年)

envelope (94年)

enviously (91年①)

environment (84, 88, 95, 97, 98年)

environmental (84, 85, 87, 88, 91①, 92②, 94, 98年)

episode (91年①)

equal (91①, 94年)

equally (90, 97年)

equator (96年)

equip (90年)

equipment (83, 86, 88, 94年)

erase (98年)

erratic (98年)

erect (87年)

escape (83, 91①②, 93, 95, 97年)

escorted (88年)

especially (89, 91②, 92②, 94, 96, 97, 98年)

essential (86, 92②, 95, 96年)

establish (83, 86, 96年)

estimate (91①, 92①②, 95, 98年)

estimated (88年)

etc. (88年)

eternal (93, 94年)

EU (94年)

(= European Union)

Europe (87, 90, 91①, 93, 94, 95, 97, 98年)

European (83, 94年)

evaluate (96年)

even (91②, 95, 96, 97, 98年)

evening (96年)

evenly (92②, 93年)

event (86, 88, 89, 91②, 92①, 97, 98年)

eventually (85, 88, 90, 91①②, 92①, 97年)

ever (88, 91②, 92①, 97, 98年)

everlasting (93, 94年)

evidence (84, 92②, 95年)

evident (94年)

evil (86, 96年)

evolution (88, 98年)

evolve (86, 93年)

exactly (84, 90, 92②, 94, 96年)

exaggerate (91年②)

examination (87年)

examine (86年)

example (96, 97, 98年)

exceed (92年①)

excel (93年)

excellent (88, 89, 96年)

except (88, 89, 91①年)

exception (88年)

exchange (86, 89, 91②, 98年)

excite (90年)

excited (88, 89年)

excitedly (92年①)

exciting (91②, 92①年)

exclamation (91年②)

exclude (93年)

excuse (84, 96年)

execute (93年)

executive (91②, 96年)

exercise (92①, 93, 95年)

exhale (87年)

exhaust (86, 94, 98年)

exhausted (88年)

exhaustion (98年)

exhibition (87, 90年)

exist (84年)

existence (93年)

existing (90, 97年)

expand (88, 93, 94, 96年)

expect (84, 87, 91②, 92②, 94, 96, 97, 98年)

expectation (92②, 97年)

expectedly (94年)

expel (84年)

expense (95, 96年)

expensive (84, 89, 92②, 94, 96年)

experience (86, 87, 88, 91②, 94, 95, 96, 97年)

experiment (95, 97年)

expert (84, 86, 91②, 93, 94, 96年)

explain (89, 90, 91①②, 92①②, 94, 95, 96, 98年)

explicit (89, 98年)

explicitly (92年②)

explode (92①, 95年)

explore (91①, 92②, 96年)

explorer (83年)

explosion (94年)

explosive (84年)

export (92年②)

expose (92②, 95, 98年)

exposure (86, 90年)

express (85, 88, 91①, 93, 94, 96年)

expression (86, 92①②, 96年)

expressive (86年)

extend (98年)

extension (87, 92②, 94, 96年)

extensive (86年)

extensively (86年)

extent (90, 95年)

external (90年)

extinct (88年)

extra (85, 86, 89, 91①②, 92①, 95年)

extraordinary (90, 95年)

extreme (92②, 95年)

extremely (85, 87年)

eyebrow (93年)

fable (91②, 98年)

fabric (96年)

face (83, 89, 93, 95年)

facial (92年②)

facilitate (84年)

fact (98年)

factor (91②, 92②, 98年)

factory (87, 92②, 94年)

factual (91年②)

fade (94年)

fail (87, 91①, 92①, 95, 96年)

failure (90, 98年)

faint (86年)

fair (91①, 94年)

fairly (84年)

fairy (93年)

faith (92年①)

fall (88, 91①, 93, 98年)

false (88, 91①, 93年)

falsify (91年①)

fame (91年①)

familiar (93, 96, 98年)

family (96年)

family-sized (93年)

famous (83, 84, 86, 90, 91①②, 92①, 94, 96, 98年)

fan (88, 90, 91②, 95年)

fantasize (91①, 94年)

fantastic (91①, 92②年)

fantasy (91年①)

far (96年)

farmland (94年)

fascinate (90, 92①年)

fascinating (91年①)

fascination (90年)

fashion (92①, 96年)

fashionable (90年)

fast (98年)

fasten (96年)

fatal (94年)

father-in-law (89年)

fatty (92年②)

faulty (85年)

favor (91①, 92②年)

favorable (92①, 95年)

favorably (90年)

favorite (90, 92①, 95, 96, 97, 98年)

fear (87年)

feat (95, 97年)

feature (84, 90, 91②, 92①, 97, 98年)

fee (85, 86年)

feed (92年②)

feel (96年)

feeling (96年)

feet (85年)

female (93, 97年)

fence (84年)

fermentation (95年)

ferment (97年)

fertilize (98年)

fever (90年)

few (97年)

fiber (92年②)

fiction (91年①)

field (85, 91②, 92②, 94, 98年)

fierce (92年②)

fifth (96年)

fight (87, 90, 91②, 92②, 94, 96, 97年)

fighter (91年②)

figure (84, 88, 95年)

file (91年②)

fill (86, 94, 98年)

film (90, 94年)

film camera (91年②)

final (90, 97, 98年)

finally (84, 87, 88, 89, 90, 91①, 92①②, 94, 95年)

finance (96年)

financial (84, 88, 91①年)

finding (96, 98 年)

fine (83, 86, 90, 95 年)

finger (97 年)

finish (83, 84, 85, 86, 88, 89, 92 ②, 97, 98 年)

firefly (93 年)

firework (94 年)

firm (92 ①, 98 年)

firmly (87 年)

first (96 年)

firstly (98 年)

firstborn (92 年②)

fisher (86 年)

fisherman (91 年②)

fishing net (91 年②)

fishing ship (91 年①)

fit (84, 85, 94 年)

fix (90, 94, 98 年)

fixed (88 年)

flash (93, 97 年)

flashlight (93 年)

flavor (93, 97 年)

flexible (88, 92 ②, 98 年)

flight (84, 85, 88, 92 ①, 93, 94 年)

float (89 年)

flock (91 年②)

flooding (93 年)

floor (83, 92 ①, 98 年)

flourish (92 年①)

flow (88, 92 ①年)

fluent (91 年①)

fluff (96 年)

flutter (89 年)

fly (98 年)

flying (98 年)

focus (86, 88 年)

fold (83, 90, 98 年)

folk (84, 86, 91 ②, 92 ①年)

folklore (98 年)

follow (85, 86, 87, 92 ②, 95, 96, 97, 98 年)

following (83, 84, 85, 86, 87, 88, 89, 90, 91 ①②, 92 ①, 93, 94, 96, 97, 98 年)

food (96 年)

foot (83, 87, 88, 91 ①, 96 年)

football (84, 95 年)

footprint (98 年)

force (91 ①, 93 年)

foreign (84, 85, 88, 94 年)

foreigner (85, 92 ②, 97 年)

foresee (97 年)

forest (86, 91 ①, 97 年)

forever (89, 92 ②, 94 年)

forget (94 年)

fork (90 年)

form (85, 87, 88, 89, 90, 91 ②, 96 年)

formal (87, 90, 91 ①, 92 ①年)

formality (90 年)

formally (87 年)

formation (96 年)

forthcoming (95 年)

fortunate (91 年①②)

fortune (86, 96 年)

forward (83, 89, 92 ②, 98 年)

found (90 年)

foundation (92 ①, 96 年)

fourth (96 年)

fragrance (84, 97 年)

franc (87 年)

France (97 年)

frankly (96 年)

fragrance (98 年)

freak (92 年①)

freely (84 年)

freeway (85 年)

French-fried (90 年)

frequent (93, 94 年)

frequently (85, 91 ②, 92 ①, 93 年)

fresh (91 ①②, 92 ②年)

fried (90, 95 年)

friendliness (97 年)

friendly (84, 88, 91 ②年)

friendship (97 年)

frighten (91 年①)

frightened (88 年)

frog (88 年)

front (89, 98 年)

frown (92 年②)

frozen (97 年)

fruit (98 年)

fruitful (90 年)

frustrating (91 年①)

fuel (96 年)

fulfill (91 ①, 94 年)

full (96, 98 年)

fully (90, 92 ①, 93 年)

function (87, 95, 97 年)

fund (90, 97 年)

funding (96 年)

fungi (88 年)

funny (86, 87, 88, 95 年)

fur (96 年)

fur-free (96 年)

furiously (92 年②)

furniture (86, 92 ②年)

furthermore (83, 84, 97 年)

future (84, 88, 90, 91 ②, 93, 94, 97, 98 年)

gadget (91 年②)

gain (89, 91 ①②, 94 年)

gallery (88 年)

gallon (84, 90 年)

game (96, 98 年)

gang (84 年)

garbage (97 年)

garden (84, 89, 92 ②年)

gash (88年)

gasoline (88年)

gather (93年)

gathering (91年①)

gaze (85, 90年)

gear (95年)

gender (93年)

gene (90年)

general (85, 89, 90年)

generality (88年)

generally (85, 91 ②, 92 ①②, 94, 98年)

generate (86, 92 ①年)

generation (91 ②, 93, 96年)

generous (83, 90, 96, 97年)

generously (86, 88, 97年)

genetic (84, 91 ①年)

genetics (93年)

genius (84, 90年)

gentle (87年)

gentleman (88, 92 ①年)

geographical (88年)

geography (93, 95, 96年)

get-together (85年)

giant (87, 91 ①, 98年)

gift (85, 90, 91 ②, 92 ②年)

given (87, 92 ②, 98年)

glacier (97年)

gladly (85, 89年)

glance (89, 90年)

glasses (84年)

glide (95年)

global (92 ①, 93, 98年)

globally (92年②)

glory (95年)

glue (98年)

goal (87, 91 ①②, 93, 94, 95年)

goat (86, 96年)

god (92①, 93年)

gold (90, 92 ②, 93年)

golden (89, 90年)

golf (95年)

goodness (91年②)

good-quality (86年)

goods (85, 90, 91 ②年)

gorgeous (84年)

gorgeously (84年)

gorilla (95年)

govern (98年)

government (83, 84, 87, 90, 91 ①, 94, 96, 97年)

governmental (96年)

grab (95, 98年)

graceful (90年)

grade (88, 98年)

grader (95年)

gradual (91年①②)

gradually (86, 87, 90, 98年)

graduate (87, 96年)

graduation (84, 87, 90年)

grain (98年)

gram (92年②)

grammar (91年②)

grandfather (93年)

grandly (87, 88年)

grandmother (85, 93年)

grandson (85, 90年)

grass (92年②)

grateful (86年)

gratefully (97年)

graze (96年)

grazing (98年)

great (96, 97, 98年)

greedy (91年②)

green (98年)

greening (98年)

greet (83, 86, 96年)

grieve (94年)

grin (93年)

grind (88年)

grit (98年)

gross (92年①)

ground (84, 91 ①, 93, 94, 98年)

group (84, 87, 88, 89, 92 ①②, 95, 98年)

grow (84, 86, 91 ②, 92 ①②, 94, 97年)

growing (90, 91 ②, 92 ②, 93, 97, 98年)

growth (93, 96, 97年)

guess (89, 93年)

guest (85, 89, 90, 94年)

guidance (96年)

guitar (92 ①, 94年)

gun (91年②)

guru (97年)

gutter (87年)

guy (91年①)

habit (86, 93, 94, 98年)

habitual (93年)

hacker (84年)

hacking (84年)

hairstyle (91年①)

half (95, 96年)

hall (83, 87, 91 ①年)

Halloween (96年)

hallway (88年)

halt (88年)

handle (92 ②, 97年)

handout (92年②)

handsome (89, 91 ①年)

handwriting (98年)

handwritten (91年②)

handy (85年)

happen (86, 87, 88, 89, 90, 91 ①, 93, 94, 96年)

happily (84, 88, 94, 96年)

happiness (94年)

happy endings (91年①)

happy-natured (85年)

hard (97, 98年)

hardly (84, 87, 88, 89, 91①, 92①, 95, 96年)

hardship (90年)

hare (98年)

harm (92②, 93年)

harmful (83, 95年)

harmony (98年)

harsh (87, 90年)

harvest (94, 97年)

hate (88年)

hateful (89年)

Hawaii (98年)

head (96, 98年)

headache (97年)

headlamp (93年)

headline (83年)

heal (92①, 96年)

healer (92年①)

healing (92①, 93, 95年)

health (87, 88, 91②, 92①②, 94, 95, 97年)

healthful (98年)

health care (91②, 92①年)

health food (92年②)

Health Ministry (93年)

healthcare (91年②)

health-conscious (92年②)

healthiest (84年)

healthy (90, 92①②, 95, 96, 98年)

hear (96年)

hearing (96年)

heart (86, 91①, 92②, 93, 97年)

heart attack (84, 86, 93年)

heart disease (92年①)

heartbeat (87年)

heartily (88年)

heat (95, 97, 98年)

heavily (89, 94年)

heavy (84, 85, 87, 88, 89, 91①, 92①年)

hectare (94年)

height (89, 96年)

help (96年)

helpful (90, 91②, 92①, 97年)

hemisphere (85, 98年)

herb (92年①②)

herd (90, 96年)

heritage (97年)

hero (83, 88, 91②, 95年)

hesitate (87年)

hesitation (91①, 96, 97年)

hidden (89, 98年)

high (96, 97, 98年)

highlight (94, 97, 98年)

highly (91①②, 92①②, 93, 96年)

high-tech (94年)

highway (84年)

highway-dividing (84年)

hike (86, 91①年)

hiking (87, 88年)

hill (89, 93, 96年)

Himalayas (96年)

hip-hop (92年①)

hire (91①, 92②年)

historic (94年)

historical (88, 91②年)

historically (93年)

history (83, 87, 89, 92①②, 93, 98年)

hit (88, 91①, 92①, 96年)

hoist (84年)

hold (85, 86, 87, 89, 93, 97, 98年)

hole (85, 95年)

holiday (86, 91②, 92①年)

holy (92年①)

home country (93年)

homeless (94年)

homesick (97年)

hometown (86年)

honesty (92年②)

honeybee (98年)

honor (83, 88, 96, 97年)

honorably (88年)

hope (96, 97, 98年)

hopeful (87年)

hormone (95年)

horn (96年)

horse (97年)

horseback (97年)

hospital (92年②)

host (83, 89, 98年)

hot dog (92年②)

hotel (97年)

hour (96年)

household (86, 91②, 93年)

house-hold (92年②)

housewife (91年②)

housing (92年②)

however (83, 84, 85, 86, 87, 88, 89, 90, 91②, 92①②, 93, 94, 96, 97, 98年)

howl (97年)

howler (97年)

hug (92年②)

huge (88, 90, 91②, 97年)

human (83, 85, 87, 90, 91②, 92②, 94, 96, 97年)

human being (83, 84, 85, 86, 96年)

humane (96年)

humanity (86年)

humble (91年②)

humor (93年)

humorous (98年)
hundred (91年②)
hunger (89年)
hungry (97年)
hunt (84年)
hurricane (88年)
hurry (88, 92②年)
hurt (83, 86, 90, 94, 97年)
husband (90年)
hymn (98年)
ice (97年)
idea (96, 97, 98年)
ideal (91②, 97年)
ideally (95年)
identical (91年①)
identify (93, 98年)
identity (88, 98年)
idiotic (89年)
ignore (87, 91①②, 92①, 94, 95, 96年)
ill (91②, 96年)
illegible (89年)
illness (86, 91②, 92①, 95年)
ill-timed (84年)
ill-treat (91年①)
illuminate (87年)
illustrate (91年①)
illustration (92年①)
image (90, 91②, 94, 98年)
imaginary land (91年①)
imagination (90, 91②年)
imaginative (91②, 93年)
imagine (91年②)
imitate (92年②)
imitation (92②, 98年)
immediate (88年)
immediately (86, 88, 92①②, 94年)
immense (83年)

immigrant (85, 98年)
immune (97年)
immune system (87年)
impact (85, 86, 91①, 98年)
impatiently (84年)
implication (85年)
imply (98年)
impolite (92年②)
impolitely (91年①)
importance (83, 85, 87, 92①, 94, 97, 98年)
important (83, 84, 85, 86, 88, 90, 91①②, 92②, 94, 95, 96, 98年)
importantly (84, 92②, 94年)
impossible (83, 85, 89年)
impossibly (84年)
impracticably (84年)
impress (84, 88, 91①, 98年)
impression (92①, 94, 95年)
impressive (94, 98年)
improper (91年①)
improve (91①②, 98年)
improvement (83, 91②年)
impulse (93年)
inadequate (89年)
inappropriate (87, 98年)
inattentive (96年)
inboard (86年)
inch (88, 89年)
incident (86, 93, 94, 96年)
inclination (90年)
incline (88年)
include (87, 88, 90, 92②, 94年)
included (85, 93年)
including (85, 86, 92②, 93, 96年)
income (92年②)
inconvenience (84年)
increase (85, 87, 91②, 94, 96, 97, 98年)

increasing (84, 93, 98年)
increasingly (90年)
indeed (86, 88, 92①, 93, 94, 96年)
India (96年)
Indian (96, 97年)
indicate (83, 85, 89, 93年)
indifferent (94年)
individual (83, 84, 85, 88, 91①②年)
individually (87, 98年)
indoor (88年)
indoors (94年)
indulge (95年)
industry (86, 88, 91①, 96, 98年)
inevitable (83年)
inexpensive (92年②)
infant (90, 92②年)
infection (87, 97年)
infectious (86年)
infer (86, 89, 90, 92①②, 94, 95年)
inferior (91年②)
infest (94年)
inflated (88年)
influence (91②, 92②, 95, 97, 98年)
influential (92①, 96年)
influentially (94年)
inform (88, 93, 94, 95, 98年)
informal (87, 89年)
information (85, 86, 88, 92①②, 94, 98年)
ingredient (91②, 93年)
initial (85年)
injure (92①, 95年)
injury (84年)
inn (85年)
inner (86年)
inning (95年)
innocent (96年)
innovative (87, 92①年)

input (98年)

inquiringly (87年)

insect (94, 95年)

insecticide (93年)

insensitive (87年)

inside (86, 88, 89, 90, 91①, 92②, 94, 95, 97年)

insist (86, 88, 90, 94年)

insomnia (97年)

inspection (94年)

inspire (86, 90, 97年)

install (87, 92①年)

instance (84, 85, 97年)

instant (91年②)

instead (83, 87, 91①, 96, 98年)

instinctive (85年)

institute (87, 98年)

instruct (95年)

instruction (86, 87, 97年)

instrument (92①, 95, 98年)

insulation (94年)

insult (90年)

insurance (88, 98年)

insure (98年)

intellectual (84年)

intellectually (91年②)

intelligence (87年)

intelligently (87年)

intelligible (84年)

intend (88, 91①, 92②, 93, 98年)

intensify (91年②)

intensity (88, 90, 97年)

intensive (91①, 92②年)

intention (93年)

intentionally (86, 98年)

interact (86, 92②年)

interaction (93, 95年)

interest (87, 88, 91①, 93, 97年)

interested (87, 88年)

interesting (84, 91①, 96, 98年)

interestingly (97年)

interference (92年①)

interfering (95年)

internal (90, 94年)

international (88, 91①, 93, 94, 95, 96, 97, 98年)

internet (95年)

inter-office (98年)

interpersonal (96年)

interpret (90年)

interpretation (95年)

interrupt (89, 92①②, 93, 98年)

interview (88, 91①年)

intimacy (86年)

intimate (86, 87, 97年)

intimately (85, 92①年)

intolerant (94年)

intonation (91年②)

introduce (83, 90, 91②, 95年)

introduction (88, 95年)

introductory (85年)

intuition (85年)

invade (94, 97年)

invariably (98年)

invent (83, 90年)

invention (83, 94年)

invest (91②, 98年)

investigate (98年)

invisible (84年)

invisibly (92年②)

invitation (95年)

invite (85, 89, 93年)

inviting (95年)

involve (85, 91②, 97, 98年)

involvement (92②, 95, 97年)

iron (87, 90, 97年)

ironic (91年②)

irritation (98年)

island (86, 87, 88, 92②, 94, 98年)

issue (83, 84, 85, 92②, 96, 98年)

itch (97年)

item (84, 86, 89, 90, 91②, 92②, 94年)

ivory (90年)

jackknife (88年)

jail (83, 93年)

Japan (97年)

jaw (92年②)

jealous (97年)

jeans (92年①)

jet (94年)

jetlag (88年)

jingle (98年)

job (96年)

jog (95年)

join (85, 88, 91②, 97年)

jointly (98年)

joke (91①, 93年)

jolly (89年)

journalism (88年)

journey (90, 91①, 94年)

joy (85年)

joyfully (88年)

judge (88, 92①年)

judgmental (94年)

June (98年)

jungle (88年)

junior (95年)

justification (93年)

justify (96年)

keen (91年①)

keep (96年)

keeper (90, 97年)

khaki (91年①)

kick (94, 95年)

kid (96, 98年)

kill (91②, 92②, 94, 95, 96, 97年)

killing (96年)

kind (97, 98年)

kindergarten (98年)

kilogram (89, 97年)

kind-hearted (90年)

kindly (87年)

kitchen (98年)

knife (91②, 97, 98年)

knock (96年)

knot (86年)

knowledge (87, 88, 91②, 92①年)

known (83, 87, 96, 98年)

label (91②, 97年)

laboratory (89, 90年)

lack (84, 90, 91②, 92①年)

lacking (92年②)

lag (94年)

lake (89, 96, 97年)

land (88, 90, 93, 94, 97年)

landing (95年)

landmark (93年)

landscape (96年)

landslide (88, 93年)

land-visa (85年)

language (83, 85, 91①②, 95, 98年)

large (96年)

largely (84, 97年)

laser (87年)

last (89, 90, 92①, 94, 96, 97年)

last name (84年)

lasting (86年)

lastly (86, 98年)

late (89, 90, 94年)

later (84, 86, 88, 89, 90, 92②, 94, 96, 97年)

latest (84, 89, 96年)

latter (89年)

laughingly (86年)

laughter (86, 87, 89年)

launch (93, 97年)

law (83, 85, 98年)

lawn (94, 98年)

lawyer (86, 92①, 98年)

lay (87年)

lazy (92年②)

lead (91①, 92①, 94, 97, 98年)

leader (87, 93, 94, 96年)

leadership (92, 98②年)

leading (86, 92①, 93, 96年)

leaf (85, 95年)

learn (96, 97年)

least (88, 95, 97年)

leather (90, 96年)

leave (86, 90, 95, 96, 97年)

lecture (92年②)

left (85年)

left-brained (85年)

leg (97年)

legal (90, 96年)

legend (91②, 92①, 93年)

legendary (93年)

legislator (94年)

leisurely (90年)

lend (89年)

length (97年)

lengthen (86年)

lengthy (89年)

less (96, 97年)

lessen (92②, 94年)

lesson (91①, 95, 98年)

let (97年)

letter (83, 88, 98年)

level (92②, 94, 96, 97年)

liberal (92年①)

liberation (89年)

liberty (86年)

librarian (92年②)

library (87, 94年)

license (95年)

lid (89年)

lie (87, 88, 89, 95年)

life (96年)

lifespan (93年)

lifetime (88年)

lift (86, 91①年)

light (84, 87, 89, 91②, 93, 97, 98年)

lighten (91①, 95, 97年)

lightly (95年)

like (97, 98年)

likely (83, 85, 89, 92①②, 94, 96, 98年)

likewise (83, 96年)

limit (83, 86, 87, 95年)

limitation (86, 91①, 95年)

limited (87, 92②, 95, 96年)

Lincoln (97年)

line (84, 92①, 94, 96, 98年)

linguist (89年)

linguistic (89年)

link (84, 88, 92②, 96年)

liquid (87, 92①年)

liquor (84年)

list (85, 86, 89, 98年)

listener (87, 88年)

literate (84年)

literature (91年①②)

litter (97年)

little (97, 98年)

live (96年)

liver (92年①)

livestock (92②, 94年)

living (86, 88, 92②, 93, 98年)

living thing (88年)

lizard (85, 98年)

load (87, 91①年)

loaf (92年②)

lobby (90年)

local (84, 91①, 94年)

localize (88年)

locally (91年①②)

locate (90, 96, 97, 98年)

location (98年)

lock (89年)

lodge (84年)

logic (85, 92①年)

logical (85, 92①年)

lonely (87, 89, 92②年)

long-awaited (94年)

long-dead (93年)

long-term (85年)

loosely (95年)

lose (86, 90, 91②, 92②, 96, 98年)

loser (98年)

loss (85年)

lost (84, 86, 94年)

loud (87, 90, 95, 97, 98年)

loudness (97年)

loved (88年)

lovely (84, 86, 91②年)

low-calorie (84年)

low-cost (92年②)

lower (85, 92②, 95年)

lowly (93年)

loyal (94年)

luck (95年)

luckily (83, 90, 91①年)

lucrative (88年)

lullaby (87年)

luminous (87年)

lunchtime (88年)

lung (83, 87, 91①②, 92①, 94, 98年)

lure (93年)

lush (96年)

luxury (92②, 95年)

M.I.T. (86年)

(= *Made In Taiwan*)

machine (97年)

madness (84年)

mafia (84年)

magazine (94, 96, 98年)

magic (91①, 92①年)

magical (91①, 94, 97年)

magically (90, 92①年)

magician (92年①)

magnetic (95, 98年)

magnetism (98年)

magnificent (96, 97年)

mail (87, 88, 89年)

mailbox (91年②)

main (83, 84, 87, 88, 90, 91①, 92①②, 94, 95, 96, 97, 98年)

mainland (86, 97年)

mainly (87, 89, 91②, 92①②, 93, 95, 96, 97, 98年)

mainsail (86年)

maintain (84, 85, 88, 90, 92①②, 96, 97年)

major (86, 88, 92①②, 93, 96, 98年)

majority (92②, 96年)

make-believe (88年)

maker (92年①)

malaria (93年)

male (93, 97年)

mammal (84, 98年)

manage (86, 89, 91①, 92①②, 95, 98年)

manageable (91①, 97年)

management (90年)

manager (91②, 96, 98年)

mankind (92年②)

manlike (90年)

manpower (92年②)

mansion (90年)

manual (98年)

manufacture (94年)

manufacturer (84, 88, 91②, 94年)

manufacturing (91年①)

manuscript (86, 91②年)

marble (93年)

march (92年②)

margin (89年)

mark (93, 94, 95, 96, 97, 98年)

market (84, 92①②, 97, 98年)

marketer (92年①)

marketing (88, 92①年)

marketplace (94年)

marriage (95年)

marvel (97年)

marvelous (94, 95, 97年)

mask (90年)

mass (90, 96年)

massage (96年)

massaging tub (96年)

master (92年②)

match (98年)

mate (93, 97年)

material (85, 86, 88, 96, 97年)

math (84年)

mating (93年)

matter (83, 84, 93, 95, 96, 98年)

maximize (98年)

maximum (85年)

maybe (87, 91②年)

mayor (83, 87, 88年)

meal (91②, 92②, 94, 96, 98年)

mean (83, 85, 86, 88, 89, 91①, 92①, 94, 95, 96, 97, 98年)

meaning (86, 87, 88, 95, 96年)

meantime (85年)

meanwhile (91②, 95年)

measure (87, 89, 92②, 93, 96, 97年)

meat (92年②)

meatball (92年②)

mechanical (90年)

medal (83年)

medical (88, 92①②, 93, 97年)

medication (91②, 93年)

medicine (86, 87, 91②, 92①, 93, 94年)

medieval (97年)

meet (97年)

meeting (93, 95, 98年)

melancholy (83年)

melt (91①, 97年)

member (86, 87, 91①, 92①②, 95, 96, 97年)

memorable (93年)

memorial (91年①)

memorize (85, 88年)

memory (85, 92②, 97年)

mental (86, 95年)

mention (85, 86, 87, 89, 91①, 92②, 93年)

menu (90年)

mercury (88年)

mere (88年)

merely (96, 97年)

merry (86年)

message (84, 91②, 92②, 94年)

metal (83, 87年)

meter (87, 91①, 95年)

method (83, 91①, 92②, 95年)

metropolitan (91①, 93年)

microgravity (95年)

microphone (89年)

Microsoft (91年②)

middle (89年)

migrate (85年)

mild (97年)

mile (84, 86, 88, 91①②, 97年)

military (88年)

milkshake (98年)

millennium (87年)

millet (92年②)

millimeter (96年)

million (83, 84, 87, 89, 90, 91①②, 92①, 94, 96, 98年)

millionaire (86, 90年)

mind (95, 97, 98年)

miniature (92年①)

minimize (98年)

minimum (92②, 97年)

ministry (85, 91①年)

minor (88年)

minority (96年)

minute (87, 97年)

mirror (92年①)

mischief (97年)

mischievous (90年)

miss (84, 87, 91②, 92①, 97年)

missing (89年)

mission (95, 98年)

mistake (95年)

mistakenly (94年)

mistreat (95年)

mistrust (94年)

misunderstanding (91年②)

mix (95年)

model (91②, 98年)

moderate (97年)

modern (90, 98年)

modern time (91年②)

modestly (90年)

modesty (88年)

modified (92年①)

mole (98年)

mollusk (88年)

moment (84, 86, 89, 94年)

monument (87, 94年)

mood (87, 98年)

moon (88年)

moral (88, 98年)

morale (91年①)

morally (89年)

moreover (84, 88, 92②, 93年)

mosque (94年)

mosquito (93年)

mostly (84, 86, 87, 92①②, 94年)

motion (92年②)

motivate (91①, 92②, 98年)

motivation (91年①)

motor (93, 98年)

motorcycle (91年②)

motorist (84年)

mound (94年)

mount (84年)

mountain (96, 97年)

mouth (92①, 96年)

movable (83年)

move (83, 84, 86, 91①, 92①②, 93, 94, 95, 98年)

movement (86, 89, 90, 95, 96年)

movie (96年)

mud (94年)

mud-brick (94年)

muddy (91年①)

multi-media (84年)

multiple (94年)

mummy (93年)

Muppet (96年)

muscle (87, 92②年)

museum (88, 90, 93, 96, 97年)

musical (87年)

must (96年)

must-have (91年②)

myrtlewood (84年)

mystery (85, 86, 89年)

naively (94年)

name (96, 97年)

naptime (96年)

narrate (98年)

narrowly (91①②, 95, 98年)

NASA (92年①)

nasty (98年)

nation (92年②)

national (84, 85, 96, 97年)

native (83, 87, 91①②, 93, 98年)

natural (88, 89, 93, 94, 97, 98年)

naturally (94年)

nature (85, 88, 89, 90年)

naughty (90年)

navigate (98年)

navigation (87年)

nearby (86, 89, 98年)

nearly (83, 88, 91①, 92②, 94, 97, 98年)

neat (91①, 92①年)

necessarily (86, 95, 98年)

necessary (85, 91①②, 92①, 95, 97年)

necessity (92年②)

necktie (91年①)

need (96, 97年)

needle (98年)

needlessly (96年)

negative (86, 91①②, 95, 96, 97年)

neglect (87, 91②, 95, 96年)

neglected (87年)

negotiate (90, 96年)

neighbor (89, 97年)

neighborhood (89年)

neither (92年②)

nephew (85年)

never (96年)

nervous (94, 98年)

nervously (89年)

nest (92②, 94年)

net (91②, 93年)

network (95, 96年)

neuroscientist (95年)

never-ending (89年)

nevertheless (84, 88, 95年)

newly (96, 97, 98年)

newlywed (88年)

news (96年)

news conference (83年)

news story (96年)

New York (97年)

next (98年)

nicotine (91年②)

niece (85, 89年)

nightclub (84年)

nightlife (88年)

nightmare (96年)

noble (93年)

nobody (90年)

noise (85, 91②, 92②, 96年)

noisy (96年)

non-dreamer (89年)

non-profit (96年)

non-rapid (89年)

nonsense (94年)

non-smoker (83年)

non-visa (85年)

noon (97年)

nor (96年)

normal (83, 90, 92②, 95, 96年)

normally (86, 91②, 98年)

north (86, 94, 97, 98年)

northeastern (86年)

northern (96, 98年)

north-south (98年)

northward (96年)

notably (87年)

note (87, 89, 98年)

notebook (91年②)

noteworthy (96年)

notice (94, 97, 98年)

noticeable (95年)

noticing (95年)

notify (87, 91①②年)

notoriously (89年)

novel (90, 91②年)

nowadays (91②, 92①, 95年)

nuclear (87, 91②年)

nuisance (94, 96年)

number (84, 89, 91②, 94, 96, 97, 98年)

numerous (85年)

nurse (90年)

nutrition (84, 89, 98年)

oblige (89年)

observation (88, 92①, 95年)

observe (92①, 93, 95年)

obtain (85, 88, 89年)

obvious (96, 98年)

obviously (85, 96, 97年)

occasion (88年)

occasionally (85, 91①年)

occupant (84年)

occupation (97年)

occur (83, 89, 91①, 94, 98年)

ocean (91②, 98年)

off-duty (89年)

offend (89年)

offer (84, 85, 86, 88, 91①②, 96年)

office wear (91①, 98年)

officer (83, 88, 91②年)

official (83, 94年)

officially (91②, 93年)

oil (98年)

Olympic (98年)
Olympics (98年)
omega (92年②)
once (87, 88, 89, 90, 91①②, 92①, 94, 96年)
onto (92年②)
onward (85年)
onwards (98年)
open (96年)
open-air (97年)
opening (89年)
opera (84, 91①年)
operate (86, 90年)
operating hour (96年)
operation (91年②)
operator (92年①)
opining (88年)
opinion (86, 88年)
opportunity (91年①)
oppose (91年①)
opposite (84, 87, 91②, 98年)
oppress (85年)
optimistic (94, 95年)
option (89年)
oral (95年)
orbit (88年)
orchestra (92年①)
order (86, 89, 90, 98年)
ordinary (83, 88, 90, 91①②, 95年)
organ (85, 90, 93年)
organic (93, 97年)
organism (86, 88年)
organization (96, 98年)
organize (92①, 98年)
orient (98年)
origin (91②, 93, 97年)
original (84, 85, 90, 91①, 92②年)
originality (84年)

originally (91②, 93, 94, 95, 97, 98年)
originate (92①, 93年)
ornament (90年)
orphanage (90年)
other (97, 98年)
otherwise (90, 92①年)
ought (88年)
outcome (83年)
outdoor (85年)
outdoors (88年)
outer space (91①, 93年)
outgoing (88, 96年)
outlook (91②, 94年)
outside (83, 88, 90, 92①②, 94, 95, 96, 98年)
outward (96年)
overall (91②, 92②, 98年)
overcome (90, 91①年)
overdo (93, 98年)
overhead (93年)
overlook (88年)
oversized (84年)
overstate (91年②)
overtired (91年①)
own (90, 98年)
owner (91年①②)
oxygen (88, 91①, 95年)
P.O. Box (88, 93年)
pace (87年)
Pacific (98年)
package (89, 90, 91①, 97年)
packet (94年)
page (83, 89, 91②, 93, 98年)
pain (94, 95, 97年)
painful (91②, 97年)
painfully (92年①)
painkiller (97年)
painting (91①, 93年)

pair (97年)
pale (86年)
palm (94年)
pamper (96年)
panic (89年)
pants (91年①)
paper-thin (90年)
parachute (95年)
parade (88年)
paradise (91①, 96, 98年)
paragraph (86, 88, 94, 95, 96, 97, 98年)
Paraguay (98年)
Paralympic (98年)
Paralympics (98年)
parent (96年)
parents (98年)
parental (92年②)
parenthood (95年)
parrot (87年)
part (97, 98年)
partial (92年②)
participant (89, 97, 98年)
participate (83, 89, 91②, 98年)
participation (86, 89年)
particular (86, 87, 93, 95年)
particularly (92①②, 96年)
partner (85, 86年)
part-time (95, 96年)
pass (84, 87, 89, 90, 91①, 92②, 93年)
passage (83, 84, 85, 86, 87, 88, 89, 90, 91②, 92①②, 93, 94, 96, 97年)
passenger (92①, 95年)
passers-by (89年)
passionate (95年)
passionately (88年)
passive (86, 95, 98年)
passport (85年)

past (84, 89, 91①, 96年)
pasta (92年②)
pasture (94年)
patchwork (96年)
path (91①, 93年)
patience (83, 89年)
patient (90, 91②, 92①, 97年)
pattern (90, 91②, 92①, 95, 97年)
pause (97年)
pave (91年②)
pay (96年)
paycheck (96年)
payment (91②, 92②年)
payoff (92年①)
peace (97, 98年)
peace-loving (90年)
peasant (98年)
peculiar (83年)
pediatric (96年)
peel (90年)
pencilwomanship (98年)
penniless (90年)
penny (83年)
per (88, 96年)
perceive (98年)
percent (89, 90, 91①②, 92①, 94, 96, 97年)
percentage (91①, 92②, 96年)
perception (88, 98年)
perfect (91①②, 92②, 98年)
perfectly (97年)
perform (91①, 92①, 93, 95, 97年)
performance (83, 92①, 93, 94年)
perhaps (85, 87, 89, 90, 92①, 94年)
period (95, 97, 98年)
perish (93年)

permanent (92年①)
permanently (86, 97年)
permission (83, 96年)
permit (83, 98年)
persist (94年)
personal (83, 84, 87, 90年)
personality (88, 92②年)
personally (85年)
personify (91年②)
personnel (88年)
persuade (92②, 94, 95, 97年)
persuasion (92年②)
persuasive (86, 87, 92②年)
pet (87, 90, 91②, 96, 98年)
petal (87年)
petroleum (84年)
pharaoh (92年①)
PhD (94年)
phenomenon (84, 91①, 95年)
photo (98年)
photograph (91②, 95, 98年)
phrase (86, 87, 96年)
physical (90, 94, 95, 97, 98年)
physically (84, 88年)
physician (92年①②)
physiological (94, 95年)
pick (92②, 95年)
picky (98年)
picture (85, 94, 98年)
piece (83, 87, 91①, 93, 96, 97, 98年)
pig (97年)
pigeon (98年)
piglet (97年)
pillar (87年)
pilot (84, 87年)
pineapple (98年)
pinewood (87年)
pitcher (96年)
pity (86, 96年)

place (98年)
plan (96年)
plane (88年)
planned (85年)
plant (86, 87, 88, 92②, 94, 95, 97, 98年)
plastic (85, 92②年)
plate (96年)
plausible (89年)
playground (89年)
playwright (89年)
pleasant (96, 98年)
please (87, 90年)
pleased (83年)
pleasure (85, 98年)
plentiful (95年)
plenty (92①, 97年)
plot (87年)
plus (88年)
poem (86, 87, 90年)
poet (89年)
point (84, 86, 91①, 96, 98年)
poison (92年②)
poisoning (92年②)
poisonous (92年②)
police (83, 86, 88, 94, 97年)
police officer (83年)
police station (89年)
policeman (84, 92①年)
policy (91年②)
politely (85, 88年)
political (87年)
politician (94年)
politics (92②, 98年)
pollute (92②, 93年)
pollution (84, 92②, 95年)
polyester (96年)
pool (84, 87年)
poor (95年)

poorly (91年②)

popular (84, 88, 90, 91②, 92①②, 95, 97, 98年)

popularity (91②, 92①年)

popularly (91年②)

population (91②, 92①②, 94, 97, 98年)

porker (89年)

port (94年)

portable (93, 98年)

porthole (85年)

portion (94年)

pose (92年②)

position (94年)

positive (83, 91②, 95年)

positively (85年)

possess (88, 91①年)

possession (86, 87, 92①年)

possibility (93, 95, 98年)

possible (83, 92②, 93, 95, 96, 97, 98年)

possibly (83, 86, 90年)

post (86, 94, 98年)

post office (89年)

postal (89, 91①年)

postpone (92①, 97年)

postwar (97年)

pot (89年)

potato chip (90, 96年)

potential (87, 96年)

pound (84, 85, 90, 94年)

pour (88年)

poverty (90, 92②年)

powder (94年)

power (97年)

powerful (98年)

power plant (91年②)

powerful (88, 90, 92①, 93, 94, 97年)

practical (88年)

practice (84, 87, 89, 92①②, 98年)

Prague (97年)

praise (83, 91①, 97年)

pray (92年①)

prayer (93年)

preceding (84年)

precious (86, 91①②, 94, 95, 97年)

precise (90年)

precisely (96年)

predator (93年)

predecessor (93年)

predicable (93年)

predict (83, 88, 91①, 98年)

prefer (84, 95, 98年)

preference (98年)

preferred (93年)

pregnant (91年①)

premature (98年)

preparation (95, 98年)

prepare (90, 91②, 92①②年)

prescribe (86年)

prescription (86, 94年)

presence (86年)

present (84, 87, 88, 90, 92②年)

preserve (96, 98年)

president (92②, 96, 97, 98年)

press (83, 85年)

pressure (93, 95年)

pretend (94, 97年)

pretty (92②, 93, 95年)

prevent (91①, 92②, 97, 98年)

prevention (92年①)

preview (85, 91②年)

previous (93年)

previously (85, 86, 91①, 97年)

prey (93年)

price (85, 91②, 94, 98年)

priceless (86年)

pride (94年)

priest (92年①)

primarily (83年)

primary (92①, 95年)

primitive (93年)

prince (83, 91②, 97年)

princess (91①年)

print (83, 91②, 92①, 94年)

printing (83年)

priority (94年)

prison (83年)

private (90, 95, 96年)

privately (91年①②)

privilege (88, 97年)

prize (91年①)

probably (83, 84, 86, 88, 89, 90, 92①②, 94, 95年)

problem (86, 87, 88, 90, 91①, 92②, 94, 95, 96, 98年)

procedure (85年)

proceed (87年)

process (83, 84, 88, 91①, 95, 97, 98年)

produce (84, 88, 91①, 92②, 93, 94, 95, 96, 97, 98年)

producer (91②, 92②年)

product (91①, 92①②, 93, 94, 98年)

production (87, 90, 92②, 94, 95, 98年)

productive (91①, 95年)

productivity (87, 91①, 94年)

profession (92年②)

professional (88, 91②, 95, 96年)

professor (89, 91②, 92①②, 94年)

profit (92①, 96, 97年)

profitable (92①, 95, 96年)

profound (83, 85年)

program (87, 88, 89, 90, 91①, 93, 95, 96年)

programmer (91年②)

programming (95年)

progress (85, 95年)

project (86, 87, 88, 90, 91①②, 92①②, 95, 98年)

projection (90年)

projector (90年)

promise (88, 92②, 94, 96, 97年)

promote (83, 86, 92①, 95, 97, 98年)

promotion (84, 89年)

pronoun (91年②)

pronounce (84, 89年)

proper (86, 91②, 92②年)

properly (90, 93, 94年)

proponent (96年)

proposal (84, 86, 87, 92②年)

propose (88, 91①年)

proposition (84年)

prosper (96年)

prosperous (90年)

protect (85, 87, 90, 94, 95, 97, 98年)

protection (84, 85, 88, 92②, 96年)

protein (92年②)

protest (91年①)

proud (85年)

prove (83, 90, 95年)

proverb (91年②)

provide (85, 87, 88, 92②, 93, 94, 95, 96, 97年)

provincial (94年)

provision (92年①)

psychological (87, 97年)

public (83, 91②, 92②, 93, 94, 95, 96年)

publicity (94年)

publish (93年)

pull (83, 89年)

pulse (97年)

punctually (98年)

punish (83, 92①年)

pupae (92年②)

puppy (96年)

purchase (92①, 93年)

pure (92②, 97年)

purify (91年①)

purpose (86, 88, 90, 92①, 94, 95, 96, 97, 98年)

purposefully (89年)

pursue (93年)

push (88, 89, 95, 96年)

pyramid (92①, 95年)

quail (94年)

quake (94年)

qualification (88年)

quality (89, 91②, 93, 96, 97, 98年)

quantity (85, 90年)

quarter (83, 88, 95, 96年)

queen (94年)

quest (91年①)

question (98年)

quick (95, 96年)

quicken (87年)

quickly (91①, 92②, 95, 96, 97年)

quiet (86, 95, 98年)

quietly (86年)

quite (83, 86, 87, 88, 89, 90, 91①②, 92②, 95, 97年)

quote (93年)

race (93, 98年)

racial (92②, 93年)

racism (90, 91①年)

radiation (95年)

radish (98年)

raft (84年)

rage (92年①)

raid (92年②)

raided (92年②)

rainbow (86年)

rainfall (88, 93, 98年)

rainforest (91年①)

rainy (83年)

raise (85, 96年)

raisin (96年)

range (91②, 92②, 96年)

rank (92年②)

rap (92年①)

rapid (84, 89, 98年)

rapidly (89, 90, 92②, 94年)

rare (88, 91①, 97年)

rarely (87, 94, 95年)

rat (98年)

rate (92①, 96年)

rather (88, 89, 90, 91①, 92①, 95, 96, 97, 98年)

razor (97年)

reach (83, 91①②, 92②, 94, 98年)

react (89, 94, 95, 97年)

reaction (83, 92①, 97年)

readable (93年)

readily (86年)

real (91①, 94, 97年)

realistic (97年)

realize (85, 92①②, 93, 94, 95年)

really (84, 87, 91①, 92②, 96年)

rear (86年)

rearrange (83年)

reason (85, 86, 87, 88, 89, 91①②, 92②, 93, 94, 95, 96, 97年)

reassurance (93年)

rebel (94, 97年)

reborn (97年)

rebuild (88, 94年)

re-built (87年)

recall (87, 88, 92②, 94年)

receive (83, 84, 88, 90, 91①, 92②, 93, 96, 97年)

recent (85, 87, 91①, 92①②, 93, 95, 96, 97年)

recently (84, 90, 91①②, 95, 96, 97, 98年)

recipe (90, 92②年)

recipient (83年)

reckless (86年)

recognition (97年)

recognize (85, 88, 91①, 92①, 93, 95, 96, 97年)

recommend (96年)

record (85, 89, 92①, 93, 95, 96, 97年)

recorded (92②, 97年)

recording (89, 97年)

recover (86, 88, 96, 97年)

recovery (93, 96年)

recreational (96年)

recycle (94, 98年)

recycling (88年)

red fire ant (94年)

redevelop (87年)

redevelopment (97, 98年)

red-faced (89年)

rediscover (92年②)

redistribute (86年)

reduce (84, 87, 92②, 95, 98年)

reevaluate (83年)

refer (87, 92②, 95, 98年)

reference (93年)

reflect (83年)

reform (94年)

refresh (97, 98年)

refreshing (95年)

refuge (90年)

refuse (89, 91②年)

regain (94年)

regard (95年)

regarding (88, 94年)

regards (83年)

region (88, 95, 98年)

regional (89年)

register (87年)

registration (87年)

regret (89年)

regular (87, 88, 91②, 93, 95, 98年)

regularity (94年)

regularly (85, 86, 92①, 93年)

regulate (85年)

reincarnated (93年)

reincarnation (93年)

reintroduce (97年)

reject (86, 96年)

rejection (83, 92②, 94年)

rejoice (97年)

relate (85, 86年)

related (97年)

relating (86, 96年)

relation (92年②)

relationship (85, 86, 89, 90, 94年)

relative (83, 87, 93年)

relatively (95, 96, 97年)

relax (87, 89, 92①, 94, 96年)

relaxation (91年①)

relaxed (91①, 92②年)

relaxing (95, 96年)

release (88, 90, 92②, 95, 97年)

relentlessly (88年)

reliable (98年)

reliably (96年)

relief (88, 89年)

relieve (91①, 92①, 94年)

religion (87年)

religious (92①, 93, 97, 98年)

reload (91年②)

reluctance (96年)

reluctant (91年②)

reluctantly (93年)

rely (94年)

remain (84, 88, 90, 91①, 92②, 93, 95, 97年)

remark (86年)

remarkable (88, 98年)

remember (86, 88, 92①, 94, 95, 98年)

remind (89, 94, 98年)

reminder (94年)

remove (91①②, 93, 96, 98年)

rename (97年)

renew (91①, 92①年)

rent (85, 86年)

repair (84, 86, 91②年)

repeat (87年)

repeatable (91年①)

repeatedly (85年)

repetition (85年)

replace (84, 86, 92②, 94, 98年)

reply (89年)

report (83, 88, 91①, 92①, 93, 94, 97年)

reporter (83, 88, 93年)

represent (86, 88, 97年)

repression (94年)

reproduce (94年)

republic (97年)

reputation (90, 91②, 94年)

request (90, 92②, 96, 98年)

require (83, 86, 87, 88, 90, 91②, 93年)

requirement (85, 88, 93年)

rescue (84, 86年)

research (86, 87, 89, 91②, 92②, 93, 95, 96, 98年)

researcher (89, 91②, 97, 98年)

resemblance (85年)

resentful (94年)

resentment (94年)

reservation (92①, 93年)

reserve (91年②)

reserved (83年)

resign (89, 96, 98年)

resist (91①, 92①, 94年)

resistance (87年)

resolution (98年)

resolve (86, 87年)

resonance (95年)

resort (88年)

resource (84, 94, 98年)

respect (93, 94, 96年)

respectably (90年)

respectfully (87年)

respiration (84年)

respond (86, 88, 91②, 93年)

response (86, 93, 95, 96年)

responsibility (92②, 95年)

responsible (84, 85, 87, 88, 91②年)

rest (89, 92①, 95, 96, 97, 98年)

restaurant (84, 88, 90, 97年)

restore (90, 94年)

restrained (88年)

restrict (89, 90, 95年)

result (84, 85, 88, 91②, 92①②, 95, 96, 98年)

resulting (98年)

resume (88年)

retain (84, 97年)

retire (88, 91②, 96年)

retreat (96年)

return (83, 84, 86, 87, 88, 89, 91①, 93, 95年)

reusable (92年②)

reuse (98年)

reused (83年)

reveal (91②, 93, 96年)

revenge (91年①)

review (94年)

revise (98年)

revive (96年)

revolution (90, 91①, 95年)

revolutionary (90年)

reward (83, 87, 92②, 96年)

rewarding (85年)

reword (90年)

rewrite (98年)

rhyme (86年)

rhythm (86年)

rice (92年②)

richness (97年)

ride (97, 98年)

riding (97年)

ridge (93年)

ridicule (91年①)

right (85, 86, 87, 90, 97年)

right-brained (85年)

rise (86, 88, 90, 91②, 92①, 93, 94, 98年)

rising (98年)

risk (83, 91②, 92②, 95, 98年)

risky (95年)

ritual (93年)

rival (98年)

river (96年)

roadhouse (84年)

roadside (84年)

roar (91年①)

roasted (92年②)

robber (84年)

robot (87年)

rock (84年)

Rococo (97年)

role (85, 90, 92①, 93年)

roll (91②, 95年)

Romanic (97年)

romantic (85年)

Rome (98年)

roof (87年)

room (96年)

root (86年)

rope (93年)

rough (85年)

roughly (89, 96年)

round (89年)

route (88, 98年)

routine (83, 97年)

row (91①, 93年)

rowboat (91年①)

rudder (86年)

rug (92年②)

rugged (88年)

ruin (91①, 95年)

rumor (92年②)

run (97年)

runway (96, 98年)

rupee (96年)

rural (92年①)

rush (83, 85, 86, 89年)

sack (91年①)

sacrifice (95年)

safety (83, 86, 87年)

sage (86年)

sail (86, 87, 98年)

sailboat (86年)

sailing (84年)

sailor (98年)

salad (92②, 98年)

salary (88, 96年)

sales (91②, 92①年)

salesman (91年②)

salesperson (92年②)

salon (96年)

salt (84, 91①年)

salute (88年)

same (96, 97, 98年)

sample (88, 98年)

sanctuary (97年)

sand (91①, 94年)

sandy (98年)

satellite (96, 98年)

satellite-based (96年)

satisfaction (94, 98年)

satisfied (83, 86, 90年)

sauna (98年)

save (83, 86, 90, 91①②, 93, 98年)

saving (95, 98年)

saw (91年①)

saying (87年)

scandal (92年②)

scanner (95年)

scanning (95年)

scarce (89年)

scarcely (96年)

scare (97年)

scared (84, 89年)

scary (88年)

scatter (98年)

scenery (88, 97年)

scenic (97年)

scent (95年)

schedule (88, 92①, 94, 97年)

scheme (86年)

scholar (91②, 92②, 93年)

scholarship (96年)

school (96年)

schoolbag (86年)

science (84, 96年)

scientific (84, 85, 89, 91②, 92①年)

scientifically (98年)

scientist (84, 85, 88, 89, 90, 94, 97年)

scoff (94年)

score (84, 85, 91②年)

scorecard (95年)

scrabble (85年)

scratch (98年)

scratch (97年)

scream (87, 97年)

screen (91年②)

script (86年)

scuba diving (88年)

sculpt (97年)

sculptor (84, 97年)

sculpture (93, 97年)

scurvy (98年)

seafood (88年)

seagoing (84年)

seal (91②, 92①年)

seaport (86年)

search (89, 93, 94, 97年)

seashell (88年)

season (87, 88, 91②, 95年)

seat (96年)

second (87, 91①, 97年)

secondary (97年)

secondly (84年)

secret (93, 97年)

section (87, 97年)

secure (92年②)

securely (90年)

securing (85年)

security (86, 92②, 94, 98年)

seed (93年)

seek (86, 90, 94年)

seeker (90年)

seem (83, 84, 85, 86, 87, 88, 89, 90, 91①, 93, 95, 98年)

segment (96年)

seize (92②, 93年)

seldom (85, 91①, 92①, 97年)

select (91①②, 97年)

selected (88年)

selection (91年②)

self (93年)

self-assurance (83年)

self-concept (83年)

self-confident (83年)

self-destructive (84年)

self-esteem (83年)

selfish (92年①)

selfless (95年)

self-protection (94年)

self-worth (94年)

sell (97, 98年)

seller (95年)

selling (88年)

senate (88年)

send (85, 86, 90, 91①②, 94, 95, 98年)

sender (86年)

senior (91年②)

sensation (94年)

sensational (85年)

sense (83, 89, 90, 93年)

senseless (91年②)

sensible (85, 98年)

sensitive (85, 89, 93, 96, 97, 98年)

sensitivity (98年)

sensory (93年)

sentence (88, 93, 98年)

sentimental (85, 87年)

Seoul (98年)

separate (96年)

separately (83, 86, 87年)

series (94年)

serious (84, 85, 87, 88, 91①②, 94年)

seriously (84, 89年)

seriousness (91②, 94年)

serve (88, 95, 98年)

service (86, 88, 91①, 96, 98年)

sesame (96年)

set (92①, 95, 96年)

setting (87年)

settle (86, 92②年)

several (84, 86, 92②, 95, 97, 98年)

several knot (87年)

severe (97年)

severely (92年①)

sex (91②, 96年)

sexual (86年)

sexuality (86年)

sexy (94年)

shabby (92年②)

shade (88年)

shake (88, 91①年)

shall (86, 89年)

shameful (96年)

shampoo (96年)

shape (88, 97年)

share (88, 91②, 92②, 93, 96, 97年)

sharp (92②, 97, 98年)

sharpen (97年)

shed (89年)

sheet (88年)

shelf (91年②)

shell (88年)

shine (89, 95年)

shivering (89年)

shock (97年)

shocked (87年)

shocking (94年)

shoot (91②, 98年)

shortcoming (85年)

shortly (92①, 98年)

short-term (85年)

shout (91年①)

show (96, 97年)

shred (86年)

shredded (88年)

shrine (92年①)

shrink (92②, 96年)

shut (89年)

shuttle (95年)

sibling (92年②)

sickness (92年①)

side (96, 98年)

sidewalk (87年)

sight (95年)

sighted (92年②)

sight-seeing (85年)

sign (87, 89, 91②, 93, 96, 98年)

signal (88, 92②, 93年)

signature (91年②)

significance (94年)

significant (85年)

signify (91年②)

silence (86, 90, 97年)

silent (97年)

Silk Road (94年)

silk worm (92年②)

silky (91年①)

silver (87, 93年)

similar (84, 86, 89, 93年)

similarity (90年)

similarly (91②, 92①, 93, 94, 95年)

simple (90, 91②, 92①, 98年)

simplify (92年①)

simply (84, 89, 91①, 95, 98年)

simulate (90年)

since (97年)

sincere (85年)

sincerely (95, 96, 98年)

sing (98年)

single (86, 90, 93, 96年)

site (86, 97年)

situate (97年)

situation (83, 84, 86, 88, 91①, 92②, 95, 98年)

sixth (98年)

sizable (91年②)

size (96, 97, 98年)

skeleton (90年)

ski (84年)

skill (83, 92①年)

skillful (93年)

skillfully (94年)

skin (85, 91①年)

skylight (93年)

slaughter (97年)

slave (90, 92①②年)

sleeping (89年)

sleep-song (87年)

slice (89, 90年)

slide (98年)

slightly (94年)

slim (98年)

slippery (93年)

slowly (96年)

slow-paced (98年)

smart (98年)

smash (86年)

smattering (88年)

smoke (98年)

smoker (83, 91②, 94年)

smoking (83, 94年)

smooth (86, 91①年)

smoothly (86年)

snack (90年)

snapper (91年②)

soap (84年)

sociable (92②, 97年)

social (86, 92②, 94, 96年)

society (84, 87, 92①②, 94, 96年)

soften (86年)

software (91年①)

soil (88, 94, 96年)

solar (98年)

soldier (90年)

solemnly (89年)

solid (84, 92①, 96年)

soloist (91年①)

solution (86, 91①年)

solve (85, 87, 92②年)

someday (85年)

somehow (91①, 94, 95年)

sometimes (98年)

somewhat (90年)

somewhere (90年)

soon (96年)

sorrow (89年)

sorrowful (87年)

sort (85, 92②, 96年)

soul (88年)

sound (86, 89, 92①, 94, 95, 96, 97, 98年)

sound basis (92年①)

source (92①②, 98年)

south (86, 94, 98年)

southeastern (88, 94年)

southern (96, 98年)

southwestern (86年)

sow (97年)

soybean (92年②)

spa (92①, 96年)

space (88, 92①, 93, 95, 97年)

space shuttle (92年①)

spaceship (89年)

spacesuit (92年①)

spaciously (92年②)

spare (91年②)

sparkling (96年)

sparse (88年)

spawning (84年)

speak (96年)

speaker (87年)

special (83, 85, 91①, 92②, 94, 97年)

specialist (95年)

species (92②, 93年)

specific (85, 93年)

specifically (89, 92②, 95, 97年)

spectator (88年)

speculate (93年)

speech (85, 87, 89, 92②年)

speed (91年①)

spell (92年①)

spice (92年②)

spiral (83年)

spirit (90, 95, 96年)

spiritual (93, 94, 95年)

spiritually (93年)

spoilt (89年)

spokeswoman (98年)

sponsor (84, 89, 92①年)

spontaneously (83年)

sport show (91年②)

sports (88, 91①, 96, 98年)

spot (84, 88, 90, 96年)

spread (90, 92②, 93, 94, 95, 98年)

sprightly (89年)

spring (93年)

square (87年)

squeeze (97年)

stab (98年)

staff (89, 96, 98年)

stage (87, 90, 93年)

stain (87年)

stair (90年)

standard (86, 88, 92②, 94年)

standpoint (94年)

start (96年)

startle (90年)

starvation (90年)

starve (88年)

starving (90年)

state (88, 91②, 94, 95年)

statement (83, 84, 85, 86, 87, 88, 90, 91①②, 92①②, 93, 96, 97年)

station (84, 95, 96年)

statistics (91年②)

statue (92年①)

stay (96, 98年)

steady (85, 91②, 95, 98年)

steak (93年)

steam (95年)

steep (93年)

step (83, 86, 98年)

sternly (89年)

stick (98年)

sticky (96年)

still (96年)

stimulating (95年)

stimulus (95年)

sting (94年)

stitch (98年)

stock (90, 98年)

stomachache (97年)

storage (91年②)

store (86, 89, 90, 91②, 92①②年)

storm (84, 96年)

story (83, 98年)

storytelling (87年)

stove (97, 98年)

straight (95年)

strand (84年)

strange (84年)

stranger (86, 90 年)

strategy (98 年)

straw (94 年)

stream (88, 91 ① 年)

strength (92 ②, 95, 98 年)

strengthen (84, 93 年)

stress (92 ①, 95, 98 年)

stressful (97 年)

stress-related (92 年 ①)

stretch (88, 89, 91 ②, 96 年)

stretchable (91 年 ①)

strict (92 年 ②)

stricter (87 年)

strictly (84, 87 年)

strike (83, 90, 91 ① 年)

striking (96 年)

strip (87, 94 年)

strive (94 年)

stroke (97 年)

strongly (89, 92 ② 年)

strong-willed (85 年)

structure (84, 87, 90, 97 年)

struggle (87 年)

stuck (96 年)

study (96, 97, 98 年)

studio (89 年)

stuff (96 年)

stunning (88 年)

stupid (85, 87, 94 年)

style (85, 86, 90, 93, 97, 98 年)

stylist (98 年)

subject (83, 92 ①, 95 年)

submit (87 年)

substance (92 年 ②)

substitute (90, 92 ②, 96 年)

substitution (92 年 ①)

suburb (95 年)

suburban (87 年)

subway (92 ①, 95 年)

succeed (84, 86, 87, 90, 91 ①, 94, 96 年)

success (86, 87, 88, 91 ①, 92 ① ②, 97 年)

successful (90, 92 ①, 93, 94, 98 年)

successfully (86, 88, 95, 97 年)

such (96, 97, 98 年)

sudden (93 年)

suddenly (83, 85, 86, 89, 97 年)

sue (83 年)

suffer (92 ① ②, 93, 94, 96, 97, 98 年)

suffering (91 ②, 94 年)

sufficient (94 年)

sugar (96 年)

suggest (91 ②, 92 ②, 97, 98 年)

suggestion (83, 84, 86, 95 年)

suicidal (84 年)

suicide (92 年 ①)

suit (91 ① ②, 92 ②, 95, 98 年)

suitable (88, 90, 97 年)

suitcase (92 年 ②)

sum (86 年)

sun (98 年)

sunny (91 ①, 94, 95, 97 年)

superficial (93 年)

super-intelligent (84 年)

superior (93, 97, 98 年)

superiority (93 年)

supervisor (88 年)

supplier (95 年)

supplies (90 年)

supply (88, 94, 95, 96 年)

support (84, 85, 86, 87, 88, 90, 93, 94, 95, 96 年)

supporter (91 年 ①)

suppose (94 年)

sure (96 年)

surface (90, 93, 94, 96, 98 年)

surgery (93, 97 年)

surplus (86 年)

surprise (83, 86, 90, 93, 95, 97 年)

surprised (90, 91 ① 年)

surprisingly (88, 91 ② 年)

surround (91 ①, 95 年)

survey (91 ②, 92 ① 年)

survive (84, 85, 88, 90, 91 ① ②, 93, 94, 95, 96 年)

survivor (84 年)

suspect (97 年)

suspend (89 年)

sustain (92 年 ①)

swallow (84 年)

swan (97 年)

sway (85 年)

swear (86, 91 ② 年)

sweat (85 年)

sweater (92 年 ②)

sweaty (95 年)

Sweden (97 年)

sweet (96 年)

swim (98 年)

swirl (88 年)

switch (87, 91 ② 年)

sword (91 年 ①)

symbol (87, 94, 96, 97, 98 年)

symbolic (89 年)

symbolically (89 年)

sympathetically (83 年)

symptom (83, 95 年)

synthetic (86 年)

system (91 ②, 94, 96, 98 年)

Tahiti (98 年)

tail (98 年)

Taiwan Strait (86 年)

Taiwanese (86, 91 ②, 97 年)

tale (91 ②, 93 年)

talent (88, 98 年)

talented (85年)

talk show (91年②)

tall tale (91年②)

tank (84年)

tannin (96年)

tape (89, 94年)

tape-recorder (89年)

target (98年)

task (95, 97, 98年)

taste (93年)

tasty (98年)

teach (96年)

team (84, 86, 88, 91①, 94, 95, 98年)

teamwork (98年)

tear (86, 98年)

tease (91年①)

technical (88, 97年)

technician (88年)

technological (90, 94年)

technically (98年)

technology (86, 87, 88, 98年)

teen (92年①)

teenage (83年)

teenager (84, 92①, 94, 95, 96年)

teens (92①, 94, 95年)

teeth (94, 96年)

tele-course (96年)

television (96年)

tell (98年)

temper (87年)

temperature (85, 91②, 96, 97年)

temple (92①, 97年)

temporary (92①, 97年)

temptation (94年)

tempted (94年)

tend (88, 92②, 96年)

tendency (92②, 98年)

tennis (91①, 95年)

tense (86年)

tent (85, 86年)

tentative (89年)

term (88, 92②, 98年)

terminal (92年①)

termite (98年)

terrible (86, 92①年)

terribly (88年)

terrific (95年)

territorial (87, 97年)

territory (97年)

textbook (90, 94年)

texture (90, 98年)

the Milky Way (89年)

the Olympic Games (90年)

the Pacific (88年)

the Pacific Ocean (91年①)

the public (89, 90年)

the red imported fire ant (94年)

the Red Sea (93年)

the Seine (87年)

the UN (91年①)

the United Nations (91年①)

the United States (96, 97, 98年)

the wild (90年)

theater (90年)

theme (88, 97年)

then (96, 97, 98年)

theory (93, 98年)

therapy (84年)

therefore (87, 88, 90, 92①, 94, 96, 97, 98年)

thick (93年)

thickly (90年)

thickness (96年)

thin (94年)

think (97年)

third (96年)

thirst (89年)

thorough (84年)

thoroughly (83, 97年)

though (96年)

thought (86年)

thousand (96, 98年)

threaten (85, 93, 94年)

thrilled (96年)

thrive (86, 88, 94年)

throat (84, 97年)

through (84, 85, 86, 88, 89, 90, 91②, 94, 97年)

throughout (87, 91①, 92②, 93, 94, 96, 98年)

throw (87, 89, 98年)

thrust (92年②)

thunderstorm (92年①)

thus (83, 89, 91②, 96, 97, 98年)

ticker-tape (88年)

tide (87年)

tide table (87年)

tie (84, 91①, 98年)

tighten (86年)

tightly (89年)

timber (87年)

time difference (94年)

time zone (94年)

time-consuming (90年)

tiny (93, 96年)

tip (86, 91②, 96年)

tire (84年)

tiredness (94年)

title (85, 88, 89, 92①, 93年)

tobacco (94年)

today (97年)

tofu (92年②)

together (98年)

toilet (92年①)

token (95年)

tolerance (92年②)

tolerant (92年①)

tolerate (83, 88, 97年)

ton (88, 90年)

tone (85, 91②, 97年)

tongue (95年)

tool (92②, 97, 98年)

tooth (90年)

topic (86, 87, 88, 91②年)

Toronto (98年)

tortoise (98年)

toss (89, 98年)

total (93年)

touch (89, 92①, 94, 95, 97年)

tour (88, 94, 97年)

tour guide (88年)

tourism (98年)

tourist (84, 97年)

tournament (91年①)

toward (88, 92②, 93, 94年)

towards (91①, 93年)

towel (96年)

tower (87年)

tow-thirds (91年②)

trace (87年)

trade (84, 85, 90, 91②, 93, 94, 95年)

trading (94年)

tradition (94, 97, 98年)

traditional (88, 91②年)

traditionally (95年)

traffic (87, 92②, 95年)

traffic jam (85年)

tragedy (92①, 94年)

tragic (92①, 96年)

trail (90, 91①年)

train (83, 88, 97年)

training (88, 93, 96年)

transfer (92②, 95, 96年)

transform (87, 96年)

translate (90年)

translation (83年)

transplant (93年)

transport (90年)

transportation (88, 95, 97, 98年)

trap (91年①②)

travel (83, 84, 86, 88, 91②, 92②, 93, 94, 95, 97, 98年)

traveler (83, 94, 97年)

treasure (88, 92②, 94年)

treat (83, 86, 87, 88, 92①②, 93, 96, 97年)

treatment (89, 92①, 95, 96, 97年)

tremble (89年)

tremendous (91年①)

trend (92①, 96, 98年)

tribal (92①, 96年)

trick (89, 91①, 92①, 97年)

trip (85, 88, 90, 94, 97年)

triumph (91①②, 96年)

trivial (96年)

tropical (88, 94, 98年)

trouble (86, 91①, 92②, 94年)

troubled (96年)

trouser (85年)

truck (85, 90年)

true (96年)

truly (96年)

trunk (89, 91①, 94年)

trust (86年)

truth (91②, 92①②, 94年)

truthful (90年)

try (98年)

tub (96年)

tubing (92年②)

tuna (91年②)

tune (98年)

tunnel (97年)

turkey (92年②)

turn (96, 97, 98年)

turnout (88年)

twice (89, 92②年)

twin (87, 93年)

twinkle (89年)

twin-mast (86年)

twist (98年)

tying (87年)

type (83, 85, 86, 92①, 94年)

typhoon (88, 91②年)

typical (85, 92①, 94, 97年)

typically (93年)

uh-huh (89年)

UK (97年)

ulcer (95年)

umbrella (83年)

unable (84, 98年)

unabridged (85年)

unanimously (89年)

unbelievable (91年②)

unborn (92年②)

unchanged (97年)

uncomfortable (86, 92②, 98年)

undeniable (92年①)

undergo (88年)

underground (94, 98年)

underline (95年)

underside (93年)

understand (84, 87, 90, 91①②, 94, 95, 96, 97年)

understandable (98年)

understanding (84, 86, 87, 91②年)

undertake (92年②)

underwater (91年②)

underwear (92年①)
undo (90年)
undoubtedly (92年②)
unexplained (91年①)
unfortunately (89, 91②, 98年)
unharmed (91年①)
unhealthy (92年②)
uniform (92年①)
union (97年)
unique (86, 87, 94年)
unit (96年)
universal (88, 90年)
university (88, 92①, 96, 97年)
unknown (84, 89, 97年)
unless (83, 84, 85, 86, 89, 92①, 94, 96年)
unlike (90, 91①, 94, 96年)
unlikely (83, 90年)
unlocked (88年)
unnamed (86年)
unnecessary (84, 91①, 94, 96, 98年)
unnoticed (95年)
unpack (88年)
unpredictable (92年②)
unprepared (90年)
unrealistic (91①, 95年)
unselfish (83年)
unsustainable (98年)
until (96年)
untouched (97年)
unusual (84, 90, 92①年)
unusually (87年)
unwanted (91②, 92②年)
upcoming (97年)
upload (96年)
upon (97, 98年)
upper (91年①②)
upset (89, 91②年)

upside (97年)
upward (91年②)
upward-slanting (93年)
urge (85, 86, 92①, 94年)
use (97年)
used (94, 97年)
useful (85年)
usefulness (98年)
useless (91②, 92②年)
user (91年②)
usual (91年①)
usually (86, 92②, 93, 94, 98年)
vacant (94年)
vacation (84, 89, 95年)
vain (94年)
Valentine's Day (93年)
valid (85年)
valley (86年)
valuable (97年)
valuably (95年)
value (86, 91②, 92②, 93年)
van (84年)
vanish (89年)
vanity (86年)
varied (98年)
variety (86, 89, 92②, 95, 98年)
various (90, 91②, 92①, 93年)
variously (91①, 96年)
vary (92②, 94, 95年)
vase (92年②)
vast (91①, 96年)
vegetable (98年)
vegetarian (92年②)
vehicle (84年)
veil (98年)
verify (84年)
verse (86年)
version (83, 98年)
vessel (86年)

vice (96年)
vicinity (92年①)
victim (86, 90, 92②年)
video (84, 92①, 96年)
view (84, 92①, 93, 94年)
viewer (83, 96年)
village (86, 90, 91①, 93年)
villager (91年①)
violation (83, 85年)
violence (94年)
violent (90, 94年)
violently (91年①)
violin (92年①)
VIP (91年②)
virginity (92年①)
virus (91年②)
visa (85年)
visibility (90年)
visible (89年)
vision (97年)
visit (84, 85, 86, 88, 89, 91②, 92①, 93, 94, 95, 97年)
visitor (84, 88, 90, 94, 96, 97, 98年)
visual (93, 97年)
vital (88, 90年)
vitamin (90, 92②年)
vivid (90, 98年)
vocabulary (91年②)
voice (87, 91①②, 96, 97年)
volcano (88年)
volunteer (86, 97, 98年)
vow (94年)
voyage (86, 98年)
vulnerable (92年②)
wagon (84, 85年)
waist-high (96年)
wake (89年)
waken (88年)
wale (89年)

Wall Street (88年)
wander (85, 89, 90, 96年)
wandering (90年)
wanted (88年)
war (97, 98年)
warm (85, 93, 95年)
warm-hearted (85年)
warmth (98年)
warn (85年)
warning (94年)
warrior (92年②)
wash (96年)
waste (91②, 92①②年)
waste matter (88年)
waterfall (86, 97年)
wave (89, 90, 92②年)
way (96, 97, 98年)
wayward (96年)
weak (83, 84, 88, 89, 92②年)
wealth (92②, 93年)
wear (90, 91①, 92①, 95, 97年)
weather (83, 85, 86, 88, 90, 93, 94, 95, 97年)
website (91②, 98年)
wedding (84, 92①, 97年)
weed (91①, 94年)
weekend (85, 92①, 95年)
week-long (93年)
weep (87, 89年)
weigh (85, 90, 91①, 94, 97年)
weight (84, 85, 87, 89, 91②, 92②, 94, 97, 98年)
weight-conscious (94年)
weight-loss (89年)
welfare (90年)
well (96年)
well-being (92年②)
well-built (88年)
well-educated (90年)

well-exercised (96年)
well-intentioned (85年)
well-known (93年)
well-trained (96年)
wellness (95年)
west (85, 86, 88, 94年)
western (92②, 98年)
west-to-east (94年)
wet (91年①)
whale (84年)
whatever (86, 97年)
wheat (92年②)
wheel (95年)
whenever (86, 93, 96, 97年)
whereabouts (97年)
wherever (97年)
whether (83, 85, 86, 89, 92①, 93, 96, 97, 98年)
while (84, 86, 87, 88, 89, 91①②, 92①, 93, 94, 97, 98年)
whoever (90年)
whole (86, 87, 90, 92①, 94, 96, 97, 98年)
wholesome (84, 86年)
wholly (97年)
wide (85, 86, 91②年)
widely (91①, 92②, 93, 94年)
widespread (84, 91①年)
wild (83, 84, 90, 97年)
wilderness (90年)
wildlife (97年)
willing (88, 91②, 95年)
willingly (88年)
win (91①, 92②, 97, 98年)
wind (86, 98年)
winding (97年)
wine (92年①)
winner (98年)
wire (89, 94, 96年)

wise (91②, 97, 98年)
wish (87, 91①②年)
wit (91年②)
within (85, 91①, 93, 95, 98年)
without (96年)
woman (97年)
wonder (83, 85, 86, 91①②, 95年)
wonderful (85, 86, 87, 91②, 98年)
wood (83, 87, 91①年)
work (97年)
workload (87年)
world (98年)
World Trade Center (83年)
world-wide (93, 95年)
worried (87年)
worry (92②, 95, 97, 98年)
worse (96年)
worsen (98年)
worst (94年)
worth (86, 90年)
worthy (90年)
wound (94, 98年)
wounded (94年)
wrinkle (91①, 98年)
wrist (92年②)
writing (92②, 93, 95年)
written (92①, 94年)
yard (97年)
yearly (93, 94年)
yell (88, 96年)
yelling (96年)
yet (84, 88, 91①②, 92①, 94, 96年)
yield (96, 98年)
yogurt (94年)
youngster (90年)
youth (92年①)
zigzag (93年)

★ 電腦統計歷屆學科能力測驗成語 ★

a bit (84, 89 年)

a couple of (91 ①, 93, 96 年)

a great deal of (97 年)

a large number of (90 年)

a large quantity of (85 年)

a large sum of (85 年)

a list of (88 年)

a lot (98 年)

a lot more (87 年)

a lot of (98 年)

a number of (86, 91 ②, 93, 94 年)

a pair of (93, 97 年)

a period of time (95, 98 年)

a piece of (89 年)

a quarter of (83, 96 年)

a range of (88 年)

a roomful of (93 年)

a series of (92 ①, 94 年)

a small percentage of (91 年②)

a third of (94 年)

a variety of (84, 89, 92 ①, 98 年)

above all (86, 96 年)

above everything (91 年①)

according to (83, 84, 86, 87, 88, 90, 91 ①②, 92 ①, 93, 94, 95, 96, 97, 98 年)

account for (92 年①)

accuse *sb*. of~ (87 年)

adapt to (98 年)

adjust to (90 年)

afford to (95 年)

after all (86, 88, 95, 98 年)

agree to (86 年)

agree with (87 年)

ahead of (83 年)

all of a sudden (91 年①)

all *one* has to do is V. (84 年)

all over (88, 90, 96, 98 年)

all over the country (96 年)

all over the world (84, 90, 92 ①, 93 年)

all right (84 年)

all the time (90, 91 ①年)

all walks of life (86 年)

all year around (96 年)

along with (97, 98 年)

anything but (91 ①, 96 年)

apart from (86, 88, 93 年)

appeal to (86, 91 ①年)

appear to V. (94, 96 年)

apply for (85, 88, 91 ①年)

around the clock (92 年①)

around the world (98 年)

arrive at (85, 89 年)

as a matter of fact (91 年①)

as a result (85, 87, 89, 91 ①②, 92 ①, 95, 98 年)

as a result of (84, 86, 88, 93 年)

as far as (85, 89, 94 年)

as for (86 年)

as good as (85 年)

as if (94, 95, 96, 98 年)

as little as (97 年)

as long as (94, 98 年)

as many (87 年)

as many as (84 年)

as much (87, 97 年)

as much as (93 年)

as of (85, 90 年)

as *one* know (84 年)

as scheduled (92 年①)

as soon as possible (91 年②)

as such (84 年)

as well (84, 92 ①年)

as well as (83, 85, 93, 98 年)

as…as ever (88 年)

as…as possible (90, 92 ①年)

as…as~ (83 年)

ask for (88, 97 年)

associate A with B (97 年)

at a glance (89 年)

at a time (83 年)

at all (86, 91 ②年)

at all cost (93 年)

at death (88 年)

at ease (91 年①)

at fault (84, 87, 91②年)

at first (96年)

at first glance (90年)

at last (94年)

at least (85, 89, 90, 94, 95, 97年)

at most (86, 96年)

at once (89年)

at one time (90, 91②年)

at other times (89年)

at sea (91年①)

at that moment (86年)

at that time (90, 92①年)

at the center of (88年)

at the cost of (98年)

at the end (89年)

at the end of (96, 98年)

at the moment (84, 94年)

at the request of (98年)

at the risk of (98年)

at the same time (91年②)

at this moment (84年)

at times (85, 90年)

at war (87年)

at will (91年①)

at work (92①, 94年)

attempt to (93年)

attend to (93年)

away from (98年)

back and forth (91年②)

based on (84, 93, 98年)

be able to V. (85, 86, 89, 90, 91①, 92①, 93, 94, 95年)

be about to (97年)

be added to (98年)

be associated with (91年②)

be attracted to (94年)

be aware of (90, 92①年)

be believed to V. (84年)

be born (91年①)

be born with (96年)

be capable of (90年)

be careful of (98年)

be characterized by (88年)

be close to (87, 89, 96年)

be closely related to (97年)

be compared with (91年②)

be composed of (97年)

be concerned with (95年)

be content to (95年)

be convinced that (94年)

be crowded with (91年①)

be described as (92年①)

be destined to (94年)

be devoid of (94年)

be different from (94年)

be disappointed at (95年)

be disposed of (92年①)

be exempted from (85年)

be exposed to (89年)

be faced with (91年①)

be familiar with (87, 96年)

be famous for (84, 86, 88, 92①, 96, 98年)

be fascinated by (92年①)

be filled with (89, 91②, 94, 98年)

be fond of (86年)

be for (91年①)

be going to V. (85年)

be good at (85, 88, 92①年)

be happy with (90年)

be home to (90年)

be inclined to (88年)

be indifferent to (94年)

be intended for (98年)

be intended to (88, 91①年)

be interested in (86, 89, 91①, 97年)

be involved in (91②, 97年)

be known as (91年①)

be known for (94, 98年)

be known to (98年)

be likely to (86, 91②, 98年)

be limited to (86年)

be linked to (92年①)

be located (90年)

be located in (96, 97年)

be made from (83, 94年)

be made into (90年)

be made of (87, 93年)

be made possible (90年)

be more than willing to V. (84年)

be named after (83年)

be named as (97年)

be obliged to (89年)

be of great importance (86年)

be on a diet (98年)

be popular with (91年②)

be proud of (85年)

be ready to (87年)

be referred to as (87年)
be related to (86年)
be responsible for (84,
　85, 93年)
be sensitive to (97年)
be sent to prison (83年)
be sick with (89年)
be similar to (89, 90, 95年)
be strange to (83年)
be stressed out (95年)
be superior (98年)
be supposed to (92①,
　94年)
be sure of (95年)
be sure to (92年①)
be taken from (94年)
be tempted to V. (94年)
be thought of as (92年①)
be to V. (93年)
be topped with (87年)
be translated into (90年)
be turned into (98年)
be unable to V. (84, 91①,
　98年)
be used to (97年)
be weighed down
　(91年①)
be well known (96, 98年)
be well received (90年)
be willing to V. (91年②)
bear in mind (86年)
because of (84, 85, 89, 91①②,
　92①, 93, 95, 96年)
become used to (84年)
before long (94年)
believe in (89, 91①年)

believe it or not (90年)
belong to (90年)
benefit from (96年)
better than (96年)
between A and B (96,
　97年)
beyond doubt (96年)
big deal (89年)
blend with (85年)
break down (84, 86, 94年)
break down into (88年)
break into (84年)
break into pieces
　(91年②)
break the rule (94年)
break up (92年①)
break up into (92年①)
bring about (90, 93年)
bring back (90年)
bring out (88年)
bring round (89年)
bring up (89年)
burst into tears (92年①)
by accident (87, 90年)
by all means (87年)
by and by (83年)
by and large (84年)
by chance (87, 88年)
by contrast (91年②)
by definition (94年)
by far (84, 91①年)
by hand (83, 90年)
by itself (87年)
by law (91年②)
by no means (91②, 93年)
by *oneself* (84, 86, 92①年)

by the name of (83年)
by the same token (95年)
by the time (91年②)
by the way (87, 89, 98年)
by then (87年)
by this time (90年)
by word of mouth
　(91年②)
call in (89年)
call into question (90年)
call off (85年)
call out (92年①)
call up (88年)
call upon (86年)
care for (92①, 96年)
carry out (90, 91①②, 95年)
catch cold (97年)
catch on (89年)
catch up (95年)
catch up with (94年)
change *one's* mind
　(88年)
check in with (97年)
check on (97年)
check out (87, 89, 97年)
cling to (96年)
close to (90, 96年)
come about (87, 93年)
come across (89年)
come along (92年①)
come around (87年)
come back (96年)
come by (85年)
come down (91年②)
come first (97年)
come from (84, 86, 88, 89年)

come in (91年②)

come off (87年)

come on (89年)

come out of (86年)

come out right (91年②)

come over (87年)

come to (83, 85, 86, 87, 88年)

come to pass (91年①)

come together (86年)

come up to (88年)

come up with (91①, 98年)

concentrate on (85, 88, 95年)

connect A with B (97年)

consist of (87, 92①, 95年)

continue with (92年①)

contribute to (93年)

cope with (97年)

could hardly (96年)

count on (96年)

crash down (91年①)

creep in (94年)

cross out (89年)

cut back (95年)

cut down (95年)

cut in (92年①)

cut off (85, 95年)

cut short (95年)

cut up (98年)

date from (92年①)

deal with (85, 89, 91①年)

dedicate *oneself* to (84年)

depend on (90, 91②, 94, 96年)

derive from (84年)

develop into (94年)

die down (90年)

die of (84, 90年)

die out (88年)

die young (90, 94年)

differ from (85年)

dispose of (86年)

do damage to (94年)

do good (86年)

do *one's* best (86, 87年)

do some fishing (86年)

do well (93年)

dozens of (91年②)

dream of (89年)

dress down (91年①)

dress up (91年①)

due to (84, 89, 94, 95, 96, 97年)

each other (90, 98年)

either…or~ (88, 95年)

end up (89, 90, 91①年)

enough to (83, 84, 87, 92①, 94年)

escape from (83, 93年)

even if (94, 95年)

even more (85, 87, 90年)

even so (83, 94, 95年)

even though (87, 90, 92①年)

ever after (94年)

ever again (90年)

ever since (90, 94, 98年)

every now and then (85年)

every once in a while (91年①)

except for (86, 94年)

expose A to B (98年)

fail to V. (91①②, 93, 95年)

fall in love (94年)

fall into (85年)

fall off (92年①)

fall short of (94年)

fall victim to (91年②)

far away (96年)

far from (84年)

far less (88年)

far more (88, 91②, 98年)

fight a war (90年)

fight for (97年)

figure out (83, 84, 89, 92①年)

fill in (89年)

find *one's* way home (90年)

find out (83, 84, 85, 86, 91①②, 92①, 95年)

first of all (89, 98年)

focus on (86年)

fold up (83年)

follow by (96, 97年)

for a long time (91①②, 96年)

for a long while (93年)

for better or worse (91年②)

for example (84, 86, 88, 91①②, 93, 94, 95, 96, 97, 98年)

for free (91年②)

for fun (84年)

for instance (83, 84, 85, 89年)

for one thing (84年)

for sale (91年②)

for sure (90年)

for that matter (96年)

for the first time (98年)

for the last time (85年)

for the rest of *one's* life
(97年)

from a distance (97年)

from case to case (94年)

from door to door (94年)

from place to place
(94年)

from then on (91年①)

from top to toe (94年)

from…to~ (89年)

gain entry to (94年)

gaze upon (85年)

generally speaking (85,
94年)

get away from (91年①)

get close to (93年)

get into (94年)

get into difficulty (90年)

get into trouble (86年)

get married to (91年①②)

get on (93年)

get on board (85年)

get *one's* way (95年)

get out of (91①, 94年)

get over (89, 94年)

get over with (92年①)

get ready to (95年)

get rid of (86, 89, 93, 96年)

get the better of (89年)

get to (83, 86, 87, 91①, 92①年)

get used to (94年)

give away (88, 90, 91②年)

give birth (97年)

give birth to (91年①)

give in (85, 87, 88年)

give off (85年)

give out (88, 93, 97年)

give over (85年)

give rise to (86年)

give *sb*. a ride (87年)

give up (85, 87, 94年)

give way to (91年①②)

go abroad (92年①)

go against (94年)

go around the world
(86年)

go away (96年)

go back to (92年①)

go beyond (90年)

go down (98年)

go hand in hand with
(96年)

go off (91年①)

go off duty (92年①)

go on (88年)

go on duty (92年①)

go *one's* way (91年①)

go out (84, 87, 96年)

go round (89年)

go through (84年)

go to (97年)

go to church (87年)

good luck (95年)

graduate with honors
(96年)

grow into (86年)

grow up (91②, 98年)

half of (91②, 96年)

hand back (93年)

hand out (95年)

hand over (93年)

hang on (88年)

hang out with (92年①)

hang up (87年)

happen to (86年)

happen to V. (88年)

hardly ever (91年①)

have a baby (89年)

have a good laugh
(87年)

have a good time (89年)

have a lot to do with
(86年)

have a way of (91年①)

have an effect on (98年)

have an impact on
(86年)

have an interest in
(88年)

have difficulty (in) +
V-ing (84年)

have no idea (88年)

have nothing in
common (87年)

have *one's* share of
(88年)

have the upper hand
(91年①)

have to V. (83, 93, 94, 98年)

have…in common
(83, 93年)

head for (91年①)

hear about (83, 91②年)

hear of (90年)

hold on (84, 90年)

hold onto (93年)

hold up (85年)

human being (96年)

hundreds of (91②, 97年)

if any (88年)

in a hurry (86年)

in a pack (91年①)

in a panic (89年)

in a way (85年)

in a word (89年)

in abundance (90年)

in accordance with (88年)

in addition (83, 84, 87, 88, 89, 95年)

in addition to (86, 88, 91②年)

in advance (90年)

in advance of (94年)

in ancient time (92年①)

in any way (93年)

in case (83, 85, 90年)

in case of (93年)

in class (96年)

in comparison (87年)

in conjunction with (93年)

in consequence (93年)

in contact (87年)

in contrast (85, 87, 88, 89, 93, 94, 95年)

in control (88年)

in defeat (90年)

in due time (84年)

in earlier days (87年)

in fact (88, 91②, 93, 94, 96, 98年)

in favor of (91年①)

in front of (83, 88, 89, 92①, 98年)

in full view (92年①)

in general (83, 89, 93年)

in height (96年)

in honor of (91年①)

in large print (94年)

in need (83年)

in no doubt that (89年)

in no sense (91年②)

in no time (91年①)

in *one's* honor (83年)

in order (88年)

in order of (83, 84, 90, 93, 94年)

in order to (95, 98年)

in other words (88, 91②年)

in part (84年)

in particular (88, 90年)

in person (83, 86年)

in place (97年)

in place of (86, 91①, 96, 98年)

in print (84年)

in public (91年①)

in relation to (93年)

in response to (86年)

in return (97年)

in search of (91年①)

in service (91年②)

in spite of (88, 89, 93年)

in terms of (98年)

in that (88年)

in the beginning (89年)

in the best interest of *sb.* (94年)

in the distance (87年)

in the end (89年)

in the face of (94年)

in the front of (86年)

in the future (86, 94, 97, 98年)

in the hope that (89年)

in the late 1930s (94年)

in the long run (93年)

in the meantime (85年)

in the middle of (89年)

in the near future (98年)

in the neighborhood (89年)

in the nick of time (91年①)

in the past (90, 91②年)

in the process of (97年)

in the sea (93年)

in the sky (93年)

in the wild (90, 97年)

in the world (98年)

in this way (86年)

in touch (96年)

in trouble (88年)

in turn (88, 89年)

in vain (88, 89, 90, 94年)

in view of (93年)

in···direction (98年)

in~form (89年)

in~way (90, 98年)

insist on (90年)

instead of (83, 85, 86, 88, 89, 92①, 93, 94, 98年)

invest in (98年)

It is believed that…
(94年)

It is said that… (89年)

it's a pity that (96年)

jump into (91年①)

just like (90年)

just the opposite (84年)

justify *oneself* (96年)

keep an eye on (93年)

keep from (95年)

keep in mind (91年②)

keep in touch (95年)

keep *sth.* off (83, 94年)

keep to (90年)

keep up (89年)

keep up with (94年)

keep~as a pet (90年)

kick out (95年)

kick the habit (94年)

knock at (96年)

knock out (89年)

know about (91年②)

known as (84年)

land on (88年)

lay out (89年)

lead a~life (90年)

lead to (89, 91②, 92①, 94, 97年)

learn from (94年)

learn the lesson (91年①)

leave a message (84年)

leave for (93年)

leave out (89年)

less than (85, 86, 92①年)

let go (93年)

let in (88年)

let off (89年)

lie in (95年)

light up (95年)

little by little (98年)

live a~live (90, 94年)

live on (95, 96, 97年)

live without (96年)

look after (85, 97年)

look down upon (86, 98年)

look for (85, 86, 89, 92①, 93年)

look forward to V-ing
(85, 89年)

look inside (94年)

look into (85年)

look over (88年)

look up (88年)

lose track of (91年①)

lose weight (94年)

lots of (98年)

lung cancer (98年)

magnetic field (98年)

make a decision (86, 89年)

make a difference to
(86, 87, 91②年)

make a fool of *oneself*
(86年)

make a fortune (86, 90年)

make a living (90年)

make a phone call (89年)

make a speech (87年)

make a trip (90年)

make an order (90年)

make ends meet (95年)

make it (90年)

make out of (96年)

make profits (96年)

make progress (85年)

make sense (90年)

make sure (85, 92①年)

make a telephone call
(88年)

make up (90年)

make up for (87, 91①年)

make up with (92年①)

make use of (91②, 96年)

millions of (90年)

more or less (85年)

more than (85, 91①, 92①, 94, 96, 98年)

more than once (85, 86, 88年)

most of the year (88年)

move about (89年)

move around (93, 98年)

move in (89年)

much less (84年)

much more (86, 91②年)

much the same (91年②)

neither…nor~ (93年)

next time (94年)

next to (85, 93年)

no doubt (88年)

no longer (88, 91①, 92①年, 95年)

no matter (89年)

no matter how (86年)

no matter what (90, 95, 98年)

no more than (95年)

no sooner than (95年)

no way (96年)

no wonder (89年)

none of *one's* business
  (89年)

not always (85, 91①年)

not at all (84年)

not exactly (96年)

not only…but also~
  (84, 90, 98年)

not until (95年)

not…any longer (85, 86年)

not…any more (84年)

not…anymore (92年①)

not…at all (87, 89, 91②年)

not…until (83, 84, 90, 98年)

not…yet (84, 86年)

now that (91②, 98年)

occur to (98年)

of course (89, 91①, 93, 94年)

off and on (91年②)

off the record (96, 97年)

on and off (93年)

on any account (92年①)

on average (87年)

on behalf of (89, 93年)

on board (87年)

on earth (86, 88, 95年)

on land (93年)

on leave (97年)

on line (91年②)

on *one's* own (84, 95年)

on *one's* tour (84年)

on *one's* way (88, 90年)

on purpose (88, 90年)

on television (87年)

on the basis of (83, 85年)

on the contrary (95年)

on the house (92年①)

on the increase (98年)

on the mark (92年①)

on the move (92年①)

on the other hand
  (85, 94, 95年)

on the side (92年①)

on the spot (92年①)

on the telephone (98年)

on the whole (84, 91①②年)

on time (90, 93年)

once and for all (85年)

once more (85年)

one day (85, 98年)

or rather (93年)

out of (84, 89, 90, 91②, 92①,
  94, 98年)

out of pity (91年①)

out of place (91年①)

out of politeness (91年①)

out of practice (91年①)

out of sorrow (89年)

out of stock (90年)

out of style (86年)

out of the question
  (91年①②)

over and over again
  (84, 94年)

over the years (91②, 92①,
  93年)

over there (84年)

owe…to~ (88年)

participate in (90, 91②年)

pass down (91年②)

pass on (87年)

pass out (90年)

pass through (94年)

pay attention (96年)

pay attention to (89年)

pay off (91年②)

pick on (89年)

pick out (97年)

pick up (87, 94年)

pick up on (92年①)

pile up (89年)

plan to V. (91年②)

play a practical joke on
  (88年)

play a~role (88, 90年)

play guitar (94年)

play roles (85年)

plenty of (91②, 92①, 97年)

point out (86, 93, 96年)

point to (90, 93年)

prefer A to B (95年)

prefer to (98年)

prepare for (91年②)

prevent…from~ (91①,
  97年)

protect from (95年)

provide *sb.* with *sth.*
  (97年)

pull down (89年)

pull out (89年)

put about (93年)

put away (90年)

put off (85, 93年)

put on (92年①)

put out (89, 92①, 95年)

put *sth.* at risk (98年)

put *sth.* on show (93年)

put together (98年)

put up (86年)

put up with (86, 92①, 96年)

quite a bit (87年)

quite a few (93年)

quite a lot (86年)

rain down (88年)

range from A to B (84年)

rather than (88, 91②, 93, 94, 97, 98年)

recover from (86年)

refer to (84, 86, 87, 91①, 92①, 95, 98年)

regardless of (86, 93年)

relate A to B (85年)

rely on (92年①)

remain unknown to (97年)

remind *sb.* of *sth.* (94年)

replace A with B (98年)

rest upon (84年)

result in (96年)

return to (84年)

right away (88, 92①年)

right now (89, 93年)

run down (89年, 91①, 93年)

run into (87年)

run off (87年)

run out of (87, 91①, 96年)

run over (87年)

run the risk of (95年)

say no to (96年)

scare away (97年)

search for (89, 94年)

seek for (86年)

seem like (90年)

seem to (87, 95年)

send on (87年)

sent out (93年)

separate from (96年)

serve as (87, 95年)

set about (93年)

set aside (83年)

set foot on (96年)

set free (84年)

set off (86, 90, 94年)

set out (91①, 95年)

set up (86, 87, 90年)

shake *one's* hand (88年)

shout at (91年①)

show off (87, 89, 91②年)

Sincerely yours, (98年)

sit around (84年)

sit down (89, 90年)

slow down (95, 97年)

so that (84, 89, 90, 93, 94, 97年)

so…that~ (84, 90, 91①, 94, 97, 98年)

some other time (84年)

speak out (90, 95年)

speak to (84年)

spend a night (87年)

split off (88年)

stand by (83, 92①, 93年)

stand for (86年)

stare at (91年①)

start out (90, 91①年)

start with (94, 96年)

stay in place (98年)

stay on board (91年①)

stay up (90年)

stop V-ing (91年①)

stop…from~ (90, 95年)

storm away (96年)

study hard (95年)

succeed in (94, 96年)

such as (84, 86, 90, 91②, 93, 94, 95, 96, 98年)

such…that~ (86年)

suffer from (94, 97年)

sum up (86年)

take a break (92年①)

take A as B (96年)

take A for B (84年)

take a message (84年)

take a rest (98年)

take a trip (91年①)

take a walk (90年)

take action (92年①)

take apart (93年)

take by surprise (97年)

take care of (90, 92①年)

take different form (83年)

take in (88年)

take medicine (86, 91②年)

take notice of (86年)

take off (85, 90, 92①, 98年)

take on (97年)

take *one's* word (89年)

take out (91年①)

take over (87, 94, 95, 97, 98年)

take part in (90, 91②, 98年)

take photos (98年)

take place (85, 86, 91①, 97, 98年)

take pride in (94年)

take revenge on (91年①)

take *sth*. for granted
(88年)

take turns (98年)

take ~ from (89年)

talk about (84, 92①年)

talk over (84年)

talk *sb*. into V-ing
(91年②)

teach *sb*. a lesson (88年)

tear down (87年)

tell about (91年②)

tell A from B (98年)

tend to V. (83, 96年)

than ever (91年①)

thank goodness (89年)

that is (86, 98年)

that way (90年)

the longer…the
stronger (97年)

the minute (88年)

the most (90年)

the other day (85年)

the rest (96年)

There is no doubt that…
(91年①)

these days (83年)

think about (83, 89, 95年)

think of (89, 92①, 98年)

think up (90年)

this time (98年)

this way (96年)

thousands of (85, 90, 91②,
94, 98年)

thrive on (88年)

throw at (98年)

throw away (89, 90, 91②,
94年)

tie A to B (98年)

to begin with (94, 95年)

to some extent (95年)

together with (90年)

travel lighter (90年)

treat A as B (83, 86年)

treat as (96年)

trick *sb*. into *sth*. (97年)

triumph over (91年①②)

try hard (92年①)

try not to V. (94年)

try to V. (83, 84, 85, 86, 89,
91①②, 92①, 94年)

turn A into B (91年②)

turn a new page (98年)

turn away (89年)

turn back (90年)

turn down (85, 86, 91①年)

turn in (89年)

turn into (83, 96年)

turn off (89, 90, 98年)

turn on (89, 93年)

turn out (89, 90, 94, 97年)

turn up (83, 89, 93年)

turn…upside down
(97年)

under control (95年)

under no circumstances
(91年①)

under the care of (90年)

unknown to (84年)

up and down (91年②)

up to (86, 87, 89, 90, 91②, 92①年)

ups and downs (92年①)

used to (83, 86, 87, 91①②,
94年)

wake up (88, 89, 90年)

want to V. (93年)

ward off (87年)

warn *sb*. of (85年)

wear out (95年)

well done (89年)

what a shame (89年)

what if (90年)

what it takes (88年)

when it come to…
(89年)

whether…or not (90年)

why not (94年)

win the hand of (91年①)

with confidence (83年)

with delight (89年)

with regard to (93年)

with relief (89年)

within reach (96年)

without fail (96年)

without hesitation
(96年)

work on (86年)

work with (84, 90, 97年)

worry about (88, 98年)

worse than (96年)

worst of all (94, 96年)

would like (97年)

would like to V. (90年)

write down (88, 90年)

you name it (96年)

劉毅英文「98年學科能力測驗」15級分名單

姓名	學校班級	姓名	學校班級	姓名	學校班級	姓名	學校班級	姓名	學校班級
何冠廷	建國中學 302	林聖凰	北一女中三眞	盧胤諮	中山女中三信	鄭旭峰	建國中學 325	曹舜皓	麗山高中 307
高儀庭	北一女中三孝	李瑋穎	薇閣中學三丁	陳禹志	建國中學 329	許軒睿	市立大同 301	趙愷文	大同高中 315
許誌珍	北一女中三勤	殷偉珊	景美女中三眞	高慈宜	北一女中三射	莊雅茵	北一女中三射	李懿軒	建國中學 322
林儀芬	北一女中三和	劉傳靖	建國中學 329	梁筠	薇閣中學三丁	康育	延平高中 312	廖祥智	松山高中 312
袁輔君	北一女中三和	王捷	建國中學 329	張耘甄	薇閣中學三丁	黃美慈	中山女中三群	簡碩麒	建國中學 314
畢源伸	成功高中 324	林庭羽	板橋中學 307	白旻樺	市立大同 305	張雅晴	師大附中1164	鍾頎	北一女中三讓
王文哲	成功高中 324	黃農茵	北一女中三眞	賴冠百	建國中學 327	林群皓	延平高中 314	傅筠	台中女中 312
曾心潔	北一女中三和	林後嶧	建國中學 315	林怡廷	北一女中三義	蕭鈺芳	松山高中 306	林志安	台中一中 324
林洺安	北一女中三公	陳羅	建國中學 315	馮偉翔	建國中學 326	侯進坤	建國中學 330	林鉦峻	台中一中 316
黃筱勻	北一女中三誠	韓羽唯	北一女中三恭	邱冠霖	師大附中1173	洪庭妤	中山女中三博	蕭漢思	師大附中1176
簡翔瀅	北一女中三誠	沈柏妏	北一女中三愛	張熏文	松山高中 304	陳昱愷	建國中學 318	張希慈	北一女中三善
王瑋慈	北一女中三誠	徐涵葳	中山女中三捷	黃彥瑄	北一女中三忠	劉彥君	師大附中1164	藍宜欣	中山女中三品
沈奕彤	北一女中三和	蔡杰辰	建國中學 315	章品萱	北一女中三良	盧宇勝	師大附中1164	邱冠霖	建國中學 318
張雅甄	北一女中三勤	鄭惟之	成功高中 317	黃詩婷	中山女中三博	洪于涵	師大附中1158	許紹倫	成功高中 324
王怡文	北一女中三誠	宋瑞祥	建國中學 330	林奎沂	北一女中三愛	林劭辰	北一女中三樂	陳佑維	師大附中1167
許凱婷	華江高中 303	謝家惠	市立大同 312	張雅喬	北一女中三勤	潘筠	聖心女中三孝	高嘉駿	松山高中 308
丘清華	進修生	黃孺雅	北一女中三讓	陳庭萱	薇閣中學三丁	鄭立群	建國中學 327	張靜婷	西松高中三誠
謝明勳	師大附中1170	陳韻婷	北一女中三恭	張亦鎮	和平高中 312	李品彥	建國中學 329	張至婷	北一女中三射
朱盈盈	北一女中三毅	鄭皓宇	師大附中1161	田顏禎	建國中學 310	王澤恩	內湖高中 305	何逸風	台中一中 303
許書瑋	內湖高中 303	郭哲好	北一女中三毅	翁上雯	中山女中三捷	陳怡安	中山女中三仁	許力權	北一女中三良
翁靖堯	內湖高中 303	郭晉廷	師大附中1162	李承翰	成功高中 314	張詩玉	北一女中三讓	林芸安	北一女中三忠
張奕浩	師大附中1172	陳姿蓉	北一女中三恭	石知田	師大附中1172	李宗叡	成功高中 318	曹曉琳	北一女中三忠
鍾秉軒	建國中學 312	林承熹	師大附中1172	蘇柏穎	北一女中三數	陳翊含	松山高中 306	王衍皓	延平高中 311
劉承疆	建國中學 311	顏傑青	建國中學 317	徐逸竹	北一女中三數	黃宣榮	成功高中 309	簡喬	內湖高中 314
吳季儒	進修生	盧宜謙	師大附中1162	李苡萱	北一女中三恭	謝昀宇	辭修高中 301	李顯洋	師大附中1165
徐銘均	北一女中三勤	林欣諭	北一女中三讓	黃上瑋	建國中學 322	高偉豪	師大附中 301	林嫻	師大附中1165
陳柏玉	北一女中三愛	林芳瑜	北一女中三恭	徐智威	建國中學 327	蔡佳珉	北一女中三眞	朱君浩	建國中學 318
阮思瑀	北一女中三勤	胡琇雯	北一女中三善	廖祥伶	辭修高中 301	張清堯	建國中學 312	劉介民	建國中學 318
張正宜	成功高中 323	曾文昇	建國中學 317	匡小琪	政大附中 301	呂馥伊	北一女中三讓	林育正	新莊高中 303
陳俊樺	板橋中學 303	廖玠智	建國中學 310	林宛頤	延平中學 312	黃柏源	建國中學 318	李晏如	北一女中三射
蔡毅任	建國中學 323	陳昱豪	成功高中 323	李育瑋	師大附中1170	阮元泰	市立大同 314	陳瑞翔	建國中學 314
蘇哲毅	建國中學 319	黃韻儒	北一女中三忠	江品慧	師大附中1156	杜昆諭	建國中學 318	蘇冠霖	建國中學 318
洪一軒	板橋中學 307	高正陽	進修生	簡捷	北一女中三孝	于恩庭	北一女中三義	王雅琦	市立大同 310
梁珈珀	市立大同 306	黃明靜	北一女中三孝	吳周駿	延平中學 308	廖苑辰	辭修高中 301	林建宇	建國中學 308
歐宜欣	中山女中三禮	呂惠文	中山女中三禮	洪以青	延平中學進修生	林韋翰	建國中學 318	徐惠儀	桃園高中 317
蔡旻珊	延平中學 301	陳利未	建國中學 310	陳柏如	北一女中三御	周姿吟	北一女中三書	鑑家慧	景美女中三美
劉盈盈	北一女中三愛	王奕云	大同高中 302	林浩存	建國中學 314	許晉衍	東山高中三忠	陳昱州	延平高中 313
劉威廷	建國中學 313	陳奕廷	建國中學 312	唐子堯	建國中學 323	許嘉偉	建國中學 323	陳柏僑	宜蘭高中 313
孫瑋駿	建國中學 330	陳欣	政大附中 122	蘇俊瑋	松山高中 319	張潤元	延平中學 312	張妤如	北一女中三良
宋佳陵	北一女中三莊	高至頤	中正高中 306	高嘉吟	北一女中三毅	張哲偉	建國中學 320	余乙玉	北一女中三良
范廷瑋	北一女中三莊	吳致逸	師大附中1161	葉芃筠	師大附中1157	鄭晏羽	格致中學普三忠	金寧煊	建國中學 314
劉怡琴	師大附中1178	吳芳育	建國中學 322	盛博今	建國中學 322	林政儒	建國中學 315	卓珈仔	北一女中三莊
蔡明辰	成功高中 307	王映萱	北一女中三數	曾以寧	北一女中三勤	吳思萱	衛理女中高三恩	劉欣瑀	北一女中三溫
卓朝崴	北一女中三讓	蕭力婷	北一女中三儉	何中誠	建國中學 318	蘇柏勳	建國中學 303	李律恩	北一女中三恭
江姵璇	北一女中三書	林瑀芸	中山女中三慧	魏士惟	建國中學 324	朱得誠	新莊高中 303	郭潤宗	師大附中1173
張祐宬	成功高中 323	魏禎瑩	師大附中1160	陳政葦	建國中學 320	葉家維	建國中學 320	陳書瀚	建國中學 314
林宸弘	建國中學 327	龔國安	師大附中1173	于志業	建國中學 325	蔡秉達	建國中學 318	謝人傑	建國中學 323
劉任軒	建國中學 311	王斯瑋	成功高中 319	林聖翔	建國中學 325	李秉浩	建國中學 310		

劉毅英文家教班成績優異同學獎學金排行榜

姓名	學校	總金額	姓名	學校	總金額	姓名	學校	總金額	姓名	學校	總金額
賴宣佑	成淵高中	144550	董家琳	中和高中	29500	徐歆閔	福和國中	21900	楊紹紘	建國中學	17600
林采蓁	古亭國中	110600	簡 棻	自強國中	28300	董澤元	再興高中	21600	趙祥安	新店高中	17500
林妍君	薇閣高中	91150	洪嘉瑗	北一女中	28150	呂亞庭	縣中山國中	21450	楊舒涵	中山女中	17350
王 千	中和高中	89900	吳書軒	成功高中	28000	許丞敔	師大附中	21400	黃偉倫	成功高中	17200
黃怡文	石牌國中	79850	蔡佳恩	石牌國中	27800	陳思涵	成功高中	21200	黃詠期	建國中學	17100
方昱傑	溪崑國中	79250	江品萱	海山高中	27800	陳柏豪	萬華國中	21100	鄭巧兒	北一女中	17000
陳泱碩	重慶國小	60800	陳 明	建國中學	27450	王鈺雯	三重國中	21100	蔡承翰	萬華國中	17000
洪湘齡	新泰國中	53700	楊博閱	華江高中	27450	張祐銘	延平高中	20950	曹欣怡	延平高中	16900
林 臻	北一女中	53300	呂咏霏	長安國中	27350	盧 安	成淵高中	20800	朱冠宇	建國中學	16900
呂芝瑩	內湖高中	51450	王于綸	中山女中	27300	楊竣宇	新莊國中	20800	劉美廷	德音國小	16900
王思云	延平高中	51200	許晏魁	竹林高中	27150	蕭允祈	東山高中	20650	林承緯	延平國中部	16900
陳師凡	師大附中	50000	邱奕軒	內湖高中	27150	牟庭辰	大理高中	20500	郭學豪	和平高中	16800
江旻儒	葡萄國中部	50000	林祐瑋	耕莘護專	27050	林曜崴	鳳山國中	20400	陳怡舜	市中正國中	16800
蔡翰林	康橋國中	50000	蔡佳容	北一女中	27050	吳元魁	建國中學	20400	周筱涵	南湖高中	16800
陳 暐	自 學	50000	詹笠坊	石牌國中	26700	蔡佳芸	和平高中	20300	劉應傑	西松高中	16700
朱庭萱	北一女中	48917	江少軒	銘傳國中	26650	韓宗叡	大同高中	20200	鄭竣陽	中和高中	16650
呂宗倫	南湖高中	47950	施宛妤	武崙國小	26500	王聖雄	金華國中	20100	莫雅晴	永和國中	16600
賴鈺錡	明倫高中	44650	黃棨翼	北一女中	26350	趙于萱	中正高中	20100	薛宜軒	北一女中	16500
張祐豪	埔墘國小	42900	施廷睿	莒光國小	26200	練冠霆	板橋高中	20000	徐子涵	新莊國中	16400
何欣蓉	蘭雅國中	41100	梁家豪	松山高中	26200	洪啓修	師大附中	20000	許志遙	百齡高中	16400
塗皓宇	建國中學	39834	陳昱勳	華江高中	26200	羅之勵	大直高中	19900	洪敏珊	景美女中	16300
林清心	板橋高中	39500	王挺之	建國中學	26100	柯穎瑄	北一女中	19800	梁齡心	北政國中	16300
楊玄詳	建國中學	38800	江采軒	銘傳國中	26000	鄭昀叡	市中正國中	19700	馬偉傑	成功高中	16300
鄭翔仁	師大附中	38450	張祐寧	建國中學	25900	蔡承儒	南山國中	19700	劉侑如	江翠國中	16300
陳冠宏	東海高中	37150	鍾佩璇	中崙高中	25900	黃靖淳	師大附中	19650	許令揚	板橋高中	16300
陳琳涵	永春高中	36850	楊哲煜	板橋高中	25800	卓晉宇	華江高中	19600	吳承叡	中崙高中	16300
謝家綺	板橋高中	36600	劉 桐	北一女中	25400	饒哲宇	北一女中	19600	許晉魁	政大附中	16250
吳品賢	板橋高中	35750	黃馨鎂	育成高中	25200	顏薇澤	華江高中	19500	趙家德	中和高中	16100
許瑞云	中山女中	34450	朱煜婷	長安國中	25150	廖祥舜	永平高中	19300	鄭家宜	成淵高中	16100
柳堅鑅	景美國中	34300	吳佳輝	仁愛國中	24900	柯姝廷	北一女中	19300	郭 權	建國中學	16100
李祖荃	新店高中	34100	林弘灝	內湖高中	24050	蔡柏晏	北一女中	19300	林于傑	師大附中	16000
蘇子陽	林口國中	33800	王芊蓁	北一女中	23850	李欣儒	江翠國中	19300	呂佾蓁	南湖高中	15950
宋 安	東湖國中	33150	林俐吟	中山女中	23750	陳冠揚	南湖高中	19300	廖婕妤	景美女中	15950
趙啓鈞	松山高中	32950	高仲鎣	百齡高中	23700	鄭瑋伶	新莊高中	19100	謝宜廷	崇林國中	15900
丁哲沛	成功高中	32150	張仲豪	師大附中	23700	劉紹增	成功高中	19000	趙勻慈	新莊高中	15900
蔡佳伶	麗山高中	31800	郭韋成	松山高中	23500	林悅婷	北一女中	19000	李姿瑩	板橋高中	15800
胡嘉杰	建國中學	31700	李秉宜	薇閣國中部	23400	位芷甄	北一女中	18850	潘柏維	和平高中	15800
吳思儀	延平高中	31500	劉家伶	育成高中	23400	陳 昕	中山女中	18700	林學典	格致高中	15800
袁妤蓁	武陵高中	31450	林瑋萱	中山女中	23300	許喬青	海山高中	18700	楊薇翼	重慶國小	15600
洪紫瑜	北一女中	31400	謝昀彤	建國中學	23167	何思緯	內湖高中	18600	翁鉦達	格致高中	15500
徐恩平	金華國中	31200	林羿懿	大直高中	22600	劉瀞允	建國中學	18300	蔡欣儒	陽明高中	15500
高行灃	西松高中	30900	匡若榆	青山國中	22600	陳怡霖	北一女中	18300	賴建元	大安高工	15500
許顯升	內湖高中	30900	徐浩芸	萬芳高中	22500	李念恩	建國中學	18050	呂胤慶	建國中學	15400
周芷儀	三重高中	30800	鄭豪文	大安高工	22200	廖珮琪	復興高中	17900	洪千雅	育成高中	15300
李芳曇	辭修高中	30650	徐柏庭	延平高中	22200	王廷鎧	建國中學	17900	羅郁善	景興國中	15300
黃詩芸	北一女中	30500	簡祥恩	桃園高中	22100	戴秀娟	新店高中	17900	賴沛恩	建國中學	15300
賴佳駿	海山高中	30100	蔡涓伍	北一女中	22000	王思僾	建國中學	17700	蔡佳好	基隆女中	15200
鄭雅涵	北一女中	30100	陳盈穎	弘道國中	22000	蘇郁芬	中山女中	17600	郭憲等	大葉大學	15200
郭珥蓁	成功高中	29500	黃筱雅	北一女中	22000	李盼盼	中山女中	17600	劉裕心	中和高中	15050

※ 因版面有限，尚有領取高額獎學金同學，無法列出。

www.learnschool.com.tw

劉毅英文教育機構

學費最低・效果最佳

高中部：台北市許昌街17號6F（捷運M8出口對面・學勤補習班）TEL：（02）2389-5212
國中部：台北市重慶南路一段10號7F（火車站前・學林補習班）TEL：（02）2361-6101
台中補習：台中市三民路三段125號7F（世界健身中心樓上）TEL：（04）2221-8861

歷屆大學學測英文試題詳解

主　　　編 / 劉　毅

發　行　所 / 學習出版有限公司　　　　☎ (02) 2704-5525

郵　撥　帳　號 / 0512727-2 學習出版社帳戶

登　記　證 / 局版台業 2179 號

印　刷　所 / 裕強彩色印刷有限公司

台　北　門　市 / 台北市許昌街 10 號 2 F　　☎ (02) 2331-4060

台灣總經銷 / 紅螞蟻圖書有限公司　　　☎ (02) 2795-3656

美國總經銷 / Evergreen Book Store　　☎ (818) 2813622

本公司網址　www.learnbook.com.tw

電　子　郵　件　learnbook@learnbook.com.tw

售價：新台幣五百八十元正

2013 年 5 月 1 日二版三刷

ISBN 978-986-231-020-5